Shifting Power Dynamics in International Relations:

From Unipolar Hegemony to Multipolarity

Merve Suna Özel Özcan
https://orcid.org/0000-0001-9027-3990
Kirikkale University, Turkey

IGI Global
Scientific Publishing
Publishing Tomorrow's Research Today

Vice President of Editorial Melissa Wagner
Director of Acquisitions Mikaela Felty
Director of Book Development Jocelynn Hessler
Production Manager Mike Brehm
Cover Design Jose Rosado

Published in the United States of America by
IGI Global Scientific Publishing
701 East Chocolate Avenue
Hershey, PA, 17033, USA
Tel: 717-533-8845 | Fax: 717-533-7115
Website: https://www.igi-global.com E-mail: cust@igi-global.com

Library of Congress Cataloging-in-Publication Data

Names: Özel Özcan, Merve, 1988- editor
Title: Shifting power dynamics in international relations : from unipolar hegemony to multipolarity / edited by: Merve Suna Özel Özcan.
Description: Hershey, PA : IGI Global Scientific Publishing, [2026] | Includes bibliographical references and index. | Summary: "This book aims to analyze the transformation within the field of international relations in the 21st century, starting from the individual level and extending to the state and the system"-- Provided by publisher.
Identifiers: LCCN 2025019823 (print) | LCCN 2025019824 (ebook) | ISBN 9798337323428 hc | ISBN 9798337323435 sc | ISBN 9798337323442 e
Subjects: LCSH: World politics--21st century | International relations--History--21st century | Hegemony
Classification: LCC D863.3 .S535 2026 (print) | LCC D863.3 (ebook)
LC record available at https://lccn.loc.gov/2025019823
LC ebook record available at https://lccn.loc.gov/2025019824

British Cataloguing in Publication Data
A Cataloguing in Publication record for this book is available from the British Library.

Table of Contents

Detailed Table of Contents

This chapter offers a critical exploration of the reconfiguration of the international political economy (IPE), focusing on the rise of heterarchical frameworks that challenge traditional, state-centric paradigms. Most discussions of IPE still rely on the assumption that states are central, cohesive entities that govern global economic relations. However, this chapter argues that recent global developments reveal a shift toward transnationalism, where the traditional dominance of nation-states is increasingly supplemented, and sometimes even challenged, by a variety of sub- and supra-national actors that are increasingly shaping global economic governance. As transnational linkages expand, the power of these actors grows, contributing to the creation of new webs of economic influence. The chapter concludes by examining the potential consequences of these changes, highlighting the implications for inclusive economic policy, sustainable development, and global governance in the evolving international political economy.

This chapter seeks to answer the fundamental research question, "How can the changing power dynamics evolving towards multipolarity in the international system be explained theoretically?" The chapter aims to test the arguments of neoclassical realism regarding the change in international power dynamics in today's international relations, where more than one great power competes. For this purpose, the breaking points that caused the international system to become multipolar are emphasized. Thus, the discussions on the end of unipolarity in connection with the structural transformation of the international system, the limitations of the neorealist explanation, and the effects of the arguments of neoclassical realism on the transformation of the international system are included. As a result of all these explanations, the study puts forward the following argument: The evolution from unipolarity to multipolarity in the international system can be understood through the balance of interests of neoclassical realism instead of the balance of power claimed by neorealism.

This chapter analyzes the shift in the global order from U.S.-led unipolar dominance to a progressively intricate multipolar framework. This analysis utilizes historical examination, theoretical models, and case studies to investigate how emerging powers, regional alliances, and the Global South are transforming power dynamics via strategic adaptation, geoeconomic tools, and normative challenges. Special emphasis is placed on the constraints of U.S. global supremacy in the 21st century, the emergence of digital sovereignty, and the reconfiguration of international institutions. The chapter delineates prospective scenarios for global governance and provides pragmatic policy proposals to foster cooperative multipolarity. It concludes that while multipolarity creates new obstacles, it also offers opportunity to cultivate a more pluralistic, sustainable, and egalitarian global order through inclusive diplomacy and adaptable governance initiatives.

Since 1944, the unipolar factor has begun to form in the world economic system. Thus, the formation of a dollar-centered currency system after the Bretton Woods Monetary Conference further deepened the unipolar economic hegemony of the United States, parallel to the unipolar political hegemony. In the research work, the author analyzed the impact of this economic hegemony on international exchange reserves. The author relied on macroeconomic proportional analysis here. As a result, although the value of the US dollar in the volume of foreign currency reserves has increased, proportional analysis shows that this indicator has not increased, but rather decreased.

The shining years of the U.S. ideological hegemony in the world tended to darken at the dawn of the twenty first century. The unipolar system waned as the U.S. grappled with sustaining democracy as a relatively accepted and appealing ideology in the world. This shift marked a pivotal moment in international relations, questioning the sustainability of American ideological hegemony. This paper attempts to address the question of how ideology serves as an indicator of American global hegemony and its subsequent decline. It also seeks to find out what are the reasons behind the diminishing influence of American ideology on the global stage. It is assumed that democracy, a cornerstone of U.S. ideology, played a pivotal role in its global rise. However, this ascent is now declining as constitutional challenges undermine democracy domestically. Simultaneously, its reduced international commitment to democracy promotion and inconsistent global actions have eroded American ideological influence, diminishing democracy as a means of its global hegemony.

NATO was established as the defense organization of the Western Bloc during the Cold War. During the Cold War period, it became functional for the political integration of the Western Bloc more than being a defense organization. The concept of the West has become synonymous with NATO over time, and NATO has become a systemic actor in the international system. Moving from the European security architecture to regional cooperation, NATO started to take part as a global actor in the fight against a wide range of security threats in the international system. The steps taken by NATO after the Cold War show that it has an understanding that demonstrates the Western approach to the system rather than a defense organization. In this direction, the chapter examines NATO's strategic, geostrategic, regional and global policies in the international system and discusses NATO's place and role in the international system and its impact on the system. As the defence organisation of the Western alliance, NATO can be said to have acted as an actor in the international system through its policies and actions in the post-Cold War era. For this reason, the study has examined NATO's policies and actions in the international system using neorealism and world systems analysis theories, which treat the system as a unit at the level of analysis, and has endeavoured to analyse them on this basis.

The South China Sea is a key area of international cooperation and conflict, serving as a crucial maritime link between the Indian and Pacific Oceans. The region is pivotal in regional and global trade and energy security, underscoring its strategic significance for global actors. Given these dynamics, this chapter examines Russia's South China Sea policies. It highlights that while Moscow officially maintains a neutral stance in its rhetoric, it has developed complex relationships with regional

Peculiarities of Russian-Turkish relations, The Black Sea Region as a Zone of Cooperation/Competition, Ideological and Value-Based Approach in Russian-Turkish Relations, The Syrian Case in Russian-Turkish Relations, Economic Cooperation in Russian-Turkish Relations.

Until the 21st century, states mostly used conventional warfare, but this has lost relevance with the rise of hybrid warfare. Initially associated with non-state actors, hybrid methods are now widely used by states. Amid rising tensions in the Russia-Ukraine conflict, the term "Collective West"—referring to NATO, the EU, and the US—gained prominence in Russian discourse. Following Russia's 2022 "special military operation," the Collective West intensified hybrid tactics against Russia. Türkiye, though a NATO member, maintained a distinct policy toward Russia, positioning itself independently. This study examines Türkiye's role in the Collective West's hybrid war against Russia in Ukraine between 2016 and 2023. Using qualitative methods and interviews with diplomats and experts, it adopts principles of credibility and objectivity to analyze Türkiye's strategic choices during this period.

Within the new multipolar international system the role of non-Western centers of power increased dramatically. The middle powers began to undergo a new stage of transformation of behavior and positioning within the international system. Against this background, Turkey began to position itself as a "transregional" power. This status of Türkiye is manifested in the spread of influence in three priority areas: Islamic, post-Ottoman and Turkic/post-Soviet. The purpose of this chapter is to examine the evolution of Türkiye's international positioning and to justify the place that it is striving for within the modern international system during the period of the Justice and Development Party (JDP) in power. An excessively ambitious foreign policy for a middle power can be considered untenable due to a number of systemic and internal factors. However, although Türkiye's attempts to change its international status are not sufficient to achieve the status of a global power, they create the basis for reconsidering the approach to Türkiye as a middle power.

Compared to the previous century, international relations in the 21st century are more intense and complex. The global order moved from multipolarity (pre-Second World War period) to bipolarity (post-Second World War period) to unipolarity (post-Cold War era). Although many believed that unipolarity would continue to exist for long under the superpower leadership of the USA, it was short-lived. Globalization, liberalization, and an open economy reshaped the international order that echoes interconnectedness and interdependence. Accordingly, the 21st century witnesses the revival of multipolarity. However, this period advances the emergence of developing countries to the global scenario, demanding active roles in policy-making and decision-making processes. The BRICS grouping is one such body. Consisting of ten emerging economies, it has a unique position to stand for the developing world's interests. From this perspective, this chapter critically examines the role of BRICS in 21st-century international relations through the lens of multipolarity.

Southeast Asia has emerged as a central arena in the evolving great-power competition between China and the Quadrilateral Security Dialogue (QUAD). As the QUAD consolidates its Indo-Pacific strategy, aimed at countering Beijing's expanding influence, China continues to entrench its economic and military presence in the region through a combination of economic statecraft, military posturing, and infrastructural expansion under the Belt and Road Initiative (BRI). This geopolitical contest has placed ASEAN in a structurally precarious position, compelling it to navigate security dilemmas, economic dependencies, and shifting alliances while striving to uphold its centrality and neutrality in regional governance. Framed Geopolitical Theory, this study examines the evolving strategic calculus of key regional actors. The QUAD seeks to construct a security and economic architecture that constrains China's ability to dictate the terms of engagement in the Indo-Pacific. In response, Beijing employs a dual-pronged strategy, combining coercive diplomacy with economic inducements to reinforce its influence. ASEAN, lacking the institutional cohesion and military capabilities of major power blocs, finds itself entangled in this strategic rivalry, with internal divisions and external pressures threatening its ability to function as a cohesive geopolitical entity.

This chapter offers a case study of the 2025 Iran-Israel War which confirms the theoretical propositions of Offensive Realism but is limited by one particular assumption - that there are no miscalculations in the pursuit of power maximization. The country's pre-conflict policy - a deliberate pursuit of regional dominance supported by a nuclear ambiguity as close to breakout capacity as possible - demonstrates the theory's prediction that in an anarchic world, states pursue maximum power for their own survival. However, the conflict also reveals a major flaw - ambiguity creates uncertainty in strategic decisions – as seen 2025 Iran-Israel war it can also bring about a sudden conflict. This paper will rely on reports from the IAEA, professional assessments and conflict data to show that while Offensive Realism can explain a state's structural motivations - it cannot accurately predict miscalculations and/or failure mechanisms. The 2025 crisis clearly shows that rational power maximizing strategies are inherently risky when the uncertainty surrounding an adversary's resolve exists.

Kazakhstan, like many other post-Soviet states, possesses a multicultural and multilingual social structure. Its long shared border with Russia and the relatively large proportion of Russian-speaking ethnic communities within its population distinguish it from other countries in the region. The status of the Kazakh language, which had been disadvantaged prior to independence, has significantly improved through language policies implemented since 1991. With the adoption of the Trilingual Education initiative in 2007, the state aimed to integrate Kazakh, Russian, and English into the national education system. However, experience and findings accumulated over time indicate that the initiative has not fully achieved its intended objectives. Adopting an interdisciplinary approach, this chapter analyzes Kazakhstan's current language policy and its implications for identity formation and geopolitics, offering a theoretical framework for understanding multilingual education in post-Soviet contexts alongside practical recommendations for policymakers.

Preface

OVERVIEW OF THE BOOK

The international system has entered a period of profound and multidimensional transformation. The post–Cold War era, which had long been defined by the unchallenged dominance of a unipolar order led by the United States, is now giving way to a far more complex and heterogeneous global structure. The foundations of the so-called "liberal order" — ideological supremacy, institutional hierarchy, and normative legitimacy — have gradually eroded, revealing the contours of a multipolar world shaped by competing powers, shifting alliances, and diversified regional mechanisms. This book, Shifting Power Dynamics in International Relations: From Unipolar Hegemony to Multipolarity, was born out of the necessity to understand these structural ruptures and to reexamine the theoretical lenses through which global change is perceived. The current transformation is not merely a transition from one polarity to another; it represents a deeper systemic reconfiguration where material, ideological, and technological dimensions intersect. Power today is neither centralised nor clearly defined — it is dispersed across regions, institutions, and networks that often operate outside traditional great-power hierarchies. The underlying motivation for this volume is to question whether the existing frameworks of international relations can still explain this complexity.

Realism, liberalism, and critical theories each provide partial insights, yet none alone can fully capture the pluralistic and dynamic nature of the emerging order. Hence, the book brings together diverse scholarly perspectives to explore both the continuities and discontinuities of power in the twenty-first century — from the resurgence of realism to the normative crisis of Western hegemony, from the rise of middle powers like Türkiye to the institutional rebalancing led by BRICS and the Shanghai Cooperation Organisation. What defines the twenty-first-century international system is not only the return of great power competition but also the emergence of new actors capable of redefining the logic of cooperation, resistance, and legitimacy. Multipolarity today embodies both the fragmentation and recomposition of global governance. It is a condition in which states navigate between competition and interdependence, where economic, ideological, and security interests constantly overlap. The book, therefore, approaches the phenomenon of systemic change through multiple dimensions — theoretical, geopolitical, financial, and normative.

Chapter 1: Great Power Competition – Structuring An Analytical Theoretical Framework for Small/ Middle Power Security Strategies (Hursid Dingil)

This chapter establishes a conceptual basis for understanding Great Power Competition, tracing its origins in U.S. strategic doctrine and exploring its implications for smaller and middle powers. Using the Iran–Israel rivalry (2017–2023) as a case study, it bridges theoretical and empirical analysis to examine how power rivalry shapes security strategies in a post-hegemonic world.

Chapter 2: The Forces of Conflict in the Twenty-First Century – States or Individuals (Yusuf Wara)

This volume concludes with Wara challenging realist assumptions by questioning whether states remain the principal agents of conflict in today's interconnected world, positing that individuals and non-state groups may now exert greater influence in global security dynamics.

Chapter 3: Reimagining IPE – From Hegemony to Heterarchy (Dana-Marie Ramjit)

Ramjit reinterprets international political economy through a heterarchical lens, arguing that transnational networks and non-state actors are reshaping global economic governance. The chapter calls for a rethinking of global order beyond the state-centric paradigm.

Chapter 4: Theoretical Framework of the International System Transforming from Unipolarity to Multipolarity – Neoclassical Realism (Emre Erdemir)

Erdemir employs neoclassical realism to explain the structural transformation of the international system, arguing that multipolarity can be better understood through the balance of interests rather than traditional balance-of-power models.

Chapter 5: The Future of International Relations – Balancing Multipolarity and Non-Polar Challenges (Ramazan Safa)

This chapter analyzes the coexistence of multipolar and non-polar trends in global politics, highlighting the growing influence of non-state actors and the importance of adaptive, multilateral governance to confront transnational threats.

Chapter 6: From Cold War Bipolarity to Unipolarity – Analyzing Contemporary System Change (Goran Roos)

Roos introduces the Multi-Dimensional Order Transformation (MDOT) Framework to map global systemic change across multiple axes—political, institutional, and economic—illustrating how regional autonomy and normative fragmentation shape today's transition.

Chapter 7: Navigating Change – Understanding the Dynamics of Global Power Transitions (Andi Asrifan & Rismawati Rismawati)

Through a blend of theory and case study, this chapter explores how emerging powers and regional alliances reshape international institutions and norms, proposing a framework for cooperative multipolarity in the 21st century.

Chapter 8: The Impact of Unipolar Hegemony on Foreign Exchange Reserves – A Macroeconomic Proportional Analysis (Aslan Azimzadeh)

Azimzadeh empirically assesses how U.S. dollar hegemony has shaped international reserve compositions since Bretton Woods, revealing subtle shifts in global financial dependency patterns.

Chapter 9: Shifting Horizons of United States Hegemony – A Normative Perspective (Ejazul Haq Ateed)

Ateed examines the ideological dimension of U.S. hegemony, arguing that America's declining global influence is closely tied to the erosion of democracy's normative appeal both domestically and internationally.

Chapter 10: International System and the West's Approach Through NATO (Cihan Günyel)

This chapter situates NATO as a systemic actor representing the Western worldview, tracing its evolution from a regional defense alliance to a global governance mechanism in the post-Cold War international order.

Chapter 11: Russia's Policy in the South China Sea – Strategic Interests and Geopolitical Maneuvers (Ezgi Şahin & Merve Suna Özel Özcan)

Şahin and Özel Özcan investigate Russia's pragmatic engagement in the South China Sea, demonstrating how Moscow balances neutrality and influence to maintain its regional foothold amidst Sino-U.S. competition.

Chapter 12: The Resurgence of Realism in International Relations – The Russia-Ukraine Conflict and Vietnam's Foreign Policy (Kiet Le, Pranjal Khare & Hiep Tran)

Using the Russia-Ukraine war as a case, this chapter underscores the enduring relevance of realism and its policy implications for smaller states like Vietnam navigating between competing great powers.

Chapter 13: Russia and Turkey After 2022 – Peculiarities of Bilateral Relations in Russian Academic Discourse (Damir Islamov)

Islamov examines Russian scholarly interpretations of post-2022 Russo-Turkish relations, identifying the dominant academic narratives shaping perceptions of cooperation and competition.

Chapter 14: Türkiye's Role in the Collective West's Hybrid War Against Russia – The Case of Ukraine (Yıldıran Acar)

Acar explores Türkiye's strategic balancing during the Russia-Ukraine conflict, analyzing its nuanced position within NATO and its independent approach to hybrid warfare and diplomacy.

Chapter 15: The Role of Middle Powers in Shaping the New International System – The Case of Türkiye (Nubara Kuliyeva)

Kuliyeva analyzes Türkiye's aspiration to act as a "transregional" power, discussing the limits and opportunities of middle powers in influencing global governance under multipolarity.

Chapter 16: The Role of BRICS in 21st-Century International Relations – A Multipolarity Perspective (Jipson Joseph)

Joseph assesses BRICS as a collective platform advancing developing countries' voices in global politics, emphasizing its contribution to redefining multipolar governance.

Chapter 17: Triple Strategic Dynamics and Contestations – QUAD, China, and ASEAN in Southeast Asia (Tin Htwe)

Tin Htwe examines Southeast Asia's strategic complexity amid great-power rivalry, analyzing the competing visions of China and the QUAD within the Indo-Pacific framework.

Chapter 18: Miscalculation in Anarchy – Iran's Strategic Ambiguity and the 2025 Iran-Israel Conflict (Mehmet Akar)

Akar's case study of the 2025 Iran-Israel conflict highlights the limitations of Offensive Realism, showing how miscalculation and uncertainty can destabilize rational power strategies.

Chapter 19: Language, Identity, and Geopolitics – Multilingual Education in Kazakhstan (Suat Beylur)

This chapter is an interdisciplinary exploration of language policy in Kazakhstan, linking multilingual education to questions of national identity, soft power, and regional geopolitics.

Each chapter contributes to this broader picture, examining how global transitions are negotiated, contested, and institutionalised in a rapidly evolving order. The guiding assumption is that the world is not witnessing the decline of power per se, but its redistribution, accompanied by the birth of new regional and ideational centres of influence. Ultimately, this volume aims to contribute to a deeper understanding of how global power transitions unfold — not as linear processes, but as multidirectional interactions among states, institutions, and ideas. By revisiting classical paradigms and integrating contemporary empirical realities, Shifting Power Dynamics in International Relations seeks to map the contours of a world that is no longer unipolar, yet not entirely multipolar — a world suspended between competition and coexistence, fragmentation and realignment, dominance and dialogue.

Merve Suna Özel Özcan
Kirikkale University, Turkey

Acknowledgment

In an era marked by rising conflicts, deepening divisions, and an ever-shifting global balance of power, the hope for peace remains the most enduring aspiration of humanity. This book was written with the belief that even amidst uncertainty and turbulence, the idea of peace—both as a moral value and as a structural principle—continues to guide the collective conscience of our world. The contributors and scholars who have shared their insights in this volume have all, in their own way, sought to understand and to reimagine a more stable, inclusive, and humane international system.

I am deeply grateful to all the authors, reviewers, and colleagues whose intellectual engagement and collaboration have enriched this project. Their efforts have transformed this volume into a meaningful academic contribution at a time when understanding power, order, and coexistence has never been more urgent. I also wish to express my heartfelt gratitude to my family for their endless patience, encouragement, and love throughout this long and demanding process. Their understanding and unwavering support have been my most significant source of strength and serenity.

Finally, this book is dedicated to all who continue to believe in dialogue over discord, understanding over indifference, and peace over power.

Merve Suna Özel Özcan
Kirikkale University, Turkey

Introduction

The international system in the twenty-first century is witnessing a historic transformation that challenges the post–Cold War unipolar order. For nearly three decades, the United States maintained a unique position as the sole hegemon, shaping the rules, norms, and institutions of global governance. Nevertheless, the erosion of that dominance—visible across political, economic, technological, and normative dimensions—has given rise to a more fragmented, pluralistic, and contested international environment. This book, Shifting Power Dynamics in International Relations: From Unipolar Hegemony to Multipolarity, examines this fundamental shift and explores the emerging architecture of global order.

Hegemony, one of the most central concepts of international relations theory, determines not only the balance of power but also the legitimacy basis of the global system. Since ancient Greece, hegemony has represented the domination of a superior power over other actors; however, in the modern era, the concept has acquired a more profound meaning through its economic, ideological, and normative dimensions. Hegemony is not merely a form of superiority achieved through coercion; rather, it is a system of legitimacy that ensures the production of consent, the construction of norms, and the continuity of international order (Gramsci, 1971).

The term denotes an actor's "rise" and "establishment of dominance" over others—an ambition that has remained at the core of traditional empires throughout history. A hegemonic power seeks to instil fear in its rivals and position itself as the most influential actor within the system. The ancient Greek city-states, notably Athens and Sparta, witnessed nearly thirty years of hegemonic rivalry. In this sense, the pursuit of hegemony has persisted since the era of city-states, manifesting as a recurring pattern in the behaviour of all actors within the international system. Hegemony is inherently linked to power: a powerful state, by achieving a dominant position, reshapes the system to serve its own interests, leaving weaker states with limited options. Consequently, both the Greek city-states and great empires such as the Achaemenids disappeared as stronger political entities emerged. The Macedonian Empire, in turn, consolidated its hegemonic superiority through imperial expansion, eliminating other political formations in the region (Özel Özcan, 2024).

Also, the concept of the international system lies at the epistemological core of modern international relations. Although inter-state relations have historically formed an interactive network, the term "system" implies the continuity of order, rules, and the distribution of power. In this respect, the system is not merely an aggregation of states but also a complex structure comprising norms, institutions, and ideological frameworks (Waltz, 1979; Bull, 1977). In Kenneth Waltz's Theory of International Politics (1979), the notion of "system" was redefined in structuralist terms. Waltz conceptualised the international system as an anarchic order—an arena lacking a central authority—where states act as rational actors striving for survival. Within this anarchic structure, hegemony emerges as a temporary equilibrium, since no power can remain permanent. Waltz's structural realism thus posits that the balance of power is inherently cyclical.

In the post-Cold War period, the idea of the permanence of liberal hegemony, symbolised by Francis Fukuyama's (1992) end-of-history thesis, faced serious challenges. The unipolar order established by the United States in the 1990s has become increasingly fragile amid the 2008 financial crisis, the rise of China, Russia's resurgence, Europe's tendencies toward fragmentation, and the growing voices of the Global South (Acharya, 2017; Ikenberry, 2018). Today, the international system is evolving beyond a single-centred hegemonic structure toward a multi-centric world order, in which multiple regional centres, civilizational spheres, and normative approaches intersect and coexist.

On the other hand, Military and technological advancements have generated power asymmetries that compel major powers to feel insecure not only toward each other but also toward lesser actors. This condition sustains the principle of self-help as a core mechanism of the international system. In the age of new empires, this dynamic can be understood through Mearsheimer's (2001) notion of the "fear factor," which drives states to pursue power accumulation as a means of survival. New empires seek to strengthen their strategic capabilities and widen the gap between themselves and the second-strongest actor in the system. Hence, the pursuit of hegemony is no longer confined to military expansion but encompasses multidimensional forms of power generation (Toft, 2005). Consequently, hegemony in the contemporary era is transforming from a centralised and hierarchical structure into a multi-layered, regional, and normatively interconnected system of interactions.

The theoretical tension between Waltz's structuralism and Bull's normative institutionalism reveals the intellectual core of the hegemonic debate. Understanding the relationship between power, order, and legitimacy requires examining not only the system's material structure but also its ideological and historical cyclicality. It is within this analytical framework that George Modelski (1987) introduces his theory of long cycles of world leadership, combining historical sociology with systemic analysis. Modelski argues that world politics undergoes a leadership cycle every 100–120 years, each driven by global wars, technological revolutions, and the establishment of new institutional orders. Every hegemonic power ascends through innovation and strategic expansion, but eventually declines under the weight of overextension and economic cost. Thus, hegemonic transitions are not merely shifts in power, but reflections of the system's evolutionary rhythm.

Modelski's cyclical theory complements Waltz's structural analysis by adding a temporal dimension, while simultaneously converging with Bull's normative insights. Each hegemonic cycle involves not only a redistribution of power but also a reconstruction of global norms and institutions. For example, 19th-century British hegemony institutionalised the norms of free trade and maritime dominance. In contrast, 20th-century American hegemony consolidated liberal internationalism through institutions such as the United Nations, the IMF, and the World Bank. Hence, hegemony is not simply a structural position—it represents the ideological and institutional redefinition of international order.

From a historical standpoint, we can identify three dominant forms of hegemonic order. First, the unipolar system, in which a single actor exercises hegemonic dominance. The post–Cold War era, characterised by the United States' global preeminence, exemplifies this type.

Second, the bipolar or dual-hegemonic system is defined by the rivalry of two major powers competing for systemic leadership. The U.S.–Soviet confrontation (1945–1990) and, in antiquity, the Athens–Sparta rivalry both illustrate this configuration. Third, the multipolar or collective hegemonic system, wherein several powers collectively shape the rules and direction of the international order. The post-1815 Concert of Europe, led by Britain, France, Prussia, Austria, and Russia, represents a historical prototype of this collective arrangement (Wallerstain, 2011). This tripartite classification demonstrates that hegemony is not merely a hierarchy of power but a mechanism for the formation of systemic stability. Beyond Waltz's notion of hegemony as a temporary equilibrium within an anarchic order, integrating Modelski's historical cyclicality and Bull's normative institutionalism offers a deeper understanding of the evolutionary logic of the international system.

As clearly shown in the table I, the 21st-century international system represents not merely a period of shifting actors, but an era of profound conceptual transformation. The defining pillars of the hegemonic order—unipolarity, liberal legitimacy, neoliberal economics, Western-centric knowledge production, and interventionist security—are steadily losing their validity. This dissolution does not signify a vacuum but rather the birth of a new phase: a transition from hegemonic stability to systemic flexibility. Power in the contemporary era is no longer concentrated along a single axis; it is increasingly network-based and polycentric. This diffusion of power has generated an intermediate space that transcends the classical "order–chaos" dichotomy in international relations. Hegemony today is not monopolised by a single state or ideology, but is instead shaped through the interaction of multiple regions, civilisations, and centres of normative production.

Table 1. Hegemonic System and Post-Hegemonic System

	Hegemonic System (20th Century)	*Post-Hegemonic System (21st Century)*
Power	Unipolar (United States)	Multipolar, network-based
Legitimacy	Liberal values and consent generation	Regional norms and relative legitimacy
Economic Model	Neoliberal globalization	Diverse development models
Knowledge Production	Western-centric epistemology	Global IR and pluralistic knowledge production
Security Perception	Interventionist stability	Sovereignty-based resilience
Institutions	Bretton Woods system	Regional and thematic networks
Systemic Balance	Maintained by the hegemon	Formed through simultaneous interactions

Legitimacy, likewise, is transforming. The liberal values of the 20th century are no longer universal but have evolved into regionally interpreted normative frameworks. The claim of "universality" has given way to the reality of pluralism. Accordingly, legitimacy can no longer be confined to a Western-defined set of values; it now demands a broader and multilayered perspective. Many core concepts—most notably the notion of security—are being redefined. The interventionist notion of stability has given way to a model of sovereignty-based resilience. State security policies are no longer oriented toward regime export but toward internal resilience, technological independence, and regional cooperation. Finally, the transformation of institutions reflects the structural decentralisation of the global system. Thematic and regional network structures are increasingly replacing the Bretton Woods framework. Platforms such as BRICS, ASEAN, the Organisation of Turkic States (OTS), and the Shanghai Cooperation Organisation (SCO) now constitute the institutional backbone of this new era.

In conclusion, hegemony should be defined not solely by military or economic capacity, but by the ability to generate legitimacy, construct norms, and institutionalise order. Thus, in the contemporary era, hegemony is no longer limited to the domination of one state over others—it represents an ongoing process of ideological, institutional, and normative reconstruction within the global system. Ultimately, the international system has evolved into a structure too complex to be controlled by a single hegemon. This transformation is not merely about shifts in the distribution of power, but also about the global redistribution of values, norms, and knowledge, which collectively redefine the very foundations of legitimacy and authority in world politics.

Within this framework, this study focuses on the reinterpretation of hegemony's transforming nature in the global system. It examines how diverse actors and international organisations influence systemic dynamics and contribute to the ongoing transformation of global order. In this context, the study brings together valuable insights from distinguished scholars and researchers to reinterpret hegemony through political, historical, theoretical, and economic perspectives, aiming to offer a multidimensional understanding of how hegemony is being reshaped in the 21st century. This volume brings together diverse theoretical and empirical perspectives that collectively illuminate how global power transitions unfold in the current era. From the revival of great power competition to the rise of heterarchic economic networks, from NATO's strategic recalibration to the assertive roles of Russia, China, and Türkiye, the chapters engage with the most critical questions facing international relations today: How is power redistributed? What new institutional and regional configurations are emerging? Moreover, can the world sustain stability without a hegemonic centre?

The book's central argument is that the ongoing transformation is not a mere return to classical multipolarity but the emergence of a hybrid global system in which traditional great-power politics coexist with transnational challenges, normative contestations, and complex interdependence. By revisiting foundational theories while incorporating contemporary empirical analyses—from macroeconomic structures to cultural and linguistic dimensions—the book aims to offer a multidimensional understanding of global systemic change.

Merve Suna Özel Özcan
Kirikkale University, Turkey

REFERENCES

Acharya, A. (2017). After liberal hegemony: The advent of a multipolar world order. *Ethics & International Affairs, 31*(3), 271–285. DOI: 10.1017/S089267941700020X

Bull, H. (1977). *The anarchical society: A study of order in world politics. London: Macmillan. Fukuyama, F. (1992). The End of History and the Last Man.* Free Press.

Gramsci, A. (1971). *Selections from the prison notebooks* (Hoare, Q., & Nowell Smith, G., Eds. & Trans.). International Publishers.

Ikenberry, G. J. (2018). After victory: Institutions, strategic restraint, and the rebuilding of order after major wars (Updated ed.). Princeton: Princeton University Press.

Mearsheimer, J. J. (2001). *The tragedy of great power politics.* W. W. Norton & Company.

Modelski, G. (1987). *Long cycles in world politics.* Macmillan. DOI: 10.1007/978-1-349-09151-5

Özel Özcan, M. S. (2024). *İmparatorluklar.* Orion Yayınları: Ankara.

Toft, P. (2005). John J. Mearsheimer: An offensive realist between geopolitics and power. *Journal of International Relations and Development*, *8*(4), 381–40. DOI: 10.1057/palgrave.jird.1800065

Wallerstein, I. (1974). *The modern world-system I: Capitalist agriculture and the origins of the European world-economy in the sixteenth century.* Academic Press.

Wallerstein, I. (1980). *The modern world-system II: Mercantilism and the consolidation of the European world-economy, 1600–1750.* New York: Academic Press.

Wallerstein, I. (1989). *The modern world-system III: The second era of great expansion of the capitalist world-economy, 1730–1840s.* San Diego, CA: Academic Press.

Waltz, K. N. (1979). *Theory of international politics.* Addison-Wesley.

Chapter 1
Great Power Competition:
Structuring An Analytical Theoretical Framework for Small/Middle Power Security Strategies

Hurşid Dingil
https://orcid.org/0000-0002-0836-0620
Independent Researcher, Turkey

ABSTRACT

The Great Power Rivalry is a strategic reality with implications at both the international and regional levels. The concept of 'Great Power Competition' (GPC), first formally identified in the 2017 US National Security Strategy, aimed to explain great power behaviors in the post-US hegemony period. While existing literature is rich in historical and global impact studies, research focusing on the conceptual and theoretical aspects of rivalry within the context of security strategies remains scarce. This chapter addresses this gap by offering a comprehensive theoretical and analytical framework for GPC. The central problem investigated is: "How does great power rivalry affect the struggles of small and middle powers, especially in the context of security strategies and doctrines?" The Iran-Israel struggle (2017 to 2023) is presented as a key illustrative case study for future analysis, demonstrating the necessity of the proposed theoretical approach.

DOI: 10.4018/979-8-3373-2342-8.ch001

GREAT POWER COMPETITION AND ITS HISTORICAL EVOLUTION

The concept of "Great Power Competition" emerged during the final years of the Obama administration, although its usage at that time was not yet widespread. In 2014, Secretary of Defense Chuck Hagel referred to Russia's assertive tendencies in Europe and China's increasingly aggressive posture in the Asia-Pacific, lamenting that these rising powers were challenging the U.S.-led international order established in the aftermath of the Second World War. Subsequently, until 2015, Deputy Secretary of Defense Robert Work employed the term "Great Power Competition" as a referential expression underscoring the United States' military superiority over its adversaries (Friedman, 2019). In this respect, Work may be considered as one of the first figures to practically integrate the notion of competition into security strategies.

Work himself observed that "during the first term of the Obama administration, the primary focus of this expression was to socialize China as a responsible stakeholder in the international community." According to Work, the term did not initially imply any form of global rivalry. However, toward the end of Obama's tenure, China began to be explicitly identified as a real competitor. As discourses such as "we need to insure ourselves against China's potentially hostile future behavior" surfaced, the concept underwent a significant semantic transformation. Consequently, both the meaning and emphasis of "competition" shifted, signaling an important conceptual evolution (Friedman, 2019).

Indeed, while the concept of "Great Power Competition" appeared in 141 news articles in the Nexis database during George W. Bush's eight-year presidency, it was cited 1,021 times during Obama's two terms, with a marked increase in frequency particularly in his second term. In the first two years of the Trump administration, following the publication of the National Security Strategy (NSS) and the National Defense Strategy (NDS), the concept surged dramatically, appearing in more than 6,500 articles (Friedman, 2019).

The rising frequency of the term reflected broader regional and global developments. Russia's intervention in Crimea and subsequent annexation of the territory, followed by its military and political entrenchment in Syria, significantly contributed to the widespread usage of the term. During this period, the United States maintained only a limited presence in Syria, thereby allowing Russia to exploit the emerging power vacuum and recalibrate its security and foreign policy strategies in order to reassert itself in the Middle East.

Despite considerable international criticism, the de facto acceptance of Russia's aggressive behavior created fertile ground for the proliferation of the "Great Power Competition" discourse. Accordingly, in 2017, the Trump administration formally incorporated the concept into the National Security Strategy for the very first time.

Nadia Schadlow, a senior analyst at the Hudson Institute, noted that the expression "Great Power Competition" had been employed since the drafting of the 2017 NSS (Friedman, 2019). She further highlighted that President Trump did not oppose its usage in strategic briefings, thereby enabling the concept to become central to the administration's strategic vision. Senior National Security Council officials as well as leaders of national security institutions also endorsed it. As Schadlow, who personally briefed the President, recalled: "in my personal experience, Trump did not object to the concept of Great Power Competition" (Friedman, 2019).

From its first official appearance in the 2017 National Security Strategy, the concept came to denote an increasingly competitive global struggle primarily among the United States, China, and Russia (U.S. NSS, 2017). When the document was released, the terminology swiftly gained acceptance in Washington, largely due to its prior circulation. With the subsequent publication of the National Defense Strategy in 2018, and following the defeat of ISIS in Mosul and Raqqa, Secretary of Defense James Mattis explicitly declared that the foremost priority of U.S. national security was no longer terrorism, but "Great Power Competition" (U.S. NDS, 2018).

Moreover, by 2019, Ali Wyne, a senior fellow at the RAND Corporation, argued that "Great Power Competition" had evolved into a key expression reinvigorating and shaping U.S. foreign policy. Both policymakers and academics were encouraged to adopt the term (Friedman, 2019). Its usage intensified further with the escalation of the U.S.–China trade wars beginning in 2018, which entailed reciprocal increases in tariffs as well as restrictions across various economic sectors, particularly in technology and industry. Allegations of intellectual property theft and espionage further deepened U.S. security concerns regarding China. Parallel to the global expansion of the Belt and Road Initiative, American assessments of China's rise adopted increasingly securitized framings. Russia's arms sales and economic engagements in the Middle East similarly exacerbated U.S. regional anxieties. Taken together, these developments firmly elevated "Great Power Competition" to the forefront of the U.S. strategic agenda.

HEGEMONIC STABILITY THEORY AND GREAT POWER COMPETITION

The concepts of hegemony and stability occupy a crucial position in understanding how the era of "Great Power Competition" began. In this regard, it can be argued that a period of stability transformed into one of competition as the balance of power among states deteriorated (Mazarr et al., 2021). The period of hegemonic stability, during which the United States emerged as the sole superpower—particularly in the wake of its victory in the Cold War—gradually gave way to an era of decline, as reflected both in academic debates and in regional as well as global developments (Report to Congress on Great Power Competition, 2021).

According to Robert Keohane, the most distinctive features of hegemonic stability can be observed in the hegemon's monopolistic and dominant control over three critical areas: finance, trade, and oil. Keohane argues that the erosion of U.S. influence in these domains has laid the groundwork for the decline of hegemonic stability (Keohane, 2005). Another defining feature of this period was the tendency of smaller and regional powers to align their policies with those of the hegemon, particularly given U.S. dominance in these three areas. Indeed, during this period, the most common strategy adopted by states was "bandwagoning."

Bandwagoning refers to a strategy in which smaller and middle powers, lacking sufficient material capacities, align themselves with the hegemon rather than pursuing autonomous policies. The widespread adoption of this strategy by middle and small powers reduced conflicts and disputes within the international system. In this sense, the hegemon's coercive dominance functioned as a stabilizing force that curtailed instability both regionally and globally. Accordingly, the concept of "Great Power Competition" emerged precisely at the juncture where hegemonic stability began to erode, shaping debates on the evolving international order.

One strand of these debates revolves around the post-hegemonic period. Scholars have critically examined the structure of the international system after hegemony, with particular attention to the behavior of rising powers, the roles of smaller actors, and the strategies of states that lose hegemonic status. Within these debates, Robert Keohane (2005) suggested that the erosion of hegemonic stability would lead to a state of anarchy and chaos. Under such conditions, however, states might still prefer cooperation over conflict, primarily because the costs of conflict in an anarchic environment would be unsustainable. Thus, the driving force behind cooperation would be the unsustainability of conflict-related costs.

Another key question in the literature concerns *how* hegemonic stability is lost. Consequently, scholarly attention has focused on how and why the United States, once the quintessential hegemon, has entered a post-hegemonic phase. Some scholars have explained this decline in terms of sociological and domestic factors (Norrlöf, 2021), whereas others—most notably Robert Gilpin and Robert Keohane—have attributed it to relative decreases in material capabilities. For instance, Norrlöf argues that America's hegemonic decline stemmed from internal social and political fractures, which eroded social cohesion and tolerance, thereby weakening the state's hegemonic role.

Alternatively, Graham Allison associated the loss of hegemonic power with the concept of the Thucydides Trap, examining historical instances in which parity of capabilities between rising powers and established hegemons led to heightened risks of military, political, and economic conflict. His assessment particularly emphasized the growing potential for conflict between the United States and China (Allison, 2017). Meanwhile, Gilpin argued that hegemonic stability is inherently linked to the hegemon's superiority in material capabilities (Webb & Krasner, 1989).

From this perspective, military and economic capacities constitute the fundamental foundations of hegemonic power. Should a hegemon experience relative decline in these areas, it creates opportunities for rising powers to pursue hegemonic aspirations, thereby fostering a competitive international environment. As a result, intensifying rivalry emerges between the declining hegemon (the United States) and rising contenders such as China and Russia. Ultimately, the absence of a clear hegemon has fueled aspirations among great powers to assume leadership, producing the conditions of global competition witnessed today.

In sum, Hegemonic Stability Theory posits that the existence of a single dominant power with superior material capacities (military and economic) ensures stability in the international system. Moreover, the hegemon is assumed to play a stabilizing role globally. However, the theory provides no adequate answer to the question of how stability can be sustained in the absence of a hegemon. Consequently, the theory fails to sufficiently explain the current international context, marked by intensifying rivalries among the United States, China, and Russia. This inadequacy has led scholars to question the continuing relevance of Hegemonic Stability Theory. In this respect, the present study engages critically with the theory, arguing instead that the concept of "Great Power Competition" offers a more compelling framework for analyzing the contemporary international environment, in which no single hegemon exists and competitive dynamics among major powers have intensified.

HEDGING THEORY IN THE CONTEXT OF GREAT POWER COMPETITION

Since its formal incorporation into the U.S. National Security Strategy documents in 2017, the concept of Great Power Competition has reshaped the international system, simultaneously exerting significant influence over sub-regional dynamics. Smaller and middle powers within these sub-regional systems (for example, Iran and Israel) have increasingly felt the repercussions of this competitive environment. The effects of a rivalry-driven international system became more visible at the sub-regional level, compelling middle and small powers to recalibrate their security strategies in line with competitive global conditions (El-Dessouki & Mansour, 2020). Accordingly, these actors began adopting hedging strategies to address their short- and medium-term security concerns (El-Dessouki & Mansour, 2020).

In essence, such behavior can be understood as protective measures undertaken by smaller and middle powers against the uncertainties inherent in a competitive international order. Within the Great Power Competition, hedging has emerged as a strategic tool through which these states seek to minimize risks and threats in order to preserve national survival. Indeed, in this period, hedging strategies reflected risk-averse tendencies designed to safeguard national security (Telci & Rakipoğlu, 2021). The increasing prevalence of cross-cutting relationships between middle and small powers and great powers—for instance, Israel's simultaneous engagements with both the United States and China, or Iran's interactions with China and Russia between 2017 and 2023—provides clear examples of such strategies (Chaziza, 2022). These patterns of behavior are analyzed in detail through case studies in the third and fourth chapters of this study.

Through such policies, middle and small powers constructed compartmentalized bilateral relationships with great powers, in which issues were separated and pursued on distinct tracks (Chaziza, 2022). Consequently, their national security strategies came to be based on dualities and cross-relationships, often shaped by hedging dynamics (Kuik, 2021). Understanding this logic of hedging facilitates an examination of the central research question of this study: how Great Power Competition affects the security dimension of the Iran–Israel rivalry. As both Iran and Israel can be categorized as middle and small powers within their respective subregional systems, their compartmentalized and cross-cutting ties with great powers illustrate how hedging strategies are operationalized in practice.

Hedging has thus been employed in this study as a theoretical lens to strengthen its conceptual foundations. The term originates in finance, where it denotes the simultaneous pursuit of contradictory strategies aimed at protecting economic assets (Hemmings, 2013). Within economics, hedging is particularly associated with actors seeking to secure their gains in uncertain environments by employing methods that mitigate potential risks (Kuik, 2021).

The concept has also been explained through metaphors. As emphasized in Yalçın's *National Security Strategies* (2017) and Kurt's *National Security Strategies in the Middle East* (2018), the most well-known saying associated with hedging is "not putting all eggs in one basket." In this metaphor, the baskets symbolize investment areas while the eggs represent assets and gains. By distributing eggs across multiple baskets, an actor minimizes the risk of total loss should one basket fall. Conversely, placing all eggs in a single basket renders the actor vulnerable to losing everything under adverse circumstances. This metaphor captures the essence of hedging: safeguarding at least part of one's gains under unfavorable conditions.

Thus, hedging requires actors to calculate and anticipate future uncertainties. As Salman and Geeraerts (2013) demonstrated in their study on China's energy security in the Middle East, hedging entails probabilistic assessments of how to maximize future returns while simultaneously insuring against potential losses. Because future conditions are inherently uncertain and unpredictable, the only known imperative for the actor is to protect its assets. In this sense, hedging reflects a preventive behavioral model, whereby actors adopt preemptive measures to limit risks and threats before they materialize (Dingil & Güven, 2021).

The ultimate goal of hedging, therefore, is to preserve gains under all circumstances. However, the pursuit of this goal involves adopting seemingly contradictory strategies, which together serve the common objective of protection. This dual-track logic represents the defining feature of the hedging model (Wang & Tan, 2021). Although the strategies employed may appear antithetical, they converge upon the same purpose: securing the actor's survival and interests amid uncertainty. The transposition of this concept from economics to international relations thus provided a framework for explaining state behavior under conditions of risk and unpredictability.

In international relations, the hedging model has been applied primarily to understand how states address foreign policy and security concerns in uncertain environments. It has been particularly useful in explaining how states attempt to safeguard their interests in high-risk contexts. Consequently, two features stand out: first, the centrality of preventing risks and threats; and second, the incorporation of context-specific conditions into the actor's calculations (Wang & Tan, 2021). For the model to be applicable in international relations, therefore, the prior condition is the existence of a state confronted with substantial risks.

Although debates in the literature remain divided over the precise definition and scope of hedging (Yue, 2021), the concept has gradually expanded beyond its original application to great powers. Given the erosion of hegemonic structures and the transformation of the global order, hedging now also provides a useful lens for analyzing the behavior of middle and small powers (Kuik, 2021). Mordechai Chaziza (2015), for instance, argued in his analysis of China–Saudi Arabia relations that hedging strategies are employed by states of all scales, from superpowers to small states. Similarly, in his study of Israel–China relations, Chaziza (2017) described Israel's limited engagement with China, despite its close ties with the United States, as an instance of "limited strategic hedging."

The erosion of the unipolar system and the subsequent emergence of multiple great powers seeking hegemonic status have led to radical changes in the strategies of small and middle powers. This process resonates with Zakaria's (2011) notion of the "rise of the rest," illustrating how shifts in the global distribution of power compel smaller states to adopt more complex and flexible strategies. The Iran–Israel rivalry, as analyzed in this dissertation, provides a clear case through which to explore how small and middle powers adapt to these structural transformations by employing hedging strategies within a competitive environment.

At the same time, this raises the question of *why* smaller and middle powers resort to such strategies. In competitive conditions where multiple great powers (e.g., the United States, China, and Russia) simultaneously aspire to hegemonic status, smaller states must incorporate the behavior and positioning of all these powers into their security calculations. The detailed case studies in the third and fourth chapters of this study address this issue empirically.

Although hedging was originally applied in non-competitive contexts, evolving global dynamics have demonstrated its utility in explaining behavior within highly competitive environments. Accordingly, this study employs hedging theory as an analytical framework for understanding how Iran and Israel, as middle and small powers, have navigated their security relations with great powers (the United States, China, and Russia) during the era of Great Power Competition.

CONCLUSION

This study affirmed Great Power Competition (GPC), formalized in the 2017 U.S. National Security Strategy, as the dominant strategic reality rooted in the post-Cold War order's erosion. This necessitated moving away from Hegemonic Stability Theory (HST), invalidated by the U.S. decline and intensified rivalry among China and Russia. The uncertain environment compels small and middle powers to fundamentally recalibrate its national security strategies. The central finding is that Hedging Theory—defined by simultaneous, seemingly contradictory strategies ("not putting all eggs in one basket")—is the most relevant framework.

Hedging serves as a strategic imperative, not a mere choice, allowing these actors to establish compartmentalized bilateral relationships with multiple great powers. This dual-track logic enables them to maximize potential gains while insuring against future threats, thereby safeguarding their national interests and survival amid the complexities of GPC.

REFERENCES

Allison, G. (2017). *Destined for war: Can America and China escape Thucydides's trap?* Houghton Mifflin Harcourt.

Chaziza, M. (2015). Strategic hedging partnership: A new framework for analyzing Sino–Saudi relations. *Israel Journal of Foreign Affairs*, *9*(3), 3–15. DOI: 10.1080/23739770.2015.1120017

Chaziza, M. (2017). Israel–China relations enter a new stage: Limited strategic hedging. *Contemporary Review of the Middle East*, *5*(1), 30–45. DOI: 10.1177/2347798917744293

Chaziza, M. (2022). Israel-China relations in an era of strategic rivalry and great power competition. A Multidisciplinary Journal on National Security, 24, 1–21.

Dingil, H., & Güven, A. (2021). ABD-Çin mücadelesi üzerine bir çözümleyici bağlam analizi örneği: Hindistan stratejik bir araç olabilir mi? *Afyon Kocatepe Üniversitesi Sosyal Bilimler Dergisi*, *23*(1), 290–302. DOI: 10.32709/akusosbil.827171

El-Dessouki, A., & Mansour, O. R. (2020). Small states and strategic hedging: The United Arab Emirates' policy towards Iran. *Review of Economic and Political Science*, *8*(5), 394–407. DOI: 10.1108/REPS-09-2019-0124

Friedman, U. (2019, Ağustos 7). The new concept everyone in Washington is talking about. The Atlantic. https://www.theatlantic.com/politics/archive/2019/08/what-genesis-great-power-competition/595405/

Hemmings, J. (2013, Mayıs 16). Hedging: The real U.S. policy towards China? The Diplomat. https://thediplomat.com/2013/05/hedging-the-real-u-s-policy-towards-china/

Keohane, R. O. (2005). *After hegemony: Cooperation and discord in the world political economy*. Princeton University Press. DOI: 10.2307/j.ctt7sq9s

Kuik, C. (2021). Getting hedging right: A small-state perspective. *China International Strategy Review*, *3*(2), 300–315. DOI: 10.1007/s42533-021-00089-5

Kurt, V. (2018). *Ortadoğuda Ulusal Güvenlik Stratejileri*. Seta Yayınları.

Mazarr, M. J., Charap, S., Casey, A., Chindea, I. A., Curriden, C., Demus, A., Frederick, B., Chan, A., Godges, J. P., Han, E., Heath, T. R., Ma, L., Treyger, E., Ulin, T., & Wyne, A. (2021). Stabilizing great-power rivalries. RAND Corporation. https://www.rand.org/pubs/research_reports/RRA456-1.html

Norrlöf, C. (2021). The Ibn Khaldûn trap and great power competition with China. *The Washington Quarterly*, *44*(1), 7–28. DOI: 10.1080/0163660X.2021.1893022

Report to Congress on Great Power Competition. (2021, Ekim 8). USNI News. https://news.usni.org/2021/10/08/report-to-congress-on-great-power-competition

Salman, M., & Geeraters, G. (2013, Eylül 25-27). The impact of strategic hedging on the foreign politics of great powers: The case of Chinese energy strategy in the Middle East [Konferans sunumu]. China Goes Global 2013, Bremen, Almanya.

Telci, İ. N., & Rakipoglu, M. (2021). Hedging as a survival strategy for small states: The case of Kuwait. All Azimuth: A Journal of Foreign Policy and Peace, 10(2), 213–229.

United States NDS. (2018). *Summary of the 2018 national defense strategy of the United States of America: Sharpening the American military's competitive edge*. Department of Defense.

United States NSS. (2017). *The national security strategy of the United States of America*. The White House.

Wang, T., & Tan, A. C. (2021). Balancing, bandwagoning or hedging: Taiwan's strategic choices in the era of a rising China. *Political Science (Wellington, N.Z.)*, *73*(1), 66–84. DOI: 10.1080/00323187.2021.1967765

Webb, M. C., & Krasner, S. D. (1989). Hegemonic stability theory: An empirical assessment. *Review of International Studies*, *15*(2), 183–198. DOI: 10.1017/S0260210500112999

Yalçın, H. B. (2017). *Ulusal Güvenlik Stratejisi: ABD-İngiltere-Fransa-Rusya-Çin*. Seta Yayınları.

Yue, W. (2021). Hedging in international relations and its implications for China. *Journal of China Studies*, *24*(2), 1–23. DOI: 10.20288/JCS.2021.24.2.1

Zakaria, F. (2011). *The post-American world: And the rise of the rest*. Penguin Books.

KEY TERMS AND DEFINITIONS

Bandwagoning: A foreign policy strategy wherein smaller and middle powers, lacking sufficient material capacity, align themselves with the policies and interests of the dominant power or hegemon rather than balancing against it. This strategy was common during the period of U.S. unipolarity.

Compartmentalized Bilateral Relationships: A feature of the hedging strategy where a middle or small power separates its relationships with great powers into distinct issue tracks (e.g., cooperating with China on trade but with the U.S. on security), thereby managing the risks associated with the GPC environment.

Great Power Competition (GPC): A strategic concept officially introduced in the 2017 U.S. National Security Strategy to describe the growing global rivalry, primarily among the United States, China, and Russia, challenging the post-Cold War U.S.-led international order. It denotes a systemic struggle for influence and dominance.

Hedging Strategy: A risk-averse security strategy employed by states, particularly small and middle powers, in uncertain or competitive international environments (like GPC). It involves the simultaneous pursuit of seemingly contradictory strategies (e.g., maintaining close ties with a hegemon while engaging with a rival) to minimize risks and ensure national survival and asset protection.

Hegemonic Stability Theory (HST): An international relations theory positing that the existence of a single, dominant power (hegemon) with superior material capabilities (military, economic, and control over finance/trade/oil) is necessary to ensure stability and reduce conflict in the international system.

Post-Hegemonic Period: The era following the relative decline of a dominant power (the United States), characterized by the erosion of hegemonic stability and the intensification of rivalry among rising and established powers.

Chapter 2
The Forces of Conflicts in the Twenty-First Century: States or Individuals

Yusuf Abubakar Wara
https://orcid.org/0000-0003-3410-6113
Kastamonu University, Turkey

ABSTRACT

The realist thinkers have posed the state as a strategic actor or force in determining who gets what, when, and how. This classification of the state as a vital actor in global politics indicates the relevance of states in maintaining peace and order in regional and universal affairs. However, it also pinpoints that the state should bear the lion's share of blame for disastrous activities worldwide. The prime question for this chapter is, in the contemporary global village, is the state still a strategic actor that could be majorly responsible for international affairs? We assume that other factors, such as individuals and groups of individuals, can be more effective than the states in most current global issues especially conflicts.

INTRODUCTION

The realist thinkers have posed the state as a strategic actor or force in determining who gets what, when, and how. This classification of the state as a vital actor in global politics indicates the relevance of states in maintaining peace and order in regional and universal affairs. However, it also pinpoints that the state should bear the lion's share of blame for disastrous activities worldwide. The prime question for this chapter is, in the contemporary global village, is the state still a strategic actor that could be majorly responsible for international affairs? We assume that other

DOI: 10.4018/979-8-3373-2342-8.ch002

factors, such as individuals and groups of individuals, can be more effective than the states in most current global issues especially conflicts.

Conflicts have been rampant since the beginning of human history. In other words, conflicts have always existed in all the world's nations and at every level of society throughout history (Lomia, 2020: 927). The struggle for survival, territories, resources, and rights have always been the basic reasons for empires, states, kingdoms, and villages to go against each other fiercely. In ancient times, empires and kingdoms representing modern nation-states had always been the center of affairs in conflict or peace processes. After the treaty of Westphalia, nation-states began to replace empires' relevance as the principle of Westphalian sovereignty led to a significant rise in the importance of states in the global arena (Mack, 2025).

In the 21st century, however, states' traditional relevance and influence in international politics are mitigating, which led to the emergence of non-state actors such as civil societies, multinational corporations, and individuals to take center stage. Through grassroots movements, social media channels, and even violent extremism, these non-state actors surpass the state in shaping a series of global affairs in several aspects. Several of these examples can be listed as the relevance of scientists in global health and climate issues; business moguls determining international negotiations; and terrorists affecting international security policies compelling states to act in a manner that they would otherwise not have done (Arts, 2003: 1-3).

This paper explains why individual-centric, compared to weak and failing governments with strong-armed organizations, define the leading causes of conflicts that determine most international affairs in the twenty-first century. These emerging global players uses erratic strategies to influence stability, changing the emphasis from conventional state-centric paradigms to complicated and multifarious confrontations. Just like the states, individuals are now engaging in different global interactions- legally and even otherwise. Several groups of individuals are shaping the international environment through several means, such as engaging in grassroots movements, social media channels, and even becoming members of extremist associations.

CONFLICT

Several ideas have been put forward in an attempt to define Conflict's meaning. It is often defined by opposing values, interests, or goals. It is defined as a condition of disagreement or confrontation. It can show up as political, social, financial, or personal conflicts and develop locally and worldwide. From the world wars to modern civil wars, conflicts have defined world history. Knowing historical trends helps one see how past grievances and power struggles still affect present conflicts, especially territorial disputes and ideological differences. This is a significant reason for analyzing conflicts and crises worldwide.

Notwithstanding the lack of a general definition of Conflict, different researchers define it based on their viewpoints. It is defined, for example, by an analyst as processes occurring inside a group in several forms, including hostility, reduced communications, mistrust, sabotage, verbal abuse, and coercive tactics. From a different perspective, a scholar sees Conflict as discord occurring within an organization, between communities and individuals from varying ideas, beliefs, or feelings (Kelly, 2006: 22-23).

This inseparable part of humanity can be classified into four different types: intrapersonal Conflict, which is known as the conflict we fight inside ourselves, usually centers on the uncertainty of making a decision or several decisions, which may have several barriers and factors of attractiveness and unattractiveness. Usually, it involves only the concerned individual (Silverman, 2020: 19-22); interpersonal conflict describes any conflict involving two or more people. It is not like an intrapersonal conflict—an inner struggle with yourself; intra-group conflict results and grows mainly from intellectual differences among group members. Furthermore, this kind of Conflict is based on the emotional responses of group members to a circumstance; and intergroup conflict which develops between groups, formal or informal. These are conflicts between different groups depending on one another in an activity whereby discontent is voiced and opposition results (Zlatkova, 2023: 256-258).

Regarding the causes of conflicts in the international system, distribution, and access to resources remain prime factors that create discord between states, groups, and individuals. Four vital areas need to be scrutinized to highlight the causal factors regarding conflict. Inequality is a major causal factor of conflict in most underdeveloped societies. For example, nations with extreme economic, political, and social inequalities—Afghanistan, Nigeria, Togo, Sudan, and Central African Republic—witness more violent conflict than those with less series of inequalities. In other words, disparities between groups defined by religion, ethnicity, or regional identities have been linked to a relatively higher risk of armed conflict (Nygård, 2018).

Identifying factors that entail possessing ethnic, ideological, or religious identities is also a major cause of conflicts in states, regions, and the global arena. The existence of different identities such as ethnic identity, race identity, religious identity, sexual orientation identity, ability identity, gender identity, and socioeconomic status identity in a common society often leads to conflicts as each group of identity competes with the others in resource allocation and power sharing. Within this competition emerges the fear of losing political cum economic status from one to the other, which results in tensions and conflicts in a given community (Bahouli, 2023: 440-450).

The political factor hinges on the weaknesses of states' institutions, and crises in states' legitimacy are a vital facet of conflicts in the international atmosphere. It is a public display of opposition, or conflict, between two or more social groups. Political conflict is usually differentiated from social conflicts that only involve individuals in social settings (Marshall, 2005, p. 89).

The economic factor, the fourth and essential component of conflict, arises due to the unequal distribution of scarce resources. Several underdeveloped countries are battling with numerous conflicts and crises despite their abundant natural resources because these resources are not equitably distributed (Dar, 2011: 73). The extreme desire to accumulate capital by human beings has been a significant cause of disputes and wars between states, group of individuals and among different sections of societies. This is buttressed by the slogan attributed to Socrates and George Orwell: “All wars are fought for money” (Schneider, 2010: 284). Much literature has justified the relevance of 'money' in wars and conflicts, proving that even wars for independence were triggered by economically disadvantaged societies.

The occurrences of incessant pockets of conflicts in the history of humanity led him to design an effective strategy for resolving them. Conflict resolution, which entails the application of techniques to restrict the negative features of conflicts and boost the positive ones at a level equal to or higher where the conflict is in progress (Umana, 2019: 661), is adopted to mitigate the effect of conflict or even proffer solutions to an existing crisis. The most adopted conflict resolution strategies include negotiation, mediation, conciliation, and arbitration.

Negotiation occurs when an individual, group of individuals, regions, or states cannot achieve their goals single-handedly without the help of others (Thompson, Wang, & Gunia, 2010: 493). It is an appealing and engaging approach encompassing multiparty, multi-company, multinational, and international engagements aiming to achieve a specific objective collectively. In peacebuilding, negotiation is the process of ending disputes and disagreements that would be mutually acceptable.

Mediation, which is triadic in structure, is a technique of conflict resolution defined as any action taken by an actor not a direct party to the crisis, intended to reduce or eliminate one or more of the problems of the bargaining relationship and so help to enable the termination of the crisis itself (Bercovitch & Jackson, 2009: 33). Mediation is different from negotiation in that a third party must do it—that is, it occurs when a third party resolves a conflict or offers a suitable settlement. Conversely, negotiation is the process by which the involved parties reach an agreement or concession on which both sides approve.

In conciliation, which is more formal than mediation in conflict resolution, the conciliators have the authority to issue formal orders on the decision taken or agreed upon. Moreover, conciliation differs from mediation in that the third party-conciliator has the right to submit recommendations to all that have a stake in the issues (Valenzuela Rendón, 2017: 168). Conciliation is a negotiation of conflict done through a guide of an impartial third party(s) that can be a reconciliatory or a conciliatory commission.

Arbitration generally refers to a method of dispute resolution between two parties by a decision rendered by a third party to either natural or legal persons (Vlahna, Krasniqi, Krasniqi, & Vlahna, 2020: 160). Article 37 of 1907 of the Hague Convention for the peaceful settlement of international disputes defines arbitration as aims to resolve disputes between states by judges of their own choice and based on respect for international law (Bercovitch & Jackson, 2020: 98).

GLOBAL ACTORS OF CONFLICT

Several actors have engineered crises in the international environment due to numerous factors, including competition over scarce resources, ideological differences, political competition, and ethnic and religious factors. These actors act fiercely against each other to outpower one another in achieving common goals. Traditionally, the state has been the most prevailing actor in whatever perspective in global politics. However, other actors, such as individuals, have become relevant and vital in global affairs in the twenty-first century.

State as a Primary Actor in Global Conflicts

The institutional capacity of states determines their ability to manage conflicts and, according to realists, maintain their status and relevance in global politics (Douma, 2003: 12). As a pillar of the international system, state sovereignty shapes perceptions of and solutions for conflicts. Even in humanitarian crises, states claiming sovereignty might object to outside intervention. Strategic interests between countries sometimes cause geopolitical tensions, from which disputes over territory and resources follow. Two examples are the conflicts in the South China Sea and growing Eastern European tensions (Frans-Paul, 2017), where the United States, China, and other Pacific Countries are tackling each other to achieve their common goals.

A state, an entity with military might, is always susceptible to conflicts, considering the continuous discord over resources, territory, or ideologies. The struggle for geopolitical and global power to maintain or increase status also led to disagreements and confrontations among states in an international environment. While Russia is battling Ukraine to reduce Western influence in the region, the United States of America is threating trade wars against China to gain certain global economic advantages. States thus often get involved in both internal and external conflicts.

During the war, they directly participate in military operations or employ diplomatic channels to forward shared objectives (Dennana, 2024).

Individual as Emerging Actor in Global Conflicts

Determining the individual as a primary actor in international conflicts hinges on the general notions of human rights and ethnonational identities. Individual-centric drivers challenge the state in many ramifications by emphasizing the importance of individual rights and humanitarian concerns (Lovane, 2018: 205-207). Individual groups, including civil societies and pressure groups, challenge authoritarian regimes, especially those that violate human rights and are corrupt. In doing this advocacy, the state tries to intervene, often leading to societal conflict. The agent of state tends to counter the actions of pressure and activist individuals mostly by interfering with their advocacy roles that they perceive as detrimental to their whims and caprices. On the other hand, these individuals resist the temptation of the states by organizing demonstrations and protests that usually lead to clashes and skirmishes between the state's security personnel and members of the general public.

In the modern era, people have positioned themselves in the echelon of conflict that emphasizes the need for individual responsibility in both creating and stopping violence, implying that personal actions can have more general consequences for international law and humanitarian endeavors (Welsh, Akande, & David, 2023: 1-6). Recent confrontations show how state and personal factors interact. For example, the Arab Spring brought about notable sociopolitical changes around the region using broad individual activism challenging established state powers.

Civil Action and Conflict Dynamics

Individuals, just like states, do not only create conflicts. They also assist in managing conflict created by them or other actors in a global environment. As case studies from Syria and Colombia show, civil action has either delayed or stopped escalations, and community groups and NGOs are vital in reducing violence during conflicts (Avant, 2019: 3-6). Peace advocacy civil societies in conflict-stricken societies are always at the forefront of adopting conflict resolution strategies to ensure a peaceful, harmonious, coexisting society.

The world has witnessed famous, talented peacekeepers who are highly talented in conflict management due to their productive capacity, expertise, and knowledge in resolving conflicts. Among these peace-promoting individuals the world has come across is Nelson Mandela, who applied tactics, patience, perseverance, pragmatism, empathy, and emotional intelligence to end the racial segregation in South Africa, becoming a master of negotiators whose legacies continue to inspire both states and individuals conflict resolutions experts around the world (Adristanbul, 2024).

The 26th President of the United States, Theodore Roosevelt, was another tactful negotiator who, besides ending the disastrous coal strike in Pennsylvania in 1902, was able to resolve the Russo-Japanese War, which earned him the Nobel Peace Prize in 1906 (Borkowski, 2023). He was known for his peaceful conflict resolution strategies through skillful diplomacy, which earned him respect and made him worthy of emulation in the contemporary world.

Henry Kissinger is another important diplomat whose conflict resolution strategy and peaceful negotiation techniques have left an indelible mark on the earth's surface. He was well known for practical discussions during the Cold War and the peace talks in Vietnam. He has also been accoladed for his role in the Paris Peace Accords, which earned him the 1973 Nobel Peace Prize (Sebenius, Mnookin, & Burns, 2018: 1-10).

Madeleine Albright, the first female U.S. secretary of state, was the epitome of virtue and an exemplary example of how effectively an individual could manage conflict in the international arena. She has shown great diplomatic talent and exceptional negotiation skills in ensuring peace during the Kosovo War (Overvest, 2025). Albright led several complex negotiations, including campaigns to admit Central European countries to the North Atlantic Treaty Organization (NATO) and to respond militarily to the 1999 Kosovo crisis. Her diplomatic skills and tough but sympathetic negotiating style are praised.

A Major in Global Conflict: State or Individual

Considering the contemporary shifts in global affairs where modern technologies, especially with the introduction of artificial intelligence, other actors rather than the state have begun to take center stage in most cases better than what most states can do. The distinction between states and individuals regarding power prowess in international affairs has become a critical topic for discussion in the modern era. While states can still capitalize on their military capabilities, individuals are banking on the power of modern gadgets and digitalization to challenge states and their apparatus in many aspects. Often working via military and diplomatic channels, state authorities enforce laws and sovereignty. On the other hand, grassroots movements and digital platforms allow individual forces—such as activists and organizations—to influence change by often confronting state authority.

In modern days, the advancement of technology coupled with the increasing relevance of artificial intelligence has been helping to empower private individuals in many ramifications around the world, individual through grassroots movements, social media channels, and extremism that includes but is not limited to radical rights, religious and ethnic extremists and terrorists are shaking the affairs of the global village beyond what most states can control in several regions on the surface of the earth.

In conflict dynamics, grassroots movements have become essential and sometimes result in significant political changes. Notable instances of how group individual action might inspire state response and change societal standards are the Civil Rights Movement in the United States and the Arab Spring. A grassroots movement bases its political or continental movement on the people living in a particular district, region, or community. To bring about local, regional, national, or worldwide change, grassroots movements and organizations mobilize volunteers locally. Grassroots movements have become relevant in the past two decades to ensure a just world order that could not be obtained and maintained by the traditional power of the states (Batliwala, 2002: 393).

Grassroots activists have accentuated a series of global protests in the past few years, even in some developed countries, and have indicated the relevancy of individuals in conflict over states in the contemporary global village. These citizen's movements in industrialized countries and the global south, driven by several unfavorable factors, are now defining the characteristics of global politics more than any other actor, including states. Public anger has led to numerous protests in several countries in the past three years, including China, the Democratic Republic of Congo, Denmark, Iraq, Norway, Nigeria, Sudan, Myanmar, Kenya, Pakistan, Bangladesh, and even in France, the United Kingdom and the United States where cost of living protests ensued (Velpillay, 2025).

Several factors and reasons are said to be responsible for these grassroots activism or social movements that have led to clashes between state security agents and private individuals or groups of individuals. In developing countries like Nigeria, masses fill the streets to protest against the high cost of living, often leading to violent clashes between protesters and police officials (Aljazeera, 2024). In 2020, Nigeria was slopped into violent protests against police brutality, extrajudicial killing, and ill-treatment against humanity that later turned brutal, leading to several loss of lives and the destruction of numerous properties.

In modern conflicts, social media channels are essential tools for mobilization since they let people share knowledge and plan appropriately. Movements like #MeToo show how digital environments might magnify voices and change public opinion. The movement, founded in 2006 by Tarana Burke, aims to support sexual harassment survivors worldwide; it has been capitalizing on social media channels to ensure massive campaigns across borders. #MeToo and its associate campaigns around the world, such as # in China, #Sex4Grades in Kenya, and uykularınkacsın in Türkiye are seen as typical examples where individual challenges a specific trauma in the society better than the state (Burke, 2025).

Individuals or groups are now benefiting from social media- Facebook, X, TikTok, and several others to facilitate protest activities, which states may find difficult to undermine and control. Around the world, activists organize demonstrations against certain wrongdoings or unwanted policies by mobilizing their members on social media meeting points, medical and food services distribution, actions to be taken, and warnings against police action. Social media are the channels where protest organizers trigger protests and conflict by exchanging motivational information, emphasizing anger, bad government policies, and concerns about justice, corruption, maltreatment, and societal brutality (Jost et al., 2018: 85-6).

Conflicts organized by individuals or civil activists generally begin with social media campaigns with hashtags shared to reach larger societies. Protests with hashtags #OWS in 2011 in the United States, #EndSARS in 2020 in Nigeria, #Jan25 in 2011 in Egypt, #direngeziparkı in 2013 in Turkiye, #Euromaidan in 2013 in Ukraine pinpoint the relevance of social media and power of the individual in organizing protests and conflicts to iron out specific issues around the world (Kara, 2013). The world has witnessed a series of protests and demonstrations that are mobilized through several social media channels, becoming so intense that most of them influence government decisions, indicating the relevance of individuals in conflict organization rather than state action in a given state or region.

Individuals can organize protests and conflicts to register their discord with the constituted authority, even through illegitimate means. People are turning to terrorism and extremism more and more as means of expression of disagreement or ideological pursuit. The emergence of lone-wolf attacks challenges state authorities and increases public fear by highlighting how one person's actions might have more general consequences. This illegal means of countering existing establishments is seen as a significant way of justifying that individuals rather than states play a crucial role in causing and managing conflict.

In recent times, the world has witnessed the emergence and wanton activities of several terrorist groups and organizations, dwindling the developmental efforts of states and international organizations that are aiming to fight poverty, uplift the standard of living, standardized education, and improve the health and well-being of the general public. For instance, al-Shabab has been carrying out several attacks to undermine its rival - “The Islamic State in Somalia” (ISS), as well as carrying out offensive attacks in Kenya, all of which contribute to the chronic insecurity and the rise of the level of conflicts in the two countries' societies (Birhane, 2025). The military operations to retake Mosul and the surrounding areas from the armed group claiming to be Islamic State (IS) are another instance of individual groups inciting conflicts rather than the state, putting civilians in danger as they are caught in the crossfire or, in certain situations, are being used as human shields by IS fighters (Wedel, 2025).

Today, we have witnessed the rampant growth and attack of terrorist individuals and groups around the world, especially in fragile economies. Such individuals and groups even take over certain territories and enact their prescribed rules and regulations, replacing states' orders and presence in the regions. For example, Al-Qaeda in Iraq (AQI) increased its visibility in provinces such as al-Anbar, Ninawa, Diyala, and Salah ad-Din. It even gained control over some towns. For instance, starting in 2012, the organization exerted substantial control over As-Sa'diyah, northeast of Baghdad in Diyala province. This resulted in Baghdad losing control over key areas of al-Anbar province in 2014 (Kaválek, 2015: 12), indicating the effectiveness of individuals and their groups in conflict creation compared to inter and intra-state struggles.

Islamic State of Iraq and the Levant (ISIS) is also another stronger organization that has been waging its tail and tentacles controlling vast territory inhabited by over five million people in Syria and Iraq. This is similar to status once Boko Haram reached in Nigeria, where it occupied and controlled a large territory almost the size of Belgium. The organization has been attacking Nigeria and its neighbors- Niger, Chad, and Cameroon. The group proclaimed an "Islamic caliphate" in parts of the northeastern Nigerian states of Adamawa, Borno, and Yobe in the middle of 2014 (Ajakaye, 2014).

The above and several other examples of terrorists and extremists that include Islamophobic and xenophobic influences around the world have testified to the relevance of individuals in conflicts in the contemporary global village.

CONCLUSION

Based on realists' perspectives, states are the primary instruments in determining the major affairs in an international environment. However, the emerging influence of non-state actors, especially determined individuals, raises many questions on whether the states are still the most relevant organ in global politics. Undoubtedly, states and people shape global affairs through conflict creation or conflict management in the twenty-first century. However, the area of contrast has been the conventional function of state sovereignty, growing personal activism, and the powerful character of social media that changes the dynamics of conflicts in global environment.

The state has been at the forefront of global affairs owing to its inevitable connection with conflict in sharing scarce resources, differences in ideologies, and the struggle for global control. From the World War era to the Cold War period, states had been the major agents of conflicts in global affairs and, by implication, determining what should be done in region, continent, or global environment. Nevertheless, with the fading of the Cold War and the emergence of strong individual-legitimate or otherwise, the power and influence of states began to dwindle and be replaced by the influence of such individuals.

Individuals and groups now influence most state and international actions in regions or worldwide. Policy-making procedures are now much influenced by the interactions between state actions and personal movements. Climate change shows that activity influencing global agreements and successful grassroots movements can force states to implement new policies. Legitimate strong individuals or groups of individuals such as human rights activists, pressure groups advocating for a greener environment, campaigning against global warming, and calling for a just world order are challenging undemocratic states in several parts of the world-justifying the relevance of individual rather than just the state in global affairs.

Besides legitimate influential individuals, illegitimate individuals such as extremist terrorists' individuals and groups are also magnificent in shaping global affairs, in most cases, far more than the states. These individuals challenge states in many ramifications, even making states redirect their approach, change their policies, and act in a way they would otherwise not have done. Several terrorist individuals and groups, especially after the Cold War, have been causing conflict that compels states and international organizations to respond from several perspectives. Al-Qaida, AL Shabab, Boko Haram, ISIS, and several terrorist groups have been challenging states' orders to the extent that they even occupy some parts of some states' territories where they impose their rugged rules, whims, and caprices. They make the states' power obsolete, showcasing their prowess better than government in such occupied regions.

Legal and illegal individuals, through actions and inactions, define the nature of the contemporary international system, which is even making the states redesign their policies. While legal individuals and groups challenge the corrupt system through advocacy, illegal individuals and groups, such as terrorists, create unnecessary conflicts in society, compelling the government to modify its mode of operandi. Future conflicts will probably show a more complex interaction between state and personal players. Practical understanding and resolution of upcoming conflicts depend on a multidisciplinary approach combining political science, sociology, and technology. In whatever case, individuals and groups will continue to play a significant role in shaping the international system, and in some cases, more effectively than in most states.

REFERENCES

Adristanbul (2024). *Nelson Mandela: Lessons from a Master Negotiator*. adristanbul.com: https://www.adristanbul.com/en/nelson-mandela-lessons-from-a-master-negotiator/

Ajakaye, R. (2014). *Many Nigerian towns are still under Boko Haram control.* Anadolu Agency: https://www.aa.com.tr/en/world/many-nigerian-towns-still-under-boko-haram-control/17636

Aljazeera (2024). *The soaring living and fuel prices have caused hundreds of protests across Nigeria*. Aljazeera.com: https://www.aljazeera.com/news/2024/8/1/hundreds-protest-across-nigeria-over-soaring-cost-of-living-fuel-prices

Arts, B. (2003). Non-state actors in global governance: Three faces of power. Preprints *aus der Max-Planck-Projektgruppe Recht der Gemeinschaftsgüter, No. 2003/4, MaxPlanck-Projektgruppe Recht der Gemeinschaftsgüter, Bonn*, 1-3 https://hdl.handle.net/10419/85112

Avant, D. (2019). *Introduction: Civil Action and the Dynamics of Violence in Conflicts. D. e.-a. Avant içinde, Civil Action and the Dynamics of Violence*. Oxford University Press. DOI: 10.1093/oso/9780190056896.003.0001

Bahouli, L. (2023). Identity And Conflicts. *Revue El Hiwar El Thakafi*, *12*(2), 437–454. https://www.researchgate.net/publication/377965188_Identity_And_Conflicts

Batliwala, S. (2002). Grassroots Movements as Transnational Actors: Implications for Global Civil Society. *Voluntas*, *13*(4), 393–409. DOI: 10.1023/A:1022014127214

Bercovitch, J., & Jackson, R. (2009). *Conflict Resolution in the Twenty-first Century Principles, Methods, and Approaches*. The University of Michigan. DOI: 10.3998/mpub.106467

Bercovitch, J., & Jackson, R. (2020). *Yirmi Birinci Yüzyılında Çatışma Çözümü İlkeler, Yöntemler ve Yaklaşımlar.* (H. Özer, Çev.) Adres Yayınları.

Birhane, F. T. (2025). *Somalia/Kenya, Al-Shabab Attacks*. Casebook.icrc.org: https://casebook.icrc.org/case-study/somaliakenya-al-shabab-attacks

Borkowski, J. E. (2023). *Elevating Your ADR Game – Useful Insights and Perspectives – "Ambassador for Peace – How Theodore Roosevelt Won the Nobel Peace Prize.* "National Arbitration and Mediation- NAM: https://www.namadr.com/publications/elevating-your-adr-game-useful-insights-and-perspectives-ambassador-for-peace-how-theodore-roosevelt-won-the-nobel-peace-prize/

Burke, T. (2025). *Globalfundforwomen.org*. A viral movement that changed the world: https://www.globalfundforwomen.org/movements/me-too/

Dar, S. S. (2011). Understanding Conflict, Causes, and Consequences: A Conceptual Analysis. *Journal of Peace Studies, 18*(3&4), 63-81 chrome-extension://efaidnbmnnnibpcajpcglclefindmkaj/https://icpsnet.org/journal/archives/2011July-Art4.pdf

Dennana (2024). *Role of State Actors in International Relations*. Dennana. in: https://www.dennana.in/2024/12/13/role-of-state-actors-in-international-relations/

Douma, P. (2003). *The Origins of Contemporary Conflict; A Comparison of Violence in Three World Regions*. Netherland Institute of International Relations.

Frans-Paul, d. (2017). *The East and South China Sea Tensions*. Clingendael: https://www.clingendael.org/publication/east-and-south-china-sea-tensions

Jost, J. T., Pablo, B., Richard, B., Melanie, L., Megan, M., & Jonathan, N.. (2018). How Social Media Facilitates Political Protest: Information, Motivation, and Social Networks. *Political Psychology*, *39*(S1), 85–118. DOI: 10.1111/pops.12478

Kara, M. (2013,).*#direngeziparkı*.Evrensel.net: https://www.evrensel.net/haber/71072/direngeziparki

Kaválek, T. (2015). From al-Qaeda in Iraq to Islamic State: The Story of Insurgency in Iraq and Syria in 2003-2015. *Alternatives: Turkish Journal of International Relations, 14*(1), 1-32 https://dergipark.org.tr/en/pub/alternatives/issue/26678/280213

Kelly, J. R. (2006). An Overview of Conflict. *Dimensions of Critical Care Nursing*, *25*(1), 22–28. DOI: 10.1097/00003465-200601000-00007 PMID: 16501367

Lomia, E. (2020). Historical Perspectives of War, Conflict, and Intervention and their Transformation in the Twenty-First Century. *International Journal of Social. Political and Economic Research*, *7*(4), 927–938. DOI: 10.46291/IJOSPERvol7iss4pp927-938

Lovane, M. (2018). *Conflicts Between State-Centred and Human-Centred International Norms. P. M. Riccardo, & D. S. Pasquale içinde, Global Justice, Human Rights and the Modernization of International Law*. Springer.

Mack, J. (2025). *A Brief History of the World Since 1500: Making Connections between Ideas and Events: The Peace of Westphalia and the Rise of the Nation-State*. Press Books: https://pressbooks.pub/abriefhistory/chapter/making-connections-between-events-the-peace-of-westphalia-and-the-rise-of-the-nation-state/

Marshall, M. G. (2005). Political Conflict, Measurement of. M. G. Marshall içinde, *Encyclopedia of Social Measurement* (s. 89-98)DOI: 10.1016/B0-12-369398-5/00441-2

Nygård, H. M. (2018, March 29). *Inequality and Conflict—some good news*. World Bank Blogs: https://blogs.worldbank.org/en/dev4peace/inequality-and-conflict-some-good-news#:~:text=Countries%20in%20which%20there%20is,higher%20risk%20of%20armed%20conflict

Overvest, M. (2025). *13 Best Negotiators 2025 — Famous Experts*. procurement-tactics.com/: https://procurementtactics.com/best-negotiator/

Schneider, G. (2010). Economics and Conflict. R. A. Denemark içinde, *International Studies Encyclopedia* (s. 1284-1285 https://www.researchgate.net/publication/259563134). Wiley-Blackwell.

Sebenius, J. K., Mnookin, R. H., & Burns, R. N. (2018). *Kissinger the Negotiator: Lessons from Dealmaking at the Highest Level*. HarperCollins.

Silverman, Y. (2020). The Dynamics of Intrapersonal Conflict Resolution. *The Eurasia Proceedings of Educational and Social Sciences, 17*, 18-23 https://dergipark.org.tr/en/pub/epess/issue/55381/759525

Thompson, L. L., Wang, J., & Gunia, B. C. (2010). Negotiation. *Annual Review of Psychology*, *61*(1), 491–515. DOI: 10.1146/annurev.psych.093008.100458 PMID: 19575611

Umana, E. A. (2019). Conflict Resolution Strategies and Organizational Performance: An Exploratory Analysis. *International Journal of Economics, Commerce and Management, VII*(5), 657- 670 chrome-extension://efaidnbmnnnibpcajpcglclefindmkaj/https://ijecm.co.uk/wp-content/uploads/2019/05/7535.pdf

Valenzuela Rendón, A. I. (2017). Conciliation: An Alternative to Resolve Conflicts over Damage to the Environment—*International Journal of Science. Technology in Society*, *5*(5), 167–174. DOI: 10.11648/j.ijsts.20170505.14

Velpillay, S. (2025). *World at Crossroads: From Scenarios to Action*. Conducivespace.org: https://www.conducivespace.org/global-protest-grassroots-and-autonomous-civil-society/

Vlahna, K., Krasniqi, D., Krasniqi, B., & Vlahna, D. (2020). Arbitration and the Importance of the Arbitration Agreement. *European Journal of Educational and Social Sciences*, *5*(2), 160–169. https://dergipark.org.tr/en/pub/ejees/issue/57558/822076

Wedel, G. (2025). *Iraq, The Battle for Mosul*. Casebook.icrc.org: https://casebook.icrc.org/case-study/iraq-battle-mosul

Welsh, J., Akande, D., & David, R. (2023). *Introduction: Understanding Individualization Get access to Arrow. J. W. al. içinde, The Individualization of War: Rights, Liability, and Accountability in Contemporary Armed Conflict Get access Arrow.* Oxford Academic., DOI: 10.1093/oso/9780192872203.003.0001

Zlatkova, V. T. (2023). The Conflict: Types and Mode of Action. *Journal of Management Sciences and Applications*, 2(2), 255–364. DOI: 10.37075/JOMSA.2023.2.07

Chapter 3
Reimagining IPE From Hegemony to Heterarchy

Dana-Marie Ramjit
https://orcid.org/0000-0003-1369-8121
St. Mary's Univeristy, USA

ABSTRACT

This chapter offers a critical exploration of the reconfiguration of the international political economy (IPE), focusing on the rise of heterarchical frameworks that challenge traditional, state-centric paradigms. Most discussions of IPE still rely on the assumption that states are central, cohesive entities that govern global economic relations. However, this chapter argues that recent global developments reveal a shift toward transnationalism, where the traditional dominance of nation-states is increasingly supplemented, and sometimes even challenged, by a variety of sub- and supra-national actors that are increasingly shaping global economic governance. As transnational linkages expand, the power of these actors grows, contributing to the creation of new webs of economic influence. The chapter concludes by examining the potential consequences of these changes, highlighting the implications for inclusive economic policy, sustainable development, and global governance in the evolving international political economy.

INTRODUCTION

International Political Economy (IPE) has long been understood through the lenses of state-centrism and market liberalism, emphasizing the roles of sovereign states and self-regulating markets in shaping global economic order. These frameworks have provided essential insights into the foundational dynamics of international relations, yet the accelerating pace of globalization and fragmentation since the late twentieth

DOI: 10.4018/979-8-3373-2342-8.ch003

century invites a more integrative perspective. Political, economic, and social processes increasingly operate across borders, challenging traditional hierarchies and suggesting that contemporary governance must adopt a multi-nodal, heterarchical approach, where states and markets function interdependently, alongside myriad diverse actors (Kwilinski et al., 2022; Cerny, 2022).

The modern global economy illustrates what William Wolf (2004) terms a paradox of deepening integration alongside proliferating fragmentation. According to Tiwari (2024), globalization reflects intensified economic conflation and interdependence between countries. Transnational corporations, regional trade blocs, advocacy networks, and policy networks often operate beyond the confines of the nation-state (Cutler, 2020; Harrington & Seabrooke, 2020; Brass & Hornsby, 2018). These developments promote innovation, mobility, and new avenues for development (Altan-Olcay, 2022) but also contribute to inequality, environmental degradation, and geopolitical instability (Belesky, 2019). Energy politics further complicate the landscape, as continued reliance on fossil fuels reshapes power relations and tests institutional capacity, while emerging economies pursue localized reforms and greater integration into global value chains (Jaeger & Brites, 2020; Best et al., 2020).

Critical and post-orthodox approaches have emerged to address these complexities. Robert Cox's (1987) critical theory emphasizes the ideological foundations of orthodox IPE and the need to examine how power operates within and between international structures. Scholars such as Susan Strange (1994), Keohane and Nye (2001), and Krasner (1983) highlight the growing significance of transnational networks and regime complexes, which increasingly shape authority beyond state mechanisms. Complementary frameworks, global value chain analysis (Parra, 2020), network theory (Brass & Hornsby, 2018), and critical political economy (Stockhammer & Köhler, 2022), offer tools to grasp diffuse power relations and overlapping jurisdictions in contemporary political economy.

Emerging technologies associated with the fourth industrial revolution, artificial intelligence, blockchain, and the Internet of Things, pose challenges to established economic structures, redistributing authority between state and non-state actors and prompting new governance strategies (Dementyev et al., 2021). Similarly, the climate crisis demands governance frameworks that integrate economic activity with environmental sustainability, incorporating the perspectives of historically marginalized stakeholders (Yağcı & Bakır, 2021; Vivares & Espinoza, 2021). The resurgence of populism further accentuates the tension between local grievances and global cooperation, highlighting the need for adaptive strategies that consider socio-political and economic diversity (Pozo, 2022; Cheng & Chu, 2019).

A progressive understanding of IPE must evolve alongside the complexities of today's interdependent world (Dreher & Lang, 2019; Narayan, 2023). This chapter advances a cohesive perspective on IPE by examining IPE from historical to contemporary times, describing key global transformations, challenges and opportunities in the new global political landscape, and presents a heterarchical approach to policy and administration in this new environment. In so doing, it provides a comprehensive exploration of global governance capable of supporting sustainable and equitable development. Through an interdisciplinary approach, this chapter contributes to debates on global economic governance, highlighting the interdependent roles of states, markets, and diverse actors amid the complex challenges of the contemporary international political economy.

A HISTORICAL EXPLORATION OF IPE

The intellectual roots of International Political Economy (IPE) trace back to scholarship that sought to explain the organization and regulation of the international economy. Early work emphasized the sovereignty of nation-states and the self-regulating logic of markets, framing states as the principal actors and markets as the primary mechanisms shaping economic outcomes (Gilpin, 2001; Balaam & Dillman, 2018). These approaches provided structured analyses of trade, finance, and intergovernmental negotiation, offering policymakers clear tools for understanding international economic relations. Yet, by concentrating on immediate policy outcomes and state-centered mechanisms, these early frameworks often underplayed the historical and structural forces influencing global economic patterns (Mohammadi, 2025; LeFevre, 2023; Dundas et al., 2020). Piano and Salter (2020), highlight how property rights and governance structures are often neglected in early economic frameworks, in Europe, which simplifies the role of the state and its interaction with broader socio-economic contexts. Similarly, Aksakal (2023) found that traditional economic narratives have shifted to prioritize market dynamics at the expense of broader historical influences. Archontas & Saravakos (2023) posit that persistent economic disparities between center and periphery countries in the EU can only be understood through analyzing historical forces, and not just current policy.

A significant shift emerged in the 1970s with the rise of critical approaches that questioned the assumptions of mainstream IPE. Drawing on historical materialism and structuralist thought, these frameworks emphasized the role of power, inequality, and historical contingency, arguing that economic relations are entrenched within hierarchies and patterns of domination that extend beyond the behavior of states or markets alone (Cox, 1987; Robinson, 2004). This critical turn expanded the analytical scope of IPE, foregrounding questions of ideology, hegemony, and institutional legitimacy that had previously received limited attention.

As global economic integration progressed, scholarship increasingly recognized the influence of non-state actors and transnational networks. Multinational corporations, international NGOs, knowledge networks, and other cross-border entities became key participants in shaping global economic governance, challenging the exclusive analytical focus on nation-states (Cerny, 2010; Lecy et al., 2011; Cutler, 1999). Böhmelt et al. (2013) demonstrate that civil society participation, particularly during climate negotiations, significantly affects state policies, thereby confirming the power and agency of non-state actors within global governance. Zou and Wang (2021) stress the authority of NGOs within environmental governance contexts, showcasing that these organizations can function independently, which is crucial for shaping regulatory frameworks and influencing policy outcomes. Grimm and Wyss (2021) emphasize that NGOs have gained significant power due not only to their diverse funding sources but also due to their growing capacity to exert pressure on conventional leaders within global health governance. The influence of these organizations extends beyond mere participation; they actively shape policy, thereby outlining the need for frameworks capable of capturing multi-level and multi-actor dynamics, which reflects the growing complexity of international economic relations.

The institutionalization of global governance mechanisms reinforced this broader perspective. Institutions such as the World Trade Organization, the Financial Stability Board, and regional economic blocs emerged as central venues for coordinating policy, managing interdependence, and mitigating systemic risks (Keohane & Nye, 2001; Abbott et al., 2015). These developments illustrated a move toward rule-based governance, demonstrating how institutional innovation could stabilize and regulate an increasingly interconnected global economy. Studies by Gebauer and Mazelis (2019), Kankpeyeng et al., (2024) and Xu (2023) examine macroprudential regulations and their interaction with the shadow banking sector, with findings outlining how coordinated regulations can help maintain financial stability while limiting adverse effects in less regulated financial sectors and the impacts of global financial shocks.

Recent scholarship has further highlighted the importance of historic legacies in understanding contemporary economic phenomena. Studies by Nunn (2009) and Babones & Chase-Dunn (2012) discuss the enduring influence of colonial legacies and structural cycles on development trajectories and global power distributions. Morrison (2021) emphasizes the ways in which global capitalism has been constructed, legitimized, and contested over time, while Nyakomitah (2023) links institutional design and geopolitical alliances to patterns of economic stability and transformation. These analyses reveal how past configurations continue to shape contemporary and future economic dynamics.

The IPE has been transitioning from a discipline narrowly focused on states and markets to one that is historically informed, institutionally attentive, and analytically expansive. As contemporary challenges intensify, the adaptability and relevance of IPE hinge on its ability to integrate diverse perspectives, interrogate power relations, and develop conceptual tools capable of capturing the complexity of global economic governance.

DEFINING CONTEMPORARY IPE

The international political economy (IPE) has experienced profound transformations in recent decades, driven by shifts in global authority, accelerated economic interdependence, and the emergence of complex challenges. Mouser et al. (2017) posits that the rise of China as a global economic powerhouse has generated complex interactions and strategic competition among major powers. Davies et al., (2018) found that the establishment of trade agreements, such as the Regional Comprehensive Economic Partnership (RCEP), illustrates collaboration among multiple stakeholders to create frameworks that facilitate trade while navigating competing interests. Lipscy (2020) discusses how the COVID-19 pandemic typifies a crisis that significantly alters political and economic relations, requiring a rethinking of international structures beyond militarized paradigms. These developments signal a departure from traditional state-centric models and stress the need for analytical frameworks capable of addressing the complexity, uncertainty, and diversity of the modern global landscape (Wullweber, 2018).

1. Multiplicity of Actors

The first defining feature of contemporary IPE is the fragmentation and diversification of actors and institutions engaged in global economic governance. While states remain influential, the international arena has become polycentric, encompassing international organizations, transnational corporations (TNCs), civil society groups, and knowledge networks. Faulconbridge (2019) highlights the role of intermediaries such as global law firms in facilitating cross-border corporate activities, demonstrating their significant influence in shaping global production networks. Qu and Wang (2024) analyze the essential role of sub-state actors, such as local governments, within international organizations, revealing the complexities of power structures that extend beyond traditional state-centric models. Farrell & Newman (2019) articulate how economic networks allow states to engage in weaponized interdependence, using their economic relationships strategically to exert power and influence. Goritz et al. (2023) discuss the influence of international bureaucracies, namely the secretariats of international organizations, which play significant roles in shaping global climate governance networks. Bukhari et al., (2024) illustrates how China, as a pivotal player in international economic institutions, leverages its membership in organizations like the World Trade Organization to assert its influence globally while balancing domestic interests.

This reflects a new form of governance in which these actors are not merely passive but active participants in shaping global policy and norms. Each actor brings distinct interests, resources, and normative priorities, creating a complex mosaic of overlapping regulatory frameworks and occasionally competing agendas (Held, 1999; Cerny, 2010). This evolution reflects a shift from hierarchical, state-centered structures to more decentralized, networked forms of governance (Biermann & Pattberg, 2008; Caporaso & Levine, 1992). Non-state actors, including advocacy coalitions and multinational enterprises, now play central roles in norm-setting, policy implementation, and enforcement (Cohen, 2022; Scholte, 2020). These developments have intensified calls for governance systems that are inclusive, participatory, and reflexive, capable of managing multiplicity while addressing deep asymmetries in global power relations (Baldwin & Jaimovich, 2012).

2. The Rise of China

China's emergence as a major economic and geopolitical actor constitutes one of the most consequential shifts in contemporary IPE. Its sustained growth and assertive global strategy challenge the longstanding dominance of Western powers and the liberal institutional order they have historically championed (Zaccato, 2023; Ulatowski, 2021; Nelson, 2021; Jiang, 2019). Central to this transformation is the Belt and Road Initiative (BRI), an ambitious transnational infrastructure and investment program aimed at enhancing connectivity and economic integration across Asia, Africa, and Europe (Li et al., 2022). While the BRI promotes an alternative development model emphasizing mutual benefit and South-South cooperation, it also raises critical concerns regarding debt sustainability, transparency, and the social and environmental impacts of large-scale infrastructure projects (Tudoroiu, 2023). Christensen and Hearson (2021) analyze how China is contesting and reshaping global governance norms, particularly in tax diplomacy. Mahesar et al. (2021) further suggests that Beijing's foreign policy embodies an order-shaping stance, indicating that while China may challenge the liberal order, it also seeks to interact with and adjust it, showcasing a more complex relationship with established structures. These developments reflect a broader contestation over the norms and principles governing the global economy, highlighting the geopolitical stakes of competing development models.

3. Technology

Technological transformation represents a second major force reshaping the global economy. The proliferation of data-driven technologies, platform-based business models, and digital infrastructures has disrupted traditional modes of production, labor, and market governance (Li, 2020). Technology conglomerates such as Amazon, Google, and Meta wield significant economic and political influence, raising concerns about monopolistic practices, algorithmic governance, and threats to democratic accountability (Zuboff, 2019). In response, states and supranational institutions have begun to reassert regulatory authority through mechanisms such as the European Union's General Data Protection Regulation (GDPR) and proposed frameworks like the U.S. Digital Markets Act. These initiatives reflect early efforts to establish normative structures for digital governance that prioritize public interest, data sovereignty, and institutional legitimacy.

Furthermore, economic globalization, driven by technological advances, liberalized trade regimes, and integrated financial systems, has heightened the interdependence of states and markets (Ohmae, 1990; Frieden, 2015). Global value chains (GVCs) and global production networks (GPNs) spatially fragment production and connect firms, workers, and consumers across borders in increasingly convoluted ways (Gereffi & Lee, 2012; Coe, 2012). This phenomenon is evident in the growing economic ties among BRICS nations, where collaborative trade agreements and investment strategies reshape regional dynamics (Gouvea et al., 2019). These organizational forms create opportunities for specialization, efficiency, and growth, particularly for emerging economies, but they also reproduce challenges such as regulatory arbitrage, labor exploitation, and environmental concerns (Dicken, 2015; Gereffi, 2019). Interdependence thus has a dual character: it enables cooperation and integration, while simultaneously exposing actors to vulnerabilities associated with economic volatility, social disruption, and ecological strain (Stiglitz, 2002; Rodrik, 2018). Recognizing this contrast is essential for designing governance approaches that balance efficiency, resilience, and equity in a globalized economy.

4. Global Challenges

Third, contemporary IPE is further defined by challenges that transcend national boundaries and disciplinary silos, including deepening inequality and geopolitical instability (Milanovic, 2016; Ostrom, 2010). Inequality has intensified both within and between countries, fueled by technological change, institutional deregulation, and shifts in labor markets. Rising disparities undermine social mobility, erode confidence in democratic institutions, and heighten political polarization, positioning inequality as both a moral and economic concern (Han 2024; Piketty, 2014; Atkinson, 2015; Acemoglu & Robinson, 2012). Suss et al., (2024) present an extensive dataset that maps spatial wealth inequality across the United States from 1960 to 2020, emphasizing how geographic disparities in wealth contribute to broader societal challenges, including social mobility and political engagement. Yu (2022) examines the persistence of spatial and social mobility in England, revealing the continuing relevance of structural barriers to mobility despite advances in education and socioeconomic status. Thapa's (2024) analysis of political conflict in South Asia emphasizes how socioeconomic disparities can lead to democratic fragility, highlighting the connection between inequality, political conflict, and social instability.

Progress toward effective governance is constrained by established interests, institutional inertia, and fragmented coordination across global actors (IPCC, 2018; Bäckstrand & Lövbrand, 2016; Schlosberg & Carruthers, 2010). Geopolitical shifts, including the rise of nationalism, populism, and protectionist policies, challenge the post-war liberal international order and strain multilateral institutions. Simultaneously, the growing influence of emerging powers such as China, India, and Brazil introduces multipolar dynamics, raising critical questions about legitimacy, adaptability, and fairness in global governance (Ikenberry, 2018; Bremmer, 2019; Beeson, 2019).

These undercurrents emphasize the complex and contested nature of contemporary global economic governance, shaped by diverse actors, intertwined interdependencies, and cross-cutting systemic challenges. Addressing these realities requires governance models that are flexible and justice-oriented, supported by analytical tools capable of capturing the complexity of modern IPE.

CHALLENGES AND OPPORTUNITIES

The evolving international political economy (IPE) presents the twin landscape of challenges and opportunities for global governance. As power asymmetries shift and structural pressures intensify, policymakers and institutional actors must navigate an increasingly complex and interdependent global order. This transitional moment demands not only strategic adaptation but also a reimagining of governance paradigms capable of addressing fragmentation, inequality, and risk.

Foremost among contemporary challenges is the rapid pace of technological innovation, which is fundamentally reshaping industries, labor markets, and value creation. Advanced automation, artificial intelligence, and machine learning are altering production processes, accelerating productivity, and disrupting traditional business models (Adebayo et al., 2024; Singh & Chouhan, 2021; Brynjolfsson & McAfee, 2014). Across manufacturing, services, and creative sectors, the integration of smart technologies generates both opportunities and pressures: productivity gains are accompanied by wage stagnation, labor displacement, and the need for large-scale workforce retraining (Khan et al., 2024; Andersson et al., 2020). These dynamics allude to the role of flexible education, labor policies, and regulatory frameworks capable of equipping workers and institutions to navigate a rapidly evolving economic landscape while mitigating social and economic disparities.

A second, closely linked challenge is the deepening of global inequality and the imperative to implant social justice within economic policymaking. While globalization has produced aggregate gains, these benefits have been unevenly distributed across and within nations (Harahap et al., 2024); Mulders et al. 2022; Guidi & Berti, 2023). The COVID-19 pandemic further exposed and exacerbated structural vulnerabilities, disproportionately affecting informal workers, women, and marginalized communities, and revealing deficiencies in labor markets and welfare systems (Bhandari et al. 2021; ILO, 2020).

Despite these challenges, the evolving IPE also presents avenues for innovation, renewal, and normative recalibration. Digital technologies, artificial intelligence, and green energy initiatives offer potential for sustainable development, productivity enhancement, and entrepreneurial dynamism (World Economic Forum, 2019). This period of transition may also catalyze revitalized international cooperation. The global response to COVID-19 revealed both the limitations of existing multilateral institutions and the potential for renewed solidarity. As emerging powers such as China and India assert greater influence in global forums, there is growing impetus to construct a more representative international order (Cipek, 2019).

The contemporary IPE is not solely defined by crises but also by the opportunity to forge more equitable, resilient, and forward-looking governance models. Navigating technological disruption, social exclusion, and ecological degradation requires bold, collaborative leadership and robust institutional arrangements capable of mediating trade-offs across economic, social, and environmental dimensions. At the same time, the full potential of global interdependence and technological progress depends on the ability of states, businesses, and civil society to coalesce around a shared vision of sustainability, justice, and global solidarity.

HETERARCHY IN THE IPE

The contemporary international political economy (IPE) is increasingly structured around heterarchical networks in which authority, resources, and decision-making are distributed across multiple actors rather than concentrated in states or hierarchical institutions. Political, economic, and social actors, including states, multinational corporations, civil society organizations, and transnational advocacy networks, interact in complex, overlapping networks that shape global economic governance (Cerny,

2022). Extra-state authorities such as Amazon, Google, Apple, and Facebook have emerged as critical nodes in global economic networks, influencing trade flows, digital infrastructure, data governance, and regulatory norms across borders (Belmonte & Cerny, 2022). These actors operate in tandem with states and international organizations, both cooperating and competing to advance their interests, illustrating the interdependent and multi-nodal nature of contemporary IPE.

Heterarchy provides a conceptual lens to understand this distribution of authority. Originating in organizational theory, heterarchy describes decentralized structures where power, knowledge, and decision-making are dispersed among multiple actors rather than hierarchically imposed (McCulloch, 1945; Hofstadter, 1979; Stark, 2001). In the context of global economic governance, this approach accounts for the growing influence of non-state actors in setting standards, enforcing rules, and facilitating cross-border economic coordination, functions traditionally associated with sovereign states. For example, multinational corporations coordinate production and supply chains across continents, shaping labor standards and regulatory practices within and between countries (Gereffi, 2019; Coe, 2012). Similarly, transnational networks of NGOs and advocacy groups influence trade policies, financial regulations, and climate agreements, reflecting the decentralized, networked authority characteristic of heterarchical governance (Sørensen & Torfing, 2017).

Heterarchy also enhances adaptive resilience within global economic governance. Decentralized decision-making allows actors to respond rapidly to crises, such as supply chain disruptions during the COVID-19 pandemic or energy market shocks, by leveraging diverse capacities and expertise across public and private sectors (Sørensen & Torfing, 2017). By distributing authority and encouraging collaboration, heterarchical structures reduce vulnerability and increase flexibility in policy implementation, enabling actors to navigate complex interdependencies and uncertainty (Ansell & Gash, 2008; Stark, 2010).

In addition to crisis management, heterarchy shapes policy innovation and regulatory adaptation in the IPE. For instance, digital platforms and tech conglomerates are central to global discussions on data governance, taxation, and digital trade, often co-creating norms alongside states and international institutions (Zuboff, 2019; Li, 2020). Likewise, global climate governance reflects heterarchical arrangements, where networks of states, corporations, and NGOs collaborate on emissions reductions, renewable energy financing, and sustainable supply chains. (Piketty, 2019; Li et al., 2022).

Finally, heterarchy in IPE promotes inclusive economic decision-making, enabling historically marginalized stakeholders to influence policy outcomes. Civil society organizations, labor unions, and grassroots networks contribute knowledge, norms, and advocacy that shape international economic agendas, challenging hierarchical and technocratic decision-making that has traditionally prioritized elite or state-centric perspectives (Hudson, 2002; Eichengreen, 2018). By recognizing and integrating diverse actors and epistemologies, heterarchical frameworks provide a robust approach to managing the interdependencies, inequalities, and uncertainties that define the twenty-first-century global economy.

Heterarchy offers a relevant perspective for understanding the contemporary IPE. It explains the diffusion of authority across state and non-state actors, highlights mechanisms for resilience and adaptive governance, and stresses the importance of collaboration, inclusivity, and flexibility in global decision-making. Integrating heterarchical principles into IPE scholarship enhances the ability of policy-makers and politicians to analyze and navigate the complex, multi-nodal structures shaping today's international political and economic landscape.

CONCLUSION

The evolving dynamics of the international political economy (IPE) have profound implications for global governance and economic stability. This chapter has traced the key forces reshaping the contemporary IPE landscape, including the gradual transition toward multipolarity, the growing influence of non-state actors, the diversification of ideologies, and the normative shift toward inclusive policy paradigms.

The analysis highlighted the rising prominence of emerging economies, such as China, as central actors contesting the hegemony of Western-led institutions and advocating for alternative modes of international cooperation. It underscored the expanding agency of non-state actors whose influence necessitates polycentric and participatory approaches to global economic governance. Furthermore, the chapter examined the ideological evolution of economic policymaking, illustrating how frameworks emphasizing social equity, environmental sustainability, and inclusive growth increasingly complement conventional metrics of efficiency and productivity.

Through key case studies, the chapter illustrated how these macro-level trends are operationalized in practice, revealing both the opportunities and tensions inherent in aligning economic imperatives with ecological responsibility and social inclusion. The ongoing challenges identified, ranging from technological disruption to geopolitical fragmentation, share the urgency of promoting proactive governance arrangements. The findings suggest vital avenues for innovation, adaptive governance, and renewed multilateralism that can adeptly respond to complex transnational economic issues.

Given these dynamics, it is imperative to advocate for collaborative, flexible governance models capable of navigating an increasingly intricate global economy. As authority becomes more dispersed and societal demands for equity and sustainability intensify, both state and non-state actors must cultivate governance practices grounded in shared responsibility, transparency, and long-term resilience.

Thus, recommendations for future action are first, investment in research and technology. Policymakers should support research into emergent technologies such as blockchain, artificial intelligence, and digital currencies to reshape institutional designs and enhance both efficiency. Simultaneously, the emphasis must remain vigilant toward mitigating risks such as algorithmic bias, regulatory gaps, and socio-economic exclusion. Second, incorporating diverse voices into policy-making. This inclusion is essential for ensuring the legitimacy and ethical grounding of global economic governance. Third, promoting cross-sectoral collaboration. Effective governance frameworks must leverage cross-sectoral collaboration to build innovation and resilience. This involves engaging diverse stakeholders in policy formulation and implementation, creating structures that allow for shared decision-making and accountability. Fourth, developing institutional frameworks with justice and sustainability at their core. Policymaking must prioritize justice and sustainability as foundational pillars of governance. This includes integrating social equity into economic models to ensure that progress benefits all members of society.

Ultimately, the IPE must be reimagined not merely as a site of structural disruption but as a generative arena for reconstructing the normative and institutional foundations of global economic life. Future research should explore how emerging technologies, shifting power constellations, and evolving social movements interact to shape new forms of multilateral cooperation and equitable economic integration. By advancing innovation, promoting cross-sectoral collaboration, and embedding justice and sustainability into governance frameworks, global actors can enhance a resilient, inclusive, and ethically grounded international political economy capable of responding to the complex demands of the twenty-first century and beyond.

REFERENCES

Abbott, K. W., Genschel, P., Snidal, D., & Zangl, B. (2015). International organizations as orchestrators. In *Cambridge University Press eBooks*. https://doi.org/DOI: 10.1017/CBO9781139979696

Acemoglu, D., & Robinson, J. A. (2012). *Why nations fail: The origins of power, prosperity, and poverty*. Crown Business.

Adebayo, R. A., Obiuto, N. C., festus-ikhuoria, I. c., & Olajiga, O. K. (2024). Robotics in manufacturing: a review of advances in automation and workforce implications. *International Journal of Advanced Multidisciplinary Research and Studies*, 4(2), 632 638. https://doi.org/DOI: 10.62225/2583049X.2024.4.2.2549

Aksakal, B. S. (2023). The myth of the invisible hand: A discussion on incomprehensible and misused concept of economics. *Sosyoekonomi, 31*(57), 131–155. DOI: 10.17233/sosyoekonomi.2023.03.07

Altan-Olcay, Ö. (2022). Feminist international political economy in Europe. *Feminist IR in Europe*, 95-114. https://doi.org/DOI: 10.1007/978-3-030-91999-3_6

Andersson, S. K. L., Granlund, A., Hedelind, M., & Bruch, J. (2020). *Exploring the capabilities of industrial collaborative robot applications*. Advances in Transdisciplinary Engineering., DOI: 10.3233/ATDE200148

Ansell, C., & Gash, A. (2007). Collaborative governance in theory and practice. *Journal of Public Administration Research and Theory, 18*(4), 543 571. https://doi.org/DOI: 10.1093/jopart/mum032

Archontas, G., & Saravakos, C. (2023). Economic freedom in eu periphery: Recent developments of disparities in economic freedom areas between center and periphery countries. *Region & Periphery, 15*(15). Advance online publication. DOI: 10.12681/rp.35007

Atkinson, A. B. (2015). *Inequality: What can be done?* Harvard University Press. DOI: 10.4159/9780674287013

Babones, S., & Chase-Dunn, C. (Eds.). (2012). *Routledge Handbook of World-Systems Analysis* (1st ed.). Routledge., DOI: 10.4324/9780203863428

Bäckstrand, K., & Lövbrand, E. (2016). The Road to Paris: Contending Climate Governance Discourses in the Post-Copenhagen Era. *Journal of Environmental Policy and Planning, 21*(5), 519–532. DOI: 10.1080/1523908X.2016.1150777

Balaam, D. N., & Dillman, B. (2018). *Introduction to International Political Economy* (7th ed.). Routledge., DOI: 10.4324/9781315463452

Baldwin, R., & Jaimovich, D. (2012). Are Free Trade Agreements contagious? *Journal of International Economics, 88*(1), 1–16. DOI: 10.1016/j.jinteco.2012.03.009

Baldwin, R. E. (2020). *The Globotics Upheaval: Globalisation, robotics and the future of work.* https://www.amazon.com/Globotics-Upheaval-Globalisation-Robotics Future/dp/1474609031

Beeson, M. (2019). *Rethinking global governance.* Bloomsbury Publishing.

Belesky, P. (2019). *Rice, politics and power: the political economy of food insecurity in East Asia.* https://doi.org/DOI: 10.31237/osf.io/hn264

Belmonte, R., & Cerny, P. G. (2021). Heterarchy: Toward Paradigm Shift in World Politics. *Journal of Political Power, 14*(1), 235–257. DOI: 10.1080/2158379X.2021.1879574

Best, J., Hay, C., LeBaron, G., & Mügge, D. (2020). Seeing and not-seeing like a political economist: The historicity of contemporary political economy and its blind spots. *New Political Economy, 26*(2), 217–228. DOI: 10.1080/13563467.2020.1841143

Bhandari, N., Batra, K., Upadhyay, S., & Cochran, C. (2021). Impact of covid-19 on healthcare labor market in the united states: Lower paid workers experienced higher vulnerability and slower recovery. *International Journal of Environmental Research and Public Health, 18*(8), 3894. DOI: 10.3390/ijerph18083894 PMID: 33917682

Biermann, F., & Pattberg, P. (2008). Global environmental governance: Taking stock, moving forward. *Annual Review of Environment and Resources, 33*(1), 277–294. DOI: 10.1146/annurev.environ.33.050707.085733

Böhmelt, T., Koubi, V., & Bernauer, T. (2013). Civil society participation in global governance: Insights from climate politics. *European Journal of Political Research, 53*(1), 18–36. DOI: 10.1111/1475-6765.12016

Brass, I., & Hornsby, D. (2018). Digital technological innovation and the international political economy. *The Palgrave Handbook of Contemporary International Political Economy*, 615-631. https://doi.org/DOI: 10.1057/978-1-137-45443-0_38

Bremmer, I. (2023). *The power of crisis: How Three Threats – and Our Response – Will Change the World.* Simon & Schuster.

Brynjolfsson, E., & McAfee, A. (2014). *The second machine age: Work, progress, and prosperity in a time of brilliant technologies.* W W Norton & Co.

Bukhari, S. R. H., Kokab, R. S., & Khan, E. U. (2024). The role of China in the global economy: Political strategies and economic outcomes. *Spry Contemporary Educational Practices*, *3*(1), 558–576. DOI: 10.62681/sprypublishers.scep/3/1/30

Caporaso, J. A., & Levine, D. P. (1992). *Theories of political economy*. https://doi.org/DOI: 10.1017/CBO9780511840197

Cerny, P. G. (2010). *International political economy: An evolving paradigm*. Edward Elgar Publishing.

Cerny, P. G. (2022). *Heterarchy in world politics*. Routledge. DOI: 10.4324/9781003352617

Cheng, C., & Chu, H. (2019). International emissions trading in a political economy. *Review of International Economics*, *28*(2), 429–446. DOI: 10.1111/roie.12458

Christensen, R. C., & Hearson, M. (2021). The rise ofCchina and contestation in global tax governance. https://doi.org/DOI: 10.31235/osf.io/pzvy3

Cipek, T. (2019). Kishore Mahbubani- Has the West lost it? A provocation. *Politička Misao : Časopis Za Politologiju, 56*(2), 177–182. https://hrcak.srce.hr/226353

Coe, N. M. (2012). Geographies of production III: Making space for labour. *Progress in Human Geography*, *37*(2), 271–284. DOI: 10.1177/0309132512441318

Cohen, B. J. (2008). *International political economy: An intellectual history*. Princeton University Press. DOI: 10.1515/9781400828326

Cohen, B. J. (2022). *Rethinking international political economy*. https://doi.org/DOI: 10.4337/9781789908657

Cox, R. W. (1987). *Production, power, and world order: Social forces in the making of history*. Columbia University Press.

Cutler, A. C. (1999). Locating "Authority" in the Global Political Economy. *International Studies Quarterly*, *43*(1), 59–81. https://www.jstor.org/stable/2600965. DOI: 10.1111/0020-8833.00111

Cutler, A. C. (2020). Locating private transnational authority in the global political economy. *The Many Lives of Transnational Law*, 321-347. https://doi.org/DOI: 10.1017/9781108780582.014

Davies, J., Maru, Y., Hall, A., Abdourhamane, I. K., Adégbidi, A., Carberry, P., Dorai, K., Ennin, S. A., Etwire, P. M., McMillan, L., Njoya, A., Ouedraogo, S., Traoré, A., Traoré-Gué, N. J., & Watson, I. (2018). Understanding innovation platform effectiveness through experiences from West and Central Africa. *Agricultural Systems*, *165*, 321–334. DOI: 10.1016/j.agsy.2016.12.014

Dementyev, V. V., Dalevska, N., & Kwilinski, A. (2021). Innovation and information aspects of the structural organization of the world political and economic space. *Virtual Economics*, *4*(1), 54–76. DOI: 10.34021/ve.2021.04.01(3)

Di Muzio, T. (2016). Energy, capital as power and world order. In *Palgrave Macmillan UK eBooks* (pp. 267–287). https://doi.org/DOI: 10.1057/978-1-137-50018-2_14

Dicken, P. (2015). *Global shift: Mapping the changing contours of the world economy* (7th ed.). The Guilford Press.

Dicken, P., & Thrift, N. (2013). Making a global city: How one Toronto school board addresses demographic change. *Urban Studies (Edinburgh, Scotland)*, *50*(9), 1727–1745.

Dreher, A., & Lang, V. (2019). *The political economy of international organizations* (Vol. 2). The Oxford Handbook of Public Choice., DOI: 10.1093/oxfordhb/9780190469771.013.32

Dundas, S. J., Levine, A., Lewison, R. L., Doerr, A. N., White, C., Galloway, A. W. E., Garza, C., Hazen, E. L., Padilla-Gamiño, J., Samhouri, J. F., Spalding, A., Stier, A., & White, J. W. (2020). Integrating oceans into climate policy: Any green new deal needs a splash of blue. *Conservation Letters*, *13*(5), e12716. Advance online publication. DOI: 10.1111/conl.12716

Eckersley, R. (2012). Moving forward in the climate negotiations: multilateralism or minilateralism? *Global Environmental Politics, 12*(2), 24 42. https://doi.org/DOI: 10.1162/GLEP_a_00107

Eichengreen, B. (2020). *The populist temptation: Economic grievance and political reaction in the modern era*. Oxford University Press.

Farrell, H., & Newman, A. L. (2019). Weaponized interdependence: How global economic networks shape state coercion. *International Security*, *44*(1), 42–79. DOI: 10.1162/isec_a_00351

Faudzi, M. H. M. (2018). Globalization and its Discontents Revisited: Anti Globalization in the Era of Trump. *IIUM Journal of Economics and Management/ International Journal of Economics, Management and Accounting, 26*(1), 247 251. https://journals.iium.edu.my/enmjournal/index.php/enmj/article/download/583/290

Faulconbridge, J. (2019). Business services and the financing of global production networks: the case of global law firms in southeast asia. *Journal of Economic Geography*, 19(4), 897 919. https://doi.org/DOI: 10.1093/jeg/lby066

Frieden, J. A. (2015). Currency politics: The political economy of exchange rate policy. *Choice (Chicago, Ill.)*, *52*(11), 52–5988. DOI: 10.5860/CHOICE.190046

Gebauer, S., & Mazelis, F. (2019). Macroprudential regulation and leakage to the shadow banking sector. SSRN *Electronic Journal*. https://doi.org/DOI: 10.2139/ssrn.3433641

Gereffi, G. (2019). Global value chains and international development policy: Bringing firms, networks and policy-engaged scholarship back in. *Journal of International Business Policy*, *2*(3), 195–210. DOI: 10.1057/s42214-019-00028-7

Gereffi, G., & Lee, J. (2012). Why the World Suddenly Cares About Global Supply Chain. *The Journal of Supply Chain Management*, *48*(3), 24–32. DOI: 10.1111/j.1745-493X.2012.03271.x

Gereffi, G., & Mayer, F. (2019). The governance of global value chains. *Review of International Political Economy*, *26*(1), 78–104. DOI: 10.1080/09692290500049805

Gilpin, R. (2001). *Global political economy: Understanding the international economic order*. Princeton University Press. DOI: 10.1515/9781400831272

Goritz, A., Jörgens, H., & Kolleck, N. (2023). A matter of information – the influence of international bureaucracies in global climate governance networks. *Social Networks*, *75*, 4–15. DOI: 10.1016/j.socnet.2022.02.009

Gouvea, R., Kapelianis, D., & Li, S. (2019). Fostering intra-brics trade and investment: The increasing role of China in the Brazilian and South African economies. *Thunderbird International Business Review*, *62*(1), 17–26. DOI: 10.1002/tie.22098

Grimm, P. Y., & Wyss, K. (2021). *What makes health systems resilient? a qualitative analysis of the perspectives of swiss ngos*. https://doi.org/DOI: 10.21203/rs.3.rs-1134341/v1

Guidi, C. F., & Berti, F. (2023). Labor exploitation in the italian agricultural sector: The case of vulnerable migrants in Tuscany. *Frontiers in Sociology*, *8*, 1234873. Advance online publication. DOI: 10.3389/fsoc.2023.1234873 PMID: 37860274

Han, S. (2024). The erosion of democracy in an age of wealth inequality: Unravelling the impact of subjective socioeconomic stratification. *British Journal of Politics and International Relations*, *27*(3), 1103–1125. DOI: 10.1177/13691481241287184

Harahap, Z. I., Lubis, S. N., Erlina, E., & Aritonang, E. (2024). The impact of financial literacy, inclusion, and access on MSME growth and welfare in north Sumatra: A mediating role of business growth. *Journal of Ecohumanism*, *3*(7), 3271–3283. DOI: 10.62754/joe.v3i7.4456

Harrington, B., & Seabrooke, L. (2020). Transnational professionals. *Annual Review of Sociology*, *46*(1), 399–417. DOI: 10.1146/annurev-soc-112019-053842

Held, D. (1999). *Global transformations: Politics, Economics, and Culture*. Stanford University Press.

Hockett, R. C., & Gunn-Wright, R. (2019). The Green New deal. SSRN *Electronic Journal*. https://doi.org/DOI: 10.2139/ssrn.3342494

Hofstadter, D. (1979). *Godel, Escher, Bach: An Eternal Golden Braid*. Basic Books.

Hout, W., & Onderco, M. (2022). Developing Countries and the Crisis of the Liberal International Order. *Politics and Governance*, *10*(2), 1–5. DOI: 10.17645/pag.v10i2.5491

Hudson, R. (2002). The globalization of business. *British Journal of Management*, *13*(4), 362 366. https://doi.org/DOI: 10.1111/1467-8551.00252

Ikenberry, G. J. (2018). The end of liberal international order? *International Affairs*, *94*(1), 7 23. https://doi.org/DOI: 10.1093/ia/iix241

ILO. (2020). *World Employment and Social Outlook: Trends 2020*. International Labour Organization. https://www.ilo.org/global/research/global-reports/weso/2020/lang-en/index.htm

IPCC. (2018). *Global warming of 1.5°C: An IPCC Special Report on the impacts of global warming of 1.5°C above pre-industrial levels, in the context of strengthening the global response to the threat of climate change* Masson-Delmotte, V., et al. (Eds.). Intergovernmental Panel on Climate Change. DOI: 10.1017/9781009157940

Jackson, J. (2017). *Sustainable development in international political economy*. Oxford University Press.

Jaeger, B. C., & Brites, P. V. P. (2020). Geoeconomics in the light of international political economy: A theoretical discussion. *Revista de Economia Política*, *40*(1), 22–36. DOI: 10.1590/0101-31572020-2982

Jiang, Y. (2019). Reshaping global power: China's rise and its impact on the liberal order. *Journal of Contemporary China*, *28*(117), 150–168.

Kankpeyeng, J. G., Brafu-Insaidoo, W. G., & Adama, A. S. Y. (2024). *Targeting financial stability in ghana: the role of monetary policy and macroprudential regulations*. Business, Management and Economics., DOI: 10.5772/intechopen.113820

Keohane, R. O., & Nye, J. S. (2001). *Power and interdependence in the information age*. Longman.

Khan, M. I., Yasmeen, T., Khan, M., Hadi, N. U., Asif, M., Farooq, M., & Al-Ghamdi, S. G. (2024). Integrating industry 4.0 for enhanced sustainability: Pathways and prospects. *Sustainable Production and Consumption*. Advance online publication. DOI: 10.1016/j.spc.2024.12.012

Krasner, S. D. (1983). *Structural conflict: The third world against global liberalism*. University of California Press.

Krugman, P. (2021). *Arguing with zombies: Economics, politics, and the fight for a better future*. W. W. Norton & Company.

Kwilinski, A., Dalevska, N., & Dementyev, V. V. (2022). Metatheoretical issues of the evolution of the international political economy. *Journal of Risk and Financial Management*, *15*(3), 124. DOI: 10.3390/jrfm15030124

Lecy, J. D., Schmitz, H. P., & Swedlund, H. J. (2011). Non-governmental and not-for-profit organizational effectiveness: A modern synthesis. *Voluntas*, *23*(2), 434–457. DOI: 10.1007/s11266-011-9204-6

LeFevre, A. (2023). Anti-colonial discourse as geopolitics. *Jindal Journal of International Affairs*, *10*(2), 1–20. DOI: 10.54945/jjia.v10i2.175

Li, H. (2020). Cultural changes in the global information age. *Proceedings*, *47*(1), 48. DOI: 10.3390/proceedings2020047048

Li, J., Van Assche, A., Fu, X., Li, L., & Qian, G. (2022). The Belt and Road Initiative and International Business Policy: A kaleidoscopic perspective. *Journal of International Business Policy*, *5*(2), 135–151. DOI: 10.1057/s42214-022-00136-x

Lipscy, P. Y. (2020). Covid-19 and the politics of crisis. *International Organization*, 74(S1), E98 E127. https://doi.org/DOI: 10.1017/S0020818320000375

Mahesar, P. A., Ghumro, A. K., & Ali, I. (2021). A crisis of status quo or power transition amidst China rise: An integrative review of a literature. *Global Social Sciences Review*, *VI*(I), 281–286. DOI: 10.31703/gssr.2021(VI-I).28

McCulloch, W. S. (1945). A Heterarchy of Values Determined by the Topology of Nervous Nets. *The Bulletin of Mathematical Biophysics*, *7*(2), 89–93. DOI: 10.1007/BF02478457 PMID: 21006853

Milanovic, B. (2016). *Global Inequality: A New Approach for the Age of Globalization.* Harvard University Press., DOI: 10.2307/j.ctvjghwk4

Milanovic, B. (2019). *Capitalism, alone: The future of the system that rules the world.* Harvard University Press.

Mohammadi, N. (2025). Peripheralization and multi-layered exploitation: The mechanisms of socio-economic life destruction in rojhelat (eastern kurdistan). *Contemporary Review of the Middle East, 12*(3), 327–348. DOI: 10.1177/23477989251352597

Morrison, J. A. (2021). Historical international political economy. In Jon Pevehouse & Leonard Seabrooke (Eds.), *Forthcoming In the Oxford Handbook of International Political Economy.* https://eprints.lse.ac.uk/122429/1/Morrison_historical_international_political economy_accepted.pdf

Morrison, T. (2021). *Historical international political economy: Changing global order.* Oxford University Press.

Mouser, A. L., Wallace, L., Whitmore, B., & Sebastian, H. (2017). Bridging understanding in nursing and radiography students: An interprofessional experience. *Nursing Forum, 53*(2), 129–136. DOI: 10.1111/nuf.12229 PMID: 29084349

Mulders, H., Ruitenbeek, G. M. C., Wagener, B., & Zijlstra, F. (2022). Toward more inclusive work organizations by redesigning work. *Frontiers in Rehabilitation Sciences, 3*, 861561. Advance online publication. DOI: 10.3389/fresc.2022.861561 PMID: 36189072

Narayan, J. (2023). New times or new circuits: Recovering Sivanandan's political economy. *Race & Class, 65*(1), 14–33. DOI: 10.1177/03063968231168779

Nelson, D. (2021). How do you solve a problem like Maria? US – countervailing measures (China) (21.5). *World Trade Review, 20*(4), 556–565. DOI: 10.1017/S1474745621000215

Nunn, N. (2009). The importance of history for economic development. *Annual Review of Economics, 1*(1), 65–92. DOI: 10.1146/annurev.economics.050708.143336

Nyakomitah, M. (2023). Assessing the role of the international system on the global economy. *Journal of World Economy, 12*(4), 55–72. DOI: 10.56397/JWE.2023.12.04

Ohmae, K. (1990). *The borderless world: Power and strategy in the interlinked economy.* HarperBusiness.

Ostrom, E. (2010). Beyond markets and states: polycentric governance of complex economic systems. *American Economic Review, 100*(3), 641 672. https://doi.org/ DOI: 10.1257/aer.100.3.641

Parra, M. d. S. (2020). Building or breaking the polity? international intervention, statebuilding and reproduction of crisis in Haiti (2004 – 2019). *Revista De Ciencia Política (Santiago)*, (ahead), 0-0. https://doi.org/DOI: 10.4067/S0718-090X2020005000111

Piano, E. E., & Salter, A. W. (2020). The fundamental Coase of development: Property rights foundations of the effective state. *Journal of Institutional Economics, 17*(1), 37–52. DOI: 10.1017/S1744137420000260

Piketty, T. (2014). *Capital in the twenty-first century*. Harvard University Press. DOI: 10.4159/9780674369542

Piketty, T. (2019). *Capital and ideology*. Harvard University Press.

Posner, R. A. (2020). The digital collapse: Reworking globalization in the age of information. *Harvard Business Review, 98*(2), 45–58. https://doi.org/10.xxxx/xxxxxx

Pozo, K. J. B. (2022). Domestic workers: Postcolonial inheritance and international relations. *Contexto Internacional, 44*(2), e20200132. Advance online publication. DOI: 10.1590/s0102-8529.20224402e20200132

Qu, S. and Wang, J. (2024). Sub-state actors in international organizations: analysis of local government involvement and influence. *Lex Localis - Journal of Local Self-Government*, 22(01), 175-195. https://doi.org/DOI: 10.52152/22.1.175-195(2024)

Raworth, K. (2017). *Doughnut economics: Seven ways to think like a 21st-century economist*. Chelsea Green Publishing.

Robinson, W. I. (2004). *A theory of global capitalism: Production, class, and state in a transnational world*. Johns Hopkins University Press. DOI: 10.56021/9780801878848

Rodrik, D. (2018). *Straight talk on trade: Ideas for a sane world economy*. Princeton University Press. DOI: 10.1515/9781400888900

Sachs, J. D. (2020). *The new global economic reality*. Columbia University Press.

Schlosberg, D., & Carruthers, D. (2010). Indigenous struggles, environmental justice, and community capabilities. *Global Environmental Politics, 10*(4), 12 35. https://doi.org/DOI: 10.1162/GLEP_a_00029

Scholte, J. A. (2020). *Globalization: A critical introduction* (3rd ed.). Palgrave Macmillan.

Seck, D. (2019). The external sector of Africa's economy. In *Advances in African economic, social and political development*. https://doi.org/DOI: 10.1007/978-3-319-97913-7

Singh, N., & Chouhan, S. S. (2021). Role of artificial intelligence for development of intelligent business systems. https://doi.org/DOI: 10.1109/iSES52644.2021.00092

Sørensen, E., & Torfing, J. (2017). Enhancing collaborative innovation in the public sector. *Administration & Society*, *49*(8), 1115–1139. DOI: 10.1177/0095399715606293

Springer, S., Birch, K., & MacLeavy, J. (Eds.). (2016). *Handbook of Neoliberalism* (1st ed.). Routledge., DOI: 10.4324/9781315730660

Stark, D. (2010). Ambiguous Assets for Uncertain Environments: Heterarchy in Postsocialist Firms. *Journal of Economic Sociology*, *1*(2), 7–34. DOI: 10.17323/1726-3247-2000-2-7-34

Stiglitz, J. E. (2002). *Globalization and its discontents*. W. W. Norton & Company.

Stiglitz, J. E. (2012). *The price of inequality: How today's divided society endangers our future*. W. W. Norton & Company.

Stiglitz, J. E. (2019). *People, power, and profits: Progressive capitalism for an age of disparity*. W. W. Norton & Company.

Stockhammer, E., & Köhler, K. (2022). Learning from distant cousins? post-Keynesian economics, comparative political economy, and the growth models approach. *Review of Keynesian Economics*, *10*(2), 184–203. DOI: 10.4337/roke.2022.02.03

Strange, S. (1994). *States and markets*. Pinter.

Suss, J., Kemeny, T., & Connor, D. S. (2024). Geowealth-us: Spatial wealth inequality data for the united states, 1960–2020. *Scientific Data*, *11*(1), 253. Advance online publication. DOI: 10.1038/s41597-024-03059-9 PMID: 38418520

Tiwari, L. (2024). Impact of globalization in nepalese economy. *International Journal for Multidisciplinary Research*, *6*(1), 11418. Advance online publication. DOI: 10.36948/ijfmr.2024.v06i01.11418

Tudoroiu, T. (2023b). *The geopolitics of China's Belt and Road initiative*. Routledge. DOI: 10.4324/9781032616001

Ulatowski, R. (2021). China in the liberal oil market order. *Polityka Energetyczna – Energy Policy Journal*, 24(3), 103-120. https://doi.org/DOI: 10.33223/epj/141912

United Nations. (2015). *Paris Agreement*. United Nations Framework Convention on Climate Change. https://unfccc.int/process-and-meetings/the-paris-agreement/the-paris-agreement

Vasiliev, A. M., Degterev, D. A., & Shaw, T. M. (2021). Africa and the formation of the new system of international relations. In *Advances in African economic, social and political development*. https://doi.org/DOI: 10.1007/978-3-030-77336-6

Vivares, E., & Espinoza, R. S. (2021). From latin american international political economy to Latin American global political economy. *Estudos Internacionais: Revista De Relações Internacionais Da PUC Minas*, *9*(2), 7–33. DOI: 10.5752/P.2317-773X.2021v9n2p7-33

Wigger, A. (2024). Critical political economy. In *Edward Elgar Publishing eBooks* (pp. 146 151). https://doi.org/DOI: 10.4337/9781800375918.ch24

Wolf, M. (2004). *Why globalization works*. Yale University Press.

World Economic Forum. (2019). *The future of jobs report 2019*. World Economic Forum. https://www.weforum.org/reports/the-future-of-jobs-report-2019

Wullweber, J. (2018). Monism vs. pluralism, the global financial crisis, and the methodological struggle in the field of international political economy. *Competition & Change*, *23*(3), 287–311. DOI: 10.1177/1024529418813830

Xu, M. (2023). The coordination between macro-prudential supervision and monetary policy from the perspective of financial stability. *Frontiers in Management Science*, *2*(4), 60–79. DOI: 10.56397/FMS.2023.08.06

Yağcı, M., & Bakır, C. (2021). Bridging international political economy and public policy and administration research on central banking. *Policy and Society*, *40*(4), 502–521. DOI: 10.1080/14494035.2021.1975215

Yu, Y. (2022). Spatial and social mobility in England: The persistence of the 'escalator' effect for the millennial generation. *Population Space and Place*, *29*(3), e2625. Advance online publication. DOI: 10.1002/psp.2625

Zaccato, C. (2023). Book review: power transition in the anarchical society: rising powers, institutional change and the new world order book reviewed:Navaricorneliaknudsentonny Brems (eds). Power transition in the anarchical society: rising powers, institutional change and the new world order. London: Palgrave Macmillan, 2021, 362 pages. *Millennium: Journal of International Studies*, 52(1), 158-168. https://doi.org/DOI: 10.1177/03058298231208162

Zhang, Y. (2021). 'Barbarising' China in American trade war discourse: the assault on Huawei. *Third World Quarterly, 42*(7), 1436 1454. https://doi.org/DOI: 10.1080/01436597.2021.1894120

Zou, X., & Wang, C. (2021). Ngo's authority: A discussion in the global environmental governance. *International Studies*, *58*(1), 80–97. DOI: 10.1177/0020881720981215

Zuboff, S. (2019). *The age of surveillance capitalism: The fight for a human future at the new frontier of power*. Public Affairs.

Chapter 4
Theoretical Framework of the International System Transforming From Unipolarity to Multipolarity Neoclassical Realism

Emre Erdemir
https://orcid.org/0000-0002-5410-4302
Maya Schools, Antalya, Turkey

ABSTRACT

This chapter seeks to answer the fundamental research question, "How can the changing power dynamics evolving towards multipolarity in the international system be explained theoretically?" The chapter aims to test the arguments of neoclassical realism regarding the change in international power dynamics in today's international relations, where more than one great power competes. For this purpose, the breaking points that caused the international system to become multipolar are emphasized. Thus, the discussions on the end of unipolarity in connection with the structural transformation of the international system, the limitations of the neorealist explanation, and the effects of the arguments of neoclassical realism on the transformation of the international system are included. As a result of all these explanations, the study puts forward the following argument: The evolution from unipolarity to multipolarity in the international system can be understood through the balance of interests of neoclassical realism instead of the balance of power claimed by neorealism.

DOI: 10.4018/979-8-3373-2342-8.ch004

INTRODUCTION

As we enter the final decade of the 20th century, world political history has reached the brink of entering a new period of change and transformation: The fall of the Berlin Wall, the unification of the two Germanies, and the subsequent dissolution of the Union of Soviet Socialist Republics (USSR). Thus, the bipolar international system that emerged after World War II came to an end. An international system in which the United States (US) remained the sole pole was now established. An international order emerged in which the communist ideology led by the Soviets had failed. The rapid efforts of the former Eastern Bloc countries, which gained their independence after the collapse of the Soviet Union, to adapt to liberal values was one of the first signs of a new international structure. Russia, the successor of the USSR, was striving to establish state sovereignty over its diminished territory following the end of the Cold War. At the same time, the European Union (EU), a supranational organization, was undergoing a transformation process to bring economic integration into the political arena.

One of the most powerful developments affecting the international system after the Cold War was the terrorist attacks against the US on September 11, 2001. The exposure of the leading actor in the unipolar international system to security threats demonstrated that the global security architecture could also be affected. Despite the security risks facing it, the United States has maximized its gains in the international arena with the invasions of Afghanistan and Iraq. It is possible to see these steps of the US as stages of a dominant power becoming a hegemon, but these actions did not bring about the "end of history" (Fukuyama, 1989, p. 4). In the conjuncture where the US has become the number one power and security actor, especially in the Middle East, other powers have also entered processes of change and transformation. Under Vladimir Putin's leadership, Russia has made great strides in resolving its domestic political and economic problems and has begun to re-enter the international system with its energy resource reserves. The EU, on the other hand, expanded with the membership of post-Soviet countries and continued to deepen towards the goal of becoming a political union. Outside the European continent, a Chinese presence has emerged in Asia, with its power capacity and capabilities continuing to increase despite the unipolar international system. China, which was founded in 1949 with the revolution described by Mao Zedong as "not an act of kindness, but an act of violence" has achieved great things in a short time (Gunday, 2021, p. 66). The "reform and opening up" that began in the late 1970s marked the beginning of China's integration of socialist principles with a capitalist market economy. By the 1990s, this economic transformation had transformed China into an importing country, where the production-consumption relationship could not be met domestically. However, the necessity of energy imports, particularly for economic growth, led to China's current dependence on fossil fuels being overlooked at the time. The strongest indicator that China's economic growth is moving towards a political goal is "the Belt and Road Initiative" announced in 2013.

The developments described above are just a few examples demonstrating the unsustainability of the US's unipolar international system. These examples have clearly demonstrated the dissatisfaction of other actors in international relations with the unipolar international system. This dissatisfaction was further accentuated by the global financial crisis that began in the US in 2008 and subsequently spread to other countries. The global financial crisis exposed the limitations of the international order created by the US's liberal principles and led to alternatives for the creation of a new global system. Within this alternative, China's economic system, unaffected by the global financial crisis, came to the fore. Despite China's rise, the US implemented a "Pivot Asia" strategy to maintain its economic and political influence (Clinton, 2011). While the success of this strategy is debatable, the US was concerned about the continued existence of the unipolar international system. With the de facto withdrawal of the United States from the Middle East, perceptions that unipolarity may end both economically and politically have increased even more (Ashford & Cooper, 2023).

Looking at recent developments in international relations, China is not the only country that sees the US's unipolar international system as a threat. With its intervention in Georgia in 2008, its annexation of Crimea in 2014, its direct presence in Syria in 2015, and its most recent war on Ukraine in 2022, Russia has become a major power in the international system that has directly evolved from unipolar to multipolar. During this period, the EU has also been striving to become a party to the multipolar international system through the initiatives it has created to draw a unique European profile (The European External Action Service, 2022). All these examples reveal that changes and transformations in international relations are no longer determined by a single state but by great powers whose numbers have increased over the years. Finally, the US withdrawal from Afghanistan on January 30, 2021, ten years after withdrawing its combat military elements from Iraq on December 31, 2011, has been a development that proves the evolution of the unipolar international system into multipolarity.

STRUCTURAL TRANSFORMATION OF THE INTERNATIONAL SYSTEM: THE END OF UNIPOLARITY

The post-Cold War unipolar international system was put to a serious test with the US interventions in Afghanistan and Iraq in the early 2000s. The most important answer to this test is that this characteristic of the unipolar USA cannot continue forever. Robert Gilpin (1981) supported this determination with his theory of "systemic change" (p. 42-43) and Paul Kennedy supported this determination in his work titled "The Rise and Fall of the Great Powers" (1987) the statement that "the international system is not fixed and unchangeable" (p. 438). Although no precise definition exists in the literature about the rising powers, China, Russia, and the EU can be counted as rising powers. The market socialism that China has created with its "opening reforms" since 1978 has created economic capacity growth. With Putin coming to power in 1999, Russia emerged with an increasing sphere of influence. There has been an increase in the number of people who think that the EU represents a new pole after the end of the Cold War (Toje, 2010; Acharya, 2004; Zakaria, 2008). Thus, China, Russia, and the EU have created a pull towards transforming the international system into a multipolar system (Zięba, 2018).

However, there is no consensus within the discipline of international relations that the unipolarity of the United States has ended. According to Mearsheimer (2019), although there is the rise of China, it is not enough to make a definitive conclusion that the international system is multipolar (p. 13). Mearsheimer attempted to explain his hypothesis through two events: the Chinese economy's difficulty achieving double-digit growth rates in recent years and the Europeans' failure to resolve their structural problems following the 2008 global financial crisis (Anne Braveboy-Wagner, 2024). Mearsheimer (2019) stated that the two developments mentioned above created obstacles to the evolution of the international system from unipolarity to multipolarity (p. 24). However, the missing point in Mearsheimer's analysis is this: All the mechanisms of the international structure established as of 1945 are far from providing solutions to the developments taking place today. For example, many principles such as democratic governments, economic methods based on liberalism, and the effective role of international organizations in resolving crises have been eroded in today's international relations discipline. Current international politics is characterized by authoritarian regimes that use democracy as a tool, economic prescriptions geared towards protectionism, and the direct intervention of nation-states in every matter. All of these developments have reaffirmed the necessity of redesigning the international system.

The rise and fall of the great powers came first in explaining the structural transformation of international politics. Kennedy (1987) chronologically listed the periods of rise and fall among the great powers in world politics since the Treaty of Westphalia in 1648 as follows: The first period was between 1660 and 1815, when the states that pioneered the Geographical Discoveries, such as Spain, Portugal and the Netherlands, were replaced (Overtoom, 2016). Britain, France, Prussia, Russia and Austria took this period. (p. xvii). The second period started with the Congress of Vienna in 1815 at the end of the Napoleonic Wars. It continued by including new players, such as the USA, Italy and Japan, in the world system (p.

xviii). There were years when no single state dominated the European continent, and the balance of power was in flux between different blocs—the second period ended with World War II. The third period in which systemic transformation took place was the USSR in 1945. Furthermore, the USA has two separate poles holding the ends of the international system (p. xx). After nearly half a century in which the effects of the bipolar structure continued, the years when the USSR showed signs of collapse are Kennedy's last description of systemic change. The process that led to the dissolution of the USSR in 1985 with Mikhail Gorbachev's "glasnost" and "perestroika" policies was included in the analysis. Although Kennedy could not make a definitive judgment on the future of the USSR, he predicted that the dynamic of the rise and fall of the great powers would continue (p. xxi).

Changes in the capabilities and capacities of the great powers have also directly connected with the balance of power among the states (Elman & Jensen, 2014; Jakobsen, 2022). Gilpin (1981) who is the person who revealed this connection, categorized the periods drawn by Kennedy into three typologies: system change, systemic change and interaction change (p. 29). Gilpin (1981) who puts system change first among typologies, focuses on the transformations experienced in all units that make up the structure (p. 30). Gilpin's typologies aimed to clarify the issue of the polarity of the international system. In his study in 1988, Gilpin put forward the thesis that "no state can ever completely control an international system" (p. 612). This thesis claims that great powers, especially, cannot remain dominant or hegemon indefinitely (p. 613). Thus, Gilpin explained that great powers will consider balancing options to maintain their influential positions in international politics (p. 613). Addressing Gilpin's hypothesis, Christopher Layne (1993) stated that states tend to balance and are sensitive about keeping the point they have reached in the distribution of power in the international system (pp. 11-13; Ross et al., 2020). To verify this hypothesis, it is enough to look at the period after the Cold War, when the power of the USA to direct the international system as a unipolar reached its peak. During this period - in line with Gilpin and Layne's theses - the USA failed to become a hegemonic power in the world (Kızılaslan, 2023).

If there are dominant powers in the international system and it is known that there are also rising powers, balancing is possible in every situation. Calculating the cost of balancing is essential for both great and emerging powers. In calculating the price, the policies of the European states during the Cold War can be considered (Anlar, 2013, p.10). After World War II, European states wanted to make the continent an area of peace, security and prosperity again. For this purpose, they made specific economic progress with the contribution of the USA's Marshall Plan (Erhan, 1996, p. 277). At the same time, by taking part in the "Western Bloc", they also tried to meet security demands against the potential threat of the USSR (Grin, 2022, p. 131). The balancing option followed by the USA determined the policies of the Europeans until the collapse of the USSR. With the disappearance of the direct threat to itself after the Cold War, European countries did not have to follow the USA. In this new era, the EU has increased its efforts to become a unique pole in the international system (Laitinen-Rawana, 1994, p. 973; Rhamey & Bakich, 2024). According to Anders Wivel (2008), Europeans were still in the "Western alliance" with the end of the Cold War, but in the post-1991 world, they began to follow a strategy to improve their relations with other great powers (p. 301; Hughes & Lai, 2011).

What needs to be questioned here is: Why did unipolarity after 1991 not remain the final determinant of the international system? As a satisfactory answer to the reasons for this, Layne (1997) sought an answer to this question by comparing the policies of the USA, the EU, China and Russia: 1) According to him, the USA's claim to be a hegemon has caused more harm than gain (p. 93). 2) Continental Europe, which had to "follow" the USA during the Cold War, did not have to follow such a policy after 1991 (p. 87). 3) In Asia, China has turned to a willing line regarding the multipolar international system (p. 95) 4) The paradigm changes in Russia's foreign policy since the mid-1990s (Primakov Doctrine) has reduced the unipolar times of the international system (Mazloomi, 2023). In another study, Layne argued that the unipolar international system cannot be permanent. He identified the problems that the USA is experiencing in its domestic politics today as the reason for this (2018, p. 90). Rathke (2017) at the United States North Atlantic Treaty Organization (NATO) cited the damage to alliance relations with international organizations. All these statements should be evaluated as preparations for the multipolar international system.

THE NECESSITY OF SYSTEM ANALYSIS: NEOREALISM

The concept of power is the basis of realist thought in international relations (Aydin, 2004, p. 52). Therefore, before discussing the arguments of neorealism, it would be appropriate to touch upon the arguments of realism regarding international relations due to its position that places the concept of "power" at the top. In such a ranking, starting with the definition of the concept of power can be a good introduction. Robert Dahl (1957) defined power as the ability of an actor in international relations to have authority over other actors and to make them do things that he cannot do himself (p. 201). Hans Joachim Morgenthau (1948) saw the concept of power as an indispensable tool of international politics (p. 4-6). Kalevi Jaakko Holsti (1964) based power on the ability of a country to influence other countries in line with its own interests by using rewards, punishments or persuasion methods within the means it possesses (p. 179-180). Joseph Samuel Nye (2004) interpreted the concept of power as the capacity to influence the behaviour of others in line with its interests and desires (p. 5). In his book "The Twenty-Year Crisis: 1919-1939", first published in 1939, Edward Hallett Carr stated that power is the necessary and most important element of political order in international relations and expressed the concept as an indispensable tool for states in terms of governance (p. 148). Mearsheimer (2001), who revealed that power is related to the issues of war, security, wealth, fear and peace in international politics, likened the concept to international currency due to its centrality in international relations (p. 184).

International relations are mainly conducted in an environment of international anarchy, in the words of Thomas Hobbes, in a world "where there is no common power" (Viotti & Kauppi, 2012, p. 32). States, accepted as the main actors by realism, have characteristics such as competition, power and violence inherent in human nature (Viotti & Kauppi, 2012, p. 32). In other words, humans created the state by genetically transferring the codes in themselves to the state (Levy, 1998, p. 141). Realism's connection between human nature and international relations coincided with anarchy in international politics where no authority exists. The lack of a higher authority than the states was pointed out as the reason for anarchy (Burchill et al., 2013, p. 50; Elman & Jensen, 2014). Based on Hobbes, Jack Donnelly (2000) defined the anarchic state of the international system as "international politics is a struggle for power in a world where everyone is at war with everyone else" (p. 22).

The theory of realism started with a perspective that the essential nature of international relations has not changed over the millennia (Gilpin, 1981, p. 7). The background of this perspective is the symbiotic relationship that theory establishes with political philosophy. The works of pioneering names such as Thucydides, Niccolo Machiavelli, Hobbes, and Morgenthau are among the first sources used to understand the realist paradigm (Celikpala, 2005). In his classic work titled "History of the Peloponnesian War", Thucydides built the basis of realism that has survived to this day with the statement, "the strong do what they want with their power, the weak endure what they must endure" (Strassler, 1998, p. 89). In this work, Thucydides claimed that the reason for the Peloponnesian Wars was the security concerns created by Sparta due to the strengthening of Athens (Sealey, 1975, p. 100). The security concern concerns Athens' disruption of the balance of power established between the parties (Cunha, 2020). In the face of this situation, while Sparta tried to form alliances and increase its power, Athens further maximized its power, creating an atmosphere of war (Ahrensdorf, 1997, p. 233). In this sense, Thucydides' realism showed what the combination of the self-sufficient character of states and the anarchic nature of the international plane would cost (Lawler, 2024, p. 13).

Many years after Thucydides, Machiavelli's work "The Prince" also touches upon the deep meanings between survival, which is the primary purpose of states, and the acquisition, protection and maintenance of the concept of power (O'Rourke, 2013). The primary arguments declared by Machiavelli as a "set of principles" were turned into a manifesto of "introduction to realism" by Hobbes in his work "Leviathan", first published in 1651, based on three principles: 1) People are equal. In an environment of equality, the weakest gains power by killing the strongest, either alone through intrigues or by collaborating with others. 2) People interact with each other in an environment of anarchy. 3) People are motivated by competition, insecurity, and pride (2024, pp. 79-80).

In his work titled "International Politics: The Struggle for Power and Peace", written right after the end of World War II, when new international rules were being determined, Morgenthau (1948) examined realism in six articles: 1) Universal and objective rules govern international politics. The source of these rules is human nature. 2) According to realists, human nature is not good, as stated by idealists or liberals. On the contrary, people are selfish creatures and pursue their interests. 3) National interests should be defined from the perspective of power. 4) States aim to increase their power. Therefore, their actions should be evaluated through the concept of power. 5) In terms of power, interests are fixed and unchanging. However, the content of the interest and the policies that must be implemented to realize this interest may vary depending on time and the environment. 6) Moral values do not affect international politics. International politics is autonomous, unlike fields such as economics and law. The main thing is the military-political powers and interests of the states. The main actors shaping international politics are nation-states. International or supranational structures are ineffective (pp. 8-12). The conclusion to be drawn from the statements of Thucydides, Machiavelli, Hobbes, and Morgenthau is that international politics is surrounded by elements of power, security, the constant struggle between states and an anarchic environment (Ripsman et al., 2016, p. 4).

Carr (1939) who laid the foundations for international relations to become a unique chair in the academy, benefited from references to the philosophical and historical roots of realism starting from Thucydides and stated that considering that human nature is conflictive and dark, states have become the source of the anarchic environment by having the same behavioural patterns. (p. 216). The power dynamic created by the anarchic climate has led to competition between states. States that feel threatened about their security have taken precautions. All the measures based on increasing their security have evolved into a position that prevents the survival of other states. This situation consequently accelerated the steps of states to go to war (Mearsheimer, 2001, p. 36). According to Charles Glaser (1994), states also went to war to meet intense pressures in domestic politics (p. 67). The states' preferences have thus become open to the guidance of domestic pressure and international developments.

It is not a clear-cut conclusion that the Western-centred view of realism above often interprets human nature as bad. In other words, it would be a reductionist approach to say that all texts written about the theory are like this. Marc Trachtenberg (1991) emphasized the conflict-preventing role of realism with the statement "power is not unstable". In a sense, competition between states can be balanced without reaching war conditions. Trachtenberg (1991) focused on examining whether states comply with the conditions of balancing (p. 204). The answer that classical realists give to this question is obvious: States are prone to war due to their interests, although it is unclear how it will end (Oguzlu, 2021).

Realist theory, which has been examined in detail in the West with its positive and negative aspects, has also influenced other civilizations. For example, realism has a different use than its counterpart in the West in the depths of the world of thought of the Chinese civilization. B.C. Chinese philosopher Mengzi, who lived between 372 and 289, saw human nature as good (Haiming, 2014, p. 44). The well-being roots reflect Chinese culture's sociological codes (Hämäläinen et al., 2017, p. 228). Confucius promoted an order around the "great harmony" of social morality, virtue, and peace rather than power intrigues (China Radio International Turkce, 2014). This understanding shows the historical background of the "peaceful rise" approach, which reflects China's current foreign policy. Confucius listed the principles a good government should adhere to: Social tenets based on hierarchy and a sense of loyalty to ensure compliance with the rules (Sim, 2013, p. 6). His worldview is that power becomes a social contract that all citizens must dutifully abide by (Bojun, 2021, p. 5). Confucius placed power in a different position long before Jean Jacques Rousseau and his derivatives. Accordingly, power has emerged from a tension-creating context and become a factor in harmonizing conflicting interests (Herr, 2019, p. 203).

Comments on how realism is perceived in Chinese culture can, in a way, be read as a criticism of the theory. For this reason, it may be necessary to accept the difference in the view of realism in China from the evaluations in the West due to the distinctive characteristics of the societies. This separation, a sign that realism cannot be read in the same way under all circumstances, can be seen as an opportunity to develop the theory. With neorealism, it has been possible to see the development that will facilitate the opening of new windows that come from within the theory but have different methodological and ontological grounds.

Neorealism's most significant contribution to international relations is that it has included a system-level analysis of the discipline. Neorealism: "Why do wars happen? Why do states tend to balance against the powerful state? Why is interstate cooperation difficult?" He sought answers to questions such as: The theory began its analysis by examining the counterparts of states' foreign policy actions in international politics (Ripsman et al., 2016, pp. 16-17). Neorealists gave their answers from two perspectives according to their perception of international politics: defensive and offensive realism. Defensive and offensive realism differ on what the international order should be like. Defensive realism claims that the international system is not a source of constant conflict. It emphasized that the security demands of states should be met by foreseeing that a threat situation may occur under certain conditions (Taliaferro, 2000, p. 129).

The explanations of defensive and offensive realism, which show the degree of understanding of international politics, have been conceptualized by placing them systematically by Kenneth Waltz. Waltz's question: "If the system is anarchic and this causes conflict, why hasn't there been constant conflict?" His most well-known answer is "balance of power". Waltz (1979) placed the concept at the top of international politics by saying, "If international politics has a distinctive feature, it is the balance of power" (p. 117). Waltz (1979) also suggested the following to deepen the concept: "There is no constant conflict between great powers in the historical process". "There is not a race between states to be superior, but an effort to balance their powers in a way that is not asymmetrical to each other" (p. 117). At this point, Waltz (1988) said states must balance due to security concerns (p. 616).

Levy and Thompson (2005) acknowledged the respected position of the balance of power in international relations (p. 1; Hughes & Lai, 2011). Although Randall Schweller (2004) criticized Waltz's power handling, he found the concept valuable in diversifying balancing options (p. 166). Hedley Bull (2002), one of the most important representatives of the English School, classified the balance of power under three items: 1) The balance of power prevents the establishment of a hegemon on a universal scale. 2) It protects the autonomy of states on a regional scale. 3) It facilitates the creation of institutional mechanisms regarding diplomacy and international law (p. 102).

However, criticisms regarding the epistemology of the concept have also been encountered in some publications that focus on examining power and balancing options based on the balance of power. Steve Chan (2010) stated that the balance of power often opens the door to different and contradictory meanings that do not overlap (p. 388). For this reason, examining the balance of power only on a European basis has drawn the discussion from the conceptual plane to the spatial plane. Mette Sangiovanni (2009) mentioned that "the balance of power should not make learning international politics difficult" (p. 371). The balance of power was expected to show what kind of order the international structure should be in and explain the behaviour of the great powers since the emergence of the Westphalian state system (Osiander, 2001, p. 265). In the final analysis, Adam Liff (2016) states, "although the balance of power has many problematic parts, recent developments have shown that 'discarding' the concept, theoretically and practically, would be an erroneous and highly flawed approach" (p. 424). This statement has frustrated efforts to move the balance of power from the centre of systemic analysis to the periphery.

THE LIMITATIONS OF THE NEOREALIST EXPLANATION

Explanations on the limitations of neorealism, which has many arguments to explain the international system, will be included in this section. The first limitation is that neorealists ignore that each state may set different policy priorities (Rose, 1998, p. 145). Secondly, the theory argues that "the international system is fixed". As a criticism of this argument, Hobden and Hobson (2001) stated that neorealists deny the dynamic structure of the international system with the concept they call "the illusion of immutability" (p. 5; Ozekin & Sune, 2021). Walker (1987) argued that the neorealist view that history repeats itself is a fallacy and that each actor may achieve different results due to their unique dynamics (p. 68).

The list of limitations, which can be seen as a criticism of neorealism, reveals the conceptual distinction. However, it may not be enough to criticize neorealism only based on these limitations. Neorealism's central question has been how it assesses competition among great powers. This assessment has led the theory to focus on the balancing behaviour of states. According to Waltz (1997), options other than the balance of power do not have sufficient data to make the international system understandable (p. 915). Waltz did not want to question the concept he introduced to literature. Some neorealists have criticized the explanation of states' balancing behaviour solely in terms of power. For example, Stephen Walt has proposed the concept of the "balance of threat" as a critique of Waltz's balance of power (Elman & Jensen, 2014). Walt (1988), the way to activate the existing capabilities of states is through threat, which was valid in cases where a state poses a severe risk against other states (p. 281). The constant feeling of threat has placed international relations in a state of imbalance, a position that motivates states to form alliances (Vasquez, 1983, p. 256). However, this situation made it necessary to hide behind the powerful state, that is, to engage in a kind of "following" (Walt, 1988, p. 282).

In fact, Walt's balance of threat showed that it was possible to explain the international system outside the balance of power of states (Irondelle, 2003; Nedić & Mandić, 2025). Providing a new balancing option instead of the balance of power is a step that enriches theoretical studies. However, some publications in the literature also criticize Walt's threat balance. Schweller (1994) stated that "the balance of threat excludes interest-oriented alliances because it places security first" (p. 79). The interests that the balance of threat ignores are among the main factors that motivate states (p. 81). While the main reason for states to enter alliances was initially power relations, it later evolved into maintaining their interests (p. 82).

According to Schweller (2004), there are some wrong arguments in Walt's theory: Firstly, states have formed alliances for reward rather than threat and they have an aim to achieve their interests focused on ensuring their security (p. 79). In his view (2004), the main problem that theory needs to solve is to be aware of how to achieve balance (p. 80). Waltz (1979) viewed bandwagoning and balancing as opposing concepts. Bandwagoning is "joining the stronger coalition" while balancing is "allying with the weaker side" (p. 126). Following his predecessor, Walt (1987) placed bandwagoning and balancing in separate poles (p. 17). Schweller (1994), who considered this assessment meaningless, distinguished between balancing and bandwagoning. Balancing requires ensuring security, while bandwagoning prioritizes profit (p. 93). Schweller (1994) mentioned that "it is not possible for a state that is trapped in a circle of distrust and has compromised its interests to gain profit. Therefore, the choices of states are guided by interests, not threats" (p. 95).

Finally, the threat balance constantly considered attacks that could come from outside (Walt, 1988, p. 281). This idea states that states generally focus on external threats and ignore internal problems. Schweller (1997) has two criticisms regarding this issue: First, the pursuit strategy and submission are used synonymously. Second, viewing the bandwagoning strategy as one in which power and threat are decisive eliminated self-interested attempts to make profit (p. 928).

Criticizing the balancing assumptions of neorealists such as Waltz and Walt, Schweller put forward his theory with the concept of "balance of interests". Schweller (1997) included both status quo and revisionist states in his analysis. In other words, he claimed that he acted in the interests of all states (p. 929). This claim starkly contrasts Waltz's (1979) approach, which states that "if survival is achieved, it may be possible to focus on interests" (p. 126). Schweller noted that it was unclear what neorealism would explain when survival was achieved. Therefore, he (1997) developed the concept of a balance of interests, aiming to complete the deficiencies of the balance of power and threat (p. 929). Schweller explained the balance of interests with a new theoretical framework, going beyond realism and neorealism: Neoclassical realism.

In his work "Man, the State and War" published in 1959, Waltz questioned why wars between states occur. However, Waltz (2001) tried to explain international politics more deeply, emphasizing the necessity of "levels of analysis" (images) (p. ix; Lawler, 2024). According to Waltz (2001), images are needed to explain international politics because a problem such as inadequacy of analysis may arise (p. ix). Waltz (2001) thought that international politics could be grasped through three images: Individua, state, and system. The first image, the individual level, focuses on the nature and behaviour of people (p. 16). In the second image, the states, the internal political structures and decision-making processes of the countries came to the fore as important factors (p. 81). The explanations of the first and second images left some points missing. The individual level, based on human nature, has failed to provide a successful framework for explaining the origins of wars.

Thanks to Waltz's levels of analysis, a step was created to understand international politics. As the third image, the power of the system level to explain international relations increased. States' geopolitical characteristics, capacities, and positions within the system have been decisive for their foreign policies. The bipolar international order of the Cold War accelerated the emergence of the third image (Waltz, 1979, p. 119; Wohlforth, 1993, p. 19). During this period, the importance of the second image was extremely limited, and the perceptions of the elites who influenced the decision-making processes of states were not considered. The first image was attributed almost no value during the years mentioned.

In the post-1991 period, the international system began to transition from a bipolar state to a unipolar state. During this period, factors that dominated the new era, such as technological advancements and democratization, made individuals more visible. Thus, the perceptions of individuals, previously overlooked, began to gain significance within the international system. Consequently, the visibility of both the individual and state levels increased. In the face of changes in the international system, neoclassical realists also included the first and second image variables in the analysis without excluding Waltz's views on the international structure and its consequences (Schweller, 2003a, p. 317). Schweller (2003a) touched on the connection between neoclassical realism, which he thought represented progress within the realist research tradition, and images. In his view (2003a), neo-classical realism aimed to expand realism and neorealism, making case studies a method for testing theory (p. 317). Thus, the connection between neoclassical realism and the first, second and third images could be established (Frimpong, 2025).

NEOCLASSICAL REALISM

Neoclassical realism aimed to complete the missing points of realism and neorealism's explanations of the international system (Rathbun, 2008, p. 313). For this purpose, neoclassical realism aimed to transform the system readings of neorealism into foreign policy analysis (Ripsman et al., 2016, p. 9). However, reducing neoclassical realism only to foreign policy analysis is wrong. Neoclassical realism first addressed the behaviour of executive heads who represent the decision-making mechanism of states. Secondly, the theory included in its analysis the institutional mechanisms of states and the bureaucracy organization within this mechanism (Erdemir, 2023, p. 227). Finally, social classes such as pressure and interest groups that shape the decision-making processes of the ruling elite, which determines the country's domestic and foreign policies, are also included in the scope of neoclassical realism (Rose, 1998, pp. 146-147). In other words, not all segments of the country are excluded from the analysis in a top-down classification that goes down to individuals.

The first question that needs to be asked about neoclassical realism is: Why was neoclassical realism needed? A good place to start would be to revisit Waltz's theory of international politics. Waltz (1979) defined international politics as follows:

> *A theory of international politics can describe the range of possible outcomes of the actions and interactions of states within a given system and show how the range of expectations changes as systems change. It can tell us what pressures are exerted and what possibilities are opened by systems of different structures. However, it cannot tell us how and how effectively the units of a system will respond to these pressures and possibilities a theory of international politics does not focus on the foreign policies of nations. While relying on it, he claims it only explains certain aspects (pp. 71-72).*

In another study, Waltz (1996) stated that "neorealism, as a theory, explains very little in international relations; most of the rest is included in the analysis" (p. 55). The "analyses" to which Waltz refers can, in a sense, be made through neoclassical realism. Neoclassical realism was inspired by the balance of power and its extension, the balance of threat, that Waltz brought to literature (Erdemir, 2023, p. 231). In his article titled "Neoclassical Realism and Foreign Policy Theories", known as the constitution of neoclassical realism, Rose (1998) defined the principles of the theory as follows:

> *Neoclassical realism combines internal and external variables and systematizes by updating some views drawn from classical realist thought. The theory argues that the scope and purpose of a country's foreign policy is determined above all by its place in the international system, especially its relative material power capabilities. That's why he's a realist. However, he argues that the impact of force capabilities on foreign policy is indirect and complex because systemic pressures must be translated through intervening variables, say at the unit level. This is also neoclassical (p. 146).*

Rose's thought (1998), it becomes clear that neoclassical realism also respected the concept of power (p. 146). However, the theory opposed creating a privileged space for power, like realists and neorealists (Strassler, 1998, p. 352). Understanding who distributes power and how it is distributed is more important. According to neoclassical realists, leaders who have gained legitimacy to govern a state for a certain period of time determine how to utilize power, prioritize national interests, and shape their foreign policy within the framework of the country's available material resources. However, since "looking between the lips of leaders" would pose a risk, the perceptions of structures such as pressure and interest groups and bureaucracy organizations have also gained an active role in decision-making. Zakaria (1998) drew attention to the power of a country's state apparatus and its relationship with the culture surrounding it (p. 39). Christensen (1996) drew attention to the importance of the people's ability to direct governments (p. 20).

According to Schweller (2003b), neoclassical realism aims to expand realism and neorealism, making case study a method to test the theory; it seeks to holistically explain states' national and foreign policy behaviours (p. 317). For this reason, the theory closely examines domestic and foreign policies to establish the connection between power and the international system. It criticized the features of realism and neorealism that privilege systemic variables (Thelen & Steinmo, 2010, p.11). According to neoclassical realists, an excellent international relations theory "should discuss the impact of the international system on national behaviour while also showing the role of local factors in external developments" (Schweller, 1998, p. 11). The empirical prediction of the theory is not to assume that states seek security. It shows that they need to control their internal and external environments against the uncertainties of international anarchy (Rose, 1998, p. 152). As a result of all these explanations, neoclassical realism has brought a different methodological formation. This methodological formation linked the internal power possibilities of the states with their foreign policy outputs.

Schweller (1998) suggested that states could change their domestic and foreign policy strategies, thus criticizing the stability of neorealism (p. 19). In his view, states continued the decision-making processes that started at the local level in international politics depending on the changes in their relative power (p. 20). Agreeing with Schweller, Rose (1998) argued that "the increasing trend in the relative power of a state creates an expansion in the country's foreign policy" (p. 167). The ups and downs in the power of states thus placed neoclassical realism in a focus that combined local and international levels of analysis (Wohlforth, 1993, p. 19). Neoclassical realism believes states have different interests rather than being standardized by balancing against power (James, 2022, p. 417).

Schweller (1994) made the following classification to separate the balance of interests from power and threat: At the system level, states' capabilities alone are insufficient to understand their behaviour. In addition, it is also essential to know what states' goals are and what tools they will use to realize these goals. A state must first decide what to do on two issues: Will it spend its power to manage the system or to destroy it? Will it use its power to threaten other states or to make them feel safe? (p. 104; Erdemir, 2023, p. 239). Compared to the balance of power and threat, the balance of interests' states that states' policy changes become a chain of local reasons and affect their foreign policies (Miller & Toritsyn, 2005, p. 353). The system was stable when status quo states were much more robust than revisionist states (Anlar, 2013, p.15). The system eventually changed when a revisionist state or coalition became more potent than the defenders of the status quo (Anlar, 2013, p. 25). For neoclassical realists, what causes states' foreign policies to differ is interests. For this reason, Schweller focused on leaders' behaviour to understand states' interests. According to him, leaders are pragmatic and do not hesitate to consider the balance of interests to achieve their goals (James, 2022, p. 420).

CONCLUSION

Understanding the structure of the international system evolving towards multipolarity today can be possible with the help of the explanatory and predictive powers of international relations theories. The most important requirement for writing the study based on the arguments of the realist paradigm is the ongoing power relations and competition among all actors in the international system, regardless of their capacity and abilities. The dominance of the realist school in the discipline of international relations has brought neorealism one step forward in the literature, especially in explaining the bipolar system of the Cold War years. In this period, the inability to control the behaviour of states brought about by the anarchic state of the international structure has increased the visibility of neorealism's system analysis. The strong positions of the balance of power and threat in explaining the competition between states have caused neorealism to prioritize the system level, ignoring the individual and state levels.

However, after the end of the Cold War, a new phenomenon has emerged in the discussions about the international system. The international system is no longer bipolar, but unipolar, and international developments have begun to be determined by a single great power. In this new period, the communication channels that have accelerated with the advancement of technology and the development of democratization processes have led to the individual and state levels gaining importance again. Therefore, it is not enough to look only at systemic factors to understand the policies of states in the international arena. A current conjuncture has begun to be seen where variables in the domestic policies of states, namely local factors, can also affect the international system. Aware of the momentum created by this environment, neoclassical realists have argued that international relations can be explained by simultaneously including systemic and local factors in the analysis. Neoclassical realists have based their claims on the discourse that "changes in the domestic policies of great powers will also lead to transformations in the international system." The economic and political strengthening of China, Russia and the EU, and the US's loss of its dominant power in the Middle East, have strengthened the arguments of neoclassical realists. Developments in international relations, especially after the 2008 global financial crisis, are surrounded by examples showing that the international system has become multipolar and that this is due to the internal dynamics of great powers.

The main research question of this chapter, "How can the changing power dynamics evolving towards multipolarity in the international system be explained theoretically?" is aimed to be answered by neoclassical realism under the guidance of realist theory. According to neoclassical realism, without considering the perceptions and approaches of the elites, starting from the executive heads who are in the decision-making positions of the states, including the public opinion, pressure and interest groups and the bureaucracy organization, neither the quality of the analyses related to foreign policy, nor the international system can be explained correctly. Thus, neoclassical realism has facilitated the understanding of the international system towards multipolarity by establishing the relationship between local variables and the international structure. First, neoclassical realism discovered the limitations of realism and neorealism in predicting the international system. In the light of these limitations, neoclassical realism presented its own arguments regarding the international system. Although the aspects left by the theory are possible since the evolution process of the international system towards multipolarity is a completed phenomenon, neoclassical realism has drawn an analysis framework in which the individual, state and system levels can be used together. The chapter has presented the theoretical infrastructure of the change in power dynamics experienced within the discipline of international relations in terms of all explanations.

REFERENCES

Acharya, A. (2004, December). Regional Security Arrangements in a Multipolar World? The European Union in Global Perspective. Friedrich Ebert Stiftung. Retrieved May 1, 2025, from https://library.fes.de/pdf-files/iez/global/50101.pdf

Ahrensdorf, P. J. (1997). Thucydides' Realistic Critique of Realism. *Polity, 30*(2), 231–265. DOI: 10.2307/3235218

Anlar, A. (2013). *Security in the Black Sea Region: continuity and change* [PhD Dissertation]. Middle East Technical University.

Anne Braveboy-Wagner, J. (2024). *Diplomatic Strategies of rising nations in the Global South: The search for leadership and influence*. Springer. DOI: 10.1007/978-3-031-52629-9

Ashford, E., & Cooper, E. (2023, October 5). Yes, the world is multipolar. Foreign Policy. https://foreignpolicy.com/2023/10/05/usa-china-multipolar-bipolar-unipolar/

Aydin, M. (2004). Uluslararası İlişkilerin "Gerçekçi" Teorisi: Kökeni, Kapsamı ve Kritiği. *Uluslararası İlişkiler Dergisi, 1*(1), 33–60.

Bojun, Y. (2021). *Konuşmalar* (4th ed.). (Fidan, G., Trans.). Türkiye İş Bankası Kültür Yayınları.

Bull, H. (2002). *The Anarchical Society: A Study of Order in World Politics* (3rd ed.). Palgrave Macmillan.

Burchill, S., Linklater, A., & Devetak, R. (2013). *Theories of international Relations* (5th ed.). Red Globe Press. DOI: 10.1007/978-1-137-31136-8

Carr, E. H. (1939). The Twenty Years' [*An Introduction to the Study of International*. Palgrave Macmillan.]. *Crisis*, 1919–1939.

Celikpala, M. (2005). Geçmişten Günümüze Vazgeçilemeyen Bir Kavram: Ulusal Çıkar. *Hacettepe Üniversitesi İktisadi ve İdari Bilimler Fakültesi Dergisi, 23*(1), 439–461.

Chan, S. (2010). An odd thing happened on the way to balancing: East Asian states' reactions to China's rise. *International Studies Review, 12*(3), 387–412. DOI: 10.1111/j.1468-2486.2010.00944.x

China Radio International Turkce. (2014, September 30). *Konfüçyüs her geçen gün yeniden doğuyor*. Retrieved May 5, 2025, from http://turkish.cri.cn/882/2014/09/30/1s163388.htm

Christensen, T. J. (1996). *Useful adversaries: Grand Strategy, Domestic Mobilization, and Sino-American Conflict, 1947-1958*. Princeton University Press.

Clinton, H. (2011, October 11). America's Pacific Century. *Foreign Policy*. https://foreignpolicy.com/2011/10/11/americas-pacific-century/

Cunha, J. F. P. E. (2020). *Exploring the political chessboard of Syria: An analysis of the role of the US, Russia, Iran and Turkey through the lens of Realism(s)"* [PhD Dissertation, University of Lisbon]. https://repositorio.iscte-iul.pt/bitstream/10071/21103/1/master_joana_prata_cunha.pdf

Dahl, R. A. (1957). The concept of power. *Behavioral Science*, *2*(3), 201–215. DOI: 10.1002/bs.3830020303

Donnelly, J. (2000). *Realism and international relations*. Cambridge University Press. DOI: 10.1017/CBO9780511612510

Donnelly, J. (2012). The Elements of the Structures of International Systems. *International Organization*, *66*(4), 609–643. DOI: 10.1017/S0020818312000240

Elman, C., & Jensen, M. (2014). *The Realism Reader*. Routledge. DOI: 10.4324/9781315858579

Erdemir, E. (2023). EU-China relations in an evolving multipolar international system: A Comparative Analysis of Neo-classical Realism and Neo-realism. *Marmara Journal of European Studies*, *31*(2), 221–241. DOI: 10.29228/mjes.449

Erhan, C. (1996). Ortaya Çıkışı ve Uygulanışıyla Marshall Planı. *Ankara Üniversitesi SBF Dergisi*, *51*(1), 275–287.

Frimpong, I. O. (2025). *China's emerging security diplomacy in Africa*. Springer. DOI: 10.1007/978-981-96-4364-6

Fukuyama, F. (1989). The End of History. *National Interest*, *16*, 3–18. https://www.jstor.org/stable/24027184

Gilpin, R. (1981). *War and Change in World Politics*. Cambridge University Press. DOI: 10.1017/CBO9780511664267

Gilpin, R. (1988). The theory of hegemonic war. *The Journal of Interdisciplinary History*, *18*(4), 591–613. DOI: 10.2307/204816

Glaser, C. L. (1994). Realists as Optimists: Cooperation as Self-Help. *International Security*, *19*(3), 50–90. DOI: 10.2307/2539079

Grin, G. (2022). European Integration A Continent of Revolution. In *Fondation Jean Monnet Pour L'Europe*. Fondation Jean Monnet Pour L'Europe. Retrieved May 5, 2025, from https://jean-monnet.ch/wp-content/uploads/2022/03/22-04-european-integration-g--grin-cdd-n-24.pdf

Gunday, H. (2021). *Zamir*. Dogan Kitap.

Haiming, W. (2014). *Chinese Philosophy*. Source Publications.

Hämäläinen, J., Chen, H., & Zhao, F. (2017). The Chinese prosperity philosophy in the light of the traditional concept of family. *International Social Work*, *62*(1), 224–239. DOI: 10.1177/0020872817721736

Herr, R. S. (2019). Confucian democracy as popular sovereignty. *Asian Philosophy*, *29*(3), 201–220. DOI: 10.1080/09552367.2019.1653529

Hobbes, T. (2024). *Leviathan*. Oxford University Press.

Hobden, S., & Hobson, J. M. (2001). *Historical Sociology of international Relations*. Cambridge University Press.

Holsti, K. J. (1964). The concept of power in the study of international relations. *Background*, *7*(4), 179–194. DOI: 10.2307/3013644

Hughes, C. W., & Lai, Y. M. (2011). *Security Studies: A Reader*. Routledge. DOI: 10.4324/9780203422144

Irondelle, B. (2003). Civil-Military relations and the end of conscription in France. *Security Studies*, *12*(3), 157–187. DOI: 10.1080/09636410390443116

Jakobsen, J. (2022). *The geopolitics of U.S. overseas troops and withdrawal*. Springer. DOI: 10.1007/978-3-030-94488-9

James, P. (2022). *Realism and international relations: A Graphic Turn Toward Scientific Progress*. Oxford University Press. DOI: 10.1093/oso/9780197645024.001.0001

Kennedy, P. (1987). *The Rise and Fall of the Great Powers: Economic Change and Military Conflict from 1500 to 2000*. Random House.

Kızılaslan, K. T. (2023). *The rise of China: the Taiwan question, the Belt and Road initiative and offensive structural realism* [MA Thesis]. Middle East Technical University.

Laitinen-Rawana, S. K. M. (1994). Creating a Unified Europe: Maastricht and Beyond. *The International Lawyer*, *28*(4), 973–993.

Lawler, P. (2024). *International Relations theories*. Oxford University Press. DOI: 10.1093/hepl/9780198784890.001.0001

Layne, C. (1993). The Unipolar Illusion: Why New Great Powers will Rise. *International Security*, *17*(4), 5–51. DOI: 10.2307/2539020

Layne, C. (1997). From Preponderance to Offshore Balancing: America's Future Grand Strategy. *International Security*, *22*(1), 86–124. DOI: 10.1162/isec.22.1.86

Layne, C. (2018). The US–Chinese power shift and the end of the Pax Americana. *International Affairs*, *94*(1), 89–111. DOI: 10.1093/ia/iix249

Levy, J. S. (1998). The Causes of War and The Conditions of Peace. *Annual Review of Political Science*, *1*(1), 139–165. DOI: 10.1146/annurev.polisci.1.1.139

Levy, J. S., & Thompson, W. R. (2005). Hegemonic Threats and Great-Power Balancing in Europe, 1495-1999. *Security Studies*, *14*(1), 1–33. DOI: 10.1080/09636410591001465

Liff, A. P. (2016). Whither the balancers? The case for a methodological reset. *Security Studies*, *25*(3), 420–459. DOI: 10.1080/09636412.2016.1195624

Mazloomi, E. (2023). *From status inconsistency to revisionism: A study of Russian foreign policy from 1991 to the Colour Revolutions* [PhD Dissertation]. University of Malaya.

Mearsheimer, J. J. (2001). *The Tragedy of Great Power Politics*. W. W. Norton & Company.

Mearsheimer, J. J. (2019). Realism and Restraint. *Horizons: Journal of International Relations and Sustainable Development*, *14*, 12–31.

Miller, E. A., & Toritsyn, A. (2005). Bringing the leader back in: Internal Threats and alignment Theory in the Commonwealth of Independent States. *Security Studies*, *14*(2), 325–363. DOI: 10.1080/09636410500234079

Morgenthau, H. J. (1948). *Politics Among Nations: The Struggle for Power and Peace*. Alfred A. Knopf.

Nedić, P., & Mandić, M. (2025). Serbia's foreign policy strategic goals and the issue of Kosovo and Metohija in the conditions of the diminished clarity of the international system. In Pietrzak, P. (Ed.), *International Relations Theory and Philosophical political insights into conflict management* (pp. 85–112). IGI Global. DOI: 10.4018/979-8-3693-9626-1.ch005

Nye, J. S. (2004). Soft power: The Means To Success. In *World Politics*. Public Affairs.

O'Rourke, J. (2013, February 6). *Machiavelli's The Prince: Still Relevant after All These Years | BU Today | Boston University*. Boston University. Retrieved May 5, 2025, from https://www.bu.edu/articles/2013/machiavelli-the-prince-still-relevant-after-all-these-years/

Oguzlu, T. (2021, March 22). *Principled realism: A foreign policy balance*. Daily Sabah. https://www.dailysabah.com/opinion/op-ed/principled-realism-a-foreign-policy-balance

Osiander, A. (2001). Sovereignty, international relations, and the Westphalian myth. *International Organization, 55*(2), 251–287. DOI: 10.1162/002081801551140577

Overtoom, N. (2016). *Challenging Roman Domination: The End of Hellenistic Rule and the Rise of the Parthian State from the Third to the First Centuries BCE* [PhD Dissertation, Lousiana State University]. DOI: 10.31390/gradschool_dissertations.2802

Ozekin, M. K., & Sune, E. (2021). *Critical approaches to international relations: Philosophical Foundations and Current Debates*. Brill.

Rathbun, B. (2008). A Rose by Any Other Name: Neoclassical Realism as the Logical and Necessary Extension of Structural Realism. *Security Studies, 17*(2), 294–321. DOI: 10.1080/09636410802098917

Rathke, J. (2017, May 24). America's NATO Problem: We've Forgotten Why We're a member. *Center for Strategic and International Studies*. https://www.csis.org/analysis/americas-nato-problem-weve-forgotten-why-were-member

Rhamey, J. P., & Bakich, S. D. (2024). *The sources of great power competition: Rising powers, grand strategy, and system dynamics*. Routledge. DOI: 10.4324/9781003396420

Ripsman, N. M., Taliaferro, J. W., & Lobell, S. E. (2016). *Neoclassical realist theory of international politics*. Oxford University Press. DOI: 10.1093/acprof:oso/9780199899234.001.0001

Rose, G. (1998). Neoclassical Realism and Theories of Foreign Affairs Policies. *World Politics, 51*(1), 144–172. DOI: 10.1017/S0043887100007814

Ross, R. S., Wang, D., & Tunsjø, Ø. (2020). *US-China foreign relations: power transition and its implications for Europe and Asia*. Routledge. DOI: 10.4324/9781003056683

Schweller, R. L. (1994). Bandwagoning for profit: Bringing the revisionist state back in. *International Security, 19*(1), 72–107. DOI: 10.2307/2539149

Schweller, R. L. (1997). New Realist Research on alliances: Refining, not refuting, Waltz's balancing proposition. *The American Political Science Review, 91*(4), 927–930. DOI: 10.2307/2952176

Schweller, R. L. (1998). *Deadly imbalances: Tripolarity and Hitler's Strategy of World Conquest*. Columbia University Press.

Schweller, R. L. (2003a). New Realist Research on Alliances: Refining, Not Refuting, Waltz's Balancing Proposition. In Vasquez, J. A., & Elman, C. (Eds.), *Realism and the Balancing of Power: A New Debate*. Pearson.

Schweller, R. L. (2003b). The progressiveness of neoclassical realism. In Elman, C., & Elman, M. F. (Eds.), *Progress in International Relations Theory: Appraising the Field* (pp. 311–348). MIT Press. DOI: 10.7551/mitpress/5627.003.0012

Schweller, R. L. (2004). Unanswered Threats: A Neoclassical Realist Theory of Underbalancing. *International Security, 29*(2), 159–201. DOI: 10.1162/0162288042879913

Sealey, R. (1975). The causes of the Peloponnesian War. *Classical Philology, 70*(2), 89–109. DOI: 10.1086/366154

Sim, M. (2013). Confucian values and human rights. *The Review of Metaphysics, 67*(1), 3–27.

Strassler, R. B. (1998). *The Landmark Thucydides: A Comprehensive guide to the Peloponnesian War*. Free Press.

Taliaferro, J. W. (2000). Security Seeking Below Anarchy: Defensive realism revisited. *International Security, 25*(3), 128–161. DOI: 10.1162/016228800560543

The European External Action Service. (2022). A Strategic Compass for Security and Defence: For a European Union that protects its citizens, values and interests and contributes to international peace and security. In The European External Action Service. Retrieved May 5, 2025, from https://www.eeas.europa.eu/sites/default/files/documents/strategic_compass_en3_web.pdf

Thelen, K., & Steinmo, S. (2010). Historical Institutionalism in Comparative Politics. In Steinmo, S., Thelen, K., & Longstreth, F. (Eds.), *Structuring Politics: Historical Institutionalism in Comparative Analysis* (pp. 1–32). Cambridge University Press.

Toje, A. (2010). *The European Union as a Small Power*. Palgrave Macmillan. DOI: 10.1057/9780230281813

Trachtenberg, M. (1991). The Past and Future of Arms Control. *Daedalus*, *120*(1), 203–216.

Vasquez, J. A. (1983). *The Power of Power Politics: From Classical Realism to Neotraditionalism*. Cambridge University Press.

Viotti, P. R., & Kauppi, M. V. (2012). *International Relations and world Politics*. Pearson.

Walker, R. B. J. (1987). Realism, Change, and International Political Theory. *International Studies Quarterly*, *31*(1), 65–86. DOI: 10.2307/2600660

Walt, S. M. (1987). *The Origins of Alliances*. Cornell University Press.

Walt, S. M. (1988). Testing theories of alliance formation: The case of Southwest Asia. *International Organization*, *42*(2), 275–316. DOI: 10.1017/S0020818300032823

Waltz, K. N. (1979). *Theory of International Politics*. Random House.

Waltz, K. N. (1988). The Origins of War in Neorealist Theory. *The Journal of Interdisciplinary History*, *18*(4), 615–628. DOI: 10.2307/204817

Waltz, K. N. (1996). International politics is not foreign policy. *Security Studies*, *6*(1), 54–57. DOI: 10.1080/09636419608429298

Waltz, K. N. (1997). Evaluating Theories. *The American Political Science Review*, *91*(4), 913–917. DOI: 10.2307/2952173

Waltz, K. N. (2001). *Man, the state, and war: A Theoretical Analysis*. Columbia University Press.

Wivel, A. (2008). Balancing against threats or bandwagoning with power? Europe and the transatlantic relationship after the Cold War. *Cambridge Review of International Affairs*, *21*(3), 289–305. DOI: 10.1080/09557570802253419

Wohlforth, W. C. (1993). *The Elusive Balance: Power and Perceptions During the Cold War*. Cornell University Press. DOI: 10.7591/9781501738081

Xinhua. (2004). *Peaceful Rise: Strategic Choice for China*. 20 January 2022. Retrieved from http://www.china.org.cn/english/features/93939.htm

Zakaria, F. (1998). *From Wealth to Power: The Unusual Origins of America's World Role*. Princeton University Press.

Zakaria, F. (2008). *The Post-American World*. W. W. Norton & Company.

Zięba, R. (2018). *The Euro-Atlantic security system in the 21st century*. Springer. DOI: 10.1007/978-3-319-79105-0

KEY TERMS AND DEFINITIONS

Elite Cohesion: Elite cohesion refers to the extent to which a central government's political leadership is fragmented by persistent internal divisions.

Elite Consensus: Elite consensus is the proximate cause of a state's response or failure to respond to external threats. If there is consensus among policy makers, decision-making leaders will strike a balance.

Glasnost: Glasnost is the Soviet policy of open discussion of political and social issues.

Government and Regime Vulnerability: Government or regime vulnerability asks what the likelihood of the current leadership being removed from political office is. Government or regime vulnerability has attempted to capture the relationship between the rulers and the ruled at any given moment.

Perestroika: Perestroika is the program initiated to restructure Soviet economic and political policy.

Social Cohesion: Social cohesion describes the relative strength of the ties that bind individuals and groups together into the core of a given society. The key to social cohesion is that all members of a society accept the same rules of the game; that is, they support the institutions of society as legitimate and appropriate mechanisms for resolving disagreements among themselves, no matter how deep their disagreements or grievances.

The English School: English School theory has attempted to explain developments in international relations through methodological pluralism, historicism and the interconnection of three key concepts: international system, international society and world society. The school has been seen to challenge the theoretical fragmentation affecting international relations and to build the foundations of a return to grand theory.

The 2008 Global Financial Crisis: The 2008 financial crisis, also called the mortgage crisis, led to a serious liquidity contraction in global financial markets all over the world because of the collapse of the housing market in the United States. It is considered the largest economic crisis in world history after the Great Depression (1929-1939).

The Belt and Road: It is a global infrastructure development strategy adopted by the Chinese government in 2013 to invest in approximately 70 countries and international organizations.

The Primakov Doctrine: The Primakov Doctrine has been described as the 'Near Abroad Doctrine', which determines Russia's relations with its geography, especially with neighbouring countries. The doctrine included determinations about multipolarity, regional alliances, and the disadvantages of the US being a hegemon. Yevgeny Primakov, who served as Russian Foreign Minister between January 1996 and September 1998, proposed a multipolar international system named after the doctrine.

Chapter 5
The Future of International Relations:
Balancing Multipolarity and Non-Polar Challenges

Ramazan Safa
https://orcid.org/0000-0002-1629-5283
Adam Mickiewicz Univesity, Poland

ABSTRACT

This study analyzes the evolving dynamics of the international system in the post-9/11 era, focusing on the interplay between multipolarity and non-polarity. It explores the historical transition from multipolar and bipolar frameworks to a unipolar world dominated by the U.S., and the recent re-emergence of multipolar structures with rising powers like China, India, and the EU. The research highlights the growing role of non-state actors such as multinational corporations and NGOs in shaping global governance. Employing a qualitative methodology, the study integrates literature reviews and case studies to examine how global security and cooperation have been redefined by transnational challenges like climate change, cyber threats, and pandemics. It argues for adaptive, inclusive, and collaborative strategies in international relations, emphasizing regional organizations and multilateral efforts as essential to addressing modern complexities and achieving sustainable global stability.

DOI: 10.4018/979-8-3373-2342-8.ch005

THE FUTURE OF INTERNATIONAL RELATIONS: BALANCING MULTIPOLARITY AND NON-POLAR CHALLENGES

Historically, global power balance has been heavily predicated on military strength, enabling nations to expand territories, enforce policies, and project influence. While military capability remains a crucial element of national security and international stature, the modern geopolitical landscape has evolved significantly. Today, economic power, political stability, ideological influence, diplomatic networks, and strategic leadership play equally vital roles (Markowitz & Fariss, 2017). These factors, amplified by the far-reaching impacts of globalization, have transformed the architecture of global governance and the nature of power relations. Over the past century, the world has moved through distinct phases: from multipolarity to bipolarity during the Cold War, and then into a brief unipolar moment dominated by the United States following the Soviet Union's collapse (Han, 2018). However, the events of September 11, 2001, marked a watershed moment that redefined global security paradigms and accelerated the transition toward a more complex, multipolar, and in some respects, non-polar world. This shift brought non-state threats to the forefront of security agendas, fundamentally altered U.S. foreign policy, and led to the formation of new alliances and coalitions aimed at combating terrorism.

This study aims to examine how 9/11 served as a catalyst for these changes, transforming not only the concept of national and global security but also the roles of both state and non-state actors in shaping international relations. In exploring these developments, the essay will address several key dimensions: the immediate and long-term foreign policy consequences for the United States, the rise of new power centers—including regional powers such as Brazil, India, and South Africa—and the growing influence of entities such as the European Union, multinational corporations, and NGOs in global governance. Moreover, the research will assess how regionalism, exemplified by organizations like the European Union (EU), The Association of Southeast Asian Nations (ASEAN), the Organization of Turkic States (OTS) and the African Union (AfU), has shifted the global power balance and introduced new dynamics in international cooperation and competition. These developments are particularly salient in the face of modern challenges such as cybersecurity threats, climate change, and global pandemics, which further complicate the traditional state-centric model of international relations.

This essay employs a qualitative methodology, drawing on a wide range of academic literature, policy documents, and case studies to analyze the evolution of global governance in the post-9/11 world. Particular attention will be given to recent conflicts, the response to COVID-19, and climate change negotiations, as these serve as key indicators of how multipolar and non-polar dynamics manifest in practice. The significance of this study lies in its ability to elucidate how contemporary global governance must adapt to an era marked by distributed power, diverse actors, and evolving threats. By examining the intersection of traditional power structures and emergent global forces, this analysis aims to offer strategic insights for policymakers, scholars, and international institutions navigating an increasingly interconnected—and unpredictable—world.

The structure of the essay is as follows: it begins with a discussion of the pre-9/11 global order and the Cold War's residual geopolitical structures. It then explores the transformative impact of 9/11 on security, emphasizing the rise of new state and non-state actors. Following this, the essay delves into the complexities of a multipolar and non-polar world, analyzing the roles of regional organizations, international institutions, and global trends such as technological innovation and climate change. Finally, it presents future scenarios for global governance, identifying emerging powers and proposing adaptive strategies for an evolving international system.

POLARITY AND THE INTERNATIONAL ORDER

World orders describe the way power is distributed across the globe, influencing political, economic, and security relations among countries (Goddard & Nexon, 2016). Polarity theory is generally credited to Kenneth Waltz, a prominent figure in the neorealism school of thought. In his influential 1979 work, Theory of International Politics, Waltz used the concept of polarity to analyze the distribution of power in international relations (Waltz, 1979). Waltz, while conducting a structural analysis of the international system, classified the distribution of power into three main types: Unipolarity, where one hegemon dominates the world; Bipolarity, where there is a balance and competition between two major powers; and Multipolarity, where a balance exists among multiple great powers.

The unipolar world order is a system that emerged after the Cold War, especially with the rise of the United States to the position of absolute power. In this order, a single superpower has the capacity to largely steer international policies, institutions, and norms. As Yaqing (2013) notes, the dominance of centralized power can bring stability because a small number of rival actors can directly threaten the authority of the leading country. Indeed, in the 1990s, US military and economic supremacy led to the expansion of NATO, the liberalization of global trade, and the spread of liberal democratic values across the globe. However, this situation has serious drawbacks as well as advantages. First, unipolarity weakens pluralism in decision-making processes and can open the door to unilateral interventions that disregard international law. For example, the US military intervention in Iraq in 2003 without United Nations approval demonstrated the lack of democratic legitimacy of this order. Moreover, the cultural influence of the hegemonic power can impose a dominant lifestyle and way of thinking on other societies through media and technology. This can lead to the erosion of local identities and cultural diversity, while at the same time triggering global backlash, anti-Americanism, and resistance from regional powers. Indeed, the growing economic and military capacities of actors such as China and Russia are among the developments that question the sustainability of unipolarity.

On the other hand, the bipolar world order refers to a structure in which the global balance of power is divided between two major states and these two actors have a similar degree of influence on the international system. The most striking historical example of this order is the rivalry between the United States and the Soviet Union during the Cold War. This struggle between the United States, representing capitalism and liberal democracy, and the Soviet Union, based on socialist ideology, shaped world politics around two separate blocs for many years (Hidayat, 2023). Although these two superpowers did not engage in a direct war, they fought through proxy wars instead of direct confrontation due to the principle of "mutually assured destruction" caused by the mutual nuclear threat. Wars in Vietnam, Korea and Afghanistan stand out as concrete examples of this indirect competition (Baig, 2020). Although this structure has provided stability on a global scale, it has been maintained in a state of constant tension and arms race, and international relations have become highly fragile due to the sensitivity of the parties to each other's spheres of influence. At the same time, this order made it difficult for small and medium-sized states to remain neutral, pushing them to join either the Western or the Eastern bloc. Nevertheless, the bipolar structure created a relative equilibrium in terms of preventing large-scale wars and maintaining the balance of power to a certain extent. In this respect, it provides an example of an international order in which stability and tension coexist.

In contrast, a multipolar world order refers to a structure shaped by multiple influential states or blocs, none of which can unilaterally dominate (Baig, 2020). One of the distinctive features of the multipolar world order is that the balance of power in international relations is flexible and dynamic. Another feature is that the multipolar order encourages more multilateral cooperation. International organizations, diplomatic forums and trade agreements allow for greater cooperation between countries from different poles. This leads to broader efforts to solve global problems. Each pole is composed of powerful states with different geopolitical, economic and military influences. Today, this emerging structure includes powers such as the United States, China, the European Union and Russia (Acharya et al., 2023). Before World War I, Europe was an example of a multipolar order, with multiple empires struggling for control. While multipolarity can provide a balance of power, it increases the complexity of international relations, as multiple rivalries and alliances can lead to instability and increase the likelihood of conflict (Posen, 2009). Instead of ensuring peace, this order risks creating more conflict. Conflicting interests of states at different poles can lead to the spread of conflicts or the emergence of new crises. In particular, the mutual rivalry of great powers with closely aligned interests can increase tensions at the regional and global levels. This shows that the multipolar world offers both advantages and challenges.

Lastly, the non-polar world order describes a structure in international relations in which there is no hegemony of a particular power and power centers are dispersed. Such an order implies a world in which there is no hegemony between the traditional poles and a plurality of actors are influential in global affairs. Such an order implies an environment in which global powers are more evenly distributed, hegemonic dominance is absent, and the relationship structures between states are more complex and multifaceted. Zartman (2019) defines a non-polar world order as a system in which power exists not only among states but also among non-state actors such as multinational corporations, international organizations and influential individuals. This results in a wider range of power dynamics across the globe. One of the major advantages of a non-polar world order is that no single hegemonic power dominates international relations, and the balance of power can be distributed more equitably. This can provide more opportunities for global cooperation. In a world without the dominance of powerful states, smaller states and developing countries can also make their voices heard and have more influence at the global level. Another advantage is that international relations will become more flexible. In a world without polarized conflicts, countries can form different alliances and have more diverse strategic options. At the same time, in a world where many actors are influential, more cooperation and solidarity can emerge to solve global problems. This allows a multi-actor structure to generate broader and more inclusive solutions in global decision-making processes (Koppel & Пархомчук, 2021). However, the non-polar world order also has some negative aspects. First of all, it may create more uncertainty. The disintegration of power centers may lead to less predictable relations between states. This may make international cooperation and dispute resolution more difficult.

Non-polar and multipolar world orders define the distribution of power in global politics in different ways. Non-polar world order refers to a structure in which there is no clear hegemonic state or strong central power, and many actors are influential in global politics. In this order, power is more widely dispersed and there is no single state or a few powerful states dominating others. Multipolar world order, on the other hand, describes a structure in which more than two major powers are influential in world politics and international relations. This order implies power-sharing and more than one state having a significant influence at the global level. For example, in the late 19th century, Europe was dominated by great powers such as Britain, France, Germany, and Russia, leading to a multipolar structure.

Each world order has its advantages and risks. Unipolarity offers stability through concentrated power, while bipolarity involves competition between the two poles, preventing uncontrolled conflicts. Multipolarity provides balance but also competition, while non-polarity offers greater adaptability, responding more flexibly to global challenges that require cooperation beyond individual states. Each system shapes global relations in different ways and responds to international pressures and crises in its unique way.

COLD WAR RIVALRY: STABILITY THROUGH BIPOLARITY

The Cold War era (1947–1991) was defined by a bipolar power structure that influenced almost every aspect of global politics (Baig, 2020; Keersmaeker, 2017; Wagner, 1993). This structure has led to intense ideological, military, and economic competition. The United States of America (US) and the Union of Soviet Socialist Republics (U.S.S.R.) emerged as superpowers, representing competing ideologies—capitalism and communism, respectively—each leading opposing bloc (Thies, 2012). The ideological and strategic competition between the US and the USSR was the main determinant of the international system (Hopf, 1991). This contributed to the "long peace" process, especially through the use of nuclear weapons as a stabilizing deterrent (Väyrynen, 1995). Third actors such as China have also influenced the direction and intensity of this rivalry, demonstrating that the bipolar structure is not absolute (Yazid, 2014). This rigidly divided world order affected economic policies, military alliances, and even domestic politics worldwide. The "Iron Curtain" dividing East and West symbolized not only a physical boundary but also a profound ideological rift, structuring global strategies and alliances for decades (Oates-Indruchová & Mueller, 2017). These two actors, which differed markedly from all other states in terms of military, economic, and political capacity, formed the main axis of the system (Keersmaeker, 2017; Wagner, 1993). However, this structure was based not only on the balance of material power but also on a deep ideological rivalry. This polarization between the capitalist West and the communist East was embodied in foreign policy strategies such as the Truman Doctrine, while the USSR's socialist solidarity efforts constituted the opposite leg of this struggle (Thies, 2013; Yazid, 2014). This ideological and military rivalry led to the clustering of states around alliances such as NATO and the Warsaw Pact, institutionalizing bipolarity and strengthening inter-bloc clustering (Keersmaeker, 2017; Suporn et al., 2021). On the other hand, the proliferation of nuclear weapons and deterrence doctrines that guarantee mutual annihilation prevented direct wars, while intra-system competition continued through proxy wars, crises, and low-intensity conflicts (Hopf, 1991; Kim, 2009). The functioning of the international system is shaped not only by military and economic parameters, but also by norms, identities, and values, which are defined as ideational elements. These elements have assumed an explanatory role in understanding the foreign policy behavior of states (Thies, 2013; Yazid, 2014). All these factors brought relative stability to the Cold War system. While the concentration of power in two centers increased the predictability of the system, the price of this stability was civil wars, coups, and foreign interventions, especially in third-world countries (Suporn et al., 2021; Väyrynen, 1995). In this process, it became more visible how states' domestic political regimes influenced their foreign policy choices, as the democratic structure of the US and the centralist rule of the USSR significantly determined foreign policy behavior and patterns of international engagement (Väyrynen, 1995). Likewise, alliance systems and international institutions were deeply affected by this bipolarity. Structures such as NATO, COMECON, and even the United Nations have lost their neutrality under the influence of superpowers and have often been instrumentalized (Keersmaeker, 2017; Suporn et al., 2021; Yazid, 2014).

On the one hand, nuclear deterrence and bloc discipline prevented direct great-power war. On the other hand, proxy conflicts in Vietnam, Korea, and Afghanistan revealed the instability produced by rigid ideological competition. Bipolarity provided stability through balance, but it also forced smaller states into hierarchical alignments, leaving little room for independent action. Thus, while the system contained major wars, it reproduced insecurity on the periphery and institutionalized ideological polarization.

With the Soviet Union's collapse in 1991, this bipolar system was replaced by a unipolar world order dominated by the United States, as the sole superpower (Wohlforth, 1999). The US wielded considerable influence across global institutions and policies, guiding international relations toward liberal democratic values (Han, 2018). This era was marked by optimism regarding the spread of democracy and open markets, with the United States leading both diplomatically and economically. In order to maintain this advantage, the US has sought a balance in its relations with other great powers and pursued competitive policies in the economic arena (Kapstein & Mastanduno, 2000; Sheetz & Mastanduno, 1997). However, this absolute power position does not correspond to hegemony in the classical sense. Rather than providing global public goods, the US has often preferred unilateral decision-making processes, which has led to criticism from both allies and rivals (Wilkinson, 1999). In this context, the conceptualization of "unipolarity without hegemony" draws attention. International institutions played an important role in maintaining US influence in this process. Steps such as the eastward expansion of NATO and the redefinition of the effectiveness of organizations such as the United Nations reveal the US quest for international legitimacy and its instrumental multilateralism strategy (Catley, 1999; Bert, 1997). Although these efforts gave the appearance of multilateralism, in practice they served the construction of an international order in line with US interests. Different regions have reacted differently to this hegemonic approach. While the European Union sought a more egalitarian partnership with the US, states in East Asia, while welcoming the US military presence from a security perspective, were critical of unilateralist tendencies (Fukui & Fukai, 1998; Rubin & Keaney, 2001). The US role in the unipolar order has also been decisive in the economic sphere. The Washington administration assumed the role of the architect of the global economic order with policies such as the expansion of free trade, liberalization of capital movements and support for liberal democracies (Catley, 1999; Hawthorn, 1999). In this process, the US, acting in line with the hegemonic stability theory, consolidated its economic supremacy through institutions such as the International Monetary Fund (IMF) and the World Bank (Sheetz & Mastanduno, 1997; Khalilzad, 1995). However, this absolute dominance also brought with it competition from rising economic powers such as Japan and Germany. The US responded to this competition with national economic mobilization strategies and efforts to shape global trade rules in its favor (Kapstein & Mastanduno, 2000; Sheetz & Mastanduno, 1997). In this context, the "Washington Consensus" aimed to expand neoliberal reforms on a global scale, but with consequences that deepened social and economic inequalities in various regions (Catley, 1999; Amin, 1992).

In terms of military strategies, the US has developed comprehensive policies to maintain its unipolar position. The 1992 Pentagon draft strategy aimed to prevent the emergence of any global rival and to preserve the unipolar order (Wohlforth, 1999; Khalilzad, 1995). The practical extension of this strategy has been to maintain a permanent military presence in regions such as East Asia and the Middle East. Although this presence sometimes had the effect of enhancing regional stability, unilateral US interventions in these regions were met with serious criticism (Fukui & Fukai, 1998; Rubin & Keaney, 2001). The Gulf War is one of the most striking examples of this period; the intervention of the US-led coalition with UN approval demonstrates an attempt to strike a balance between multilateralism and military effectiveness. However, the structures that emerged after the war brought new debates questioning the unlimited power of the US (Herrmann, 1991; Amin, 1992). In this context, NATO's expansion to the east was an important turning point in both the consolidation of US influence and the restructuring of relations with Russia (Bert, 1997).

On the cultural dimension, the United States continued to position itself as an "exceptional" nation and continued its mission to spread values such as freedom and democracy around the world as universal norms (Catley, 1999; Hawthorn, 1999). These values were disseminated on a global scale not only through diplomatic discourse but also through media, education and cultural export channels. The rise of American popular culture and the shaping of global consumption patterns around the American lifestyle have also brought up the debate on cultural homogenization (Catley, 1999; Amin, 1992). In this process, the presentation of liberal democracy and the free market economy as the only valid system was met with resistance in some regions. Especially in the Middle East and Asia, US cultural and political interventions were perceived as a threat to the preservation of local identities, which fueled anti-Americanism (Hansen, 2000; Herrmann, 1991). As a result, the process of cultural hegemony building, although supported by soft power elements, has not been able to suppress the existence of differences and identities at the global level, on the contrary, it has triggered conflicts from time to time.

However, this unipolar phase proved relatively short-lived as regional powers and alliances, such as the EU and Asia-Pacific Economic Cooperation (APEC), began to rise, signaling a gradual shift away from unipolarity (Peters, 2022). Emerging actors like China, India, and Russia began to assert themselves, leading to a more complex multipolar international system with several influential centers (Acharya et al., 2023).

SEPTEMBER 11 AS A CATALYST FOR CHANGE

The September 11, 2001, attacks on the United States marked a critical turning point in this evolving structure. These attacks highlighted vulnerabilities even within the most powerful states and demonstrated that threats could arise from unconventional sources—not just from rival states (Mueller & Stewart, 2012). This event led to a global reassessment of security, emphasizing the importance of counterterrorism and accelerating the trend toward multipolarity. Analysts recognized the growing influence of other global powers, such as China, Russia, India, and the European Union, as well as the rise of regional actors like Turkey, Brazil, and Iran (Dal, 2018). This newly diversified power landscape began to shift international relations from a singular focus on U.S.-centric diplomacy to a more Afro-Eurasian axis, where economic and strategic interests across regions played central roles (Arkhipov & Yeletsky, 2015). In addition to multipolar dynamics, some scholars began to see features of a non-polar world order emerging, characterized by the diffusion of power not just among several states but also among influential non-state actors (Koppel & Пархомчук, 2021). In a non-polar world, global power is widely distributed beyond national governments to include multinational corporations, international organizations, non-governmental organizations (NGOs), and even influential individuals (Bormann et al., 2018). Unlike a multipolar world, where several major powers still compete for influence, a non-polar structure involves various entities whose influence cuts across borders, affecting international relations on issues ranging from climate change to digital security and human rights. In this order, states cannot singlehandedly control outcomes on global issues without the cooperation of these non-state actors (Oidtmann & Mokry, 2020). This contrasts sharply with the hierarchical power distribution seen in unipolar, bipolar, or even multipolar frameworks.

The post-9/11 era amplified both multipolar and non-polar characteristics within the global order. As new powers emerged, they often aligned their influence through regional organizations like the Shanghai Cooperation Organization (SCO), the Union of South American Nations (UNASUR), and the Organization for Democracy and Economic Development (GUAM) (Larson, 2018). These alliances not only focused on economic and military objectives but also reflected diverse strategic interests, giving regional powers leverage in areas that the U.S. might not directly influence (Dittmer, 2014). Meanwhile, non-state actors and multinational corporations expanded their roles, particularly in addressing cross-border challenges like climate change, economic development, and cybersecurity.

Security perceptions have similarly evolved to accommodate both multipolar and non-polar dynamics. The end of the Cold War broadened the scope of security concerns to include economic instability, globalization, and environmental pressures, while the September 11 attacks underscored the importance of non-traditional threats, such as terrorism, human trafficking, (Langhorne, 2005) and cyber risks (Jang et al., 2016). Responding to these challenges, the United States adopted a more aggressive counter-terrorism strategy, exemplified by the 2002 National Security Strategy, which prioritized countering rogue states and terrorist networks (Daalder et al., 2002). This policy expanded the focus of NATO and other international alliances to encompass both traditional and unconventional security risks, signaling a broader, more comprehensive approach to collective security. In this complex blend of multipolar and non-polar elements, global stability depends increasingly on collaboration among a wider array of actors. Today, both state and non-state players shape security strategies, economic development, and environmental policy (Gill, 2010). Multinational corporations, with their transnational operations, play significant roles in economic and technological developments, while international NGOs influence humanitarian policies and environmental regulations. These actors, alongside regional alliances, illustrate the growing non-polar dimension of the world order, where cooperation and networks drive outcomes on issues beyond any single nation's control. The rise of non-state actors reveals how state-centric approaches are insufficient to address interconnected issues such as cyberterrorism, climate change, and global health crises.

On the other hand, Russia and China have often emerged as a counterweight to US hegemony, while regional powers such as Turkey, India and the EU have also dealt a blow to US hegemony. Russia is putting more effort into global networking and promoting a multiple world order, while China is focusing on expanding its influence through regional partnerships (Marassiro, 2022; Turner, 2009). Through strategic projects such as the Green Deal, the EU has assumed a leadership role in the face of new security threats such as global warming and environmental problems. The EU's approach demonstrates its continued importance in global governance (Janković & Mitić, 2024). India seeks to establish itself as a great power through strategic partnerships and multilateral engagements. Trying to balance its relations with the US, Russia and China, India seeks to strengthen its position without unduly antagonizing any major power (Velichkin, 2024). In addition, the rise of non-traditional security threats allows medium-sized powers like Turkey and civil societies to play a greater role in global governance. These actors are increasing their influence in a polarized world (Howe, 2022).

The terrorist attacks of September 11, 2001, marked a watershed in international relations, exposing vulnerabilities even at the core of U.S. power. Systemic indicators of transition became visible:

-*Security expansion:* NATO's mission in Afghanistan and the U.S. National Security Strategy of 2002 redefined security to include counter-terrorism, pre-emptive strikes, and unconventional threats.
-*Emerging rivals:* Russia reasserted itself through military interventions in its neighborhood, China launched the Belt and Road Initiative to reshape global connectivity, and India consolidated its role in BRICS and regional diplomacy.
-*Rise of non-state actors:* Al-Qaeda, later ISIS, as well as NGOs and multinational corporations, demonstrated that global governance was no longer state-centric.
-*New transnational challenges:* Cybersecurity breaches, climate change, and pandemics blurred the line between domestic and international threats.

These developments show that 9/11 did not merely inaugurate a "war on terror" but catalyzed a systemic restructuring. Power became more diffused across multiple states and non-state actors, accelerating the movement toward both multipolarity and non-polarity.

The systemic transition after 9/11 can be observed through several concrete indicators that reshaped global governance. The 2002 U.S. National Security Strategy, known as the Bush Doctrine, introduced the principle of pre-emptive war and emphasized unilateral action against perceived threats, marking a decisive shift in U.S. foreign policy. NATO's mission in Afghanistan demonstrated how traditional security alliances were redefined to address non-traditional threats, extending their role beyond territorial defense to global counter-terrorism operations. Simultaneously, new security paradigms emerged, incorporating concepts such as cyber resilience, biosecurity, and energy security into the mainstream of international relations. Rising powers also seized this momentum: China expanded its influence through the Belt and Road Initiative, Russia reasserted its geopolitical weight in Georgia and Ukraine, and India strengthened its role in BRICS as a voice for the Global South. These developments illustrate how 9/11 catalyzed a multidimensional restructuring of the international order.

NON-STATE ACTORS AND THE TRANSFORMATION OF GLOBAL GOVERNANCE

The multipolar world order has led to a greater role for new actors in international politics. When the international system was unipolar or bipolar, global security was shaped under the control of more centralized actors. During the Cold War, two superpowers, the United States and the Soviet Union, tightly controlled their spheres of influence, greatly restricting the space for non-state actors. Similarly, in the post-Cold War unipolar order, the military and intelligence capacity of the United States created a relatively stronger and more direct response to global terrorist threats. However, during these periods, terrorism was seen as a security problem that was largely limited to the geopolitical balance and resonated more at the regional level. In contrast, in the multipolar world order, the distribution of power has become more dispersed and different regional powers have become more independent in determining their own security policies. In a multipolar world, gaps created by state weakness or collapse create fertile ground for terrorist networks to operate and evolve. Conflicts of interest between states and incompatibilities in the perception of common threats allow terrorist organizations to take advantage of these gaps and act more easily. Since one state's counterterrorism efforts may conflict with the interests of another, it is becoming increasingly difficult to formulate a unified strategy at the global level. Weak states lack the capacity to provide security and this creates opportunities for terrorist groups to base and recruit. Failed states, particularly in the Middle East and Africa, have become hotbeds of terrorist activity due to their inability to fight corruption and redress historical grievances (Piazza, 2008; Plummer, 2011).

Moreover, multipolarity can cause different states to develop different attitudes towards the same terrorist network. While some states may see these groups as strategic tools, for others these organizations may pose a direct threat. This fragmented approach creates a wider geopolitical space for terrorist organizations to both shelter and operate. Terrorist groups often operate across borders, with recruitment, planning and implementation taking place in different countries. They form alliances with other groups to expand their operational reach and resources, complicating counterterrorism efforts (Wright & D'Amato, 2023). Therefore, in a multipolar order, terrorist networks can take advantage of not only security gaps but also the weak coordination environment created by inter-state competition.

In a multipolar world system, multinational corporations (MNCs) are another non-state actor increasing its influence. The growing influence of multinational corporations in a multipolar world is directly related to their capacity to utilize and benefit from the structure of global capitalism effectively. With the evolution of the international system from unipolarity to multipolarity, MNCs have become decisive actors not only in economics but also in the political and social spheres. Through their cross-border operations, these companies can seize global market opportunities, shape regulatory structures, and drive technological innovation. These capabilities, coupled with their capacity to benefit from a multipolar structure, further increase the influence of MNCs at the international level. By restructuring international production structures, trade, and investment flows, MNCs deepen global economic integration and increase their influence in many regions (Liu, 2025). Their access to low-cost production inputs and flexible regulatory environments allow them to expand their markets and consolidate their economic power (Roach, 2005). Their establishment of production facilities, especially in developing countries, leads to an increase in foreign direct investment in these countries, but this also increases the external dependence of local economies. MNCs exert pressure on governments, demanding tax reductions, incentive packages and regulatory relief, and create competition among countries in line with these demands (Roach, 2005). Especially through free trade agreements, they indirectly overcome the sovereignty of many nation-states and have a say in decision-making processes. This process leads to the weakening of local laws and labor protection measures, while at the same time increasing corporate power on a global scale (Roach, 2005).

MNCs make significant contributions to technological development and the increase of production capacities in host countries, thus becoming strategic actors in industrial development processes (Oleynik, 1981). Activities such as technology transfer and the development of new products and processes not only increase the competitiveness of companies, but also play an important role in the structural transformation of the multipolar world (Oleynik, 1981). However, this technological transformation does not always serve the development of local capacity and in some cases reproduces dependency relations. The growing influence of MNCs in the multipolar world brings with it specific challenges. Competition between global powers and the mechanisms of exploitation inherent in capitalist relations of production can trigger monopolization tendencies and disruption of the local economic order. Especially in the countries of the Global South, the strong ties of local elites to transnational capitalism limit their economic and political independence and further consolidate the influence of MNCs (Liu, 2025; Harris, 2024). In this context, an effective governance mechanism and binding regulations at the international level are needed for a more just, sustainable and balanced global structure. A multipolar capitalist world system devoid of economic regulation has the potential to increase the number of exploiting countries and undermine the economic development of the countries of the Global South.

In a multipolar world, not only specific states, terrorist organizations, or MNCs but also non-governmental organizations (NGOs) have become important actors in global governance and policy-making processes. Through diplomatic engagement and policy advocacy, NGOs are able to influence decision-making at local, national and international levels. In this context, the strategies and mechanisms used by NGOs to increase their influence in this complex geopolitical landscape should be carefully examined.

NGOs often establish Transnational Advocacy Networks to increase their influence. These networks bring together NGOs, state actors, and international organizations united around common goals. An example is the International Campaign to Abolish Nuclear Weapons (ICAN), which played a major role in the implementation of the Treaty on the Prohibition of Nuclear Weapons (TPNW). By combining advocacy with direct diplomacy, ICAN demonstrated how NGOs can be effective in shaping international agreements in a multi-polar world (Mikhaylenko, 2022). NGO diplomatic engagement is based on working directly with governments and international organizations. Thanks to their expertise and moral authority, NGOs can exert significant influence on government policies, especially in environmental negotiations and human rights issues (Albin, 1999; Lucas et al., 2023). During the formation of agreements such as the Paris Climate Agreement and the Kunming-Montreal Global Biodiversity Framework, NGOs have contributed to the negotiation process by providing technical information as well as mobilizing public support (Betsill & Corell, 2008; Albin, 1999). NGOs engage in policy advocacy by bringing global or humanitarian issues to the forefront, thereby becoming agenda-setters. This non-state actor can influence international political discourse by framing issues, setting goals, and imposing norms.

NGOs have specialized knowledge and expertise that decision-makers often lack. This knowledge gives them the power to guide decision-making in areas that require technical know-how (Betsill & Corell, 2008; Albin, 1999). Public opinion mobilization is also one of the most effective strategies of NGOs. They put pressure on governments by raising public awareness and garnering support. This strategy also includes interaction with the media. Media campaigns on issues such as deforestation and whaling have led to policy changes by raising public awareness (Albin, 1999; Lucas et al., 2023). With the opportunities brought by the digital age, NGOs are using digital advocacy effectively. Social media platforms are widely used for functions such as recruiting supporters, organizing campaigns and forming public opinion. Digital campaigns have been particularly effective in raising awareness about human rights violations and environmental crises (Hall et al., 2019). NGOs play a functional role by filling governance gaps in areas not adequately covered by states and international organizations. Their capacity to act quickly in times of crisis and their influence at the local level make them critical in areas such as humanitarian aid and human rights defense (Weaver, 2020). Thus, NGOs increased their influence in a multipolar world by building transnational networks, conducting strategic diplomacy, engaging in policy advocacy, leveraging expertise, and mobilizing public support. Their ability to adapt to changing circumstances and maintain their independence will be decisive for the future of their effect on global politics.

The post-9/11 era vividly illustrates how non-state actors have transformed global security dynamics. Terrorist organizations provide one of the most direct examples: al-Qaeda's worldwide operations, from the 2004 Madrid train bombings to the 2005 London attacks, demonstrated the ability of non-state groups to destabilize even advanced democracies. Later, ISIS exploited state failure in Iraq and Syria to establish territorial control, creating an unprecedented hybrid threat that combined terrorism with quasi-state governance. Multinational corporations also became decisive actors in global politics. Pfizer and Moderna, through the rapid development of COVID-19 vaccines, not only shaped global health responses but also acquired bargaining power in international diplomacy. At the same time, technology giants such as Google and Meta influenced political processes worldwide through their control over data and digital platforms, making them critical players in cybersecurity and information warfare. Non-governmental organizations, too, have been essential: Greenpeace and Friends of the Earth played significant roles in pushing states toward the Paris Climate Agreement, while ICAN's advocacy culminated in the Treaty on the Prohibition of Nuclear Weapons in 2017. Even individual actors such as Elon Musk, who provided Ukraine with Starlink satellite services during the 2022 war, highlight how personal influence can alter strategic outcomes. These examples underscore the diffusion of power in a non-polar system, where state authority coexists with the growing leverage of non-state entities.

In conclusion, the evolution of the international system into a multipolar structure has enabled non-state actors to gain more decisive roles in global politics. These actors, ranging from terrorist organizations to MNCs and NGOs, clearly demonstrate that international relations are not only an inter-state arena. The more dispersed distribution of power has led to a lack of coordination in global security and differences in threat perceptions, which has created a fertile ground for terrorist organizations. At the same time, multinational corporations have seized the opportunities offered by global capitalism and increased their influence not only in economic but also in political and social spheres. On the other hand, NGOs have become more visible in global governance and have gained an active position in international decision-making processes with their technical expertise, norm-creating roles, and effectiveness in mobilizing public opinion. Expanding their spheres of influence with the opportunities offered by the digital age, these organizations fill important gaps in areas where states fall short.

REGIONALISM IN A FRAGMENTED WORLD

In today's multipolar global political order, regional organizations such as the EU, AfU, ASEAN, and the OTS have become increasingly decisive actors in international relations. The influence of these organizations is mainly shaped by three factors: economic impact, political stability, and conflict resolution. it is necessary to explain why these three elements are important. Economic impact is one of the cornerstones of the power of regional organizations in the international system. By promoting economic integration and cooperation, they create powerful economic blocs that influence global trade, investment, and economic policies. On the other hand, political stability is vital for the effectiveness of regional organizations. Stable political environments strengthen trust and cooperation and increase the capacity to jointly tackle global challenges. Moreover, one of the most important functions of regional organizations is conflict resolution. These organizations contribute to global peace and security by addressing conflicts in their respective regions.

The European Union is one of the largest economies in the world and has a highly institutionalized and legalized structure that facilitates economic integration among member states. Its economic influence is not limited to Europe but is expanding to enhance competitiveness in dynamic regions such as the Indo-Pacific. For example, the EU's economic cooperation with ASEAN demonstrates its desire to maintain global economic competitiveness (Chytopoulou, 2024; Páldi, 2020). Political stability plays a decisive role in the EU's international influence. While challenges such as Brexit and migration crises have tested the unity of the union, the EU is still seen as an important example of political stability and regional solidarity (Bharti & Aryal, 2023; Ewers-Peters, 2018). The 2021 European Recovery Fund was as much a message of political unity as economic recovery. Moreover, the EU plays an active role in resolving conflicts within and beyond Europe. In particular, its interventions in the Ukraine-Russia war show the union's importance to peace and stability (Bharti & Aryal, 2023; Ewers-Peters, 2018).

Another regional organization, ASEAN, has become an important hub for European goods and a critical player in regional supply chains. Its economic growth and integration efforts have led the region to become the focus of strategic competition between global powers. ASEAN's role in free trade initiatives has prompted the EU to forge stronger economic ties with the region (Sutanto & Priyanto, 2023; Islam, 2015). For example, ASEAN countries have formed the world's largest free trade bloc with the signing of the RCEP (Regional Comprehensive Economic Partnership) in 2020. Despite the political and cultural diversity among its members, ASEAN has made significant strides in maintaining stability. Consensus-based decision-making and strategic engagement with major powers support the political stability of the organization (Mirza et al., 2024; Sutanto & Priyanto, 2023). ASEAN seeks to resolve disputes in Southeast Asia through mediation and strategic balancing and aims to manage disputes in the South China Sea and ensure maritime security. For example, the Code of Conduct in the South China Sea (CoC) negotiated with China to reduce tensions between the parties in the South China Sea is a concrete reflection of this mission. These efforts demonstrate the importance of the organization in conflict resolution (Mirza et al., 2024; Sutanto & Priyanto, 2023).

The economic impact of the African Union, which is growing in importance on the African continent, is based on its efforts to promote regional integration and development. Although the continent faces serious challenges, initiatives such as the African Continental Free Trade Area (AfCFTA) aim to increase economic cohesion and strengthen Africa's global economic position (Massoni, 2020; Piccolino, 2014). Initiatives such as the AfCFTA aim to increase economic cohesion and strengthen Africa's global economic position. For example, the AfCFTA, which entered into force in 2021, aims to increase continental trade by 60%, covering a market of 1.2 billion people. The African Union faces significant political challenges, including conflicts, weak institutions and external interference. Despite this, AfU contributes to political stability on the continent through peacekeeping missions, mediation and international partnerships (Birhan, 2024; Musau, 2023).The diplomatic mediation efforts during the Tigray conflict in Ethiopia demonstrated the capacity of the organization to ensure stability. Moreover, the AfU peacekeeping force deployed in Mali has played an important role in the fight against radical groups. The AfU is at the forefront of conflict resolution on the continent, countering security threats through tools such as early warning systems and peacekeeping missions. Despite the challenges, significant progress has been made (Birhan, 2024; Musau, 2023).

The Organization of Turkic States, which consists of Turkic-speaking countries, has gained momentum in recent years due to geopolitical changes. By promoting trade, investment and economic cooperation, it has become an important actor in regional socio-economic development (Guliyev, 2024). For example, the transport links between Azerbaijan and Turkey developed under the Zangezur Corridor project support intra-organizational economic integration. The OTS strengthens regional ties to enhance political stability among member states. Cooperation developed through common ethnocultural ties promotes regional cohesion and political solidarity (Guliyev, 2024). The "Vision 2040 of the Turkic World" adopted at the Istanbul Summit in 2021 formed the basis for long-term strategic plans to support political integration. Cooperation and solidarity among the member states stands out as an important element that enhances regional stability (Guliyev, 2024).

Economic integration and political stability are mutually reinforcing processes. Stable political environments facilitate economic cooperation, while economic development increases the global effectiveness of regional organizations. For example, the EU's economic strength is supported by its political stability, while ASEAN's growth is closely linked to regional stability (Chytopoulou, 2024; Sutanto & Priyanto, 2023). Political stability is essential for effective conflict resolution. Politically stable regional organizations have a more competent capacity to resolve conflicts and maintain peace. The AfU's efforts to combat conflicts prioritize political stability in this context (Birhan, 2024; Musau, 2023). Economic power can be an effective tool for conflict resolution. Through economic sanctions or incentives, regional organizations can manage conflicts. The EU's economic influence plays an important role in conflict resolution in Europe and other regions (Bharti & Aryal, 2023; Ewers-Peters, 2018).

As can be seen, the multipolarity trend, which has gained momentum since the beginning of the 21st century, has brought about a fundamental restructuring not only in the balancing act between great powers but also in global governance structures. In this context, there has been a noticeable shift from global to regional governance. This transition is taking place in a context where the effectiveness of universal institutions such as the United Nations and the World Trade Organization is being questioned, while regional actors are emerging as more functional, inclusive, and conjunctural responsive structures. This transformation reflects fundamental changes not only at the normative level but also at the structural level. No longer mere implementing bodies, regional organizations have become multi-layered actors shaping normative arrangements, intervening in conflicts, determining economic strategies and conducting diplomatic engagement. In this context, regional governance can be defined as an "intermediate scale" form of governance that has implications not only at the regional level but also at the global level.

The global order is no longer a structure driven from a single center (i.e. the West), but rather a structure with multiple centers of governance located in different geographies. Organizations such as the EU, ASEAN, the AfU and the OTS claim to have a say not only in their own regions but also in global affairs. These organizations not only adapt to existing international norms but also generate regional norms and practices that are informed by their own historical, cultural and political contexts. While the limitations of transatlantic structures such as NATO are becoming evident in the field of security, the African Union's peacekeeping missions or ASEAN's mediating role in the South China Sea crisis reveal the rise of regional security architectures. Similarly, in the economic sphere, the EU's digital tax regimes or the AfCFTA's efforts to liberalize continental trade point to the construction of alternative models of economic governance. In this framework, the structural character of the global system is changing. Governance is no longer shaped solely by the interests of nation-states, but by the strategic visions and collective capacity building of regional actors. Therefore, today, the term "crisis of global governance" as well as the concept of "rise of regional governance" is becoming as central to the international relations literature.

CASE STUDIES AND FUTURE TRENDS

The transition from a unipolar to a multipolar world order has led to fundamental changes in global conflicts. Shaped by the rise of new power centers such as China, Russia, and India, this transformation has profoundly affected not only the balance of power in international relations but also the way national security strategies are structured. This polycentric structure has further complicated the classical security dilemma, where every move to enhance the security of states is perceived as a potential threat by other actors. The deepening of the security dilemma is particularly evident in geopolitically sensitive regions such as Eastern Europe, the Indo-Pacific, and the Middle East (Loza et al., 2024; Baghdasaryan, 2025).

Today, the security dilemma is not limited to interstate threats, but has evolved into a "composite security dilemma" involving non-state actors. New forms of threats such as cyber-attacks, transnational terrorism, and economic pressures further complicate the international security environment (Wilson et al., 2020). In this context, Russia and China's drive towards nuclear weapons modernization has put the risk of nuclear proliferation back on the agenda (Alkanalka, 2023). For instance, the war in Ukraine has made the classic security dilemma even more salient, with Russia's military intervention leading to NATO's eastward expansion and military buildups within the alliance (Alkanalka, 2023; Prorokovic, 2023). Similarly, China's rising power has led countries such as Australia and India to develop balancing policies against Beijing (Gore, 2015; Baghdasaryan, 2025). The Middle East, on the other hand, remains an arena of proxy wars, with actors such as Iran, Saudi Arabia, and Turkey struggling for influence (Loza et al., 2024; Baghdasaryan, 2025).

In order to adapt to this multipolarity, states are reshaping their national security strategies. These reconfigurations are characterized by changes in military posture, alliance policies, and economic/technological strategies. For instance, the United States is strategically prioritizing the Indo-Pacific region to balance China's influence in the Asia-Pacific region, while maintaining its commitment to NATO (Kopylov et al., 2024; Elamiryan, 2023). China, on the other hand, is expanding its military capacity and seeking to form a strategic bloc against US influence, especially by strengthening its relations with countries in the Global South (Eisenman & Heginbotham, 2019; Marassiro, 2022). Russia, on the other hand, uses its energy resources and military capacity as strategic tools to increase its geopolitical influence (Roseira, 2023; Prorokovic, 2023).

Another fundamental dimension of national security strategies is economic and technological competition. The US and China are engaged in intense competition for global supremacy in areas such as artificial intelligence, semiconductor technologies, and quantum computing (Slawotsky, 2024; Eisenman & Heginbotham, 2019). This situation reveals that national security is no longer defined only by military capabilities, but also by economic and technological capabilities. Peace-building requires strengthening international cooperation and dialogue processes, taking confidence-building steps, and establishing effective mechanisms for conflict resolution. States should develop policies to ensure mutual trust while pursuing their national interests. In this process, economic and technological cooperation, regional alliances, and multilateral diplomacy should take center stage. Furthermore, the root causes of conflicts, such as inequalities, resource-sharing problems and human rights violations, should be addressed to ensure a just order, and an approach based on international law and human rights norms should be adopted. For lasting peace, not only military solutions but also social reconciliation, cultural dialogue, and sustainable development should be promoted.

A multipolar world is also manifesting itself in issues such as the COVID-19 pandemic and climate change, profoundly affecting international cooperation and global governance structures. The COVID-19 pandemic and climate change constitute two of the most significant global crises of the 21st century, both requiring unprecedented levels of international cooperation. However, the emergence of a multipolar world, where power is distributed among many state and non-state actors, has created both opportunities and challenges for global cooperation. The pandemic has exposed weaknesses in international health systems, while climate change has exposed the fragility of environmental agreements. In a multipolar world, the capacity to deal with these crises depends on the willingness of countries to transcend geopolitical rivalries and prioritize collective action. The pandemic has highlighted the need for strong global health governance, particularly in areas such as vaccine distribution, data sharing and equitable access to health services. However, responses have often been fragmented, with countries prioritizing national interests over global solidarity (Cole & Dodds, 2021; Bauernfeind et al., 2024). Climate change requires long-term, coordinated efforts to reduce greenhouse gas emissions and adapt to its impacts. However, the multipolar nature of global politics has led to uneven progress as some countries prioritize economic growth over environmental sustainability (Umamah et al., 2024; Asad et al., 2023).

The multipolar world has reshaped the dynamics of global health governance, particularly in the context of COVID-19. While some argue that multipolarity encourages diversity in the production of solutions, others argue that it leads to fragmentation and inefficiency. One opportunity is that multipolarity offers diverse perspectives and innovative solutions that can strengthen health initiatives. For example, China and India have played critical roles in vaccine production and distribution during the pandemic (Montgomery, 2024). Moreover, the rise of new global health leaders such as the Coalition for Epidemic Preparedness Innovations (CEPI) has shown that multipolarity can contribute to more inclusive decision-making processes (Kheir-Mataria et al., 2024). However, multipolarity is not without its challenges. The absence of strong implementation mechanisms in most environmental agreements creates significant gaps between commitments and actual emission reductions (Umamah et al., 2024; Asad et al., 2023). In addition, the multipolar world has deepened inequalities between developed and developing countries. While developing countries feel the impacts of climate change more severely, they do not receive sufficient support for adaptation and mitigation efforts (Nazareth et al., 2024; Zhang, 2024). Moreover, geopolitical tensions between major powers such as the US and China hinder cooperation on global issues. Competition in areas such as vaccine diplomacy and green technology often prevents collective action (Góes, 2024; Montgomery, 2024).

It is essential to strengthen global cooperation on health and environmental initiatives to meet the challenges posed by a multipolar world. Institutions such as the World Health Organization (WHO) and the United Nations Framework Convention on Climate Change (UNFCCC) should increase their capacity to ensure adaptation and coordinate global responses (Youde, 2024; Burci, 2024). Climate change statistics also reveal systemic vulnerabilities: despite repeated commitments, G20 countries were responsible for nearly 80% of global emissions in 2022, with only a handful on track to meet the Paris Agreement targets. Governments should support social dialogue mechanisms that promote cooperation between different stakeholders, such as civil society and the private sector. The COVID-19 pandemic has highlighted the importance of equitable access to vaccines and other health commodities. Future health initiatives should prioritize adequate support to low- and middle-income countries (Bauernfeind et al., 2024; Kheir-Mataria et al., 2024). Recent data further reinforce the significance of non-polar challenges in shaping international relations. According to COVAX reports, by mid-2021 less than 2% of people in low-income countries had received a COVID-19 vaccine, illustrating the deep inequalities in global health governance. These figures highlight that today's challenges are not confined to interstate rivalries but are embedded in complex, cross-border problems requiring inclusive governance. Incorporating empirical data into the analysis demonstrates not only the urgency of addressing these issues but also the necessity of integrating non-state actors into sustainable solutions. Developing countries need financial and technical support to tackle climate change.

Fulfillment of climate finance commitments by developed countries is critical to achieving global climate goals (Nazareth et al., 2024; Yang, 2023). Global solidarity is essential to tackle crises such as pandemics and climate change. This requires a shift from nation-centered approaches to a more collaborative mindset (Cole & Dodds, 2021; Umamah et al., 2024). By capitalizing on the strengths and mitigating the limitations of multipolarity, the global community can move towards a more resilient and sustainable future.

CONCLUSION

In the 21st century, the international system entered an evolutionary process characterized by multipolarity. Accelerated by landmark global crises such as the 9/11 attacks, this transformation reflects a world increasingly characterized by complexity, interdependence, and shifting balances of power. What was once a relatively stable bipolar or unipolar structure has evolved into a diversified and decentralized constellation of power, comprised of both state and non-state actors, influencing global affairs. The emergence of a multipolar world represents a significant break with the unipolar American dominance of the post-Cold War era. While the United States is still a central actor, it no longer enjoys undisputed supremacy. China, Russia, the European Union, India, Brazil, Russia, Russia, the European Union, India, Brazil and even medium-sized countries such as Turkey and South Africa are increasingly asserting their strategic interests in global governance. Their growing influence stems not only from their military or economic power but also from their ability to shape regional norms, participate in multilateral structures, and forge strategic alliances. This distribution of power has diversified the sources of authority in international politics and brought new dynamics to global cooperation and competition.

Multipolarity necessitates a rethinking of international relations theory and practice. Traditional state-centered models are insufficient to respond to contemporary challenges such as climate change, cybersecurity, global health crises, and economic inequality. These issues transcend borders and require the collective efforts of multiple stakeholders. The COVID-19 pandemic has highlighted the inadequacy of nationalistic and isolated responses, reinforcing the importance of global cooperation mechanisms based on resource and knowledge sharing. Similarly, climate change has exposed the shortcomings of fragmented environmental governance and highlighted the need for long-term, holistic strategies.

One of the most striking consequences of this new global order is the transformation of security paradigms. While the classical understanding of security emphasized territorial integrity and military deterrence, today's security agenda has become much broader and multi-layered. Human security, public health, economic stability, environmental protection, and digital security are now part of the security discourse. The security dilemma, which used to encompass only interstate threats, now includes issues as diverse as cyber warfare, terrorism, resource scarcity, and disinformation. In a multipolar world, the diverging threat perceptions of powerful actors complicate efforts to develop a common understanding of risk and a collective response. This lack of consensus can lead to delayed or inadequate responses in times of crisis. Moreover, strategic competition between great powers such as the US, China, and Russia has reintroduced elements of the Cold War into modern geopolitics: arms races, proxy wars, and ideological polarization. But today's rivalries are intertwined with economic interdependence and shared global responsibilities, rather than a clear ideological distinction between capitalism and communism. For example, the US and China are strategic military and technological rivals, yet they work together, however inconsistently, on issues such as climate change, trade regulations, and public health. This contradiction highlights the need for flexible and multifaceted foreign policies that balance competition and cooperation.

This study also reveals that regionalism has become an important feature of contemporary global governance. Organizations such as the European Union, ASEAN, the African Union, and the Organization of Turkic States serve as both buffers and bridges in the management of global uncertainties. These structures are taking on more and more of the roles that have traditionally belonged to universal institutions, such as conflict resolution, economic integration, disaster response, and norm-building. Their growing influence reflects the decentralization of authority and a pragmatic trend towards regional solutions to the gridlock of universal structures. But regionalism is not without its challenges. Differences among member states in terms of political culture, level of economic development, and strategic priorities can undermine unity and effectiveness. Moreover, the imbalance in the capacity of regional organizations leads to an uneven distribution of their influence globally. While the EU is an example of successful integration, many other organizations face internal divisions, lack of resources, or external interference. Despite these limitations, regional governance remains an indispensable layer of the international system, offering context-sensitive and complementary approaches to global efforts.

Another important element in this transforming order is the rise of non-state actors. Simultaneously, the rise of non-polarization, characterized by the diffusion of power not only among states but also among non-state actors, has further complicated the landscape. The evolution of global governance is no longer defined solely by inter-state interactions, but by the interconnected roles of civil society, the private sector, and decentralized networks. Multinational corporations have become global political actors, shaping everything from labor policies to digital surveillance systems. NGOs play vital roles in areas such as humanitarian aid, environmental advocacy, and human rights protection. Through cross-border advocacy networks and digital mobilization, they are able to influence state behavior, shape public opinion, and contribute to the formation of international norms. However, this growing influence raises questions of legitimacy, accountability, and the risk of global discourse capitulating to institutionalized or Western-centric agendas.

In light of these transformations, the future of international relations requires innovative approaches to governance, diplomacy, and policymaking. States must adopt adaptive strategies to encompass the multiple actors and diverse interests that shape the world today. This requires reforming international institutions in line with the current balance of power, strengthening regional cooperation, promoting multilateral diplomacy, and creating inclusive platforms to engage non-state actors. Policymakers should adopt a holistic understanding of security and development in terms of its social, environmental, economic, and technological dimensions.

Ultimately, navigating this complex environment requires resilience, foresight, and a commitment to shared solutions. From pandemics to climate change, from digital transformation to ideological conflicts, the challenges of our time are not issues that can be solved by a single actor or traditional methods. Success depends on the ability to build coalitions across sectors and borders, build trust between different actors, and balance sovereignty, solidarity, and sustainability. The future of international relations lies not in returning to old hierarchies but in embracing the dynamic interaction of multiple centers of power and influence. In this way, the international community has the potential to build a more inclusive, just, and stable world order.

REFERENCES

Acharya, A., Estevadeordal, A., & Goodman, L W. (2023, November 6). Multipolar or multiplex? Interaction capacity, global cooperation and world order. Oxford University Press, 99(6), 2339-2365. https://doi.org/.DOI: 10.1093/ia/iiad242

Albin, C. (1999). Can NGOs enhance the effectiveness of international negotiation? *International Negotiation*, *4*(3), 371–387. DOI: 10.1163/15718069920848534

Alkanalka, M. (2023). *Towards a nuclear multipolar world and its spillover effects.* Afyon Kocatepe Üniversitesi İktisadi ve İdari Bilimler Fakültesi Dergisi., DOI: 10.33707/akuiibfd.1275045

Amin, S. (1992). U.S. Militarism in the New World Order. *Social Justice (San Francisco, Calif.)*, *19*(1), 1. https://www.questia.com/library/journal/1G1-14142925/u-s-militarism-in-the-new-world-order

Arkhipov, A., & Yeletsky, A N. (2015, June 1). Various Aspects of the Multipolarity within the World Economic System. Mediterranean Center of Social and Educational Research. https://doi.org/.DOI: 10.5901/mjss.2015.v6n3s6p59

Asad, S., Feldes, M. L., Schmid, J., Schmidt, L., Sommer, L., Stöcker, M., & Khalifa, M. S. (2023). A confluence of global crises: An unprecedented learning moment for climate change from the COVID-19 pandemic. DOI: 10.22541/au.168897273.35390913/v1

Baghdasaryan, S. (2025). The new world order and the strategic security situation in the greater middle east and indo-pacific regions. 2(28), 109–122. .DOI: 10.46991/ai.2024.2.28.007

Baig, T. (2020, September 15). Re-setting World Order. *World Politics in Transition.*, *4*(III), 389–402. DOI: 10.35484/pssr.2020(4-III)29

Bauernfeind, A., Reíd, J. A., McCallum, A., Sheek-Hussein, M., Magid, A., Lopes, H., Cunningham, C., Green, M. S., Koivusalo, M., Sarkar, A., Middleton, J., & Davidovitch, N. (2024). No time to lose: Pandemic agreement—Urgency over complacency; unity over fragmentation. *The International Journal of Health Planning and Management*, *39*(6), 1810–1818. Advance online publication. DOI: 10.1002/hpm.3847 PMID: 39133762

Bert, W. (1997). *The United States and the Post-Cold War International System.* Palgrave Macmillan., DOI: 10.1057/9780230372764_1

Betsill, M. M., & Corell, E. (2008). NGO diplomacy : the influence of nongovernmental organizations in international environmental negotiations. MIT Press. http://ci.nii.ac.jp/ncid/BA83676394

Bharti, S. S., & Aryal, S. K. (2023). *The Global Aspirations of the European Union and Dealing With Regional Conflicts*. Brill., DOI: 10.4018/979-8-3693-2837-8.ch011

Birhan, A. T. (2024). *The African Union and Conflict Resolution: Challenges and Prospects*. Social Science and Humanities Journal., DOI: 10.18535/sshj.v8i03.958

Bormann, N., Cederman, L., Gates, S., Graham, B A., Hug, S., Strøm, K., & Wucherpfennig, J. (2018, December 6). Power Sharing: Institutions, Behavior, and Peace. Wiley, 63(1), 84-100. .DOI: 10.1111/ajps.12407

Burci, G. L. (2024). The COVID-19 pandemic and the development of global health law: Managing crises or achieving structural changes? *Journal of Global Health Law*, *1*(1), 8–25. DOI: 10.4337/jghl.2024.01.01

Catley, B. (1999). Hegemonic America: The Arrogance of Power. Contemporary Southeast Asia: A Journal of International and Strategic Affairs, 21(2), 157–175. https://doi.org/.DOI: 10.1355/CS21_2A

Chytopoulou, E. (2024). ASEAN and European Union addressing the challenges of the 21st century. *Economic and Regional Studies*, *17*(3), 373–407. DOI: 10.2478/ers-2024-0021

Cole, J., & Dodds, K. (2021). Unhealthy geopolitics: Can the response to COVID-19 reform climate change policy? *Bulletin of the World Health Organization*, *99*(2), 148–154. DOI: 10.2471/BLT.20.269068 PMID: 33551508

Daalder, I H., Lindsay, J M., & Steinberg, J B. (2002, December 1). Hard Choices: National Security and the War on Terrorism. University of California Press, 101(659), 409-413. https://doi.org/.DOI: 10.1525/curh.2002.101.659.409

Dal, E P. (2018, December 2). Rising powers in international conflict management: an introduction. Taylor & Francis, 39(12), 2207-2221. .DOI: 10.1080/01436597.2018.1503048

Dittmer, L. (2014, January 1). Asian Alliances. *Chinese and Japanese Experiences Compared.*, *38*(1), 1–29. DOI: 10.1353/apr.2014.0000

Eisenman, J., & Heginbotham, E. (2019). Building a More "Democratic" and "Multipolar" World: China's Strategic Engagement with Developing Countries. China Review-an Interdisciplinary Journal on Greater China, 19(4), 55–83. https://muse.jhu.edu/article/743120/pdf

Elamiryan, R. (2023). World Order and Shifting Regional Security Landscapes. *Jindal Journal of International Affairs*, *11*(1), 1–20. DOI: 10.54945/jjia.v11i1.186

Ewers-Peters, N. M. (2018). The EU as an Interorganizational Influencer. *European Foreign Affairs Review*, *23*(3), 365–380. https://dialnet.unirioja.es/servlet/articulo?codigo=6864767. DOI: 10.54648/EERR2018031

Fukui, H., & Fukai, S. N. (1998). The Role of the United States in Post-Cold War East Asian Security Affairs. *Journal of Asian and African Studies*, *33*(1), 114–133. DOI: 10.1177/002190969803300107

Gill, B. (2010, November 1). Diffuse Threats, Frail Institutions: Managing Security in the New Era. University of California Press, 109(730), 329-335. .DOI: 10.1525/curh.2010.109.730.329

Goddard, S E., & Nexon, D H. (2016, February 1). The Dynamics of Global Power Politics: A Framework for Analysis. Oxford University Press, 1(1), 4-18. .DOI: 10.1093/jogss/ogv007

Góes, G. S. (2024). Poder de estado e governança global na era pós-covid. *Revista Da Escola Superior de Guerra*, *38*(82), 29–48. DOI: 10.47240/revistadaesg.v38i82.1313

Gore, L. L. P. (2015). Between the Giants in Pursuit of Asian Prosperity: Dilemmas of Australia's National Security Strategy. .DOI: 10.1142/9789814632874_0003

Guliyev, V. (2024). The Reinvigoration of the Organization of Turkic States amid Ongoing Geopolitical Unrest and Economic Uncertainty. *Khazar Journal of Humanities and Social Sciences*, *27*(2), 37–54. DOI: 10.5782/2223-2621.2024.27.2.37

Hall, N., Schmitz, H. P., & Dedmon, J. M. (2019). Transnational Advocacy and NGOs in the Digital Era: New Forms of Networked Power. *International Studies Quarterly*, *64*(1), 159–167. DOI: 10.1093/isq/sqz052

Han, L C. (2018, September 3). When the World Seemed New: George H. W. Bush and the End of the Cold War. Taylor & Francis, 46(5), 137-137. .DOI: 10.1080/03612759.2018.1489685

Hansen, L. (2000). Past as Preface: Civilizational Politics and the 'Third' Balkan War. *Journal of International Students*, *29*(3), 1–28.

Harris, J. (2024). Is multi-polarity the new non-alignment? .DOI: 10.1177/03063968231217397

Hawthorn, G. (1999). Liberalism since the Cold War: An enemy to itself? *Review of International Studies*, *25*(5), 145–160. DOI: 10.1017/S026021059900145X

Herrmann, R. K. (1991). The Middle East and the New World Order: Rethinking U.S. Political Strategy After the Gulf War. *International Security*, *16*(2), 42–75. DOI: 10.2307/2539060

Hidayat, F. (2023, January 1). Escape from the Cold War Mindset to Set Up a Post-Cold War History of Philosophy. *Escape from the Cold War Mindset to Set Up a Post-Cold War History of Philosophy.*, *09*, 00006–00006. DOI: 10.29037/digitalpress.409438

Hopf, T. (1991). Polarity, the offense-defense balance, and war. *The American Political Science Review*, *85*(2), 475–493. DOI: 10.2307/1963170

Howe, J. (2022). New actors in global governance and non-traditional security threats. *International Journal of Global Politics*, *34*(2), 123–141.

Islam, S. (2015). *A new momentum in EU–ASEAN relations: drivers, risks, the way forward.* Routledge., DOI: 10.4324/9781315744193-31

Jang, J., McSparren, J. J., & Rashchupkina, Y. (2016, January 19). Global governance: Present and future. *Palgrave Communications*, *2*(1), 15045. Advance online publication. DOI: 10.1057/palcomms.2015.45

Janković, M., & Mitić, M. (2024). The European Union's strategy in a multipolar world. *European Political Review*, *58*(3), 45–67.

Kapstein, E. B., & Mastanduno, M. (2000). Unipolar politics: Realism and state strategies after the Cold War. *Foreign Affairs*, *79*(2), 158. DOI: 10.2307/20049663

Keersmaeker, G. D. (2017). *Polarity, balance of power and international relations theory: Post-Cold War and the 19th century compared.* Springer. DOI: 10.1007/978-3-319-42652-5

Khalilzad, Z. (1995). From Containment to Global Leadership?: America and the World After the Cold War. https://www.rand.org/content/dam/rand/pubs/monograph_reports/2006/MR525.pdf

Kim, W. B. (2009). Power transitions and great power war from Westphalia to Waterloo. *World Politics*, *61*(4), 573–596. DOI: 10.1017/S0043887109990064

Koppel, O., & Пархомчук, О С. (2021, September 21). Megatrends of the world politics., 192(7-8(2)), 4-14. .DOI: 10.21003/ea.V192-01

Kopylov, A. V., Likhonosov, A. G., & Pivovarov, Y. (2024). Influence of Geopolitical Concepts on the US National Security Strategy. Obŝestvo: Politika, Èkonomika. *Pravo*, *12*(12). Advance online publication. DOI: 10.24158/pep.2024.12.1

Langhorne, R. (2005, June 1). The Diplomacy of Non-State Actors. Taylor & Francis, 16(2), 331-339. .DOI: 10.1080/09592290590948388

Larson, D W. (2018, May 25). New Perspectives on Rising Powers and Global Governance: Status and Clubs. Oxford University Press, 20(2), 247-254. .DOI: 10.1093/isr/viy039

Liu, Y. (2025). The dual impact of multinational corporations: Drivers of growth and challenges to sovereignty in a globalized economy. *Advances in Economics Management and Political Sciences, 152*(1), 207–214. DOI: 10.54254/2754-1169/2024.19459

Loza, V., Myronenko, V., Myronenko, P., Smolianiuk, V., & Chelak, O. (2024). *The escalation of military threats as a reality of modern geopolitics.* Multidisciplinary Science Journal., DOI: 10.31893/multiscience.2024ss0223

Lucas, K., Hanegraaff, M., & De Bruycker, I. (2023). Lobbying the Lobbyists: When and Why Do Policymakers Seek to Influence Advocacy Groups in Global Governance? (pp. 165–196). DOI: 10.1007/978-3-031-27864-8_6

Marassiro, M. J. (2022). Seizing the multipolar moment? Russia in the new world disorder (pp. 17–30). Edward Elgar Publishing eBooks. https://doi.org/DOI: 10.4337/9781788977692.00007

Marassiro, T. (2022). China's global influence and regional partnerships. *Global Policy Review, 18*(4), 77–98.

Massoni, M. (2020). *Integration dynamics between the African Union (AU) and the Regional Economic Communities (RECs) in light of a newly oriented Euro-African geopolitics.* Routledge., DOI: 10.4324/9781003030621-14

Mikhaylenko, E. (2022). From Advocacy to Diplomacy: The Case of the International Campaign to Abolish Nuclear Weapons. *International Trends, 20*(1), 55–79. DOI: 10.17994/IT.2022.20.1.68.5

Mirza, I. M. M., Panjaitan, O. D. A., & Pratama, A. A. (2024). Adopting European Union Legal Frameworks for Restructuring ASEAN: Pathways to Regional Stability. Dialogia Iuridica, 16(1), 001–026. https://doi.org/.DOI: 10.28932/di.v16i1.8663

Montgomery, R. M. (2024). The Impact of Pandemics on the World Power Axis. DOI: 10.20944/preprints202409.0193.v1

Mueller, J., & Stewart, M G. (2012, July 1). The Terrorism Delusion: America's Overwrought Response to September 11. The MIT Press, 37(1), 81-110. .DOI: 10.1162/ISEC_a_00089

Musau, S. M. (2023). Regional Intergovernmental Organizations to Conflict Prevention and Resolution: The Case of the African Union in the Nile River Conflict. *Open Journal of Social Sciences*, *11*(01), 361–400. DOI: 10.4236/jss.2023.111026

Nazareth, A., Kim, D., & Shawoo, Z. (2024). External power dynamics and international climate governance in a crises-constrained world. *Climate and Development*, *16*(10), 1–11. DOI: 10.1080/17565529.2024.2330984

Oates-Indruchová, L., & Mueller, W. (2017, April 19). From the Iron Curtain to the Schengen Area: Memory Cultures of Bordering Communist and Postcommunist Europe. *Eastern European Politics and Societies*, *31*(2), 227–233. DOI: 10.1177/0888325416688764

Oidtmann, R., & Mokry, S. (2020, July 7). Future dis(order). https://journals.sagepub.com/doi/10.1177/2336825X20935243

Oleynik, I. S. (1981). The influence of multinational corporations on industrial development: A preliminary analysis of the problem (IIASA Working Paper No. WP-81-151). International Institute for Applied Systems Analysis. https://pure.iiasa.ac.at/1610

Páldi, Z. (2020). The EU-ASEAN Ties: A Strategic Partnership? : Assessing the Development of Relations through the Lens of Political and Economic Cooperation. 13, 96–113. .DOI: 10.47706/KKIFPR.2020.13.96-113

Peters, M A. (2022, December 5). The emerging multipolar world order: A preliminary analysis. Taylor & Francis, 55(14), 1653-1663. .DOI: 10.1080/00131857.2022.2151896

Piazza, J. A. (2008). Incubators of Terror: Do Failed and Failing States Promote Transnational Terrorism? *International Studies Quarterly*, *52*(3), 469–488. DOI: 10.1111/j.1468-2478.2008.00511.x

Piccolino, G. (2014). The European Union and the promotion of regional integration: a viable approach to the resolution of regional conflicts in Sub-Saharan Africa? Social Science Research Network. https://doi.org/DOI: 10.2139/SSRN.2455061

Plummer, L. (2011). Failing States in the Middle East and Africa: Terrorist Group Formation and Terrorist Attacks Over Time. https://repository.lib.ncsu.edu/handle/1840.16/7314

Posen, B R. (2009, November 1). Emerging Multipolarity: Why Should We Care?. University of California Press, 108(721), 347-352. .DOI: 10.1525/curh.2009.108.721.347

Prorokovic, D. (2023). Russia's position in the multipolar world and Serbia's strategic options. *Srpska Politička Misao*, *79*(1), 41–64. DOI: 10.5937/spm79-42705

Roach, B. (2005). *Leviathans: A Primer on Multinational Corporations*. Cambridge University Press., DOI: 10.1017/CBO9780511512025.002

Roseira, A. M. (2023). *O mundo tripolar – geopolítica russa no século xxi e a nova ordem internacional*. Geographia., DOI: 10.22409/GEOgraphia2023.v25i54.a55146

Rubin, B., & Keaney, T. (2001). US allies in a changing world, Besa Studies in International Security, http://ci.nii.ac.jp/ncid/BA50607760

Sheetz, M. S., & Mastanduno, M. (1997). Debating the Unipolar Moment. *International Security*, *22*(3), 168–174. DOI: 10.2307/2539361

Slawotsky, J. (2024). Conceptualizing National Security in an Era of Great Power Rivalry: Implications for International Economic Law. *East Asia (Piscataway, N.J.)*. Advance online publication. DOI: 10.1007/s12140-024-09434-y

Suporn, S., Chanlett-Avery, E., Nikitin, M. B. D., Rennack, D. E., & Williams, B. R. (2021). *Strategic competition and foreign policy*. Congressional Research Service.

Sutanto, R., & Priyanto, P. (2023). *The roles of asean in building a strategic equilibrium with major powers to strengthen sustainable stability, and maritime security in the region*. Jurnal Diplomasi Pertahanan., DOI: 10.33172/jdp.v9i3.14513

Thies, C G. (2012, August 21). The Roles of Bipolarity: A Role Theoretic Understanding of the Effects of Ideas and Material Factors on the Cold War. Oxford University Press, 14(3), 269-288. .DOI: 10.1111/j.1528-3585.2012.00486.x

Thies, C. G. (2013). The construction of international relations: Social norms and domestic practices. *International Studies Quarterly*, *57*(1), 11–20.

Turner, D. (2009). Multipolarity and global governance: The Russian and Chinese perspective. *International Relations Journal*, *28*(1), 11–28.

Umamah, M., Mufti, A., Ali, K., Jilani, S., Farooqi, I., Khan, M. A., Khan, P. R., & Dhupper, R. (2024). Navigating the Nexus: Insights from the COVID-19 Pandemic for Climate Change Mitigation. *Asian Journal of Water, Environment and Pollution*, *21*(3), 27. Advance online publication. DOI: 10.3233/AJW240031

Väyrynen, R. (1995). Post-hegemonic theories of international relations: The decline of the Soviet Union and the end of the Cold War. *World Politics*, *48*(1), 31–52.

Velichkin, A. (2024). India's balancing strategy in a multipolar world. *Asian Politics and Strategy*, *22*(1), 33–56.

Wagner, R. H. (1993). The causes of peace. In Wagner, R. H. (Ed.), *War and the state: The theory of international politics* (pp. 237–262). University of Michigan Press.

Weaver, J. J. (2020). Nongovernmental Organizations and the Global Governance Institutional Gap. *Nongovernmental Organizations and the Global Governance Institutional Gap.*, *12*(1), 9. DOI: 10.5590/JOSC.2020.12.1.09

Wilkinson, D. (1999). Unipolarity Without Hegemony. *International Studies Review*, *1*(2), 141–172. DOI: 10.1111/1521-9488.00158

Wilson, I., Iii, S., & Scott, A. (2020). The Compound Security Dilemma: Threats at the Nexus of War and Peace. *Parameters*, *50*(2), 3. https://press.armywarcollege.edu/cgi/viewcontent.cgi?article=1014&context=parameters. DOI: 10.55540/0031-1723.1014

Wohlforth, W. C. (1999). The Stability of a Unipolar World. *International Security*, *24*(1), 5–41. DOI: 10.1162/016228899560031

Wright, J., & D'Amato, S. (2023). Transnational terrorism as a threat: Cross-border threats. In Handbook for management of threats (pp. 193–208). First Online: 27 December 2023.

Yang, C. (2023). Strengthening International Legal and Institutional Systems Governing Climate Change and Pandemic Disease. *Lecture Notes in Education Psychology and Public Media*, *2*(1), 218–229. DOI: 10.54254/2753-7048/2/2022416

Yaqing, Q. (2013, January 1). Power Shift, Governance Deficit and a Sustainable Global Order. Taylor & Francis, 1(1), 89-106. .DOI: 10.1080/20954816.2013.11673871

Yazid, S. (2014). Cold War international politics and the emergence of the bipolar system. *Journal of International Relations*, *10*(2), 65–79.

Youde, J. (2024). 24. Global health governance and COVID-19. 453–471. .DOI: 10.1093/hepl/9780192863072.003.0024

Zartman, I W. (2019, January 1). Systems of World Order. Springer International Publishing, 271-291. https://doi.org/.DOI: 10.1007/978-3-030-06079-4_16

Zhang, S. (2024). Exploration of International Climate Governance Mechanisms from the Perspective of Social Dialogue. *Lecture Notes in Education Psychology and Public Media*, *77*(1), 70–75. DOI: 10.54254/2753-7048/2024.18145

Chapter 6
From Cold War Bipolarity to Unipolarity:
Analysing Contemporary System Change

Goran Roos
https://orcid.org/0000-0003-0943-3585
University of Adelaide, UK

ABSTRACT

This chapter introduces the Multi-Dimensional Order Transformation (MDOT) Framework, addressing gaps in understanding international system change. Unlike traditional approaches assuming uniform transformation, the framework disaggregates change into five dimensions: material power distribution, institutional architecture, normative contestation, economic integration, and regional autonomy. Each includes measurable thresholds whilst modelling dynamic interactions. Applied to contemporary politics, the framework reveals differentiated transformation characterised by institutional layering, normative fragmentation, and expanding regional autonomy rather than simple multipolarity. Case studies of Sweden, Australia, and Turkey illustrate varying state responses. The analysis demonstrates partial system change approaching transformation thresholds, suggesting substantial change without complete breakdown.

INTRODUCTION

The contemporary international system confronts an unprecedented transformation challenge that defies existing theoretical frameworks for understanding global order change. While scholars increasingly recognise the transition from unipolarity

DOI: 10.4018/979-8-3373-2342-8.ch006

toward a more complex global configuration, conventional approaches remain inadequate for capturing the multifaceted nature of this transformation (Parrat, 2024; Davies, 2024). Traditional polarity analysis, focused primarily on material power distribution, fails to account for the asynchronous and multi-dimensional character of contemporary order change, where different aspects of international relations transform at varying speeds and in divergent directions (Zala, 2017; Röhren, 2024).

This chapter addresses a fundamental gap in international relations theory by introducing the Multi-Dimensional Order Transformation (MDOT) Framework, a novel analytical approach that transcends conventional frameworks to provide more precise identification of transformation indicators whilst acknowledging that global order change is neither uniform nor unidirectional. The framework responds to what scholars identify as a paradigm shift in international relations, moving from multilateral cooperation toward "pragmatic inclusivity" characterised by multiple centres of power pursuing varied and sometimes contradictory approaches to global governance (Luo, 2024; Acharya, 2024).

The central research question driving this analysis concerns how we can systematically measure and understand international order transformation when different dimensions of the global system change at different rates and directions simultaneously. Existing scholarship provides insufficient guidance on "when international society furthers transformation, and when it furthers stability" (Parrat, 2024, p. 416). Contemporary debates about the decline and future of the "liberal" international order have produced increasing interest in the concept and sources of disorder in world politics, yet these discussions often lack analytical clarity and theoretical precision about transformation thresholds (Ikenberry, 2018; Cooley & Nexon, 2020).

The MDOT Framework addresses this limitation by disaggregating systemic change into five distinct but interconnected dimensions, establishing measurable threshold indicators, and modelling dynamic interactions between dimensions. This theoretical innovation builds upon established analytical frameworks whilst offering original perspectives on system change that synthesise realist attention to material capabilities with liberal institutionalist emphasis on rules and procedures and constructivist insights about ideational change.

Scope and Theoretical Contribution

Unlike approaches that assume uniform systemic change, the MDOT Framework posits that different aspects of international order experience varying transformation trajectories, creating complex patterns of continuity and change requiring multi-dimensional analysis. The framework contributes to international relations theory through three primary innovations addressing current limitations in order transformation analysis.

First, it recognises asynchronous transformation dynamics, where different dimensions can simultaneously experience stability, incremental change, or rapid transformation. This insight explains why some periods of apparent change produce system stability whilst others generate rapid transformation. Traditional power transition theory assumes linear progression from one configuration to another, but contemporary transformation involves complex patterns that existing theories struggle to explain (Zhou, 2019; Lemke, 1997).

Second, the framework establishes measurable threshold indicators for distinguishing between stability, adaptation, and systemic transformation, providing analytical precision about when change constitutes fundamental system alteration. Existing approaches often rely on subjective assessments or post-hoc analysis to identify system change, whilst the MDOT Framework enables real-time assessment of transformation patterns (Parrat, 2024; Davies, 2024).

Third, it models dynamic interactions between dimensions, explaining how changes in one area can reinforce, compensate for, or contradict changes in others. This dynamic interaction modelling explains why transformation patterns vary across historical cases and contexts, providing theoretical tools for understanding variation in system change patterns that traditional approaches overlook.

Contemporary Relevance and Empirical Application

The framework's relevance becomes particularly apparent when examining contemporary global developments that transcend simple polarity models. The end of the Cold War marked a watershed in international relations, transforming a bipolar order into an unprecedented unipolar moment dominated by the United States (Krauthammer, 1990/1991; Wohlforth, 1999). However, the 21st century has witnessed systematic challenges to this order that resist categorisation within traditional analytical frameworks.

Contemporary transformation involves institutional layering rather than replacement, normative contestation rather than consensus breakdown, economic diversification rather than complete decoupling, and regional autonomy expansion rather than fragmentation. These patterns require analytical tools capable of capturing multi-dimensional change whilst maintaining theoretical precision and policy relevance.

The MDOT Framework's application to current global politics reveals that rather than experiencing uniform change toward multipolarity or bipolar competition, the international system undergoes differentiated transformation characterised by partial system change approaching system-wide transformation thresholds. This represents substantial systemic change without complete order breakdown, suggesting that managing transformation requires understanding its multi-dimensional character and developing strategies that account for varying transformation speeds across different aspects of international relations.

Chapter Structure and Methodology

This chapter employs a multi-level analytical approach drawing upon Kenneth Waltz's (1959) levels of analysis framework whilst extending it to capture contemporary complexity. The analysis integrates individual-level factors (leadership choices and perceptions), state-level factors (domestic politics, economic systems, national identities), and system-level factors (power distribution, institutional arrangements, normative frameworks) whilst recognising their operation across multiple interconnected dimensions.

The empirical analysis draws upon multiple methodological approaches including comparative case studies, statistical analysis of transformation indicators, and process tracing of dynamic interactions between dimensions. Primary sources include government documents, official statements, and policy papers from major powers and international organisations. Secondary sources encompass peer-reviewed academic literature from leading international relations journals, reports from credible think tanks and research organisations, and analysis from international financial institutions.

Three detailed case studies—Sweden, Australia, and Turkey—illustrate how different types of states navigate contemporary transformation dynamics through the MDOT Framework lens. These cases represent different approaches to strategic autonomy and alliance relationships, providing empirical validation of the framework's analytical utility whilst demonstrating its capacity to explain variance in state responses to systemic change.

The chapter concludes by assessing implications for international relations theory and policy practice, identifying limitations and future research directions, and evaluating the framework's contribution to understanding complex system change in contemporary international relations.

LITERATURE REVIEW AND THEORETICAL FOUNDATIONS

Existing Approaches to Order Transformation

International relations scholarship offers several established approaches to understanding order transformation, each contributing valuable insights whilst suffering from analytical limitations that the MDOT Framework addresses. Realist theories emphasise material power shifts and balance-of-power dynamics, but neglect institutional, normative, and economic dimensions of transformation (Waltz, 1979; Mearsheimer, 2001). Power transition theory provides sophisticated analysis of hegemonic challenges but focuses primarily on bilateral relationships between rising and declining powers whilst overlooking complex multilateral dynamics and non-material factors (Organski, 1958; Zhou, 2019).

Liberal institutionalist frameworks emphasise formal institutions and cooperative arrangements but often overlook informal power dynamics, regional autonomy patterns, and the role of dissatisfied powers in challenging existing arrangements (Keohane, 1984; Ikenberry, 2001). These approaches tend to assume that institutional effectiveness depends primarily on great power support whilst underestimating the capacity of middle powers and regional organisations to create alternative arrangements.

Constructivist analyses examine normative change and ideational contestation but often lack systematic measurement criteria for transformation thresholds whilst struggling to specify conditions under which normative change produces systemic transformation rather than adaptation (Finnemore & Sikkink, 1998; Reus-Smit, 2013). Critical theories highlight ideological dimensions of hegemony and resistance but frequently lack analytical precision about transformation indicators and policy implications.

Power Transition Theory: Contributions and Limitations

Power transition theory represents the most influential approach to understanding systemic change in international relations, providing sophisticated analysis of relationships between material power shifts and conflict propensity. The theory's core proposition holds that systemic war becomes most likely when rising challengers approach parity with declining hegemons, particularly when challengers are dissatisfied with existing arrangements (Organski, 1958; Tammen et al., 2000).

Recent scholarship has refined power transition theory to address contemporary challenges. Zhou (2019) incorporates prospect theory and nuclear deterrence considerations to explain strategic competition between the United States and China, arguing that states take diplomatic actions not only to seek gains but also to avoid losses during power transition processes. Lemke (1997) extends the theory to regional contexts, demonstrating its applicability beyond global power transitions whilst recognising that different levels of analysis may experience transformation at different rates.

However, power transition theory suffers from several limitations that constrain its applicability to contemporary transformation dynamics. First, it focuses primarily on bilateral relationships between rising and declining powers whilst overlooking complex multilateral dynamics involving multiple powers, regional organisations, and non-state actors (Zala, 2017; Alterman & McElwee, 2024). Second, it assumes relatively uniform change across different aspects of international relations whilst contemporary transformation involves asynchronous change across multiple dimensions.

Third, power transition theory privileges material capabilities whilst underestimating the importance of institutional arrangements, normative frameworks, economic interdependence, and regional autonomy patterns in shaping transformation outcomes. Fourth, it tends to focus on conflict propensity rather than broader questions of order transformation, limiting its analytical utility for understanding complex systemic change processes.

Polarity and System Structure

Polarity analysis provides another established approach to understanding international system change, focusing on the distribution of capabilities among major powers and its implications for system stability and conflict patterns. Traditional approaches distinguish between unipolar, bipolar, and multipolar systems whilst debating their relative stability characteristics (Waltz, 1979; Wohlforth, 1999; Layne, 2012).

Recent scholarship has identified significant limitations in conventional polarity analysis. Zala (2017) argues that "depictions of a current multipolarity are found alongside discussions of the longevity of US-led unipolarity, while others point to the early stages of US-Sino-dominated bipolarity" (p. 2), reflecting analytical confusion arising from definitions focused solely on material capabilities whilst assuming all actors perceive polarity objectively.

Contemporary polarity analysis faces additional challenges. Röhren (2024) contends that "unipolarity is not over yet" despite widespread assumptions about American decline, arguing that the United States maintains significant advantages that complicate simple power transition predictions. Conversely, other scholars argue for emerging multipolarity or even "apolarity" characterised by diffusion of power without clear hierarchy (Haass, 2008; Acharya, 2017).

These disagreements reflect deeper theoretical problems with polarity analysis that the MDOT Framework addresses. Traditional approaches assume that polarity determines other system characteristics whilst overlooking feedback effects from institutional, normative, economic, and regional dimensions. They also assume uniform change across all dimensions whilst contemporary transformation involves complex patterns of continuity and change that resist simple categorisation.

International Order Theory

Broader international order theory provides additional perspectives on systemic transformation that inform the MDOT Framework's development. Ikenberry (2001, 2011) argues that hegemonic powers can create durable constitutional orders that outlast their own dominance through institutional embedding and legitimacy cultivation. This liberal institutionalist perspective emphasises the importance of consent and mutual benefit in maintaining international order.

Critical perspectives challenge liberal assumptions about order construction and maintenance. Cox (1983) argues that hegemony operates through both coercive and consensual mechanisms, requiring ideological dominance alongside material capabilities. Neo-Gramscian approaches suggest that American hegemony has endured through securing consent for Western-centric arrangements, but this consent can erode if arrangements are perceived as illegitimate or if alternative ideas gain traction.

Recent scholarship has expanded international order theory to address contemporary challenges. Acharya (2017) proposes the concept of a "multiplex world" featuring multiple centres of power and cross-cutting networks rather than simple multipolarity. This perspective recognises that contemporary order involves layered arrangements where no single power dictates outcomes whilst various actors maintain influence in different domains.

Cooley and Nexon (2020) analyse the "exit from hegemony" through examining how American-led order is unravelling without clear replacement arrangements. They emphasise gradual erosion rather than sudden collapse, highlighting institutional decay, legitimacy challenges, and the emergence of alternative arrangements that supplement rather than replace existing structures.

Gaps in Existing Literature

Despite these valuable contributions, existing literature suffers from several gaps that limit understanding of contemporary transformation dynamics. First, most approaches focus on single dimensions of change—whether material power, institutions, norms, economics, or regional dynamics—whilst overlooking interactions between dimensions and their combined effects on systemic transformation.

Second, existing frameworks struggle to specify transformation thresholds with analytical precision, often relying on subjective assessments or post-hoc analysis rather than systematic indicators. This limits their utility for real-time assessment of transformation patterns and policy applications.

Third, current approaches tend to assume uniform change across all aspects of international relations whilst contemporary transformation involves asynchronous patterns that require more sophisticated analytical tools. Fourth, existing literature lacks systematic analysis of middle power strategies and regional autonomy dynamics that increasingly shape global politics.

The MDOT Framework addresses these gaps through disaggregating systemic change into five distinct but interconnected dimensions, establishing measurable threshold criteria, and modelling dynamic interactions between dimensions. This approach enables more precise analysis of when, how, and why international orders transform whilst capturing the complexity of contemporary change processes.

THEORETICAL INNOVATION: THE MULTI-DIMENSIONAL ORDER TRANSFORMATION FRAMEWORK

Conceptual Foundation and Analytical Innovation

The Multi-Dimensional Order Transformation Framework represents a significant theoretical advance beyond existing approaches to international system change. Rather than treating order transformation as uniform change across all aspects of international relations, the framework recognises that different dimensions can evolve independently whilst maintaining interactive relationships. This disaggregation enables more precise analysis of transformation patterns whilst acknowledging the complexity of contemporary change processes.

The framework builds upon three foundational insights about international system change that existing theories inadequately address. First, transformation occurs across multiple dimensions simultaneously, with different aspects of international relations experiencing varying rates and directions of change. This asynchronous transformation dynamic explains why some periods of apparent change produce system stability whilst others generate rapid transformation.

Second, systemic change involves threshold effects where incremental changes accumulate until reaching critical points that trigger more fundamental transformation. These thresholds operate differently across dimensions, creating complex patterns where some aspects of the system experience rapid change whilst others remain stable.

Third, dimensions interact dynamically through reinforcing, compensatory, and contradictory relationships that shape overall transformation trajectories. Understanding these interactions is essential for explaining variation in transformation patterns and predicting future developments.

The Five Dimensions of Order Transformation

The MDOT Framework disaggregates international order transformation into five dimensions that capture the most significant aspects of systemic change whilst remaining analytically manageable. Each dimension includes specific indicators, transformation thresholds, and measurement criteria that enable systematic analysis and cross-case comparison.

Figure 1. Multi-Dimensional Order Transformation (MDOT) Framework. Dynamic interactions between five dimensions of international order change

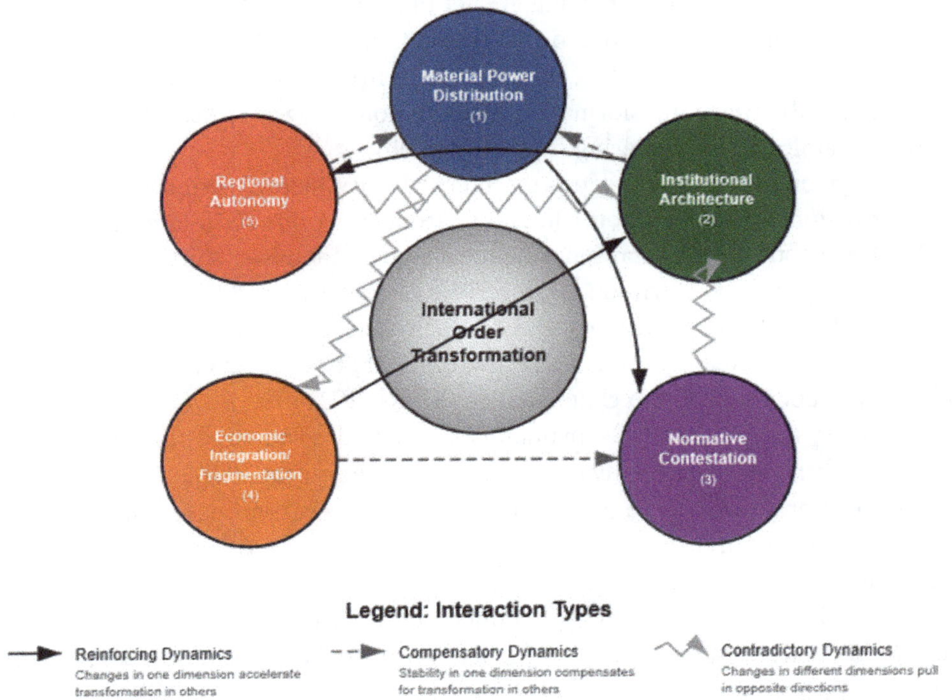

Dimension 1: Material Power Distribution

The material power dimension encompasses traditional realist concerns with relative capabilities among major powers, extending beyond simple GDP or military expenditure comparisons to include technological capabilities, demographic factors, resource control, and comprehensive measures of national power. This dimension recognises that power involves multiple components that may change at different rates, creating complex patterns of capability distribution.

Material power indicators include economic capabilities measured through GDP, GDP per capita, manufacturing output, technological innovation indices, and trade volumes. Military capabilities encompass defence spending, force structure, technological sophistication, power projection capacity, and nuclear arsenals. Demographic factors include population size, age structure, education levels, and human capital development. Resource control involves access to critical materials, energy resources, food security, and supply chain dominance.

Transformation thresholds are defined as primary transformation when new peer competitors emerge (states achieving greater than 70% of hegemon's aggregate capabilities), secondary transformation when significant capability shifts occur among existing powers (greater than 15% relative change in comprehensive national power rankings), and tertiary transformation when regional power redistributions affect global dynamics without altering overall hierarchy.

Contemporary evidence suggests the international system experiences secondary transformation in this dimension. China's rise from the world's sixth-largest economy in 2000 to second largest represents the most significant power shift, with Chinese GDP growing from $1.2 trillion to over $17 trillion between 2000 and 2023 (IMF, 2023; World Bank, 2024). Military spending has risen correspondingly, with China's defence budget increasing from $22 billion in 2000 to over $250 billion in 2023, making it second only to the United States (SIPRI, 2024).

However, the United States maintains substantial advantages that complicate simple power transition analysis. American military capabilities, particularly global force projection through carrier battle groups, overseas bases, and alliance networks, remain unmatched. Technological leadership in critical sectors including semiconductors, artificial intelligence, biotechnology, and aerospace provides enduring advantages. The dollar's continued dominance in international finance and the attractiveness of American higher education and innovation ecosystems reinforce soft power advantages.

India represents another significant power shift, with GDP growing from $468 billion in 2000 to over $3.7 trillion in 2023, whilst defence spending increased from $13 billion to $76 billion over the same period (World Bank, 2024; SIPRI, 2024). However, India's power remains primarily regional rather than global, with limited force projection capabilities and technological dependence in critical sectors.

Russia's position illustrates the complexity of power measurement. Despite economic stagnation and technological limitations, Russia maintains significant military capabilities, nuclear arsenals, and resource control that provide influence disproportionate to its economic size. The Ukraine conflict has revealed both Russian military limitations and continued capacity for regional disruption.

Dimension 2: Institutional Architecture and Legitimacy

The institutional dimension examines changes in formal international institutions, their effectiveness, perceived legitimacy among member states, and the emergence of alternative institutional arrangements that challenge existing governance structures. This dimension addresses both institutional adaptation within existing frameworks and the creation of parallel structures that supplement or compete with established arrangements.

Institutional indicators include membership patterns in international organisations, compliance rates with international agreements, effectiveness measures such as goal achievement and problem-solving capacity, and legitimacy assessments through surveys and diplomatic behaviour. Reform initiatives, voting patterns in international organisations, and the creation of alternative institutions provide additional measures of institutional change.

Transformation thresholds comprise primary transformation when widespread institutional bypassing or creation of parallel systems occurs (greater than 30% of major powers establishing alternative arrangements), secondary transformation when significant reform of core institutions takes place, and tertiary transformation when regional institutional proliferation affects global governance patterns without fundamentally altering existing structures.

The expansion of BRICS exemplifies secondary transformation in institutional architecture. The 2024 expansion to include Egypt, Ethiopia, Iran, and the United Arab Emirates, followed by Indonesia in 2025, demonstrates growing attraction of alternative institutional arrangements. BRICS+ now comprises eleven members representing 37.3% of global GDP and 45% of world population, providing substantial economic and demographic weight (Council on Foreign Relations, 2025; Banque de France, 2024).

The New Development Bank (NDB) and Asian Infrastructure Investment Bank (AIIB) represent significant institutional innovations that supplement rather than replace existing structures. The NDB has approved over $30 billion in loans since 2015, whilst the AIIB has provided over $40 billion in financing across more than 100 projects (AIIB, 2024; NDB, 2024). These institutions demonstrate capacity to mobilise substantial resources whilst operating according to different governance principles than Western-dominated institutions.

However, BRICS faces significant limitations that constrain its institutional effectiveness. The organisation lacks formal charter, secretariat, or common funds, relying on consensus-based decision-making that constrains collective action capacity. Internal divisions over issues including Russia's invasion of Ukraine demonstrate challenges in developing coherent alternative governance frameworks. The heterogeneity of members—ranging from democratic India and Brazil to authoritarian China and Iran—complicates consensus formation on sensitive political issues.

Established institutions demonstrate resilience whilst adapting to changing power distributions. The United Nations system continues functioning despite increasing gridlock in the Security Council, with General Assembly and specialised agencies maintaining significant activities. The World Trade Organisation has survived the Doha Round stalemate and trade wars whilst continuing to adjudicate disputes and facilitate negotiations. International financial institutions have accommodated new members and adjusted governance structures whilst maintaining core functions.

NATO expansion and adaptation demonstrate institutional evolution in response to changing security environments. The alliance has added fourteen new members since 1999, including Sweden and Finland in 2023-2024, whilst developing new capabilities and strategic concepts to address contemporary challenges. The alliance's ability to maintain cohesion whilst expanding geographically and functionally illustrates institutional adaptability.

Dimension 3: Normative and Ideational Contestation

The normative dimension captures struggles over fundamental principles governing international relations, including sovereignty interpretations, intervention norms, human rights standards, development models, and governance frameworks. Contemporary analysis reveals systematic challenges to liberal norms across multiple domains, reflecting ideational competition between different governance models and international order conceptions (Chen et al., 2024; Davies, 2024).

Normative indicators include frequency and intensity of normative disputes in international forums, promotion of alternative governance models through diplomatic initiatives and institutional arrangements, changes in international law interpretation and application, and ideological coalition formation patterns. Survey data on norm acceptance, voting patterns on normative issues, and policy convergence provide additional measures of normative change.

Transformation thresholds encompass primary transformation when competing normative frameworks emerge with substantial state support (greater than 40% of states endorsing alternative principles), secondary transformation when systematic challenge to existing norms through practice occurs, and tertiary transformation when gradual norm evolution through reinterpretation and adaptation takes place.

Evidence suggests secondary transformation in normative contestation through sophisticated challenges to Western liberal norms rather than complete normative breakdown. China's normative entrepreneurship represents systematic challenge to liberal internationalism through promoting alternative concepts of governance, development, and international order. The concept of "democracy with Chinese characteristics" provides alternative governance model emphasising economic development and social stability over individual rights and electoral democracy (Chen et al., 2024).

Chinese officials and scholars promote "common values" versus "universal values," challenging Western claims about human rights universality whilst maintaining commitment to international cooperation. The Belt and Road Initiative embodies alternative development principles emphasising infrastructure investment, economic connectivity, and state-led development rather than liberal market reforms and democratic conditionality. This approach has attracted support from over 140 countries, demonstrating significant appeal for alternative development models.

Russia's normative contestation emphasises "traditional values," "multipolarity," and sovereignty principles whilst rejecting Western intervention and democracy promotion. Russian actions in Ukraine challenge post-Cold War norms regarding territorial integrity and peaceful settlement of disputes, but frame these actions through sovereignty and self-determination principles rather than rejecting international law entirely. Russian officials argue for "sovereign democracy" and traditional values as alternatives to Western liberal models.

The international response to Ukraine illustrates normative fragmentation without complete breakdown. Western states imposed comprehensive sanctions and provided military support to Ukraine, demonstrating commitment to territorial integrity and rule of law. However, much of the Global South maintained neutral positions, with major democracies including India, Brazil, and South Africa abstaining on certain UN resolutions whilst supporting humanitarian assistance.

This pattern indicates autonomous decision-making rather than clear bloc allegiance, suggesting normative multipolarity rather than ideological division. Countries increasingly make independent assessments of normative issues based on national interests and regional considerations rather than automatic alignment with great power preferences.

Dimension 4: Economic Integration and Fragmentation

The economic dimension examines the tension between continued economic interdependence and growing geoeconomic fragmentation, reflecting what scholars describe as coexistence of "geopolitical tensions and economic interdependence" (Luo, 2024, p. 128). Analysis reveals accelerating "geoeconomic fragmentation" with measurable impacts on trade, investment, and technology flows whilst maintaining substantial economic relationships (Aiyar et al., 2023).

Economic indicators include trade flow patterns and supply chain restructuring, financial system integration or fragmentation, technology transfer restrictions and export controls, investment flow redirections and screening mechanisms, and currency usage patterns. Specific measures encompass bilateral trade volumes, foreign direct investment flows, technology licensing agreements, and participation in international economic institutions.

Transformation thresholds comprise primary transformation when distinct economic blocs form with limited interconnection (less than 30% cross-bloc trade), secondary transformation when substantial decoupling occurs in critical sectors, and tertiary transformation when diversification of economic partnerships occurs without bloc formation.

The International Monetary Fund documents accelerating geoeconomic fragmentation driven by policy decisions rather than technological or preference shifts. Friend-shoring and near-shoring have increased trade among politically aligned countries by 4-6% whilst reducing trade between geopolitical rivals (Aiyar et al., 2023). Technology restrictions have created bifurcation in critical sectors, with semiconductor supply chains showing approximately 40% reduction in China-US interdependence since 2019.

However, complete economic decoupling remains limited, suggesting tertiary rather than secondary transformation. China and the United States maintain trade relationships worth approximately $690 billion annually despite tariffs and restrictions (US Trade Representative, 2024). China holds approximately $859 billion in US Treasury securities as of 2024, down from peak holdings of $1.3 trillion in 2013 but still representing substantial financial interdependence (US Treasury, 2024).

Financial system fragmentation shows modest changes rather than fundamental restructuring. The dollar's share of global foreign exchange reserves declined from 71% in 2000 to 59% in 2023, but no clear alternative has emerged to challenge dollar dominance (IMF, 2024). The euro accounts for approximately 20% of reserves, with the Chinese yuan at only 2.7% despite China's economic size.

BRICS proposals for alternative payment systems and potential reserve currency face substantial technical and trust barriers limiting implementation. The New Development Bank primarily uses dollars for lending, whilst the BRICS Contingent Reserve Arrangement has never been activated. These limitations reflect the complexity of financial systems and network effects favouring established arrangements.

Supply chain diversification accelerated during the COVID-19 pandemic and subsequent geopolitical tensions, but complete reshoring remains limited by cost considerations and technical requirements. Multinational corporations pursue "China plus one" strategies whilst maintaining significant Chinese operations. This suggests managed diversification rather than complete decoupling.

Dimension 5: Regional Autonomy and Governance

The regional autonomy dimension assesses the capacity and willingness of regional powers to manage local affairs independently of global powers, reflecting the emergence of increasingly influential "middle powers" pursuing "strategic autonomy" strategies (Alterman & McElwee, 2024; Aran et al., 2025). Regional autonomy represents a crucial aspect of contemporary order transformation as powers seek to carve autonomous space amid great power competition.

Regional autonomy indicators include regional conflict management without great power involvement, independent diplomatic initiatives, regional integration processes and institutional development, autonomous responses to global challenges, and the development of regional security complexes. Specific measures encompass the number of regional organisations, their membership and activity levels, regional trade integration, and diplomatic coordination on global issues.

Transformation thresholds encompass primary transformation when regional powers consistently manage major regional issues independently without great power involvement, secondary transformation when autonomous regional security complexes form with minimal external influence, and tertiary transformation when increased regional coordination on global issues occurs whilst maintaining dependence on great powers for major challenges.

China's mediation of Saudi-Iranian rapprochement in 2023 exemplifies growing regional autonomy through indigenous diplomatic solutions that bypass traditional Western intermediation. The March 2023 agreement restored diplomatic relations between Riyadh and Tehran after seven years of hostility, demonstrating China's capacity to act as international mediator in regional conflicts (Batrawy, 2023). This success showcases Beijing's growing influence in regions historically under strong American sway whilst providing regional powers with alternatives to Western mediation.

Middle power diplomacy reveals sophisticated strategies for maintaining autonomy amid great power competition. India simultaneously participates in the Quad (with United States, Japan, and Australia), BRICS (with China and Russia), and Shanghai Cooperation Organisation, demonstrating strategic autonomy through multiple alignments. This "multi-alignment" strategy enables India to pursue diverse partnerships whilst avoiding exclusive dependence on any single power or bloc.

Turkey's strategic autonomy illustrates both opportunities and constraints in regional governance. Ankara has attempted to carve autonomous space from Western allies through building ties with non-Western actors, pursuing independent policies in Syria, Libya, and the Eastern Mediterranean whilst maintaining NATO membership. However, geopolitical imperatives and domestic priorities often contradict autonomy-seeking policies, demonstrating structural limitations on regional autonomy (Aran et al., 2025).

Regional organisations demonstrate increasing capacity for autonomous action whilst remaining constrained by great power interests. ASEAN has developed the ASEAN Outlook on the Indo-Pacific as hedging tool against various uncertainties resulting from US-China competition, proposing to move evolution of Indo-Pacific concept away from dominance by any single country (Anwar, 2020). The African Union has enhanced peacekeeping capabilities and conflict mediation capacity, though major interventions still require external support.

However, regional powers remain constrained by structural factors limiting autonomous action. Major security challenges continue requiring great power involvement or backing, as demonstrated by ongoing conflicts in Ukraine, Gaza, and other regions. Economic dependence on great powers constrains political autonomy, whilst regional institutions remain relatively weak compared to global frameworks.

Dynamic Interaction Model

The MDOT Framework recognises that the five dimensions interact dynamically rather than evolving independently. Understanding these interactions is crucial for explaining transformation patterns and predicting future developments. Three types of inter-dimensional relationships characterise these interactions, providing insights into how transformation patterns emerge and evolve.

Reinforcing Dynamics

When changes in one dimension accelerate transformation in others, reinforcing dynamics emerge that can trigger rapid systemic change. The BRICS expansion illustrates this pattern, where institutional developments (Dimension 2) strengthen regional autonomy (Dimension 5) by providing platforms for coordination and alternative governance arrangements. This institutional development also enables normative contestation (Dimension 3) by offering forums for promoting alternative governance models and challenging Western-dominated frameworks.

Economic fragmentation (Dimension 4) reinforces alternative institutional arrangements (Dimension 2) by creating demand for non-Western financial mechanisms and reducing dependence on established systems. Countries experiencing sanctions or financial restrictions seek alternative arrangements, increasing support for institutions like the New Development Bank and potential BRICS payment systems.

Material power shifts (Dimension 1) reinforce normative contestation (Dimension 3) by providing rising powers with resources and confidence to challenge existing norms. China's economic growth enables promotion of alternative governance models and development paradigms, whilst providing resources for institutional alternatives and regional influence operations.

These reinforcing dynamics explain why contemporary transformation appears accelerating despite continued American dominance in many areas. Changes in multiple dimensions create momentum for further transformation whilst reducing system inertia and creating new possibilities for autonomous action.

Compensatory Dynamics

When stability in one dimension compensates for transformation in others, compensatory dynamics provide system stability that prevents complete breakdown whilst enabling partial change. Economic interdependence (Dimension 4) moderates normative contestation (Dimension 3) and material power competition (Dimension 1) by creating shared interests in maintaining stable relationships despite political disagreements.

China and the United States maintain substantial economic relationships despite strategic competition, preventing complete systemic breakdown. Trade relationships, financial interdependence, and shared challenges create incentives for cooperation even amid political tensions. This economic integration constrains both powers from pursuing maximally confrontational policies that could trigger economic decoupling with severe costs for both sides.

Institutional resilience (Dimension 2) compensates for normative fragmentation (Dimension 3) by providing forums for dialogue and cooperation despite ideological differences. The United Nations system continues functioning despite increasing disagreements about intervention and sovereignty, whilst international economic institutions adapt to accommodate new members whilst maintaining core functions.

Regional autonomy (Dimension 5) compensates for great power competition (Dimension 1) by providing alternative channels for conflict resolution and cooperation. Regional organisations and middle powers create buffers reducing direct confrontation between major powers whilst maintaining communication channels and opportunities for face-saving solutions.

Contradictory Dynamics

When changes in different dimensions pull in opposite directions, contradictory dynamics create system tension and unpredictable outcomes that complicate policy planning and strategic forecasting. Growing regional autonomy (Dimension 5) conflicts with attempts to maintain global institutional effectiveness (Dimension

2) as regional solutions bypass multilateral frameworks and reduce incentives for global cooperation.

China's Belt and Road Initiative and regional mediation efforts enhance regional autonomy whilst challenging established Western-led institutional arrangements. Regional powers pursuing strategic autonomy resist pressure to choose sides in great power competition, complicating alliance formation and global governance efforts.

Material power diffusion (Dimension 1) contradicts institutional resistance to reform (Dimension 2), creating legitimacy deficits that undermine institutional effectiveness. Rising powers demand greater representation in international institutions whilst established powers resist changes threatening their influence, generating institutional gridlock and alternative arrangement creation.

Economic interdependence (Dimension 4) contradicts security competition (Dimension 1) by creating vulnerabilities that states seek to reduce through diversification and friend-shoring. This generates economic fragmentation despite continued trade relationships, creating complex patterns where economic and security logics pull in different directions.

Normative contestation (Dimension 3) contradicts institutional cooperation (Dimension 2) when states challenge fundamental principles underlying international institutions whilst maintaining membership and participation. This creates tensions between institutional effectiveness and normative coherence that complicate collective action.

Transformation Thresholds and Systemic Change

The MDOT Framework establishes that systemic transformation occurs when critical masses of dimensions experience primary or secondary transformation simultaneously. This threshold approach provides analytical precision about when change constitutes fundamental system alteration rather than adaptation within existing arrangements.

Specific thresholds include system-wide transformation when primary transformation occurs in three or more dimensions or secondary transformation occurs in four or more dimensions, partial system change when primary transformation occurs in 1-2 dimensions or secondary transformation occurs in 2-3 dimensions, and system stability when predominantly tertiary transformations occur across all dimensions.

This approach addresses scholarly observations about contemporary international relations featuring "disagreement over the principles and rules that should govern the behaviour and define the obligations of sovereign states" whilst providing analytical precision about when such disagreements constitute systemic change (Parrat, 2024, p. 416).

Figure 2. Transformation Threshold Matrix

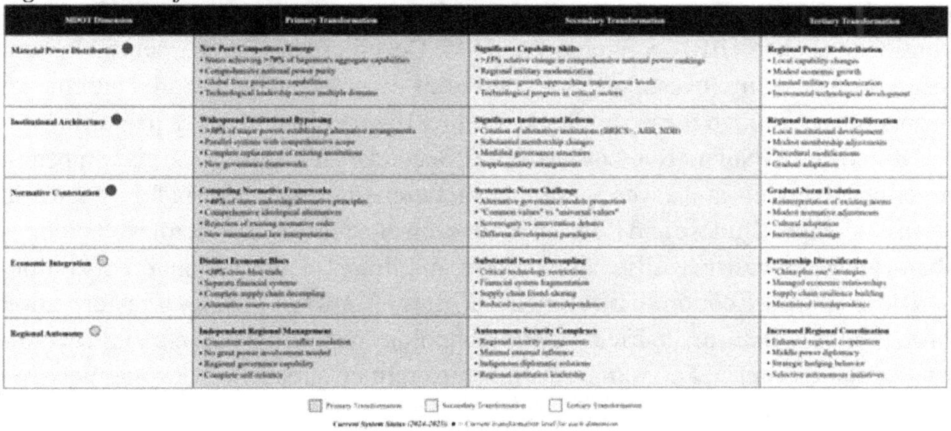

The threshold-based analysis enables identification of transformation trajectories and potential tipping points before they manifest across all dimensions. Unlike approaches that assume uniform change or rely on single indicators, the MDOT Framework captures complexity whilst maintaining analytical precision for policy applications.

Application to Contemporary Global Order

Applying the MDOT Framework to the current international system reveals complex transformation patterns that transcend simple polarity models whilst providing systematic analysis of change dynamics across multiple dimensions. The analysis demonstrates that rather than experiencing uniform change toward multipolarity or bipolar competition, the international system undergoes differentiated transformation creating complex patterns of continuity and change.

Current Threshold Assessment

The framework's application to contemporary global politics reveals that the international system experiences partial system change approaching system-wide transformation thresholds. The assessment of each dimension demonstrates:

Dimension 1 (Material Power Distribution): Secondary transformation characterised by China's rise and relative American decline without emergence of clear peer competitors. China's economic growth and military modernisation represent significant capability shifts, but the United States maintains substantial advantages in global force projection, technological innovation, and alliance networks.

Dimension 2 (Institutional Architecture): Secondary transformation through alternative institution creation and expansion meeting criteria for significant institutional change. BRICS expansion, New Development Bank operations, and Asian Infrastructure Investment Bank activities demonstrate substantial alternative arrangements, though these supplement rather than replace existing institutions.

Dimension 3 (Normative Contestation): Secondary transformation via competing governance models and sovereignty interpretations meeting criteria for systematic norm challenge. Chinese and Russian promotion of alternative principles challenges liberal internationalism whilst maintaining commitment to international cooperation.

Dimension 4 (Economic Integration/Fragmentation): Tertiary transformation through supply chain diversification and technology restrictions not meeting secondary threshold criteria. Economic relationships remain substantial despite managed fragmentation in critical sectors.

Dimension 5 (Regional Governance): Tertiary transformation with increased regional diplomatic initiatives not meeting secondary threshold criteria. Regional autonomy has expanded but remains constrained by dependence on great powers for major challenges.

This pattern indicates the international system experiences partial system change characterised by substantial transformation in multiple dimensions without reaching system-wide transformation thresholds. The analysis suggests that continued secondary transformation in additional dimensions could trigger system-wide transformation, whilst compensatory dynamics might stabilise the system at current levels.

DETAILED DIMENSION ANALYSIS

Material Power Distribution: Secondary Transformation Dynamics

The material power dimension demonstrates secondary transformation through significant capability shifts among existing powers whilst avoiding the emergence of peer competitors that would constitute primary transformation. This pattern reflects the complexity of contemporary power measurement and the multifaceted nature of national capabilities.

China's economic transformation represents the most dramatic power shift since the end of the Cold War. Chinese GDP grew from $1.2 trillion in 2000 to $17.7 trillion in 2023, increasing its share of global output from 3.6% to approximately 18% (World Bank, 2024; IMF, 2023). This growth trajectory has been accompanied by systematic efforts to develop comprehensive national power through technological innovation, military modernisation, and global influence operations.

Chinese military spending increased from $22 billion in 2000 to $296 billion in 2023, enabling substantial force modernisation including development of anti-ship ballistic missiles, hypersonic weapons, advanced fighter aircraft, and naval expansion (SIPRI, 2024). The People's Liberation Army has developed capabilities that challenge American military advantages in the Western Pacific, though global force projection remains limited compared to American capabilities.

Technological development represents a crucial aspect of Chinese power accumulation. China has achieved leadership in several emerging technologies including 5G telecommunications, renewable energy systems, and electric vehicles whilst making substantial progress in artificial intelligence, quantum computing, and biotechnology. However, dependence on foreign semiconductors and advanced manufacturing equipment constrains technological autonomy in critical sectors.

India's rise provides additional evidence of power diffusion without peer competitor emergence. Indian GDP grew from $468 billion in 2000 to $3.7 trillion in 2023, whilst defence spending increased from $13 billion to $76 billion (World Bank, 2024; SIPRI, 2024). India has developed significant military capabilities including nuclear weapons, advanced fighter aircraft, and space technology, but power projection remains primarily regional.

The United States maintains substantial advantages that prevent emergence of peer competitors despite relative decline. American defence spending of $816 billion in 2023 exceeds Chinese spending by nearly three-to-one, whilst technological advantages in critical sectors including semiconductors, aerospace, and biotechnology provide enduring benefits (SIPRI, 2024). The global network of military bases, alliance relationships, and intelligence partnerships enables power projection capabilities that remain unmatched.

American economic advantages include the dollar's continued dominance in international finance, the attractiveness of American capital markets, and leadership in innovation ecosystems. Despite China's economic growth, the United States maintains higher GDP per capita ($76,330 versus $12,720 in 2023), superior productivity levels, and demographic advantages including immigration attraction (World Bank, 2024).

Russia's position illustrates the complexity of power measurement under contemporary conditions. Despite economic limitations—Russian GDP of $2.2 trillion ranks eleventh globally—Russia maintains disproportionate influence through nuclear capabilities, resource control, and willingness to use force (World Bank, 2024). The Ukraine conflict has revealed both Russian military limitations and continued capacity for regional disruption, demonstrating that power involves multiple dimensions beyond simple economic measures.

Figure 3. Contemporary Global Power Distribution (2023)

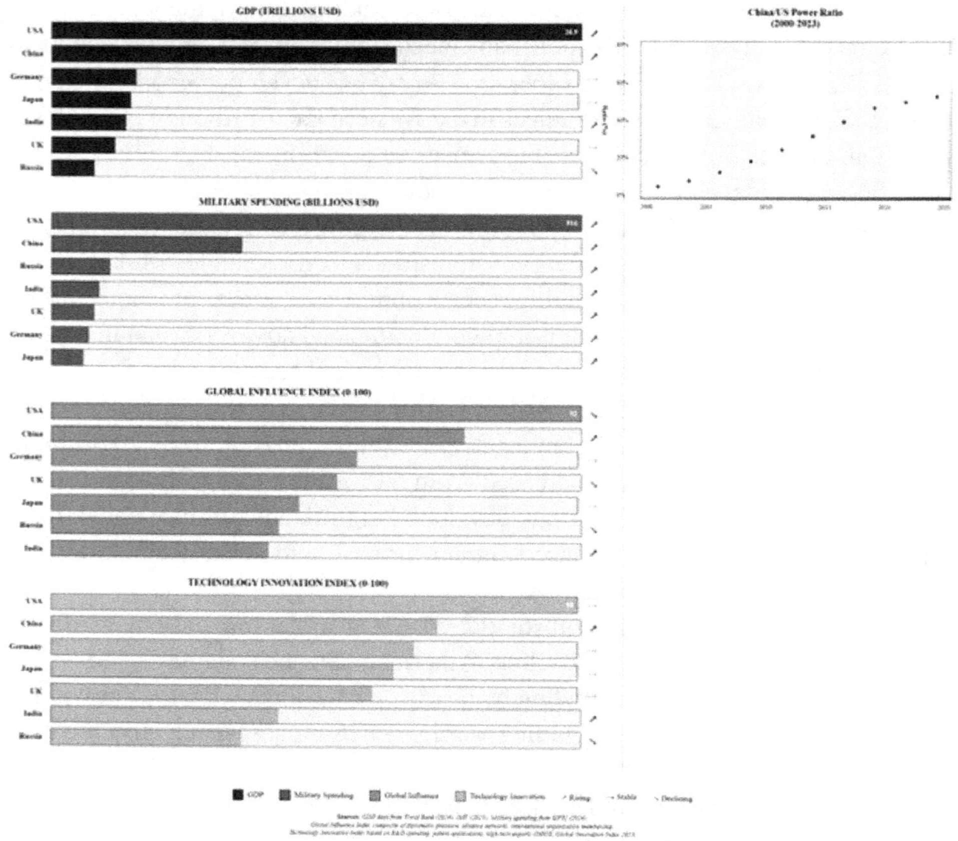

Institutional Architecture: Alternative Arrangements and Adaptation

The institutional dimension experiences secondary transformation characterised by significant alternative institution creation whilst established frameworks maintain substantial influence. This pattern reflects institutional layering rather than replacement, with new arrangements supplementing rather than supplanting existing institutions whilst creating alternative governance options.

BRICS expansion represents the most significant institutional development challenging Western-dominated arrangements. The 2024 expansion to include Egypt, Ethiopia, Iran, and the United Arab Emirates, followed by Indonesia in 2025, increased the organisation's economic and demographic weight whilst demonstrating growing appeal of alternative institutional arrangements. BRICS+ now comprises approximately 37% of global GDP and 45% of world population, providing substantial potential influence (Council on Foreign Relations, 2025).

The New Development Bank has emerged as significant alternative to World Bank lending, approving over $30 billion in loans since 2015 across 96 projects in member countries and others (NDB, 2024). The bank's emphasis on infrastructure development, renewable energy, and sustainable development provides alternative development finance operating according to different principles than traditional institutions. Local currency lending and simplified approval processes offer advantages for borrowing countries.

The Asian Infrastructure Investment Bank demonstrates capacity to attract broad membership including American allies despite Washington's initial opposition. With 109 members and over $40 billion in approved financing, the AIIB has established credibility as alternative development finance institution whilst maintaining high operational standards (AIIB, 2024). British, German, and other European participation indicates recognition of potential benefits despite American concerns.

However, BRICS faces significant limitations constraining institutional effectiveness and challenging its capacity to provide comprehensive alternative to existing arrangements. The organisation lacks formal charter, permanent secretariat, or common funding mechanisms, relying on consensus-based decision-making that constrains collective action. Internal divisions over issues including Russia's invasion of Ukraine, China's relations with India, and economic policy differences complicate coordination.

The 2024 BRICS summit in Kazan demonstrated both potential and limitations of alternative institutional arrangements. Whilst the summit attracted participation from over 30 countries and addressed economic cooperation, payment systems, and global governance reform, concrete achievements remained limited. Proposals for BRICS currency and comprehensive payment system face substantial technical and political obstacles that prevent near-term implementation.

Established institutions demonstrate resilience whilst adapting to changing power distributions and emerging challenges. The United Nations system continues functioning despite Security Council gridlock, with General Assembly activities, specialised agencies, and peacekeeping operations maintaining significant global influence. Reform initiatives including expansion of Security Council membership remain stalled, but institutional adaptation continues through other mechanisms.

The World Trade Organisation survived the Doha Round collapse and recent trade wars whilst maintaining core dispute resolution functions and facilitating plurilateral agreements. WTO adaptation includes new agreements on telecommunications, government procurement, and trade facilitation that demonstrate institutional evolution despite broader negotiation failures.

International financial institutions have accommodated new members and adjusted governance structures whilst maintaining core functions. The International Monetary Fund increased Chinese quotas whilst expanding lending facilities and surveillance functions. The World Bank has incorporated climate change considerations and adjusted lending priorities whilst maintaining substantial operations.

NATO expansion and adaptation demonstrate institutional evolution in response to changing security environments. The alliance added Sweden and Finland in 2023-2024, bringing membership to 32 countries whilst developing new strategic concepts addressing cyber warfare, space security, and hybrid threats. NATO's ability to maintain cohesion whilst expanding geographically and functionally illustrates institutional adaptability under changing conditions.

Figure 4. BRICS+ Expansion Impact Visualisation (2009-2025)

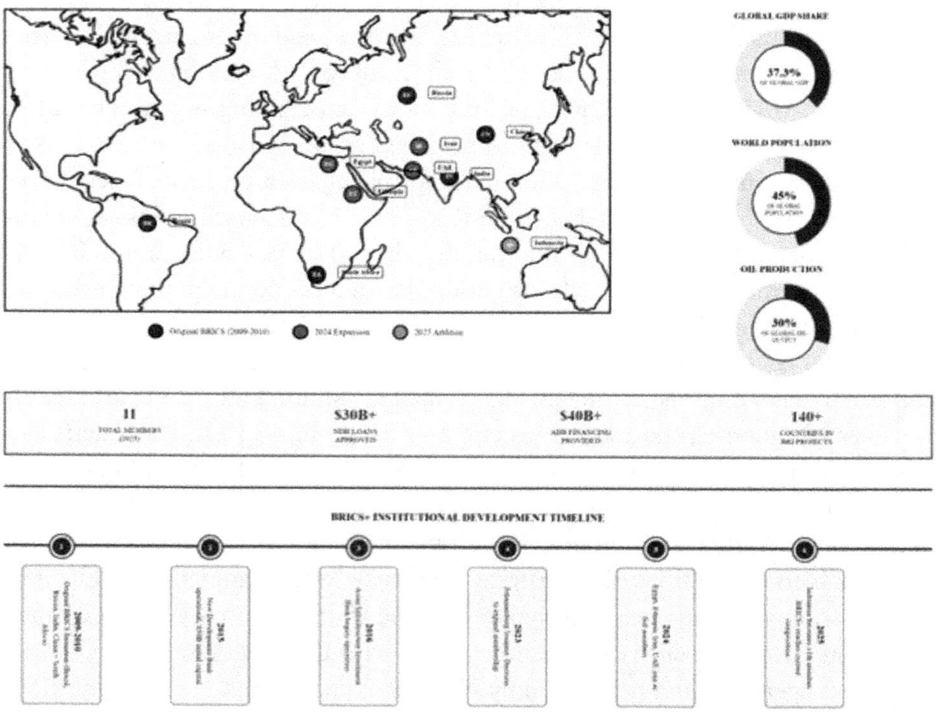

Normative Contestation: Systematic Challenges Without Breakdown

The normative dimension experiences secondary transformation through systematic challenges to liberal internationalism whilst avoiding complete normative breakdown or emergence of entirely alternative frameworks. This pattern reflects sophisticated contestation that reinterprets existing principles rather than rejecting international cooperation entirely.

Chinese normative entrepreneurship represents sophisticated challenge to Western liberal norms through promoting alternative governance concepts that maintain commitment to international cooperation whilst rejecting liberal democracy and human rights universality. The concept of "democracy with Chinese characteristics" provides alternative governance model emphasising economic development, social stability, and party leadership rather than electoral competition and individual rights (Chen et al., 2024).

Chinese officials and scholars promote "common values" versus "universal values," challenging Western claims about human rights universality whilst arguing for cultural relativism and state sovereignty in determining domestic arrangements. This approach maintains engagement with international human rights frameworks whilst rejecting external pressure for political reform.

The Belt and Road Initiative embodies alternative development principles emphasising infrastructure investment, economic connectivity, and state-led development rather than liberal market reforms and democratic conditionality. With over 140 countries participating in BRI projects worth more than $1 trillion, this approach demonstrates significant appeal for alternative development models that prioritise economic growth over political liberalisation.

Russian normative contestation emphasises sovereignty, traditional values, and multipolarity whilst challenging Western intervention norms and democracy promotion. Russian officials argue for "sovereign democracy" that rejects external interference whilst maintaining domestic legitimacy through different mechanisms than Western electoral systems. This approach resonates with authoritarian governments whilst providing intellectual framework for resistance to Western pressure.

Russian actions in Ukraine challenge post-Cold War norms regarding territorial integrity and peaceful settlement of disputes, but frame these actions through sovereignty and self-determination principles rather than rejecting international law entirely. Russian justifications emphasise protection of ethnic Russians, resistance to NATO expansion, and defence against Western encroachment rather than territorial conquest or imperial expansion.

The international response to Ukraine illustrates normative fragmentation without complete breakdown. Western states imposed comprehensive sanctions and provided military support to Ukraine, demonstrating commitment to territorial integrity and rule of law. However, much of the Global South maintained neutral positions whilst supporting humanitarian assistance, indicating autonomous decision-making rather than automatic alignment with great power preferences.

Major democracies including India, Brazil, and South Africa abstained on certain UN resolutions condemning Russian actions whilst supporting humanitarian measures and peaceful resolution. This pattern reflects complex calculations balancing normative commitments with geopolitical interests and historical relationships rather than simple ideological alignment.

ASEAN's response to various regional challenges demonstrates alternative approaches to normative issues that emphasise consensus, non-interference, and gradual progress rather than confrontational advocacy for liberal principles. The ASEAN Way provides alternative model for international cooperation that accommodates diverse political systems whilst maintaining regional stability.

Economic Integration: Managed Fragmentation Without Decoupling

The economic dimension experiences tertiary transformation characterised by supply chain diversification and technology restrictions whilst maintaining substantial interdependence. This pattern reflects managed fragmentation in critical sectors rather than comprehensive economic decoupling, with states pursuing security objectives whilst preserving economic benefits from integration.

The International Monetary Fund documents accelerating geoeconomic fragmentation driven by policy decisions rather than technological or preference shifts. Friend-shoring and near-shoring have increased trade among politically aligned countries by 4-6% whilst reducing trade between geopolitical rivals, but these changes remain modest compared to overall trade volumes (Aiyar et al., 2023).

Technology restrictions represent the clearest evidence of economic fragmentation, with semiconductor supply chains showing approximately 40% reduction in China-US interdependence since 2019. American export controls on advanced semiconductors, manufacturing equipment, and related technologies aim to constrain Chinese technological development whilst encouraging domestic production and allied sourcing.

However, complete economic decoupling remains limited by cost considerations and technical requirements. China-US trade reached $690 billion in 2023 despite tariffs and restrictions, demonstrating continued economic relationship despite political tensions (US Trade Representative, 2024). Chinese manufacturing remains integrated into global supply chains, whilst American companies maintain significant Chinese operations.

Financial interdependence persists despite political tensions. China holds $859 billion in US Treasury securities as of 2024, down from peak holdings of $1.3 trillion in 2013 but still representing substantial financial relationship (US Treasury, 2024). Chinese financial institutions remain integrated into global banking systems, whilst dollar-denominated transactions continue dominating Chinese international trade.

Currency fragmentation shows modest changes without fundamental restructuring of international monetary system. The dollar's share of global foreign exchange reserves declined from 71% in 2000 to 59% in 2023, but alternative currencies have not gained correspondingly (IMF, 2024). The euro accounts for approximately 20% of reserves, whilst the Chinese yuan represents only 2.7% despite China's economic size.

BRICS proposals for alternative payment systems face substantial technical and political obstacles. The New Development Bank primarily uses dollars for lending, reflecting practical constraints of international finance rather than ideological preference. The BRICS Contingent Reserve Arrangement has never been activated, indicating limited confidence in alternative mechanisms during actual crises.

Supply chain diversification accelerated during COVID-19 pandemic and subsequent geopolitical tensions, but reshoring remains limited by cost considerations. Multinational corporations pursue "China plus one" strategies that maintain Chinese operations whilst developing alternative sources, reflecting risk management rather than complete decoupling. Manufacturing relocation focuses on labour-intensive sectors whilst advanced manufacturing remains concentrated in established centres.

European responses to economic security challenges demonstrate similar patterns of managed diversification rather than complete separation. The European Union's economic security strategy emphasises reducing dependence in critical sectors whilst maintaining openness and international cooperation. Measures include supply chain diversification, domestic capacity building, and enhanced screening of foreign investment without comprehensive decoupling.

Figure 5. Economic Fragmentation vs Interdependence Trends (2018-2024)

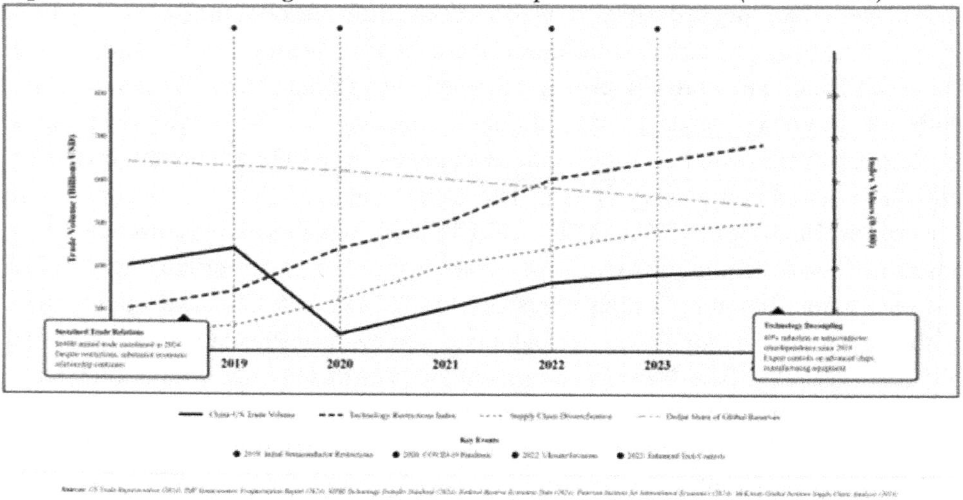

Regional Autonomy: Expanding Influence Within Structural Constraints

The regional autonomy dimension experiences tertiary transformation characterised by increased regional coordination and diplomatic initiative without fundamental alteration of global power structures. Regional powers demonstrate growing capacity for autonomous action whilst remaining constrained by dependence on great powers for major security challenges and economic relationships.

China's mediation of Saudi-Iranian rapprochement in March 2023 exemplifies growing regional autonomy through indigenous diplomatic solutions that bypass traditional Western mediation. The Beijing-brokered agreement restored diplomatic relations between Riyadh and Tehran after seven years of hostility, demonstrating China's capacity to act as international mediator in regional conflicts whilst advancing its Middle Eastern influence (Batrawy, 2023).

This diplomatic success illustrates China's systematic approach to regional influence through economic incentives, diplomatic engagement, and strategic patience. The agreement built upon years of Chinese economic investment in both countries whilst providing face-saving mechanism for rivals to reduce tensions that threatened regional stability and Chinese interests.

Middle power diplomacy reveals sophisticated strategies for maintaining autonomy amid great power competition through multiple alignments and strategic hedging. India simultaneously participates in the Quad (with United States, Japan, and Australia), BRICS (with China and Russia), and Shanghai Cooperation Organisation, demonstrating capacity to pursue diverse partnerships whilst avoiding exclusive dependence on any single power or bloc.

This "multi-alignment" strategy enables India to balance relationships with competing powers whilst preserving decision-making autonomy on critical issues. India's response to the Ukraine conflict illustrates this approach, with New Delhi abstaining on condemnatory UN resolutions whilst purchasing discounted Russian energy and maintaining defence cooperation, whilst simultaneously strengthening ties with Western partners through Quad activities and bilateral initiatives.

Turkey's strategic autonomy illustrates both opportunities and constraints in regional governance under contemporary conditions. Ankara has attempted to carve autonomous space from Western allies through building ties with non-Western actors, pursuing independent policies in Syria, Libya, and the Eastern Mediterranean whilst maintaining NATO membership (Aran et al., 2025).

Turkish policies demonstrate capacity for autonomous action within alliance frameworks through leveraging geographical advantages, military capabilities, and diplomatic relationships. Turkey's operation of Russian S-400 air defence systems despite NATO objections, mediation efforts between Russia and Ukraine, and independent Middle Eastern policies illustrate scope for autonomous action even within alliance constraints.

However, structural factors limit regional autonomy in significant ways. Geopolitical imperatives and domestic priorities often contradict autonomy-seeking policies, preventing effective implementation of independent strategies. Economic dependence on major powers constrains political autonomy, whilst security challenges require great power backing or acquiescence.

Regional organisations demonstrate enhanced capacity for autonomous action whilst remaining limited by institutional weaknesses and member state divergences. ASEAN has developed the ASEAN Outlook on the Indo-Pacific as hedging tool against US-China competition, proposing to move evolution of Indo-Pacific concept away from domination by any single country (Anwar, 2020).

The African Union has enhanced peacekeeping capabilities and conflict mediation capacity through initiatives including the African Peace and Security Architecture and Continental Early Warning System. However, major interventions still require external support, as demonstrated by French involvement in Sahel operations and international assistance for peacekeeping missions.

Latin American regional autonomy has expanded through initiatives including the Union of South American Nations (UNASUR), Community of Latin American and Caribbean States (CELAC), and Pacific Alliance, but institutional effectiveness remains limited by political polarisation and economic dependence on external markets. Brazilian and Mexican leadership provides regional influence whilst remaining constrained by domestic priorities and global economic integration.

Dynamic Interactions in Contemporary Transformation

The MDOT Framework's application reveals complex patterns of interaction between dimensions that explain why contemporary transformation differs from historical precedents. Rather than uniform change across all dimensions characteristic of previous systemic transitions, current patterns involve reinforcing, compensatory, and contradictory dynamics that create novel configurations requiring new analytical approaches.

Reinforcing Dynamics Accelerating Change

Several reinforcing dynamics operate across dimensions to accelerate transformation whilst creating momentum for further change. Institutional developments (Dimension 2) strengthen regional autonomy (Dimension 5) by providing platforms for alternative governance arrangements that enable regional powers to coordinate responses to global challenges whilst developing alternatives to Western-dominated frameworks.

BRICS expansion creates forums for regional powers to coordinate policies on global issues whilst developing alternative financial mechanisms, technology transfer arrangements, and diplomatic coordination. This institutional platform enables countries like India, Brazil, and South Africa to pursue autonomous policies whilst maintaining relationships with great powers, expanding their strategic options whilst reducing dependence on established arrangements.

Material power shifts (Dimension 1) reinforce normative contestation (Dimension 3) by providing rising powers with resources and confidence to challenge existing norms whilst developing alternative frameworks. China's economic growth enables promotion of alternative governance models and development paradigms through providing successful example of non-democratic development whilst offering resources for countries adopting similar approaches.

Chinese success in maintaining rapid economic growth whilst rejecting political liberalisation provides empirical challenge to liberal assumptions about relationships between democracy and development. This example gains credibility through China's capacity to provide alternative development finance, technology transfer, and market access without political conditionality.

Economic fragmentation (Dimension 4) reinforces alternative institutional arrangements (Dimension 2) by creating demand for non-Western financial mechanisms and reducing dependence on established systems. Countries experiencing sanctions or financial restrictions seek alternative arrangements, increasing support for institutions like the New Development Bank whilst developing bilateral currency arrangements and trade mechanisms.

Russian exclusion from SWIFT banking systems following Ukraine invasion accelerated development of alternative payment mechanisms including expanded use of Chinese yuan, bilateral currency arrangements, and barter systems. This fragmentation creates network effects that encourage additional countries to develop alternative arrangements as insurance against potential restrictions.

These reinforcing dynamics explain why contemporary transformation appears accelerating despite continued American dominance in many areas. Changes in multiple dimensions create momentum for further transformation whilst reducing system inertia and enabling new possibilities for autonomous action.

Compensatory Dynamics Maintaining Stability

Compensatory dynamics provide system stability despite significant changes in individual dimensions by creating buffers that prevent complete breakdown whilst enabling partial transformation. Economic interdependence (Dimension 4) moderates normative contestation (Dimension 3) and material power competition (Dimension 1) by creating shared interests in maintaining stable relationships despite political disagreements.

China-US economic relationship exemplifies these compensatory dynamics, with trade relationships, financial interdependence, and shared challenges creating incentives for cooperation even amid strategic competition. Economic integration constrains both powers from pursuing maximally confrontational policies that could trigger economic decoupling with severe costs for both sides.

Chinese dependence on American markets, technology, and financial systems constrains confrontational policies that could provoke severe economic retaliation. American dependence on Chinese manufacturing, supply chains, and consumer markets similarly constrains policies that could trigger complete economic separation. This mutual dependence creates space for managed competition rather than zero-sum confrontation.

Institutional resilience (Dimension 2) compensates for normative fragmentation (Dimension 3) by providing forums for dialogue and cooperation despite ideological differences. International institutions continue functioning despite increasing disagreements about fundamental principles, enabling practical cooperation on technical issues whilst avoiding confrontation over normative differences.

The United Nations system demonstrates this compensatory effect through continued operation of specialised agencies, humanitarian programmes, and technical cooperation despite Security Council gridlock. Countries maintain participation in

UN activities whilst disagreeing about intervention principles, sovereignty interpretation, and political arrangements.

Regional autonomy (Dimension 5) compensates for great power competition (Dimension 1) by providing alternative channels for conflict resolution and cooperation. Regional organisations and middle powers create buffers reducing direct confrontation between major powers whilst maintaining communication channels and opportunities for face-saving solutions.

ASEAN's approach to South China Sea disputes illustrates this compensatory dynamic through providing forum for dialogue between China and Southeast Asian countries without requiring great power involvement. This regional approach enables conflict management without forcing choices between competing great powers whilst maintaining stability in contested areas.

Contradictory Dynamics Creating Tension

Contradictory dynamics generate system tension and unpredictable outcomes by pulling different dimensions in opposite directions, creating complex challenges for policy coordination and strategic planning. Growing regional autonomy (Dimension 5) conflicts with attempts to maintain global institutional effectiveness (Dimension 2) as regional solutions bypass multilateral frameworks whilst reducing incentives for global cooperation.

Regional organisations increasingly address challenges that previously required global institutional responses, creating parallel governance structures that may compete with established arrangements. This regional preference reflects frustration with global institutional gridlock whilst enabling more flexible responses to local challenges.

Material power diffusion (Dimension 1) contradicts institutional resistance to reform (Dimension 2), creating legitimacy deficits that undermine institutional effectiveness whilst generating pressure for alternative arrangements. Rising powers demand greater representation in international institutions whilst established powers resist changes threatening their influence, creating institutional gridlock that encourages alternative arrangement development.

United Nations Security Council reform exemplifies this contradiction, with emerging powers demanding permanent membership whilst existing permanent members resist changes that would dilute their influence. This gridlock undermines institutional legitimacy whilst encouraging countries to pursue alternative forums for addressing security challenges.

Economic interdependence (Dimension 4) contradicts security competition (Dimension 1) by creating vulnerabilities that states seek to reduce through diversification and friend-shoring. This generates economic fragmentation despite continued trade relationships, creating complex patterns where economic and security logics operate according to different principles.

Supply chain security concerns drive diversification efforts that increase costs whilst reducing efficiency, creating tension between economic and security objectives. Countries must balance economic benefits from integration against security risks from dependence, generating complex policy trade-offs without clear solutions.

Normative contestation (Dimension 3) contradicts institutional cooperation (Dimension 2) when states challenge fundamental principles underlying international institutions whilst maintaining membership and participation. This creates tensions between institutional effectiveness and normative coherence that complicate collective action whilst generating pressure for institutional reform or alternative arrangements.

These contradictory dynamics explain why contemporary transformation generates significant uncertainty whilst creating opportunities for creative policy solutions that address multiple objectives simultaneously. Managing these contradictions requires sophisticated approaches that acknowledge complexity whilst pursuing realistic objectives within structural constraints.

Figure 6. Dynamic Interactions Between MDOT Dimensions

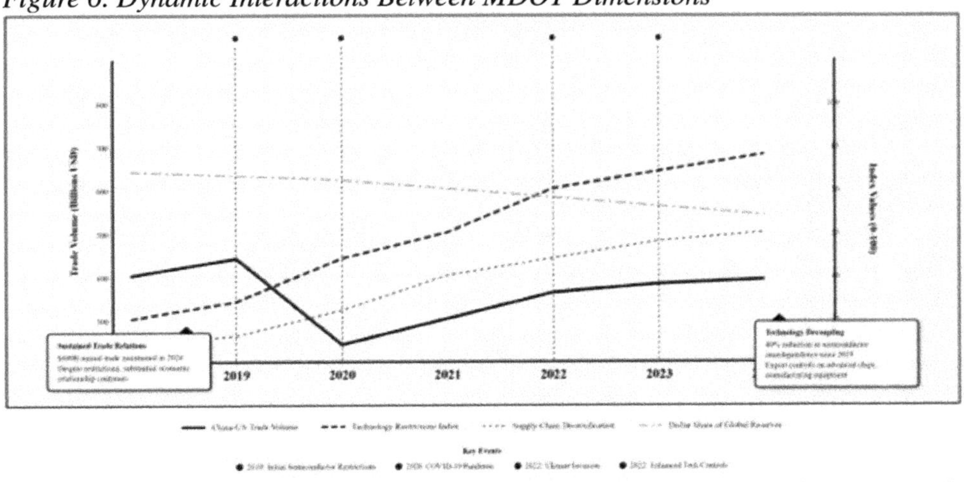

CASE STUDIES: STATE RESPONSES TO MULTI-DIMENSIONAL TRANSFORMATION

The following three case studies illustrate how different types of states navigate contemporary transformation dynamics through the MDOT Framework lens. Sweden, Australia, and Turkey represent distinct approaches to strategic autonomy and alliance relationships, providing empirical validation of the framework's analytical utility whilst demonstrating variance in state responses to systemic change.

Figure 7. Case Studies Transformation Trajectories (2010-2024)

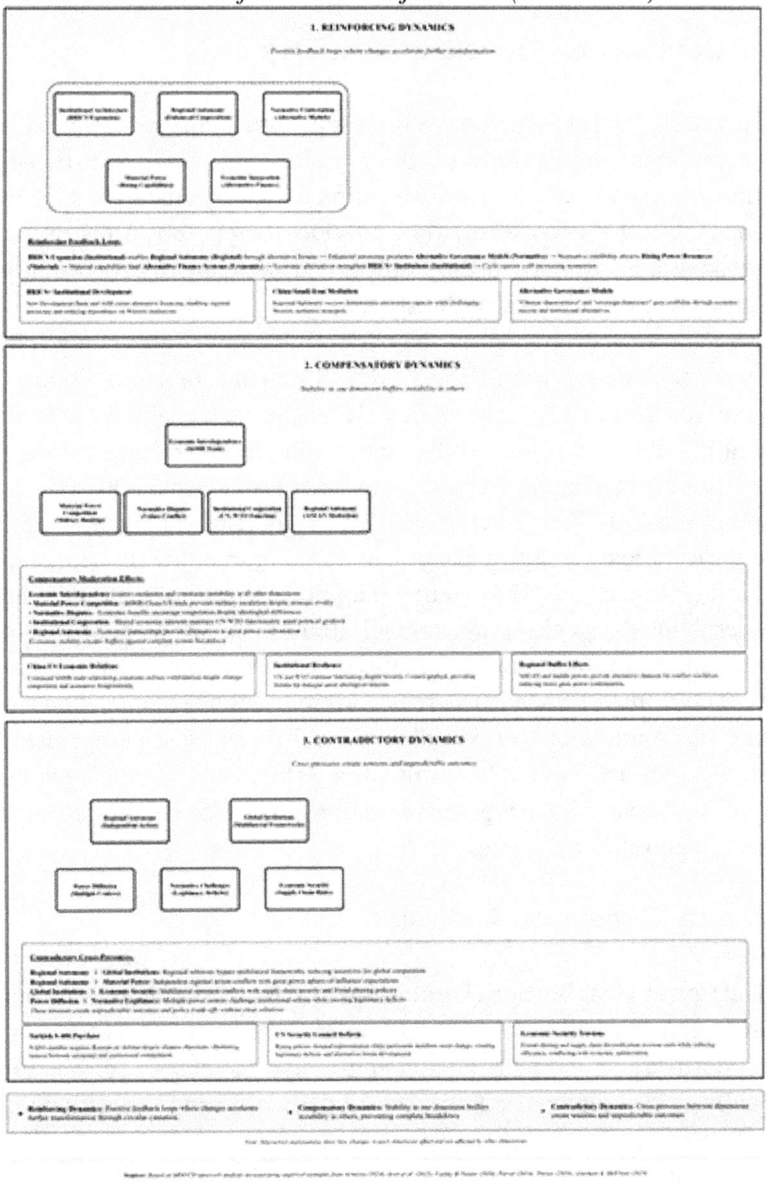

Case Study 1: Sweden - From Neutrality to NATO Membership

Historical Context and Transformation Trajectory

Sweden's 2024 NATO membership represents one of the most dramatic foreign policy reversals in recent European history, ending over two centuries of military non-alignment that had defined Swedish national identity since 1812 (Government of Sweden, 2024). This transformation provides compelling illustration of how systemic change can override deeply embedded national role conceptions when security imperatives reach critical thresholds.

Swedish neutrality originated in the early 19th century following military defeats and territorial losses, with King Karl XIV Johan establishing non-alignment as foundation for Swedish security policy. This approach enabled Sweden to avoid involvement in both world wars whilst maintaining independence during the Cold War through careful balancing between superpowers (Kaynak, 2023).

The end of the Cold War initially seemed to vindicate Swedish neutrality, with reduced security threats enabling continued non-alignment whilst pursuing deeper European integration through EU membership in 1995. Sweden participated extensively in international peacekeeping, humanitarian assistance, and conflict resolution whilst maintaining military non-alignment as core principle of national identity.

However, systematic changes across multiple MDOT dimensions gradually undermined the foundations of Swedish neutrality whilst creating pressures for fundamental policy revision. The cumulative effect of these changes eventually reached threshold levels that triggered rapid transformation despite strong domestic attachment to neutrality principles.

Dimension-by-Dimension Analysis

Material Power Distribution (Dimension 1): Changes in regional power balance created direct security challenges that traditional neutrality could not address. Russia's military modernisation and increasingly aggressive policies under Vladimir Putin systematically eroded regional stability whilst demonstrating Swedish vulnerability to potential coercion or attack.

The 2008 war with Georgia marked initial warning of Russian willingness to use force against neighbouring states, whilst the 2014 annexation of Crimea and intervention in Eastern Ukraine demonstrated systematic challenge to European security order. These actions directly threatened Swedish security by suggesting potential Russian actions against other neutral or NATO-adjacent states.

Russian military activities in the Baltic Sea region increased pressure on Sweden through submarine incursions, airspace violations, and cyber attacks that demonstrated both capability and intent to intimidate Swedish decision-makers. The 2014 submarine incident in Stockholm archipelago particularly highlighted Swedish vulnerability whilst raising questions about deterrence effectiveness under neutrality arrangements.

Institutional Architecture (Dimension 2): Changes in European security institutions created pressures for Swedish alignment whilst demonstrating limitations of alternative arrangements. NATO adaptation to address Russian threats provided credible deterrence framework that neutrality could not match, whilst EU security capabilities remained limited despite integration efforts.

NATO's Enhanced Forward Presence in Baltic states demonstrated alliance capability to provide credible deterrence through collective defence arrangements that individual states could not achieve independently. Swedish military cooperation with NATO through Partnership for Peace and Host Nation Support agreements provided insight into alliance benefits whilst highlighting limitations of non-membership status.

EU efforts to develop Common Security and Defence Policy remained constrained by institutional limitations and member state preferences, providing insufficient security guarantee for Swedish requirements. The 2016 EU Global Strategy emphasised strategic autonomy but lacked mechanisms for credible defence against major power threats.

Normative Contestation (Dimension 3): Russian challenges to European security norms undermined Swedish assumptions about international law effectiveness whilst demonstrating limitations of neutrality in deterring norm violations. Russian actions in Ukraine directly challenged post-Cold War settlement that had enabled Swedish neutrality through assumption of stable regional order.

Swedish commitment to international law, human rights, and peaceful conflict resolution created normative incentives for supporting Ukraine against Russian aggression. Maintaining neutrality whilst witnessing systematic violations of international law created cognitive dissonance that undermined policy sustainability.

NATO's role in defending democratic values and international law provided normative justification for membership that aligned with Swedish identity whilst offering mechanism for effective action. This normative alignment proved crucial for domestic acceptance of membership despite traditional neutrality commitments.

Economic Integration (Dimension 4): Swedish economic integration with EU and NATO countries created asymmetric vulnerabilities that neutrality could not address whilst demonstrating economic benefits from security cooperation. Trade relationships, investment flows, and technological dependencies created interests in maintaining stable relationships with Western partners.

Russian economic coercion against other European states demonstrated potential vulnerabilities from energy dependence and trade relationships that neutrality could not prevent. Swedish observation of Russian actions against other states provided lessons about economic vulnerability under neutrality arrangements.

Economic benefits from defence cooperation with NATO allies provided additional incentives for membership through access to collaborative development programmes, technology sharing, and cost reduction through standardisation and interoperability.

Regional Autonomy (Dimension 5): Nordic cooperation created pressures for alignment through Finnish NATO membership and Norwegian concerns about regional security arrangements. Finland's decision to join NATO following Russian invasion of Ukraine created strategic isolation for Sweden whilst demonstrating regional consensus about threat assessment.

Baltic state vulnerability highlighted Nordic responsibility for regional security that neutrality complicated whilst NATO membership could address effectively. Swedish military capabilities provided significant contributions to regional defence that neutrality prevented from full utilisation whilst membership could enhance through alliance integration.

Transformation Process and Outcomes

The transformation process demonstrates how systemic changes across multiple dimensions can accumulate to overcome domestic resistance whilst creating momentum for rapid policy change. Public opinion shifted dramatically following Russian invasion of Ukraine, with support for NATO membership increasing from approximately 35% in early 2022 to over 60% by May 2022 when application was submitted (Kaynak, 2023).

However, the transformation process also revealed constraints on autonomous action through Turkish objections to Swedish membership that delayed accession for nearly two years. Turkey's demands regarding Kurdish organisations, arms embargoes, and diplomatic recognition demonstrated how middle power strategies can constrain even major power policies whilst illustrating complexity of contemporary alliance relationships (Alterman & McElwee, 2024).

The eventual resolution through diplomatic negotiations, policy adjustments, and trilateral cooperation with Finland demonstrated adaptive capacity whilst highlighting interdependence between alliance relationships and broader geopolitical considerations. Swedish concessions on Turkish concerns while maintaining core policy principles illustrated compromise possibilities within alliance frameworks.

MDOT Framework Insights

Sweden's transformation illustrates several key insights about contemporary order change. First, deeply embedded national role conceptions can change rapidly when systemic pressures reach critical thresholds across multiple dimensions simultaneously. Swedish neutrality survived two world wars and the Cold War but could not withstand combined pressures from material power shifts, institutional changes, normative challenges, economic vulnerabilities, and regional transformation.

Second, transformation involves interaction effects between dimensions that create reinforcing dynamics leading to rapid change. Material power shifts in the region (Russian aggression) combined with institutional developments (NATO adaptation), normative challenges (international law violations), economic vulnerabilities (sanctions and coercion), and regional transformation (Finnish membership) to create irresistible pressure for policy change.

Third, middle power strategies can significantly influence great power policies whilst illustrating complexity of alliance relationships under multipolarity. Turkish capacity to delay Swedish membership despite broad alliance support demonstrates how contemporary transformation creates opportunities for autonomous action even within established institutional frameworks.

Case Study 2: Australia - Middle Power Strategic Alignment

Historical Context and Strategic Evolution

Australia's foreign policy evolution illustrates how middle powers navigate contemporary transformation through strategic alignment with major powers whilst pursuing autonomous capabilities and regional influence. As a medium-sized power with significant capabilities but global dependencies, Australia exemplifies middle power strategies under changing international conditions.

Australia's strategic culture historically combined alliance relationships with major powers (Britain, then United States) whilst developing autonomous capabilities for regional influence and defence. The ANZUS alliance with United States became central to Australian security policy following World War II, providing security guarantee whilst enabling regional leadership in Southeast Asia and Pacific regions.

However, contemporary transformation dynamics have created pressures for strategic adaptation that move beyond traditional middle power approaches. Australia's recent policies demonstrate shift from "strategic ambiguity" to "strategic alignment" with United States whilst developing enhanced autonomous capabilities for regional deterrence (Abbondanza, 2022).

Dimension-by-Dimension Analysis

Material Power Distribution (Dimension 1): China's rise as regional power presents direct challenge to Australian security interests whilst creating economic opportunities that complicate strategic relationships. Chinese military modernisation and regional assertiveness threaten Australian assumptions about regional stability whilst demonstrating limitations of traditional deterrence approaches.

Australia's response involves substantial defence investment aimed at developing autonomous deterrence capabilities whilst strengthening alliance relationships with United States. The 2024 National Defence Strategy prioritises "deterrence by denial" through maintaining ability to hold adversary forces at risk during sustained operations whilst achieving situational awareness across relevant operational areas.

AUKUS partnership with United States and United Kingdom represents major enhancement of Australian capabilities through nuclear submarine acquisition, advanced technology sharing, and enhanced interoperability. This partnership enables Australia to contribute significantly to regional deterrence whilst maintaining dependence on allied technology and support systems.

Defence spending increases from 1.9% of GDP in 2020 to projected 2.4% by 2034 demonstrate commitment to capability development whilst illustrating resource constraints on autonomous action. Australia's defence budget of approximately AUD 50 billion annually provides significant regional capabilities whilst remaining limited compared to major power spending levels.

Institutional Architecture (Dimension 2): Australia has strengthened institutional relationships with United States and regional partners whilst engaging selectively with alternative arrangements. Quad partnership with United States, Japan, and India provides framework for regional cooperation on security, technology, and economic issues whilst avoiding formal alliance commitments.

AUKUS represents unprecedented level of institutional integration with United States and United Kingdom through technology sharing arrangements that extend beyond traditional alliance relationships. This partnership creates new institutional framework for advanced capability development whilst maintaining Australian sovereignty over key decisions.

Regional institutional engagement demonstrates Australian commitment to maintaining influence through multiple frameworks including East Asia Summit, ASEAN Regional Forum, and Pacific Island Forum. Australia's approach emphasises maintaining relationships across different institutional arrangements whilst prioritising those aligned with strategic interests.

Normative Contestation (Dimension 3): Australia advocates for "rules-based international order" whilst adapting to challenges from alternative governance models. Australian officials emphasise international law, democratic values, and peaceful dispute resolution whilst developing capabilities for deterrence and defence against norm violations.

China's challenges to regional norms through South China Sea claims, economic coercion against trading partners, and authoritarian governance model create normative tensions that Australia addresses through alliance cooperation and institutional engagement. Australian responses emphasise rules-based approaches whilst building capabilities for alternative scenarios.

Australian advocacy for democratic values and human rights provides normative foundation for alliance relationships whilst creating tensions with economic interests in Chinese markets. This normative positioning enables coalition building with democratic partners whilst potentially constraining economic relationships.

Economic Integration (Dimension 4): Australia maintains substantial economic relationships with China whilst developing supply chain diversification and economic security measures. Chinese trade represents approximately 30% of Australian exports, creating significant economic interdependence despite strategic competition concerns.

Australian approaches to economic security emphasise diversification rather than decoupling, developing alternative markets whilst maintaining profitable Chinese relationships where possible. Critical minerals development, renewable energy cooperation, and technology partnerships provide alternative economic foundations whilst reducing dependence on single markets.

Defence industry development represents major economic security initiative aimed at reducing import dependence whilst creating export opportunities. Australian defence exports increased from AUD 1.5 billion in 2015 to over AUD 4 billion in 2023, demonstrating growing autonomous capabilities whilst remaining constrained by technological dependencies.

Regional Autonomy (Dimension 5): Australia pursues enhanced regional influence through Pacific leadership, Southeast Asian engagement, and Indian Ocean cooperation whilst maintaining alliance relationships with United States. Pacific Step-up initiative demonstrates Australian commitment to regional leadership through increased aid, diplomatic engagement, and security cooperation.

Regional autonomy involves balancing alliance commitments with autonomous regional interests that may diverge from American priorities. Australian Pacific policies emphasise development assistance, climate change response, and governance support whilst avoiding great power competition frameworks that could alienate regional partners.

Australian approaches to Southeast Asian engagement demonstrate sophisticated middle power diplomacy that maintains relationships across different political systems whilst advancing shared interests in regional stability and economic development.

ASEAN engagement provides alternative frameworks for regional cooperation that supplement alliance relationships.

Strategic Implications and Adaptations

Australia's strategic evolution demonstrates how middle powers can enhance their capabilities and influence whilst remaining embedded within alliance frameworks. The shift from strategic ambiguity to strategic alignment enables Australia to contribute significantly to regional deterrence whilst maintaining decision-making autonomy on issues not affecting core security interests.

However, Australian approaches also reveal constraints on middle power autonomy under contemporary conditions. Alliance relationships provide essential capabilities and security guarantees that Australia cannot achieve independently, whilst creating dependencies that constrain policy options on issues affecting alliance relationships.

Regional leadership aspirations must balance great power interests with local partner preferences, creating complex diplomatic challenges that require sophisticated policy coordination. Australian success in Pacific engagement demonstrates middle power capacity for regional influence whilst highlighting limitations when regional interests conflict with alliance priorities.

MDOT Framework Insights

Australia's case illustrates several important insights about middle power strategies under contemporary transformation. First, middle powers can enhance their capabilities and influence through strategic alignment whilst maintaining significant autonomy on issues not affecting core alliance interests. Australian approaches demonstrate sophisticated balancing between alliance commitment and regional leadership that enables multiple objectives simultaneously.

Second, middle power strategies require substantial resource commitments to maintain credibility whilst remaining constrained by structural limitations. Australian defence spending increases and capability development demonstrate commitment to autonomous deterrence whilst acknowledging continued dependence on alliance relationships for advanced capabilities.

Third, economic interdependence creates complex trade-offs between security and prosperity that require careful management to avoid forced choices between competing interests. Australian economic relationships with China whilst maintaining strategic alignment with United States demonstrate sophisticated approaches to managing conflicting pressures.

Case Study 3: Turkey - Strategic Autonomy and Alliance Constraints

Historical Context and Policy Evolution

Turkey's foreign policy evolution over the past two decades illustrates complex dynamics of strategic autonomy pursuit within alliance frameworks whilst navigating competing domestic and international pressures. As NATO's second-largest military and geopolitically significant bridge between Europe, Asia, and Middle East, Turkey represents unique case of middle power attempting to carve autonomous space amid great power competition.

Turkish foreign policy under the Justice and Development Party (AKP) since 2002 demonstrates dramatic transformation from "logic of interdependence" in the first decade to "quest for strategic autonomy" in the second decade, accompanied by interventionism, unilateralism, and coercive diplomacy (Kutlay & Öniş, 2021). This evolution reflects both systemic changes and domestic political imperatives that interact to shape policy outcomes.

The concept of strategic autonomy in Turkish foreign policy involves both structural orientation toward non-Western powers to balance US-led hierarchical order and domestic political motives to organize regime support through external accomplishments and identity appeals (Aran et al., 2025). This dual character creates tensions between geopolitical imperatives and domestic priorities that often contradict effective autonomy implementation.

Dimension-by-Dimension Analysis

Material Power Distribution (Dimension 1): Turkey's strategic autonomy reflects adaptation to changing regional power balance whilst attempting to enhance its relative position through diversified partnerships and military capability development. Turkish military capabilities including indigenous defence industry, regional intervention capacity, and geopolitical position provide leverage for autonomous policies.

Turkish defence industry development represents major component of autonomy strategy, with domestic production increasing significantly whilst arms imports declining by 59% between 2011-2015 and 2016-2020 periods. Indigenous systems including Bayraktar drones, MILGEM corvettes, and Altay tanks demonstrate technological progress whilst reducing Western dependence.

However, Turkish economic limitations constrain material power capabilities compared to major regional actors. Turkish GDP of approximately $820 billion ranks sixteenth globally, providing middle power resources whilst remaining far below major power levels. Economic vulnerabilities including currency instability and energy dependence limit autonomy options whilst creating pressure for external support.

Regional military interventions in Syria, Libya, and elsewhere demonstrate Turkish capacity for power projection whilst revealing limitations in sustained operations against major adversaries. Turkish military effectiveness in specific contexts provides regional influence whilst acknowledging structural constraints on autonomous action against superior forces.

Institutional Architecture (Dimension 2): Turkey maintains NATO membership whilst developing alternative institutional relationships that provide additional policy options and leverage within alliance frameworks. This institutional diversification enables Turkey to pursue policies that might otherwise face alliance constraints whilst maintaining security guarantees.

Turkish participation in Shanghai Cooperation Organisation, observer status in BRICS discussions, and membership in various regional organisations provide institutional alternatives whilst maintaining Western alliance relationships. This institutional hedging creates policy flexibility whilst generating tensions with alliance partners concerned about Turkish reliability.

NATO membership provides essential security guarantees whilst constraining Turkish policies that conflict with alliance preferences. Turkish acquisition of Russian S-400 air defence systems despite NATO objections illustrates both autonomy capacity and alliance tensions that such policies create. Resolution of these tensions requires complex negotiations that balance autonomy objectives with alliance commitments.

Regional institutional leadership through Organisation of Islamic Cooperation, Turkic Council, and various Middle Eastern frameworks provides platforms for Turkish influence whilst demonstrating capacity for autonomous initiative. These institutions enable Turkish policy coordination with diverse partners whilst maintaining flexibility for independent action.

Normative Contestation (Dimension 3): Turkish foreign policy combines Islamic identity appeals with sovereignty principles and traditional values to challenge Western liberal norms whilst maintaining commitment to international cooperation. This normative positioning provides domestic legitimacy whilst creating tensions with Western allies concerned about democratic backsliding.

Turkish officials argue for "Turkish model" that combines Islamic values with democratic governance and economic development, offering alternative to both Western liberal democracy and authoritarian alternatives. This model provides normative foundation for regional leadership whilst creating tensions with EU partners emphasising liberal democratic standards.

Ottoman historical references and neo-Ottoman discourse provide narrative framework for regional influence whilst challenging Western-imposed boundaries and arrangements. These historical appeals resonate with domestic audiences whilst potentially alienating regional partners concerned about Turkish intentions.

Syrian refugee policy demonstrates Turkish humanitarian leadership whilst creating leverage for European cooperation and Middle Eastern influence. Turkish hosting of over 3.5 million Syrian refugees provides moral authority whilst generating domestic political costs that require external support and recognition.

Economic Integration (Dimension 4): Turkish economic relationships demonstrate complex balancing between Western integration and diversification toward non-Western partners. EU economic integration remains substantial through customs union and trade relationships whilst Turkish economic partnerships with China, Russia, and regional powers have expanded significantly.

Turkish trade with EU countries represents approximately 40% of total trade, maintaining substantial economic integration despite political tensions over democratic governance and foreign policy differences. This economic relationship provides mutual benefits whilst creating constraints on policies that could trigger economic retaliation.

Economic partnerships with Russia include energy cooperation, tourism, and trade relationships that provide alternatives to Western dependence whilst creating new vulnerabilities to sanctions and political pressure. Turkish balancing between Western sanctions on Russia and economic interests demonstrates complex calculations required for autonomy policies.

Chinese economic engagement through Belt and Road Initiative, investment projects, and technology cooperation provides additional diversification whilst raising concerns about strategic dependence and technology transfer. Turkish approaches emphasise maintaining beneficial relationships whilst avoiding excessive dependence on any single partner.

Regional Autonomy (Dimension 5): Turkey pursues regional leadership through military interventions, diplomatic initiatives, and economic partnerships that demonstrate autonomous capacity whilst creating tensions with alliance partners and regional competitors. Turkish regional policies illustrate both opportunities and constraints for middle power autonomy under contemporary conditions.

Syrian intervention demonstrates Turkish capacity for autonomous regional action whilst revealing limitations when facing superior forces or international opposition. Turkish support for Syrian opposition and subsequent accommodation with Russian and Iranian preferences illustrates adaptation requirements under structural constraints.

Libyan intervention provides additional example of Turkish regional reach whilst generating tensions with European partners concerned about migration and stability implications. Turkish military support for Government of National Accord demonstrated projection capabilities whilst requiring careful coordination to avoid escalation with other regional actors.

Eastern Mediterranean policies including drilling activities and maritime claims illustrate Turkish assertions of sovereign rights whilst creating tensions with EU partners and regional competitors. These policies demonstrate autonomy capacity whilst generating costs through diplomatic isolation and economic sanctions threats.

Challenges and Contradictions

Turkish strategic autonomy faces significant challenges that illustrate broader constraints on middle power policies under contemporary conditions. Geopolitical imperatives and domestic priorities often contradict each other, preventing effective implementation of autonomy-seeking policies whilst generating tensions with both alliance partners and regional competitors.

Economic constraints limit Turkish capacity for sustained autonomous policies whilst creating pressure for external support that may compromise autonomy objectives. Currency crises, inflation pressures, and development financing requirements create dependencies that constrain foreign policy options whilst providing leverage for external actors.

Democratic governance concerns create tensions with EU partners whilst potentially limiting Turkish capacity for regional leadership and alliance cooperation. Democratic backsliding allegations undermine Turkish soft power whilst creating obstacles for EU integration and NATO cooperation that Turkish autonomy strategies seek to overcome.

Regional competitor responses to Turkish policies create security dilemmas that may require alliance support whilst potentially undermining autonomy objectives. Greek, Egyptian, and other regional responses to Turkish policies create complex challenges that autonomous policies alone cannot address effectively.

MDOT Framework Insights

Turkey's case provides several important insights about strategic autonomy pursuit under contemporary transformation conditions. First, middle powers can pursue significant autonomous policies within alliance frameworks whilst remaining constrained by structural limitations and partner reactions. Turkish capacity for autonomous action demonstrates middle power agency whilst revealing costs and limitations of such strategies.

Second, domestic political imperatives and geopolitical requirements often contradict each other, creating policy tensions that may undermine autonomy effectiveness whilst generating costs for alliance relationships. Turkish experiences illustrate complexity of managing multiple objectives simultaneously whilst maintaining coherent strategic direction.

Third, economic constraints significantly limit autonomy capacity whilst creating dependencies that may compromise autonomous policies when external pressure increases. Turkish economic vulnerabilities demonstrate importance of resource base for autonomous action whilst illustrating constraints on middle power strategies.

Fourth, regional autonomy efforts may generate competitive responses that require alliance support whilst potentially undermining autonomy objectives. Turkish regional policies illustrate both opportunities for autonomous action and constraints when such policies generate opposition from superior forces or alliance partners.

Comparative Analysis and Broader Implications

Cross-Case Patterns and Variations

The three case studies reveal important patterns about state responses to contemporary transformation whilst demonstrating variation in strategies and outcomes that illuminate different pathways for adaptation under changing international conditions. These cases represent different approaches to strategic autonomy and alliance relationships that provide insights about middle power strategies under multipolarity.

Sweden's transformation demonstrates how deeply embedded national role conceptions can change rapidly when systemic pressures reach critical thresholds across multiple dimensions simultaneously. The abandonment of neutrality after over two centuries illustrates threshold effects where accumulated pressures overcome domestic resistance whilst creating momentum for fundamental policy change.

Australia's strategic alignment illustrates sophisticated middle power diplomacy that enhances capabilities and influence through alliance relationships whilst maintaining autonomy on issues not affecting core security interests. Australian approaches demonstrate capacity for multiple objective achievement whilst acknowledging structural constraints on autonomous action.

Turkey's strategic autonomy pursuit reveals both opportunities and constraints for middle power policies within alliance frameworks whilst highlighting tensions between domestic imperatives and geopolitical requirements. Turkish experiences illustrate complexity of managing multiple relationships simultaneously whilst maintaining policy coherence.

Strategic Autonomy Under Multipolarity

All three cases demonstrate growing emphasis on strategic autonomy as states adapt to changing international conditions whilst maintaining different approaches to balance relationships and capability development. Strategic autonomy represents common response to multipolarity whilst taking different forms depending on state capabilities, geographical position, and domestic constraints.

Sweden's NATO membership paradoxically represents autonomy enhancement through alliance integration that provides security guarantees whilst enabling independent decision-making on non-security issues. This approach demonstrates how alliance relationships can enhance rather than constrain autonomy under specific conditions.

Australia's strategic alignment enables enhanced regional influence whilst maintaining alliance security guarantees that provide foundation for autonomous regional policies. Australian approaches illustrate sophisticated balancing between alliance commitment and regional leadership that enables multiple objectives simultaneously.

Turkey's autonomy pursuit within NATO frameworks demonstrates both opportunities and limitations for independent action whilst maintaining alliance membership for security guarantees. Turkish experiences reveal tensions between autonomy objectives and alliance commitments that require careful management to avoid forced choices.

Alliance Relationships and Transformation

Contemporary transformation creates new dynamics in alliance relationships that differ from Cold War patterns whilst enabling greater flexibility for autonomous action within cooperative frameworks. Alliance relationships increasingly involve diverse partnerships rather than hierarchical arrangements whilst accommodating different approaches to regional and global challenges.

NATO's accommodation of diverse member approaches to China, Russia, and regional issues demonstrates alliance adaptability whilst maintaining core security functions. Swedish and Turkish experiences within NATO illustrate range of approaches that alliance frameworks can accommodate whilst maintaining collective defence commitments.

AUKUS partnership represents new form of alliance relationship that combines capability sharing with maintained sovereignty whilst enabling enhanced deterrence and technological cooperation. This institutional innovation demonstrates alliance evolution toward more flexible arrangements that accommodate different strategic requirements.

Quad partnership provides framework for cooperation without formal alliance commitments whilst enabling coordination on regional challenges and shared interests. This institutional flexibility demonstrates alternative approaches to cooperation that supplement traditional alliance arrangements whilst maintaining strategic autonomy.

Economic Security and Strategic Competition

All three cases demonstrate growing attention to economic security considerations that balance prosperity objectives with security requirements whilst managing relationships with competing powers. Economic security represents crucial dimension of strategic autonomy whilst creating complex trade-offs between different objectives.

Swedish approaches to economic security emphasise European integration whilst developing resilience against economic coercion and supply chain vulnerabilities. Swedish participation in EU economic security initiatives demonstrates collective approaches to economic challenges whilst maintaining national decision-making autonomy.

Australian economic security strategies emphasise diversification whilst maintaining beneficial relationships with major trading partners including China. Australian approaches demonstrate sophisticated management of competing economic and security pressures whilst maintaining prosperity and security simultaneously.

Turkish economic diversification illustrates both opportunities and constraints for economic autonomy whilst revealing tensions between different partnership requirements and domestic economic pressures. Turkish experiences demonstrate complexity of economic security management under resource constraints and external pressures.

Regional Leadership and Global Engagement

Middle power strategies increasingly emphasise regional leadership as pathway for global influence whilst maintaining relationships with major powers that provide capabilities and access beyond regional scope. Regional leadership provides foundation for autonomous action whilst remaining constrained by global power structures.

Swedish regional leadership in Nordic cooperation and Arctic development provides foundation for global influence whilst remaining embedded within broader European and transatlantic frameworks. Swedish approaches demonstrate capacity for regional initiative whilst maintaining global partnerships.

Australian Pacific leadership illustrates sophisticated middle power diplomacy that addresses regional development challenges whilst maintaining strategic relationships with major powers. Australian success in Pacific engagement demonstrates middle power capacity for regional influence whilst acknowledging limitations when regional interests conflict with global pressures.

Turkish regional leadership aspirations reveal both opportunities and constraints for autonomous action whilst generating competitive responses that may require external support. Turkish experiences illustrate complexity of regional leadership under competitive conditions whilst maintaining relationships with competing major powers.

Broader Implications for International Relations Theory

The MDOT Framework's application to contemporary global politics and empirical validation through case studies provides several important contributions to international relations theory that extend beyond existing approaches whilst offering new analytical tools for understanding complex system change.

Theoretical Advances Beyond Existing Approaches

The framework's recognition of asynchronous transformation challenges linear progression assumptions in power transition theory whilst providing more sophisticated analysis of change dynamics. Rather than inevitable conflict between rising and declining powers, multi-dimensional transformation creates opportunities for accommodation and adaptation that existing theories struggle to explain.

Traditional power transition theory focuses primarily on bilateral relationships between rising and declining hegemons whilst overlooking complex multilateral dynamics involving middle powers, regional organisations, and alternative institutions. The MDOT Framework addresses these limitations through comprehensive analysis of transformation across multiple dimensions whilst recognising interactive effects between different aspects of system change.

The framework's threshold-based analysis provides specific, measurable criteria for distinguishing between different levels of transformation whilst enabling real-time assessment of change patterns. Traditional approaches often rely on subjective assessments or post-hoc analysis rather than systematic indicators, limiting their utility for policy applications and comparative analysis.

Dynamic interaction modelling explains why transformation patterns vary across historical cases and contexts whilst providing theoretical tools for understanding variation in system change patterns. Traditional approaches assume uniform change whilst contemporary transformation involves complex patterns that require more sophisticated analytical frameworks.

Methodological Innovations and Contributions

The framework provides systematic indicators for measuring transformation across dimensions whilst enabling cross-dimensional comparison through standardised threshold criteria. This methodological innovation addresses widespread analytical problems in determining when change becomes transformation whilst providing tools for comparative analysis across different cases and time periods.

The multi-dimensional approach enables more accurate assessment of systemic outcomes whilst identifying potential tipping points before they manifest across all dimensions. Unlike approaches that rely on single indicators or assume uniform change, the MDOT Framework captures complexity whilst maintaining analytical precision for policy applications.

Cross-dimensional comparison through standardised threshold criteria enables systematic analysis of transformation patterns across different historical periods and geographical contexts whilst facilitating theory testing and refinement through comparative analysis. This methodological contribution provides foundation for future research applications and theoretical development.

Policy Implications and Applications

The framework's insights about asynchronous transformation and dynamic interactions provide policy guidance for managing system change whilst suggesting strategies for different types of actors under varying conditions. Understanding that transformation occurs across multiple dimensions simultaneously suggests policy approaches must address multiple aspects of international relations rather than focusing solely on material power balances.

Compensatory dynamics suggest opportunities for maintaining stability through strengthening dimensions experiencing less transformation whilst managing tensions generated by rapid change in other areas. Economic interdependence and institutional cooperation can moderate competition in material power and normative dimensions whilst providing buffers against complete system breakdown.

Regional autonomy patterns suggest middle powers play crucial roles in system transformation whilst providing opportunities for influence beyond traditional great power management. Regional solutions to global challenges might provide alternatives to direct great power confrontation whilst enabling creative approaches to complex problems.

The framework's application to contemporary global politics suggests that managing transformation requires sophisticated approaches that acknowledge complexity whilst pursuing realistic objectives within structural constraints. Successful management depends on understanding multi-dimensional character of change whilst developing strategies that account for varying transformation speeds across different aspects of international relations.

Future Research Directions and Applications

The MDOT Framework provides foundation for extensive future research applications that could advance understanding of international system change whilst addressing limitations and expanding analytical scope. Several research priorities emerge from the framework's development and initial application.

Historical case studies applying the framework to previous order transitions would enable theory testing and refinement whilst providing baseline comparisons for contemporary analysis. Systematic application to cases including the Concert of Europe, interwar period, and early Cold War would illuminate transformation patterns under different conditions whilst validating framework utility.

Comparative analysis across different regional systems could reveal variation in transformation patterns and threshold dynamics whilst providing insights about how global transformation manifests differently across geographical contexts. Regional applications might generate insights about sub-global transformation processes whilst contributing to broader theoretical development.

Longitudinal studies tracking transformation patterns over extended periods would enhance understanding of dynamic interactions whilst enabling validation of threshold criteria and interaction modelling. Panel studies of multiple cases experiencing different transformation patterns would facilitate comparative theory development whilst testing framework predictions.

Quantitative analysis of transformation indicators could enhance framework precision whilst providing statistical validation of threshold criteria and interaction effects. Development of composite indices for transformation assessment could enable large-scale comparative analysis whilst maintaining analytical sophistication.

Integration with other theoretical approaches could enhance framework comprehensiveness whilst addressing limitations in current scope. Incorporation of domestic politics variables, transnational networks, and non-state actor roles could expand analytical capacity whilst maintaining focus on systemic transformation dynamics.

LIMITATIONS AND METHODOLOGICAL CONSIDERATIONS

Framework Limitations and Constraints

The MDOT Framework faces several limitations that require acknowledgment whilst suggesting directions for future theoretical development and empirical research. Recognition of these limitations is essential for appropriate application whilst avoiding overextension of framework claims and maintaining analytical humility about complex phenomena.

The framework requires extensive data collection across five dimensions, creating measurement challenges for historical cases where comprehensive data may be unavailable whilst generating resource requirements that may limit application scope. Historical analysis faces particular challenges given data limitations for earlier periods whilst contemporary analysis must balance comprehensiveness with resource constraints.

Threshold determination, whilst based on systematic criteria, retains subjective elements requiring refinement through additional case studies and comparative analysis. Different analysts might reach different conclusions about threshold achievement whilst cultural and theoretical biases could influence assessments of transformation levels.

The framework's complexity may limit predictive precision compared to simpler models focusing on single variables whilst generating more variables and potential outcomes that reduce forecast accuracy for specific events. Complexity provides analytical richness whilst potentially compromising parsimony and predictive clarity.

Dynamic interaction modelling, whilst theoretically sophisticated, requires further development to specify conditions under which different types of interactions occur whilst current understanding of when reinforcing, compensatory, or contradictory dynamics emerge remains incomplete.

Measurement and Validation Challenges

Measuring transformation across multiple dimensions presents significant methodological challenges that require sophisticated approaches whilst acknowledging inherent limitations in quantifying complex political phenomena. Different dimensions involve different types of indicators whilst requiring different measurement approaches that complicate systematic comparison.

Material power measurement faces long-standing challenges in international relations regarding appropriate indicators and weighting schemes whilst contemporary analysis must address technological change, cyber capabilities, and economic complexity that traditional measures inadequately capture.

Institutional effectiveness measurement requires assessment of both formal characteristics and practical outcomes whilst accounting for different institutional purposes and membership characteristics that complicate cross-institutional comparison. Legitimacy assessment presents particular challenges given subjective elements and cultural variation in institutional evaluation.

Normative change measurement involves identifying shifts in abstract concepts whilst distinguishing between rhetorical change and behavioural modification that reflects genuine normative evolution. Survey data, voting patterns, and policy convergence provide indicators whilst requiring interpretation that acknowledges cultural and political differences.

Economic integration measurement must account for complex interdependence patterns whilst distinguishing between policy-driven and market-driven changes that may have different implications for transformation analysis. Supply chain complexity and financial integration present particular measurement challenges.

Regional autonomy measurement requires assessment of both capacity and willingness for independent action whilst accounting for structural constraints and situational variation that affect autonomy expression. Comparative measurement across different regions presents additional challenges given varying institutional arrangements and power distributions.

Validity and Reliability Considerations

Establishing framework validity requires demonstration that MDOT dimensions actually capture essential aspects of international order transformation whilst providing accurate assessment of change patterns. Construct validity involves ensuring that dimension definitions correspond to theoretical concepts whilst content validity requires comprehensive coverage of transformation aspects.

External validity requires demonstration that framework insights apply beyond specific cases whilst enabling generalisation to other contexts and time periods. The current application focuses primarily on contemporary Western and major power cases whilst requiring expansion to diverse contexts for broader validation.

Reliability requires consistent application across different analysts and contexts whilst ensuring that framework application produces similar results when applied to same cases by different researchers. Intercoder reliability testing and systematic application procedures could enhance framework reliability whilst reducing subjective bias.

Temporal validity requires demonstration that framework remains applicable over time whilst accounting for changing international conditions that might affect dimension relevance or interaction patterns. Framework validation requires testing across different historical periods whilst acknowledging potential need for adaptation.

Scope and Boundary Conditions

The framework focuses primarily on state-centric analysis whilst potentially underestimating non-state actor roles and transnational processes that increasingly shape international relations. Non-state actors including multinational corporations, international organisations, and civil society groups may influence transformation in ways that state-focused analysis inadequately captures.

The framework emphasises systemic transformation whilst potentially underestimating regional variation and sub-global transformation processes that may not conform to global patterns. Regional transformation may occur according to different logics whilst requiring different analytical approaches than global system change.

Cultural and ideational factors receive attention through normative dimension whilst potentially requiring more sophisticated treatment that accounts for civilisational differences and alternative worldviews that challenge Western-centric theoretical assumptions.

The framework addresses contemporary transformation whilst requiring historical validation that demonstrates applicability to different eras and conditions. Framework utility for historical analysis remains untested whilst historical differences may require significant adaptation for earlier periods.

CONCLUSION

The Multi-Dimensional Order Transformation Framework provides a sophisticated analytical tool for understanding global order transition that transcends existing approaches to international system change whilst addressing fundamental limitations in current theoretical frameworks. Through disaggregating systemic transformation into five distinct but interconnected dimensions, establishing clear threshold indicators, and modelling dynamic interactions, the framework enables more precise analysis of when, how, and why international orders transform.

The framework's application to contemporary global politics reveals complex transformation patterns that defy simple polarity models whilst providing systematic analysis of change dynamics across multiple dimensions. Rather than experiencing uniform change toward multipolarity or bipolar competition, the international system undergoes differentiated transformation characterised by institutional layering, normative fragmentation, economic diversification, and regional autonomy expansion.

This analysis demonstrates that the international system currently experiences partial system change approaching system-wide transformation thresholds, with secondary transformation in three dimensions (material power, institutions, norms) combined with tertiary transformation in two dimensions (economics, regional autonomy). This pattern suggests substantial systemic change underway without complete order breakdown whilst indicating potential trajectories for future development.

Theoretical Contributions and Innovations

The MDOT Framework makes several significant contributions to international relations theory that advance understanding beyond existing approaches whilst providing new analytical tools for scholars and practitioners. The framework's recognition of asynchronous transformation provides crucial insight that different aspects of international order can transform at different speeds and directions simultaneously, explaining why some periods of apparent change produce system stability whilst others generate rapid transformation.

This insight challenges linear progression assumptions in power transition theory whilst providing more sophisticated analysis of change dynamics that accounts for complex patterns of continuity and change. Traditional approaches assume inevitable conflict between rising and declining powers, but multi-dimensional transformation creates opportunities for accommodation and adaptation that existing theories struggle to explain.

The framework's threshold-based analysis provides specific, measurable criteria for distinguishing between different levels of transformation whilst enabling real-time assessment of change patterns. This methodological innovation addresses widespread analytical problems in determining when change becomes transformation whilst providing tools for comparative analysis across different cases and time periods.

Dynamic interaction modelling explains why transformation patterns vary across historical cases and contexts whilst providing theoretical tools for understanding variation in system change patterns. The framework's identification of reinforcing, compensatory, and contradictory dynamics between dimensions offers new insights about how complex systems evolve whilst enabling more sophisticated forecasting approaches.

Empirical Insights and Policy Implications

The framework's application generates several important empirical insights about contemporary international relations that inform both scholarly understanding and policy development. Contemporary order transformation represents neither Western decline nor Eastern rise, but rather systemic adaptation to changing power distributions, technological capabilities, and governance demands that creates new configurations requiring adaptive strategies.

The analysis reveals that managing transformation requires understanding its multi-dimensional character whilst developing strategies that account for varying transformation speeds across different aspects of international relations. Successful adaptation involves sophisticated approaches that acknowledge complexity whilst pursuing realistic objectives within structural constraints.

Case study analysis demonstrates that states pursue various strategies for managing transformation depending on their capabilities, geographical position, and domestic constraints. Sweden's NATO membership, Australia's strategic alignment, and Turkey's autonomy pursuit illustrate different approaches to adaptation whilst revealing common patterns in state responses to systemic change.

These insights suggest policy implications for different types of actors under contemporary conditions. Great powers must acknowledge limits of unilateral action whilst developing cooperative approaches that accommodate other actors' interests and capabilities. Middle powers can enhance influence through strategic positioning whilst remaining constrained by structural limitations that require careful management.

Regional organisations and international institutions face pressures for adaptation whilst maintaining core functions that provide stability and cooperation opportunities. Institutional innovation and reform become essential for maintaining relevance whilst addressing new challenges and accommodating changing power distributions.

Future Research Directions

The MDOT Framework provides foundation for extensive future research that could advance understanding of international system change whilst addressing current limitations and expanding analytical scope. Several research priorities emerge from the framework's development and initial application.

Historical validation through systematic application to previous order transitions would enhance theoretical credibility whilst providing baseline comparisons for contemporary analysis. Cases including the Concert of Europe, interwar system, and early Cold War would illuminate transformation patterns under different conditions whilst testing framework applicability across various contexts.

Comparative regional analysis could reveal variation in transformation patterns whilst providing insights about how global transformation manifests differently across geographical contexts. Regional applications might generate insights about sub-global transformation processes whilst contributing to broader theoretical development.

Quantitative analysis of transformation indicators could enhance framework precision whilst providing statistical validation of threshold criteria and interaction effects. Development of composite indices for transformation assessment could enable large-scale comparative analysis whilst maintaining analytical sophistication.

Integration with other theoretical approaches could enhance framework comprehensiveness whilst addressing limitations in current scope. Incorporation of domestic politics variables, transnational networks, and non-state actor roles could expand analytical capacity whilst maintaining focus on systemic transformation dynamics.

Final Assessment and Implications

The Multi-Dimensional Order Transformation Framework represents a significant advance in international relations theory that addresses fundamental gaps in understanding complex system change whilst providing practical tools for analysis and policy development. The framework's innovations—asynchronous transformation theory, threshold-based analysis, and dynamic interaction modelling—offer new analytical capabilities whilst maintaining empirical grounding and policy relevance.

Contemporary international order transformation involves complex patterns that transcend traditional analytical frameworks whilst requiring sophisticated approaches that acknowledge multidimensional change dynamics. The MDOT Framework provides conceptual tools for understanding these patterns whilst suggesting strategies for managing transformation that account for varying speeds and directions of change across different dimensions.

As the international system continues evolving toward greater complexity, frameworks capable of capturing multi-dimensional transformation dynamics become increasingly essential for theoretical understanding and policy analysis. The MDOT Framework represents important progress in this direction whilst providing foundation for continued theoretical development and empirical research.

The framework demonstrates that international order transformation is neither inevitable nor uniform, but rather a complex process involving multiple dimensions changing at different rates and in different directions. Understanding this complexity is essential for developing effective strategies for managing system change whilst maintaining international stability during periods of transformation.

Future scholarship applying and refining the MDOT Framework will enhance understanding of international order transformation whilst contributing to broader theoretical development in international relations. The framework's emphasis on multi-dimensional analysis and dynamic interactions provides foundation for continued innovation in addressing the challenges of understanding complex system change in contemporary international relations.

The analysis suggests that the current period represents a crucial juncture in international relations where policy choices made by major powers, middle powers, and international institutions will significantly influence transformation trajectories. Understanding transformation dynamics through sophisticated analytical frameworks becomes essential for developing policies that promote stability whilst accommodating necessary change in response to evolving global conditions.

Figure 8. Current International System Status Dashboard (2024-2025)

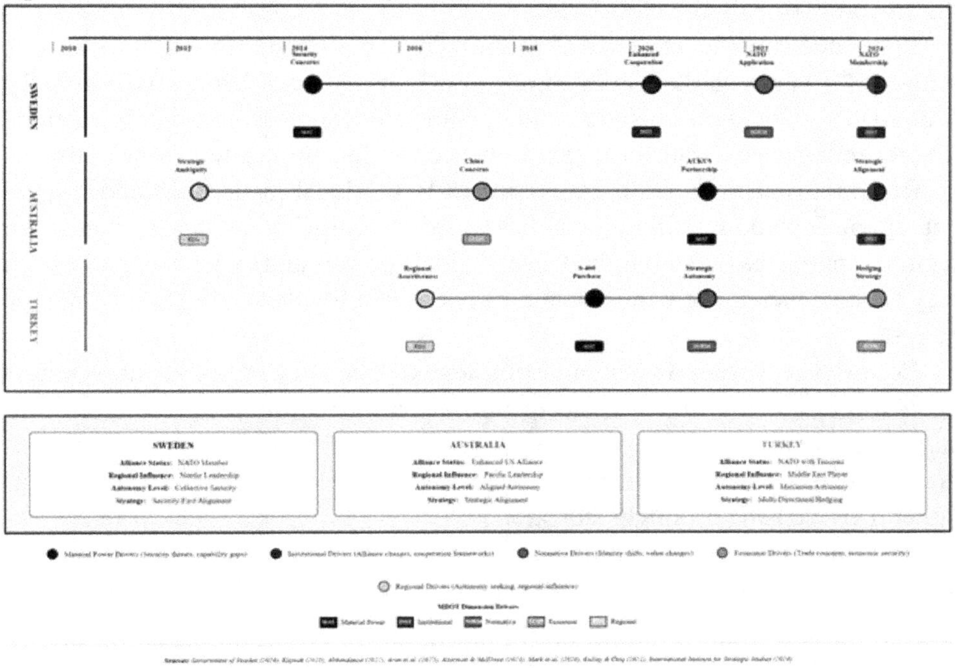

The Dashboard in figure 8 Reveals a Critical Juncture: The international system stands at 75% progress toward system-wide transformation—close enough to fundamental change that small shifts could trigger cascading effects, yet stable enough that current policies still matter enormously for shaping outcomes.

Policy Urgency: With three dimensions already experiencing secondary transformation, policymakers face a narrow window for proactive adaptation. Waiting for "clearer signals" risks being overtaken by events, while premature responses to uncertain trends could prove counterproductive. The rising trend arrows across four of five dimensions suggest momentum is building.

Strategic Choices Matter More, Not Less: Paradoxically, approaching transformation thresholds makes individual state choices more consequential. Sweden's rapid shift from neutrality to NATO membership demonstrates how quickly established policies can change when systemic pressures reach critical mass. Similarly, middle powers like Australia and Turkey show how strategic positioning during transformation can enhance or constrain future options.

No Return to Previous Order: The absence of any primary transformations suggests we're not witnessing complete system breakdown, but the presence of three secondary transformations indicates the post-Cold War unipolar moment is definitively ending. The question is not whether change will occur, but what form the emerging order will take.

Economic Interdependence as Stabilizer: The economic dimension's tertiary status (40%) represents the system's strongest stabilizing force. Maintaining substantial China-US trade relationships and avoiding complete economic blocs may be essential for preventing partial transformation from accelerating into system-wide upheaval.

Regional Solutions Gain Importance: With global institutions under stress but regional autonomy still limited (35%), there's significant untapped potential for regional approaches to global challenges. Middle powers and regional organizations may become increasingly important for system stability during the transformation period.

Confidence Intervals Signal Complexity: The varying uncertainty ranges (±5% to ±12%) reflect that transformation is neither uniform nor predictable. This complexity demands adaptive strategies rather than rigid doctrines, and suggests that successful navigation requires understanding multi-dimensional interactions rather than focusing on single indicators.

Bottom Line: The international system is undergoing substantial but manageable change. Current transformation levels create both risks and opportunities that require sophisticated responses acknowledging complexity while maintaining strategic coherence. The next 3-5 years will likely determine whether partial system change stabilizes at current levels or accelerates toward complete transformation.

REFERENCES

Abbondanza, G. (2022). Australia's Indo-Pacific strategy: From strategic ambiguity to strategic clarity? *Australian Journal of International Affairs*, *76*(4), 402–420.

Acharya, A. (2017). After liberal hegemony: The advent of a multiplex world order. *Ethics & International Affairs*, *31*(3), 271–285. DOI: 10.1017/S089267941700020X

Acharya, A. (2024). The multiplex world order and global governance. *Global Studies Quarterly*, *4*(2), ksae021. Advance online publication. DOI: 10.1093/isagsq/ksae021

AIIB. (2024). *Annual report 2023: Growing impact.* Asian Infrastructure Investment Bank.

Aiyar, S., Chen, J., Ebeke, C. H., Garcia-Saltos, R., Gudmundsson, T., Ilyina, A., Kangur, A., Kunaratskul, T., Rodriguez, S. L., Ruta, M., Schulze, T., Soderberg, G., & Trevino, J. P. (2023). *Geoeconomic fragmentation and the future of multilateralism (IMF Staff Discussion Note SDN/2023/001).* International Monetary Fund.

Allison, G. (2017). *Destined for war: Can America and China escape Thucydides's trap?* Houghton Mifflin.

Alterman, J. B., & McElwee, L. (2024). Pursuing global order in the twenty-first century. Center for Strategic and International Studies. https://features.csis.org/pursuing-global-order/

Anwar, D. F. (2020). Indonesia and the ASEAN outlook on the Indo-Pacific. *International Affairs*, *96*(1), 111–129. DOI: 10.1093/ia/iiz223

Aran, A., Kutlay, M., & Yilmaz, S. (2025). Strategic autonomy in Turkish foreign policy in an age of multipolarity: Lineages and contradictions of an idea. *International Politics*, *62*(1), 142–168. DOI: 10.1057/s41311-024-00638-w

Asmus, R. D. (2002). *Opening NATO's door: How the alliance remade itself for a new era*. Columbia University Press.

Batrawy, A. (2023, March 10). Rivals Saudi Arabia and Iran restore ties, with China's help. *NPR*.

Bush, G. H. W. (1991). Toward a new world order. *Vital Speeches of the Day*, *57*(24), 730–733.

Byman, D., & Pollack, K. (2001). Let us now praise great men: Bringing the statesman back in. *International Security*, *25*(4), 107–146. DOI: 10.1162/01622880151091916

Chen, D. (2016). Institutional balancing and the AIIB. *International Affairs, 92*(5), 1161–1178.

Chen, D., Zhang, W., & Li, Y. (2024). Reconceptualizing international order: Contemporary Chinese theories and their contributions to global IR. *International Organization, 78*(3), 543–578. DOI: 10.1017/S0020818324000158

Clinton, W. J. (2000). *Speech on China trade bill, March 8, 2000*. Presidential Speeches Archive.

Cooley, A., & Nexon, D. H. (2020). *Exit from hegemony: The unraveling of the American global order*. Oxford University Press. DOI: 10.1093/oso/9780190916473.001.0001

Council on Foreign Relations. (2025). What is the BRICS group and why is it expanding? https://www.cfr.org/backgrounder/what-brics-group-and-why-it-expanding

Cox, R. W. (1983). Gramsci, hegemony and international relations: An essay in method. *Millennium, 12*(2), 162–175. DOI: 10.1177/03058298830120020701

Davies, T. (2024). World order transformation from the grassroots: Global South social movements and the transcendence of established approaches to international change. *International Political Sociology, 18*(1), olad023. Advance online publication. DOI: 10.1093/ips/olad023

de France, B. (2024). Expansion of BRICS: What are the potential consequences for the global economy? *Bulletin*, (250), 2.

Dossani, R., Cooper III, C. A., & Chang, J. (2024). *Middle-power equities in a cross-strait conflict*. RAND Corporation, RR-A3108-1.

Economy, E. (2018). *The third revolution: Xi Jinping and the new Chinese state*. Oxford University Press.

Finnemore, M., & Sikkink, K. (1998). International norm dynamics and political change. *International Organization, 52*(4), 887–917. DOI: 10.1162/002081898550789

Fofack, H. (2023, August 23). Piece by piece, the BRICS really are building a multipolar world. *Atlantic Council - New Atlanticist*. https://www.atlanticcouncil.org/blogs/new-atlanticist/piece-by-piece-the-brics-really-are-building-a-multipolar-world/

Fukuyama, F. (1992). *The end of history and the last man*. Free Press.

Gill, S. (1993). *Gramsci, historical materialism and international relations*. Cambridge University Press. DOI: 10.1017/CBO9780511558993

Gill, S., & Law, D. (1989). Global hegemony and the structural power of capital. *International Studies Quarterly, 33*(4), 475–499. DOI: 10.2307/2600523

Gilpin, R. (2001). *Global political economy: Understanding the international economic order*. Princeton University Press. DOI: 10.1515/9781400831272

Government of Sweden. (2024, April 16). Why Sweden joined NATO - a paradigm shift in Sweden's foreign and security policy. Speech by Minister for Foreign Affairs Tobias Billström at Selwyn College, Cambridge. https://www.government.se/speeches/2024/04/why-sweden-joined-nato---a-paradigm-shift-in-swedens-foreign-and-security-policy/

Haass, R. (2008). The age of nonpolarity. *Foreign Affairs, 87*(3), 44–56.

Hirsh, M. (2025, February 19). The new meaning of "Munich". *Foreign Policy*.

Howorth, J. (2019). *Strategic autonomy: Why it's not about Europe going it alone*. Wilfried Martens Centre for European Studies.

Huntington, S. P. (1991). *The third wave: Democratization in the late 20th century*. University of Oklahoma Press.

Huntington, S. P. (1999). The lonely superpower. *Foreign Affairs, 78*(2), 35–49. DOI: 10.2307/20049207

Huntington, S. P. (2003). America in the world. *The Hedgehog Review, 5*(1), 7–18.

Ikenberry, G. J. (2001). *After victory: Institutions, strategic restraint, and the rebuilding of order after major wars*. Princeton University Press. DOI: 10.1515/9781400823963

Ikenberry, G. J. (2011). *Liberal Leviathan: The origins, crisis, and transformation of the American world order*. Princeton University Press. DOI: 10.2307/j.ctt7rjt2

Ikenberry, G. J. (2018). The end of liberal international order? *International Affairs, 94*(1), 7–23. DOI: 10.1093/ia/iix241

IMF. (2023). *World economic outlook database*. International Monetary Fund. https://www.imf.org/en/Publications/WEO/weo-database/2023/October

IMF. (2024). *Currency composition of official foreign exchange reserves*. International Monetary Fund.

International Institute for Strategic Studies. (2024). Mexico's foreign policy under new leadership. *Strategic Comments, 30*(10), i–iv. DOI: 10.1080/13567888.2024.2438556

Kaynak, A. B. (2023). How neutrality lost its appeal as a political strategy: Sweden and Finland's accession to NATO. *Journal of Applied And Theoretical Social Sciences, 5*(3), 236–250. DOI: 10.37241/jatss.2023.91

Keohane, R. (1984). *After hegemony: Cooperation and discord in the world political economy*. Princeton University Press.

Keohane, R., & Nye, J. (2012). *Power and interdependence* (4th ed.). Longman.

Kindleberger, C. (1973). *The world in depression, 1929-1939*. University of California Press.

Krauthammer, C. (1990/1991). The unipolar moment. *Foreign Affairs, 70*(1), 23–33. DOI: 10.2307/20044692

Kutlay, M., & Öniş, Z. (2021). Turkish foreign policy in a post-western order: Strategic autonomy or new forms of dependence? *International Affairs, 97*(4), 1085–1104. DOI: 10.1093/ia/iiab094

Layne, C. (2012). This time it's real: The end of unipolarity and the Pax Americana. *International Studies Quarterly, 56*(1), 203–213. DOI: 10.1111/j.1468-2478.2011.00704.x

Lemke, D. (1997). The continuation of history: Power transition theory and the end of the Cold War. *Journal of Peace Research, 34*(1), 23–36. DOI: 10.1177/0022343397034001003

Luo, Y. (2024). Paradigm shift and theoretical implications for the era of global disorder. *Journal of International Business Studies, 55*(2), 127–135. DOI: 10.1057/s41267-023-00659-2

Mark, M., Colley, T., & Hagström, L. (2024). Small states and the dilemma of geopolitics: Role change in Finland and Sweden. *International Affairs, 100*(1), 139–159. DOI: 10.1093/ia/iiad244

Mearsheimer, J. J. (2001). *The tragedy of great power politics*. W. W. Norton.

Merkel, A. (2017, May 28). Beer tent campaign speech in Trudering, Germany (post-G7 statement on Europe's fate in its own hands). *Süddeutsche Zeitung* (transcript).

Ministry of Foreign Affairs of PRC. (2014). Xi Jinping attends the Fourth Summit of the Conference on Interaction and Confidence Building Measures in Asia. Press Release.

Natasha. (2025). Sweden and Finland from neutrality to NATO: The strategic transformation of European security. *International Journal of Politics & Social Sciences Review*, 4(1), 282-292.

NDB. (2024). *Annual report 2023*. New Development Bank.

Nye, J. (1990). *Bound to lead: The changing nature of American power*. Basic Books.

Organski, A. F. K. (1958). *World politics*. Alfred A. Knopf.

Organski, A. F. K., & Kugler, J. (1980). *The war ledger*. University of Chicago Press. DOI: 10.7208/chicago/9780226351841.001.0001

Panda, J. (2023, January). India in a world of asymmetrical multipolarity. In *East Asia Forum Quarterly* (Vol. 15, No. 1, pp. 18-22). ANU Press.

Park, S., & Gunaydin, E. (2024). Australia as an ecocidal middle power. *Australian Journal of International Affairs*, *78*(4), 1–25. DOI: 10.1080/10357718.2024.2363386

Parrat, C. F. (2024). Change in international order? An institutional analysis. *European Journal of International Security*, *9*(3), 415–435. DOI: 10.1017/eis.2024.12

Paul, T. V. (2005). Soft balancing in the age of U.S. primacy. *International Security*, *30*(1), 46–71. DOI: 10.1162/0162288054894652

Powell, C. (1992). US forces: Challenges ahead. *Foreign Affairs*, *71*(5), 32–45. DOI: 10.2307/20045401

Putin, V. (2005, April 25). Annual address to the Federal Assembly of the Russian Federation [Transcript]. Kremlin.

Reus-Smit, C. (2013). *Individual rights and the making of the international system*. Cambridge University Press. DOI: 10.1017/CBO9781139046527

Rid, T. (2020). *Active measures: The secret history of disinformation and political warfare*. Farrar, Straus and Giroux.

Röhren, P. (2024). Unipolarity is not over yet. *Global Studies Quarterly*, *4*(2), ksae018. Advance online publication. DOI: 10.1093/isagsq/ksae018

Rutland, P. (2021). Energy and Russian Great Power Post-Crimea. In Buchanan, E. (Ed.), *Russian Energy Strategy in the Asia-Pacific: Implications for Australia* (pp. 85–104). ANU Press. DOI: 10.2307/j.ctv1prsr27.10

SIPRI. (2024). *Military expenditure database*. Stockholm International Peace Research Institute.

Stiglitz, J., & Bilmes, L. (2008). *The three trillion dollar war: The true cost of the Iraq conflict*. W.W. Norton.

Stuenkel, O. (2015). *The BRICS and the future of global order*. Lexington Books.

Tammen, R. L., Kugler, J., Lemke, D., Stam, A. C.III, Abdollahian, M. A., Alsharabati, C., Efird, B., & Organski, A. F. K. (2000). *Power transitions: Strategies for the 21st century*. Chatham House Publishers.

Trenin, D. (2011). *Post-imperium: A Eurasian story*. Carnegie Endowment for International Peace. DOI: 10.2307/j.ctt6wpjpz

Turner, M. (2024, December 25). The Global South and the Russia-Ukraine War: Nonalignment and Western responses on the cusp of a multipolar world. *Security in Context*. Retrieved April 5, 2025, from https://www.securityincontext.org/posts/the-global-south-and-the-russia-ukraine-war-nonalignment-and-western-responses-on-cusp-of-multipolar-world

U.S. Department of Defense. (2018). Summary of the 2018 national defense strategy of the United States of America. DoD.

US Trade Representative. (2024). *U.S.-China trade facts*. Office of the United States Trade Representative.

US Treasury. (2024). *Major foreign holders of Treasury securities*. U.S. Department of the Treasury.

Verma, R., & Brosig, M. (2024). The Russia-Ukraine war, the evolving global order, the Global South and emergence of non-alignment 2.0. *Global Policy*, *15*(4), 794–801. DOI: 10.1111/1758-5899.13410

Verma, R., & Düben, B. A. (2023). Russia's invasion of Ukraine: Cementing US global preeminence. *Journal of Indo-Pacific Affairs*, *6*(3), 74–91.

Vinjamuri, L. (Ed.). Aydın-Düzgit, S., Bajpaee, C., Cooley, A., de Hoop Scheffer, A., Emmers, R., Fravel, M. T., Lind, J., Nasr, V., Quencez, M., Stelzenmüller, C., Stuenkel, O. D. C., Vakil, S., & Zarakol, A. (2025). *Competing visions of international order: Responses to US power in a fracturing world*. Chatham House, The Royal Institute of International Affairs.

Walt, S. (2005). Taming American power: The global response to U.S. primacy. *Foreign Affairs*, *84*(5), 105–120. DOI: 10.2307/20031709

Waltz, K. (1959). *Man, the state and war*. Columbia University Press.

Waltz, K. (1979). *Theory of international politics*. Addison-Wesley.

Waltz, K. (2000). Structural realism after the Cold War. *International Security*, *25*(1), 5–41. DOI: 10.1162/016228800560372

Western, J. (2002). Sources of humanitarian intervention: Beliefs, information, and advocacy in U.S. decisions on Somalia and Bosnia. *International Security*, *26*(4), 112–142. DOI: 10.1162/016228802753696799

White House. (2017). National Security Strategy of the United States of America (December 2017). Washington, DC.

Wohlforth, W. C. (1999). The stability of a unipolar world. *International Security*, *24*(1), 5–41. DOI: 10.1162/016228899560031

World Bank. (2024). *World development indicators*. World Bank Group.

Yu, H. (2017). Motivation behind China's "One Belt, One Road" initiatives and establishment of the Asian Infrastructure Investment Bank. *Journal of Contemporary China*, *26*(105), 353–368. DOI: 10.1080/10670564.2016.1245894

Zala, B. (2017). Polarity analysis and collective perceptions of power: The need for a new approach. *Journal of Global Security Studies*, *2*(1), 2–17. DOI: 10.1093/jogss/ogw025

Zhou, J. (2019). Power transition and paradigm shift in diplomacy: Why China and the US march towards strategic competition? *The Chinese Journal of International Politics*, *12*(1), 1–34. DOI: 10.1093/cjip/poy019

Zoellick, R. B. (2005). Whither China: From membership to responsibility? Remarks to National Committee on U.S.-China Relations. U.S. Department of State Archive.

ADDITIONAL READINGS

Acharya, A., Estevadeordal, A., & Goodman, L. W. (2023). Multipolar or multiplex? Interaction capacity, global cooperation and world order. *International Affairs*, *99*(6), 2339–2365. DOI: 10.1093/ia/iiad242

Aiyar, S., Presbitero, A. F., & Ruta, M. (Eds.). (2023). *Geoeconomic fragmentation: The economic risks from a fractured world economy*. CEPR Press.

Bargués, P., Joseph, J., & Juncos, A. E. (2023). Rescuing the liberal international order: Crisis, resilience and EU security policy. *International Affairs*, *99*(6), 2281–2299. DOI: 10.1093/ia/iiad222

Clayton, C., Maggiori, M., & Schreger, J. (2025). Geoeconomics. *Annual Review of Economics, 17*.

Goddard, S. E., Krebs, R. R., Kreuder-Sonnen, C., & Rittberger, B. (2024). Contestation in a world of liberal orders. *Global Studies Quarterly, 4*(2), ksae026.

Juncos, A. E., & Vanhoonacker, S. (2024). The ideational power of strategic autonomy in EU security and external economic policies. *Journal of Common Market Studies*, *62*(4), 973–992. DOI: 10.1111/jcms.13597

Umar, A. R. M. (2023). The rise of the Asian middle powers: Indonesia's conceptions of international order. *International Affairs*, *99*(4), 1459–1476. DOI: 10.1093/ia/iiad167

Vinodan, C., & Kurian, A. L. (2024). Strategic autonomy and India's hedging policies in the Indo-Pacific. *International Politics*. Advance online publication.

Wijaya, T., & Jayasuriya, K. (2024). A new multipolar order: Combined development, state forms and new business classes. *International Affairs*, *100*(5), 2133–2152. DOI: 10.1093/ia/iiae135

KEY TERMS AND DEFINITIONS

Asynchronous Transformation: The process whereby different dimensions of international order experience varying rates and directions of change simultaneously, rather than uniform transformation across all aspects of the international system.

BRICS: Economic and political cooperation organisation comprising Brazil, Russia, India, China, and South Africa, expanded in 2024 to include Egypt, Ethiopia, Iran, and the United Arab Emirates, representing an alternative institutional arrangement to Western-dominated frameworks.

Compensatory Dynamics: Interactive relationships between dimensions of international order where stability in one dimension compensates for transformation in others, providing system stability that prevents complete breakdown whilst enabling partial change.

Contradictory Dynamics: Dynamic interactions where changes in different dimensions pull in opposite directions, creating system tension and unpredictable outcomes that complicate policy planning and strategic forecasting.

Economic Integration and Fragmentation: The fourth dimension of the MDOT Framework examining tensions between continued economic interdependence and growing geoeconomic fragmentation, reflecting coexistence of geopolitical tensions and economic relationships.

Friend-shoring: The practice of relocating supply chains and production to politically aligned countries to reduce dependence on geopolitical rivals whilst maintaining economic efficiency and security considerations.

Geoeconomic Fragmentation: Policy-driven reversal of global economic integration guided by strategic considerations including national security, economic security, and enhanced autonomy through reduced reliance on other countries.

Hegemonic Powers: Dominant states in the international system that possess sufficient material capabilities and influence to shape international order according to their preferences and maintain system stability.

Institutional Architecture and Legitimacy: The second dimension of the MDOT Framework encompassing changes in formal international institutions, their effectiveness, perceived legitimacy amongst member states, and emergence of alternative institutional arrangements.

International Order: The governing arrangements amongst a group of states, including fundamental rules, principles, and institutions that structure international relations and allocate rights whilst limiting the exercise of power.

Liberal International Order (LIO): A set of global, rule-based, structured relationships based on political liberalism, economic liberalism, and liberal internationalism, characterised by multilateral institutions, human rights, open markets, and democratic governance.

Material Power Distribution: The first dimension of the MDOT Framework encompassing traditional realist concerns with relative capabilities amongst major powers, including economic, military, demographic, and technological capabilities.

Middle Powers: States with significant capabilities and regional influence but lacking the comprehensive power to unilaterally shape global order, often pursuing strategic autonomy and regional leadership whilst maintaining relationships with great powers.

Multi-Dimensional Order Transformation (MDOT) Framework: A novel analytical approach that disaggregates international order transformation into five distinct but interconnected dimensions, establishing measurable threshold indicators and modelling dynamic interactions between dimensions.

Multipolarity: An international system characterised by the existence of multiple major powers with relatively similar economic, military, and political capabilities, contrasting with unipolar or bipolar configurations.

Near-shoring: The practice of relocating production and supply chains to geographically proximate countries to reduce transportation costs and security risks whilst maintaining operational efficiency.

Normative and Ideational Contestation: The third dimension of the MDOT Framework capturing struggles over fundamental principles governing international relations, including sovereignty interpretations, intervention norms, human rights standards, and governance frameworks.

Partial System Change: A level of international order transformation characterised by primary transformation in 1-2 dimensions or secondary transformation in 2-3 dimensions, representing substantial change without complete system breakdown.

Polarity Analysis: An analytical approach focusing on the distribution of capabilities amongst major powers and its implications for system stability and conflict patterns, distinguishing between unipolar, bipolar, and multipolar systems.

Power Transition Theory: A theoretical approach suggesting that systemic war becomes most likely when rising challengers approach parity with declining hegemons, particularly when challengers are dissatisfied with existing arrangements.

Primary Transformation: The highest level of change within each MDOT dimension, representing fundamental alteration of basic structures and arrangements within that dimension of international order.

Regional Autonomy and Governance: The fifth dimension of the MDOT Framework assessing the capacity and willingness of regional powers to manage local affairs independently of global powers, reflecting emergence of influential middle powers pursuing strategic autonomy.

Reinforcing Dynamics: Interactive relationships between dimensions where changes in one dimension accelerate transformation in others, creating momentum that can trigger rapid systemic change across multiple areas simultaneously.

Rules-based International Order: An international system organised around agreed-upon legal and political institutions that operate to allocate rights and limit the exercise of power through established rules and procedures.

Secondary Transformation: A moderate level of change within each MDOT dimension representing significant alteration of existing arrangements without fundamental structural change, meeting criteria for substantial institutional or normative modification.

Strategic Autonomy: The capacity and policy approach of states to maintain decision-making independence whilst pursuing diverse partnerships and avoiding exclusive dependence on any single power or bloc in international relations.

System-wide Transformation: The highest level of international order change occurring when primary transformation manifests in three or more dimensions or secondary transformation occurs in four or more dimensions simultaneously.

Tertiary Transformation: The lowest level of change within each MDOT dimension representing incremental modification through adaptation and evolution without significant structural alteration of existing arrangements.

Transformation Thresholds: Specific, measurable criteria for distinguishing between different levels of transformation within each dimension and across the international system, enabling systematic analysis of when change constitutes fundamental system alteration.

Unipolarity: An international system configuration characterised by a single dominant power possessing overwhelming material capabilities and global influence, as experienced during the American unipolar moment following the Cold War.x

Chapter 7
Navigating Change:
Understanding the Dynamics of Global Power Transitions

Andi Asrifan
https://orcid.org/0000-0002-9934-6129
Universitas Negeri Makassar, Indonesia

Rismawati Rismawati
https://orcid.org/0000-0001-8046-6764
Universitas Muhammadiyah Palopo, Indonesia

ABSTRACT

This chapter analyzes the shift in the global order from U.S.-led unipolar dominance to a progressively intricate multipolar framework. This analysis utilizes historical examination, theoretical models, and case studies to investigate how emerging powers, regional alliances, and the Global South are transforming power dynamics via strategic adaptation, geoeconomic tools, and normative challenges. Special emphasis is placed on the constraints of U.S. global supremacy in the 21st century, the emergence of digital sovereignty, and the reconfiguration of international institutions. The chapter delineates prospective scenarios for global governance and provides pragmatic policy proposals to foster cooperative multipolarity. It concludes that while multipolarity creates new obstacles, it also offers opportunity to cultivate a more pluralistic, sustainable, and egalitarian global order through inclusive diplomacy and adaptable governance initiatives.

DOI: 10.4018/979-8-3373-2342-8.ch007

1. INTRODUCTION

1.1 Conceptual Foundations of Global Power Transitions

Power is a fundamental and contentious notion in the field of international affairs. It fundamentally determines state conduct, organizes the international system, and affects the results of global disputes, cooperation, and order. Power in international relations fundamentally denotes an actor's—usually a state's—capacity to affect the actions of others to attain preferred results (Kuik, 2021; Rachmad, 2025). This influence can emerge in various forms: coercion (hard power), persuasion (soft power), or the structural structuring of the rules (structural power).

Historically, international relations theory has prioritized hard power, including military weapons and economic resources, as key markers of global influence. The realist school perceives international politics as a zero-sum competition for survival, wherein power serves as the currency of international relations (Gajdzik et al., 2024; Nye, 2023). This limited perspective has been contested by researchers such as Joseph Nye (2004), who proposed the notion of soft power, emphasizing the significance of attraction, values, culture, and legitimacy. In the contemporary globalized and interdependent landscape, the exertion of power increasingly depends on narrative construction, institutional leadership, and digital influence, in addition to command and coercion (Codagnone & Weigl, 2023; Weibel et al., 2025).

Furthermore, structural power, as articulated by Susan Strange (1996), provides a more sophisticated comprehension of how states and non-state entities influence global economic and political frameworks—rules, norms, and institutions that regulate international behavior. This type of power is particularly pertinent in examining the construction and contestation of global governance across various domains, including trade, finance, climate, and technology (Alami et al., 2023; Friel et al., 2021).

In the transition from a unipolar to a multipolar world, comprehending the multifaceted nature of power is essential. Global influence can no longer be monopolized by a singular hegemon; instead, new powers are establishing their influence through regional leadership, alternative development paradigms, and technological ecosystems. Consequently, examining power changes necessitates an extensive framework that integrates various modalities of power and acknowledges the increasingly intricate structure of global authority. This fundamental comprehension establishes the groundwork for a more profound exploration of power transition theories and their empirical representations in the next chapters of this book.

1.2 Theoretical Approaches to Power Shifts

Comprehending global power transitions necessitates interaction with essential theoretical frameworks in international relations (IR) that elucidate the mechanisms and reasons behind power transfers in various historical and geopolitical situations. The most notable ideas include realism, liberal institutionalism, and critical theories, each providing unique insights into the mechanisms of global hegemony, conflict, and institutional transformation (Morales Ruvalcaba, 2024).

Power Transition Theory, grounded on realism, posits that global conflict is most probable when an ascending power jeopardizes the supremacy of the prevailing hegemon (Knudsen, 2022). This paradigm perceives international order as hierarchical and intrinsically unstable during transitional phases. The erosion of U.S. unipolarity and the ascendance of China exemplify this trend of possible instability. Realist scholars Baciu and Knudsen (2022) assert that great nations are fated to compete, resulting in power shifts that frequently culminate in antagonism or conflict.

Liberal institutionalism asserts that the international system is not entirely anarchic but can achieve stability through norms, laws, and institutions. Power transfers, from this perspective, do not inherently lead to conflict if institutions can adjust and integrate emergent powers. The G20, WTO, and the Paris Agreement exemplify platforms where multipolar collaboration can mitigate systemic tensions (Gatto, 2022; Dupont et al., 2024). Franke & Kurthen (2023) assert that cooperation is attainable within complex interdependence, particularly when institutions facilitate interests and ensure transparency.

Critical theories, such as post-colonialism and world-systems theory, focus on structural inequities and historical legacies that influence global power dynamics (Parashar & Schulz, 2021). Edwards Jr et al. (2022) highlight, through world-systems analysis, the enduring core-periphery dynamics that perpetuate global hierarchies, irrespective of the hegemonic state's identity. Post-colonial researchers attack Western-centric power paradigms and call for epistemic pluralism, emphasizing the agency of the Global South in constructing new power narratives.

Recently, academics have included constructivist methodologies that highlight the influence of ideas, identities, and speech in establishing power relations. The perception of legitimacy is as vital as material competence in ascertaining global leadership. Every theoretical perspective provides distinct insights into the mechanisms, effects, and pathways of power transitions. A comprehensive understanding must thus integrate various frameworks to encapsulate the multifaceted and multicausal characteristics of modern global power changes.

1.3 Unipolarity, Bipolarity, and Multipolarity: A Comparative Overview

The international system is conventionally classified into three main configurations: unipolarity, bipolarity, and multipolarity. These classifications delineate the allocation of power among principal actors and significantly impact global stability, alliance formation, and conflict dynamics. Comprehending their unique attributes is crucial for understanding the nature and consequences of power transitions (Ateed and Özcan, 2025).

Unipolarity denotes a system characterized by the predominance of a singular superpower that wields unparalleled military, economic, and ideological authority. The post-Cold War period, especially from 1991 to the early 2000s, is predominantly regarded as a unipolar moment dominated by the United States (Rapanyane, 2021; Leoni, 2021). In such a system, the hegemon frequently formulates and upholds global norms, sustains institutional leadership, and prevents significant conflicts. Nonetheless, unipolarity is not intrinsically stable; detractors contend that it provokes balancing actions, results in overextension, and may diminish legitimacy over time.

Bipolarity refers to a power structure in which two predominant states or blocs vie for global dominance. The Cold War period (1947–1991) between the United States and the Soviet Union exemplify this framework. Realist theory posits that bipolarity provides relative stability by distinct authority delineation and mutual deterrence (Ali2022). Nonetheless, it also involves fierce ideological competition, proxy wars, and restricted opportunities for non-aligned entities. Strategic equilibrium is sustained through balance; nonetheless, the chances of crisis amplification remain significant (Geronik, 2024).

Multipolarity refers to a power allocation among three or more principal governments or alliances. The 19th-century European state system and the interwar period were characterized by a multipolar structure. In these systems, alliances are dynamic, power is more dispersed, and forecasting state behavior more intricate. Although multipolarity might enhance diplomatic flexibility and promote inclusive multilateralism, it may also lead to miscalculations and instability resulting from the lack of a definitive hierarchical structure (Peters, 2023).

The modern world is arguably shifting towards asymmetric multipolarity, in which emerging countries such as China and India acquire regional and global influence, although no single entity exerts supremacy across all spheres. This emerging order questions conventional notions and necessitates novel frameworks for overseeing competition and collaboration. A comparative review of polarity kinds demonstrates that each presents distinct opportunities and risks. Policymakers and scholars must comprehend these contrasts to maneuver through the intricacies of evolving global power dynamics.

2. THE DECLINE OF UNIPOLAR HEGEMONY: U.S. GLOBAL DOMINANCE IN FLUX

2.1 The Rise of American Unipolarity Post-Cold War

The conclusion of the Cold War in 1991 signified a pivotal historical moment that initiated an era of unipolarity, characterized by the unparalleled global supremacy of the United States. Following the demise of the Soviet Union, the bipolar structure of the international system transitioned to a unipolar configuration, with the U.S. emerging as the singular superpower possessing unparalleled military, economic, technological, and cultural impact. Scholars like Siegelbaum (2024) characterized this as the "unipolar moment," a period during which American dominance influenced global norms, dictated security frameworks, and shaped international institutions.

The United States exhibited predominant military strength, constituting over 40% of worldwide defense spending during the 1990s and 2000s. Its force projection capabilities, supported by worldwide base networks and superior technologies, guaranteed unimpeded strategic reach. Liberal democracy and free-market capitalism, advocated by the United States, achieved global prominence, culminating in Fukuyama's (1992) renowned assertion of "the end of history" (Tian et al., 2023).

American-led globalization intensified, characterized by trade liberalization, capital mobility, and the preeminence of institutions like the International Monetary Fund (IMF), World Bank, and World Trade Organization (WTO). U.S.-based multinational firms, the ascendance of the U.S. dollar as the global reserve currency, and the dissemination of neoliberal economic principles bolstered this hegemonic status (Goldstein & Gulotty, 2021).

The dissemination of American media, education, and technology—via entities such as Hollywood, CNN, Microsoft, and subsequently Silicon Valley companies—enhanced the United States' soft power, as articulated by Nye (2024). The liberal international order, primarily influenced by American interests, established a rules-based framework designed to safeguard U.S. strategic and economic objectives under the pretense of multilateralism and global governance (El Damanhoury & Garud-Paktar, 2022).

This unipolar structure, however, encompassed intrinsic inconsistencies. The exertion of U.S. power was frequently associated with notions of unilateralism, moral exceptionalism, and aggressive diplomacy. Subsequent chapters will examine how these inconsistencies, along with developing global developments, will eventually undermine U.S. hegemony, indicating a complicated transition to multipolarity. Comprehending the establishment and role of American unipolarity is essential for evaluating its present fall and the dynamics of the changing international order.

2.2 Challenges to U.S. Hegemony in the 21st Century

The post-Cold War era was characterized by American unipolarity; however, the 21st century has seen increasing challenges that threaten the sustainability of U.S. hegemony in various domains. The difficulties are both external, resulting from the strategic aggressiveness of emerging powers, and internal, deriving from political, economic, and social fragmentation inside the United States (Saleh and Yazdanshenas, 2023; Leoni, 2021).

The primary external challenge arises from China's emergence as a systemic competitor. China's swift economic expansion, technical progress, and military enhancement have elevated it from a regional participant to a worldwide authority. China extends its influence across Eurasia, Africa, and Latin America through initiatives such as the Belt and Road Initiative (BRI), providing alternative development and governance models (Peters, 2023; Wang & Yi, 2021). Moreover, Russia's strategic rebirth, especially its aggressive stance in Eastern Europe and the Middle East, challenges U.S. dominance, indicating a revival of great-power rivalry.

The supremacy of the U.S. is being eroded by growing demands for reform in global governance structures. The legitimacy of the post-World War II liberal international order is being challenged, particularly by Global South nations advocating for more fair representation in institutions such as the UN Security Council, IMF, and World Bank (Alami and Taggart, 2024; Lall, 2025). The creation of rival institutions, exemplified as the BRICS New Development Bank, signifies this discontent and signals a transition towards a more pluralistic society.

The United States is experiencing increasing political polarization, deterioration of democratic institutions, and a reduction in worldwide moral authority. Incidents like the 2008 financial crisis, extended military engagements in the Middle East, and domestic turmoil related to racial and electoral matters have diminished worldwide views of U.S. leadership. Moreover, economic disparity, deindustrialization, and the decline of the middle class undermine the viability of its economic framework and soft power attractiveness (Kerr et al., 2021; Lee, 2022).

U.S. technological supremacy is no longer unchallenged. Although American corporations formerly led the digital economy, China has established formidable rivals in artificial intelligence, 5G technology, and digital banking. The technological divergence between the U.S. and China exemplifies a transition towards rival digital domains of power (Segal, 2020). Collectively, these difficulties indicate the progressive decline of unipolarity and the rise of a more contested and divided international order. Comprehending these pressures is crucial for understanding the wider transition towards multipolarity.

2.3. Case Studies: Afghanistan, Ukraine, and the Limits of U.S. Power

The strategic failures encountered by the United States in Afghanistan and Ukraine exemplify the practical constraints of U.S. global dominance in the 21st century. Despite differing geopolitical dynamics, both situations underscore the decline of American credibility, strategic efficacy, and capacity to enforce desired outcomes in intricate regional wars (Grinin & Korotayev, 2021; Iksan & Soong, 2023).

The U.S. operation in Afghanistan (2001–2021)—originally characterized as a counterterrorism initiative—transformed into an extended state-building endeavor focused on establishing democratic government and liberal institutional structures. Despite two decades of military engagement and substantial financial investment, the rapid disintegration of the U.S.-supported Afghan government in August 2021 and the resurgence of Taliban authority highlighted the constraints of coercive power and liberal interventionism. This incident undermined the impression of U.S. reliability among allies and strengthened adversaries by revealing Washington's strategic exhaustion and diminishing resolve to maintain prolonged global commitments (Sharma, 2024; Gopal, 2021).

The United States has been pivotal in assisting Ukraine in its resistance against Russia's takeover of Crimea in 2014 and the comprehensive invasion initiated in 2022. Although American military and financial aid has been essential in strengthening Ukrainian resistance, Washington's failure to avert Russia's assault, despite earlier warnings and deterrent language, has exposed the limitations of deterrence in a multipolar context. Furthermore, the crisis has challenged NATO's unity, revealed Europe's energy dependency, and expedited dialogues regarding strategic autonomy inside the European Union (Szpak et al., 2023; Harris, 2024; Charap & Shapiro, 2021).

Afghanistan and Ukraine exemplify the shift from direct control to indirect influence, indicating that unipolar domination techniques are increasingly insufficient for addressing regional complexities influenced by asymmetric warfare, crises of local legitimacy, and interventions by competing powers. This also indicates a wider trend in which the assertiveness of great powers, particularly Russia and China, is altering regional dynamics, frequently in opposition to U.S. interests. Consequently, these case studies function as indicators of U.S. overreach and strategic adjustment, as well as empirical evidence of a transitioning world—characterized by contested American dominance, constricted instruments, and an increasingly challenged hegemonic status.

3. THE RISE OF MULTIPOLAR ACTORS AND EMERGING COALITIONS

3.1. Emerging Powers and Regional Blocs

The progressive decline of U.S. unipolarity has coincided with the ascent of developing countries and the consolidation of regional blocs, indicating a definitive transition to a multipolar international system. This shift is propelled by both the reconfiguration of material capabilities and the political determination of non-Western governments to assert strategic autonomy, reform global governance, and advocate for alternative development paradigms (Brooks & Wohlforth, 2023; Ali, 2022).

China is at the forefront of this transformation, with its economic ascent being unprecedented in contemporary history. Through programs such as the Belt and Road Initiative (BRI) and the creation of the Asian Infrastructure Investment Bank (AIIB), China has utilized infrastructure diplomacy to enhance its geopolitical influence throughout Asia, Africa, Latin America, and some regions of Europe. India has progressively established itself as a regional hegemon in South Asia and a significant player in the Indo-Pacific, advocating for a multipolar Asia through strategic alliances and digital diplomacy (Mearsheimer, 2021).

Despite economic limitations, Russia has reestablished itself as a military and energy giant, exerting influence in Eastern Europe, Central Asia, and the Middle East. In addition to these major countries, intermediate powers like Brazil, Indonesia, Turkey, and South Africa have strengthened their global involvement, frequently via South-South cooperation and multilateral diplomacy.

Alongside the ascent of individual nations, regional blocs have gained significant importance. Entities such as ASEAN, the African Union (AU), MERCOSUR, and the Gulf Cooperation Council (GCC) have endeavored to define shared regional interests and diminish reliance on Western-led institutions. Entities such as the Shanghai Cooperation Organization (SCO) and BRICS constitute alternative coalitions that contest the moral and institutional supremacy of the liberal international order (Liu, 2023; Kuzemko et al., 2025).

The rising actors and blocs do not constitute a unified anti-Western coalition; instead, they collectively facilitate a diffusion of power, undermining the monopoly of Western influence and broadening the scope of global decision-making. Their expanding agency signifies a structural shift in global politics characterized by pluralism, regionalism, and challenged authority in the post-unipolar era. Comprehending the evolution and interaction of these entities is crucial for understanding the essence of modern multipolarity and its ramifications for international order, stability, and governance.

3.2. Global South and the Reshaping of Multilateralism

The reemergence of the Global South as a formidable entity in international politics signifies a pivotal shift in the development of global governance. Historically marginalized within the post-World War II liberal international order, nations of the Global South—comprising Asia, Africa, Latin America, and segments of the Middle East—are presently contesting the hierarchies entrenched in current multilateral institutions and promoting a more equitable, inclusive, and pluralistic global order (Haug et al., 2021; Trajber Waisbich, 2022).

A primary criticism from Global South entities concerns the underrepresentation and unequal power dynamics in major international organizations, including the United Nations Security Council (UNSC), the International Monetary Fund (IMF), and the World Bank. Although constituting the majority of the global population and making substantial contributions to global economic output and resource distribution, countries in the Global South maintain less formal power inside these institutions. The demand for structural change, encompassing increased permanent representation in the UNSC and revision of voting rights in Bretton Woods organizations, has emerged as a significant issue in modern multilateral discussions (Haug et al., 2021).

In response, actors from the Global South have progressively invested in alternative institutional frameworks that align with their interests and development ideologies. The emergence of BRICS, the New Development Bank (NDB), the Asian Infrastructure Investment Bank (AIIB), and South-South cooperation initiatives highlights a significant shift in multilateralism from grassroots levels. These initiatives frequently underscore sovereignty, mutual respect, non-intervention, and developmental requirements—signifying a shift from the conditionalities traditionally linked to Western aid and financial support (Dutt, 2022; Bracking and Leffel, 2021).

Moreover, the Global South has emerged as a normative entrepreneur, advocating for initiatives focused on climate justice, technological fairness, vaccination accessibility, and sustainable development, especially within the context of the UN 2030 Agenda and the Sustainable Development Goals (SDGs). Coalitions like the G77 and the African Group have played a crucial role in influencing negotiations in UN forums, while regional organizations such as the African Union and CELAC are progressively exerting collective influence (Arora-Jonsson & Gurung, 2023; von Malmborg, 2024; Nisbett & Spaiser, 2023).

The rise of the Global South as a transformational entity is not solely reactive but foundational to a new global order—one that transcends unipolarity and Western-centric multilateralism. This transition highlights a profound reorganization of authority, legitimacy, and leadership in international affairs.

3.3. Technological Sovereignty and Digital Geopolitics

In the developing multipolar global system, technology has emerged as a pivotal element of geopolitical rivalry. Digital capabilities have transcended their role as mere instruments of economic progress, increasingly influencing the allocation of global power, national security plans, and normative authority. The quest for technical sovereignty—characterized as a nation's ability to autonomously build, manage, and govern its digital infrastructure, data, and innovation systems—has become a strategic necessity for both emerging and established nations (Luo & Tung, 2025; Hanson, 2021).

The rivalry between the United States and China in domains such as artificial intelligence (AI), 5G networks, quantum computing, and semiconductors illustrates the emerging paradigm of digital geopolitics. China's “Made in China 2025” policy and its worldwide Digital Silk Road program seek to diminish reliance on Western technologies while promoting Chinese standards for digital governance. Concurrently, U.S.-imposed restrictions on Chinese companies like Huawei and TikTok signify an endeavor to safeguard technical supremacy and national security interests (Liu & Miao, 2024; Segal, 2020).

This bifurcation has resulted in the fragmentation of the global digital ecosystem, frequently referred to as the emergence of a “splinternet,” characterized by the proliferation of rival digital standards and governance frameworks. The European Union, albeit not a technology superpower, has established itself as a regulatory leader via measures such as the General Data Protection Regulation (GDPR) and its promotion of digital rights and ethical artificial intelligence. These initiatives exemplify a normative power, underscoring the significance of values in the formulation of digital governance (Troitiño et al., 2024; Walter, 2024).

In addition to great powers, emerging economies are also demonstrating influence in the digital sphere. Countries like India, Brazil, and Indonesia are investing in native digital infrastructure, advocating for open-source platforms, and negotiating equitable access to global digital marketplaces and data governance frameworks. These initiatives signify overarching apprehensions regarding data colonialism, digital reliance, and algorithmic prejudice (Dote-Pardo et al., 2025; Tripathi, 2024).

Moreover, the militarization of digital domains—via cyberattacks, misinformation initiatives, and monitoring technologies—has transformed the parameters of global confrontation. Cyberspace has emerged as a realm of strategic competition and a venue for novel international collaboration, leading to proposals for a global digital compact under UN frameworks (Hofmann and Pawlak, 2023). Technological sovereignty and digital geopolitics constitute a pivotal frontier in the restructuring of global power dynamics. As nations adjust their strategic priorities, digital autonomy and influence will progressively dictate geopolitical standing in the 21st century.

4. STRATEGIC ADAPTATIONS AND INSTITUTIONAL REALIGNMENTS

4.1. Recalibration of Global Institutions

The shift from unipolarity to multipolarity in the international system is exerting greater pressure on the framework of global governance. Post-World War II institutions—namely the United Nations (UN), International Monetary Fund (IMF), World Bank, and World Trade Organization (WTO)—face pressure to adjust to evolving power dynamics, changing global objectives, and calls for inclusivity. This recalibration process transcends institutional reform, embodying a strategic negotiation of legitimacy, authority, and functionality within a more fragmented global order (Owen et al., 2022; Koepke et al., 2021).

A significant concern is the representational disparity inherent in numerous institutions. The UN Security Council is predominantly influenced by five permanent members (P5) that represent the power dynamics of 1945, rather than the contemporary realities of the 21st century. Emerging powers like India, Brazil, Germany, and South Africa have advocated for increased permanent or semi-permanent participation, referencing their escalating contributions to global peacekeeping, development, and economic advancement (Wallensteen, 2021). Voting power at the IMF and World Bank is disproportionately allocated to wealthy nations, leading the Global South to advocate for more fair decision-making processes.

Consequently, initiatives for gradual reform and institutional diversity have intensified. The G20, comprising both developed and developing economies, has evolved into a more representative forum for global economic coordination, especially after the 2008 financial crisis. Simultaneously, emerging institutions like the BRICS New Development Bank and the Asian Infrastructure Investment Bank (AIIB) exemplify how new actors are simultaneously augmenting and contesting the conventional global financial framework (Ji & Lim, 2022; Zhang and Tian, 2021).

The recalibration procedure furthermore entails normative evolution. Challenges include climate change, digital governance, global health, and migration necessitate institutional responses that beyond Westphalian state-centric frameworks. Multistakeholder frameworks, which include non-state players including civil society, the commercial sector, and epistemic communities, are becoming increasingly essential to global governance (Taggart & Abraham, 2024; Uribe, 2024; Oyenuga, 2021). This institutional heterogeneity, whilst promoting inclusivity, simultaneously engenders apprehensions over coherence and accountability. The recalibration of global institutions signifies a continuous struggle between stability and transformation. The sustainability of the liberal order will hinge on its ability to adjust to a polycentric world, where legitimacy must be acquired rather than assumed.

4.2. Geoeconomic Strategies and Trade Diplomacy

In the modern global framework, the quest for power is progressively conducted through geoeconomic strategies—utilizing economic tools to attain geopolitical aims. As military interventions grow more expensive and diplomatically perilous, nations have adjusted their foreign policy strategies to prioritize commercial diplomacy, economic pressure, and infrastructure investment as means of influence. This transition exemplifies the rationale of a multipolar economy, wherein strategic alliances are established not solely via ideology or security, but also through market access, financial influence, and supply chain interdependencies (Quitzow & Zabanova, 2025; Choer and Wigell, 2022).

The United States, historically the architect of a liberal trading system, has embraced more muscular geoeconomic strategies in the 21st century. Recent administrations have employed strategies such as tariff conflicts, sanctions, and investment limitations to curb China's ascent and safeguard critical sectors. The weaponization of interdependence, as articulated by Farrell and Newman (2019), enables dominant entities within global networks—such as SWIFT, semiconductors, or banking systems—to exert influence over adversaries by limiting access or enforcing compliance. (Olsen, 2023; Nedelcu, 2024)

Concurrently, China has progressed its Belt and Road Initiative (BRI) and Digital Silk Road as instruments of geoeconomic statecraft. These activities amplify Chinese influence via infrastructure financing, connection projects, and digital infrastructure, frequently supported by advantageous trade agreements and political alliances. Critics contend that these instruments could foster debt dependence, but others saw them as feasible alternatives to Western-centric financing approaches.

Middle powers and regional blocs have adopted economic diplomacy to navigate relations with major nations and promote regional integration. Agreements like the Regional Comprehensive Economic Partnership (RCEP), the African Continental Free Trade Area (AfCFTA), and the Mercosur-EU negotiations exemplify a concerted endeavor to realign trade alliances within a dynamic global context.

In this setting, economic statecraft is no longer only the purview of hegemonic states. Smaller governments are increasingly utilizing strategic commodities, digital rules, and normative norms to augment their bargaining strength. The COVID-19 epidemic and the Ukraine conflict have expedited initiatives aimed at supply chain resilience, strategic decoupling, and “friend-shoring,” so altering the landscape of trade and investment.

4.3. Normative Power and Competing World Orders

The competition for global leadership extends beyond raw resources, focusing increasingly on normative power—the capacity of nations and coalitions to influence global norms, values, and discourses that establish legitimacy, authority, and governance. As unipolarity diminishes, global actors are increasingly competing to establish their distinct interpretations of world order, frequently based on contrasting political ideologies and cultural traditions (Taggart & Abraham, 2024).

The liberal international order, founded on concepts like democracy, rule of law, human rights, and free markets, was historically advanced and institutionalized chiefly by the United States and its Western allies. This system disseminated Western liberal ideals as "universal" through multinational organizations, foreign aid conditionalities, and public diplomacy. Nonetheless, the validity of this normative supremacy has been progressively challenged by authoritarian regimes and disenchanted factions of the Global South, who perceive these assertions of universality as a manifestation of normative imperialism (Lake et al., 2021).

Emerging countries like China and Russia have proposed alternative frameworks of order based on the ideals of state sovereignty, non-interference, and developmental authoritarianism. China's Global Development Initiative and Russia's regional partnerships aim to undermine the normative authority of the liberal order and create alternative standards, particularly in areas such as cyber governance, media regulation, and international human rights discussions (Farrell & Newman, 2021).

Simultaneously, the European Union continues to be a principal advocate of "normative power," prioritizing environmental governance, data privacy (e.g., GDPR), and democratic principles. Nevertheless, the EU's impact is frequently constrained by internal fragmentation and the increasing allure of populist and illiberal groups within its territory.

The Global South has emerged as a significant arena for the contestation and invention of norms. Many states promote normative pluralism, prioritizing context-sensitive governance, developmental justice, and postcolonial viewpoints instead than adhering exclusively to Western or non-Western models. Initiatives from the African Union, ASEAN, and CELAC increasingly embody these hybrid frameworks (Kertcher, 2023; Kolmaš and Kolmašová, 2023; Knapp and Fritzler, 2025). The evolving global order is defined by both multipolar power dynamics and normative multipolarity. The coexistence and rivalry of several normative frameworks indicate a shift from universalism to a more intricate, contentious, and negotiated global order.

5. FUTURE PATHWAYS: STABILITY, CONFLICT, OR COOPERATION?

5.1. Scenarios for Global Order in 2040

The international system's shift from unipolarity to multipolarity renders the future of global order ambiguous. By 2040, various credible scenarios may emerge, influenced by the dynamics of great power rivalry, institutional robustness, technology evolution, and global governance capabilities. These scenarios are not deterministic; instead, they exemplify contingency pathways shaped by political decisions, structural changes, and normative conflicts (Brooks & Wohlforth, 2023; Peters, 2023).

The initial scenario is cooperative multipolarity, wherein great powers and regional blocs successfully create channels for coordination and coexistence despite ideological and geopolitical divergences. This world is defined by reformed multilateralism, institutional inclusion, and issue-based coalitions that facilitate collaborative responses to transnational concerns, including climate change, pandemics, and digital governance. Prominent characteristics encompass augmented roles for middle powers, fortified UN agencies, and a revitalized focus on collective sovereignty and the stewardship of global commons (Petrakis et al., 2024).

A second potential is competitive great-power rivalry, characterized by heightened geopolitical tensions, fragmented economic realms, and technological decoupling. In this context, the United States, China, and other emerging countries participate in zero-sum competition, leading to proxy conflicts, weapons races, and the disintegration of global norms. Institutions like the WTO or WHO may become progressively incapacitated, as regional security systems replace global structures. This situation illustrates the revival of realism power politics, wherein stability is upheld through deterrence instead of collaboration (Du, 2024).

The third scenario anticipates fragmented regionalism, when the international system transforms into a decentralized mosaic of regional orders. This concept posits that the erosion of global institutional cohesiveness results in the emergence of regional governance frameworks characterized by unique laws, values, and leadership structures. ASEAN, the African Union, MERCOSUR, and the Shanghai Cooperation Organization may assume more independent roles, leading to a landscape of multiple governance. This may improve local legitimacy and contextual governance, but it also poses concerns of normative incoherence and strategic misalignment (Wang et al., 2024).

These scenarios are not mutually exclusive; hybrid configurations are likely to arise, contingent upon the adaptation of international institutions, the constraint of great powers, and the activity of non-state actors. Preparing for these futures necessitates strategic foresight, inclusive diplomacy, and a reconfiguration of global collaboration beyond 20th-century frameworks.

5.2. Opportunities for Sustainable Global Governance

In the context of increasing geopolitical uncertainty and the waning of unipolar dominance, the shift towards a multipolar world offers distinct chances to reconceptualize and establish more sustainable frameworks for global governance. Instead of concentrating exclusively on power competitions, multipolarity—if effectively managed—can establish a basis for pluralistic, resilient, and equity-focused global cooperation (Peters, 2023; Luo & Tung, 2025).

A significant opportunity exists in the progression of the Sustainable Development Goals (SDGs), which offer a global framework for tackling poverty, inequality, climate change, and institutional instability. Multipolarity facilitates the coexistence of various developmental models, enabling contributions to common goals and transcending Western-centric paradigms. Emerging powers, like China, India, Brazil, and South Africa, are influencing development discourse via South-South collaboration, technology transfer, and infrastructure expenditures customized to local settings (Trajber Waisbich, 2022; Waisbich 2023; UNDP, 2021).

Moreover, climate governance has emerged as a strategic focal point for global cooperation, wherein even competing nations acknowledge shared interests. The Paris Agreement (2015), despite facing conflicting commitments, signifies a crucial advancement in establishing a global climate framework. In a multipolar world, leadership on environmental issues may not only reside with traditional powers but might encompass coalitions of willing nations, sub-national actors, and non-state groups, including cities, corporations, and civil society (Stranadko, 2022; Rayner et al., 2021). These actors improve governance via innovation, accountability, and experimentation.

A further pathway for sustainable governance is in inclusive digital and technological collaboration. As cyber norms, data rights, and AI governance emerge as critical global issues, there exists an opportunity for multi-stakeholder frameworks that reconcile innovation with regulation. Entities like the UN High-Level Panel on Digital Cooperation and the Global Partnership on AI illustrate efforts to establish ethical and inclusive digital frameworks (Djatmiko et al., 2025; Bühler et al., 2023).

Significantly, intermediate powers and regional organizations are adept at serving as intermediaries. Countries such as Canada, Indonesia, and Kenya, in conjunction with regional organizations like the African Union and ASEAN, have exhibited the ability to facilitate cross-bloc discussions, resolve conflicts, and promote inclusive governance standards. Sustainable global governance in a multipolar world is achievable if grounded on shared responsibility, institutional agility, and inclusive involvement. The international community should capitalize on the loss of hegemony to establish a more equitable, collaborative, and environmentally sustainable global order.

5.3. Recommendations and Policy Directions

The shift from a unipolar to a multipolar global order represents not just a structural change but also a strategic opportunity to redefine international cooperation via adaptive and inclusive policy innovation. Effectively managing this shift necessitates proactive recommendations and policy directions that emphasize legitimacy, resilience, and equity (Peters, 2023; Vlados et al., 2022).

1. Advocate for Adaptive Multilateralism

Instead of depending solely on traditional institutions, governments and non-state actors ought to cultivate adaptable, issue-oriented coalitions that facilitate varied leadership and collective duties. Entities such as the G20, the BRICS+ framework, and regional groups like the African Union and ASEAN are essential in developing multi-level governance structures that address global concerns such pandemics, migration, and climate change.

2. Enhance Middle Power Diplomacy and Facilitate Bridge-Building Initiatives

Middle powers, including Indonesia, Mexico, South Korea, and South Africa, ought to utilize their moral credibility and strategic posture to mediate tensions among great powers and promote cross-bloc consensus. Their function in facilitating inclusive discussions and spearheading matters like as global health equity, conflict resolution, and digital ethics is becoming increasingly essential in a divided world.

3. Promote Digital Sovereignty and Ethical Governance of Technology

In a time of digital multipolarity, it is essential to establish global norms to regulate artificial intelligence, data sharing, cybersecurity, and platform responsibility. A multipolar order should not reproduce analogous inequities in digital realms. Governments ought to endorse multistakeholder projects that guarantee interoperability, safeguard rights, and promote developmental inclusion, especially for the Global South.

4. Integrate Equity and Sustainability into Global Economic Reform

Global economic governance must transcend austerity-focused frameworks and incorporate social justice, ecological transition, and debt sustainability into the objectives of institutions such as the IMF, WTO, and World Bank. Debt relief methods, climate finance, and technology transfer must be used to rectify structural imbalances in the global system.

5. Invest in Norms of Peaceful Coexistence and Preventive Diplomacy

To mitigate the risks of great-power confrontation, global entities must reaffirm their dedication to preventative diplomacy, arms control, and confidence-building initiatives. The establishment of common standards of restraint, particularly in cyberspace and outer space, will be essential for preserving strategic stability in a complex multipolar system.

CONCLUSION

The global system is experiencing a significant shift characterized by the steady decline of U.S. unipolar dominance and the emergence of a more distributed, multipolar power structure. This transition is a complex and non-linear evolution that entails the realignment of institutions, the dissemination of normative authority, and the development of strategic autonomy among a wider array of players. The ascendance of China, the revival of Russia, and the increasing influence of the Global South highlight a transition towards polycentric administration.

Multipolarity entails both hazards and prospects. It introduces uncertainty, norm fragmentation, and potential instability in global governance. Conversely, it fosters more inclusiveness, diversifies leadership, and redefines global goals towards sustainability, equity, and digital ethics. The erosion of hegemonic dominance paves the way for a more democratic and representative international system, provided it is administered judiciously.

This chapter has demonstrated how emergent coalitions, technological advancements, and institutional changes are reshaping the structure and rationale of global order. Strategic competition continues to be a prominent element, while the possibility for adaptive cooperation also persists. The essential strategy for managing this shift is promoting resilient multilateralism, engaging in middle power diplomacy, and integrating ethical and inclusive frameworks inside governance structures.

The success of this shift hinges on the international community's capacity to relinquish antiquated paradigms of domination and adopt a pluralistic, collaborative, and forward-looking vision of global order. The decision between fragmentation and rejuvenation is still available—but will be influenced by leadership, foresight, and the political resolve to envision a world beyond hegemonic unipolarity.

REFERENCES

Alami, I., Alves, C., Bonizzi, B., Kaltenbrunner, A., Koddenbrock, K., Kvangraven, I., & Powell, J. (2023). International financial subordination: A critical research agenda. *Review of International Political Economy*, *30*(4), 1360–1386. DOI: 10.1080/09692290.2022.2098359

Alami, I., & Taggart, J. (2024). A partial conversion: How the 'unholy trinity' of global economic governance adapts to state capitalism. *European Journal of International Relations*, *30*(4), 867–893. DOI: 10.1177/13540661241226472

Arora-Jonsson, S., & Gurung, J. (2023). Changing business as usual in global climate and development action: Making space for social justice in carbon markets. *World Development Perspectives*, *29*, 100474. DOI: 10.1016/j.wdp.2022.100474

Baciu, C. (2022). Interpolarity: Re-visiting security and the global order. *Defence Studies*, *22*(4), 571–590. DOI: 10.1080/14702436.2022.2110482

Bracking, S., & Leffel, B. (2021). Climate finance governance: Fit for purpose? *Wiley Interdisciplinary Reviews: Climate Change*, *12*(4), e709. DOI: 10.1002/wcc.709

Brooks, S. G., & Wohlforth, W. C. (2023). The myth of multipolarity: American power's staying power. *Foreign Affairs*, *102*(3), 76–91. DOI: 10.1080/0163660X.2021.2020457

Codagnone, C., & Weigl, L. (2023). Leading the charge on digital regulation: The more, the better, or policy bubble? *Digital Society : Ethics, Socio-Legal and Governance of Digital Technology*, *2*(1), 4. Advance online publication. DOI: 10.1007/s44206-023-00033-7 PMID: 36686333

Du, M. (2024). International economic law in the era of great power rivalry. *Vanderbilt Journal of Transnational Law*, *57*(3), 723–794. DOI: 10.2139/ssrn.4701265

Dupont, C., Moore, B., Boasson, E. L., Gravey, V., Jordan, A., Kivimaa, P., Kulovesi, K., Kuzemko, C., Oberthür, S., Panchuk, D., Rosamond, J., Torney, D., Tosun, J., & von Homeyer, I. (2024). Three decades of EU climate policy: Racing toward climate neutrality? *Wiley Interdisciplinary Reviews: Climate Change*, *15*(1), e863. DOI: 10.1002/wcc.863

Dutt, D. (2022). How power and politics shape niche-regime interactions: A view from the Global South. *Environmental Innovation and Societal Transitions*, *43*, 320–330. DOI: 10.1016/j.eist.2022.04.008

Edwards, D. B.Jr, Moschetti, M. C., & Caravaca, A. (2022). *Globalization, privatization, and the state: Contemporary education reform in post-colonial contexts*. Routledge., DOI: 10.4324/9781003026792

El Damanhoury, K., & Garud-Paktar, N. (2022). Soft power journalism: A visual framing analysis of COVID-19 on Xinhua and VOA's Instagram pages. *Digital Journalism (Abingdon, England)*, *10*(9), 1546–1568. DOI: 10.1080/21670811.2021.1957969

Farrell, H., & Newman, A. L. (2021). The Janus Face of the Liberal International Information Order: When global institutions are self-undermining. *International Organization*, *75*(2), 333–358. DOI: 10.1017/S0020818320000302

Franke, U., & Kurthen, H. (2023). Still lacking self-reflection after all these years? (De)stabilizing factors of transatlantic relations according to German and U.S. foreign policy experts between 2011 and 2017. *The Journal of Transatlantic Studies*, *21*(1-2), 1–29. Advance online publication. DOI: 10.1057/s42738-023-00107-x

Gatto, A. (2022). The energy futures we want: A research and policy agenda for energy transitions. *Energy Research & Social Science*, *89*, 102639. DOI: 10.1016/j.erss.2022.102639

Geronik, A. (2024). The Cold War in retrospect: A continuous international conflict or a world war? *Cogent Social Sciences*, *10*(1), 2300527. Advance online publication. DOI: 10.1080/23311886.2023.2300527

Goldstein, J., & Gulotty, R. (2021). America and the trade regime: What went wrong? [REMOVED HYPERLINK FIELD]. *International Organization*, *75*(2), 524–557. DOI: 10.1017/S002081832000065X

Grinin, L., & Korotayev, A. V. (2021). Seven weaknesses of the U.S., Donald Trump, and the future of American hegemony. *World Futures*, *77*(1), 23–54. DOI: 10.1080/02604027.2020.1801309

Harris, P. (2024). Two cheers for Biden's Ukraine policy. *Survival*, *66*(3), 1–13. DOI: 10.1080/00396338.2024.2357474

Haug, S., Braveboy-Wagner, J., & Maihold, G. (2021). The 'Global South' in the study of world politics: Examining a meta category. *Third World Quarterly*, *42*(9), 1923–1944. DOI: 10.1080/01436597.2021.1948831

Hofmann, S. C., & Pawlak, P. (2023). Governing cyberspace: Policy boundary politics across organizations. *Review of International Political Economy*, *30*(6), 2122–2149. DOI: 10.1080/09692290.2023.2249002

Iksan, M., & Soong, J. J. (2023). The political economy of Indonesia's development strategy under China–USA power rivalry and hegemonic competition: A middle power with its hedging strategy. *Chinese Economy*, *56*(4), 304–320. DOI: 10.1080/10971475.2022.2136696

Ji, X., & Lim, G. (2022). The Chinese way of reforming global economic governance: An analysis of China's rising role in the Group of Twenty (G-20). *Chinese Economy*, *55*(4), 282–292. DOI: 10.1080/10971475.2021.1972546

Kerr, J., Panagopoulos, C., & van der Linden, S. (2021). Political polarization on COVID-19 pandemic response in the United States. *Personality and Individual Differences*, *179*, 110892. Advance online publication. DOI: 10.1016/j.paid.2021.110892 PMID: 34866723

Kertcher, C. (2023). The Global South contestation narratives and the transformation of military humanitarian interventions in the early 1990s. *Cogent Social Sciences*, *9*(1), 2251251. Advance online publication. DOI: 10.1080/23311886.2023.2251251

Knapp, A., & Fritzler, J. (2025). 'Soft Contestation' of the Responsibility to Protect? Assessing Canada and Sweden's Norm Diplomacy. In Lucenti, F., Ducci, C., Wunderlich, C., & Lantis, J. S. (Eds.), *Contestation in Prism: The Evolution of Norms and Norm Clusters in Contemporary Global Politics* (pp. 65–85). Springer Nature Switzerland., DOI: 10.1007/978-3-031-83639-8_4

Knudsen, T. B. (2022). Power transition and world order: Three rival theories and the dynamics of change. Dalam T. B. Knudsen & C. Navari (Eds.), *Power Transition in the Anarchical Society: Rising Powers, Institutional Change and the New World Order* (hlm. 31–55). Palgrave Macmillan. https://doi.org/DOI: 10.1007/978-3-030-97711-5_2

Kolmaš, M., & Kolmašová, Š. (2023). How individuals shape informal institutions: Analyzing contending norm promotion in the Global South. *Journal of International Relations and Development*, *26*(3), 557–578. DOI: 10.1057/s41268-023-00308-z

Kuik, C. C. (2021). Getting hedging right: A small-state perspective. *China International Strategy Review*, *3*(2), 300–315. DOI: 10.1007/s42533-021-00089-5

Kuzemko, C., Blondeel, M., Bradshaw, M., Bridge, G., Faigen, E., & Fletcher, L. (2025). Rethinking energy geopolitics: Towards a geopolitical economy of global energy transformation. [REMOVED HYPERLINK FIELD]. *Geopolitics*, *30*(2), 531–565. DOI: 10.1080/14650045.2024.2351075

Lake, D. A., Martin, L. L., & Risse, T. (2021). Challenges to the liberal order: Reflections on international organization. *International Organization*, *75*(2), 225–257. DOI: 10.1017/S0020818320000636

Lall, R. (2025). Making global governance accountable: Civil society, states, and the politics of reform. *American Journal of Political Science*, *69*(1), 96–117. DOI: 10.1111/ajps.12824

Lee, A. H. Y. (2022). Social trust in polarized times: How perceptions of political polarization affect Americans' trust in each other. *Political Behavior*, *44*(3), 1533–1554. DOI: 10.1007/s11109-022-09787-1 PMID: 35340916

Leoni, Z. (2021). A Post-American Geopolitical World Order: Uneven Development and the Shifting Balance of Power. In *American Grand Strategy from Obama to Trump: Imperialism After Bush and China's Hegemonic Challenge* (pp. 89–130). Springer. https://doi.org/DOI: 10.1007/978-3-030-54742-4_5

Liu, F. (2023). Balance of power, balance of alignment, and China's role in the regional order transition. In *Navigating International Order Transition in the Indo-Pacific* (pp. 35–57). Routledge., DOI: 10.4324/9781003431930-3

Liu, H., & Miao, C. (2024). Digital geopolitics in a VUCA world: China encounters a new global order. *Global Policy*, *15*(S6), 67–83. Advance online publication. DOI: 10.1111/1758-5899.13435

Luo, Y., & Tung, R. L. (2025). A multipolar geo-strategy for international business. *Journal of International Business Studies*, *56*(7), 821–829. Advance online publication. DOI: 10.1057/s41267-025-00777-z

Mearsheimer, J. J. (2021). The inevitable rivalry: America, China, and the tragedy of great-power politics. *Foreign Affairs*, *100*(6), 47–58. DOI: 10.1080/09636412.2025.2497962

Morales Ruvalcaba, D. (2024). National power in Sino-Caribbean relations: CARICOM in the geopolitics of the Belt and Road Initiative. *Chinese Political Science Review*, *10*(1), 28–48. DOI: 10.1007/s41111-024-00252-4

Nedelcu, M. R. (2024). The rise of geotechnology: A paradigm shift from geopolitics and geoeconomics in the context of Industry 4.0. In *Proceedings of the International Conference on Business Excellence, 18*(1) (pp. 1979–1988). Sciendo. https://doi.org/DOI: 10.2478/picbe-2024-0167

Nisbett, N., & Spaiser, V. (2023). Moral power of youth activists – Transforming international climate politics? *Global Environmental Change*, *82*, 102717. DOI: 10.1016/j.gloenvcha.2023.102717

Nye, J. S. (2023). *Soft power and great-power competition: Shifting sands in the balance of power between the United States and China*. Springer Singapore., DOI: 10.1007/978-981-99-0714-4

Olsen, K. B. (2023). Geoeconomic diplomacy: Reforming the instrumentalization of economic interdependencies and power. In Hare, P. W., Manfredi-Sánchez, J. L., & Weisbrode, K. (Eds.), *The Palgrave Handbook of Diplomatic Reform and Innovation* (pp. 649–671). Palgrave Macmillan., DOI: 10.1007/978-3-031-10971-3_32

Owen, J. R., Kemp, D., Harris, J., Lechner, A. M., & Lèbre, É. (2022). Fast track to failure? Energy transition minerals and the future of consultation and consent. *Energy Research & Social Science*, *89*, 102665. DOI: 10.1016/j.erss.2022.102665

Oyenuga, A. (2021). Perspectives on the impact of the COVID-19 pandemic on the global and African maritime transport sectors, and the potential implications for Africa's maritime governance. *WMU Journal of Maritime Affairs*, *20*(2), 215–245. DOI: 10.1007/s13437-021-00233-3

Parashar, S., & Schulz, M. (2021). Colonial legacies, postcolonial 'selfhood' and the (un)doing of Africa. *Third World Quarterly*, *42*(5), 867–881. DOI: 10.1080/01436597.2021.1903313

Peters, M. A. (2023). The emerging multipolar world order: A preliminary analysis. *Educational Philosophy and Theory*, *55*(14), 1653–1663. DOI: 10.1080/00131857.2022.2151896

Peters, M. A. (2024). From West to East: The unraveling of the post-Cold War liberal order and the rise of autocratic capitalism in a multipolar world. *Geopolitics, History, and International Relations*, *16*(1), 9–25. DOI: 10.22381/GHIR16120241

Petrakis, P. E., Kanzola, A.-M., & Lomis, I. (2024). Adapting to Multipolarity: Insights from Iterated Game Theory Simulations—A Preliminary Study on Hypothetical Optimal Global Cooperation. *Journal of Risk and Financial Management*, *17*(8), 370. DOI: 10.3390/jrfm17080370

Rayner, T., Oberthür, S., & Hermwille, L. (2021). A sectoral perspective on international climate governance: Key findings and research priorities. *Earth System Governance*, *8*(4), 100105. Advance online publication. DOI: 10.1016/j.esg.2021.100105

Saleh, A., & Yazdanshenas, Z. (2023). China-Iran strategic partnership and the future of US hegemony in the Persian Gulf Region. *British Journal of Middle Eastern Studies*, *51*(2), 377–400. DOI: 10.1080/13530194.2023.2215188

Stranadko, N. (2022). Global climate governance: Rising trend of translateral co-operation. *International Environmental Agreement: Politics, Law and Economics*, *22*(4), 639–657. DOI: 10.1007/s10784-022-09575-6 PMID: 35370522

Taggart, J., & Abraham, K. J. (2024). Norm dynamics in a post-hegemonic world: Multistakeholder global governance and the end of liberal international order. *Review of International Political Economy*, *31*(1), 354–381. DOI: 10.1080/09692290.2023.2213441

Tian, N., Lopes da Silva, D., Béraud-Sudreau, L., Liang, X., Scarazzato, L., & Assis, A. (2023). Developments in military expenditure and the effects of the war in Ukraine. *Defence and Peace Economics*, *34*(5), 547–562. DOI: 10.1080/10242694.2023.2221877

Trajber Waisbich, L. (2022). 'It Takes Two to Tango': South–South Cooperation Measurement Politics in a Multiplex World. *Global Policy*, *13*(3), 334–345. DOI: 10.1111/1758-5899.13086

Troitiño, D. R., Mazur, V., & Kerikmäe, T. (2024). E-governance and integration in the European Union. *Internet of Things : Engineering Cyber Physical Human Systems*, *27*, 101321. DOI: 10.1016/j.iot.2024.101321

Uribe, J. (2024). Excluding through inclusion: Managerial practices in the era of multistakeholder governance. *Review of International Political Economy*, *31*(6), 1686–1709. DOI: 10.1080/09692290.2024.2362666

von Malmborg, F. (2024). Strategies and impacts of policy entrepreneurs: Ideology, democracy, and the quest for a just transition to climate neutrality. *Sustainability (Basel)*, *16*(12), 5272. DOI: 10.3390/su16125272

Waisbich, L. T. (2023). *Who is socialising whom? How Southern powers negotiate accountability in international development cooperation. Dalam Norm Diffusion Beyond the West: Agents and Sources of Leverage (hlm.* Springer Nature Switzerland., DOI: 10.1007/978-3-031-25009-5_2

Wallensteen, P. (2021). Representing the world: A Security Council for the 21st century. In *Peter Wallensteen: A Pioneer in Making Peace Researchable: With a Foreword by Jan Eliasson and a Preface by Raimo Väyrynen* (pp. 239–251). Springer International Publishing., DOI: 10.1007/978-3-030-62848-2_12

Wang, K., Chung, C. K. L., Xu, J., & Long, Z. (2024). Reconceiving China's urban economic transition through symbiotic state-firm dynamics: An integrated perspective from urban governance and global production networks. *Cities (London, England)*, *150*, 104974. DOI: 10.1016/j.cities.2024.104974

Weibel, A., Schafheitle, S., & Van der Werff, L. (2025). Smart tech is all around us – Bridging employee vulnerability with organizational active trust-building. *Journal of Management Studies*, *62*(5), 1914–1944. DOI: 10.1111/joms.12940

Zhang, Y., & Tian, H. (2021). How G20 can better support global governance?—A Chinese perspective. In *Reform, Opening-up and China's Changing Role in Global Governance* (pp. 163–187). Springer Singapore. https://doi.org/DOI: 10.1007/978-981-33-6025-9_7

Chapter 8

The Impact of Unipolar Hegemony on Foreign Exchange Reserves:
A Macroeconomic Proportional Analysis

Aslan Azimzadeh
https://orcid.org/0000-0003-1441-440X
Odlar Yurdu University, Azerbaijan

ABSTRACT

Since 1944, the unipolar factor has begun to form in the world economic system. Thus, the formation of a dollar-centered currency system after the Bretton Woods Monetary Conference further deepened the unipolar economic hegemony of the United States, parallel to the unipolar political hegemony. In the research work, the author analyzed the impact of this economic hegemony on international exchange reserves. The author relied on macroeconomic proportional analysis here. As a result, although the value of the US dollar in the volume of foreign currency reserves has increased, proportional analysis shows that this indicator has not increased, but rather decreased.

INTRODUCTION

Since the formation of the world economic system, the factor of unipolarity has always been in the foreground. The struggle of the world countries for economic hegemony for many years has characterized the development of that unipolarity.

DOI: 10.4018/979-8-3373-2342-8.ch008

However, contemporary challenges highlight the limitations of the unipolar economic model.

It should be noted that after the Bretton Woods Monetary Conference in 1944, unipolarity was formed in the world economic system.

In fact, the activities of financial institutions that emerged based on the results of this conference also somewhat deepened this economic unipolarity. The deepening processes also had serious effects on the world financial sector. Thus, the shortcomings of the dollar-centered economic system have given rise to a new phase of structural crisis. These processes are also clearly manifested in foreign exchange reserves.

Especially in the context of globalization, even relatively small problems in the US economy can significantly influence the financial systems of other countries. Thus, the 2008 Global Financial Crisis negatively affected the economic development of most countries worldwide, reflecting the combined effects of globalization and the dollar-centric model. The study will analyze the disproportionality created in foreign exchange reserves by the unipolar world model.

If we analyze the theory of the structure of the world economic system, we will see that the new world economic system was built precisely in the direction of the development of multipolarity and regional economic integration processes. Thus, during the years 1756-1816, the leader of the first, trade-monopolistic world economic system was the Netherlands, during the years 1816-1924, the leaders of the second, colonial world economic system were Great Britain and Russia, during the years 1924-2008, the leaders of the third, imperial world economic system were the USA and the USSR, and from 2008 to the present, the leaders of the fourth, integral world economic system are organizations such as the Shanghai Cooperation Organization, the Eurasian Economic Union, etc. (Glazyev, 2019; Glazyev & Kefeli, 2022) .

These factors highlight the weaknesses of the unipolar world economic system. For many years, the main schools of economic science, including the monetarist trend of the neoclassical school, have come up with various theories related to the preservation of the unipolar and dollar-centered world economic system. These theories currently shape the foundation of mainstream economics, creating barriers to the development of alternative approaches that challenge the interests of radical capitalism.

If we analyze the hypotheses of supporters of the liberalization of the cross-border movement of capital, we will see that these theories suggest that the survival of the dollar-centered unipolar economic system has come at the expense of creating significant challenges for the financial systems of many countries. However, real experience shows that the economic development of countries restricting cross-border capital flows tends to be higher than that of countries with fully liberalized regimes. China can be an important example of this.

It is noteworthy that in many countries, higher education institutions pay limited attention to alternative schools of economic thought, focusing predominantly on the neoclassical approach, which constitutes the mainstream of economic science. As a result, the new generation of economists often approach development economics primarily through the lens of these dominant schools and their relatively simplified analytical frameworks.

All these factors can be regarded as reflections of the adverse effects of the unipolar world model on economic science, the global economic system, and international financial relations. Today, there is information about the development of foreign trade relations with national currencies in a number of countries, the formation of their own basket currencies by various international economic organizations (including BRICS). However, it must be recognized that as long as the core provisions of the Bretton Woods financial system continue to shape the framework of the world economy, attempts at dedollarization and multipolarity are likely to face significant limitations. For the future development of the world economy, convening a new currency conference and addressing these issues within a multipolar framework could provide a more sustainable path forward.

The analysis will be conducted through macroeconomic proportional analysis. This analysis tool is very necessary in obtaining more progressive indicators and achieving long-term strategic goals. Unfortunately, much of the current research relies on simplistic econometric approaches, which limit analytical depth. However, the analysis based on macroeconomic proportions promises new opportunities for an effective analysis of the current situation. It is for this reason that it is necessary to resort to the aforementioned analysis in the study. The main questions of the research are as follows:

RQ 1: Is there adequate proportionality in foreign exchange reserves?
RQ 2: How has unipolarity affected the proportionality in foreign exchange reserves?
RQ 3: Under what conditions can adequate proportionality in foreign exchange reserves be formed?

These research questions will give a serious impetus to revealing the main essence of the study. Because today, such an important direction as the analysis of the disproportionality of economic development is being neglected. Representatives of the neoclassical and Keynesian economic schools have brought to the fore various considerations related to macroeconomic balance. However, it should be clearly noted that macroeconomic balance may not serve economic development. Thus, today it is necessary to stimulate direct investments for the development of the real sector. In order to increase the share of the banking sector in direct investments, there is a need to increase the money supply in the context of implementing a soft monetary policy, which can characterize the imbalance in the money market. However, the imbalance conditions economic development. From this we can conclude that ensuring long-term economic development can be achieved not by targeting macroeconomic balance, but precisely by maintaining adequate and optimal macroeconomic proportions. Especially in the context of a deepening structural crisis, designing an economic policy aimed at preserving macroeconomic proportions can stimulate sustainable economic development, which can be characterized as an adequate response to the challenges of a period of turbulence.

The paucity of studies based on the aforementioned analysis techniques may serve to fill the knowledge gap in this area.

LITERATURE REVIEW

Overall, the theory of proportionality encompasses the main factors that characterize the balanced growth of various economic structures (Colacchio, 2005). The analysis of macroeconomic proportions can be observed in the scientific works of a number of researchers. Thus, Tugan-Baranovsky noted in his scientific works that ensuring optimal proportionality between production sectors will affect the sustainability of economic development (as cited in Colacchio, 2005).

Lewis (1954) explains the formation of capital and the development of technical progress in terms of the ratio between national income and profit. According to him, if the share of profit in the national income increases, it is possible to achieve the mentioned goals. Papanek (1964) analyzed the ratio of added value to capital stock and the ratio of investments to added value. Later, within the framework of these proportions, he analyzed the regions of Pakistan. Bassanini and Manfredi (2012) analyzed the share of labor in the business sector, excluding agriculture, mining, fuel, and real estate, and again brought the proportionality factor to the fore. On the other hand, Onegina et al. (2020) analyzed the proportionality between the cost of fixed capital and the number of employees in the agricultural sector of Ukraine.

Table 1 illustrates the works of some of the studies that analyzed proportionality as the ratio of various indicators to GDP. Following the purpose of the current work, the authors included a brief literature review of the studies examining different approaches after the 2000s. The studies focused on different indicators such as Energy, Consumption, Credit, Debt, Tax, Trade and Investment.

Table 1. Some studies conducted proportional analysis in the form of the ratio of various indicators to GDP

Author	Title of study	Ratio
Kaufmann (2004)	The mechanisms for autonomous energy efficiency increases: A cointegration analysis of the US energy/GDP ratio	Energy-to-GDP
Martins et al. (2024)	Energy and Circular Economy: Nexus beyond Concepts. Sustainability	
Cleveland & Ruth (1998)	Indicators of dematerialization and the materials intensity of use	Consumption-to-GDP
Focacci (2007)	Empirical analysis of the relationship between total consumption-GDP ratio and per capita income for different metals: The cases of Brazil, China, and India	
Edge and Meisenzahl (2011)	The unreliability of credit-to-GDP ratio gaps in real-time: Implications for countercyclical capital buffers	Credit-to-GDP
Jokipii et al. (2021)	Exploring BIS credit-to-GDP gap critiques: the Swiss case	
Gordon (2014)	A new method of estimating potential real GDP growth: Implications for the labor market and the debt/GDP ratio	Debt-to-GDP
Di Domenico et al. (2024)	Distribution, capital intensity and public debt-to-GDP ratio: an input output—stock flow consistent model	
Gaspar et al. (2016)	Tax Capacity and Growth: Is There a Tipping Point?	Tax-to-GDP
Kaneva et al. (2022)	Tax policy for economic recovery and sustainable development after covid-19	
Bleaney and Tian (2023)	The trade-GDP ratio as a measure of openness	Trade-to-GDP
Durongkaveroj (2024)	Trade Openness and the Growth–Poverty Nexus: A Reappraisal with a New Openness Indicator	
Zhu et al. (2021)	Eco-Efficiency of Industrial Investment and Its Influencing Factors in China Based on a New SeUo-SBM-DEA Model and Tobit Regression	Investment-to- change in GDP volume
Amin et al. (2023)	Nexus between energy intensity and capital-output ratio: A holistic approach	

Source: author's editing

At the same time, a number of researchers have included foreign exchange reserves, the dollar, and the multipolarity factor in their studies. For example, Dailami and Masson (2011) predicted that the US dollar could lose its dominance as an international currency between 2011 and 2025 and be replaced by the Chinese renminbi.

Campanella (2014) concluded in his scientific study that the high privileges of the dollar created difficulties in managing the US balance of payments and encouraged it to borrow, regardless of the systemic disproportionality.

Sadil and Sipko (2021) concluded in their research that China's strengthening in the global economic system could seriously affect the functioning of the current international monetary system, with the aim of creating a multipolar currency system by increasing the strength of the renminbi.

Agarwal and Parekh (2023) identify the euro, renminbi, and cryptocurrencies as the dollar's main competitors in their study. The researchers conclude that a new, multipolar currency system may emerge in which the dollar can share its hegemony in the long term.

In fact, the main factor that unites all the researchers listed is that they tell us in one way or another that the dollar-centered currency system arose from unipolar hegemony. However, in the studies conducted, it is not at all clear what percentage of the dollar in foreign reserve currency would be proportional. It is precisely in order to achieve this result that the author intends to mention the factor in question in his study.

METHODOLOGY

To conduct the aforementioned analysis, we will use macroeconomic proportionality analysis. The research database will include the International Monetary Fund indicators. The research will include the following steps.

First step: General Analysis of Foreign Exchange Reserves
Second step: Proportional Analysis of Foreign Exchange Reserves (RQ1, RQ2)
Third step: Analysis of the Adequate Proportional Distribution of Foreign Exchange Reserves (RQ3)

The method we will use is similar to the method of Kozlowski (2024a). Although Kozlovsky (2024b) in his study uses the percentage indicator in the variable normalization method, the variable normalization method proposed by the author will be based on the coefficient principle, which is more indicative.

$$X_1 + X_2 + X_3 + ... + X_n = \sum_{k=1}^{n} X_k \tag{1}$$

where, X_1 is the value of the 1st currency as a foreign exchange reserve, X_2 s the value of the 2nd currency as a foreign exchange reserve, X_3 is the value of the 3rd currency as a foreign exchange reserve, s the value of n currencies as foreign exchange reserves. $\sum_{k=1}^{n} X_k$ is the sum of the values of n currencies as foreign exchange reserves.

$$\frac{\sum_{k=1}^{n} X_k}{n} = Y_k \tag{2}$$

where n is the number of different currencies in foreign exchange reserves, and Yk is the numerical average of the total value of n different currencies in foreign exchange reserves.

$$\frac{X_1}{Y_k} = A_1 \ ; \frac{X_2}{Y_k} = A_2 \ ; \frac{X_3}{Y_k} = A_3 \dots \frac{X_n}{Y_k} = A_k \tag{3}$$

where A_1 is the ratio of the value of the first currency in the foreign exchange reserves to the numerical average of the total value of n different currencies in the foreign exchange reserves. The same interpretation can be used for other ratios.

$$A_1 + A_2 + A_3 + \dots + A_n = \text{n} \tag{4}$$

Or

$$A_1 + A_2 + A_3 + \dots + A_n = \sum_{k=1}^{n} A_k \tag{5}$$

Finally, the sum of all the obtained coefficients should give us exactly the number (n) of different currencies we will use.

RESULT AND DISCUSSION

First, let's analyze the overall situation of foreign exchange reserves. The currencies to be used for this analysis are the US dollar, the Euro, the Pound Sterling, the Chinese yuan renminbi, the Japanese yen, the Australian dollar, the Canadian dollar, the Swedish franc, and a collection of other currencies. The figure below is a graphical representation of the overall picture (Fig.1)

As can be seen from Figure 1, the share of the dollar in foreign exchange reserves has been increasing over the years. Thus, if in 2015 the value of the dollar in foreign exchange reserves was \$4,873,915.48 million, in 2024 this value was \$6,631,267.36 million, which is an increase of 36 percent. However, in parallel with the dollar, the value of other currencies is also increasing. Thus, if in 2015 the value of the euro in foreign exchange reserves was \$1,419,423.44 million, in 2024 this value was \$2,274,971.35 million, which is an increase of 60.3 percent.

A similar situation continues in other currencies. In 2015, the value of the Japanese yen in foreign exchange reserves was \$278,305.84 million, while in 2024 this figure was \$667,115.93 million, which is a 2.4-fold increase. If we look at the pound sterling, we can see that the value of this currency in foreign exchange reserves has increased by 55 percent over 10 years. The Australian dollar has increased by 80 percent over 10 years, and the Canadian dollar has increased by 2.4 times. On the contrary, the Swedish franc has decreased by 1 percent over these years.

The Chinese yuan renminbi, on the other hand, looks quite interesting. So, while in 2016 the value of the Chinese yuan renminbi in foreign exchange reserves was $90,777.37 million, in 2024 the value of the renminbi in world foreign exchange reserves was $249,675.87 million, which is a 2.75-fold increase in 10 years.

Figure 1. Dynamics of world foreign exchange reserves during 2015-2024 (in million US dollars)

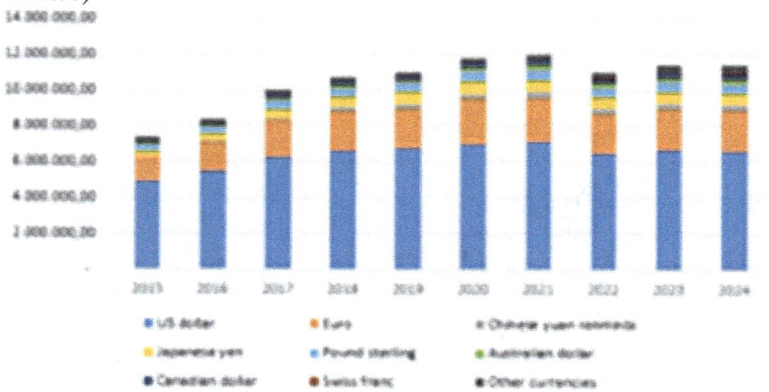

Source: Compiled by the author based on IMF indicators (https://data.imf.org/en/datasets/IMF.STA:COFER)

This analysis shows that from Bretton Woods to the present day, the unipolar world model has had a serious impact on the economic system and, in particular, foreign exchange reserves. As the simplest example, the current analysis conducted by the author, measuring the value of other currencies in terms of the US dollar, already allows us to say how this impact is integrated into everyday life. It is the hegemony of the US dollar over the world and the exploitation of the resource potential of developing countries as a result of this hegemony that in itself forms new economic development mechanisms within the framework of the multipolar world model. The analysis shows that, although the US dollar is still the leader in world foreign exchange reserves, the growth rate of foreign exchange reserves of other currencies is higher than the growth rate of the US dollar.

Although Dailami and Masson (2011) point out that the dominance of the US dollar will be lost between 2011 and 2025 as a result of the strengthening of the Chinese renminbi, this does not seem realistic in the short term. The transformation to a multipolar world is an undeniable fact. However, just as there will be new rules for this transformation politically, it is also necessary to have new rules economically.

Because it is impossible to see effective and sustainable economic development of countries as a result of the aforementioned dollar-centered Bretton Woods system.

For a more fundamental and in-depth analysis of the issue, proportional analysis is needed. The table below contains the coefficients obtained as a result of proportional analysis of foreign exchange reserves.

Table 2. Proportionality ratios of world foreign exchange reserves (2016-2024)

	2016	2017	2018	2019	2020	2021	2022	2023	2024
US dollar	5,88	5,65	5,56	5,47	5,30	5,29	5,27	5,26	5,20
Euro	1,72	1,82	1,86	1,85	1,92	1,85	1,83	1,80	1,78
Chinese yuan renminbi	0,10	0,11	0,17	0,17	0,21	0,25	0,24	0,21	0,20
Japanese yen	0,36	0,44	0,47	0,53	0,54	0,50	0,50	0,51	0,52
Pound sterling	0,39	0,41	0,40	0,42	0,43	0,43	0,44	0,44	0,43
Australian dollar	0,15	0,16	0,15	0,15	0,16	0,17	0,18	0,19	0,19
Canadian dollar	0,17	0,18	0,17	0,17	0,19	0,21	0,21	0,23	0,25
Swiss franc	0,01	0,02	0,01	0,01	0,02	0,02	0,02	0,02	0,02
Other currencies	0,21	0,22	0,22	0,23	0,24	0,28	0,31	0,35	0,42
$\sum_{k=1}^{n} A_k$	9,00	9,00	9,00	9,00	9,00	9,00	9,00	9,00	9,00

Source: author's editing

When analyzing the table, it is observed that there is no adequate proportionality in foreign exchange reserves. Thus, looking at 2024, it is seen that the proportionality coefficient of 5.20 in foreign exchange reserves falls on the US dollar. The remaining proportionality coefficient of 4.80 falls on the other 8 groups of currencies, of which the coefficient of 1.78 belongs only to the euro. However, these coefficients also show that the US dollar is actually losing value in foreign exchange reserves. Figure 1 shows the increase in the US dollar. Proportional analysis, on the other hand, showed the opposite result. This shows the real picture. For this reason, proportional analysis provides more complete and accurate information. It is precisely the increase in the value of other currencies in foreign exchange reserves that reduces the weight of the US dollar in reserves. Here, the main competitors are the Japanese yen and the Chinese yuan. The figure below will show the disproportionality more visually.

Figure 2. Box and whisker representation of proportionality coefficients for foreign exchange reserves (2016-2024)

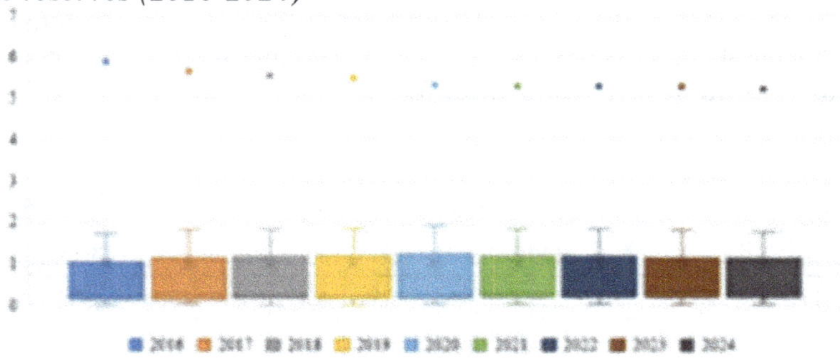

Source: author's editing

Box and Whisker shows a significant disproportionality in foreign exchange reserves. However, over the years, this disproportionality has been decreasing, as the volume of other currencies in foreign exchange reserves has increased. This indicates that the start button of the transformation processes to a multipolar world has been pressed. This once again shows that the establishment of a dollar-centered international currency system within the framework of unipolar hegemony affects the formation of serious disproportionality in the structure of foreign exchange reserves. The establishment of a dollar-centered economic model and the formation of financial institutions supporting this model direct the main line of economic science precisely towards the preservation of this system, which at least blocks scientific creative thinking. Economists, revolving around models that are simple and outside the real economy, put forward theories that do not serve economic development. This, of course, can make economic science, as Thomas Carlyle said, a "dismal science" in the long term (Şengör, 2004).

Another important question here is in which option adequate proportionality can be achieved. In response to this question, the author has put forward an estimate in the table below to ensure adequate proportionality, with greater emphasis on the US dollar, Euro, Chinese renminbi and Japanese yen.

Table 3. Adequate proportionality ratios of foreign exchange reserves presented by the author (2016-2024)

	2016	2017	2018	2019	2020	2021	2022	2023	2024
US dollar	1,7	1,9	1,9	2	2,1	1,9	1,9	1,8	1,8
Euro	1,72	1,82	1,86	1,85	1,92	1,85	1,83	1,8	1,78
Chinese yuan renminbi	1,1	1,11	1,17	1,17	1,21	1,25	1,24	1,21	1,2
Japanese yen	1,36	1,44	1,47	1,53	1,54	1,5	1,5	1,51	1,52
Pound sterling	0,83	0,76	0,73	0,71	0,67	0,71	0,71	0,73	0,71
Australian dollar	0,59	0,51	0,48	0,44	0,40	0,45	0,45	0,48	0,47
Canadian dollar	0,61	0,53	0,50	0,46	0,43	0,49	0,48	0,52	0,53
Swiss franc	0,45	0,37	0,34	0,30	0,26	0,30	0,29	0,31	0,30
Other currencies	0,65	0,57	0,55	0,52	0,48	0,56	0,58	0,64	0,70
$\sum_{k=1}^{n} A_k$	9,00	9,00	9,00	9,00	9,00	9,00	9,00	9,00	9,00

Source: author's editing

The interpretation presented here by the author may change as different currencies come to the fore. It is possible that in the long term, the Russian ruble or the BRICS basket currency (if it is formed) will come to the fore from the basket of other currencies. However, this table was compiled taking into account past years and the present. The writing of the coefficients in this form characterizes adequate proportionality. To see the proportionality in question more visually, the figure below should be considered.

Figure 3. Hypothetical box and whisker representation of adequate proportionality ratios of foreign exchange reserves presented by the author (2016-2024)

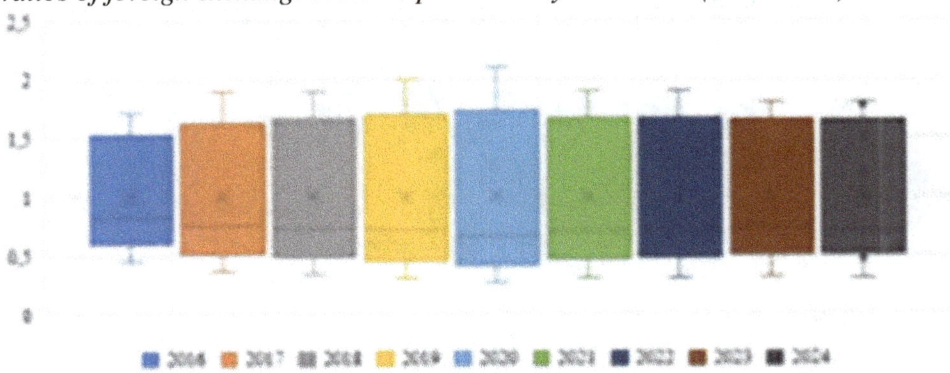

Source: author's editing

As can be seen from Box and Whisker, the proposed table is shaping adequate proportionality. If the method proposed by the author for calculating the proportionality coefficient is calculated inversely for the presented adequate proportionality indicators, a different picture may emerge.

The main principle in calculating adequate proportionality is that the share of any currency should not exceed 25 percent of the total structure. Looking at the proportionality coefficient of the US dollar in Table 3, it can be observed that in some years this indicator is given as 1.7, while in other years it appears as 2.0. A lower coefficient characterizes a sharp multipolarity scenario, whereas a relatively higher coefficient corresponds to a moderate multipolarity scenario. Thus, taking into account the 25 percent threshold, the proportionality coefficient of the dollar has been reduced, and the remaining share has been distributed among the other currencies in such a way that the total sum once again equals 9, thereby preserving the proportionality principle. Of course, alternative normative rules could also be applied, and in that case, adequate proportionality could be modeled in a different format. This is simply the author's analytical opinion and is subject to change.

A key limitation of this study lies in the absence of a more precise and sophisticated method for determining the optimal proportionality, which highlights the need for further methodological refinement in future research.

Figure 4. Value of foreign exchange reserves calculated within the framework of adequate proportionality coefficients presented by the author

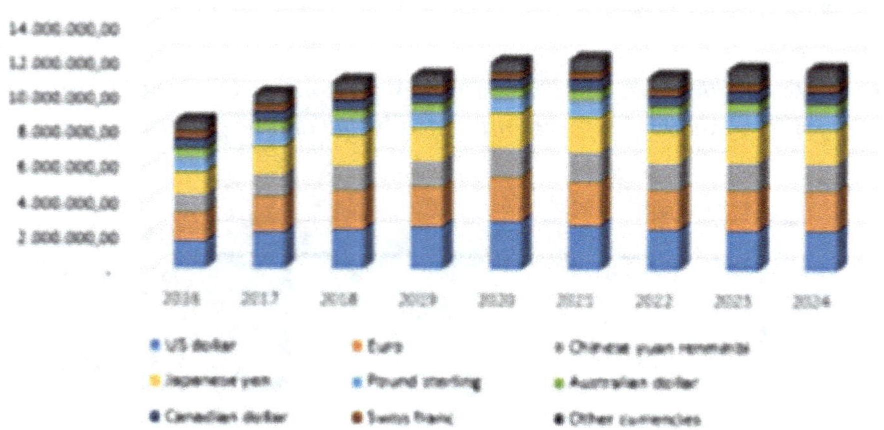

Source: author's editing

The figure characterizes what it would look like if foreign exchange reserves were adequately proportional during 2016-2024. If we analyze the year 2024, we will see that within the framework of adequate proportionality in the author's interpretation, the value of the US dollar in foreign exchange reserves should have been \$2,294,388.33 million. However, in reality, the value of the US dollar in foreign exchange reserves in 2024 is \$6,631,267.36 million, which means \$4,336,879.04 million more dollar reserves to ensure adequate proportionality. This is a very large figure. It is all these factors that characterize the existence of a serious monopoly of the US dollar in the international monetary system within the framework of the unipolar world model today.

SOLUTIONS AND RECOMMENDATIONS

It should be noted that although the unipolar world model today may have a positive impact on the political prestige of the United States, it does not have a positive impact on it economically. Although the US's retention of the dollar-centered economic model as a tool for economic development had a positive impact on the US economy in the early years, it has led to serious disproportions such as the financial sector overtaking the real sector in the following years. The radical development of the financial sector in the US within the framework of the dollar-centered economic model encourages people not to invest in the real sector, but to invest in economic sectors that promise higher profits in the short term. On the other hand, it should be noted that US expenses are constantly increasing. In order to meet these expenses, it is necessary to develop the real economy. The weakening of investment flows to the real economy is creating serious problems in the US economy. As a way out, the US leadership is increasing the dollar printing, which in turn curbs monetary inflation. These problems have a negative impact on the economies of all countries within the framework of globalization. In this case, it becomes clear that unipolar economic hegemony and the dollar-centered international monetary system are not very successful. This situation can also be described as a structural weakness of the American economy. US policymakers face a strategic choice: either prioritize the development of the real sector, which may require restructuring the financial sector, or continue preserving the dollar-centered international monetary system with potential risks to the real economy. The most successful option seems to be the first. Thus, convening a new currency conference within the framework of the collapse of the dollar-centered international monetary system and establishing a multipolar international monetary system will, on the one hand, save the US economy from the aforementioned obstacle and characterize its sustainable development, and on the other hand, stimulate the effective economic development of developing countries. In an era when regionalization and an integral world economic system are at the forefront, the continued functioning of the unipolar, dollar-centered international monetary system appears increasingly outdated. Some countries think that they will develop the dedollarization process by negotiating with national currencies in international trade. This approach is unlikely to be effective. The process of dedollarization cannot be formed through international trade in national currencies. The process of dedollarization is unlikely to be achieved solely through international trade in national currencies. It would require fundamental changes to the Bretton Woods framework and the creation of a new, multipolar international monetary system.

FUTURE RESEARCH DIRECTIONS

Although this study attempts to analyze the impact of the unipolar world model on the proportional structure of foreign exchange reserves within a general theoretical framework, a number of directions that require deeper and more specific approaches to the topic remain open for future scientific research. First of all, a comparative study of changes in the composition of foreign exchange reserves of different groups of countries - developed, developing and underdeveloped countries - may allow us to identify specific economic mechanisms of the polarity factor on an empirical basis.

In addition, the role played by geopolitical positioning and international alliances in the formation of foreign exchange reserves can also become a separate subject of research. In particular, the relationship between the level of political relations with the United States and the share of the dollar in reserve portfolios can be examined in more depth.

In the context of current global trends, the increasing role of digital currencies should also be one of the priority directions for future research. The impact of these technological innovations on the position of the US dollar as a reserve currency, as well as the economic consequences of blockchain-based assets and their legal regulation, should be analyzed with a multidisciplinary approach.

At the same time, the role of institutional and behavioral factors in central banks' reserve strategies – that is, decision-making mechanisms, political considerations, and risk assessment approaches – can be studied using qualitative methods. Finally, the long-term consequences of a possible transition to a multipolar monetary system in the world can be studied through modeling and scenario analysis. In this regard, the impact of factors such as the relative weakening of the economic influence of the United States, the strengthening of regional financial blocs, and the tendency for fragmentation due to sanctions on reserve policies should be separately examined. Future scientific research in these areas can contribute to a deeper understanding of the dynamic interactions between the balance of power and monetary sovereignty in the system of international economic relations.

It should be noted that future research should focus on developing more precise and sophisticated methodological approaches for determining optimal proportionality in foreign exchange reserves. While the present study proposes a normative framework based on diversification and concentration limits, there is a clear need for refined analytical tools—such as advanced entropy-based measures, optimization techniques, or simulation models—that can provide greater accuracy and robustness. Addressing this methodological gap will not only strengthen the theoretical foundation of proportionality analysis but also enhance its practical relevance for policymakers and international financial institutions.

CONCLUSION

The author tried to answer all three research questions posed in the study. It was determined that there is a significant disproportionality among world foreign exchange reserves. Conventional statistical analysis showed an increase in the share of the dollar in foreign exchange reserves. However, macroeconomic proportional analysis presented a completely opposite picture, showing the depreciation of the US dollar in the international currency system within the framework of the appreciation of the Chinese renminbi yuan and the Japanese yen.

After the Bretton Woods currency conference, the formation of a dollar-centered economic system based on unipolar economic hegemony stands as a barrier to the sustainability of the economic development of the world's countries. On the other hand, this system is also causing economic damage to the US economy itself.

In order to establish adequate proportionality, it is necessary for other currencies to gain value in the international currency system, in other words, the creation of a multipolar currency system. For this, it is not enough to use national currencies in foreign trade. The most important issue is to depart from the rules of the Bretton Woods system and convene a new currency conference. Addressing these disproportionalities is essential not only for the stability of the global financial system, but also for strengthening the foundations of sustainable growth within the US economy.

REFERENCES

Agarwal, M., & Parekh, J. (2023). De-Dollarisation: Emerging Alternatives to the Reserve Currency. *Available at SSRN* 4882989.

Amin, S. B., Taghizadeh-Hesary, F., Al Kabir, F., & Khan, F. (2023). Nexus between energy intensity and capital-output ratio: A holistic approach. *Energy & Environment, 34*(7), 2721–2739. DOI: 10.1177/0958305X221115489

Bassanini, A., & Manfredi, T. (2012), "Capital's Grabbing Hand? A Cross-Country/Cross-Industry Analysis of the Decline of the Labour Share", *OECD Social, Employment and Migration Working Papers*, No. 133, OECD Publishing, Paris, https://doi.org/DOI: 10.1787/1815199X

Bleaney, M., & Tian, M. (2023). The trade-GDP ratio as a measure of openness. *World Economy, 46*(5), 1319–1332. DOI: 10.1111/twec.13355

Campanella, M. (2014). The internationalization of the Renminbi and the rise of a multipolar currency system. *Journal of Self-Governance and Management Economics, 2*(3), 72–93.

Cleveland, C. J., & Ruth, M. (1998). Indicators of dematerialization and the materials intensity of use. *Journal of Industrial Ecology, 2*(3), 15–50. DOI: 10.1162/jiec.1998.2.3.15

Colacchio, G. (2005). On the origins of non-proportional economic dynamics: A note on Tugan-Baranowsky's traverse analysis. *Structural Change and Economic Dynamics, 16*(4), 503–521. DOI: 10.1016/j.strueco.2004.10.002

Dailami, M., & Masson, P. (2011). *Prospects for a multipolar international monetary system* (No. 2011: 13). DIIS Report.

Di Domenico, L., Barbieri Góes, M. C., & Gallo, E. (2024). Distribution, capital intensity and public debt-to-GDP ratio: An input output—stock flow consistent model. *Economia Politica (Bologna), 41*(2), 395–416. DOI: 10.1007/s40888-023-00318-7

Durongkaveroj, W. (2024). Trade Openness and the Growth–Poverty Nexus: A Reappraisal with a New Openness Indicator. *Asian Development Review, 41*(02), 7–29. DOI: 10.1142/S0116110524400092

Edge, R. M., & Meisenzahl, R. (2011). The unreliability of credit-to-GDP ratio gaps in real-time: Implications for countercyclical capital buffers. *International Journal of Central Banking, 7*(4), 261–298.

Focacci, A. (2007). Empirical analysis of the relationship between total consumption-GDP ratio and per capita income for different metals: The cases of Brazil, China and India. *International Journal of Social Economics, 34*(9), 612–636. DOI: 10.1108/03068290710778633

Gaspar, V., Jaramillo, L., & Wingender, M. P. (2016). *Tax Capacity and Growth: Is There a Tipping Point?* International Monetary Fund.

Glazyev, S. Y. (2019). The big Eurasian partnership as a model of a new world order: From the American to the Asian world economic paradigm. *Journal of Economic Science Research, 2*(3). Advance online publication. DOI: 10.30564/jesr.v2i3.676

Glazyev, S. Y., & Kefeli, I. F. (2022). On the question of the ideology of the Eurasian Economic Union. *Eurasian integration: economics, law, politics, 16*(1), 10-21.

Gordon, R. J. (2014). A new method of estimating potential real GDP growth: Implications for the labor market and the debt/GDP ratio (No. w20423). National Bureau of Economic Research.

Jokipii, T., Nyffeler, R., & Riederer, S. (2021). Exploring BIS credit-to-GDP gap critiques: The Swiss case. *Swiss Journal of Economics and Statistics, 157*(1), 1–19. DOI: 10.1186/s41937-021-00073-1

Kaneva, T., Chugunov, I., Pasichnyi, M., Nikitishin, A., & Husarevych, N. (2022). Tax policy for economic recovery and sustainable development after covid-19. *Problemy Ekorozwoju, 17*(2), 102–109. DOI: 10.35784/pe.2022.2.11

Kaufmann, R. K. (2004). The mechanisms for autonomous energy efficiency increases: A cointegration analysis of the US energy/GDP ratio. *The Energy Journal (Cambridge, Mass.), 25*(1), 63–86. DOI: 10.5547/ISSN0195-6574-EJ-Vol25-No1-4

Kozlovskij, V. (2024a). Assessment of smart growth indicators progress in EU: cohesion approach. In New Trends in Contemporary Economics, Business and Management. Selected Proceedings of the 14th International Scientific Conference “Business and Management 2024”, pp. 55–63. https://doi.org/DOI: 10.3846/bm.2024.1233

Kozlovskij, V. (2024b). Assessment of Baltics states regional Economic disparities according to GDP. [JEECAR]. *Journal of Eastern European and Central Asian Research, 11*(5), 887–902. DOI: 10.15549/jeecar.v11i5.1650

Lewis, W. A. (1954). Economic development with unlimited supplies of labour.

Martins, F. F., Castro, H., Smitková, M., Felgueiras, C., & Caetano, N. (2024). Energy and circular economy: Nexus beyond concepts. *Sustainability (Basel), 16*(5), 1728. DOI: 10.3390/su16051728

Onegina, V., Megits, N., Antoshchenkova, V., & Boblovskyi, O. (2020). Outcome of capital investment on labor productivity in agriculture sector of Ukraine. [JEECAR]. *Journal of Eastern European and Central Asian Research, 7*(1), 12–25. DOI: 10.15549/jeecar.v7i1.355

Papanek, G. F.G. F. Papanek. (1964). Industrial production and investment in Pakistan. *Pakistan Development Review, 4*(3), 462–490. DOI: 10.30541/v4i3pp.462-490

Sadil, V., & Sipko, J. (2021). The International Monetary System: New evidence concerning a transition to multipolarity. *Scientific Papers of the University of Pardubice, Series D: Faculty of Economics and Administration.*

Şengör, A. C. (2004). *Yaşamın evrimi sonuna fikrinin Darwin döneminin sonuna kadarki kısa tarihi*. İTÜ Yayınevi.

Tugan-Baranovsky, M. I. (2002). Studies in the theory and history of commercial crises in England. In: Hagemann, H. (Ed.), *Business Cycle Theory, Selected Texts* 1860–1939, vol. 2. Pickering and Chatto, London, pp. 3–44 (or. ed. 1901)

Zhu, C., Zhu, N., & Shan, W. U. H. (2021). Eco-Efficiency of Industrial Investment and Its Influencing Factors in China Based on a New SeUo-SBM-DEA Model and Tobit Regression. *Mathematical Problems in Engineering, 2021*(1), 5329714. DOI: 10.1155/2021/5329714

KEY TERMS AND DEFINITIONS

Macroeconomic Proportions: are quantitative relationships between different sectors of the economy

Macroeconomic Disproportionality: is the process of imbalance between proportionality coefficients

Adequate Proportionality: is the optimal distribution of macroeconomic proportions

Foreign Exchange Reserve: are globally recognized and reliable national currencies that are collected by central banks of foreign countries for reserve purposes and used as strategic assets

Bretton Woods Monetary Conference: was a monetary conference held in Bretton Woods, USA, in 1944 that shaped a new world economic order

Dollar-centric Currency System: is a currency system in which the US dollar is dominant

BRICS: An economic organization founded by Brazil, Russia, India, China, and South Africa

Cross-border Movement of Capital: is the liberal and unhindered movement of capital between countries

Radical Capitalism: is an extreme model of capitalism that disregards social justice and is based on labor exploitation

Multipolar Currency System: is a currency system characterized by the dominance of multiple currencies in foreign exchange reserves

Dedollarization Process: is the process of the dollar losing its dominant position in the international economy.

Chapter 9
Shifting Horizons of United States Hegemony: A Normative Perspective

Ejazul Haq Ateed
https://orcid.org/0000-0003-4802-2586
Kirikkale University, Turkey

ABSTRACT

The shining years of the U.S. ideological hegemony in the world tended to darken at the dawn of the twenty first century. The unipolar system waned as the U.S. grappled with sustaining democracy as a relatively accepted and appealing ideology in the world. This shift marked a pivotal moment in international relations, questioning the sustainability of American ideological hegemony. This paper attempts to address the question of how ideology serves as an indicator of American global hegemony and its subsequent decline. It also seeks to find out what are the reasons behind the diminishing influence of American ideology on the global stage. It is assumed that democracy, a cornerstone of U.S. ideology, played a pivotal role in its global rise. However, this ascent is now declining as constitutional challenges undermine democracy domestically. Simultaneously, its reduced international commitment to democracy promotion and inconsistent global actions have eroded American ideological influence, diminishing democracy as a means of its global hegemony.

INTRODUCTION

Typically, the U.S. is regarded to be synonymous with democracy as stipulated in the Declaration of Independence 'all men are created equal' and the constitution's preamble 'we the people.' There is also a dominant belief in the decisive role of

DOI: 10.4018/979-8-3373-2342-8.ch009

ideology in the consolidation of the U.S. hegemony. To highlight the importance of ideology in the U.S. political vision, some argue that the rationale behind the Cold War was ideology (Rosecrance et al., 1993, p. 48). Although Kenneth Waltz (1979, p. 172) put emphasis on the power politics over ideology in Cold War dynamics, a middle-ground view suggests that the U.S. ideological approach became significant with Ronald Reagan's presidency in the early 1980s. By establishing the National Endowment for Democracy (NED) in 1983, the U.S. embarked upon the project of democracy promotion across the globe (Fukuyama & McFaul, 2007, p. 11). The prospect of solidifying the U.S. ideological hegemony further surfaced once the history ended and the last man survived (Fukuyama, 1992).

However, Francis Fukuyama's assumption was not destined to last long. As the turn of the century approached the ideological primacy of the U.S. began to decline. The ongoing discussion about the diminishing hegemony of the U.S. is most accurately captured through an examination of the country's ideological vulnerabilities. Neo-Gramscianism is one of the dominant theories of International Relations that highlights the role of ideology in the rise and fall of hegemony. This article deals with the factors of America's ideological weakness at home and abroad by employing neo-Gramscianism theory of hegemony. In this research, liberal democracy is regarded as an ideology through which American primacy in the early post-Cold War period was maintained but later it began to decay. It is assumed that the weakness of the U.S. competency in preserving democracy as a legitimate universal ideology has contributed to its decline. In this regard, three factors made it lose its ideological primacy i.e. erosion of democracy from within, deviation from the path of post-Cold War grand strategy and contradiction in foreign behavior.

The research is delimited to the period from the year 2000 to 2024, concentrating on the normative dimension of American influence manifested through ideology. In this context, ideology is confined to liberal democracy, encompassing aspects such as voting rights, electoral freedom, civil liberties, constraints on executive power, free elections, democratic preferences, citizen participation, and the effectiveness of government. The article utilizes a descriptive-analytical research method, giving special attention to a mixed approach. The arguments presented in the research are supported by quantitative data sourced from prominent data centers, notably Freedom House, Our World in Data, Gallup, and the Pew Research Center. The article incorporates original data gathered from these sources, and the graphical representations are reproduced throughout the paper.

NEO-GRAMSCIANISM: IDEOLOGY AS A SPRINGBOARD AND SLIDE FOR HEGEMONY

Although traditional theories contain certain aspects related to hegemony that overlap with the critical theory of neo-Gramscianism, they tend to be more focused on material factors and fall short in explaining the normative aspect of the concept. When considering the emergence, maintenance, and stability of a hegemonic system, there are several theories, including Hegemonic Stability Theory (HST), the Liberal Institutional Approach and Critical Theory, which includes both neo-Gramscianism and World System Theory. Yet, in the context of this paper, the most reasoned application is the neo-Gramscian theory, which has been expanded to an international level through the contributions of Robert Cox (1983, quoted in Cox & Sinclair, 1996, p. 133).

The idea of hegemony defined by Gramsci actually connects society to each other, acts as an integrating phenomenon and restructures all institutions in terms of the dominant ideology. Thus, the use of ideology as a means of legitimization is realized by infusing the dominant political system to the minds of individuals (Gramsci, 1991, p. 69). According to Gramsci, the effectiveness of hegemony diminishes when the cohesive bonds of its control, which are rooted in ideology, weaken. Essentially, ideology serves as a tool for justifying the authority of hegemonic systems by implanting the prevailing political beliefs and values into the consciousness of individuals (Gramsci, 1991). A similar perspective to Gramsci's concept of the dissemination of the dominant ideology can be found in Louis Althusser's writings. Althusser (2020) contends that sovereign power is consistently fortifying its presence through both ideological and repressive apparatuses. The state's ideological apparatuses primarily contribute to the perpetuation of social consent, thereby establishing and consolidating hegemony.

In contrast to neo-realist theories that anchor hegemony in material power imbalances and neo-liberals who emphasize will and the supply of public goods, Cox further reinforced the nexus between ideology and hegemony. According to him, hegemony is the 'dominance of a particular kind where the dominant state creates an order based ideologically on a broad measure of consent' (Cox, 1987, p. 7). Therefore, Cox not only highlights the importance of ideology for hegemony, but also asserts that consent of other states is critical. In other words, the mere introduction of an ideology does not mean the emergence of a hegemon and hegemonic order; rather, the presented ideology should acquire audiences whose deference is willingly extended to the hegemon (Cox, 1987, p. 7).

The decline of the hegemon and its hegemonic influence can be assessed by examining the extent to which its legitimacy is preserved and the strength of its normative network's bonds. In this context, legitimacy emerges from the process of integrating leaders in peripheral regions into the prevailing norms and values. The exertion of power, and consequently the means through which cooperation is secured, revolves around the introduction of a particular set of norms by the dominant power and the willingness of leaders from other nations to embrace them (Ikenberry & Kupchan, 1990, p. 285). As this tendency weakens, it erodes the foundation of an international system built upon a dominant power.

The assessment of the legitimacy of ideology involves an examination of its dual sources i.e. structural and procedural (Rapkin & Braaten, 2009, p. 122). The first aspect involves the process of integrating others into the norms and values upheld by the dominant power. As described by Ikenberry and Kupchan (1990, pp. 290-292), this integration can be achieved through three distinct strategies. Normative persuasion, which entails the spontaneous adoption of the hegemon's norms; external inducement, encompassing economic and military threats like sanctions; and internal reconstruction, which directly involves intervening in the internal affairs of other countries. Similarly, the procedural legitimacy of the hegemon is evident in how its actions align with its established rules.

Drawing from Gramsci's political ideas, Roger Simon (1991, pp. 66-73) highlights three key aspects in the discourse on hegemonic ideology. Firstly, it is asserted that as coercion and coercive tactics increase, the capacity to secure consent diminishes and the decline of hegemony becomes more pronounced. The second pertains to ideology serving as a unifying force among diverse social classes, often referred to as common sense (Heywood, 2012, p. 12). Gramsci views ideology as the binding agent, akin to cement, that brings various classes together around a shared focal point. He challenges the notion that ideology should be assessed solely in terms of its moral value and instead regards it as outcome-oriented. If the outcomes of an ideology do not align with its fundamental purpose, which is to unite different classes, it can lead to a crisis in hegemony (Gramsci, 1971, p. 349). The third aspect involves the pluralism feature of the ruling ideology. A pluralistic ideology, on one hand, does not exclude others, and, on the other, it can incorporate historical and social elements from various groups, thus playing a crucial role in maintaining hegemony. A hegemonic system based on a non-pluralistic ideology is destined to fail. Gramsci's concept of the decline of hegemony is termed as an 'organic crisis.' This crisis occurs when the hegemonic ideology transforms into a dictatorship and disregards the ideas of other groups that were once aligned with the hegemon (Gramsci, 1991, p. 70).

DEMOCRACY'S RETREAT TO A GLOBAL LEVEL

Different democracy indexes report a decline in democratic practices across various regions over the past two decades. This trend is thought-provoking in the regions where the U.S. has been significantly involved, such as post-Soviet states in Europe, the Caucasus, Central Asia, Afghanistan, and the Middle East. Despite U.S.-backed democracy promotion efforts, these regions have experienced a democratic backslide. Shortly after the end of the Cold War, while the Baltic States quickly integrated into U.S.-aligned institutions and the Balkans began a process of liberal reforms, the outcomes have not met U.S. expectations (U.S. Department of State, 2005).

The study of Our World in Data based on the V-Dem Index, spanning 2000 to 2023, reveals a concerning decline in liberal democracy in Europe and Caucasia. The assessment considers factors like voting rights, freedom of election, civil liberties, and executive power constraints. Among 20 Soviet's ex-satellite countries excluding Kosovo, North Macedonia, and Montenegro due to their later statehood recognition, about half has experienced decreased liberal democracy scores (Our World in Data, 2023) *[Figure 1]*.

Figure 1. Backslide of Liberal Democracy in 10 Previously Socialist States in Europe and Caucasia

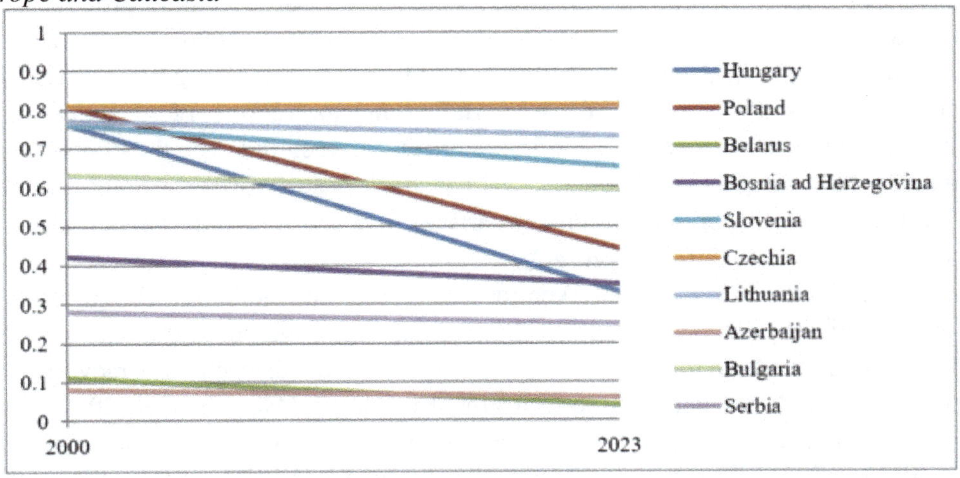

Source: Compiled from Our World in Data (2024), Retrieved from https://ourworldindata.org/democracy.

In Central Asia also backslide is observed despite U.S.' provision of $9 billion direct financial assistance to these countries, which inter alia was aimed to encourage democratic reforms. Since 1992, the U.S. financial assistance to South Caucasus surpasses its aids to Central Asia by $1 billion. Out of $10 billion, one of the main areas of expenses has been democratic reforms (U.S. Department of State, 2021).

Figure 2. State of Democracy in Central Asian Countries plus Afghanistan

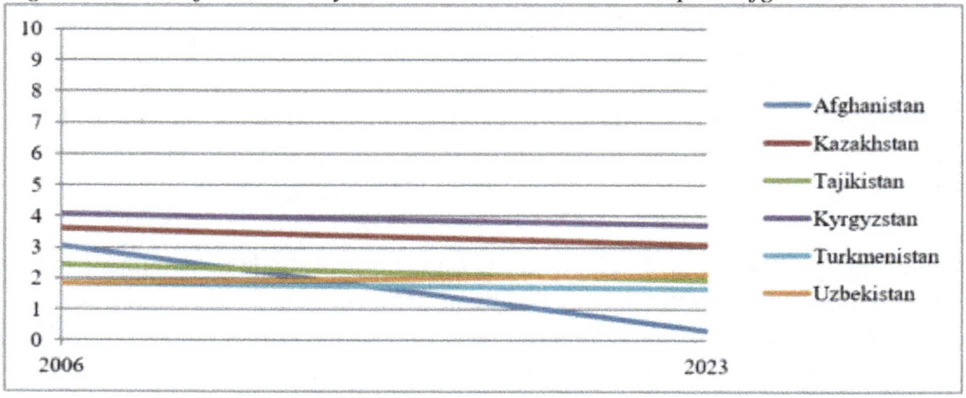

Source: Compiled from Our World in Data (2024), Retrieved from https://ourworldindata.org/democracy.

Consistent with this approach, the U.S. also advocated Color Revolution in the region (Peimani, 2009, p. 207). In Afghanistan, the U.S. failed to consolidate democracy over two decades, ultimately leading to the overthrow of the democratic government by the Taliban, a non-state actor whose founding groups and key leaders are categorized in the U.S. terrorism lists. The comparative data from 2006-2023 on Central Asian countries and Afghanistan reveals significant trends in democratic status. Four out of five Central Asian nations, except for Uzbekistan, show a decline in democracy according to the Democracy Index by the Economist Intelligence Unit (2023). This index evaluates factors such as free elections, civil liberties, democratic preference, citizen participation, and government effectiveness (Our World in Data, 2023) *[Figure 2]*.

Similarly, the U.S. direct intervention strategy in the Middle East backfired in terms of ideological assimilation of the regimes in the region. A dominant view suggests that the U.S. mission in Iraq not only failed to enhance democracy in the country but also weakened American global influence (Mearsheimer, 2019, pp. 32-33). As of 2023, Iraq's global freedom score is 30 percent where only 14 out of 60 can enjoy civil rights while political rights are scored 16 out of 40 (Freedom House, 2023). Similar patterns are observed in other Middle Eastern and North African countries like Libya, where U.S. military involvement has not translated into improved democracy; in fact, these countries rank below average in democracy indexes (Freedom House, 2023) *[Figure 3]*.

Broadly speaking, freedom tends to decline in different parts of the world. Since 2006, the number of declining countries exceeds those of improving. Among the declining countries is the U.S. itself whose score degraded -10 followed by India, commonly dubbed as the largest democracy in the world (Freedom House, 2023). Indeed, striking is the setback within those countries which are predominantly proponents and promoters of the ideology.

Figure 3. Decline of Freedom in Different Countries in the Past 10 Years

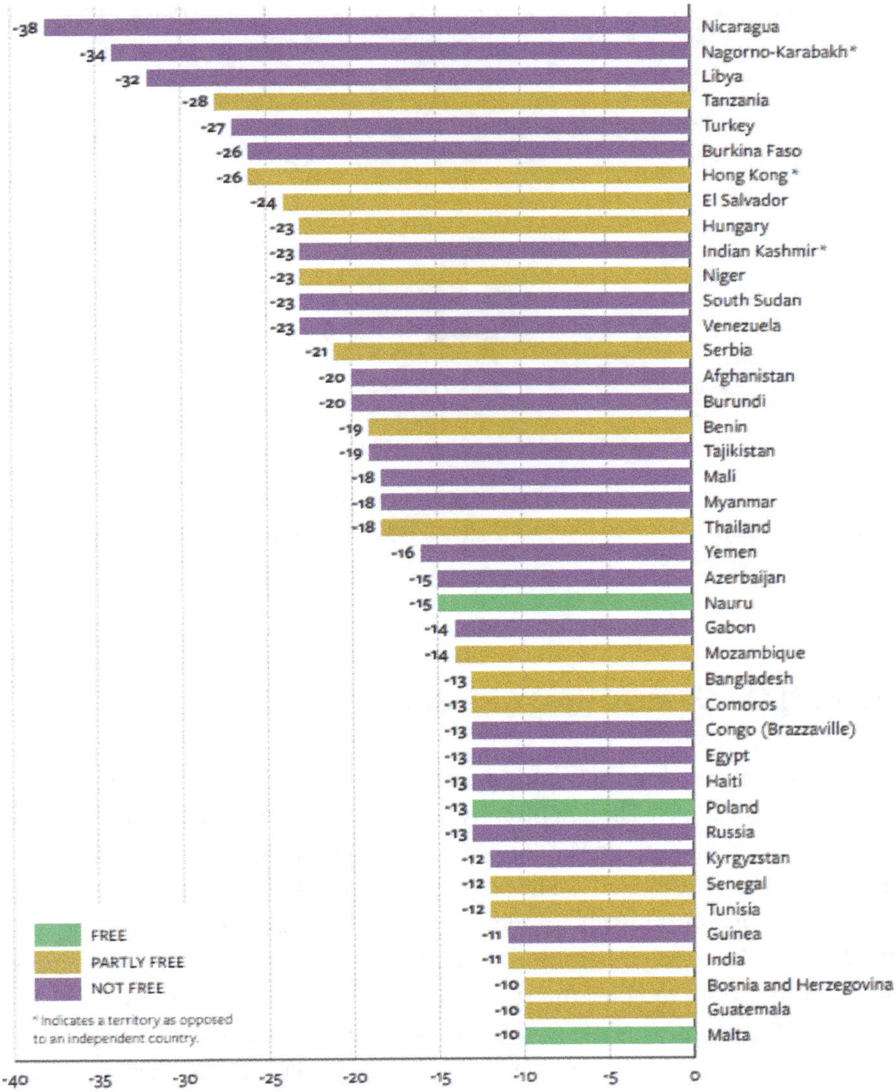

Source: Freedom House (2024), Retrieved from https://freedomhouse.org/sites/default/files/2024-02/FIW _2024_DigitalBooklet.pdf.

The BTI Transformation Index finds that in 2006 the total number of democracies in the world was 66, out of which only 20 were in consolidation, 41 defective and 5 highly defective. In contrast, autocracies accounted for 53 countries, 34 hardline and 19 moderate. Tracking back democracies in 2000, the Freedom House (2001, p. 7) report shows that 120 countries had practiced democracy. However, from 2016 to 2024 the number of autocracies dramatically increased, as 74 authoritarian regimes exceed 63 democracies (BTI Transformation Index, 2024) *[Figure 4]*.

Figure 4. Decline of Democracy and Rise of Autocracy in the World (2006-2024)

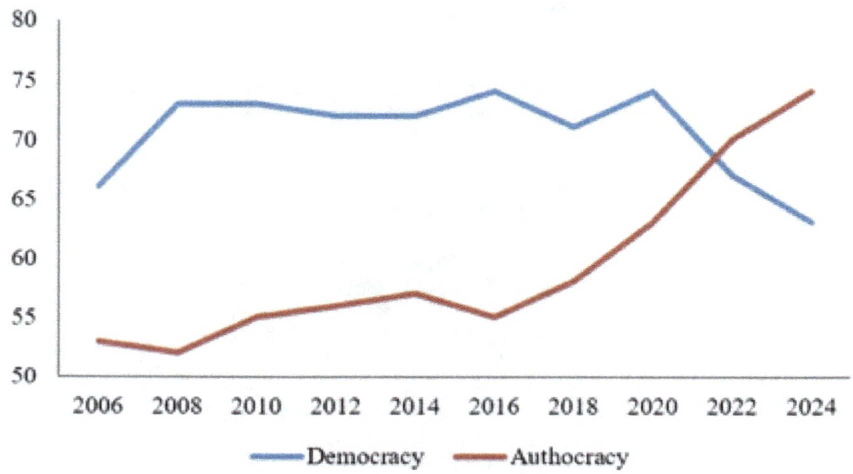

Source: Compiled from BTI Transformation Index (2024) Retrieved from https://atlas.bti-project.org/.

EROSION OF DEMOCRACY FROM WITHIN

The primary factor for American decline in terms of ideology roots in its domestic political configurations. Though literally, the U.S. is commonly considered a liberal democracy, in practice the basic foundations of democracy have tended to be undermined as it has started to lose its popularity. The critics of American democracy point to the constitution itself. In the words of Mike Lee (2020), a senior senator in the Senate, the U.S. constitution is not democratic rather it is a constitutional republic. The former denotes the rule of mob, while the later simply refers to the rule of law. Democracy in its original meaning which was used in ancient Rome refers to a political system in which people directly enacted laws. On the contrary, the republican system excludes people's direct participation in public decision-making processes (Darash, 2021, pp. 804-806). While the U.S. Constitution is one of the oldest in the world, it is considered outdated (Pears, 2021, p. 3) despite the incorporation of 27 amendments over time.

Critics highlight legal concerns within the three branches of the government. Contrary to the concept of democracy, the president is not appointed directly by the people, nor is the rule of majority ensured (Dobski, 2020). The Electoral College (EC) system has given rise to many debates in the last two decades. Due to the fault of this system, American people were ruled twice by those who could not obtain the absolute majority i.e. George W. Bush in 2000 and Donald Trump in 2016 (The American Presidency Project, 2016). This pattern has influenced public sentiment as well. According to Pew Research Center (2023), more Americans support direct presidential elections than those in favor of maintaining the current election system. Figure 5 illustrates a growing public preference for constitutional change, including an increasing number of Republicans endorsing this shift.

Figure 5. Public Opinion Supporting Amendment of Electoral System (Percentage)

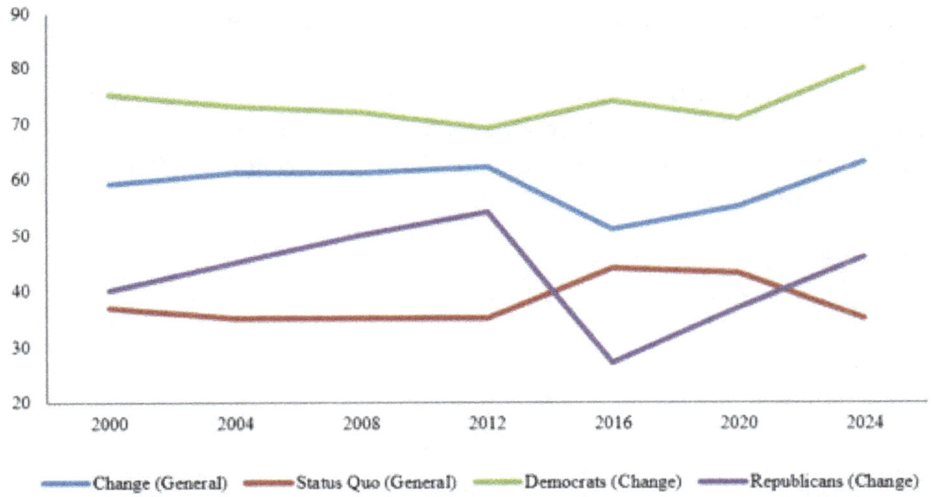

Source: Compiled from Pew Research Center (2023) Retrieved from https://www.pewresearch.org/short-reads/2024/09/25/majority-of-americans-continue-to-favor-moving-away-from-electoral-college/sr_24-09-25_electoralcollege_2/.

With respect to the U.S. legislative system, it could be argued that justice is compromised in favour of equality. For example, Article 1 of the Constitution grants each state two Senate seats regardless of population, indicating that a state's population density does not influence its decision-making process (From, 2022). This stipulation which was originally based on the biased calculations of founding fathers had to be amended after abolishment of slavery and the gradual legislative reforms to eradicate racial segregation. Nonetheless, despite legal reforms and population increase in the country, the clause remains intact.

The judiciary system of the U.S. is also subject to criticism. Constitutionally, the judges of the Supreme Court are appointed by the president with the approval of the simple majority of the senate for a lifetime. This procedure reflects a paradox as the incumbent president always nominates those who lean to his party (Zeitz, 2022). The problem gets complicated when the judges become subject to the approval of the Senate; the body itself is criticized for being undemocratic. In the words of Jill Filipovic (2022), the U.S. Supreme Court has become an 'illegitimate institution' that functions as a tool of 'minority rule over the majority.' This undemocratic nature is not only limited to the structural procedure of the Supreme Court, but it also extends to its function. Since 2005, dominated by conservative judges, the Supreme Court's national verdicts concerning civil and political rights of the citizens have contributed to the resurgence of some of the historic notorious anti-democratic laws. With respect to the right to vote, the court's 13 decisions have paved the way for the subsequent systematic racial segregation (CLC, 2022). These decisions were added by the June 2022 Supreme Court's verdict that was intended to suppress the right to abortion. Consequently, the undemocratic decisions of the Supreme Court have resulted in tremendous resentment among the American public. According to the latest Gallup (2023) report, confidence in the Supreme Court has observed a decline over the last two decades, dropping from 75 percent in 2000 to 49 percent in 2023 *[Figure 6]*.

Figure 6. Decline of People's Confidence in Supreme Court (Percentage)

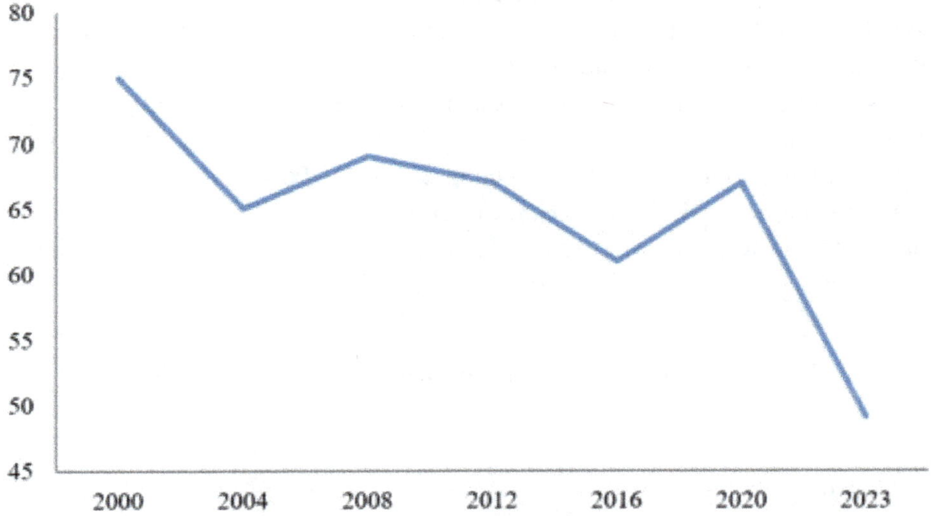

Source: Compiled from Gallup (2023) Retrieved from https://news.gallup.com/poll/511820/views-supreme-court-remain-near-record-lows.aspx.

Moreover, the report shows that only 17 percent of Americans believe that the Supreme Court is too liberal. On the other hand, the numbers of those who view the Court as too conservative rises to 39 percent while those who believe it's about right remains 42 percent *[Figure 7]*.

Figure 7. Americans' Perception of the Ideological Stance of the Supreme Court

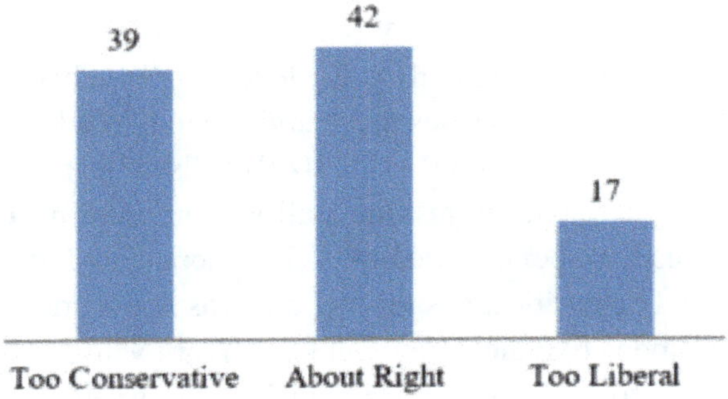

Source: Compiled from Gallup (2023) Retrieved from https://news.gallup.com/poll/511820/views-supreme-court-remain-near-record-lows.aspx.

Polarization is another major issue that has undermined American democracy at home (McCoy et al., 2018, p. 28). The practices of the two mainstream parties show that the U.S. is currently experiencing its highest level of polarization in over 150 years. The very immediate effect of this lack of consensus has been gridlock in passing bills of great importance especially those related to norms and values. The latest data issued by the GovTrack (2022) shows a tremendous decline in the number of legislations enacted by the congress since 2000.

A comparative analysis of the U.S. Congress reveals that when divided between Democrats and Republicans, the legislative process tends to slow down, causing government shutdowns and polarization *[Figure 8]*.

Figure 8. Decline of Congress's Legislative Productivity (1990-2020)

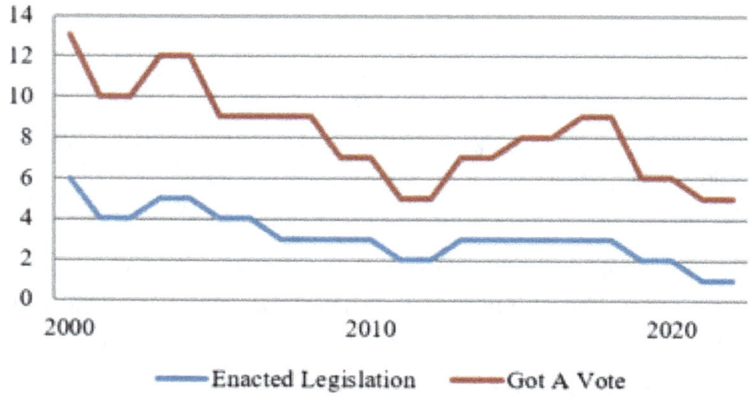

Source: Compiled from GovTrack (2022) Retrieved from https://www.govtrack.us/congress/bills/statistics.

Hence, domestically the bipartisan system in the U.S. has been disadvantageous for the legislative process (Campbell & College, 2019). This bipartisan system limits citizen choices, as other parties are marginalized. While democracy allows for some level of inequality as John Rawls (2009) calls it 'just inequality', the U.S. has been experiencing a rise in 'unjust inequality,' both in terms of legislative differences among states and social inequalities. The increasing legislative inequality, combined with social disparities, has raised concerns about societal fragility, similar to historical episodes like the American Civil War (Marche, 2022; Levitsky & Ziblatt, 2018). Normative issues such as abortion, the freedom to buy and carry arms, LGBT rights, immigration, and voting procedures further contribute to the divide (Harb, 2022). The implementation of laws in the U.S. legal system is seen as unequal and undemocratic, exemplified by varying abortion laws in different states and the enactment of laws making it harder for Americans to vote in many states.

Another fundamental issue undermining the U.S. from within is the emergence of plutocracy, where the interests of affluent corporations take precedence over those of the people. This shift was exemplified by the 2010 Supreme Court decision in Citizens United, which relaxed restrictions on financial support for presidential and congressional candidates. Despite laws prohibiting direct funding to candidates, the practice of lobbying has circumvented these regulations, enabling business corporations and economic elites to exert significant influence on American public policy through financial support and candidate backing. This crisis is so serious that in some cases the lobbies write the text of the laws themselves (O'Dell & Penzenstadler, 2019), let alone foreign funds channeled to candidates. This has led to a devaluation of public opinion in the decision-making process (Formisano, 2015, pp. 152-153).

Consequently, the foregoing issues have created a gap between the nation and the government and weakened the national trust in democracy. Several studies from prominent research centers label democracy in the U.S. as unstable. The Economist Intelligence Unit (EIU) reports that the U.S. has been demoted from a full democracy to a flawed democracy after 2016. In 2006, the U.S. was the 17th democracy in the world, while in 2023, it descended to 29th (Our World in Data, 2023).

The study of the EIU on the status of democracy in the U.S., which is compiled by Our World in Data reveals a dramatic decline of democracy in this country since 2006. The main index which includes freedom of choice, civil liberties, preference of democracy as an ideal political system, political participation and functional government has fallen from 8.22/10 in 2006 to 7.85/10 in 2023. The study also shows that the public has lost confidence in democracy as a preferred political system. This issue which is translated into democratic culture has been downgraded from 8.75/10 in 2006 to 6.25/10 in 2023 (Our World in Data, 2023) *[Figure 9]*.

Figure 9. Decline of Democracy in the US (2006-2023)

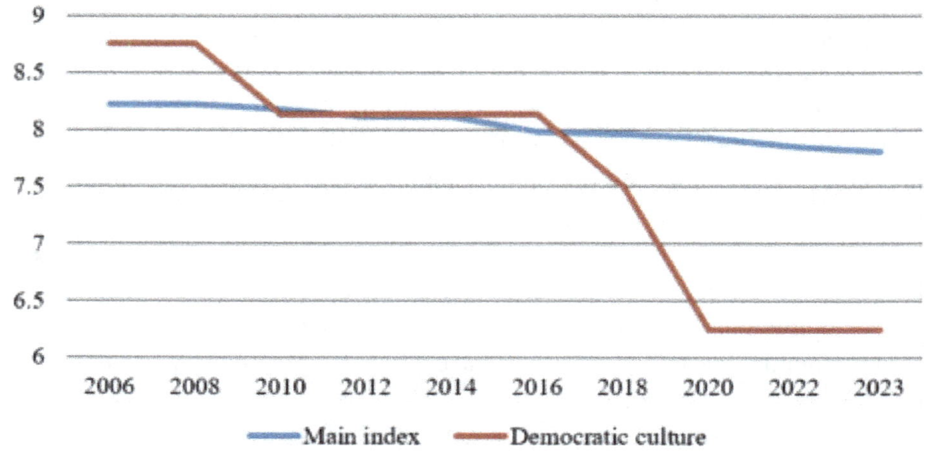

Source: Compiled from Our World in Data (2023) Retrieved from https://ourworldindata.org/democracy.

SHIFTING PRIORITIES IN FOREIGN POLICY: DEMOCRACY TAKES A BACKSEAT

The hegemon is disqualified when it refrains from undertaking the lead (Kindleberger, 1973). During the Cold War, the U.S. behavior fluctuated between pursuing strategic interests and advocating for values. At the dawn of the 21st century, the Bush Doctrine explicitly merged American values with strategic interests. In both theory and action, Bush embarked upon different initiatives to infuse democracy into the international system, either by persuasion or coercion. In the post 9/11, the White House believed that lack of democracy in most parts of Asia and the Middle East had led to Islamic radicalization. Thus, democratization was translated into de-radicalization. In order to de-radicalize the world, any aggressive act in the name of pre-emptive attack would be justified as was marked by invasion of Afghanistan and Iraq. However, this strategy backfired in a sense that - for the purpose of its realization - the U.S. had to abandon its decade-long democratic claims elsewhere. As a result, the U.S. criticism of the human rights conditions in Chechnya, Uzbekistan and the 1999 military coup in Pakistan was softened largely due to strategic interests (deRaismes Combes & Andrew L. Peek, 2021, p. 407). Heading towards both military domination and democratic promotion in the world, the U.S. also attacked Iraq and simultaneously advocated Color Revolutions in Eurasia.

But it was not until Barack Obama's administration that the U.S. foreign policy considerably abandoned its value orientations and switched towards strategic gains. As such, the word 'democracy' was also omitted from his administration's discourses as was the case with his inauguration speech and his Secretary of State, Hillary Clinton's address to the Congress (Poppe, 2020, p. 37). This was also evident in Obama's speech at Cairo University when he declared in an apologizing tone that 'No system of government can or should be imposed by one nation by any other' (The White House, 2009). Under Obama, the U.S. also abandoned ideological considerations when it inked the Joint Comprehensive Plan of Action (JCPoA) with Iran for strategic purposes and lifted some of its sanctions against the country. On the other hand, contrary to its Foreign Assistance Act, the U.S. resumed its military assistance to Egypt following the 2013 military coup that unlawfully toppled the democratic-elected government of Mohammad Morsi (Reuters, 2015). The U.S. democracy project was also overshadowed when the Obama administration chose to divert its focus from toppling the totalitarian regime in Syria to fighting ISIS. Gramsci's outcome-focused analysis suggests that the U.S. democracy initiative faltered during Obama's tenure, a period marked by the strengthening and expansion of non-state actors like the Taliban and ISIS.

The apex of the U.S. departure from its democracy project was marked under Donald Trump first administration. Indeed, he was not only committed to the mission and his actions at the national and international level also eroded democracy from within. Before assuming the presidency, he had already made it clear that the U.S. would no longer be the one who tried to spread values that were projected to be universal, but they were not (CNI, 2016). In his inaugural address in January 2017, he declared, "We do not seek to impose our way of life on anyone, but rather to let it shine as an example. We will shine for everyone to follow" (The White House, 2017). Similarly, in his speech at the United Nations General Assembly (UNGA) in September 2017, he reiterated, "We do not expect diverse countries to share the same cultures, traditions, or even systems of government...Let diverse countries with different values, different cultures, and different dreams not just coexist, but work side by side on the basis of mutual respect" (U.S. Department of State, 2017). The Trump National Security Strategy (NSS) which was published in December 2017 also implicitly affirmed the U.S. departure from its democracy promotion mission. Domestically, under his vocal approaches and systematic policies imbalance prevailed in the three branches of government and the rift between the states and the federal government began to widen (McCarthy, 2020).

Despite not abandoning bilateral relations in his foreign policy, Trump's focus remained on securing American strategic interests globally, often prioritizing them over the promotion of democracy. That is, his strategic engagement with authoritarian regimes compromised the U.S. democracy project (Kurlantzick, 2018). Certainly, withdrawal from JCPoA was not due to his inconvenience with the authoritarian regime in Tehran nor his protectionist policies against China targeted the totalitarian throne in Beijing. With regard to the former he unveiled, "We are not looking for regime change" (Washington Post, 2019) and with respect to the latter he rectified his normative antagonistic stance on 'One China Policy' (The White House, 2017).

The Doha Agreement of 2020 with the Taliban was also a setback in a sense that it emboldened the organization on the international level. The language and terms of the agreement favored the Taliban whereby they were encouraged to bypass the long-standing American-backed government in Kabul in the subsequent intra-Afghan peace negotiations. In the words of McMaster, Trump's national security advisor, the U.S. deal with the Taliban was an appeasement policy that resembled the Munich Agreement of 1938 in Europe (Society, 2020). One can conclude that Trump's peace deal with the Taliban was nothing but a retreat from American grand strategy of democracy promotion. According to the U.S. government's Special Inspector General for Afghanistan Reconstruction (SIGAR), the U.S. has failed to achieve its goals of building a democratic government in Afghanistan (2022, p. 26). However, it was Joe Biden who hammered the last nail in the coffin of democracy project in Afghanistan by the catastrophic withdrawal of forces in mid-August 2021 (Hill, 2022).

Even though Biden himself was not committed to nation-building in Afghanistan as he reiterated on several occasions, he was vocal in supporting democracy promotion elsewhere. Traumatized by Trump's anti-democratic legacy, democracy became one of the top priorities of Biden's administration. His foreign policy apparatus, however, acknowledged that democracy was being undermined from both internal and external oppositional fronts. Thus, unlike his predecessors, Biden's vision of a democracy project in the world did not follow the foregoing approaches that were mostly offensive in essence. Rather, he adopted a defensive position to protect democracy from domestic wrongdoers and rectify it abroad. As such, an initiative entitled Summit for Democracy was designed and hosted by the White House in 2021 and 2022 to defend democracy both at home and around the world. The defensive position of the U.S. in democracy project was revealed further in its NSS published in October 2022. According to the document, democracy remained America's top commitment in international relations. However, the approach would not be 'democracy promotion' but 'democratic resilience' (Wong, 2022). This democratic setback is also best seen in his regional strategies. The 2022 NSS evaded democracy in the world's most autocratic regions i.e. Middle East and Central Asia wherein the U.S. has predominantly been a critic of totalitarian regimes. The U.S. defensive retreat from democracy promotion was further unveiled when Biden's

Secretary of State Antony Blinken during his visit to Africa said that the U.S. did not want "an imbalanced or transactional relationship" (U.S. Department of State, 2022).

On the ground, too, the U.S. international behavior under Biden considerably contradicted his promises regarding democracy. During his presidency, his strategic calculations overrode U.S. long-standing value-oriented approaches. With respect to Afghanistan, the U.S. could justify its withdrawal only if the relative democratic achievements of the two-decades long were preserved. The benign hand-over of the country to the Taliban was a redo of a totalitarian regime in the region that is ripe to encourage authoritarian neighborhoods. Biden also trampled his promise on making Saudi Arabia a Pariah over American journalist Jamal Khashogji's murder, as Mohammed Bin Salman was given immunity over the case which is an evident compromise of values for strategic interests (Knickmeyer, 2022).

Trump's return to the White House in January 2025 is a continuation of his earlier agenda, as he seeks to complete his unfinished work and even expand its scope in his second term. His populist and xenophobic vision directly challenges the fundamental principles of democracy, both domestically and globally. Emphasizing the America First and MAGA policies, he swiftly halted billions of dollars in USAID funding, whose major portion went to democratic projects across the globe (The White House, 2025). As time progresses, his administration adopts increasingly isolationist policies, distancing itself from the promotion of democracy.

UNDERMINING CREDIBILITY: UNILATERAL MOVES ON THE GLOBAL STAGE

The U.S. ideological legitimacy has also been questioned to a great extent by some of its illegal practices in the last two decades. Towards the end of 1990s, the symptoms of the U.S. unilateralist international acts were observed after the U.S.-led NATO intervened in the Kosovo War. On the one hand, the intervention lacked any legal basis, on the other; it intensified humanitarian crisis in the region (Mandelbaum, 1999, p. 6). Nonetheless, the U.S. global strategic shift in the aftermath of 9/11 attacks can be regarded as a backsliding landmark of its hegemonic legitimacy in the world. Since then, the U.S. democracy project – albeit with strategic goals - was conducted by more coercive actions as it simultaneously engaged in two devastating wars i.e. Afghanistan and Iraq (Akbarzadeh, 2013, p. 3). While the U.S. attack on Afghanistan was unanimously approved by all members of the UNSC, its invasion of Iraq had little to do with legality.

The unilateral actions of the U.S. pose questions about its approach; while it encourages others to follow international law, it often does not adhere to the rules established under its own leadership. For example, the U.S. has been accusing China of violating the United Nations Convention on the Law of the Sea (UNCLOS), while itself is not signatory to the treaty (UN, 2022). The same is the case with multiple international treaties related to human rights. Furthermore, in the last twenty years the U.S. also withdrew from many key international treaties which further undermined its commitments to the common interests of the international community *[Table 1]*.

Table 1. Withdrawal of US from International Institutions

President	Year	Name	Type
Bill Clinton	1995	Pan-American Railway Congress Association	International Organization
	1995	World Tourism Organization	International Organization
	1996	United Nations Industrial Development Organization	International Organization
George W. Bush	2002	1972 Anti-Ballistic Missile Treaty	Treaty
	2005	Optional Protocol of Vienna Convention on Consular Relations	Treaty
Donald Trump	2017	Paris Agreement	Executive Agreement
	2017	Global Compact for Safe, Orderly and Regular Migration	UN Process
	2018	Global Compact on Refugees	UN Process
	2018	UN Relief and Works Agency	UN Humanitarian Agency
	2018	Joint Comprehensive Plan of Action	Political Commitment
	2018	United Nations Human Rights Council	International Organization
	2018	Universal Postal Union	International Organization
	2018	Treaty of Amity with Iran	Treaty
	2018	Optional Protocol of the Vienna Convention on Diplomatic Relations	Treaty
	2018	UNESCO	International Organization
	2019	1987 Intermediate Range Nuclear Forces (INF)	Treaty
	2020	World Health Organization	International Organization
	2020	Treaty on Open Skies	Treaty

Source: (Cooley & Nexon 2020; Hathaway 2020).

As a result, the UN, which was primarily shaped by the U.S. ideological leadership, observes erosion of its credibility in crucial issues concerning global peace and security. Instead of having a pluralistic approach to various international common threats, the U.S. unilaterally embarked upon devastating ventures i.e. the 2003 invasion of Iraq and 2013 military intervention in Syria. This process has led to the emergence of parallel political and military organizations whose founders and members were frustrated from the dysfunction of the UN (Akram, 2021, pp. 46-47). For example, the Shanghai Cooperation Organization (SCO) was established by Russia and China partly as a response to NATO (Wivel & Paul 2019, p. 95).

On the other hand, the pattern of U.S. votes in the UN has also given rise to the speculation about the legitimacy of U.S. democracy. Among many instances, its biased votes related to fundamental values such as democracy and human rights are worth mentioning. This is the case with its negative votes on resolutions on the Palestine-Israel crisis. In 2012 it voted against the resolution 67/19 of the UNGA that was proposed to upgrade the status of Palestine to a non-member observer state in the organization (UN, 2012). Surprisingly, since 2005 the U.S. has also been voting against the UNGA resolutions on the combat against racism and other forms of discrimination (Zuesse 2022). Most notably, its positive vote for the glorification of Nazism has raised serious questions on its commitment to basic tenets of democracy.

Thus, the U.S. incremental unilateral pattern of behavior in the last two decades was perceived by other states as compromising their sovereignty in the international community. As a matter of fact, the U.S. unilateralism changed the hegemonic nature of the international system by departing from setting common goals and ignoring common interests. As a result of this trend, the commitment to liberal multilateralism downgraded as states tended to recklessly embark upon military interventions, ignoring the UNSC authorization. This is truly the case with Russia's intervention in Georgia, Ukraine and Syria that was invoked by the U.S. unilateralism (Ziegler, 2021, pp. 12-13).

CONCLUSION

In examining the fragile state of American ideological hegemony through a neo-Gramscian lens, the study has unveiled a series of critical findings. Neo-Gramscianism highlights the normative dimension in understanding the rise and fall of hegemony, emphasizing the pivotal role of ideology. It is the ideology that enables a state to exert dominance by infusing its values and attracting others to its principles, while any weakening of the ideology corresponds to a decline in hegemony. The key measurements of neo-Gramscianism in examining the fall of ideological hegemony include the alignment of the hegemon's actions with its professed ideology on the global stage, the means through which ideology is disseminated (whether through consent or coercion), the outcomes of the ideology in terms of integration versus division among its audience and the commitment to engaging in ideological interactions with other states.

The core ideology of American democracy has faced challenges both domestically and globally, contributing to a decline in global democracy landscape. Domestically, constitutional paradoxes, including the Electoral College system and imbalances in the legislative and judiciary branches, have eroded democratic ideals. Intensifying political polarization and the growing influence of plutocracy are also factors contributing to the weakening of the ideology. Externally, the U.S. democracy promotion agenda suffered setbacks, particularly as it shifted towards strategic interests after 9/11. This shift, coupled with reduced emphasis during the Obama and Trump administrations, further diminished its global effectiveness. The Biden administration's current focus appears more on defending democracy than actively promoting it. Furthermore, the U.S. unilateral behaviors in the last two decades have also undermined its ideological hegemony.

In a nutshell, these factors have collectively contributed to the decline of the U.S.' global ideological hegemony with democracy as its centerpiece. The immediate implication of this decline for the world is the rise of authoritarianism, the weakening of the liberal international order initially established by the U.S., and a decline in the U.S.'s global competence. To address these challenges, the U.S. is limited to acknowledge shortcomings, re-evaluating its stance in the world.

REFERENCES

Akbarzadeh, S. (2013). *American democracy promotion in the changing Middle East: From Bush to Obama*. Routledge.

Akram, S. (2021). Case of U.S. unilateralism at the UN. *Strategic Studies, 41*(1), 41–52. https://www.jstor.org/stable/48732267

Althusser, L. (2020). *On ideology*. Verso Books.

Campbell, J. A. (2019). Political gridlock: The ongoing threat to American democracy. *Gettysburg Social Sciences Review, 3*(2), 1–38. https://cupola.gettysburg.edu/gssr/vol3/iss2/2/, accessed on May 15, 2025.

Combes, D., & Peek, A. L. (2021). Paved with good intentions: U.S. foreign policy after 9/11. In Reeder, T. (Ed.), *The Routledge history of U.S. foreign relations* (pp. 406–421). Taylor & Francis. DOI: 10.4324/9781003034889-36

Cooley, A., & Nexon, D. (2020). *Exit from hegemony: The unraveling of the American global order*. Oxford University Press. DOI: 10.1093/oso/9780190916473.001.0001

Cox, R. W. (1987). *Production, power, and world order: Social forces in the making of history*. Columbia University Press.

Cox, R. W., & Sinclair, T. J. (1996). *Approaches to world order*. Cambridge University Press. DOI: 10.1017/CBO9780511607905

Darash, J. (2021). *Government by consent*. Dorrance Publishing.

Dobski, B. (2020). *America is a republic, not a democracy*. The Heritage Foundation.

Filipovic, J. (2022, June 25). It's time to say it: The US Supreme Court has become an illegitimate institution. *The Guardian*. https://www.theguardian.com/commentisfree/2022/jun/25/us-supreme-court-illegitimate-institution, accessed on February 23, 2025.

Formisano, R. P. (2015). *Plutocracy in America: How increasing inequality destroys the middle class and exploits the poor*. Johns Hopkins University Press. DOI: 10.1353/book.49476

Freedom House. (2023). *Freedom in the world 2023*. https://freedomhouse.org/sites/default/files/2023-3/FIW_World_2023_DigtalPDF.pdf, accessed on February 19, 2025.

From, A. (2022, July 6). The challenge to democracy: Overcoming the small state bias. *Brookings Institution.* https://www.brookings.edu/blog/fixgov/2022/07/06/the-challenge-to-democracy-overcoming-the-small-state-bias/, accessed on June 26, 2025.

Fukuyama, F. (1992). *The end of history and the last man*. Free Press.

Fukuyama, F., & McFaul, M. (2007). Should democracy be promoted or demoted? *The Washington Quarterly, 31*(1), 23–45. https://muse.jhu.edu/article/224702. DOI: 10.1162/wash.2007.31.1.23

GovTrack. (2022). *Statistics and historical comparison.* (December 9, 2024). https://www.govtrack.us/congress/bills/statistics, accessed on May 28, 2025.

Gramsci, A. (1971). *Selections from the prison notebooks of Antonio Gramsci* (Q. Hoare & G. Nowell-Smith, Trans.; 5th ed.). Lawrence and Wishart.

Gramsci, A. (1991). *Gramsci's political thought: An introduction* (Simon, R., Ed.; Rev. ed.). Lawrence and Wishart.

Harb, A. (2022, October 31). US midterm elections: What are the key issues? *Al Jazeera.* https://www.aljazeera.com/news/2022/10/31/us-midterm-elections-what-are-the-key-issues- 2, accessed on March 19, 2025.

Hathaway, O. A. (2020, January 23). Reengaging on treaties and other international agreements (Part I): President Donald Trump's rejection of international law. *Just Security.* https://www.justsecurity.org/72656/reengaging-on-treaties-and-other-international- agreements-part-i-president-donald-trumps-rejection-of-international-law/, accessed on June 17, 2025.

Heywood, A. (2012). *Political ideologies: An introduction* (5th ed.). Palgrave Macmillan. DOI: 10.1007/978-0-230-36994-8

Hill, M. A. (2022). *The rise and fall of democracy promotion in US foreign policy: From Carter to Biden*. Routledge. DOI: 10.4324/9781003254799

Ikenberry, G. J., & Kupchan, C. A. (1990). Socialization and hegemonic power. *International Organization, 44*(3), 283–315. https://www.jstor.org/stable/2706778. DOI: 10.1017/S002081830003530X

Kindleberger, C. P. (1973). *The world in depression, 1929–1939*. University of California Press.

Knickmeyer, E., & Lee, M. (2022, November 13). US moves to shield Saudi crown prince in journalist killing. *Associated Press.* https://apnews.com/article/biden-business-lawsuits-journalists-jamal-khashoggi-49f3e4ce88aa21bf2ba603dcbb32277f, accessed on May 3, 2025.

Kurlantzick, J. (2018, January 23). Trump has abandoned democracy promotion. Which countries could fill the void? *World Politics Review.* https://www.worldpoliticsreview.com/trump-has-abandoned-democracy-promotion-which-countries-could-fill-the-void/, accessed on February 9, 2025.

Lee, M. (2020, October 17). Of course we're not a democracy. https://www.lee.senate.gov/2020/10/of-course-we-re-not-a-democracy, accessed on April 4, 2025.

Mandelbaum, M. (1999). A perfect failure: NATO's war against Yugoslavia. *Foreign Affairs*, *78*(5), 2–8. https://www.jstor.org/stable/20049444. DOI: 10.2307/20049444

Marche, S. (2022, January 16). The next civil war: Dispatches from the American future. *The Guardian.* https://www.theguardian.com/world/2022/jan/04/next-us-civil-war-already-here- we-refuse-to-see-it, accessed on May 8, 2025.

McCarthy, T. (2020, April 11). Trump v the states: How the president is remaking the government in his image. *The Guardian.* https://www.theguardian.com/us-news/2020/apr/11/trump- states-governors-clashes, accessed on June 2, 2025.

McCoy, J., Rahman, T., & Somer, M. (2018). Polarization and the global crisis of democracy: Common patterns, dynamics, and pernicious consequences for democratic polities. *The American Behavioral Scientist*, *62*(1), 16–42. DOI: 10.1177/0002764218759576

Mearsheimer, J. J. (2019). Bound to fail: The rise and fall of the liberal. *International Security*, *43*(4), 7–50. DOI: 10.1162/isec_a_00342

O'Dell, R., & Penzenstadler, N. (2019, February 3). You elected them to write new laws. They're letting corporations do it instead. *USA Today.* https://www.usatoday.com/in- depth/news/investigations/2019/04/03/abortion-gun-laws-stand-your-ground-model-bills- conservatives-liberal-corporate-influence-lobbyists/3162173002/, accessed on March 5, 2025.

Our World in Data. (2023, November 7). *Democracy.* https://ourworldindata.org/democracy

Our World in Data. (2023, November 7). *Democracy index.* https://ourworldindata.org/grapher/democracy-index-eiu?tab=table&country=~USA, accessed on May 7, 2025.

Pears, E. (2021). *Cords of affection: Constructing constitutional union in early American history*. University Press of Kansas.

Peimani, H. (2009). *Conflict and security in Central Asia and the Caucasus*. ABC-CLIO. DOI: 10.5040/9798400630309

Pew Research Center. (2023, September 25). Majority of Americans continue to favor moving away from electoral college. https://www.pewresearch.org/short-reads/2023/09/25/majority-of-americans-continue-to-favor-moving-away-from-electoral-college/sr23-09-25electoral-college1/, accessed on April 3, 2025.

Poppe, A. E. (2020). *US democracy promotion after the Cold War: Stability, basic premises, and policy toward Egypt*. Routledge.

Rapkin, D. P., & Braaten, D. (2009). Conceptualising hegemonic legitimacy. *Review of International Studies, 35*(1), 113–149. https://www.jstor.org/stable/20542767. DOI: 10.1017/S0260210509008353

Rawls, J. (2009). *A theory of justice* (Rev. ed.). Harvard University Press.

Reuters. (2015, April 1). Obama ends freeze on U.S. military aid to Egypt. *Reuters*. https://www.reuters.com/article/us-usa-egypt-military-idUSKBN0MR2GR20150401, accessed on June 15, 2025.

Rosecrance, R. N., & Stein, A. A. (1993). *The domestic bases of grand strategy* (Illustrated ed.). Cornell University Press.

SIGAR. (2022). *Why the Afghan government collapsed*. SIGAR.

The American Presidency Project. (2016). https://www.presidency.ucsb.edu/statistics/elections, accessed on March 6, 2025.

The White House. (2009, June 4). Remarks by the president at Cairo University. https://obamawhitehouse.archives.gov/the-press-office/remarks-president-cairo-university- 6-04-09, accessed on May 12, 2025.

The White House. (2017). Readout of the president's call with President Xi Jinping of China. https://trumpwhitehouse.archives.gov/briefings-statements/readout-presidents-call- president-xi-jinping-china, accessed on June 6, 2025.

The White House. (2017). The inaugural address. https://trumpwhitehouse.archives.gov/briefings- statements/the-inaugural-address, accessed on May 6, 2025.

The White House. (2025, January). Reevaluating and realigning United States foreign aid. https://www.whitehouse.gov/presidential-actions/2025/01/reevaluating-and-realigning- united-states-foreign-aid, accessed on March 7, 2025.

U.S. Department of State. (2005). *U.S. government assistance to and cooperative activities with Eurasia.* https://2009-2017.state.gov/p/eur/rls/rpt/55787.htm, accessed on June 22, 2025.

U.S. Department of State. (2017). *President Donald Trump addresses the 72nd session of the United Nations General Assembly*. YouTube. https://www.youtube.com/watch?v=AyttM9EnObc, accessed on June 21, 2025.

U.S. Department of State. (2021, August). *Foreign assistance fact sheet.* https://www.state.gov/wp-content/uploads/2021/08/Georgia_FY-2020-Country-Assistance-Fact-Sheet_8-26-2021_Accessible.pdf, accessed on May 15, 2025.

U.S. Department of State. (2022). *U.S. Secretary Antony J. Blinken and South African Minister of International Relations and Cooperation Naledi Pandor at a joint press availability.* https://www.state.gov/secretary-antony-j-blinken-and-south-african-minister-of-international-relations-and-cooperation-naledi-pandor-at-a-joint-press-availability/, accessed on February 7, 2025.

Waltz, K. N. (1979). *Theory of international politics.* Addison-Wesley Publishing Company.

Washington Post. (2019, December 27). Trump on Iran: 'We're not looking for regime change'. YouTube. https://www.youtube.com/watch?v=Otb7HYa-7jo, accessed on May 20, 2025.

Wivel, A., & Paul, T. V. (2019). *International institutions and power politics: Bridging the divide*. Georgetown University Press. DOI: 10.2307/j.ctvrnfqgk

Wong, E. (2022, September 6). Biden puts defense of democracy at center of agenda, at home and abroad. *The New York Times.* https://www.nytimes.com/2022/09/06/us/politics/biden-democracy-threat.html, accessed on May 28, 2025.

Zeitz, J. (2022, April 3). The Supreme Court has never been apolitical. *Politico.* https://www.politico.com/news/magazine/2022/04/03/the-supreme-court-has-never-been-apolitical-00022482, accessed on March 14, 2025.

Ziblatt, D., & Levitsky, S. (2018). *How democracies die* (Illustrated ed.). Crown.

Ziegler, C. E. (2021). A crisis of diverging perspectives: U.S.-Russian relations and the security dilemma. *Texas National Security Review, 4*(1), 11–33. http://dx.doi.org/DOI: 10.26153/tsw/11708

Zuesse, E. (2022, November 14). Why does the U.S. government support Nazis all around the world? *Counter Currents.* https://countercurrents.org/2022/11/why-does-the-u-s-government-support-nazis-all-around-the-world/, accessed on June 2, 2025.

KEY TERMS AND DEFINITIONS

Democracy: A system of government in which power originates from the people, who have the right to participate in decision-making.

Hegemony: The dominant influence of one state over others, often cultural or social, which is maintained by consent.

Ideology: A set of beliefs and values that shape the attitudes and behaviors of states and other actors.

Legitimacy: The acceptance by society of a power or government as rightful and just.

Neo-Gramscianism: This theory draws upon Antonio Gramsci's ideas about the relations between culture and power. Robert Cox, applying this theory to the international level, highlights the concepts of consent and legitimacy as essential for the realization of international hegemony.

Norm: Rules or standards of behavior expected in the international society, constituting one of the sources of power.

Chapter 10
International System and West's Approach Through NATO

Cihan Günyel
https://orcid.org/0000-0002-4431-8972
Rumeli University, Turkey

ABSTRACT

NATO was established as the defense organization of the Western Bloc during the Cold War. During the Cold War period, it became functional for the political integration of the Western Bloc more than being a defense organization. The concept of the West has become synonymous with NATO over time, and NATO has become a systemic actor in the international system. Moving from the European security architecture to regional cooperation, NATO started to take part as a global actor in the fight against a wide range of security threats in the international system. The steps taken by NATO after the Cold War show that it has an understanding that demonstrates the Western approach to the system rather than a defense organization. In this direction, the chapter examines NATO's strategic, geostrategic, regional and global policies in the international system and discusses NATO's place and role in the international system and its impact on the system. As the defence organisation of the Western alliance, NATO can be said to have acted as an actor in the international system through its policies and actions in the post-Cold War era. For this reason, the study has examined NATO's policies and actions in the international system using neorealism and world systems analysis theories, which treat the system as a unit at the level of analysis, and has endeavoured to analyse them on this basis.

DOI: 10.4018/979-8-3373-2342-8.ch010

INTRODUCTION

NATO was established in 1949 at the beginning of the Cold War as the defense organization of the Western Bloc. Despite being a defense organization during the Cold War, its civilian organs gained an important position. NATO's political organs ensured that the member countries of the Alliance were organized within the framework of collective security and common political identity, and as a defense organization, it went beyond its deterrent military power capacity and became an organization that fulfilled the political function of the Western Bloc.

NATO, which accepted Turkey and Greece as members of the alliance in 1952 during the Cold War, accepted West Germany as a member in 1955 and Spain as a member in 1986. NATO, which undertook a military approach as a defense organization against the Eastern Bloc, namely the Union of Soviet Socialist Republics (USSR), during the Cold War, expanded its allied approach within the framework of the bipolar structure in the international system by including Western European states in the alliance with the expansions during this period.

With the collapse of the Eastern Bloc in 1991, the Cold War ended, and the Western Bloc became the leading actor in the international system under the leadership of the United States (USA). NATO made a significant contribution to the West's victory in this struggle with its defense and political identity. Within the unipolar system that emerged after the Cold War, NATO first initiated an expansion process to the former Eastern Bloc European states and aimed for a common European security architecture within the framework of the NATO and Western approach. In addition, NATO's acceptance of new members meant the expansion of the West. The expansion process of the West in the international system has been one of the reasons why the Russian Federation (Russia) launched a military operation in Ukraine, especially in 2022. The military operation launched by Russia in Ukraine evolved into war, and Europe began to experience the most devastating war after World War II. The Russia-Ukraine war has taken on a character that shapes the international system today. With the war, NATO and Russia began to define each other as "threats" and "enemies". The rise of the People's Republic of China (China) in the international system and its potential to become a new challenger to the West in the international system, especially in the Asia-Pacific region, has led NATO to take steps in the context of the Asia-Pacific Policy. China's military support to Russia in the Ukraine-Russia war has led NATO to adopt the approach that Atlantic-European security is linked to the Asia-Pacific region. China was recognized as a threat for the first time at the 2024 NATO Washington Summit. However, Iran and North Korea were also evaluated within the Russia-China axis. These four countries have found a place for themselves as threats to the international system in the NATO 2030 Strategic Concept, which determines the policies that NATO will form in the coming years. NATO has accepted strategic concepts after the Cold War and how NATO's role will be shaped within the international system has been revealed. In this direction, many approaches have been adopted, from conducting out-of-area military operations to regional cooperation. Particularly recently, the NATO 2030 Strategic Concept has served as a road map for how NATO's hegemonic role in the West will be today and in the future, as an important data.

1.THEORETICAL FRAMEWORK

NATO, established as a defence organisation during the Cold War era, has also become the most important form of organisation for the West in terms of identity and agency within the international system. During the Cold War, it became an ontological reality as a deterrent force in the West's victory. During the Cold War era and today, it has not only been a defence organisation but also the cornerstone of the collective identity of the West. Within the changing structure of the international system after the Cold War, it has adopted new strategies and implemented new approaches and actions in the West's global power struggle. NATO has realised its ability to act as an actor in the post-Cold War international system.

NATO's level of being an actor in the international system will be examined in the article within the framework of systems analysis in the context of neorealism and world systems theory. Both theories approach the international system as a level of analysis and formulate their assumptions and arguments by examining the system. Both theories explain the behaviour of actors by analysing their behaviour through the system.

Neorealism emerged as a new stage in the development of realism with Kenneth N. Waltz's work Theory of International Politics (Waltz, 1979). Waltz made the international system an analysable phenomenon and identified anarchy as its defining characteristic. He approached the international system in three dimensions: structure, equally sovereign rational actors, and the struggle for survival (Tuğtan, 2016: 122).

Waltz states that wars generally stem from the anarchic structure of the international system. He states that this is something we cannot see, unlike the actors within the structure of the international system. Waltz, who addresses the variable feature in the international system as the distribution of capabilities among actors, states that a change in the system will occur if the distribution of capabilities changes. He states that the fundamental characteristic of the structure is anarchy, and that it remains fixed unless one of the actors within it establishes a hierarchical order. He argues that the anarchy of the system is caused by the homogeneity of the states, which are the dominant actors in the system, and the distribution of capabilities (Waltz, 2015: 132-133).

Although actors within the system may have different political regimes, states exhibit similar behaviours and display similar patterns of behaviour in the power struggle arising from the system's own internal order and anarchic structure. Consequently, the international system influences the formation of states' patterns of behaviour (Ersoy, 2015: 174).

Another theory at the systemic level is Immanuel Wallerstein's world-systems analysis. Emerging from dependency theory, world-systems theory can also be described as the reflection of Lenin's analysis of imperialism in international relations theory.

Wallerstein places resource distribution at the centre of understanding the international system. He states that world history has gone through periods within the framework of resource distribution. He states that resources located in the periphery flow to the centre and that market distribution occurs through the centre. He claims that in today's modern world based on capitalism, the centre is Europe-the West, and resources flow to the centre from the colonies-the periphery. It states that the centre's possession of resources determines market conditions, with the centre enjoying high levels of power and prosperity, while the periphery lags behind due to exploitation. It states that the centre acquires raw materials from the periphery at low prices and then sells processed products back to the periphery at high prices, and that within this hierarchy, the periphery, lacking technology and means of production, is dependent on the centre.(Wallerstein,2014:99-109). The international system is based on a hierarchy of centre-periphery-semi-periphery, where the centre is developed and possesses the means of production, while the periphery has become dependent on the centre and is economically and politically weaker than the centre. The semi-periphery is neither fully central nor fully peripheral. The semi-periphery is in a relatively better position than the periphery in terms of power and economic distribution. Semi-periphery countries enjoy a certain degree of stability and possess a certain level of industrial production and tourism revenue (Wallerstein, 2014: 99-109).

This section of the book will analyse NATO within the framework of neorealism's power struggle within the system and world systems analysis, based on the centre-periphery-semi-periphery framework, and will examine NATO's policies and actions within the international system.

2. NATO'S EXPANSION WITHIN THE FRAMEWORK OF THE EUROPEAN SECURITY ARCHITECTURE AFTER THE COLD WAR AND ITS REFLECTIONS ON THE INTERNATIONAL SYSTEM

The period from the end of the Second World War to the dissolution of the USSR in 1991 is called the Cold War Period. During this period, a bipolar international system emerged (Lebow, 1999: 29). A bipolar international and global system emerged, with the Western Bloc, the Atlantic and European wing led by the United States and comprising mainly Western European states, including Turkey, and the Eastern Bloc, led by the Soviet Union and comprising mainly Eastern European states (Truman Library, 2025). NATO was established in 1949 as the defense organization of the Western Bloc (NATO, 2022). NATO, which functions as a deterrent defense organization on the basis of defense, has two pillars, including its political function. On the civilian side, the North Atlantic Council (NAC) and the General Secretariat have been more prominent than the defense side (NATO, 2025).

In terms of its civilian pillar or function, NATO has sought to create a collective identity not only militarily but also politically for the member states of the Alliance. Today, the idea of the West has created a perception that represents political, economic and liberalism rather than geographical terms. Although it is a discussion of another topic, democracy, free market economy (capitalist production model) and individual rights have come to represent an identity that the West has constructed starting from the discourse (Sijursen, 2004: 687). During the Cold War, Turkey and Greece were admitted to the Alliance in 1952, West Germany joined NATO in 1955 and Spain became a member in 1982. NATO, which underwent three membership processes during the Cold War, expanded the Western Bloc with the new members (NATO, 2025).

With the end of the Cold War in 1991, the USSR disintegrated and the Western Bloc emerged victorious from this power struggle. NATO played an important role in this struggle with its ability to create a collective identity and as a deterrent defense organization (Sümer, 2020: 129). As of 1991, a new global system emerged under the leadership of the United States and the international system assumed a unipolar structure (Yılmaz, 2008: 45). Immediately after the Cold War, the Western Bloc began to think about how to chart a course within the framework of NATO. In 1991, a "New Strategic Concept" was adopted at the NATO Rome Summit. Under the New Concept, the "North Atlantic Cooperation Council" (NACC) (NATO,2022) and later the "Partnership for Peace" programs were established. In this way, it was aimed to ensure the integration of the former USSR member states with the West and to provide a single approach to the European security architecture by the West on the basis of NATO. The emergence of new threats that could jeopardize security in Europe, instability and state reconstruction in the former Eastern Bloc states, the risk of border problems between the disintegrated states turning into conflicts and threats such as internal conflict led NATO to adopt the alliance's expansion approach in the European continent within the scope of the Western approach (NATO, 2025).

NATO realized its first expansion in 1999 by admitting Poland, Hungary and the Czech Republic as members in the new membership process on the basis of the Western collective identity of the European security architecture. In the process of eastward expansion, Romania, Bulgaria, Estonia, Latvia, Lithuania, Lithuania, Slovakia and Slovenia became NATO members in 2004, thus the former Soviet sphere of influence became part of the West. After the NATO membership of Romania and Bulgaria, the alliance expanded along the Black Sea coastline with Turkey (NATO, 2025). In addition to Russia's defense and security approach, the fact that the Black Sea is Russia's gateway to the world has started to trigger Russia's threat perception from the West. NATO's enlargement process, especially in 2004, began to be perceived by Russia as a "new containment policy" (Oğuzlu, 2019: 4). Focusing on state reconstruction in the 1990s, Russia was unable to deal with Eastern Europe, one of its former spheres of influence. In 2000, after Vladimir Putin became the President of Russia, Russia started to complete the state-building process to a great extent and could not oppose the 2004 NATO membership.

In 2004, the enlargement of the Alliance with new memberships in Europe initiated a period of strained NATO-Russia relations. In 2008, at NATO's Bucharest Summit, it was stated that Ukraine and Georgia could become members of the Alliance in the Future (NATO Bucharest Summit, 2008), which led Russia to perceive a threat perception with historical roots and a new containment policy (Alkanalka, 2023: 61). The expansion of NATO's sphere of influence on the Black Sea through Ukraine and Georgia and the fact that Russia will have a narrow coastline in this context, the possibility of NATO's sphere of influence in the Caucasus and Central Asia through the Black Sea, and the possibility that Russia's sphere of influence will shrink in these regions have revealed the possibility that Russia's sphere of influence will shrink in these regions, and NATO-Russia relations have begun to strain and turn into a chess game (Özkan, 2010: 14). In this context, Russia intervened militarily in Georgia and recognized the independence of the Georgian breakaway regions of Ossetia and South Abkhazia and deployed military forces (Wilson Center, 2008). In 2008, Russia reacted by cutting off gas to Europe via Ukraine (The Economist, 2024).

In 2009 Croatia and Albania, in 2017 Montenegro and in 2020 North Macedonia joined the NATO Alliance (NATO, 2025). With these accessions, NATO expanded in the Balkans region and started to emerge as the new playmaker in Russia's historical sphere of influence (Sıvış, 2020: 88). 2014 marked the beginning of a period in which relations between NATO and Russia rose to a threatening level. In the process that started with the uprising of Russian separatists in Ukraine, Russia invaded Crimea and later annexed it. Russia recognized the separatist Donbas and Luhansk regions of Ukraine as autonomous republics and provided military and defense support (Ketenci & Nas, 2014: 70). Since 2014, NATO has increased its military deployment in the Baltic region and Eastern Europe, to which Russia has responded in kind. In the Baltic region, both sides have engaged in particularly harassing flights and mutually increased the level of missile deployment on the borders of Eastern Europe (McNamara, 2016).

The European security architecture and NATO's Western collective identity suffered a major blow in 2022 when Russia launched a military operation in Ukraine. The fact that the international system is based on the hegemonic supremacy of the West and that European security is handled within the framework of NATO has created a new area of conflict in the international system with Russia's military operation in Ukraine (Tskhovrebadze, 2023: 524). Starting in 2022, Russia's military operation in Ukraine started to turn into an occupation and the conflictual process has turned into a war today. For the first time since the Second World War, the European continent has seen a large-scale war (Charap & Priebe, 2024). In this process, NATO provided Ukraine with military ammunition and equipment as well as political support, and both NATO and the European Union (EU) imposed sanctions on Russia. NATO, which was not de facto a party to the war, de facto became a party to the war with military and political support. After 2014, NATO and Russia mutually emphasized the threat discourse and started to define each other as enemies with the 2022 Ukraine war.

Russia's invasion of Ukraine triggered the threat perception of the European wing of the Alliance and new defense plans with new defense budgets started to be implemented within the framework of both the Alliance and the EU (The Economist, 2022). In 2023, Finland became a member of the NATO Alliance and in 2024 Sweden became a members (NATO, 2025). In the face of the security threat they perceived from Russia, they decided to come under the NATO security umbrella. Both countries, which had followed a policy of neutrality for a long time, abandoned the policy of neutrality by becoming a member of NATO within the framework of the perceived threat of Russian invasion with the war (Seyaz, 2024: 136).

The war in Ukraine has had a profound impact on European security and changed NATO and the EU's approach to Europe within the framework of Western identity. The European members of the alliance have now started to implement new defense budgets and to formulate new defense plans. With the war, NATO and Russia mutually implemented a process that was reflected in the discourse around the concept of enemy (Racz, 2023: 74). This situation has brought along a process that has also had an impact on the global system. While the embargoes imposed on Russia negatively affected world trade, the interruption of grain exports to the rest of the world as a result of the conflicts between Russia and Ukraine, the main producers of world grain, over the Black Sea also created a food crisis. The regional and global rivalry between the West and the US, the dominant actor of the global system, with the People's Republic of China (China), Iran and North Korea, in addition to Russia, has reached a new dimension with the war in Ukraine (Breuer, 2022: 202). As a result of Russia's circumvention of the embargoes through China, Iran and North Korea, and its transfer of military and technological products and information from these countries, Russia started to be perceived as a threat by the West, especially by the US, and this situation was reflected in NATO's 75th Anniversary Summit Text. In the text of the summit held in Washington on July 11-12, 2024, China, Iran and North Korea were included as states threatening the international system on the basis of the United Nations (UN) (NATO Washington Summit Declaration, 2025). The West's threat perception approach in the international system, which includes not only Russia but also China, Iran and North Korea, has sparked the debate on a new polar system. The "New Cold War" debates started to come to the agenda (Kimmage, 2024).

Russia's invasion of Ukraine has also led to a significant increase in military spending among NATO members. Under the criterion of NATO members allocating 2 percent of their gross domestic product (GDP) to defense budgets, Alliance members have allocated a total defense spending budget of $1.47 trillion in 2024. In 2014, three Alliance members met NATO's 2 percent of GDP defense spending budget criterion, while twenty-three members met this figure in 2024 (Anadolu Ajansı, 2025). In 2023, NATO members with budgets of $875.603 billion, the United Kingdom $77.384 billion, Germany $74.384 billion, France $57.815 billion, Italy $32.75 billion, Poland $31.165 billion, Canada $28.140 billion, Spain $19.638 billion, Turkey $18.965 billion, Norway $8.788 billion, and Greece $7.495 billion were the Alliance members with the highest military expenditures (Anadolu Ajansı, 2024). NATO members spent a total of 1.5 trillion dollars on military spending in 2024, accounting for 55 percent of global spending. In Europe, military spending increased by 17 percent to $693 billion. Among NATO members, 18 countries increased their military spending to at least 2 percent of their GDP in 2024 (BBC,2025).

During the Cold War era, NATO adopted the doctrine of area defence as its strategy, assuming the role of protecting the territories of its member states. Following the Cold War, with its expansion into Eastern Europe, it developed a concept centred on what could be termed semi-peripheral and peripheral regions. Furthermore, in the 1990s, it intervened in Bosnia-Herzegovina (1994-1995) and Kosovo (1999) with an "out-of-area" security concept. The aim was to prevent threats that could come from the periphery to the centre and to prevent other actors in the system from establishing spheres of influence in Eastern Europe. In particular, expansion into Eastern Europe and out-of-area interventions gave rise to two approaches. The first is to stabilise the periphery and bring it into alignment with the centre, and the second is NATO's desire to expand its sphere of influence as an actor in the international system through new memberships.

3. COOPERATION AND DIALOGUE PROGRAMS WITHIN THE FRAMEWORK OF THE POST-COLD WAR NATO'S EUROPEAN SECURITY ARCHITECTURE

3.1. Partnership for Peace Program

At the 1994 NATO Summit in Brussels, an approach was adopted to ensure the future membership of Eastern European states in NATO through a program. The Partnership for Peace Program (PfP) was adopted and implemented at the Summit. In particular, the aim was to ensure the military and political integration of the former Eastern Bloc countries into NATO and the West through the PfP. The states invited to the PfP also took steps towards future NATO membership through NATO's adoption of the Membership Action Plan (MAP). Within the framework of the PfP and the MAP, countries wishing to join the Alliance were prepared for membership within the framework of the responsibilities and obligations that NATO membership would bring. Within the framework of the PfP, the current Alliance memberships were accepted. In 1999, Hungary, the Czech Republic and Poland first became members of the Alliance (NATO, 2024). In 2004, Bulgaria, Estonia, Latvia, Lithuania, Romania, Slovenia, Latvia, Lithuania, Romania, Slovenia and Slovakia became NATO members, making it the largest membership process in NATO history. In 2009, Croatia became a NATO member, Montenegro in 2017, North Macedonia in 2020, Finland in 2023 and most recently Sweden in 2024 (NATO, 2025).

The PfP has been an important pillar of NATO's Western alliance, European security architecture and NATO-based common European collective security and defense approach in the post-Cold War international system. In the post-Cold War global system, NATO focused primarily on the European security architecture and the expansion of a collective security identity as well as a Western identity in continental Europe. In the context of the PfP, NATO prepared the former Eastern Bloc countries for NATO's political and defense identity (NATO, 2025).

We can also describe the PfP as a means of developing relations with the periphery and semi-periphery and integrating them into the centre. It also functions in terms of implementing the political-military and economic discourse and instruments that NATO has placed at the core of the West's claim in the international system within member countries.

3.2. Mediterranean Dialogue

In 1994, NATO focused on the European security and political architecture within the framework of the PfP, while also targeting Europe's immediate geography and the stability of European security through the Mediterranean Dialogue Program. In particular, North Africa's historical ties with continental Europe and its geographical proximity to the continent led NATO to focus on this issue. The Mediterranean Dialogue, which aims to develop cooperation with North African countries through counter-dialogue, aims to ensure that both continental Europe and North African countries develop stable relations on the basis of mutual cooperation. While regional security has been one of the main objectives, another objective has been to establish NATO's influence in the Mediterranean, especially among the Alliance members bordering the Mediterranean. Accordingly, Morocco, Mauritania, Egypt, Tunisia, Jordan, Israel and Algeria became members of the Dialogue over time (NATO, 2025).

In 1997, the Mediterranean Dialogue was permanently transformed into a permanent forum. The "Mediterranean Cooperation Group" was established in 2002, and by 2002, cooperation was developed with the member countries in areas such as defense reform, counter-terrorism, border security, defense economics, and disaster management. With the Mediterranean Dialogue, NATO also aimed to change the negative perception of the West in the perceptions of Islamic Countries (Lesser, 2018).

The Mediterranean Dialogue, like all other NATO partnership relationships, started as a bilateral initiative and has evolved into what today can be described as a multilateral initiative. It allows for multilateral political consultations and also regional cooperation through the NATO+n formula agreed at the 2002 NATO Prague Summit. This means that two or more countries from the Mediterranean Dialogue can come together for specific cooperation projects that they propose to NATO. Since 1997, practical cooperation measures between NATO and the countries of the Mediterranean Dialogue are set out in an annual Work Programme, which aims to build trust through cooperation in a range of activities: Information and Media, Civil Emergency Planning, Airspace Management, Science and Environment, Small Arms and Light Weapons, Crisis Management and Military activities (Santis, 2024).

The Mediterranean Dialogue can be regarded as an initiative by NATO to establish relations between the centre and its immediate surroundings within the international system. It is particularly significant in terms of its geographical proximity to the Alliance's European wing and its strategic and historical relations dating back to the past. NATO's desire to establish a sphere of influence in North Africa and the Mediterranean geopolitics has also made the Dialogue important.

3.3. Istanbul Cooperation Initiative

The 2004 NATO Istanbul Summit adopted the Istanbul Cooperation Initiative, similar to the Mediterranean Dialogue. Due to NATO's presence in Afghanistan and Iraq, it was aimed to overcome the negative opinions of Muslim countries about NATO. The image of the US-West and NATO, which was damaged by the US invasions of Afghanistan in 2001 and Iraq in 2003, was tried to be corrected in this way. In addition, relations were tried to be developed on the basis of regional stability. Accordingly, the member states of the Gulf Cooperation Council were invited to the Initiative. Today, Bahrain, Kuwait, Qatar and the United Arab Emirates are participating in the Istanbul Cooperation Initiative (NATO, 2024).

With the Initiative, NATO aimed to improve the relations of the Middle East region with the West. With geographies close to continental Europe, stability in terms of security was aimed, as well as the desire for the West to become an effective power, especially through these interconnected regions. The geopolitical and geostrategic location of the Middle East, which connects Asia, Africa and Europe, its rich energy resources and the fact that it is a transit route for important trade routes such as the Suez Canal, is a factor that determines the Western view of the region through NATO. Accordingly, the West, under the leadership of the United States, aims to become the dominant actor in the region within the global system in the Middle East-Mediterranean-Europe triangle.

The Istanbul Cooperation Initiative, while regulating the relationship between the centre and the periphery, can be described as a strategy to establish a sphere of influence in the Middle East and North Africa, which are strategically important regions for the West within the international system, and to maintain a competitive advantage over rival actors within the system. The region's geopolitics, energy resources and important trade routes are of such strategic importance that they bring competition within the system to the region today.

4. NATO-AFRICAN UNION RELATIONS

In June 2005, NATO started to support the African Union*. Founded in 2002 with 55 members, the African Union aimed to prevent conflicts between states in the African continent and to establish a stable area in the continent by developing economic, cultural and political unity (African Union, 2025). In 2005, the African Union, which wanted to develop relations with NATO, aimed to create stability in the continent, especially in terms of security. In this context, NATO has also started to improve its relations with the African Union (NATO, 2023).

At the 2016 NATO Warsaw Summit, NATO committed to deepen relations with the African Union, in November 2019 the African Union and NATO signed an agreement to strengthen the political and practical partnership, and in March 2020 NATO and the African Union approved additional cooperation initiatives aimed at gradual steps from ad hoc support to a broader practice-based Partnership (NATO, 2025).

NATO supported the African Union Mission in Sudan in 2005 and provided strategic airlift support in Sudan in 2007 at the request of the African Union (The African Union, 2019). This support continues today. In addition, African Union personnel attend courses at NATO's schools and defense colleges in Europe, and are permitted to participate in NATO's centers of excellence to improve their knowledge and skills. As of 2015, African Union officers are also attending specialized courses at NATO. NATO has opened the NATO Liaison Point Embassy in Addis Ababa, the capital of Ethiopia, the seat of the African Union, and conducts relations with the African Union through this embassy (Atlantic Council, 2014).

By establishing diplomatic, political and military relations with the African Union, NATO not only seeks to develop relations through NATO with states that were historically colonial areas of the alliance members and gained their independence in the decolonization process after the Second World War, but also demonstrates the continent's aim to be a Western sphere of influence. In the global playing field of the international system, NATO does not only target continental Europe and its immediate geography, but also seeks the continuation of the collective political and security hegemony of the Western identity in geographies where other actors of the system may be active.

NATO-African Union relations can be interpreted in terms of centre-periphery relations, but it can also be seen that NATO has assumed a regulatory and constitutive role in shaping its relations with the continent as an actor in the post-Cold War international system.

5. NATO'S ASIA-PACIFIC POLICY

After the US invasion of Afghanistan in 2001, NATO started to take part in the UN peace mission in Afghanistan. As a result of its involvement in state-building, particularly in training Afghan security forces, NATO's relations with Asian countries began to improve (Bağbaşlıoğlu, 2014: 91). Australia, Singapore and New Zealand sent troops to the International Security Assistance Force (ISAF) in Afghanistan, while Japan and South Korea contributed directly and indirectly to NATO's mission in Afghanistan. As a result, these countries have been referred to as "partners around the world" (Tsuruoka, 2010). Russia's military action in Ukraine, China's rising power in the Asia-Pacific region, and the close relations between Russia-China-North Korea-Iran have led to new steps in the US-West-NATO triangle in terms of determining cooperation and common approaches between their allies in the Asia-Pacific. NATO has established an expert working group between NATO and Australia, New Zealand, Japan and South Korea. Unofficially, Japan, New Zealand, Australia and South Korea are now referred to as the Indo-Pacific Four (IP4) (United States Institute of Peace, 2024). In the early 2010s, NATO signed formal partnership agreements with the Indo-Pacific Four (Glaser, 2024). The four countries participated in the most recent Washington Summit in 2024, which celebrated NATO's 75th anniversary (Brunnstorm & Martina, 2024).

Australia, New Zealand, Japan, South Korea, South Korea, the Philippines and Taiwan stand out in Asia as countries that have developed military and political cooperation with NATO. Since the Cold War period, the realization of the US and Western policies in Asia and the production of an effective policy in the continent have been realized especially through these countries. In addition, these countries have been seen as members of the Western Identity and alliance. Japan, as a Western ally, provided Ukraine with $12 billion in financial aid, while South Korea started to develop cooperation with NATO on issues such as anti-terrorism, arms trafficking and cyber-attacks. In addition, with the outbreak of the Russian-Ukrainian war, South Korea has become a major global producer and exporter of military equipment. New Zealand and Australia have begun to develop military technology cooperation with NATO and have become key players in providing technical assistance to Ukraine (Goto, 2024).

In its relations with NATO and the West, Japan has sought alliances to prioritize Asian security and to counter China (Pohlkamp, 2023). New Zealand and Australia emphasize operational military power in their relations with NATO and see it as an international framework (Tsuruoka, 2025). South Korea has adopted the approach of creating a military balance against North Korea through the US and NATO. Similarly, the Philippines, with its historical ties to the United Kingdom (UK) and the US, has been part of the West and has developed relations with Western institutions. The Philippines falls under the US security umbrella, especially due to its military, commercial and political ties with the US (Albert, 2016).

Traditionally, the Asia-Pacific region constitutes the sphere of influence of the United States as the dominant actor in the international system. Especially in the post-Cold War era, China's emergence as a rising power in the international system as a rival to the United States has led NATO and the West in the Asia-Pacific region to take steps towards becoming an effective power in regional politics under the leadership of the United States. Japan's historically rooted regional rivalry with China (Calder, 2016), the alliance between North Korea and China since the Cold

War, South Korea's military and political alliance with the US and the West for the balance of power (Nemeth & Kim, 2024: 626-627), similarly the Philippines' regional foreign policy and Taiwan's cooperation with the US against China have led to NATO's visible influence in the Asia-Pacific (CRS, 2025). China's cooperation with the US and the West, as well as NATO, has created the perception that the US and the West want to contain and encircle it regionally. Tensions between China and Taiwan have risen to an alarming level in recent Years (Sputnik, 2024). China's alliance approach and cooperation with Russia-North Korea and Iran in the global system has also turned into a threat perception by the West. Since 2022, China's support for Russia in the ongoing Ukraine-Russia war has been perceived as a threat by NATO alliance members, particularly the US. In addition, the relations between the US and China have been reflected not only in the Asia-Pacific but also in global economic competition, which has initiated a process of competition in a wide range of economic areas, such as the US's high tax restrictions on Chinese products (Korkmaz, 2023).

The Final Declaration of the 2023 Madrid Summit, NATO's first ever, stated that China posed challenges to Euro-Atlantic security (İletişim Başkanlığı, 2025). The Declaration committed to increasing cooperation with partners sharing peace and security in the Asia-Pacific (Weaver, 2023). The 2024 NATO Washington Summit Final Declaration for the first time recognized China as a threat to the security of the NATO alliance (NATO Washington Summit Declaration, 2024). NATO's 2030 Strategic Concept also recognizes that developments in the Asia-Pacific region affect the international system and Atlantic-European security (NATO, 2025). In particular, the arms trade between Russia and North Korea was highlighted as one of the factors threatening European and Asian security (James & Capie, 2024). In this context, NATO has recently started to strengthen its dialogue and cooperation with its partners in the Asia-Pacific region, namely Australia, Japan, the Republic of Korea and New Zealand. On the basis of the complex security environment in the international system, relations with like-minded partners, cross-cutting security issues and addressing global challenges, the possibility that developments in the Asia-Pacific region could directly affect Euro-Atlantic security has occupied an important place in NATO's Summit and Concept document (NATO, 2022).

NATO, which positions the military element of the approach defined in the strategic concept on integration and deterrence in the alliance relationship, also aims to ensure that its allies are stable actors by taking steps in the field of military defence cooperation, both economically and politically. The military and defence-security approach is also used as a tool to contain competitors in the region and establish a policy of pressure. The Asian continent has gained an important place in the current systemic developments in this struggle within the international system, which also influences NATO's policies in this context.

6. NATO STRATEGIC CONCEPT 2030

On December 4, 2019, NATO's Secretary General was tasked by NATO Heads of State and Government at the Leaders' Meeting in London to launch an assessment to strengthen the strategic and political role of the Alliance (T.C. Dış İşleri Bakanlığı, 2019). In June 2020, NATO Secretary-General Jens Stoltenberg stated that the new concept is primarily about ensuring that NATO remains militarily strong, becomes politically stronger and adopts a more global approach (NATO, 2021). Following this development, at the NATO Brussels Summit in June 2021, national leaders agreed on a new strategic concept to be adopted at the Alliance Summit in Madrid in 2022 (Simon, 2022). The Summit emphasized the need for a new Strategic Concept to help NATO adapt to increased global competition, terrorism, cyber-attacks, disruptive technologies, climate change, the challenging role of Russia and China in challenging the rules-based international order, and more unpredictable threats (NATO Strategic Concept, 2023).

The NATO 2030 Strategic Concept was adopted at the NATO Summit in Madrid, Spain, on June 28-30, 2022 (NATO Madrid Summit, 2022). Russia's military operation in Ukraine in February 2022 was also an important factor behind the adoption of the Strategic Concept (Arslan, 2022). In addition to Russia, the rise of China in the international system was another important factor in the adoption of the new Strategic Concept. NATO's new Strategic Concept emphasized the importance of the Indo-Pacific for Allied security and endorsed growing cooperation with like-minded partners in the region. This partnership has become increasingly important today as the world's geopolitical center of gravity shifts towards the Indo-Pacific region (Perestrello, 2022).

NATO's Strategic Concept is designed to diagnose a dynamic international security environment, identify the main threats and challenges to Euro-Atlantic security, and outline ways to address them. The 48-point Strategic Concept lists Russia as the greatest threat to Atlantic-European security. Russia's aim is to destabilize the European security architecture. It is stated that Russia and China seek to undermine the international system based on rules and order and that the Alliance will fight against this. Emphasizing the unstable nature of Africa, Sub-Saharan Africa and the Middle East, it was stated that humanitarian crises exist in these regions and that sub-state actors emerge as a result of unstable structural problems. The concept highlights a wide range of global challenges and threats, including North Korea and Iran's efforts to acquire nuclear weapons, terrorism, human trafficking, environmental crises, cyber threats and threats to the world's democracies (NATO Strategic Concept, 2023).

The concept emphasizes that NATO will continue to contribute to global peace and stability, guarantee Atlantic-European security and guarantee democracy, peace and freedom within the Alliance's borders. It was stated that cooperation will be made more ready in the face of crises. It was stated that the Alliance will be prepared for the future in order to respond to crises more quickly and effectively, and that the collective security approach will be further strengthened (NATO, 2023).

In its Strategic Concept 2030, NATO outlined its approach to the international system and the European security architecture. In particular, Russia and China were identified as threats to the international system, and Iran and North Korea were also mentioned in the Concept. While the position of the West as the dominant actor in the international system was put forward, the steps to be taken for the continuation of the Western leadership in the system were emphasized. NATO's New Strategic Concept is a document that defines how NATO perceives the global system and what role NATO wants the West to play in the global Order (Arslan, 2022).

CONCLUSION

Although NATO was established as the defense organization of the Western Bloc during the Cold War, it has also been at the forefront with its civilian institutions. It has been involved in the construction of collective security among its members and, in parallel, in the construction of a political identity within the framework of common values. After the end of the Cold War and the victory of the Western Bloc, NATO became almost the main actor in the adoption and implementation of new Western approaches in the international system. With the dissolution of the USSR, the former Eastern Bloc countries were brought into the alliance to create a European security architecture dominated by NATO. This was NATO's first post-Cold War priority, and through programs such as the PfP and MAP, it prepared the members for military and political integration into the West.

NATO has also started to take steps to ensure the continuity of the West as the dominant actor in the post-Cold War international system. In particular, NATO, seeking to create a stable structure for the Alliance's European borders, has developed cooperation and dialogues with countries in North Africa and the Middle East. These steps were taken through the Mediterranean Dialogue and the Istanbul Cooperation Initiative programs. In developing relations with North Africa, the Alliance not only aimed at European security stability but also wanted to create a dominant space in the Mediterranean. With the Istanbul Cooperation Initiative with Middle Eastern countries, NATO, which had a negative image in the Middle East and Muslim countries, especially after the US invasion of Afghanistan in 2001 and the 2003 invasion of Iraq, not only corrected this, but also took part as a supporting force in the Middle East policies developed by the US in line with its leadership in the global system. NATO aimed to maintain the West's sphere of influence over the Middle East, which is a key point of geostrategic, energy supply and world trade.

Developing cooperation with the African Union and its allies in Asia, NATO has taken steps to maintain the Western leadership in the global system. Today, the wide range of security threats in the international system has led NATO to adopt a new strategic concept. In 2022, after Russia's military operation in Ukraine, the Alliance named Russia as a threat to both the European and global system. With the new Strategic Concept adopted in 2022, the Alliance addressed Russia and China as threats and challengers to the global system. North Korea and Iran were also included in the Concept as threats, and the steps to be taken for the stability of the international system and the European security architecture were determined.

Rather than being a post-Cold War defense organization, the NATO alliance has built a collective political and military identity among its members since its inception, and has taken steps aimed at the continuity of the West as the dominant actor in the global system on the basis of this post-Cold War approach. Focusing not only on the Atlantic-European security and defense architecture, the Alliance has also implemented approaches and actions in Africa, Asia and the Middle East geographies to maintain the hegemonic power of the West.

Although NATO exists as a defence organisation, it has adopted a non-territorial strategy for defence and security since the end of the Cold War. It has expanded beyond the transatlantic area into the former Soviet sphere of influence, expanding from the centre to the periphery. In doing so, it has broadened its Western identity and alliance. The concept of out-of-area action has been implemented as a strategy to address security risks at the front line. New memberships, the concept of out-of-area intervention, and the development of relations with all regions in the global system have demonstrated that NATO acts as an actor on behalf of the West in the international system. The West's positioning itself as the dominant actor in the system has been instrumentalised by NATO. Today, NATO shapes peripheral and semi-peripheral relations from a position centred on the West, while also continuing power-centred struggles within the system's structure.

REFERENCES

Africa's Strategic Partnership with Other Parts of the World. (2024. August 01). Retrieved from https://au.int/en/partnerships/intro#:~:text=These%20include%20Africa%2DEurope%20Partnership,regional%20Organisations%20Conference%20(AASROC)

Albert, E. (2016. October 21). The U.S.-Philippines Defence Alliance. Retrieved from https://www.cfr.org/backgrounder/us-philippines-defense-alliance

Alkanalka, M. (2023). The Path to War: Ukraine's NATO Membership. *Journal of International Relations and Political Science Studies*, (7), 55–75.

Arslan, E. (2022. July 04). NATO 2030: Yeni Stratejik Konsept. Retrieved from https://strasam.org/ua-iliskiler/uluslararasi-orgutler/nato-2030-yeni-stratejik-konsept-955#google_vignette

A Short History of NATO. (2022. June 03). Retrieved from https://www.nato.int/cps/en/natohq/declassified_139339.htm

Asya, NATO ve Ortakları: Karmaşık İlişkiler. (2010. February 10). Retrieved from https://www.nato.int/docu/review/tr/articles/2010/02/10/asya-nato-ve-ortaklari-karmasik-iliskiler/index.html

Bağbaşlıoğlu, A. (2014). Beyond Afghanistan NATO's Partnership with Central Asia and South Caucasus: A Tangled Partnership? *Journal of Eurasian Studies*, *5*(1), 88–96. DOI: 10.1016/j.euras.2013.10.001

Breuer, C. (2022). The New Cold War and the Return of History. *intereconomics*, 57(4), 202-203.

Brunnstarom, D., & Martina, M. (2024. July 10). Why Indo-Pacific Countries are joining the NATO Summit. Retrieved from https://www.reuters.com/world/why-indo-pacific-countries-are-joining-nato-summit-2024-07-10/

Bucharest Summit Declaration. (2008. April 03). Retrieved from https://www.nato.int/cps/en/natohq/official_texts_8443.htm

Calder, K. E. (2024. August 28). China and Japan's Simmering Rivalry. Retrieved from https://ciaotest.cc.columbia.edu/olj/fa/fa_marapr06/fa_marapr06j.html

Charap, S., & Priebe, M. (2024. February 09). Planning for the Aftermath. Retrieved from https://www.rand.org/pubs/research_reports/RRA2510-2.html

Çin. Asya Ülkeleri, NATO'yu Bölgede Güçlendirme Girişimlerine Direnecek. (2024. July 10). Retrieved from https://anlatilaninotesi.com.tr/20240710/asya-ulkeleri-natoyu-bolgede-guclendirme-girisimlerine-direnecek-1085720703.html

Congressional Research Service. (2024). Taiwan: Background and USA Relations, CRS Reports, May 23 2024.

Cooperation with the African Union. (2023. April 27). Retrieved from https://www.nato.int/cps/en/natohq/topics_8191

Ersoy, E. (2015). *Uluslararası İlişkiler Teorileri*. Ramazan Gözen (Ed.). Realizm. İstanbul: İletişim Yayınları.

Glaser, S. B. (2024. July 02). The Washington Summit and the Indo-Pacific. Retrieved from https://www.gmfus.org/news/nato-washington-summit-and-indo-pacific Erişim: 06.09.2024.

Goto, S. (2024. July 15). Indo-Pacific Expectations for NATO. Retrieved from https://www.wilsoncenter.org/article/indo-pacific-expectations-nato

How much do Nato members spend on defence? (2024. February 18). Retrieved from https://www.bbc.com/news/world-44717074

Istanbul Cooperation Initiative (ICI). (2024. October 03). Retrieved from https://www.nato.int/cps/en/natohq/topics_52956.htm

Jones, P. S., & Capie, D. (2024. September 02). NATO Emerges as a Platform for Coordinating Indo-pacific Security Policies. Retrieved from https://www.rusi.org/explore-our-research/publications/commentary/nato-emerges-platform-coordinating-indo-pacific-security-policies

Ketenci, A., & Nas, Ç. (2014). A Constructivist Perspective: Russia's Politics on Ukraine and Annexation Crimea (2014). *Bilge Strateji*, *12*(22), 53–88.

Kimmage, M. (2024. July 15). From the Cold Wat to Cold Wars. Retrieved from https://www.csis.org/analysis/cold-war-cold-wars

Korkmaz, H. (2023. August 16). NATO Neden Çin'e Yöneliyor? Retrieved from https://tasam.org/tr-TR/Icerik/72388/nato_neden_cine_yoneliyor

Lebow, R. N. (1991). The Rise of and Fall of the Cold War in Comparative Perspective. *Review of International Studies*, *25*(5), 21–39. DOI: 10.1017/S0260210599000212

Lesser, I. (2018. June 27). The Future of NATO's Mediterranean Dialogue. Retrieved from https://www.gmfus.org/news/future-natos-mediterranean-dialogue

Madrid Summit Declaration. (2022. June 29). Retrieved from https://www.nato.int/cps/en/natohq/official_texts_196951.htm

McNamara, E. M. (2016. March 17). Nordik-Baltık Bölgesinin Güvenliği. Retrieved from https://www.nato.int/docu/review/tr/articles/2016/03/17/nordik-baltik-boelgesinin-guevenligi/index.html

Mediterranean Dialogue. (2024. December 06). Retrieved from https://www.nato.int/cps/en/natohq/topics_52927.htm

NATO 2022 Strategic Concept. (2023. March 03). Retrieved from https://www.nato.int/cps/en/natohq/topics_210907.htm

NATO 2030. (2021. June 14). Retrieved from www.nato.int/nato_static_fl2014/assets/pdf/2021/6/pdf/2106-factsheet-nato2030-en.pdf

NATO 2030: Making A Strong Alliance Even Stronger. (2021. June 10). Retrieved from https://www.nato.int/nato2030/

NATO 2030: Yeni Bir Çağ için Birliktelik. (2019. December 04). Retrieved from https://www.mfa.gov.tr/nato-2030.tr.mfa

NATO-African Union Cooperation. (2025. April 10). Retrieved from https://jfcnaples.nato.int/operations/nato-support-to-african-union

NATO and Indo-Pacific Partners. Understanding Views Interests. (2024. September 05). Retrieved from https://www.usip.org/programs/nato-and-indo-pacific-partners-understanding-views-and-interests

NATO and the African Union Increase Cooperation. (2014. May 13). https://www.atlanticcouncil.org/blogs/natosource/nato-and-the-african-union-increase-cooperation/

NATO müttefikleri, 2024'te savunma harcamalarını önceki yıla göre yüzde 10 civarında artırdı. (2025. April 24). Retrieved from https://www.aa.com.tr/tr/dunya/nato-muttefikleri-2024te-savunma-harcamalarini-onceki-yila-gore-yuzde-10-civarinda-artirdi/3547778

NATO Nedir. (2025. March 12). Retrieved from https://www.nato.int/nato-welcome/index_tr.html

Nemeth, B., & Saeme, K. (2024). South Korea and NATO: From Unlikely Companions to Key Partners. *International Affairs, 100*(2), 609–629. DOI: 10.1093/ia/iiae007

North Atlantic Cooperation Council. (1991-1997). (2022. September 09). Retrieved from https://www.nato.int/cps/en/natohq/topics_69344.htm#:~:text=The%20North%20Atlantic%20Cooperation%20Council,NATO's%20former%20Warsaw%20Pact%20adversaries

Oğuzlu, T. (2019). NATO-Rusya ilişkileri. *Güvenlik Yazıları Serisi*, *27*, 1–6.

Özkan, G. (2010). Georgia's NATO Membership within Context of Black Sea Dimension of "New Great Game". *Karadeniz Arastirmalari*, (7), 1–22.

Partnership for Peace Programme. (2024. June 28). Retrieved from https://www.nato.int/cps/en/natohq/topics_50349.htm

Perestrello, M. (2022. December 07). NATO and the Indo-Pacific Region. Retrieved from https://www.nato-pa.int/document/2022-nato-and-indo-pacific-region-report-krimi-021-pcnp

Pohlkamp, E.-K. (2023. June 01). The New Central Front: Japan's Special Role in the West's Strategic Rivalry with China. Retrieved from https://ecfr.eu/article/the-new-central-front-japans-special-role-in-the-wests-strategic-rivalry-with-china/

Racz, A. (2023). Europe and the War in Ukraine. Laszlo A. ve Optenhögel U. (Ed.), "Sanctions and the Russian War Economy", (pp 70-79). Foundation for European Progressive Studies, Brussels.

Regional Perspectives Report on the Indo-Pacific. (2022. August 02). Retrieved from https://www.act.nato.int/article/strategic-foresight-regional-perspectives-report-on-the-indo-pacific/

Relations with Partners in the Indo-Pasific Region. (2024. July 16). Retrieved from https://www.nato.int/cps/en/natohq/topics_183254.htm

Santis, de N. (2024. August 23). Mediterranean Countries through the Mediterranean Dialogue. Retrieved from https://www.nato.int/cps/en/natohq/topics_52927.htm

Seyaz, A. (2024). Change and Continuity in North European Security: Finland and Sweden's Membership in NATO. *Marmara Üniversitesi Sosyal Bilimler Dergisi*, *12*(1), 129–141. DOI: 10.14782/marmarasbd.1431218

Simon, L. (2022. June 2). The Madrid Strategic Concept and the Future of NATO. Retrieved from https://www.nato.int/docu/review/articles/2022/06/02/the-madrid-strategic-concept-and-the-future-of-nato/index.html

Sıvış, E. (2020). Foreign Policy Perpectives and Superpower Politics: Competition of U.S. and Russia over Kosovo. *Journal of Social Sciences*, *4*(7), 87–101.

Sjursen, H. (2004). On the Identity of NATO. *International Affairs*, *80*(4), 687–703. DOI: 10.1111/j.1468-2346.2004.00411.x

Stoltenberg: Bu Yıl NATO Ülkelerinin Üçte İkisi Savunma Harcamalarında Yüze 2 Hedefini Tutturacak. (2024. March 14). Retrieved from https://www.aa.com.tr/tr/dunya/stoltenberg-bu-yil-nato-ulkelerinin-ucte-ikisi-savunma-harcamalarinda-yuzde-2-hedefini-tutturacak/3164512

Sümer, G. (2020). The Impact of the Cold War Legacy on US-Russia Bilateral Relation. *Bölgesel Araştırmalar Dergisi*, *4*(1), 116–142.

The African Union and NATO Call for Clozer Collaboration and Support in the Operationalization of the African Standby Forces (ASF). (2019. April 03). Retrieved from https://au.int/en/pressreleases/20190403/african-union-and-nato-call-closer-collaboration-and-support Erişim: 13.08.2024.

The Economist. (2022, 22 Mart). Russia's Invasion of Ukraine Pushes the West Re-arm, https://www.economist.com/united-states/2022/03/28/russias-invasion-of-ukraine-pushes-the-west-to-re-arm?utm_medium=cpc.adword.pd&utm_source=google&ppccampaignID=18151738051&ppcadID=&utm_campaign=a.22brand_pmax&utm_content=conversion.direct-response.anonymous&gad_source=1&gclid=Cj0KCQjwrp-3BhDgARIsAEWJ6SwhvpkIM-H4dwV3JikRuCagxQro7AegyiIMBJLGPIYv8G1miiO2YSMaAhYNEALw_wcB&gclsrc=aw.ds Erişim: 18.07.2024.

The Economist. (2024, 29 Ocak). A Short History of Russia and Ukraine, https://www.economist.com/graphic-detail/2024/01/29/a-short-history-of-russia-and-ukraine?utm_medium=cpc.adword.pd&utm_source=google&ppccampaignID=18151738051&ppcadID=&utm_campaign=a.22brand_pmax&utm_content=conversion.direct-response.anonymous&gad_source=1&gclid=CjwKCAjw6JS3BhBAEiwAO9waF9UpTN1zKntU-AtKBEIghxQCDeww5DJOnvliTx3yIQ5OCiC4_ekZUBoC4cAQAvD_BwE&gclsrc=aw.ds Erişim: 15.06.2024.

The Russia-Georgia Conflict: What Happened and Future Implications for US Foreign Policy. (2008. September 12). Retrieved from https://www.wilsoncenter.org/event/the-russia-georgia-conflict-what-happened-and-future-implications-for-us-foreign-policy

Tskhovrebadze, T., Putkaradze, K., & Zerekidze, Z. (2023). Rethinking European Security: The Strategic Nexus After Russian-Ukraine War. *Journal of Liberty and International Affairs*, *9*(3), 518–530. DOI: 10.47305/JLIA2393629t

Ülkeleri Savunma Harcamalarını Artırdı, N. A. T. O. (2024. May 19). Retrieved from https://www.aa.com.tr/tr/dunya/nato-ulkeleri-savunma-harcamalarini-artirdi/3253418

Washington Summit Declaration. (2024. July 10). Retrieved from https://www.nato.int/cps/en/natohq/official_texts_227678.htm

Weaver, J. (2023. July). Retrieved from 2023 NATO Zirvesinin Ardından, https://www.nato.int/docu/review/tr/articles/2023/07/27/2023-nato-zirvesinin-ardindan/index.html

Yılmaz, M. E. (2008). "The New World Order": An Outline of the Post-Cold War Era. *Alternatives: Turkish Journal of International Relations*, *7*(4), 44–58.

ENDNOTE

* The African Union was established in 2002 in Durban, South Africa. The main goal was to establish a pan-African union. It was aimed to decolonize the continent, to end apertheid regimes, to direct the growth and economic development of the continent, to increase the cooperation of the states in the continent, and to ensure integration between countries. "The African Union has set as its core principle to be governed by an integrated, prosperous and peaceful vision, driven by its own citizens and representing a dynamic force in the global arena". For detailed information see: www.au.int

Chapter 11
Russia's Policy in the South China Sea:
Strategic Interests and Geopolitical Maneuvers

Ezgi Şahin
https://orcid.org/0009-0002-6368-8669
Kirikkale University, Turkey

Merve Suna Ozel Ozcan
https://orcid.org/0000-0001-9027-3990
Kirikkale University, Turkey

ABSTRACT

The South China Sea is a key area of international cooperation and conflict, serving as a crucial maritime link between the Indian and Pacific Oceans. The region is pivotal in regional and global trade and energy security, underscoring its strategic significance for global actors. Given these dynamics, this chapter examines Russia's South China Sea policies. It highlights that while Moscow officially maintains a neutral stance in its rhetoric, it has developed complex relationships with regional states. This study analyzes Russia's military exercises, energy policies, and diplomatic rhetoric in the South China Sea, emphasizing Moscow's strategy of maintaining balanced relations with regional actors. Lastly, Russia's policy in the South China Sea demonstrates that, despite its official claims of neutrality, it remains a significant player in the region's balance of power.

DOI: 10.4018/979-8-3373-2342-8.ch011

INTRODUCTION

For centuries, Russia has been recognized as a predominantly land-based continental power. However, its vast geography has rendered maritime dominance essential for ensuring strategic access to global trade routes and security networks. Since the reign of Peter the Great, Russia has sought to pursue a naval-oriented policy that would link its maritime domains, including those in the Far East, to warm-water ports. Historically, Russia's eastward orientation has often developed in response to conflicts or exclusion from Western geopolitical frameworks. This trajectory became especially evident after the Russo-Japanese War of 1905, when Russia suffered a decisive defeat (Ozel Ozcan & Goziev, 2019). The outcome curtailed Russia's influence in the Far East, limited its leverage within the global power configuration of the early twentieth century, and undermined its ability to shape the evolving great-power competition.

Within this broader context, the South China Sea holds significant strategic importance for Russia, shaping both geopolitical and economic dynamics within the international system. The South China Sea is a semi-enclosed maritime space situated along the historic Maritime Silk Road and is today regarded as one of the most heavily trafficked sea lines of communication in the world. Geographically, it lies south of China and Taiwan, east of Vietnam, and northwest of the archipelagos that include the Philippines, Malaysia, and Indonesia. Spanning approximately 1.4 million square miles, the South China Sea contains more than 200 islands, reefs, shoals, coral formations, and atolls. These features are clustered into three principal archipelagos, namely the Spratly Islands, the Paracel Islands, and the Pratas Islands, along with Macclesfield Bank and Scarborough Shoal. The littoral states of the South China Sea include China, Taiwan, Cambodia, Vietnam, Thailand, the Philippines, Singapore, Malaysia, Brunei, and Indonesia. Among these countries, China, Taiwan, Vietnam, the Philippines, Malaysia, and Brunei maintain overlapping claims to sovereignty over islands and maritime zones. China asserts control over nearly the entire sea, while the other claimants dispute various features and waters. These rivalries have been identified as one of the most volatile geopolitical flashpoints in Asia (Fravel, 2011, p. 304).

In recent years, the militarization of disputed islands, primarily through the establishment of permanent naval bases, has transformed the region into a focal point of episodic military confrontations (Corr, 2018). The South China Sea functions as a crucial maritime corridor that enables the transportation of nearly one third of global crude oil exports. It also facilitates the flow of strategic goods and raw materials from Europe and Africa to Asia (Guan, 2010, p. 56). The geopolitical importance of the South China Sea intensifies maritime disputes among coastal states, particularly with respect to territorial waters and the delimitation of Exclusive Economic Zones (EEZs).

Many areas of power struggle in the international arena demonstrate the importance of the risk factor in cooperation and partnerships between parties. In this context, when the situation in the South China Sea is examined in the context of hedging theory, the picture becomes clear. Hedging refers to the complex strategies developed by states in international relations literature to counter uncertainty, perceived threats, and shifts in the balance of power. This approach differs from classical alliance-building (balancing) or bandwagoning strategies, as it involves the simultaneous implementation of both deterrence and engagement policies. This situation highlights the importance of security perception and defence capabilities in the balancing strategy of actors. In parallel, it may also involve Actor A allying with Actors B or C, who share a similar perception of threat. While this study will specifically focus on hedging regarding security and regional policies, it is essential to recognise that a comprehensive understanding of hedging as a human behaviour requires considering it alongside the concept of "risk." From this perspective, while risks in the field of international politics are addressed in three main categories (security, economic, and political) existing risks/risks can be decisive in the actions of actors, global developments, or systemic changes in internal political collapse and power distribution (Cheng-Chwee, 2004: 163).

When Russia's stance on the South China Sea is examined, the strategies of balancing, neutrality, and hedging emerge as central components of its approach. In an unpredictable global environment, hedging represents a strategic technique through which states adopt several, at times contradictory, policies in order to mitigate risks and maximize potential gains. In contrast, great powers generally employ balancing to counter the system's principal rivals or threats. Hedging is a flexible tactic that can be employed by both large and small states, as it entails the implementation of adaptable policies across diverse sectors of national interest without directly confronting any dominant power (Korolev, 2018). In the case of Russia's South China Sea policy, hedging signifies maintaining relations with major regional actors, particularly the United States, China, and Vietnam, while refraining from full alignment with any of them.

This study adopts a qualitative methodology to analyze official statements, military activities, and energy partnerships by drawing on secondary sources, including policy reports, academic journals, and governmental publications. The chapter provides a comprehensive assessment of Russia's policy in the South China Sea. Russia's approach rests on a pragmatic and multidimensional strategy. Within this framework, the study examines Russia's pragmatic and anti-Western balancing policies in the region by analyzing its strategic positioning and interactions with regional actors. The analysis further explores how Russia maneuvers within the geopolitical landscape of the South China Sea while reinforcing its economic and security partnerships to preserve its strategic presence. It also considers the ways in which Russia manages complex regional power dynamics by leveraging defense cooperation, energy interests, and strategic alignments.

1. GEOPOLITICAL AND ECONOMIC SIGNIFICANCE OF THE SOUTH CHINA SEA AND CONFLICTS

The South China Sea is one of the world's most strategically significant maritime regions, serving as a vital conduit for global trade and energy transportation. Connecting the Indian and Pacific Oceans, the SCS is a critical maritime passage, linking major trade routes via Sunda, Malacca, and Lombok Straits. These maritime corridors collectively facilitate an estimated $5 trillion annual trade volume (Raine, 2007). Furthermore, the SCS is integral to the energy security of East Asian economies, as it serves as a primary transit route for oil and natural gas shipments from the Persian Gulf (Morton & Blackmore, 2021). The United States also has substantial regional economic interests, with $1.2 trillion in annual trade passing through the SCS, underscoring its geostrategic relevance (Morton & Blackmore, 2021).

Figure 1. Map I: South China Sea

Source: The Economist, 2024.

Beyond its role in global trade, the SCS is significant due to its proven and potential hydrocarbon reserves. The region remains underexplored due to territorial disputes, with most confirmed oil and gas fields located near uncontested coastal areas (Rahman & Tsamenyi, 2013). According to the U.S. Energy Information Administration (EIA) (2023), the SCS holds an estimated 3.6 billion barrels of proven oil reserves and 40.3 trillion cubic feet of natural gas. This resource wealth further intensifies regional disputes, making the SCS a focal point for geopolitical competition and energy security concerns. On the other hand, to proven thepotential hydrocarbon reserves, the United States Geological Survey (USGS, 2023) has analyzed the undiscovered conventional oil and natural gas resources in the South China Sea (SCS). The USGS estimates that across the 13 basins of the SCS, the region holds between 2.4 billion and 9.2 billion barrels of undiscovered oil and between 62 trillion and 216 trillion cubic feet of natural gas (USGS, 2023). Furthermore, the SCS plays a vital role in global fisheries, accounting for approximately 12% of the world's total fish catch.

The SCS is a focal point of great power military strategies and alliance dynamics. China's increasing defense expenditures in the region primarily aim to counter potential U.S. military interventions. The United States considers the Spratly Islands part of international waters and regards the region's strategic maritime routes as critical to its naval and military operations (Sibuet, Yeh & Lee, 2016). The U.S. Seventh Fleet regularly operates in the Indo-Pacific, underscoring the SCS's role in ensuring maritime security and freedom of navigation.

In a potential large-scale military conflict, the SCS would serve as China's critical strategic military base. The artificial islands and military installations constructed by China provide defensive capabilities against potential U.S. strikes while enabling counteroffensive measures (Raine, 2017). These installations enhance China's coercive leverage during peacetime and offer strategic advantages in firepower, situational awareness, and logistical support during wartime. Additionally, the location of these fortified islands allows for the deployment of anti-ship and anti-air missiles, forming a defensive barrier to restrict enemy naval access. Their small size makes them challenge targets, necessitating high-precision strikes (Houlden et al., 2021).

The disputes in the SCS primarily pertain to the ownership and jurisdiction of islands, islets, reefs, and rock formations situated in the central region of the sea. These controversies regarding territorial and maritime jurisdiction have given rise to sovereignty disputes among several nations, namely Brunei, China, Indonesia, the Philippines, Malaysia, Taiwan, and Vietnam. The Paracel Islands and the Spratly Islands represent two principal areas of contention within these disputes. Both China and Vietnam claim the Paracel Islands, each asserting full sovereignty over the archipelago. Meanwhile, the Spratly Islands dispute involves China, Vietnam, Malaysia, the Philippines, and Brunei. While China and Vietnam claim the entirety of the Spratly archipelago, Malaysia, the Philippines, and Brunei assert sovereignty over specific portions of the islands. Taiwan's territorial claims largely align with China's stance, making it an additional party to the dispute (Raditio, 2015, pp. 323-326).

2. RUSSIA'S POSITION ON THE SOUTH CHINA SEA: DIPLOMACY AND MILITARY

Russia approaches the SCS dispute by balancing its strategic partnership with China and its longstanding relationships with Southeast Asian nations. In this regard, Russia has consistently maintained a neutral and "middle-ground" stance on the dispute at the official level (McLaughlin, 2022). Since Moscow is not directly involved in the territorial conflict, it has neither officially recognized nor explicitly supported any country's sovereignty claims. Russia's official rhetoric promotes a peaceful resolution among the involved parties, emphasizing that all sides should exercise restraint and seek diplomatic and political solutions (Denisov et al., 2021). While refraining from taking a position on the legitimacy of territorial claims, Moscow supports adherence to the 1982 United Nations Convention on the Law of the Sea (UNCLOS). Additionally, Russia endorses the 2002 Declaration on the Conduct (DOC) of Parties in the SCS signed between ASEAN and China, emphasizing the importance of transitioning from SCS DOC to a binding and comprehensive Code of Conduct (Korolev, 2018: Druzhinin & Lachininskii, 2021). Russian Foreign Minister Sergey Lavrov has emphasized that disputes in the South China Sea should be resolved exclusively among the directly involved parties, without the intervention of third parties or attempts to internationalize the issue (Tsvetov, 2016).

Table 1. Russia's Strategic Involvement in the South China Sea

Aspect	Details
Military Cooperation	Joint naval exercises with China
Balancing Act	Maintains ties with Vietnam and China
Economic Interests	Diversifying energy markets (Rosneft involved in Vietnamese)

Source: Created by the authors.

Consistent with these principles, Russia opposes the involvement of external actors in the dispute and argues that regional mechanisms should be used to resolve the issue, similar to its approach in the Arctic region (Şahin & Özel Özcan, 2024). These principles are consistently articulated on various international platforms, with Russia attempting to reinforce them both to the global community and to China and its regional rivals in the SCS dispute. Responding to a journalist's question on the issue, President Vladimir Putin articulated Russia's position as follows: "Regarding the South China Sea [...] the Russian Federation adheres to the principle that every country in the region should have the opportunity to resolve arising disputes without the intervention of external powers." (Ing, Anas, & Wihardja, 2022).

On the other hand, contrary to the UN's general stance, Russia has not publicly questioned the legitimacy of China's "Nine-Dash Line"[2] claim. This stance has, at times, been interpreted as indirect support for Beijing (McLaughlin, 2022). A key event in the South China Sea dispute took place in 2016 when the Permanent Court of Arbitration (PCA) ruled in favor of the Philippines. The court rejected China's historical claims over the Spratly and Paracel Islands and declared that the Nine-Dash Line lacked legal foundation. and competing sovereignty assertions. Despite its stated neutrality, Russia quickly aligned with China following the ruling. At the G20 Summit, President Vladimir Putin publicly expressed support for China's rejection of the PCA decision, stating: "Regarding the Hague Arbitration Court and its ruling, we support China's position in refusing to recognize the tribunal." (Druzhinin & Lachininskii, 2021).

Figure 2. Map II: South China Sea

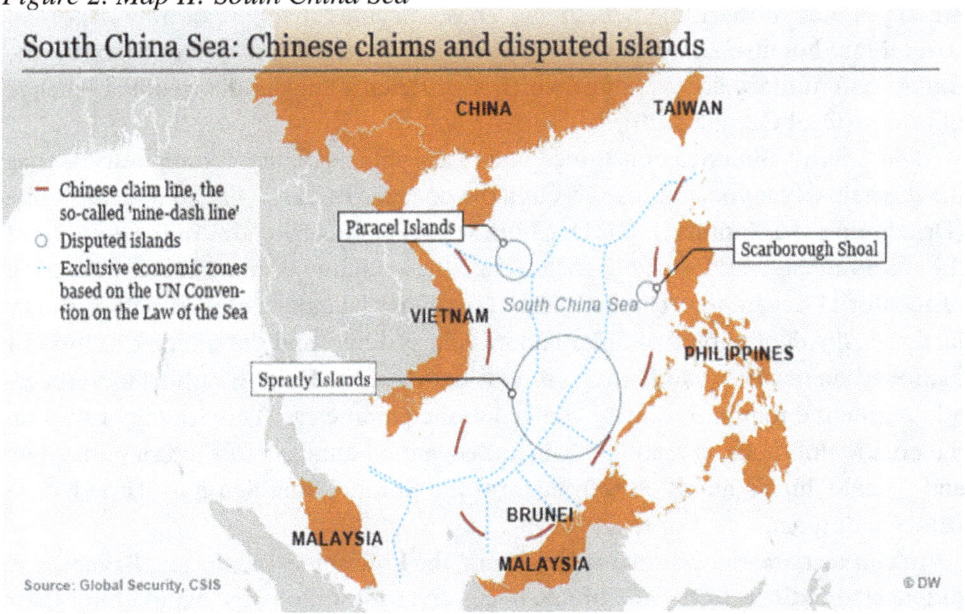

Source: *Hamilton, 2025.*

Territorial hegemony can be defined as the capacity of a state not only to establish sovereignty over a particular geographical area but also to shape the political, economic, and security parameters of that space (Şahin, 2025). The concept goes beyond the mere exercise of physical control, reflecting the ability of states to act as order-setters in strategically significant regions by restricting the maneuverability of other actors and imposing their own normative frameworks. Territorial hegemony therefore encompasses the consolidation of military presence, the management of economic resources, the regulation of maritime routes, and efforts to secure legitimacy within the framework of international law. It implies not simply the projection of power but the comprehensive reconfiguration of a region in line with the hegemon's strategic objectives (Şahin, 2025).

In the South China Sea, China's power dynamics are evident through the Nine-Dash Line, artificial islands,and militarised outposts, all aimed at redefining regional governance.China's goal is to reshape maritime hierarchies and limit the strategic autonomy of neighbouring states within a hegemonic framework.While the South China Sea is often analysed in the context of the Russia–China axis,it also attracts significant attention from multiple actors, especially Japan, due to the dynamics surrounding Taiwan. he hegemonic approach and current conditions in the region highlight a distinct struggle for hegemony alongside ongoing territorial and maritime disputes.The Kuril Islands dispute and the Senkaku Islands conflict are key issues in maritime hegemony. These disputes involve not only historical sovereignty but also strategic concerns over energy resources, fisheries, maritime routes, and military access, all of which significantly impact the regional balance of power (Özel Özcan, 2020).

The South China Sea constitutes one of the most salient contemporary arenas in which this dynamic unfolds. Through the doctrine of the so-called nine dash line (Druzhinin & Lachininskii, 2021), China asserts claims over almost the entirety of the maritime area and seeks to materialize these claims through the construction of territorial hegemony. The building of artificial islands equipped with military facilities, the deployment of radar and missile systems, and the monopolization of hydrocarbon reserves and fishing grounds demonstrate Beijing's effort to unilaterally define the region's security and economic parameters. This strategy relies on the creation of de facto realities that challenge the boundaries of international law and reveal China's ambition to transform the South China Sea into its own core strategic domain.

In contrast, the littoral states of Vietnam, the Philippines, Malaysia, Brunei, and Indonesia continue to resist China's hegemonic aspirations by maintaining their sovereignty claims. Yet their limited economic and military capacities render them insufficient to counterbalance Beijing on their own. At this juncture, the United States intervenes by providing strategic backing to regional allies and by conducting freedom of navigation operations that seek to constrain China's attempt to establish territorial hegemony (Şahin, 2024). The involvement of the United States elevates the contest from a regional maritime dispute to a broader arena of systemic rivalry, thereby transforming the South China Sea into a geopolitical laboratory where the future balance of power in the international order is being tested.

While the South China Sea dispute has primarily been framed as a contest between China and the United States alongside its regional partners, the role of other major powers has also attracted attention. In particular, Russia's stance has been a subject of debate, as its broader strategic partnership with China raised questions regarding whether Moscow might extend support to Beijing's maritime claims. This led to speculation that Russia was leaning towards a pro-China stance in the dispute. However, in response, Russian Foreign Ministry Spokesperson Maria Zakharova reaffirmed on July 14, 2016, that Russia remains neutral in the SCS dispute and adheres to the principle of not taking sides (Adelinet, 2024). Subsequent statements by Russian diplomats in Thailand, China, and other countries further confirmed Moscow's commitment to maintaining neutrality and distancing itself from the conflict (Ing et al., 2022). In this context, Russia has refrained from using its political capital to actively support either China or other claimants. Instead, Moscow has opted to stay outside the complex geopolitical equation of the SCS, reinforcing its non-interventionist approach to regional disputes.

But Russia and China have developed a comprehensive strategic partnership based on equality, mutual trust, support, and long-term cooperation (Portyakov, 2015). President Vladimir Putin has described China as Russia's "natural partner and ally" (Kaczmarski, 2023). The two countries have strengthened ties through major energy agreements (2014-2015) and the 2016 Joint Declaration, which emphasized mutual support for sovereignty and territorial integrity. Additionally, Russia-China joint naval exercises in the South China Sea (SCS) have expanded, notably the Joint Sea-2016 drill following the Permanent Court of Arbitration's ruling against China's Nine-Dash Line claim (Marcus, 2015; Buckley, 2016). These exercises fueled speculation about Russia's potential military backing for China in the SCS.

In summary, Russia's geopolitical strategy in the South China Sea is characterized by hedging strategy. It seeks to avoid becoming involved in disputes, supports China's preference against external interference, and aims to maintain good relationships with all parties to safeguard its regional interests and influence. However, despite its deepening cooperation with Beijing, Russia has maintained a strong strategic partnership with Vietnam, demonstrating that its stance is not entirely pro-China. In 2012, Russia and Vietnam upgraded their relations to a "comprehensive strategic partnership", "reaffirming their traditional ties and mutual priorities (Kobelev, 2014). During Putin's visit to Hanoi in 2013, he identified Vietnam as Russia's key partner in the Asia-Pacific, leading to enhanced military and energy cooperation (Denisov et al., 2021). Russia has also supported Vietnam's defense modernization, facilitating the transfer of advanced weaponry and defense technology. Moreover,

Russia played a crucial role in Vietnam's naval expansion by assisting in developing the Cam Ranh Bay submarine base and ship repair facilities. A 2014 agreement granted Russian naval and air forces privileged access to these facilities, strengthening bilateral military cooperation (Druzhinin & Lachininskii, 2021). While Vietnamese officials clarified that this did not constitute a Russian military base, it underscored Russia's strategic presence in the region (Lokshin, 2014).

Since 2014, Russia has significantly expanded its naval presence in Southeast Asia, signaling a deliberate strategic shift toward the Indo-Pacific region. This expansion is reflected in joint military exercises conducted with regional states, including operations with the Philippines and within the Coral Sea, as well as notable port visits to Malaysia, Singapore, and Indonesia (McLaughlin, 2022). In March 2023, Russia's newly articulated Foreign Policy Concept defined the country as both a Eurasian and a Euro-Pacific power. The document identified China and India as primary partners in Eurasian policy, while characterizing Russia's Asia-Pacific orientation as more reactive in nature. Although Russia claims to support an open regional order and to promote what it terms "non-politicized" engagement, it also alleges that external actors-implicitly the United States and its allies-are seeking to foster divisions (Kuo, 2023).

The deepening military cooperation between Moscow and Beijing is illustrated by joint naval patrols in the Indo-Pacific, which form part of a wider pattern of diplomatic and economic collaboration. As the region increasingly aligns into two distinct blocs, one led by the United States and its allies and the other centered on China with support from Russia, the Sino-Russian partnership appears particularly robust compared to other theaters of interaction. Both powers hold vital interests in the Indo-Pacific, a region that is central to global trade flows. For Russia, the significance of this maritime domain has grown especially after the loss of its European markets following the invasion of Ukraine. The prominent military presence of the United States in the region has often had the unintended effect of reinforcing the strategic alignment between Beijing and Moscow (Hamilton, 2025).

A pivotal moment in Russia's maritime engagement occurred during the G20 Summit in Brisbane in November 2014, when the Russian Pacific Fleet conducted operations off the coast of Queensland, Australia (Korolev, 2018). In the subsequent years, particularly 2015 and 2016, Russia demonstrated its naval capabilities in the South China Sea through a series of drills, transits, and the deployment of forces to strategically sensitive areas (Ing et al., 2022). These initiatives highlight Russia's intention to consolidate its operational footprint and to assert its strategic interests within the increasingly contested Indo-Pacific region.

3. RUSSIA'S STRATEGIC APPROACHES IN THE INDO-PACIFIC

When discussing the South China Sea, China emerges as the most dominant actor and Russia's key strategic ally. Observing their actions in this maritime region is crucial to understanding the broader geopolitical landscape. In the military domain, the importance of strategic interests becomes particularly evident, especially in the face of external actors such as the UN. In this context, Russia perceives itself as engaging in an existential struggle with the West, particularly with the U.S. This perception reinforces Russia's view of China as a natural partner in countering Western influence. As NATO's profile in the Indo-Pacific continues to rise, Russia's alignment with China has become even more pronounced. The shared perception of NATO as a security threat has fostered greater convergence in how Moscow and Beijing assess the regional security environment. Their mutual interest in countering Western military influence in Asia has strengthened their strategic coordination, particularly in joint military exercises, diplomatic coordination, and security cooperation in the SCS (Hamilton, 2025).

Despite its substantial Asian territory—comprising two-thirds of its landmass—and a historical ambition among Russian and Soviet leaders to enhance their influence in the Asia-Pacific region, economic challenges in the Russian Far East have persistently obstructed these goals. Also, Russia eschews the term "Indo-Pacific," perceiving it as a U.S.-led effort to undermine its ties with India and to exert pressure on China, its strategic partner (Kuo, 2023). Beijing pursues critical strategic interests in the Indo-Pacific, primarily driven by two fundamental imperatives: the restoration of China's territorial integrity and the establishment of a geographic sphere of influence across much of the region (Torkunov & Streltsov, 2023). Both objectives inherently carry the potential for conflict with the UN, which China perceives as a key obstacle to achieving these goals. Among China's territorial concerns, Taiwan remains the foremost priority (McLaughlin, 2022). Of the four contested regions where China's territorial integrity remains incomplete or challenged, Taiwan is the only one that continues to actively resist Beijing's control. While China has demonstrated sensitivity toward criticism regarding the other three regions, the Chinese Communist Party (CCP) leadership considers Taiwan's reintegration a vital national interest and has explicitly stated its willingness to use military force if necessary. Tensions surrounding Taiwan have escalated further as U.S.-China relations deteriorate. Additionally, the emergence of a new generation of political leaders in Taiwan has led to a stronger rejection of the "one country, two systems" model, signaling a more assertive stance against Beijing's influence (Druzhinin & Lachininskii, 2021).

Despite being a historically significant actor in Asia, Russia has not traditionally played a leading role in the region. Russia's most critical political, economic, and military relations have historically been centered on Europe. Since the time of Peter the Great, Russian leaders have recognized the strategic and economic value of the Far East. However, Russia's pivot to the East has often responded to tensions with the West or a perceived exclusion from Western affairs (Putra, 2021). The current shift towards Asia gained momentum after the 2014 annexation of Crimea, which led to Western-imposed sanctions on Russia. This trend accelerated further following Russia's full-scale military intervention in Ukraine in 2022. Unlike previous China-centric pivot strategies, Moscow seeks to diversify its regional engagement. Russia's 2023 Foreign Policy Concept reflects this strategic shift, emphasizing its Eurasian and Euro-Pacific power role. It also highlights that two-thirds of Russian territory lies within the Asian continent (Adelinet, 2024).

Russia's interests in the Indo-Pacific are characterized by structural contradictions. On the one hand, Moscow views China as a strategic partner, particularly within the context of its existential rivalry with the West, especially the UN. The expanding influence of NATO in the region has further reinforced this cooperation (Panda, 2016). China and Russia share a common threat perception regarding regional security dynamics, particularly in their efforts to limit NATO's presence in the Indo-Pacific. On the other hand, Russia has historically maintained strategic relations with China's regional rivals. This dual approach—forming partnerships with anti-China regional actors while simultaneously aligning with Beijing—creates geopolitical challenges and balancing difficulties (Druzhinin & Lachininskii, 2021).

Initially, Russia supported Vietnam's territorial claims in the South China Sea, but in 2015, it abruptly shifted its stance in favor of China. This change was largely driven by the warming relations between Washington and Hanoi. While Russia backed China's regional sovereignty claims, it also condemned U.S. interventions. Despite its apparent alignment with Beijing, Russia has continued its strategic cooperation with Vietnam in other areas, such as arms sales and energy collaboration. Notably, Russian oil companies have engaged in joint exploration projects with Vietnam within the area that China claims as its Nine-Dash Line, which has led to tensions with Beijing (Kaczmarski, 2023).

China has responded with concern and opposition to Russia's activities. Following Beijing's protests, Russia withdrew some of its ships from disputed waters. Additionally, China has deployed Coast Guard vessels to monitor Russian-Vietnamese oil and gas exploration efforts (McLaughlin, 2022). While some Chinese analysts argue that Russia is using Vietnam to counter China, others suggest that Moscow seeks to expand its regional influence, which could pose challenges to China's strategic interests. As a result, Beijing has become increasingly cautious about Russia's actions in the region, especially when they contradict China's geopolitical priorities (Denisov et al., 2021).

Therefore, it is crucial to emphasize one final consideration. Russia's policy concerning the Kuril Islands is fundamentally shaped by its historical claims, strategic military considerations, and diplomatic relations with Japan. The dispute over the Kuril Islands has been a notable source of tension between Russia and Japan since the conclusion of World War II. The Soviet Union assumed control over the islands in 1945, in accordance with the Yalta and Potsdam agreements. Despite Japan's ongoing claims to the four southernmost islands—Iturup, Kunashir, Shikotan, and Habomai—Russia has upheld its full sovereignty over this region. (Özel Özcan, 2020).

Moscow perceives the Kuril Islands as of significant strategic importance due to their geographic location, which affords naval access to the Pacific Ocean. The islands are vital to Russia's defense strategy in the Far East, housing military installations and surveillance systems that facilitate control over critical maritime routes. Recently, Russia has escalated its military presence in the region, including the deployment of advanced missile systems and the conduct of military exercises. These actions have prompted strong objections from Japan, which continues to advocate for negotiations regarding the status of the islands.

It is also essential to analyze Russia's relationship with Vietnam, as Vietnam is one of the key regional players in the South China Sea and shares historical ties with Moscow. In 2016, Nguyen Phu Trong, General Secretary of the Communist Party of Vietnam, introduced the concept of "Bamboo Diplomacy," emphasizing flexibility in foreign policy. Since 2021, this approach has been increasingly evident, reflecting Vietnam's resilience, adaptability, and strategic positioning in international affairs (Ha & Nhung, 2023). Following the Cold War, the evolving international system has led Vietnam to seek new partnerships to navigate global shifts. While Russia is not Vietnam's strongest trade partner today, it would be misleading to assume that bilateral relations are weak. Vietnam relies heavily on Russian-made military equipment and cooperates with Russian energy companies in oil exploration activities in the South China Sea. This dynamic can manifest Bamboo Diplomacy's flexibility, demonstrating the pragmatism of Vietnam's foreign policy and the enduring strength of historical ties between the two nations. As part of Russia's strategic expansion in the Asia-Pacific, defense industry cooperation between Russia and Vietnam has gained significant momentum. Defense agreements signed between 2012 and 2022 have substantially enhanced Vietnam's military capabilities, with key acquisitions including six Kilo-class submarines, thirty-two Su-30MK2 fighter jets, ten Tarantul-class corvettes, two Gepard-class frigates, and S-300 air defense systems (Adeline, 2024). These high-budget defense procurements have strengthened Vietnam's military deterrence, mainly supporting its territorial claims in the South China Sea.

Given the capabilities provided by these systems, Vietnam's military capacity has expanded significantly. The country has developed strike capabilities capable of targeting mainland China, enhanced anti-access/area-denial (A2/AD) strategies, and established a naval force capable of conducting operations in shallow waters (Torkunov & Streltsov, 2023). This force, centered around strategic operations from Cam Ranh Bay, holds the potential to influence regional power dynamics. From Russia's perspective, these defense agreements have generated significant economic benefits; however, they remain relatively modest compared to Russia's arms trade with China. Between 2018 and 2022, Russia's defense exports to China reached a total trade value of $5.194 billion, whereas defense trade with Vietnam amounted to only $622 million (Adeline, 2024). Consequently, Russia's arms sales to Vietnam cannot be solely attributed to economic motivations; these transactions pose certain strategic risks for Russia's broader security cooperation with China.

Beyond its arms exports to Vietnam, another key indicator of Russia's military presence in the SCS is its participation in joint military exercises. Russia participated in the "Joint Sea" drills with China in 2014 and 2016, reinforcing its strategic maritime posture. These exercises involved large-scale naval assets and included amphibious warfare scenarios, delivering a strong strategic message regarding power projection (Gady, 2016). Conducted in a manner that implicitly supports China's territorial claims within the Nine-Dash Line, these exercises have also deepened Russia-China security cooperation. Russia's military strategy in the SCS is relevant within the context of regional security dynamics and plays a critical role in global power balances. In particular, Russia's expanding military ties with China can be viewed as a counter-strategy to the U.S. role as a balancing power in the Indo-Pacific (Adelinet, 2024).

4. RUSSIA'S ENERGY ENGAGEMENT IN THE SOUTH CHINA SEA

Energy remains one of Russia's most significant foreign policy instruments, with its role becoming particularly evident during the Russia-Ukraine war. The chaos caused by Western sanctions and disruptions in European energy markets highlighted how Russia's energy policies impact global energy prices and geopolitical stability. In this context, Russia's energy strategy is a crucial element in the geopolitical significance of the SCS. Russia has actively pursued energy cooperation with ASEAN countries, particularly in subsea natural gas exploration and liquefied natural gas (LNG) projects. Among these partnerships, Vietnam holds a key position as a significant energy partner of Russian firms and a country highly dependent on energy imports (Torkunov & Streltsov, 2023). Russia's growing focus on energy collaboration in the region suggests that its interests in the SCS extend beyond military and diplomatic concerns. The abundance of hydrocarbon resources in the SCS is a critical factor driving Russia's strategic engagement in the region. The increasing global competition for these resources further enhances Russia's regional influence, making the SCS a focal point of Moscow's broader geopolitical interests. In this regard, energy security and resource-sharing negotiations are important in Russia-China relations, as both countries seek to expand their influence in the region (Druzhinin & Lachininskii, 2021).

Russia's energy partnerships with Vietnam represent a core element of its SCS strategy. Given that hydrocarbon reserves lie at the center of sovereignty disputes, the exploration and exploitation of these resources constitute a highly sensitive geopolitical issue. Conflicting maritime claims, overlapping exclusive economic zones (EEZs), and competing sovereignty assertions—including China's Nine-Dash Line claims—have led to political and diplomatic pressure on energy exploration projects (Panda, 2016). Moreover, the state-owned Russian energy giant Rosneft has actively explored gas in the SCS. Since becoming the operator of Block 06.1 in the Nam Con Son Basin in 2013, Rosneft has expanded its projects within Vietnam's EEZ, drilling two additional wells since 2018. However, with China asserting its claims over the SCS, Rosneft's activities in the disputed area have faced increasing scrutiny and diplomatic tensions (Thu & Cao, 2019).

Vietnam seeks to leverage its seabed hydrocarbon reserves for economic gain by attracting foreign energy companies to invest in offshore exploration. However, China's strong opposition and coercive tactics have significantly hindered this process. Despite these challenges, Russia has continued its hydrocarbon activities within China's claimed Nine-Dash Line, conducting offshore energy operations on Vietnam's behalf. Russian state-owned energy companies Zarubezhneft and Vietsovpetro are actively involved in multiple offshore energy projects (Korolev, 2018: Kuo, 2023). The critical importance of these operations is underscored by the fact that Block 06-01 alone accounts for approximately 30% of Vietnam's total natural gas demand. Through Zarubezhneft, Vietgazprom, and Vietsovpetro, Russia has emerged as the largest foreign energy actor operating within the disputed Nine-Dash Line, surpassing other external stakeholders such as the United Kingdom and India (McLaughlin, 2022). This places Russia in a pivotal position in defending Vietnam's rights to exploit natural resources within its Exclusive Economic Zone (EEZ). By facilitating the exploration and extraction of hydrocarbons, Russia strengthens Vietnam's de facto presence in the region, which in turn reinforces Hanoi's sovereignty claims on both political and legal grounds

However, as with Russia's arms sales to Vietnam, its energy cooperation should not be viewed solely through an economic lens. While the hydrocarbon sector is highly profitable, deep-sea exploration and extraction involve significant financial and operational risks. Russian energy giants, particularly Gazprom and Zarubezhneft, have historically encountered high operational costs in offshore drilling (Denisov et al., 2021). Consequently, Russia's SCS energy activities are not merely profit-driven;

rather, they serve as a geopolitical balancing mechanism to counter China's regional dominance. Upon examining Russia's stance in the SCS, it becomes apparent that Moscow pursues an ostensibly neutral position while simultaneously engaging in military and energy partnerships with Vietnam—a policy that at times appears contradictory to its strategic alignment with China. Russia has been cautious in its political rhetoric, aligning with China's narrative of non-external intervention in the dispute while avoiding being perceived as a direct external actor. However, Russia's military and energy engagements with Vietnam have produced outcomes that conflict with China's strategic interests.

The sale of advanced Russian weaponry to Vietnam has enhanced Hanoi's military capacity in the SCS, though it has not yet achieved parity with China's superior naval forces. Nevertheless, these arms transfers have strengthened Vietnam's power projection capabilities and bolstered its diplomatic leverage. Additionally, Russia's leadership in Vietnam's hydrocarbon exploration and extraction efforts has amplified Vietnam's influence in the SCS dispute, as control over maritime energy resources remains a critical factor in sovereignty claims (Denisov et al., 2021).

CONCLUSION

The South China Sea dispute stands as one of the most volatile and strategically consequential arenas of contemporary international politics, where geopolitical, economic, and security dynamics converge. The analysis of Russia's policy in this maritime domain demonstrates that Moscow's engagement is shaped by a multifaceted strategy that combines hedging, balancing, and pragmatic neutrality. While Russia has traditionally been recognized as a continental power, its historical quest for maritime access and strategic presence underscores the enduring importance of naval projection in its foreign policy. Against this background, the South China Sea emerges not only as a regional flashpoint but also as a theater where Russia's global orientation toward the Asia-Pacific and Indo-Pacific becomes visible. Power shifts in the global system also influence the behaviour of actors. In this context, the South China Sea serves as a notable example, where Russia and China are not only challengers but have also assumed a new central role on a global scale. From this perspective, within the restructuring of the system, existing alliances and expanding spheres of influence have led to the emergence of new security arrangements across multiple domains of the global order, stretching from the Arctic to the Antarctic. At this very point, the role of the South China Sea in the context of hegemony has noticeably increased.

The empirical evidence presented highlights that Russia's South China Sea policy is neither entirely aligned with China nor fully committed to supporting other claimants such as Vietnam. Instead, Moscow has deliberately crafted a hedging strategy that allows it to preserve strategic flexibility. This approach is visible in its official rhetoric of neutrality, which emphasizes the principles of non-intervention, peaceful dispute resolution, and adherence to UNCLOS. Simultaneously, Russia has deepened its defense cooperation and energy partnerships with Vietnam, thereby reinforcing Hanoi's capacity to sustain its sovereignty claims. These dual policies have occasionally produced contradictions with Moscow's proclaimed neutrality, yet they also reflect Russia's pragmatic attempt to safeguard its long-term interests in Southeast Asia. At this point, hedging, strategic alliances, economic interests, and an anti-Western geopolitical posture form the cornerstones of Russia's South China Sea policy. Moscow is willing to work with regional actors such as Vietnam, even while maintaining strong relations with China. The energy industry is one of the clearest domains where this dual influence is evident. Russia's strategy also reflects its perception of the United States as a hegemonic intruder. The U.S. military presence in these waterways is seen in Moscow as part of a broader pattern of systemic interference. In response, Russia has made a concerted effort to strengthen its strategic partnership with China in order to present a united front against Western dominance. Joint naval exercises have become more frequent, enhancing military coordination and symbolizing this shared commitment to countering external influence.

The broader implication of this study is that Russia's engagement in the South China Sea should be conceptualized within the framework of territorial hegemony and hedging theory. While China pursues territorial hegemony by militarizing artificial islands, asserting expansive sovereignty claims, and unilaterally shaping the security order, Russia employs hedging as a strategic response to systemic uncertainty. In doing so, Moscow avoids entanglement in sovereignty disputes while maintaining sufficient involvement to protect its interests and enhance its presence in the Indo-Pacific. This duality captures the paradox of Russia's position: a declared neutrality coexisting with policies that materially affect the regional balance of power. Russia's South China Sea policy illustrates its pragmatic and multidimensional strategy in contemporary international politics. By balancing cooperation with China against sustained ties with Vietnam, Moscow demonstrates an ability to maneuver within the shifting dynamics of great-power competition. This policy reflects not only Russia's adaptation to the evolving geopolitical landscape of Asia but also its aspiration to redefine itself as both a Eurasian and a Euro-Pacific power. As systemic rivalries deepen and regional disputes in the South China Sea intensify, Russia's strategic choices will remain a significant factor shaping the future balance of power in the Indo-Pacific and the broader international system.

Finally, it should be noted that although the South China Sea currently constitutes a focal area of hegemonic contestation, Taiwan's position at the intersection of the East China Sea and the South China Sea may transform this space into a significant point of contention between China and Japan in the near future. While the linkages may initially appear distant, the conflict dynamics of the Asia-Pacific region render this region a potential "frozen conflict" zone that must be assessed with particular caution. Although Taiwan is not geographically situated within the South China Sea, it functions as the strategic gateway to the region, effectively serving as a "gateway area"

REFERENCES

Adelinet, A. L. (2024). Navigating ambiguities: Unravelling Russia's hedging strategy in the South China Sea.

Cheng, J. Y. (2004). Challenges to China's Russian policy in early 21st century. *Journal of Contemporary Asia*, *34*(4), 480–502. DOI: 10.1080/00472330480000231

Cheng-Chwee, K. (2008). The Essence of Hedging: Malaysia and Singapore's Response to a Rising China. *Contemporary Southeast Asia*, *30*(2), 159–185. https://www.jstor.org/stable/41220503. DOI: 10.1355/CS30-2A

Denisov, I., Paramonov, O., Arapova, E., & Safranchuk, I. (2021). Russia, China, and the concept of Indo-Pacific. *Journal of Eurasian Studies*, *12*(1), 72–85. DOI: 10.1177/1879366521999899

Druzhinin, A. G., & Lachininskii, S. S. (2021). Russia in the World Ocean: Interests and lines of presence. *Regional Research of Russia*, *11*(3), 336–348. DOI: 10.1134/S2079970521030035

Fravel, M. T. (2011). China's strategy in the South China Sea. *Contemporary Southeast Asia*, *33*(3), 292–319. DOI: 10.1355/cs33-3b

Gady, F.-S. (2016, August 31). *Russia to send anti-submarine warfare destroyers to South China Sea. The Diplomat.* https://thediplomat.com/2016/08/russia-to-send-anti-submarine-warfare-destroyers-to-south-china-sea

Hamilton, R. E. (2025, January 28). *Setting the Stage: An Oveview of Chinese and Russian Interest and Inflluence in the Indo-Pacific.* https://www.fpri.org/article/2025/01/setting-the-stage-an-overview-of-chinese-and-russian-interests-and-influence-in-the-indo-pacific/

Ing, L. Y., Anas, T., & Wihardja, M. M. (2022). *2022/72 "Digital transformation under Indonesia's G20 presidency: What can it deliver?" by Lili Yan Ing*. Titik Anas, and Maria Monica Wihardja.

Kaczmarski, M. (2023). The Sino-Russian relationship and the west. In *Survival December 2020–January 2021: A World After Trump* (pp. 199–212). Routledge.

Korolev, A. (2018). Russia in the South China Sea: Balancing and Hedging1. *Foreign Policy Analysis*. Advance online publication. DOI: 10.1093/fpa/orx015

Kuo, M. A. (2023). "Russia's Asia-Pacific Interests: Insights from Elizabeth Wishnick," *The Diplomat*, May 30, 2023, https://thediplomat.com/2023/05/russias-asia-pacific-interests/

McLaughlin, R. (2022). The law of the sea and PRC gray-zone operations in the South China Sea. *The American Journal of International Law, 116*(4), 821–835. DOI: 10.1017/ajil.2022.49

Özel Özcan, M. S. (2020, May 18–20). Rus–Japon ilişkilerinde jeopolitik düello: Kuril Adaları sorunu. Paper presented at the Congress on Scientific Researches and Recent Trends.

Özel Özcan, M. S., & Goziev, R. (2019). XIX. yüzyılda Doğu Asya'da Rus-Japon imparatorluklarının güç mücadelesi: 1905 Rus-Japon Savaşı. Türkiye Rusya Araştırmaları Dergisi, (2), 46–65.

Putra, B. A. (2021). Comprehending Brunei Darussalam's vanishing claims in the South China Sea: China's exertion of economic power and the influence of elite perception. *Cogent Social Sciences, 7*(1), 1858563. DOI: 10.1080/23311886.2020.1858563

Şahin, E. (2024). Güney Çin Denizi'nde Jeopolitik Dinamikler: Ofansif Realizm Teorisi Çerçevesinde ABD-Çin Rekabeti. *Terörizm ve Güvenlik Araştırmaları Dergisi, 1*(1), 63–78. DOI: 10.29329/tegad.2024.1111.4

Şahin, E. (2025). *Arktik Bölgesinde Teritoryal Hegemonya: Rusya ve ABD Rekabeti. Yüksek Lisans Tezi. Kırıkkale Üniversitesi Sosyal Bilimler Enstitüsü.* Kırıkkale.

Şahin, E. & Özel Özcan, M. S. (2024). Bölgesel Güvenlik Kompleksi Bağlamında Artan Arktik Rekabeti ve Askeri Güvenlik. *Paradigma: İktisadi ve İdari Araştırmalar Dergisi,* 13(Özel Sayı), 90-111.

Thu, H. L. & Cao, S. (2019, Dec 18). *Russia's growing interests in the South China Sea.* Russia's growing interests in the South China Sea | The Strategist.

Torkunov, A., & Streltsov, D. (2023). Russian policy of turning to East: Problems and risks. *World Economy and International Relations, 67*(4), 5–16. DOI: 10.20542/0131-2227-2023-67-4-5-16

Tsvetov, A. (2016, November 1). *Russia's Tactics and Strategy in the South China Sea.* https://amti.csis.org/russias-tactics-strategy-south-chinasea/#:~:text=Such%20fears%20increased%20as%20the,Russia%20was%20leaning%0toward%20China.

Tsvetov, A. (2016, April 22). *Did Russia Just Side With China on the South China Sea?.* https://russiancouncil.ru/en/analytics-and-comments/analytics/did-russia-just-side-with-china-on-the-south-china-sea/#:~:text=The%20South%20China%20Sea%20is,partners%20%E2%80%93%20China%20and%20Vietnam.

ADDITIONAL READING

Aznar, J. (2024, September 10). *The scary new map of the South China Sea.* https://www.economist.com/asia/2024/09/10/the-scary-new-map-of-the-south-china-sea

Campagnol, L. (2022, March 4). *China's rising assertiveness in the South China Sea.* IARI Institute of Asia-Pacific Studies. https://iari.site/2022/03/04/chinas-rising-assertiveness-in-the-south-china-sea/

Korolev, A. (2016). Systemic balancing and regional hedging: China–Russia relations. *The Chinese Journal of International Politics, 9*(4), 375–397. DOI: 10.1093/cjip/pow013

KEY TERMS AND DEFINITIONS

Balancing Strategies: Here, a state seeks to preserve the balance of power in the international system by enhancing its own capabilities (internal balancing) or forming alliances (external balancing) in response to emerging power concentrations. This approach reflects the state's intention to limit hegemonic pressure and secure a stabilising position within the system.

Great Power and Military Conflict: Great powers are actors capable of projecting power within the international system through extensive military capacity, global influence, and the ability to shape crisis zones; therefore, any military tension between them carries the potential to generate strategic ruptures at the systemic level, far beyond the scope of regional conflicts.

Hedging: In international relations, hedging refers to a state's strategic behaviour aimed at distributing risks in the face of uncertainty or perceived threats, avoiding both complete alignment and outright opposition. This approach enables the state to maintain relations with multiple major powers simultaneously, thereby expanding its room for manoeuvre and generating strategic flexibility.

Nine-Dash Line: The Nine-Dash Line represents China's claim to sovereignty in the South China Sea, based on alleged historical rights that encompass nearly the entire maritime region as part of its area of influence. This demarcation overlaps with the exclusive economic zones of several neighbouring states, heightening geopolitical tensions and prompting ongoing discussions about international law.

Territorial Hegemony: Territorial hegemony denotes a state's capacity to establish uncontested dominance over a specific geographical area through military, political, and economic instruments, and to shape the regional order in line with its strategic interests.

United Nations Convention on the Law of the Sea (UNCLOS): UNCLOS is a comprehensive international convention that defines states' maritime jurisdiction, navigation rights, and the use of marine resources, forming the core framework of global maritime law; by doing so, it establishes the legal boundaries of sovereignty claims and geopolitical competition at sea, creating a regulatory balance mechanism.

ENDNOTES

1 In preparing this chapter, AI-based tools (DeepL and ChatGPT) were employed for translation and proofreading purposes. These AI tools were used exclusively as supportive instruments to improve linguistic clarity and coherence.

2 China initially published an Eleven-Dash Line map in 1947 to outline its territorial claims but later reduced it to Nine Dashes in 1952. However, the Nine-Dash Line lacks a clear legal definition, and its coordinates have never been officially specified. China uses this line to reinforce its sovereignty claims in the SCS (Zha, 2001).

Chapter 12
The Resurgence of Realism in International Relations:
Examining the Russia–Ukraine Conflict and Its Implications for Vietnam's Foreign Policy

Kiet Hoang Le
https://orcid.org/0009-0002-9968-1952
University of Social Sciences and Humanities, Vietnam National University, Hanoi, Vietnam

Pranjal Khare
https://orcid.org/0000-0002-9937-9588
O.P. Jindal Global University, India

Hiep Xuan Tran
The University of Da Nang, University of Science and Education, Vietnam

ABSTRACT

This research examines how the Russia-Ukraine conflict has challenged the liberal institutional order that has governed international relations since 1991. Using realism theoretical frameworks, the study analyzes the limitations of international law in regulating the behavior of great powers when core security interests are threatened. The Russia-Ukraine conflict demonstrates how traditional geopolitical considerations can override institutional constraints despite decades of economic interdependence. Through analysis of Ukraine's geostrategic position and Russia's security perceptions, the study demonstrates the continued relevance of realism in

DOI: 10.4018/979-8-3373-2342-8.ch012

explaining power dynamics in the international system. Using Vietnam as a case study, the research proposes strategic policy recommendations for small states navigating geopolitically sensitive positions amid great power competition. Finally, this study contributes to international relations discourse by illustrating the enduring explanatory power of realism while offering practical foreign policy approaches for small states seeking to maintain autonomy in an increasingly competitive great power environment.

INTRODUCTION

In the context of the third decade of the 21st century, deep globalization has created a multidimensional network of international relations and "interdependence" between nations and regions (Kiet & Tuyen, 2023). In this context, international law and multilateral institutions were expected to become tools to restrain the use of "hard power" by major powers against states with more limited capabilities (Cai, 2013). On this foundation,liberalism became the dominant theoretical framework for explaining contemporary international political interactions (Searle, 1992). However, the Russia-Ukraine conflict that erupted on February 24, 2022, created a significant turning point in contemporary international relations, considered the most serious geopolitical disaster since the end of the Cold War in 1991. Notably, the occurrence of this conflict in Europe - traditionally considered the "bastion of liberalism in the era of globalization" - has posed fundamental challenges to the rules-based world order led by the US and Western allies and the effectiveness of collective security mechanisms within the United Nations framework.

This development reflects the declining effectiveness of international law in controlling the behavior of major powers in the context of increasingly intense power competition between major powers. Particularly, in regions within the strategic spheres of influence of superpowers like the United States, China, and Russia, the principles of international law are often challenged by traditional geopolitical arguments, as Khan (2023) describes:

> *"The most concerning impact of the Russia-Ukraine conflict is the reorientation of the global security order back to its traditional concept, established after World War II, dominated by military action, alliances, agreements, large-scale arms races, military industrial production, and increased defense budgets".*

This trend has led to a fundamental restructuring in the international relations system, with geopolitical factors and traditional security playing an increasingly important role in nations' foreign policies (Grano, 2023). This is reflected in the increase in global defense spending, the formation of new strategic alliances, and the trend toward militarization in resolving international disputes (Lobell, 2016).

Consequently, the global governance model based on institutional liberal principles is facing increasingly complex challenges, requiring a fundamental reassessment of the effectiveness of multilateral cooperation mechanisms in maintaining international peace and security.

In this context, realism has reaffirmed its role as a key theoretical framework in explaining and analyzing the impact of the Russia-Ukraine conflict on global security architecture. In particular, structural realism's arguments about the role of power and balance of forces in international relations have been demonstrated through the conflict's developments (Kiet et al., 2024). The consequences of this situation pose serious security challenges for states with limited capabilities, especially countries in sensitive geopolitical zones between competing powers. Notable examples include Vietnam in US-China relations, the Taiwan (China) issue in regional strategic competition, or Cuba's position in the Latin American geopolitical context. On this basis, this study focuses on analyzing three core aspects: (i) Evaluating the limitations of international law in regulating the behavior of major powers in the context of increasing strategic competition; (ii) Analyzing the geopolitical and strategic dynamics leading to the Ukraine crisis from an international security perspective; and (iii) Proposing strategic directions in Vietnam's foreign policy to adapt to the volatile international security environment in the post-Russia-Ukraine conflict period.

The Russia-Ukraine conflict represents a watershed moment in post-Cold War international relations, fundamentally challenging the liberal institutional order that has governed international relations since 1991. This research's timeliness stems from its examination of how this conflict has exposed the limitations of international law and multilateral institutions in protecting small states' sovereignty when great powers pursue their strategic interests. This is particularly relevant as the global order appears to be shifting from a unipolar to a multipolar system, characterized by intensifying great power competition.

The research gains additional significance through its theoretical application of realism principles to analyze contemporary security challenges facing small states. By examining how traditional geopolitical considerations have reasserted themselves despite decades of economic interdependence and institutional cooperation, the study provides valuable insights into the enduring relevance of realism theory in explaining international behavior. This theoretical framework becomes especially pertinent as small states must navigate an increasingly complex security environment where great power competition intersects with regional tensions. Furthermore, the research's focus on Vietnam's strategic position carries substantial practical implications. As a small state situated within a geopolitically sensitive region amid US-China strategic competition, Vietnam's experience offers a compelling case study for understanding how similar states can maintain their security and autonomy. The research's analysis of Vietnam's situation alongside other comparable cases like

Cuba and Taiwan (China) provides valuable comparative insights into small states' strategic options in regions of great power contestation.

The study's emphasis on the diminishing effectiveness of international law and multilateral institutions in regulating great power behavior holds particular contemporary relevance. As traditional geopolitical considerations increasingly override institutional constraints, small states must adapt their foreign policy approaches accordingly. This research's examination of this trend offers crucial insights for policymakers in small states working to protect their national interests in an evolving international environment. Additionally, the research's investigation of the structural changes in international relations following the Russia-Ukraine conflict provides important analytical value. By examining how this conflict has catalyzed increased global defense spending, the formation of new strategic alliances, and the militarization of international dispute resolution, the study helps illuminate the emerging patterns in international security dynamics that small states must navigate.

The research's practical significance is further enhanced by its policy implications for Vietnam's foreign relations. As Vietnam seeks to maintain its strategic autonomy while managing relations with competing great powers, the insights derived from this analysis can inform the development of more effective foreign policy strategies. This makes the research particularly valuable for Vietnamese policymakers and analysts working to adapt national security approaches to changing international circumstances. Lastly, the research contributes to the broader academic discourse on international relations by examining how traditional realism principles interact with contemporary global challenges. This theoretical contribution helps bridge the gap between classical realism thinking and modern international relations, providing a more nuanced understanding of how small states can navigate an increasingly complex and contested global order.

LITERATURE REVIEW

The theoretical foundations of this research are deeply rooted in the extensive body of realism scholarship that has evolved since the end of the Cold War. Kenneth Waltz's seminal work "Theory of International Politics" (1979) provides the structural realism framework that underpins much of the analysis, particularly his assertion that in an anarchic international system, states prioritize national security interests and relative power over adherence to international legal principles. This foundational argument remains central to understanding contemporary great power behavior, as demonstrated by recent geopolitical developments. Building upon Waltz's structural foundations, John Mearsheimer's contributions to offensive realism theory offer crucial insights into great power competition dynamics. Mearsheimer's analysis in "The False Promise of International Institutions" (1996) challenges liberal institutionalist assumptions about the constraining power of international organizations, arguing that states will pursue their security interests regardless of institutional frameworks when vital concerns are at stake. His more recent work on the Ukraine conflict (Mearsheimer, 2022a, 2022b) directly applies these theoretical principles to contemporary events, demonstrating the enduring relevance of realism logic in explaining state behavior during crisis situations.

The evolution of international law and institutional effectiveness has been extensively examined through both liberal and realism lenses. Cai's (2013) comprehensive analysis of international law in the 21st century provides a nuanced understanding of how legal frameworks operate within the context of great power competition, while acknowledging their limitations in constraining state behavior when core interests are threatened. This perspective is further developed by Moses (2013), who critiques the liberal notion of sovereignty as responsibility, arguing from a realism standpoint that the asymmetrical distribution of power fundamentally undermines the effectiveness of international legal mechanisms.

Contemporary scholarship has increasingly focused on the practical implications of realism theory for understanding current conflicts. Edinger's (2022) analysis of Putin's war on Ukraine through both structural and classical realism frameworks demonstrates how traditional realism concepts remain highly relevant for explaining contemporary interstate conflict. Similarly, Smith and Dawson (2022) provide a thorough examination of how Mearsheimer's realism predictions about the Ukraine crisis proved prescient, highlighting the analytical value of realism theory in forecasting geopolitical developments. Besides, the literature on small state behavior within great power competition frameworks has been particularly influential in shaping this research. Walt's (2017) comprehensive analysis of realism and security provides theoretical grounding for understanding how smaller states navigate complex security environments dominated by great power rivalry. This theoretical foundation is complemented by regional studies that examine specific cases of small state adaptation strategies.

Recent scholarship has also addressed the broader implications of changing international order dynamics. Lobell's (2016) work on balance of power theory and power transitions offers valuable insights into how structural changes in the international system affect state behavior patterns. This theoretical framework becomes particularly relevant when analyzing how the Russia-Ukraine conflict has accelerated shifts toward a multipolar international system. The regional dimension of great power competition has received significant scholarly attention, particularly regarding Asia-Pacific dynamics. Shambaugh's (2022) analysis of US-China strategic competition in Southeast Asia provides crucial context for understanding how small states like Vietnam must navigate between competing great powers. This work is complemented by specialized studies examining ASEAN's role in managing regional tensions, such as Hu's (2021) analysis of the organization's effectiveness in handling South China Sea disputes. Historical perspectives on international organization effectiveness provide important comparative context for contemporary analysis. Young's (1968) foundational work on the United Nations and the international system, along with Weiss's (2015) comprehensive examination of UN evolution, offer crucial insights into the structural limitations of international institutions in constraining great power behavior. These historical analyses help illuminate the continuities and changes in international institutional effectiveness over time.

In conclusion, the synthesis of these diverse theoretical and empirical contributions creates a robust foundation for analyzing contemporary international relations through a realism lens, while acknowledging the complex interplay between traditional power politics and modern institutional frameworks.

METHODOLOGY

This study employs a qualitative research methodology grounded in the relism paradigm of international relations to analyze the Russia-Ukraine conflict and its implications for small states, particularly Vietnam. Our methodological approach combines theoretical analysis, case study investigation, and comparative evaluation within a neorelism framework. The research methodology is structured around three interconnected analytical levels.

First, the paper conduct a systematic analysis of the limitations of international law in regulating great power behavior by examining historical cases where security interests have superseded legal constraints. This analysis draws primarily on structural realism as articulated by Kenneth Waltz and offensive realism as developed by John Mearsheimer, focusing on how the anarchic structure of the international system shapes state behavior when core security interests are threatened.

Second, the paper apply geopolitical analysis to examine Ukraine's strategic position between Russia and NATO. This involves evaluating primary sources including official statements from the Russian government, policy documents, and speeches by key decision-makers. The paper analyze these materials through the lens of the security dilemma concept and balance of power theory to understand how Russia's perception of NATO expansion triggered security concerns that ultimately led to military intervention despite international legal prohibitions.

Third, the paper employ comparative case study methodology to draw parallels between Ukraine's position and that of other small states in geopolitically sensitive regions, particularly Vietnam. This comparative approach helps identify generalizable patterns in how small states navigate great power competition while maintaining strategic autonomy. The paper supplement this analysis with process tracing to establish causal mechanisms between great power competition and small state foreign policy responses.

Finally, the methodological framework allows paper to test several key relism propositions: (i) That states prioritize security over adherence to international norms when vital interests are threatened; (ii) That the distribution of power in the international system significantly influences state behavior regardless of institutional constraints; and (iii) That small states must adopt flexible, pragmatic approaches to foreign policy to survive in an anarchic international environment dominated by great power competition.

RESULTS

1. The Binding Effect of International Law in the Realist Lens

The establishment of the League of Nations on January 10, 1920, based on 26 articles in its Covenant, marked a significant turning point in efforts to create a multipolar world order. This organization was expected to serve as the first institutional foundation to promote global cooperation and maintain international peace (Young, 1968). However, from the perspective of realism, the founding of the League of Nations clearly reflected the power-balancing actions of the victorious powers after World War I, particularly Britain and France, as they sought to maintain their dominant position in the postwar world order (Mearsheimer, 1994). The transition from the League of Nations to the United Nations in 1945 signaled an attempt to restructure the global governance system following the disaster of World War II. Nevertheless, the bipolar structure of the Cold War, characterized by ideological and geopolitical confrontation between the United States and the Soviet Union, significantly weakened the effectiveness of multilateral mechanisms. According to Kenneth Waltz (1979, p. 66), in an anarchic international system, states prioritize national security interests and relative power over adherence to international legal principles.

The end of the Cold War ushered in a new era for the role of the United Nations and international law. In the context of globalization, which has blurred the boundaries of traditional nation-states, non-traditional security challenges such as transnational terrorism, climate change, illegal migration, and global pandemics require multilateral solutions and transnational legal frameworks. According to Cai's (2013) definition, international law is "a system of binding norms and principles governing relations among international actors, particularly sovereign states". This view has been consistently supported by liberalists and pacifists, who see the United Nations and international law as the foundation for maintaining a peaceful global political environment, restraining and preventing the likelihood of "hot" conflicts between major powers, as well as between states. However, realism theorist Edinger (2022) counters this argument, asserting that:

> *"In an anarchic international system, an institution that functions like a state (i.e., the United Nations) does not exist, as the asymmetrical distribution of power results in national security being under constant threat. This forces each political actor to ensure its security by balancing power".*

According to realism theory, the practical effectiveness of international law is facing fundamental challenges stemming from the characteristics of the contemporary international system. Three main obstacles that limit the effectiveness of international law can be systematically analyzed as follows:

(i) The absence of an effective coercive enforcement mechanism creates a significant gap in ensuring compliance with international law. Unlike national legal systems, where law enforcement agencies with clear coercive powers are present, the international environment lacks a "global executive authority" with the jurisdiction and capacity to enforce international rulings and resolutions. This leads to a situation where states can choose whether to comply with international regulations without facing serious legal consequences.

(ii) The principle of national sovereignty continues to serve as a major barrier to the effectiveness of international law (Moses, 2013). In the context of the Westphalian system still dominating international relations, states, particularly great powers, often invoke this principle as a legal tool to justify non-compliance with international obligations when such obligations conflict with their core national interests. This reflects the fundamental conflict between national sovereignty and the binding nature of international law.

(iii) The asymmetrical power structure in the modern international system creates profound inequalities in the application and enforcement of international law. This is most clearly illustrated by the veto power mechanism of the five permanent members of the United Nations Security Council—namely, the United States, Russia, China, the United Kingdom, and France. This mechanism creates a "two-tier" system in the application of international law, in which great powers can avoid international sanctions by exercising their veto power.

In the context of deepening globalization, although international law has made significant progress in regulating state behavior, realisms argue that its binding power is effective only in areas that do not directly threaten the national security of great powers (Mearsheimer, 2022a). When the "red line" of national security is crossed, great powers are willing to break the framework of international law to pursue countermeasures, including both traditional military conflict (hot wars) and non-traditional forms of confrontation, such as economic warfare and cyber warfare (cold wars). This practice significantly undermines the effectiveness of the United Nations and the international legal system in regulating the behavior of great powers, especially in situations involving strategic competition and conflicts of national security interests. This weakness partially arises from the internal structure of the United Nations, an organization composed of member states but dominated by the five permanent members of the Security Council. As a result, the international legal system is often rendered ineffective at the most critical moments—when it is needed to prevent conflict and maintain international order.

The shift in the methods of power enforcement by major powers from the 19th century to the present reflects fundamental changes in the structure of the international system. Before the wave of globalization in the 1980s, great powers often employed hard power through strategies like the British Empire's "Splendid Isolation" or the United States' "Offshore Balancing". However, the advent of globalization, along with the increasing role of the United Nations and international law, has created significant barriers to the direct use of hard power. In this new context, rising powers such as China have had to adjust their geopolitical strategies. While still pursuing the goal of expanding influence, they are forced to operate within the framework of international law, though sometimes through controversial "claims". This creates a more favorable environment for smaller nations to protect their sovereignty and national interests. However, instead of abandoning hegemonic ambitions, the great powers have shifted toward using new tools of power that are more suited to the era of globalization. "Economic power" and "soft power" have become important strategic tools. A notable example is China's "debt trap" strategy within the framework of the Belt and Road Initiative (BRI), as well as the use of economic and political leverage to build alliances and influence in regional organizations. A specific example is China's influence over Cambodia, which resulted in the exclusion of the South China Sea issue from the ASEAN discussion agenda in 2012 (Hu, 2021). Furthermore, recent events such as NATO's military intervention in Yugoslavia (1999), the Iraq War (2003), the Russia-Georgia conflict (2008), and particularly the ongoing Russia-Ukraine conflict have highlighted the limitations of international law in controlling the behavior of great powers when their core security interests are at stake. This presents a major challenge for countries with sensitive geopolitical positions in formulating and implementing their foreign policy strategies.

From a realism perspective, there is a discernible trend shifting from the use of traditional hard power to more complex forms of power, combining both "coercive" and "persuasive" tools. This requires smaller nations to develop stronger strategic analysis and forecasting capabilities, while also establishing flexible mechanisms for prevention and response to multidimensional influence from great powers. In this context, the development of a multilateral, balanced, and adaptable foreign policy strategy becomes more important than ever. Nations must leverage multilateral mechanisms and international law as tools to protect their interests, while maintaining the flexibility to adjust policies in response to changes in the global geopolitical environment. The Russia-Ukraine conflict, along with other recent conflicts between nations and ethnic groups, has demonstrated the ineffectiveness of international law in controlling the behavior of major powers when core interests and national security are directly involved. Therefore, smaller nations with significant and sensitive geopolitical positions in relation to the great powers must adopt flexible foreign policies to avoid compromising their own national interests.

2. The Geostrategic Position of Ukraine through the Lens of Realism

From the perspective of geopolitics and realism in international relations, Ukraine plays a pivotal role as a buffer state between the Russian Federation and the Western bloc (Mearsheimer, 2022b). Located in Eastern Europe, Ukraine occupies a strategic geographic position with an area of 603,700 km^2, making it the second-largest country in Europe after Russia. This geographical feature grants Ukraine a unique geostrategic advantage, as it shares borders with several influential countries: to the east, it borders Russia, the world's largest nuclear power; to the north, it borders Belarus, a close ally of Moscow; to the west, it shares borders with three NATO member states—Poland, Slovakia, and Hungary; to the southwest, it borders Romania (another NATO member) and Moldova, while to the south, Ukraine has access to the Black Sea and the Sea of Azov, both of which are strategically important for security and maritime trade (IMO, 2023).

From a historical-cultural perspective, Ukraine and Russia share deep-rooted ties that trace back to ancient Slavic civilization. The Kievan Rus' Empire, with its capital in Kyiv (now Ukraine), is considered the cultural cradle of both nations. However, the Mongol Empire's invasion (1223–1240) marked a significant historical turning point, forcing a portion of the Slavic population to migrate eastward, eventually giving rise to the Russian Empire. According to the perspective of Kiet et al. (2024), this historical-cultural factor has been used by Moscow as a "soft power" tool to maintain geopolitical influence over Ukraine. The collapse of the Soviet Union in 1991 marked a watershed moment in bilateral relations when Ukraine declared independence, officially becoming a sovereign state. However, from a relism viewpoint, Ukraine's increasing alignment with the West has posed a security threat to Russia's geopolitical interests (Smith & Dawson, 2022). This partially explains the outbreak of the Russia-Ukraine conflict on February 24, 2022, which is regarded as the most serious geopolitical crisis since the Cold War. The conflict has not only shattered the "brotherly" relationship between the two nations but also fundamentally altered Europe's security structure, with profound implications for the emerging multipolar world order.

With its unique geostrategic position between the Russian Federation and the "old continent" of Europe, Ukraine serves a dual role as both a "buffer zone" and a geopolitical bridge between these two powerful entities. However, the complex historical legacy, especially the traumas from the Cold War era, has left a deep impact on the strategic perceptions of the parties involved. Eastern European countries, once part of the former Soviet Union, still maintain a high level of vigilance toward Moscow. This has driven the European Union to pursue a policy of detaching from Russian influence in Europe's geopolitical space. Walt and Belfer (2017) provided a thorough analysis, stating: "The historical memories of wartime experiences strongly influence the psychology of a nation's ruling elite. Even the most rational leaders are affected by the power of collective memory." This argument explains why European nations consistently express deep concerns about Russia's potential to restore geopolitical influence, while also emphasizing Ukraine's strategic importance to both Moscow and Brussels.

Renowned geopolitical strategist Zbigniew Brzezinski made a critical observation: "Ukraine is a strategically positioned country, playing a key role in NATO's eastward expansion, forming a defensive and encircling stance against Russia" (Brzezinski, 2019, p.185). Brzezinski's analysis is particularly relevant when considering Ukraine's vast plains that border Russia's western frontier. In this context, the prospect of Ukraine joining NATO poses a serious strategic challenge to Moscow's geopolitical influence in Europe. From the Kremlin's perspective, Ukraine is viewed as a crucial geopolitical space within Russia's traditional sphere of influence in the post-Soviet region. This view is clearly articulated in President Vladimir Putin's declaration: "For us, Ukraine is not just a neighboring country, but an inseparable part of our history, culture, and spirit" (Kremlin, 2022). This statement reflects Russia's historically and culturally grounded geopolitical approach toward Ukraine, going far beyond the conventional framework of neighborly relations.

In Russia's geopolitical thinking, Ukraine plays a dual role of vital significance. On one hand, Ukraine is viewed as a strategic "buffer zone" that allows Moscow to maintain a geopolitical connection with Europe. On the other hand, Ukraine's territory serves as a "natural defense line" protecting Russia's western region, where key political, economic, and cultural centers are located. According to Robert Kaplan, this geographical feature is crucial to Moscow's strategic mindset (Kaplan, 2018, p. 155). In this context, the prospect of Ukraine joining NATO is seen by the Kremlin as an existential threat to national security. This perception is clearly reflected in Russia's "New Foreign Policy", in which Moscow accuses:

"The United States and its satellites have used the measures taken by Russia to protect its vital interests concerning Ukraine as a pretext to escalate their long-standing anti-Russian policies and initiate a new kind of hybrid war. This hybrid war seeks to weaken Russia by any means possible, including undermining its military, economic, and technological potential, as well as aiming to restrict Russia's sovereignty in foreign and domestic policy and erode its territorial integrity" (Kremlin, 2023).

Kyiv's determination to pursue NATO integration has crossed the "red line" in Moscow's strategic perception. From President Vladimir Putin's perspective, this development poses a direct threat to Russia's core security interests. Although Moscow attempted diplomacy by submitting the Security Guarantees Agreement on December 17, 2021, NATO's rejection of these proposals led to a deadlock. As the prospect of Ukraine joining NATO became increasingly relismic, coupled with a perception of national security being seriously threatened, Moscow decided to launch a special military operation against Ukraine, disregarding the constraints of international law and the risk of facing comprehensive sanctions from the international community. This event, in part, highlights the importance of national security perceptions for a great power—continuously challenging a "red line" can lead to severe consequences for weaker nations, where international law cannot enforce actions against great powers.

In analyzing the Russia-Ukraine tensions, John Mearsheimer—one of the leading theorists of the relism school in international relations—provided a profound observation: "Russia does not want a Western wall right on its doorstep, which is entirely reasonable from Russia's point of view" (Kalus, 2022). This argument reflects the nature of geopolitical thinking in international relations, where national security is always a top priority for any nation, regardless of its size. Mearsheimer asserts that when a nation's vital interests are severely threatened without an appropriate diplomatic solution, the risk of armed conflict becomes difficult to avoid. This analysis is further supported by Walt's (2017) perspective—another influential scholar of the relism school: "All nations strive to survive, while acknowledging that some may have more ambitious goals. However, because these nations exist in an anarchic system, they must rely on their own resources and strategies for survival". This point emphasizes the anarchic nature of the international system, in which each nation must fend for itself in the absence of a supreme authority.

The Russia-Ukraine conflict has illustrated the strong resurgence of relism logic in contemporary international relations. According to Milan (1984), in an anarchic international system, nations are willing to use all necessary means, including military power, to protect their core security interests. Moscow's decision to intervene militarily in Ukraine precisely reflects this logic—it was a final act aimed at halting NATO's eastward expansion, which the Kremlin viewed as an existential threat to Russia's strategic security. In this context, the use of force is seen by Moscow as an unavoidable tool to maintain regional power balance and prevent the risk of strategic encirclement.

3. Implications for Vietnam's Foreign Policy

Milan (1984) once argued that the fundamental difference between large and small nations lies in their ability to ensure their own survival. According to him, small nations cannot guarantee their own survival independently and must always rely on external factors, while large nations possess the resources to control international affairs. Although in the 21st century, with the rise of globalization and the presence of international law, smaller countries have gained more tools and mechanisms to protect their interests against larger powers—especially when their actions do not directly infringe upon the core interests of great powers—the Russia-Ukraine conflict has shown that great powers still persist in their struggle for dominance. The existing international legal institutions are still not strong enough to fully shield smaller nations from international conflicts. This has led to the continued vulnerability of smaller states, particularly when collective security systems and international law remain limited in their ability to constrain the actions of major powers.

The statement by Malaysian Prime Minister Mahathir Mohamad on July 24, 1996, also reflects this reality when he addressed the challenges of globalization for smaller nations:

> *"Since gaining freedom, the former Western colonies have realized the emptiness of the independence they achieved. They found that they are even more dependent than when they were colonies. From politics, economics, social systems, to their behaviors, they are directly or indirectly influenced by former colonial masters or other great powers" (Weiss, 2015).*

In the current context, as power competition between major nations like the United States and China in the Indo-Pacific region intensifies (Shambaugh, 2022, pp. 14), smaller nations like Vietnam need to build a proactive and flexible foreign policy strategy. To achieve the goal of "strategic autonomy" and avoid becoming passive in international relations, Vietnam needs to carefully shape its foreign policy through the following measures:

First, Vietnam needs to establish a comprehensive system for collecting information and continuously evaluating the situation to promptly capture the complex developments on the international stage, particularly amid the increasingly intense United States-China strategic competition in the Indo-Pacific region. To achieve this, Vietnam must build an extensive information-gathering system that combines official and unofficial sources, utilizing various channels of information from diplomatic missions, international organizations, experts, and researchers both domestic and foreign. This system should operate professionally, with clear roles and responsibilities to avoid overlap and waste of resources. Moreover, the process of evaluating and analyzing information requires a team of experienced experts who possess a deep understanding of regional and global issues. These experts must be capable of synthesizing, comparing, and cross-referencing different sources to produce accurate assessments and forecasts. In addition, updating information is essential in the digital age and in the era of social media. Therefore, the information collection and analysis system must be digitized, applying modern technology to enhance timeliness and accuracy. This will help Vietnam closely monitor critical developments on the international stage, particularly the United States-China competition in the region, allowing for timely and accurate assessments and forecasts to guide the country's foreign policy decisions effectively.

Second, building a high-quality diplomatic corps is a key factor for Vietnam to successfully implement its foreign policy in the face of complex and challenging international conditions. This team needs to be systematically and comprehensively trained in fields such as international relations theory, international law, foreign economics, national security, and the socio-cultural aspects of other nations. Alongside in-depth expertise, the diplomatic team must possess strong analytical, synthesis, and forecasting skills. They must regularly update themselves with the latest information and data, staying attuned to regional and global trends to make accurate judgments and assessments. This will serve as an important foundation for providing practical and effective policy recommendations to senior leaders. Additionally, diplomats should be equipped with negotiation, dialogue, problem-solving, intercultural communication, and multilingual skills. These capabilities will enable them to build relationships and promote cooperation with international partners effectively. A high-quality diplomatic team will allow Vietnam to proactively seize opportunities, respond effectively to challenges, and shape international issues in ways that align with the country's national interests. This is crucial to ensuring that Vietnam does not fall into a passive position, overly dependent on other countries in its foreign relations.

Third, strengthening connections with countries in the region and the world is an effective solution for Vietnam to mitigate risks and challenges arising from the current unpredictable and complex international situation. Diversifying and multilateralizing diplomatic relations will help Vietnam avoid over-reliance on any single partner or group of partners, thus preventing domination or pressure from any side (such as China or the United States). At the regional level, Vietnam needs to continue promoting comprehensive cooperation with ASEAN countries, an organization in which Vietnam is an active member with many strategic interests. At the same time, Vietnam should deepen relationships with key partners such as Japan, South Korea, India, and Australia to balance influence and resources among different parties. On the global stage, Vietnam should actively participate more deeply in multilateral forums and organizations to elevate its position and counterbalance the major powers. Additionally, Vietnam should strengthen strategic partnerships with other important players such as the EU, Russia, Brazil, and others. Diversifying relationships will create a balance of power, reducing the risk of Vietnam becoming dependent or losing strategic autonomy. Alongside diversifying relations, Vietnam should proactively put forth trust-building initiatives, promote dialogue, and consult with major powers both regionally and globally. This will not only enhance bilateral relations but also build confidence among partners that Vietnam is committed to pursuing a foreign policy of peace, regional stability, and cooperative development. This is a crucial foundation for Vietnam to maintain and enhance its role and position on the international stage.

Fourth, enhancing economic and defense self-reliance is a crucial issue for Vietnam to strengthen its autonomy and minimize external dependence and influence in the current context of escalating tensions between major powers. Economically, Vietnam needs to continue advancing its economic development while transitioning its growth model, improving competitiveness, and building self-reliance in key sectors such as technology, energy, and semiconductors. This will help Vietnam avoid over-reliance on external sources and be more proactive in responding to shocks and fluctuations in the international environment. In terms of defense, Vietnam must build a modern, elite armed force with strong deterrence and defense capabilities to safeguard national security and territorial integrity against non-traditional security challenges and external threats. Additionally, it is important to enhance the nation's defense industry potential, ensuring a sufficient supply of weapons and equipment with minimal reliance on external sources. Along with strengthening its economic and defense capacities, Vietnam must also consolidate national unity, which serves as a powerful internal force and a solid foundation for the country to overcome difficulties and protect its core interests, no matter the challenges or tensions it faces. Fostering national pride and confidence in the socialist path is a top priority. With growing economic and defense strength and national unity, Vietnam will be capable of achieving self-reliance, avoiding excessive dependence or external control, and securing national interests against new challenges.

Fifth, maintaining the "four no's" policy is a suitable and necessary approach for Vietnam in the increasingly complex and unpredictable international environment today. Consistently upholding this policy will allow Vietnam to affirm its position as a country that supports peace and stability in the region and the world. This helps build trust and respect from the international community, making it easier for Vietnam to establish and expand relationships with various partners without raising suspicion or facing threats. At the same time, the "four no's" policy helps Vietnam preserve a peaceful and stable environment, avoiding unnecessary conflicts, and focusing its resources on socio-economic development. It clearly demonstrates Vietnam's firm stance on protecting its sovereignty and territorial integrity without resorting to confrontation or force. In the context of escalating United States-China tensions, which risk dragging smaller countries into choosing sides, the "four no's" policy becomes even more beneficial, enabling Vietnam to maintain its autonomy and position as a trusted partner of all parties (Kiet et al., 2025). This policy serves as both leverage for developing relationships and a shield protecting Vietnam from negative external influences. Especially given Vietnam's geographical reality of being located next to a powerful giant, maintaining the "four no's" policy is essential to avoid suspicion and maintain balance.

CONCLUSION

The Russia-Ukraine conflict has had far-reaching impacts on the national security of small countries worldwide. This event has exposed the limitations and gaps in the United Nations' mechanisms for maintaining peace and security, as well as the ineffectiveness of international law in restraining major powers, particularly when their strategic interests and national security are threatened. The power struggle between superpowers is not only playing out on political and military fronts but also tends to escalate and easily break into armed conflict when tensions accumulate to a certain threshold. This puts small countries in a vulnerable position, susceptible to being drawn into power struggles as "proxy battlefields" or suffering disadvantages due to the significant disparity in national strength compared to the major powers.

Amid the increasingly intense strategic competition between the United States and China in the Indo-Pacific region, it is more urgent than ever for small countries like Vietnam to correctly identify their geopolitical position between these two superpowers. This is a decisive factor for the survival and sustainable development of the nation. To adapt to the complex situation and protect national interests, Vietnam must proactively grasp the trends and challenges in international relations while building a high-quality diplomatic corps capable of flexibly and effectively responding to new developments. Vietnam also needs to strengthen regional and international cooperation and enhance its economic and defense self-reliance to ensure its ability to defend itself against unpredictable international fluctuations. Moreover, Vietnam's foreign policy should continue to adhere to the principle of the "four no's" (no military alliances, no aligning with one country to oppose another, no foreign military bases on Vietnamese soil, and no use or threat of force in international relations). This policy not only helps Vietnam maintain its independence and autonomy but also reinforces its position as a reliable partner to all sides, thereby securing national security and interests in the long term.

In general, current international law is still insufficient to fully control the actions of great powers when their vital interests are challenged. Therefore, self-reliance and the proactive development of flexible strategies are essential for small countries, including Vietnam, Taiwan, and Cuba, to adapt to the complex and unpredictable developments of the world. Vietnam must remain steadfast in its principles of independence and autonomy, avoiding dependence or influence from any power if it wishes to sustain and protect its national interests in a sustainable way. With these ongoing efforts, Vietnam will continue to maintain its position as a peaceful and stable nation, acting as a mediator and actively contributing to regional and international peace and stability.

REFERENCES

Brzezinski, Z. (2019). *The Big Chessboard*. Omega Publisher.

Cai, C. (2013). New Great Powers and International Law in the 21st Century. *European Journal of International Law, 24*(3), 755–795. DOI: 10.1093/ejil/cht050

Edinger, H. (2022). Offensive ideas: Structural realism, classical realism and Putin's war on Ukraine. *International Affairs, 98*(6), 1873–1893. DOI: 10.1093/ia/iiac217

Grano, S. A. (2023). China-US Strategic Competition: Impact on Small and Middle Powers in Europe and Asia. In Grano, S. A., & Huang, D. W. F. (Eds.), *China-US Competition*. Palgrave Macmillan. DOI: 10.1007/978-3-031-15389-1_1

Hu, L. (2021). Examining ASEAN's effectiveness in managing South China Sea disputes. *The Pacific Review, 36*(1), 119–147. DOI: 10.1080/09512748.2021.1934519

IMO. (2023). Maritime Security and Safety in the Black Sea and Sea of Azov. https://www.imo.org/en/MediaCentre/HotTopics/Pages/MaritimeSecurityandSafetyintheBlackSeaandSeaofAzov.aspx, accessed on February 8, 2025.

Kalus, V. D. (2022). Die Nato hat mit dem Feuer gespielt und sich verbrannt. https://www.welt.de/politik/ausland/plus236575311/Der-Westen-hat-nicht-verstanden-dass-Putin-nach-anderen-Regeln-spielt.html?source=puerto-reco-2_AAA-V6.C_test, accessed on January 11, 2025.

Kaplan, R. B. (2018). *The Clarity of Geography*. Writers Association Publishing House.

Khan, T. (2023). Russia-Ukraine Conflict: The Global Security Order and Its Future. https://valdaiclub.com/a/highlights/russia-ukraine-conflict-the-global-security-order/, accessed on January 13, 2025.

Kiet, L.H., Minh, N.A., & Hiep, T.X. (2024). The origins of the Russia-Ukraine conflict: a geopolitical approach. Journal of Science and Technology - University of Danang, 22(2), pp. 26–31.

Kiet, L. H., Phuc, N. H., Tran, H. X., & Nguyen, B. T. (2025). Vietnam's Balancing Strategy in the US-China Rivalry in Southeast Asia. In Zreik, M. (Ed.), *Innovations and Tactics for 21st Century Diplomacy* (pp. 271–302). IGI Global Scientific Publishing.

Kiet, L.H., & Tuyen, N.V. (2023). Vietnam's geopolitical position with the US in its strategy to prevent China's hegemonic ambitions. Journal of Science and Technology - University of Danang, 21(8.1), pp. 63-69.

Kremlin (2022). Обращение Президента Российской Федерации (Address by the President of the Russian Federation). http://www.kremlin.ru/events/president/news/67843, accessed on January 5, 2025.

Kremlin (2023). Указ об утверждении Концепции внешней политики Российской Федерации (Decree on approval of the Concept of Foreign Policy of the Russian Federation). http://kremlin.ru/events/president/news/70811, accessed on February 12, 2025.

Lobell, S. E. (2016). Realism, balance of power, and power transitions. In Paul, T. V. (Ed.), *Accommodating Rising Powers: Past, Present, and Future*. Cambridge University Press. DOI: 10.1017/CBO9781316460191.002

Mearsheimer, J. J. (2022a). Playing With Fire in Ukraine The Underappreciated Risks of Catastrophic Escalation. https://www.foreignaffairs.com/ukraine/playing-fire-ukraine, accessed on January 24, 2025.

Mearsheimer, J. J. (2022b). The causes and consequences of the Ukraine war. Horizons. *Journal of International Relations and Sustainable Development*, *21*, 12–27.

Milan, K. (1984). *The tragedy of Central Europe*. Amsterdam University Press.

Moses, J. (2013). Sovereignty as irresponsibility? A Realist critique of the Responsibility to Protect. *Review of International Studies*, *39*(1), 113–135. DOI: 10.1017/S0260210512000113

Searle, G. R. (1992). The Rise of the Liberal Party. In *The Liberal Party*. British History in Perspective. Palgrave. DOI: 10.1007/978-1-349-22165-3_2

Shambaugh, D. (2022). *Southeast Asia: Convergence of US-China Superpowers (translation)*. National Politics Truth Publisher.

Smith, N. & Dawson, G. (2022). Mearsheimer, Realism, and the Ukraine War. Analyse & Kritik, 44(2), pp. 175-200.

Walt, S. M. (2017). Realism and Security, https://oxfordre.com/internationalstudies/display/10.1093/acrefore/9780190846626.001.0001/acrefore-9780190846626-e-286;jsessionid=C33AB7C17AFFA7DE0A48D1CC2D0218DE, accessed on January 25, 2025.

Waltz, K. N. (1979). *Theory of International Politics*. Addison-Wesley Publishing Company.

Weiss, T. G. (2015). The United Nations: Before, during and after 1945. *International Affairs*, *91*(6), 1221–1235. DOI: 10.1111/1468-2346.12450

Young, O. (1968). The United Nations and the International System. *International Organization*, *22*(4), 902–922. DOI: 10.1017/S0020818300013850

Chapter 13
Russia and Turkey After 2022:
Peculiarities of Bilateral Relations in Russian Academic Discourse

Damir Islamov
https://orcid.org/0000-0003-1338-3277
Mediterranean Studies Center, Faculty of World Economy and International Affairs, HSE University, Russia

ABSTRACT

The new stage of the Ukrainian crisis in 2022 has significantly influenced Russian-Turkish relations, which are defined by a complex interplay of cooperation and competition. This dynamic has drawn considerable attention from Russian scholars, shaping academic discourse on the subject. This chapter explores the dominant discourses articulated by Russian experts concerning the evolution of Russian-Turkish relations since 2022. The study outlines several primary frameworks for examining Russian-Turkish relations through the lens of Russian academic discourse: Peculiarities of Russian-Turkish relations, The Black Sea Region as a Zone of Cooperation/Competition, Ideological and Value-Based Approach in Russian-Turkish Relations, The Syrian Case in Russian-Turkish Relations, Economic Cooperation in Russian-Turkish Relations.

INTRODUCTION

Russian-Turkish relations have attracted significant attention from Russian scholars, particularly following the rise to power of the Justice and Development Party under the leadership of Recep Tayyip Erdoğan. In the 2000s, Moscow and Ankara's

DOI: 10.4018/979-8-3373-2342-8.ch013

interactions largely developed along pragmatic lines, expanding trade, economic, and investment relations. During the 2010s, Turkey ceased to place exclusive emphasis on the West, opening up opportunities for broader cooperation with Russia. During the Ukrainian crisis of 2013–14 and the reunification of Crimea with the Russian Federation, unlike Western countries, Turkey has not joined sanctions imposed against Russia. In fact, it continued or initiated the implementation of large-scale projects such as the Akkuyu Nuclear Power Plant and the TurkStream gas pipeline.

Meanwhile, the steady improvement in relations between the two countries came to an abrupt end in November 2015 when a Turkish F-16 fighter jet shot down a Russian Su-24 bomber. Turkey claimed that the Russian Su-24 had violated its airspace on the border with Syria. Russia, in turn, denied the allegations (Tandon, 2021). This incident led to a deterioration in Russian-Turkish relations. Following an apology from the Turkish side and recognition of the harmful nature of such trends in bilateral relations, cooperation between Moscow and Ankara commenced to recover. Furthermore, during the attempted coup in 2016, Vladimir Putin and the Russian leadership publicly endorsed Turkey's legitimate authorities and R.T. Erdoğan personally.

Notably, Russia and Turkey have engaged in competition with elements of tactical cooperation in several regions, particularly in Syria, Libya, and Nagorno-Karabakh. The new phase of the Ukrainian crisis, which began in 2022, marked a further stage in the development of Russian-Turkish relations, with Ankara seeking to act as a mediator between Moscow and Kiev. Consequently, Russian researchers are greatly interested in the interaction between Russia and Turkey after 2022, which has shaped the academic discourse on the matter.

This chapter attempts to identify and examine the key discourses developed by Russian scholars in academic and analytical publications released since 2022. From a methodological standpoint, this paper draws on the theory of critical geopolitics (as developed by G. O'Tuathail, S. Dalby, and J. Agnew), which distinguishes between different types of discourses, including formal discourse – a perspective particularly valuable for this publication. Formal geopolitics refers to what is usually considered "geopolitical thought" or "the geopolitical tradition" (O'Tuathail, 1999). It concerns the intellectuals, institutions, and forces that shape geopolitical thought in particular places and contexts. In this regard, it appears sensible to use discourse analysis as the primary research method.

The research is based on materials written by experts from leading Russian academic institutions, such as Moscow State Institute of International Relations (MGIMO University), Lomonosov Moscow State University (MSU), National Research University Higher School of Economics (HSE University), Institute of Oriental Studies of the Russian Academy of Sciences, Institute of Scientific Information on Social Sciences of the Russian Academy of Sciences, Institute of World Economy and International Relations of the Russian Academy of Sciences, Diplomatic Academy of the Ministry of Foreign Affairs of the Russian Federation, Peoples' Friendship University of Russia, Financial University under the Government of the Russian Federation, and others.

The study outlines the main tracks for analyzing Russian-Turkish relations through the lens of academic discourse from Russian scholars: Peculiarities of Russian-Turkish relations, The Black Sea Region as a Zone of Cooperation/Competition Between Russia and Turkey, Ideological and Value-Based Approach in Russian-Turkish Relations, The Syrian Case in Russian-Turkish Relations, Economic Cooperation in Russian-Turkish Relations. Within each track, the key discourses formulated by Russian experts in the context of the development of Russian-Turkish relations after 2022 are explored.

1. PECULIARITIES OF RUSSIAN-TURKISH RELATIONS

The assessment of Russian-Turkish relations, especially following the escalation of the Ukrainian crisis in 2022, is built upon several key discourses. The first discourse focuses on the idea that Russia and Turkey serve as crucial resources for each other in strengthening their sovereignty and international standing. Pavel Shlykov emphasizes that Turkey leverages its relations with Russia, as well as the Ukrainian crisis, as instruments of strategic autonomy and as an opportunity to elevate its international status beyond what its actual capabilities might otherwise permit (Shlykov, 2023).

In turn, Inessa Ivanova underscores the significance of the personal dimension in bilateral relations, wherein the presidents of both countries, who came to power in the 2000s and faced limited approval in the West, have actively engaged in dialogue, positioning themselves as central figures in the reassertion of Russia and Turkey on the global stage (Ivanova, 2023). Additionally, for Turkey, Russia represents a potential resource for reinforcing its sovereignty, while for Russia, Turkey serves as a means of bolstering its influence and eroding the cohesion of the Western bloc.

The first discourse is further complemented by the fact that since the 2010s, both Russia and Turkey have increasingly expressed dissatisfaction with the West's disregard for their national interests, perceiving Western efforts as attempts to subordinate them to its will. In this context, Moscow and, to a lesser extent, Ankara have shown growing interest in non-Western international organizations.

Irina Svistunova argues that although Russia and Turkey maintain ties with Western countries, they [Western countries] don't view Moscow and Ankara as part of the so-called Western world, often ignoring their respective national interests (Svistunova, 2025). From her perspective, both Russia and Turkey pursue a multi-dimensional foreign policy, as evidenced by Russia and Turkey's engagement with alternative international platforms, such as the Shanghai Cooperation Organization (SCO) and the BRICS.

In highlighting one of the reasons for the rapprochement between Moscow and Ankara in both political and international-institutional terms, Pavel Shlykov points out that Turkey experienced disillusionment with its alliance with the West, accompanied by a realization of the limited prospects for European integration (Shlykov, 2023). Moreover, the expert emphasizes that since the mid-2010s, Turkey has distanced itself from relying on Western models for economic modernization and the maintenance of friendly relations with the West as a cornerstone of its foreign policy strategy. Ankara sought to elevate its status within international organizations, demonstrating an increasing interest in the BRICS, the SCO, and the G20, while still maintaining connections with Western institutions such as NATO, the European Union, and others.

A number of scholars argue that Russian-Turkish relations contribute to the strengthening of a multipolar world, supported by mechanisms of regional, interregional, and global cooperation (Gadzhiyev, 2022). Furthermore, cooperation between Russia and Turkey in certain areas has reached a strategic level, signaling a progressive move toward a full-scale strategic partnership.

Another discourse within this framework is that after the escalation of the Ukrainian crisis in 2022, according to some Russian experts, Turkey's policy was ambivalent towards Russia's actions.

Dmitry Grafov believes that Ankara combined a "window of cooperation" with Russia in exchange for concessions threatened by the possibility of expanded arms supplies to Ukraine and pressure in Syria (Grafov, 2022). Additionally, Ilya Vedeneev characterizes Turkey's foreign policy after February 2022 as a policy of "equidistance". Ankara has developed relations with both Moscow and Kiev and was not ready to abandon either side (Vedeneev, 2023). This position was quite acceptable to the Russian side, with its expert defining it as a "benevolent neutrality".

Aslambek Mozloyev particularly emphasizes the "two-chair" or "multi-chair" nature of Turkey's foreign policy (Mozloyev, 2024). On one hand, Turkey is a NATO member, and on the other hand, it seeks to become a regional leader in the Eastern Mediterranean and the Middle East while maintaining partnership relations with Russia.

This discourse is further supplemented by the fact that such partnership relations between the countries have triggers for escalating competition in different regions of the world. Several Russian scholars have highlighted that bilateral relations can also lead to competition and military-political confrontation between the two countries (Irkhin et al., 2023). Nevertheless, part of this competition takes place through intermediaries, thereby mitigating the risks associated with direct confrontation between Moscow and Ankara.

Moreover, in the presence of foreign policy zones for competition, both countries, to some extent, try to find compromises to avoid direct clashes. Vladimir Avatkov and Alina Sbitneva believe that after the incident involving the downing of a Russian Su-24 aircraft over Syria in 2015, Turkey learned not to test Russia's patience and to seek compromises (Avatkov & Sbitneva, 2023).

Thus, within the promoted discourses, key risks and issues that could affect Russian-Turkish relations can be identified. First and foremost, Turkey uses Russia to strengthen its own position on the international stage, while the question remains as to how well Turkey will be able to maintain these partnership relations with Russia as it becomes stronger. Additionally, Ankara seeks to maintain a policy of "equidistance" to gain maximum foreign policy and economic benefits, which, on the one hand, satisfies the Russian authorities, but on the other hand, limits the potential for more comprehensive relations. Ultimately, the question arises as to how long Russia and Turkey will be able to avoid the topical issues that exist in their relationship, especially against the backdrop of latent competition in the South Caucasus, the Middle East, Central Asia, and Africa.

2. THE BLACK SEA REGION AS A ZONE OF COOPERATION/COMPETITION

The new stage of the Ukrainian crisis after 2022 has brought the issue of the Black Sea and the emerging order in the region to the forefront, which has also attracted the attention of Russian scholars. In this context, the Black Sea region is becoming an area for the formation of a new system of international relations. Russian-Turkish relations remain complex and multifaceted. Since 2014, Ankara, as a NATO member, has joined the "containment" of Russia in the Black Sea. However, in 2022, after the new stage of the Ukrainian crisis, Turkey closed the Black Sea straits under the Montreux Convention (Irkhin et al., 2023). Moreover, the issue of the straits has become increasingly pressing, as NATO member states seek to "open" the Black Sea to increase their physical presence. At the same time, Moscow and Ankara, in this case, are more likely to act as allies, as they both wish to maintain their regional leadership.

Furthermore, Russian authors have noted Turkish President Erdogan's desire to establish himself as a mediator between Moscow and Kiev, while maintaining the status of a special member within the Alliance. According to Sergey Markedonov, no matter how intensively cooperation between Ankara and Kiev develops, Erdogan doesn't seek to step out of the role of a "mediator" between Russia and

Ukraine (Markedonov, 2022). Turkey has developed special relations with Russia, which allows it to raise its stakes in dialogue with the US and the EU. Based on this, Turkey doesn't seek to escalate into confrontation with Russia to preserve its "special" status within NATO.

At the same time, for Russia, Istanbul is an acceptable platform for negotiations on the Ukrainian crisis (Islamov, 2025). First, for Russia, Istanbul is a symbolic location for continuing negotiations that were interrupted in the spring of 2022. Second, despite all the complexities, Ankara has proven its relative reliability, and Moscow is ready to cooperate. Despite external pressure, Turkey adheres to the provisions of the Montreux Convention, closing the Black Sea straits, not joining the sanctions against Russia, and continuing to engage in key economic projects. Third, Turkey emphasizes the need for a strong foreign policy, implementing an insightful and agile diplomacy. It could be argued that Russia provides a kind of "bonus" to its Turkish counterparts, something that Turkish President Erdogan and his inner circle need in light of domestic political instability.

A special focus was placed on the Black Sea Grain Initiative. The academic discourse in Russia correlated with the statements made by official Russian authorities. It is known that in July 2022, a Memorandum of Understanding was signed in Istanbul between Russia, Turkey, Ukraine, and the UN (Deryugina, 2023). This document facilitated the promotion of Russian food products and fertilizers on global markets and was followed by the "Initiative on the Safe Transportation of Grain and Foodstuffs from Ukrainian ports". As noted by Viktor Nadein-Raevskij, the second document was fully implemented, but the promised conditions for food exports from Russia under the Memorandum were not fulfilled (Nadein-Raevskij, 2023).

A similar position was taken by Irina Deryugina, who added that Turkey highly valued Russia's steps to extend the "grain deal" because Ankara was one of the largest recipients of food under this initiative and was also approaching the 2023 general elections (Deryugina, 2023). Additionally, Ilya Vedeneev points out the importance of the electoral cycle in Turkey in terms of which political forces would remain or come to power (Vedeneev, 2023). In his opinion, the outcome of the elections could also influence the extension of the Black Sea Grain Initiative.

Despite Turkey's foreign policy efforts in July 2023, Russia withdrew from the initiative. At the same time, as noted by Russian researchers, Turkey sought the renewal of the "grain deal" by putting forward a new package of proposals (Nadein-Raevskij, 2023). However, the issue of bilateral relations was not limited to this initiative and encompassed a broader range of issues.

Therefore, the Russian academic discourse was based on the following approaches. Firstly, Turkey aimed to maintain its special role within NATO, having close relations with Russia to increase its significance within the Alliance. Secondly, both Moscow and Ankara wished to preserve their regional leadership, relying on the Montreux

Convention, and did not plan to allow NATO's presence in the Black Sea region to grow. Thirdly, Russia's willingness to participate in and then extend the "grain deal" greatly benefited Turkey, as Ankara was one of the largest recipients under this initiative, and it also played an important role for R.T. Erdogan and the Justice and Development Party ahead of the presidential and parliamentary elections in 2023.

3. IDEOLOGICAL AND VALUE-BASED APPROACH IN RUSSIAN-TURKISH RELATIONS

An important role in Russian-Turkish relations is played by the ideological and value-based approach. One of the main discourses supported by Russian scholars is that both countries should foster the development of cultural and humanitarian ties. However, in several regions, particularly in Central Asia and the South Caucasus, areas of competition between Moscow and Ankara are emerging. This issue is particularly emphasized by Vladimir Avatkov, who believes that Turkey has several organizations that help form a Turkish lobby (Avatkov, 2023). In turn, Russia needs to reverse this trend by developing a long-term internal and external strategy.

The second discourse is related to the fact that Turkey's cultural and humanitarian policy towards Russian regions poses a threat to Russia's national security. This is further complemented by the fact that Ankara has formed Turko-centric integration structures. Maria Mayorova and Alina Sbitneva argue that Turkey's actions don't contribute to preserving the uniqueness of the Turkic peoples living both within Russia and other post-Soviet states, as Turkish authorities aim to unify them according to Turkish norms (Mayorova & Sbitneva, 2023). Based on this, it is Turkey that seeks to define the movement of the so-called "Turkic (de facto, Turkish) world".

The third discourse addressed by Russian scholars concerns the effectiveness of the cultural and humanitarian policies of Russia and Turkey in a comparative context. Several Russian researchers acknowledge the greater effectiveness of Turkey's "soft power", which is more comprehensive and has a well-developed network of institutions (Belous, Kulieva & Khasanov, 2023). At the same time, as previously mentioned, the Turkish approach includes attempts at unification, particularly in the Turkic space. In this regard, the Russian approach could differ by not involving ethnolinguistic and religious issues, instead focusing on expanding the target audience as a whole.

Hence, Russian experts have expressed the greatest concern regarding Turkey's cultural and humanitarian policies, especially in Central Asia. At the same time, Turkey seeks to become the "leader" of the Turkic space, aiming to bring ethnolinguistic, cultural, and historical spheres closer to the Turkish vision of the world. Despite this, representatives of Central Asian states are also cautious about these trends. In turn, this creates an opportunity for Russia to offer a more attractive and equitable framework for cooperation in the cultural and humanitarian fields.

4. THE SYRIAN CASE IN RUSSIAN-TURKISH RELATIONS

Russian-Turkish relations in the context of cooperation/competition in different regions of the world have also been analyzed by Russian scholars. These include post-Soviet space, the Middle East, North Africa, the Sahel, and others. Since February 2022, however, the focus has increasingly been directed toward Syria (especially before the fall of Assad's regime).

The Syrian case was partially compared to the situation in Karabakh. Igor Matveev and Yeghia Tashjian point out that in Syria, Moscow and Ankara demonstrated an "understanding" of each other's actions in the country (Matveev & Tashjian, 2023). However, the escalation of the situation in the South Caucasus in the early 2020s put bilateral relations to a serious test. Moreover, Russia and Turkey sought to balance their advantages and disadvantages. Specifically, Russia took a defensive position in the South Caucasus, while its air force carried out strikes on the positions of various groups in Idlib. At the same time, Turkey strengthened its actions in the South Caucasus.

In the diplomatic arena, according to the authors, Turkey attempted to act in the "Astana style" regarding Nagorno-Karabakh. This scenario was not acceptable to Russia, as Moscow had not wanted to grant Ankara the status of an equal partner in an area of its foreign policy interests.

Moreover, according to Irina Svistunova, Russia and Turkey demonstrated their ability to maintain a dialogue on international issues and find common interests, gaining experience in cooperation in Syria, Libya, and Nagorno-Karabakh (Svistunova, 2025).

The second discourse, noted by several researchers, was that since Turkey began supporting Syrian opposition groups, it had adopted an aggressive and revisionist foreign policy aimed at revising the balance of power in the Middle East. According to Dmitry Grafov, Russian-Turkish relations in Syria could be characterized as a "veiled" struggle, in which each side sought to deprive the other of the opportunity for retaliatory actions (Grafov, 2022).

The third discourse concerned the issue of determining which groups should be recognized as terrorist organizations and which should not. Russian experts points out the differences in Russian and Turkish approaches to distinguishing terrorists from non-terrorists, especially in northern Syria (Avatkov & Sbitneva, 2023).

The key discourse addressed the creation and functioning of the so-called "Astana Process", initiated to resolve the Syrian crisis with the assistance of Russia, Turkey, and Iran. This process should be divided into the following main tracks. Firstly, a non-Western-centric negotiation format for conflict resolution was established, excluding Western actors from the process (Avatkov & Guzaerov, 2023). Secondly, Russia, with Iran's participation, tried to keep Turkey within the framework of the negotiation process, including discussions on de facto spheres of influence in Syria (Grafov, 2022). Thirdly, Russian-Turkish cooperation in Syria elevated bilateral relations to a new level, not only in the economic sphere but also in the areas of military-technical cooperation and security (Svistunova, 2025).

A side discourse, from 2022 to December 2024, concerned the potential meeting between R.T. Erdogan and B. Assad and its preparation by Russian diplomacy. According to some Russian scholars, such a meeting would have been a significant moment in restoring relations between Turkey and Syria (Vedeneev, 2023).

However, after the fall of B. Assad's regime, Russian researchers note that Turkey has become the main external actor in Syria, even though just a few months earlier it was overshadowed by the Russia-Iran tandem. Based on this, the issue of the future of Russian military bases in Syria remains an important discourse. The absence of statements from the new Syrian authorities regarding the immediate withdrawal of Russian forces from Syria suggests that Ankara is not pressuring Damascus on this matter and is willing to reach a compromise with Moscow (Gasanov, 2025).

5. ECONOMIC COOPERATION IN RUSSIAN-TURKISH RELATIONS

The economic aspect of the relationship between Russia and Turkey is of particular importance, especially after February 2022. The initial discourse among Russian researchers was that Turkey tried to distance itself as much as possible from the sanctions imposed on Russia. This enabled trade turnover between the two countries to double in 2022 compared to 2021 (Shlykov, 2023). Moreover, Russia viewed Turkey as a link to Europe in solving transportation, logistical, goods, and energy-related issues (Shlykov, 2024).

The second discourse focused on the potential establishment of a gas hub in Turkey, an idea previously suggested by Russian President Vladimir Putin. It was specifically noted that the establishment of such a hub is possible primarily if Russia decides on ways to redirect its natural gas exports (Menshov, 2024). To achieve this goal, Moscow needs to assess the feasibility of building parallel branches to the TurkStream and developing other routes. On the other hand, the construction of the Trans-Caspian gas pipeline could make the Turkish hub more attractive, but it would reduce Russia's interest in the project. At the same time, the existence of the TurkStream project itself has allowed Ankara to become one of the key players in the global energy market, despite not having substantial reserves, and to play a role as a transit country for the export of hydrocarbons to Europe (Shlykov, 2023).

The third discourse focuses on the development of the Akkuyu nuclear power plant project. Ivan Starodubtsev points out that the Russian Federation owns this station, which is planned to operate for at least the next 60–65 years, with the possibility of extending this period (Starodubtsev, 2024). According to the expert, there are no precedents for such investment projects worldwide, so this model has inevitably caught the attention of the Turkish authorities. Based on various estimates, the nuclear power plant will generate approximately 10% of Turkey's installed capacity (Ulchenko & Ivanova, 2023). In addition to implementing the Akkuyu NPP construction project, Russia and Turkey are discussing the potential construction of a new nuclear power plant in Sinop on Turkey's Black Sea coast.

The next discourse addressed the issue of military-technical cooperation between the two countries. Several Russian scholars observe that Turkey has used its military-technical cooperation with Russia, particularly with regard to the acquisition of the S-400 missile system, as a means of political bargaining with the United States. According to Dmitry Grafov, the Turkish leadership has reason to be concerned that American weapon systems might prove "ineffective" in the event of a potential armed conflict with Greece (Grafov, 2022). Meanwhile, the United States has toughened its stance towards Turkey by imposing sanctions under CAATSA and excluding Ankara from the F-35 programme.

In addition, the instability of military-technical cooperation between Russia and Turkey can be seen in the Turkish-Ukrainian relations in this sphere. Ankara has long-standing ties with Kiev in the field of defence cooperation. According to various sources, Turkey continued to deliver arms to Ukraine even after February 2022 (Boldyrev, 2023).

CONCLUSION

Thus, since the 2010s, the rapprochement between Russia and Turkey was partially built on the fact that leading Western actors ignored the national interests of both countries. Additionally, both countries use each other to strengthen their status on the international stage, with this being especially relevant for Ankara.

Despite this, after the escalation of the Ukrainian crisis in 2022, Turkey's foreign policy towards Russia took on an ambivalent character. On the one hand, Ankara hasn't joined the sanctions against Russia, but on the other hand, it continued its cooperation with Kiev. At the same time, both the Russian and Turkish sides were ready to seek compromises not only on the Ukrainian issue but also on other potentially conflict-ridden areas in the Middle East, North Africa, the South Caucasus, Central Asia, etc.

Undoubtedly, the Wider Black Sea region is an important area for Russian-Turkish relations. The closure of the Black Sea Straits by Turkey under the Montreux Convention caused problems for Russia. However, this also prevented non-regional NATO member countries from entering the Black Sea.

In this regard, the interests of Moscow and Ankara converge, as both countries seek to preserve their status as leading regional powers, despite Turkey's NATO membership. Furthermore, Turkey is seeking to establish itself as a mediator between Russia and Ukraine through active diplomatic engagement. This is further reinforced by its desire to undertake significant international initiatives, such as the grain deal. All of this fits into Turkey's concept of Turkey as the centre of "peace diplomacy" ("Turkiye evolves," 2025).

A significant role in the assessments of Russian scholars was played by the ideological and value-based approach in Russian-Turkish relations. Particular emphasis was placed on the importance of developing cultural and humanitarian ties between the two countries. Alongside this, Russian experts expressed concern that Turkey's soft power conflicted with the interests of the Russian Federation, particularly with regard to attempts to establish a Turkish lobby in the post-Soviet region, particularly in Central Asia.

Russian scholars have addressed the issues of cooperation and competition between Russia and Turkey in various regions of the world, particularly in the post-Soviet space, the Middle East, North Africa, and the Sahel. However, one of the main topics remained Syria, particularly before the collapse of the Assad regime. In this case, the main focus was on the functioning of the "Astana Process" as a non-Western negotiation platform, created by Russia, Turkey, and Iran, as well as Turkey's support for various groups opposed to Assad. Following the fall of the Assad regime, one of the key issues became the preservation and operation of Russian military bases in Syria.

Indeed, economic cooperation has played a significant role in Russian-Turkish relations, particularly given the presence of major projects such as the TurkStream and the Akkuyu nuclear power plant. Furthermore, Russian scholars have paid attention to the possibility of establishing a gas hub in Turkey, highlighting both opportunities and risks for Russia.

The relations between Russia and Turkey have therefore been of great interest to the Russian academic community. It has been observed that Moscow and Ankara have learned to reach foreign policy compromises in many areas, thereby avoiding direct confrontation in various regions of the world. The key question is how long Russia and Turkey can maintain this balance and prevent attempts by various global and regional actors to deteriorate bilateral relations.

REFERENCES

Avatkov, V. A. (2023). *Rossiya, Turtsiya i Postsovetskiy Vostok v ideyno-tsennostnoy kartine mirovoy politiki* [Russia, Turkey and the Post-Soviet East in the Ideological and Value Picture of World Politics]. Prospect Publishing House.

Avatkov, V. A., & Guzaerov, R. I. (2023). Siriyskiy krizis vo vneshney politike Turtsii [The Syrian crisis in Turkey's foreign policy]. *Pathways to Peace and Security*, *1*(64), 111–125. DOI: 10.20542/2307-1494-2023-1-111-125

Avatkov, V. A., & Sbitneva, A. I. (2023). Tureckaya Respublika v preddverii stoletiya: Era R. T. Erdogana [The Republic of Turkey on the eve of the centenary: The era of R. T. Erdogan]. *RUDN Journal of International Relations*, *23*(4), 595–608. DOI: 10.22363/2313-0660-2023-23-4-595-608

Belous, Yu. A., Kulieva, N. S., & Khasanov, K. A. (2023). Osobennosti gumanitarnogo aspekta vneshney politiki sovremennoy Turtsii [The features of the humanitarian aspect of modern Turkey's foreign policy]. *Russia and the Contemporary World*, *1*, 115–136. DOI: 10.31249/rsm/2023.01.07

Boldyrev, A. V. (2023). Rossiya i Turtsiya: aspekty voenno-tekhnicheskogo sotrudnichestva v XXI veke [Russia and Turkey: Aspects of military-technical cooperation in the 21st century]. In A. G. Gadzhiyev (Ed.), *Vneshnyaya politika Turtsii v period pravleniya Partii spravedlivosti i razvitiya (2002–2023 gg.) [Turkey's foreign policy under the Justice and Development Party (2002–2023)]* (pp. 104–117). Institute of Oriental Studies RAS.

Deryugina, I. V. (2023, March 15). Chto stoit za «Chernomorskoj zernovoj iniciativoj» [What is behind the Black Sea Grain Initiative]. *Russian International Affairs Council*. https://russiancouncil.ru/analytics-and-comments/analytics/chto-stoit-za-chernomorskoy-zernovoy-initsiativoy/

Gadzhiyev, A. G. (2022, September 28). New role of Ankara in the global politics through the lens of Russian-Turkish relations development. *Caspian Institute*. https://caspian.institute/product/amur-gadzhiyev/new-role-of-ankara-in-the-global-politics-through-the-lens-of-russian-turkish-relations-development-38314.shtml

Gasanov, K. N. (2025, February 17). Sohranit li Turciya svoyo vliyanie v Sirii? [Will Turkey retain its influence in Syria?]. *Valdai Discussion Club*. https://ru.valdaiclub.com/a/highlights/sokhranit-li-turtsiya-svoye-vliyanie-v-sirii/

Grafov, D. B. (2022). Strategiya balansirovaniya vo vneshnej politike Turcii [Strategy of balancing in Turkish foreign policy]. *MGIMO Review of International Relations*, *15*(3), 115–142. DOI: 10.24833/2071-8160-2022-3-84-115-142

Irkhin, A. A., Moskalenko, O. A., Kabanova, N. E., & Demeshko, N. E. (2023). Imperskoe vozrozhdenie: sopernichestvo i sotrudnichestvo Rossii i Turcii v Chernomorskom regione (politiko-istoricheskij analiz) [The rebirth of empires: Contest and cooperation of Russia and Turkey in the Black Sea region (Political and historical analysis)]. *Russian Journal of Regional Studies,* 31(2), 214–237. DOI: 10.15507/2413-1407.123.031.202302.214-237

Islamov, D. R. (2025, June 4). Tureckij diplomaticheskij shpagat: po sledam vizitov Hakana Fidana [Turkish diplomatic twine: Following the footsteps of Hakan Fidan's visits]. *Russia in Global Affairs.* https://globalaffairs.ru/articles/tureczkij-shpagat-islamov/

Ivanova, I. I. (2023). Dvustoronnee politicheskoe sotrudnichestvo. [Bilateral political cooperation] In Gadzhiyev, A. G. (Ed.), *Vneshnyaya politika Turtsii v period pravleniya Partii spravedlivosti i razvitiya (2002–2023 gg.)* [Turkey's foreign policy under the Justice and Development Party (2002–2023)]. (pp. 69–92). Institute of Oriental Studies RAS.

Markedonov, S. M. (2022, February 9). Turciya v Chernomorskom regione: riski dlya Rossii? [Turkey in the Black Sea region: Risks for Russia?]. *Russian International Affairs Council.* https://russiancouncil.ru/analytics-and-comments/analytics/turtsiya-v-chernomorskom-regione-riski-dlya-rossii/

Matveev, I. A., & Tashjian, Y. (2023, March 13). Ot Sirii do Nagornogo Karabaha: ocenka rossijsko-tureckogo «sotrudnichestva/sopernichestva» [From Syria to Nagorno-Karabakh: Assessing Russian-Turkish "co-opetition"]. *Valdai Discussion Club.* https://ru.valdaiclub.com/a/highlights/ot-sirii-do-nagornogo-karabakha/

Mayorova, M. A., & Sbitneva, A. I. (2023). Ideologicheskoe vliyanie Turcii v regionah Rossii: Tyurkskij faktor [Turkish ideological influence in Russian regions: The Turkic factor]. *RUDN Journal of Political Science, 25*(1), 134–149. DOI: 10.22363/2313-1438-2023-25-1-134-149

Menshov, A. V. (2024). Turetskiy gazovyy khab: Vozmozhnosti dlya Evropy i Turtsii [Turkish gas hub: Opportunities for Europe and Turkey]. *Contemporary Europe, 1*, 206–215. DOI: 10.31857/S0201708324010169

Nadein-Raevskij, V. A. (2023, September 5). Otnosheniya Rossii i Turcii – eto ne tol'ko zernovaya sdelka [Russia-Turkey relations are not just a grain deal]. *NG.* https://www.ng.ru/kartblansh/2023-09-05/3_8818_kb.html

O'Tuathail, G. (1999). Understanding critical geopolitics: Geopolitics and risk society. *The Journal of Strategic Studies, 22*(2–3), 107–124. DOI: 10.1080/01402399908437756

Shlykov, P. V. (2023). Tureckij kul'bit [The Turkish gambit]. *Russia in Global Affairs, 21*(3), 142–159. DOI: 10.31278/1810-6439-2023-21-3-142-159

Shlykov, P. V. (2024). Otnosheniya Rossii i Turcii v nachale XXI veka: Transformaciya modelej vzaimodejstviya [Russia and Turkey in the early 21st century: Transformation of bilateral interaction models]. *Novaya i Novejshaya Istoriya, 68*(6), 179–193. DOI: 10.31857/S0130386424060145

Starodubtsev, I. I. (2024, May 28). Rossiya i Turtsiya obsuzhdayut stroitel'stvo vtoroy AES [Russia and Turkey discuss construction of second nuclear power plant]. *Smotrim*. https://smotrim.ru/article/3972742

Svistunova, I. A. (2025, February 8). Çok kutuplu dünyada Turkey-Rusya ilişkilerini değerlendirdi. Röportaj [Evaluated Turkey-Russia relations in a multipolar world. Interview]. *Uluslararası Diplomatik İlişkiler, Akademik Araştırmalar ve Eğitim Derneği*. https://udiad.org/rusya-bilimler-akademisi-uluslararasi-iliskiler-ve-dunya-ekonomisi-enstitusu-imemo-turkiye-uzmani-sayin-dr-irina-svistunova-cok-kutuplu-dunya-ve-turkiye-rusya-iliskilerini-degerlendirdi/

Tandon, K. (2021, November 10). Movie based on F-16 fighter jet's clash with Russian Su-24 near Syria-Turkey border ready for release. *EurAsian Times*. https://eurasiantimes.com/hero-of-russian-federation-movie-based-on-f-16-fighter-jets-clash-with-su-24-near-syria-turkey-border-ready-for-release/

Ulchenko, N. Yu., & Ivanova, I. I. (2023). Ekonomicheskie aspekty rossiysko-turetskikh otnosheniy. [Economic aspects of Russian-Turkish relations] In Gadzhiyev, A. G. (Ed.), *Vneshnyaya politika Turtsii v period pravleniya Partii spravedlivosti i razvitiya (2002–2023 gg.)* [Turkey's foreign policy under the Justice and Development Party (2002–2023)]. (pp. 92–104). Institute of Oriental Studies RAS.

Vedeneev, I. N. (2023). Vliyanie SVO na Ukraine na otnosheniya mezhdu Rossiej i Turciej v 2022 g [Impact of the special military operation in Ukraine on relations between Russia and Turkey in 2022]. *Eastern Analytics, 14*(2), 40–53. DOI: 10.31696/2227-5568-2023-02-040-053

Chapter 14
Türkiye's Role in the Collective West's Hybrid War Against Russia in the Case of Ukraine

Yıldıran Acar
https://orcid.org/0009-0008-2602-0401
RUDN University, Russia

ABSTRACT

Until the 21st century, states mostly used conventional warfare, but this has lost relevance with the rise of hybrid warfare. Initially associated with non-state actors, hybrid methods are now widely used by states. Amid rising tensions in the Russia-Ukraine conflict, the term "Collective West"—referring to NATO, the EU, and the US—gained prominence in Russian discourse. Following Russia's 2022 "special military operation," the Collective West intensified hybrid tactics against Russia. Türkiye, though a NATO member, maintained a distinct policy toward Russia, positioning itself independently. This study examines Türkiye's role in the Collective West's hybrid war against Russia in Ukraine between 2016 and 2023. Using qualitative methods and interviews with diplomats and experts, it adopts principles of credibility and objectivity to analyze Türkiye's strategic choices during this period.

INTRODUCTION

Until the 21st century, states generally used conventional warfare. However, this method is losing its value day by day. This change has led to the emergence of hybrid warfare. Hybrid warfare originally referred to irregular non-state actors with

DOI: 10.4018/979-8-3373-2342-8.ch014

advanced military capabilities. But nowadays states are favouring this method of warfare. Therefore, hybrid warfare plays a very important role in the 21st century.

In recent years, with the onset and escalation of tensions between Russia and Ukraine, the term 'Collective West' has been used in the Russian media and the speeches of Russian statesmen. If we look at the place and content of the term 'Collective West', we see that it includes NATO, the EU and America. In 2022, when Russian President Vladimir Putin Announced a 'special military operation' in Ukraine, the Collective West intensified its hybrid warfare methods against Russia and used them markedly effectively (Мингазов, 2022).

In this process, we observe that Türkiye, a NATO country, does not share relations with the bloc of the collective West and pursues its policy towards Russia. Therefore, Türkiye's role in the collective West's hybrid war against Russia is significant.

Definition and Characteristics of Hybrid Warfare

Today we often hear the term 'hybrid warfare' in the media, on social platforms, on television channels and even in the academic environment. We can say that in the 21st century, this term has become popular. Recently, attempts to define the concept of 'hybrid warfare' have become more frequent. For this reason, in the literature, you can find many attempts at definition, some of which are similar, and others, on the contrary, are different. To mention here each of these definitions would be tedious and would go beyond the scope of this study. For this reason, we will focus on the definitions and opinions of Western, Russian and Turkish experts. In addition, an attempt will be made to briefly outline the points common to all attempts at definition.

Although the term 'hybrid warfare' started to be used in the 21st century, some argue that this warfare is not a new method and that hybrid warfare methods have been used in history. Although the term 'hybrid' is not used in the concept of hybrid warfare, the fact that 'war is a deceptive business,' emphasised by Sun Tzu in his work The Art of War, parallels modern hybrid warfare methods. For example, in 1806 during the Peninsular War, a mixed force of Spanish guerrillas joined with British and Portuguese regular troops and succeeded against Napoleon's great army (Aras & Yıldırım, 2022: 500).

As defined by the Hybrid Threat Centre of Excellence (Hybrid CoE), which was established in 2017 by NATO and the EU in Helsinki, the capital of Finland, with the participation of 9 European and NATO countries and currently has 34 member states, hybrid threats aim to damage, wear down and collapse states and institutions through a variety of means (Hybrid CoE, d.n.). These means include information manipulation, cyber-attacks, intelligence services, economic embargoes, private military companies, coercive diplomacy or military force (Hybrid CoE, d.n.).

According to retired Colonel John McQueen, hybrid warfare is a combination of symmetric and asymmetric warfare in which friendly forces conduct conventional military operations against enemy forces while seeking to secure indigenous populations and maintain stable control. Thus, hybrid wars are full-fledged wars that have both physical and conceptual dimensions (Mccuen, 2008:108).

Hoffman defines hybrid warfare as the coordinated use of traditional military methods together with irregular asymmetric methods and all other methods, discovering the enemy's weaknesses and directing efforts to address them. This is why Hoffman, in defining the term hybrid warfare, emphasises that conflicts and wars are multifactorial and variable and therefore not as clear-cut as black and white, there are many grey areas and uncertainties, making them complex (Hoffman, 2009:35).

In Western literature, Frank Hoffman is considered the father of the concept of hybrid warfare. Moreover, according to Western experts, the concept of hybrid threats is the only one that explicitly advocates a comprehensive approach that assumes civil-military cooperation from the outset and systemic vulnerabilities of democratic systems as specific targets. It is in this area that the West sees Russia as the greatest threat. They argue that the Russians are attacking the democratic systems of Western states through hybrid warfare. After outlining the views of Western experts, let us look at the views of Russian experts on the concept of hybrid warfare (Giannopoulos, et al.,2021:9)

When analysing the academic literature, it can be seen that the concept of hybrid warfare is mostly identified with Russia's activities in Ukraine. However, given that the studies are usually of Western origin, we can say that reducing hybrid warfare only to Russia's activities can be misleading. Today, it can be said that every state in all conflict environments of the world, especially in the Middle East, uses its methods of hybrid warfare. Therefore, one of the objectives of this study is to examine and reveal the concept of 'hybrid' in Turkish and Russian sources (Özer, 2018:50).

Although the term 'hybrid warfare' is widely used in academic discussions, it is not explicitly mentioned in Russian official documents. One of the main reasons for this is disagreement among Russian military experts over the definition of hybrid warfare. Some Russian political scientists point to the ambiguity of the term and argue that hybrid warfare is not an operational concept and is unproductive in military-professional discourse. They also argue that focusing only on preparations for hybrid warfare will lead to forgetting the basic principles of military strategy and tactics, which could lead to bad consequences if the country and the army are not fully prepared for a possible war. However, according to Russian political scientist Pavel Tsygankov, the concept of 'hybrid warfare' has become a new perspective and reality that is hard to deny, and therefore, to protect the national interests of the Russian Federation, it is necessary to focus and work on preparing for and countering hybrid threats (Бартош, 2016).

The components of hybrid warfare are intelligence organisations, economics, mercenary companies, information, social networks, and cyber attacks. These components, together with classic military operations, are used to conceal facts, prepare a legitimate cover and conceal the participants and states involved in these operations. In terms of strategy, hybrid warfare is a type of interstate conflict that utilises the latest technologies and methods and is likely to be actively and increasingly effective in the future. In addition, economic sanctions, as one of the components of hybrid warfare, often lead to the escalation of conflicts into a hot phase and also open the way to the application of military elements through the use of destructive socio-political technologies. In connection with the use of these components, Russian experts advocate the need for legal regulation of such sanctions (Васильевич, 2020:38-43).

According to Oleg Batsilievich Tikhanchev, the theory and concept of hybrid warfare is not a military 'know-how', but a type of interstate conflict that has long been used in history, is somewhat differently applied in modern conditions and is likely to be actively used in the future. He also argues that today hybrid warfare methods are used by third states to be involved in conflict zones under the pretext of establishing peace, the best and most modern example of which is the war in Syria (Васильевич, 2020:38-43).

Russian experts believe that Gerasimov's article in the Military-Industrial Courier is generally interpreted by Western researchers and politicians according to their own interests. For their part, Russian experts use examples from Russian literature to explain that the term 'hybrid warfare' is a concept used against Russia created in the West. Gerasimov's article draws attention to the methods used by Western states in conflict zones. At the same time, Western experts want to associate the concept of 'hybrid warfare' with Russia through Gerasimov, meaning that Russia is using hybrid warfare methods against the West. On the other hand, we see that there are researchers who objectively and unbiasedly analyse the work of V. V. Gerasimov. V. Gerasimov. For example, according to the British researcher O. Friedman, Western experts and commentators share the views they want to see, not what Gerasimov wants to say. This reasoning and commentary have led to a misunderstanding of Russian military strategy. As an example, research by the Austrian National Defence Academy documented differences in definitions of the Gerasimov Doctrine in the EU, the UK and China. The researchers concluded that Western experts interpreted the Gerasimov Doctrine in their interests, extracting from the Gerasimov text those parts that suited their purposes (Манойло & Гончаренко, 2023: 85-86).

There is no doctrine. There is only an article expressing the desire of the chief of the Russian General Staff to draw the attention of his military scientists to the new methods and ways of warfare used by the West in conflict zones. According to Russian experts, Western politicians and specialists have popularised the terms

'Gerasimov doctrine' and 'Russian hybrid warfare', which they use in their foreign policy as anti-Russian. Using these terms, they justify to their populations the need for war with Russia and increased attention to defence spending. In doing so, they manage to divert the attention of their citizens from domestic politics and economic problems. Already in 2019, Gerasimov openly stated at the Moscow International Security Conference that the concept of 'hybrid warfare' was not developed by us (Манойло & Гончаренко, 2023: 85-86).

In the final section, let us examine the Turkish military-scientific community's opinion and views on the concept of hybrid warfare. Over the past 10 years, since the concepts of hybrid warfare and hybrid threats have entered the international relations and security literature, academic research in this field and the awareness of Turkish state institutions have grown day by day. The Turkish academic community holds conferences, sessions and publications under the auspices of the National Defence University to fully understand the concept of hybrid warfare that is often discussed in the literature, to develop policies against hybrid threats and to prepare a solid knowledge base for national security policymakers (Yıldız & Ateş, 2022:5-6).

According to Turkish historian Gültekin Yıldız, although the term 'hybrid warfare' began to be used after 2000, hybrid warfare methods are not a new method of warfare in terms of world military history. Because, he said, the components of hybrid warfare have been largely used and present in the past. We see that psychological actions, disinformation, propaganda, and terrorist attacks against critical infrastructures existed before 2000. New areas have emerged due to the rapid change and development of changing, evolving and rapidly transforming communications, artificial intelligence, the internet, etc. Due to the development of technology, we can say that cyberspace and the Internet can be spoken of as a new concept in the field of security and defence, as well as in all spheres of our life, not only in large states but also in non-state armed groups (Yıldız & Ateş, 2022:5-6).

According to some Turkish scholars, since the components of hybrid warfare include not only military but also civilian elements, harmonising the civil-military structure and coordinating between them will strengthen political and state will in dealing with hybrid threats, and more rational decisions will emerge as a result of such cooperation. Thus, if a unique and national structure is formed in the management of hybrid warfare, more accurate and dynamic decisions will be made according to the state's own interests and needs. It is necessary to analyse the methods of hybrid warfare by different players in the world and create a 'Turkish Hybrid Warfare' doctrine and decision-making mechanism. This will be formed by a new structure composed of civilian and military personnel and they emphasise the need to form a single supreme mind to manage hybrid warfare by providing intellectual knowledge and accumulating experience (Şahin & Mercimek, 2022:149-150).

To better understand the Turkish perspective, this study interviewed Lieutenant General Ismail Hakki Pekin, former Chief of Intelligence of the General Staff. According to Ismail Hakki Pekin (2024):

''Hybrid warfare is a type of war that includes almost all the elements of war, waged by completely different means. But this war is waged on a certain scale. All elements are intertwined and countries use armed groups and terrorist organisations to their advantage without fighting each other. An example is guerrilla warfare, which is an element of irregular warfare used in the war in Afghanistan. Examples of hybrid warfare include the Arab Spring, the conflicts between Hamas and Israel, the war in Syria, etc. In all these conflict zones we see examples of hybrid warfare. In hybrid warfare, the core elements are not fighting, they are just providing the supply chain. One of the best examples of this today is the conflict between Russia and Ukraine, which can be characterised as hybrid warfare. Russia and the Western bloc can be said to be the main elements in this war. NATO and the EU are using Ukraine as a subcontractor against Russia.''

Today, hybrid wars, according to Pekin (2024), *''delay and prevent World War 3, the outbreak of a major war and the spread of wars on major fronts.' That's because states use hybrid warfare methods instead of waging war directly against each other. Because of the nature of hybrid warfare, states prefer hybrid methods of warfare because the enemy is uncertain and difficult to prove, and it is less costly than other elements of warfare.''*

Hulusi Akar, former Minister of National Defence and Chief of General Staff, believes that World War 3 started under the concept of hybrid warfare and that under this concept there is no declaration of war, but it is not clear whether there is a war or not, i.e. there is a blurred military situation. Akar (2024) explained as follows:

''In the Russia-Ukraine conflict, the whole world is at war, but thanks to the methods of hybrid warfare, we don't see anyone explicitly declaring war. Can Ukraine go to war against Russia alone? No, of course not! We see that other states are behind it. But we see that they resort to hybrid methods of warfare. To give another example: what can the PKK/YPG do against Türkiye alone? Nothing! Who is behind them? All the states! But there is no one.''

To understand the Turkish point of view, we have cited the opinions of Turkish academy experts and military experts on this issue. Finally, for a better understanding of the topic, we provide the opinion of Ibrahim Kalın, the head of the National Intelligence Organisation, who is currently on active duty. According to Ibrahim Kalin, one of the most important reasons why hybrid warfare is widespread is that the instability and insecurity caused by the transition to a multipolar world system gives rise to hybrid threats. The current international system is unable to address this uncertainty and instability, and it is deepening every day (Kalın, 2024:1-13).

The unipolar world order that the United States has led since the end of the Cold War is not so much an order as a self-centred and unilateral power politics. We are dealing with a global order that has no internal coherence, where the powerful determine the rules. We see that they are using this scheme, which they created, in their interests with components of their hybrid warfare. The conflict between Russia and Ukraine is just one of the latest examples of countries in favour of international law remaining silent in one case in another as during the Israeli attacks on Gaza. The concepts of democracy, rule of law, human rights and freedom of speech are instrumentalised by the powers that hold them and used against their opponents in hybrid wars (Kalın, 2024:1-13).

Hybrid warfare is a war of attrition to slow, stop, and deplete the energy of rival and enemy states or non-state actors and spread it over a long period. The most concrete example is the ongoing war of attrition, in other words, the hybrid war between the West and Russia over Ukraine. Instead of directly intervening in countries that they perceive as a threat to their national interests, hegemonic powers initiate proxy wars, one component of hybrid warfare. For example, in the hybrid war between the West and Russia, Ukraine is used by Western powers to wear Russia down (Kalın, 2024:1-13).

Because in hybrid warfare it is very difficult to determine where threats and attacks will come from, we must think multi-dimensionally and on multiple levels. Hybrid threats require hybrid solutions. In warfare, where traditional and modern methods are used together, transitions are intense, and adaptation and reaction times are accelerated, the intelligence organisations of states play an increasingly important role (Kalın, 2024:1-13).

In the first part of this study, in which we analyse the concept of hybrid warfare and its characteristics, we focused more on the definitions and thoughts of Turkish, Russian and Western experts about the concept. In general, we can identify the common points in the definitions of the concept as follows; The most important and obvious point common to all inclusive definitions is that states use all available means such as paramilitary forces, special military elements, terrorist organisations, other illegal structures, economy, technology, diplomacy, media, etc. in addition to military measures in hybrid warfare in a coordinated manner, in different ways and at different times (Gökçe & Şengönül, 2017: 478-479).

The Concept of the Collective West

After the annexation of Crimea to Russia, the concept of 'Collective West' began to be used in the media and in the speeches of politicians. Since the beginning of the current Ukrainian crisis, this definition has been frequently used in social media, on television and in speeches of political leaders. For this reason, in this section, we will focus on what the notion of 'collective West' means and what it expresses.

A few years before Crimea's annexation to Russia, a new concept entered the sphere of international relations. It is most often used in Russian public opinion and political discourse. This notion of 'collective West' is often used in a negative sense in the Russian media and the speech of political figures. Despite this, this definition of the 'Collective West' has spread very quickly in Russian political and media discourse. One of the main reasons for its rapid spread is that this term is very convenient when politicians and journalists want to talk about Western countries as a whole, rather than referring to them individually (Chimiris, 2022:1-2)

One of the reasons for the use and emergence of such a term is the increasing global instability of the current international situation based on the ideological clash of two views on the world order, i.e. the beginning of the transition from a unipolar to a multipolar world order. Another reason for using the concept of collective West is that it is used as a diplomatic discourse to accurately and completely reflect the Russian state's point of view on international problems, protect its interests and regulate the interlocutor's activities. In addition, the genre diversity of diplomatic discourse determines the interaction of institutional, media and other features within the discourse. This is most clearly manifested in the public speeches of official representatives of the Ministry of Foreign Affairs, where such texts are included in the composition of political communication in the broad sense (Балашова, 2022:25-26).

The notion of the collective West is used in the Russian media, in speeches of state and political figures of the Russian Federation, in general designation of representatives of the 'unipolar' ideology of the United States and its allies, primarily EU and NATO countries. For example, Russian Foreign Minister Lavrov stated: ''In his speech, he defined the collective West as 'the United States and its satellites'. In speeches by Russian politicians and statesmen, this notion includes the US, the Anglo-Saxon world, NATO and the EU (Балашова, 2022:25-26).

Irina Svistunova, an expert on Türkiye at the Russian Academy of Sciences, believes that the concept of collective West is not a historical but geopolitical and political. Besides, if we consider the concept of the West historically, it includes Russia, and the concept of the collective West is expressed as a group of countries hostile to Russia. According to Irina Svistunova, the concept of 'collective West' includes EU, NATO and US countries (Свистунова, 2024)

TÜRKIYE'S ROLE IN THE UKRAINIAN CRISIS IN THE COLLECTIVE WEST'S HYBRID WAR AGAINST RUSSIA

To achieve the purpose of this study, this section will examine Türkiye's role in the current Ukrainian crisis. First of all, let us briefly explain how the parties in this crisis view what is happening. The Russian side does not consider it a war and prefers to use the term 'special military operation'. If we look at the Ukrainian side and the side of the collective West, we see that this military operation is an attempted occupation, and they characterise it as a war.

It can be argued that the Russian-Ukrainian crisis has divided the international political atmosphere into two poles. Some 140 states characterise the military operation organised by Russia as an invasion of Ukraine and take a pro-Ukrainian stance, considering it contrary to international law. However, Syria, Belarus, Eritrea and North Korea, which have close relations with the Moscow government, did not support the Russian thesis and did not take a position against the invasion. On the other hand, some states such as India and China refrained from taking a clear position between the two blocs. Some states, especially in Africa, which have recently co-operated with Russia on security issues, did not vote against Russia in the UN vote (Çınar, 2024:25).

Despite the harsh reactions of the collective Western countries to Russia's actions, Türkiye tried to establish a constructive dialogue with both sides to end the crisis and violence. In the early days of the crisis, the Turkish Foreign Ministry issued a statement saying that Ukraine's territorial integrity, sovereignty and political unity had been violated by Russia and that the Moscow administration's decision was unacceptable. However, during the current process, when the issue of Western sanctions against Russia came up on the agenda, Türkiye distanced itself from these sanctions. As the crisis escalated, President Erdoğan stated the issue and stressed that *''Türkiye does not want to choose favour of Russia or Ukraine in its foreign policy.''* (Çınar, 2024:25).

Thanks to its policy of balance and neutrality, Türkiye has become a transit country for the TurkStream pipeline from Russia to the Balkans. Russia can now bypass Ukraine and export gas to Europe via Türkiye. While economic relations defined Türkiye's foign policy towards Russia, with the acquisition of the S-400, co-operation has extended to strategic issues. These include the purchase of an air defence system from Russia and Russia's construction of the Akkuyu nuclear reactor in Türkiye (Aydın, 2022:10-11).

Amid harsh rhetoric and tensions between the collective Western countries and NATO and the Moscow administration, Türkiye, as an actor engaged in an open dialogue with Russia, has taken a strong stance in mediation processes. Türkiye's intentions to mediate an end to tensions between Kiev and Moscow have been strongly expressed by the president, foreign ministry officials and the presidential spokesman (Çınar, 2024:25-27).

Following these events, Türkiye brought together representatives of Russia and Ukraine twice at the request of the opposing sides. First, at the Diplomatic Forum in Antalya, Russian Foreign Minister Sergey Lavrov and his Ukrainian counterpart Dmytro Kuleba held a meeting in the presence of Turkish Foreign Minister Mevlüt Çavuşoğlu. Secondly, on 29 March 2022, the Russian and Ukrainian delegations held a meeting in the Working Cabinet of the President of Dolmabahçe. During this meeting, Ukrainian officials expressed their desire to see Türkiye as one of the guarantor states in the process of working towards a diplomatic settlement (Çınar, 2024:25-27).

Since February 2022, Türkiye has repeatedly made mediation attempts to stop the war between Ukraine and Russia. For instance, on 22 September 2022, 215 Ukrainian prisoners of war were released under the mediation of President Recep Tayyip Erdoğan. After the release of the prisoners, the head of the Ukrainian Presidential Chancellery Adriy Yermak emphasised the importance of Türkiye's position in the prisoner exchange operation. One of Türkiye's most important roles in the Ukrainian crisis is its cooperation with Russia and the implementation of the grain corridor agreement, which is considered a very important development both for the opposing sides and for global food security (Çınar, 2024:25-27).

As is well known, Russia and Ukraine are the world's most important exporters of grain and fertilisers. The outbreak of war between these two countries and the subsequent closure of grain export sea routes has hurt both the belligerents and the countries importing grain from these states. Especially in some African states, which are already vulnerable in terms of food security, the situation has reached a critical level due to the disruption of grain supplies. Both Russia and Ukraine point to each other as the cause of the growing food crisis in these countries (Çınar, 2024:25-27).

As a result of initiatives by Türkiye and the UN, triggered by the excessive rise in global food prices, Russia and Ukraine separately signed the 'Black Sea Grain Corridor Agreement' on 22 July 2022. The Grain Corridor Agreement aims to ensure the safe passage of grain, food and fertilisers through ports closed due to hostilities that disrupt grain shipments. Before the signing of the Grain Corridor Agreement, the Kyiv administration objected to the inclusion of Russian agricultural products in the scope of the agreement, but the agreement included them. Following the Grain Corridor Agreement, the UN and Russia signed another memorandum of understanding on the transport of Russian food products and fertilisers to international markets (Çınar, 2024:25-27).

According to the Joint Coordination Centre headquartered in Istanbul, the grain corridor agreement moved more than 32 million tonnes of grain to world markets between July 2022 and July 2023, reducing world food prices to pre-war levels. The agreement has been extended several times due to the expiry of its implementation period. However, in July 2023, Russia announced its withdrawal from the agreement due to its failure to remove obstacles to the sale of its food products. Following this announcement, President Recep Tayyip Erdoğan met with Putin and tried to persuade Russia to continue the grain corridor agreement (Çınar, 2024:25-27).

As a result, Türkiye has become an important player actively involved in initiatives to peacefully end the Russian-Ukrainian war and mitigate its global consequences. Although Türkiye has periodically experienced tensions with the Moscow administration over its relations with Ukraine and the West, it has been able to maintain a close dialogue with both sides. On the other hand, despite the military conditions, the embassy has been able to strengthen cooperation with Ukraine, with which it has deep historical and cultural ties (Çınar, 2024:25-27).

On 8 December 2023, the Embassy of Ukraine in Ankara and the Türkiye-Ukraine Friendship Association organised a reception on the occasion of the 100th anniversary of the founding of the Republic of Türkiye and the 32nd anniversary of Ukraine's independence. At this meeting, Ambassador Bodnar described Türkiye as an important partner in ending war and restoring peace and stability. This once again underlines the importance of Türkiye in world politics, emphasising its decisive position in ensuring international peace in the context of the Russian-Ukrainian war (Çınar, 2024:25-27).

Immediately after Russia's military operation, Türkiye, viewing the situation as a war between coastal states, activated Article 19 of the Montreux Straits Convention. The straits were closed to Russian and Ukrainian warships. In addition, Ankara de facto recommended other non-coastal states, including NATO members, to refrain from transiting warships to the Black Sea for a certain period, thus triggering the restrictions under Article 21 of the Convention, which states that 'Türkiye may close the straits to all warships in the event of an imminent threat of war.' Thus, from March 2022, the Black Sea became a kind of closed sea. By concluding the Montreux Treaty, Türkiye prevented a major war that could have spread to the Black Sea (Celikpala, 2023)

Another bright spot in bilateral relations has been the increase in trade between the two countries. Türkiye's trade volume with Russia, which is under severe sanctions from Western countries, has increased by almost 50 per cent due to the fact that Ankara is not a party to the sanctions. Energy imports from Russia account for a significant share of this growth. The volume of oil products that Ankara buys from Russia has doubled. This growth, which is seen as a result of sanctions imposed by Western countries, means that Türkiye has become an alternative market and supplier for Russia, whose trade with the West has been severely restricted (Celikpala, 2023)

Similarly, Türkiye's gas purchases from Russia have continued to grow since TurkStream became operational in 2022, and announcements made during the year suggested that Türkiye could become one of Russia's main routes for Russian gas to the West. This would remove Ukraine from the equation and open the door for Türkiye to become a major route for Russian gas. However, it should be borne in mind that it is too early to take this step. The construction of the Akkuyu nuclear power plant, which is one of the main elements of the two countries' energy co-operation, has been delayed, but the first unit of the plant should be operational in 2025 (Celikpala, 2023)

Another issue is the positive results of the revitalisation of tourism, which was disrupted during the Covid-19 pandemic. Although the indicators stated in the tourism strategy formed in 2021 were not achieved due to the escalation of hostilities, it can be seen that mobility is there. This is also because Türkiye has become Russia's only exit point to the Western world due to the transport embargo imposed on Russia. It should also be added that tens of thousands of Russians and Ukrainians who were forced to leave their countries due to the announcement of mobilisation have settled in Türkiye (Celikpala, 2023)

Russia sees Türkiye's aspirations for greater autonomy and independence in the international arena. However, at the same time, Moscow understands Ankara's attachment to its Western partners and NATO and thus pursues its policy in relations with its partner. This causes some disagreements between the two countries. However, despite the pressure, Moscow appreciates the fact that Ankara pursues its national interests, does not join anti-Russian sanctions and establishes mutually beneficial cooperation with Russia (Çebi, 2024).

For example, Russia announced a list of friendly and hostile countries. The list of hostile countries included all Western collective countries and NATO countries, while the list of friendly countries included only Türkiye. Overall, the dynamics of relations between the two countries can be characterised as positive. Finally, we can see that Türkiye has played a very important role and is a very important state by not fulfilling the embargo and not following NATO's strategy in the Ukrainian crisis against Russia (TRT Haber, 2023)

CONCLUSION

In the 21st century, the concept of 'hybrid warfare' is very popular and is one of the most frequently used methods of warfare between states. In our study, by conducting a comparative analysis of Russian, Turkish and Western literature, we concluded that there are more common sides in the definition of this concept. We also concluded that every state today must develop a defence system against hybrid threats according to its interests and that it is necessary to make its security and military system compatible with this system of warfare. Finally, we concluded that hybrid warfare techniques have been used in the past, but they were not defined as hybrid warfare, and today this concept has emerged with the development of technology.

Another concept in our study is the concept of ‘Collective West’. We came to the conclusion that the concept of 'Collective West' is not historical and is used as a political concept, and we also saw that the definition of the concept changes depending on the political conjuncture. As an example, based on the foreign policy of the Turkish state in the Ukrainian crisis, we concluded that Türkiye is hardly included in this concept. When we consider the countries that comprise the Collective West: NATO, EU, and America, we concluded that Türkiye, which is a member of NATO, is not included in this definition because of the political conjuncture, but it can be included in case of policy changes.

We conclude that Türkiye's influence and role in the collective West's hybrid war against Russia is significant, that Türkiye plays an important role both regionally and globally in the Ukrainian crisis, and that Türkiye is a very complex geostrategic and political actor that is difficult to give up for both the Western bloc and Russia. We conclude that Türkiye's policy of balance and neutrality in the Ukrainian crisis has led to a positive development of both commercial and strategic relations with Russia.

REFERENCES

Бартош, А. А. (2022). *Серая Зона: Театр Гибридной Войны.* Горячая Линия – Телеком.

''Гибридные войны А.А. Бартош'', https://nvo.ng.ru/concepts/2016-09-16/1_war.html, (дата обращения: 07.09.2024).

Манойло, А. В. (2023). *Гончаренко А.Р., "Докрина Герасимова: Российский Ответ На Западные Концепции Гибридной Войны", Научные Труды Ученых 1 Отделения Общих Проблем Войны.* Мира И Академии Военных Наук.

"Путин объявил о специальной военной операции на Украине" [Электронный ресурс] / Режим доступа: https://www.project- syndicate.org/commentary/modern-warfare-defense-planning-by-joseph-s--nye-2015-02?barrier=accesspaylog (дата обращения:06.09.2023).

Васильевич, Т. О. (2020). "Гибридные войны: новое слово в военном искусстве или хорошо забытое старое?", Вопросы безопасности. 2020. – No 1.

Aydın Filiz Tutku. (2022). ''Turkey's Policy On The Russian-Ukrainian Crisis'', SETA/ANALYSIS, February 2022, No. 77.

Çınar Huriye Yıldırım. (2024). ''Rusya-Ukrayna Savaşının Türkiye-Ukrayna İlişkilerine İzdüşümü'', İstanbul Kent Üniversitesi İnsan ve Toplum Bilimleri Dergisi, Cilt: 5, Sayı: 1, Yıl: 2024.

Georgios, G., Hanna, S., & Marianthi, T. (2021). *The landscape of Hybrid Threats: A conceptual model.* European Union and Hybrid CoE.

Gültekin, Y., & Ateş, B. (2022). *Hibrit Tehditleri Anlamak.* Milli Savunma Üniversitesi Yayınları.

Güngör, Ş., & Aslı, M. (2022). *Savaşın Değişen Karakteri Bağlamında Hibrit Tehditler ve Askeri Eğitim.* Hibrit Tehditleri Anlamak, Milli Savunma Üniversitesi Yayınları.

Harun, A., & Yusuf, Y. (2022). *"Rusya'nın 2014 Ukrayna Krizi'ndeki Hibrit Savaş Stratejisi", YÖNETİM VE EKONOMİ, Yıl: 2022, Cilt: 29 Sayı: 3.* Manisa Celal Bayar Üniversitesi İ.İ.B.F.

Hoffman Frank, G. (2007). *Conflict in the 21st Century: The Rise of Hybrid Wars.* Potomac Institute for Policy Studies.

Hoffman Frank, G. (2009). Hybrid Warfare and Challanges. *JFQ*, (52), 2009.

''Hulusi Akar 3. Dünya Savaşı'', https://www.youtube.com/watch?v=HbaOQpl-Pjc, (erişim tarihi: 06.09.2024).

''Hybrid CoE'' https://www.hybridcoe.fi/who-what-and-how/ (erişim tarihi: 07.09.2024).

''Hybrid CoE'', https://www.hybridcoe.fi/hybrid-threats-as-a-phenomenon/(erişim tarihi: 07.09.2024).

Kalın İbrahim. (2024). ''Belirsizlik Çağında Hibrit Tehditler ve Stratejik Öngörü'', Milli İstihbarat Teşkilâtının 97. Kuruluş Yıl Dönümü, 2024.

Mccuen John, J. (2008). Hybrid Wars. *Military Review*, (March-April), 2008.

Çelikpala Mitat, (2019). "Bugüne Tarih olarak Bakmak: Türkiye-Rusya İlişkilerinin Serencamı ve Geleceği", Dış Politika & Güvenlik, Nisan 2019.

Mülakat: İsmail Hakkı Pekin, ''Hibrit Savaşlar''(Yıldıran Acar, Video Arama, 01.03.2024).

Orhan, G., & Abdullah, Ş. (2017). "Ukranya Krizi Işığında Hibrit Savaş", 2. Mediterranean International Congress on Social Sciences (MECAS II), International Vision University Ohrid, October 10-13, 2017, 478-479.

Chapter 15
The Role of the "Middle Powers" in Shaping the New International System:
The Case of Türkiye

Nubara Kuliyeva
https://orcid.org/0000-0001-5709-320X
National Research University Higher School of Economics, Russia

ABSTRACT

Within the new multipolar international system the role of non-Western centers of power increased dramatically. The middle powers began to undergo a new stage of transformation of behavior and positioning within the international system. Against this background, Turkey began to position itself as a "transregional" power. This status of Türkiye is manifested in the spread of influence in three priority areas: Islamic, post-Ottoman and Turkic/post-Soviet. The purpose of this chapter is to examine the evolution of Türkiye's international positioning and to justify the place that it is striving for within the modern international system during the period of the Justice and Development Party (JDP) in power. An excessively ambitious foreign policy for a middle power can be considered untenable due to a number of systemic and internal factors. However, although Türkiye's attempts to change its international status are not sufficient to achieve the status of a global power, they create the basis for reconsidering the approach to Türkiye as a middle power.

DOI: 10.4018/979-8-3373-2342-8.ch015

INTRODUCTION

With the formation of a new multipolar model of the international system conditions for the increasing role of non-Western centers of power have emerged. In addition, middle powers, began to undergo a new stage of transformation of behavior and positioning within this new international system (Gilley & O'Neil, 2014; Cooper, 2013). Türkiye is one of the most illustrative examples of this process. Against this background, Türkiye began to position itself as a "transregional" power (Larrabee & Lesser, 2003). This status of the Türkiye is manifested in the spread of influence in three priority areas: Islamic area mainly consisting of the MENA countries, post-Ottoman area meaning the Balkan countries and some of the MENA states and Turkic/post-Soviet area primarily the countries of Central Asia, as well as the Republic of Azerbaijan.

The purpose of this chapter is to examine the evolution of Türkiye's international positioning and to justify the place that Türkiye is striving for within the modern international system during the period of the Justice and Development Party (JDP) in power.

During this period the Western-centric Turkish foreign policy model that emerged by the early 2000s, based on the positioning of Türkiye as a middle power and a status quo power pursuing a reactionary foreign policy, was reimagined. Ankara's new foreign policy course, formed under the JDP, is distinguished, on the one hand, by the diversification of foreign policy relations primarily through non-Western countries or countries of the "global South". On the other hand, Türkiye is expanding its foreign policy instruments both through cultural and humanitarian policy instruments and military force (Öniş & Uluyol, 2025). First of all, it is increasingly active involvement in international conflicts not only as one of the parties, but also as a successful mediator. On the one hand, Türkiye effectively expands its actual military presence by establishing military bases, for example, in Qatar and Somalia, conducting military operations as in the cases of Syria, Iraq and Libya, and strengthening military-technical cooperation and arms trade like with Azerbaijan (Gasparetto, 2021). On the other hand, Türkiye is pursuing an active cultural and humanitarian policy through the provision of humanitarian aid, the promotion of the Turkish language and culture and maintaining ties with related communities, the implementation of infrastructure and social projects, etc. Thus, we can talk about the formation of a new transitional model of foreign policy, expressed in the combination of traditional and non-traditional instruments of military and humanitarian foreign policy, which is determined by the principle of "moral realism" (Shlykov, 2019, p. 44).

On the eve of the 100th anniversary of the Turkish Republic, R.T. Erdogan announced a new concept for the development of Türkiye and its foreign policy for the next hundred years, which he called the "Century of Türkiye". This concept is of particular importance, implying the consolidation of an autonomous model of foreign policy aimed at achieving Türkiye's status as a leading power capable of realizing its own ambitions at the global level. The following can be identified as the main mechanisms for achieving this goal: 1) diversification of foreign policy relations; 2) reducing the importance of the external element in priority sectors such as energy and the military-industrial complex; 3) unilateral actions that go beyond bloc interests (Aktürk, 2020). All this seems to confirm the evolution of Türkiye's international status from a middle power to a new type of power.

The study is based on the results of the analysis of official documents, as well as academic and analytical materials mainly in English and Turkish. Particular attention is paid to the study of the initiative of Türkiye to reform the UN system "The World is Greater Than Five", reflecting the Turkish vision of the development of the modern international system. This model is based on the thesis that it is necessary to change the international system that was formed as a result of the Second World War, primarily by reforming the UN, in order to create a more "just" world. Türkiye today seeks to advance its own vision of a "fair" international order, that is, one marked by a real distribution of influence in the international arena. And the function of shaping the international order is the prerogative of the great powers.

The author comes to the conclusion that despite the intensification of Türkiye's actions in the international arena during the period under review, an excessively ambitious foreign policy for a middle power can be considered untenable due to a number of systemic, such as growing conflict potential of the international system, destabilization of regional development and internal like economic crisis, polarization of society, instability of the domestic political system factors. However, although Türkiye's attempts to change its international status are not sufficient to achieve the status of a global power, they create the basis for reconsidering the approach to Türkiye as a middle power in the full sense of the term.

KEY APPROACHES TO UNDERSTANDING TÜRKIYE'S ROLE IN THE INTERNATIONAL SYSTEM

There is no single approach to understanding the term middle power. This term has its roots in the works of Italian thinkers, among whom it is worth noting G. Botero (Botero, 1956), who identified a separate group of states between the great and small powers, capable of independent existence (Zhukovskaya, 2018). However, this term began to be used as a political concept only at the end of World War II. This was due to the growth of diplomatic activity of a group of states headed by Canada and Australia in the process of creating the UN, striving to limit the predominant influence of the great powers in the post-war system of international relations. Thus, the Canadian diplomat R.G. Riedel attempted to give one of the first definitions of a middle power as a state "close to the great powers in its size, material resources, readiness and ability to assume responsibility, influence and stability" (Riddell, 1948).

There are several main approaches to defining a middle power. The first one is rationalist or hierarchical approach (Holbraad, 1984) based on material indicators such as economic power in terms of GDP, etc., population, military potential in terms of army size, military expenditure, etc. Within this approach a middle power is considered as a positional status that globally determines the place of a state within the international system between great and small powers (Holbraad, 1971). The potential of such countries exceeds the capabilities of small states but is limited in comparison with great powers. Firstly, this is due to the fact that their actions are most effective only with the mediation of some institutions such as international organizations, informal groups of states, etc., whose opinions they can express (Efstathopoulos, 2017). Secondly, the influence of the actions of middle powers is often local within a certain sphere or issue of development of the international system, and not the mechanism of its functioning as a whole (Cooper, 1997). Thirdly, the options for possible strategies of behavior in the international arena that middle powers can implement are considered limited, primarily balancing and adjoining (Vershinina, 2020). The advantage of this approach is the ability to rank and compare states based on common criteria. However, the hierarchical approach also has its drawbacks, primarily the lack of a fixed group of criteria, differences in the methodology for determining them, etc. In this regard, the distribution of states based on the identified criteria may seem subjective.

The second approach is behavioral, based on the model of state behavior in the international arena, which determines its foreign policy instruments and positioning (Cooper, 1993). Firstly, within this approach, it is generally accepted that middle powers tend to implement foreign policy initiatives within multilateral formats as initiators and coordinators of diplomatic platforms, processes and coalitions, as well as creators and managers of international institutions on individual problematic issues. They use their management skills, material resources and international prestige to promote such multilateral initiatives (Youde & Hoffman Slagter, 2013). Secondly, in terms of the behavioral approach, it is noted that the main place in the foreign policy arsenal of middle powers is occupied by soft power tools, positioning themselves as a mediator and balancer within the framework of international processes. Thirdly, it is important to implement a foreign policy course that fits in or is part of the policy of great powers and supports the existing international order as a good international citizen (Cooper et al., 2004). This approach puts into the concept of a middle power, first of all, not the comparative power of a state, expressed in material indicators, but its capabilities and forms of influence on international processes. The main limitation of this approach is that any state that follows the above-mentioned determinants of foreign policy behavior, regardless of any objective indicators of territory, population, economic and military power, etc., actually becomes a middle power.

The last approach is constructivist, based on the country's self-determination and positioning (Carr, 2014). This approach assumes that middle power status is merely a social construct shaped by political elites to advance national interests (Cox, 1989). Within this approach states pursue multi-vector policies and advance their own interests through the use of international institutions and consensus-based decisions in order to secure their middle power status. Often, the foreign policy model of these states is quite flexible, depending on historical realities.

For a long time, the dominant approach in studies of Turkish foreign policy was to classify Türkiye as a middle power (Cooper, 1997; Hale, 2000). Initially, this was justified, first of all, from the point of view of the hierarchical approach based on an assessment of material indicators. In this case, the following factors were distinguished: 1) a growing population with a high proportion of youth; 2) high rates of economic growth and GDP indicators for the 2000s; 3) the second most powerful army in NATO and a significant share of military spending; 4) a favorable geographical position in terms of organizing transport and logistics routes (Yalçın, 2012). All this was sufficient to define Türkiye as a middle power in the early 2000s. However, at various times this argumentation weakened in terms of one or another criterion, such as during periods of economic recession.

Since the mid-2000s, Türkiye's positioning within the international system as a middle power has also been justified from the point of view of a behavioral approach. The main argument for this was the change in the goal-setting of Turkish foreign policy with the implementation of A. Davutoglu's "strategic depth" doctrine. Thus, during this period, Türkiye's foreign policy activity was characterized by: 1) the dominance of soft power instruments in the foreign policy toolkit (expanding economic, cultural and humanitarian cooperation and minimizing military activity; 2) implementing the concept of "zero problems with neighbors"; 3) a proactive diplomatic agenda (Ongur & Zengin, 2016); 4) active participation in the activities of global governance institutions and multilateral cooperation formats (Süsler, 2019); 5) positioning as a socio-economic development model not only within the region, but also beyond its borders (Öniş & Kutlay, 2017).

However, despite the fact that from the point of view of material indicators and behavioral model, Türkiye was characterized as a middle power, from the point of view of the constructivist approach, the element of Türkiye's positioning as a middle power was missing. During this period, within the framework of the doctrinal basis of Turkish foreign policy, which was "Strategic Depth", Türkiye was positioned as a central power, which significantly exceeded the capabilities of a middle power in the classical sense (Guzaerov, 2023). Moreover, after the events of the "Arab Spring", Türkiye faced a number of regional threats, the overcoming of which seemed possible only through a proactive foreign policy with the active use of hard power. This also contributed to the pursuit of a more independent foreign policy and the adoption of unilateral decisions that do not take into account the interests of Western allies (Cagaptay, 2020). Thus, from the point of view of the behavioral approach, Türkiye's actions began to go beyond the policy usual for middle powers. In this context, traditional and new (emerging) (Jordaan, 2003) middle powers began to emerge, with structural differences such as political system, period of positioning as a middle power, economic indicators and regional influence, etc. and behavioral differences like the presence of a regional dimension of influence, attitude towards integration processes and positioning in the international arena etc. (Vershinina, 2020).

It is worth noting that the number of individual studies analyzing Türkiye 's place within the international system began to grow in proportion to the strengthening of the country's foreign policy ambitions and the emergence of deviations in the country's foreign policy from the point of view of the middle power model of behavior. Before that, the number of individual studies on Türkiye was quite limited. Thus, Türkiye's growing foreign policy activity in the second half of the 2010s was interpreted as inconsistent with the existing material base, and the change in the parameters of its international status was characterized as partial in terms of the behavioral approach (Sucu et al., 2021). At the same time, the country's foreign policy, which is "uncharacteristic" (Kutlay & Öniş, 2021b) for a middle power, was, on the one hand, justified by a set of internal prerequisites - 1) centralization of power and transformation of the domestic political regime under the AKP; 2) popularity of nationalist ideas among the population and the use of foreign policy initiatives within the framework of populist policy; 3) the need to change the focus of the population from domestic problems to foreign policy successes. On the other hand, a number of systemic factors in the transformation of Türkiye's foreign policy behavior were identified, including: 1) a change in the balance of power within the international system and the emergence of new, predominantly non-Western centers of power; 2) an increase in the potential for conflict in relations with traditional allies and an improvement in relations with non-Western countries; 3) the emergence of the opportunity to pursue an autonomous foreign policy course in the context of increasing international instability.

The main factors of Türkiye's status as a "modified" (Benli Altunışık, 2023) middle power included, firstly, the historical legacy of the empire. On the one hand, it is expressed in the imperial syndrome that led to the claim to transregional influence and status. On the other hand, in the Sevres syndrome which means the securitization of regional development and interaction with external actors and ethnic minorities within the country. Secondly, the country's unique geographical position at the crossroads of Europe, Asia and Africa with control of the straits, access to the eastern Mediterranean, proximity to the hydrocarbon-rich areas of the Persian Gulf and the Caspian region, which all enhances Türkiye's international significance. Thirdly, its multifaceted identity, which makes it simultaneously part of various cultural traditions and political systems of geographic regions.

While situate Türkiye's trajectory within other middle power it can be mentioned that unlike Ankara Seoul has consciously embraced a middle power identity as part of its national role conception (O'Neil, 2014). At the same time Türkiye stands out for its reliance on hard power and strategic autonomy as the core of its modified middle power profile. Unlike Indonesia or Brazil, which emphasize multilateralism and normative leadership, Ankara often deploys unilateral military interventions and coercive diplomacy, while simultaneously promoting universalist rhetoric such as "The World is Greater Than Five."

When justifying the transformation of Türkiye's international status at the present stage from the point of view of the behavioral approach, special attention should be paid to the Turkish agenda of reforming the UN and promoting the thesis "the world is greater than five". This is Türkiye's bid to form a global dimension of its influence and one of the elements of modern Türkiye's foreign policy, which does not fit into the framework of the middle power agenda (Baklanov, 2022). Today, Türkiye strives to promote its own vision of a "fair" international order, that is, one marked by a real distribution of influence in the international arena (Shlykov, 2019). And the function of forming an international order is the prerogative of great powers. If earlier this kind of revisionist approach of Türkiye to the international system was justified by the fact that Türkiye is rather an "emerging", that is, a new, rather than a traditional middle power. In view of this, on the one hand, it criticizes the existing liberal order, in which the great powers dominate. On the other hand, Türkiye seeks to be part of this international order, but in a more advantageous position. Today, it can be said that Türkiye positions itself as a "new/rising" global/great power, which is reflected above all in the rhetoric of the Turkish leader.

Some scholars emphasize the need to reconceptualize the notion of middle powers not as a fixed analytical category defined by material indicators, but as a category of practice employed by states in their efforts to navigate the international hierarchy (de Bhal, 2023). In this case argues, the term functions less as an objective description of power and more as a status-seeking tool through which states distinguish themselves from "small states" while avoiding the expectations placed upon "great powers." Thus, Türkiye's claim to a position beyond the traditional middle power framework can be interpreted as a deliberate practice of status assertion within a stratified international order, rather than a simple reflection of material capacity.

EVOLUTION OF TÜRKIYE'S FOREIGN POLICY VISION

After JDP came to power in Türkiye, the country's traditional foreign policy has undergone significant transformations. These changes affected both the core goals and directions, as well as the instruments used to implement them. The following key stages in the evolution of conceptual foundations of Türkiye 's foreign policy during this period can be identified: 1) 2002–2011; 2) 2011–2016; 3) 2016–2020. One of the justifications for this periodization is the gradual shift away from a Western-oriented foreign policy toward Turkish-style "Eurasianism" (Arı, 2021). However, it would be more accurateto characterize the specifics of this periodization in terms of the transition from the "Davutoglu Doctrine" to the "Erdogan Doctrine," taking into account the accompanying process of establishing a presidential system.

This doctrinal transition is expressed in the transformation of the approach to foreign policy instruments from the "soft power" of the "zero problems with neighbors" period to "smart power," grounded in the concept of "moral realism" (Keyman, 2017; Shlykov, 2019). Despite the change in implementation methods, the conceptual foundations of foreign policy retain a certain degree of continuity in terms of Türkiye's positioning in the region and the world (Benli Altunışık, 2020).

The first of these stages (2002–2011) lasted until the events of the "Arab Spring." During this period, Türkiye relied on implementing Ahmet Davutoğlu's "strategic depth" doctrine, which emphasized the preferential implementation of non-military foreign policy instruments, primarily "soft power" and economic influence (Davutoglu, 2001). An important element of this doctrine was the "zero problems with neighbors" concept, which was based on the idea of overcoming the crisis in relations with Türkiye 's neighboring countries in the short term and building a new regional network of cooperative ties. In accordance with the tenets of this doctrine, Türkiye did not employ military foreign policy instruments. The remaining use of military force was limited to participation in international peacekeeping missions, post-conflict resolution, and humanitarian aid.

After 2011, Türkiye faced challenges requiring a more flexible foreign policy approach capable of responding to new regional threats. First, the results of the "Arab Spring" made it impossible to maintain the achieved level of interaction with both regional and global actors. Second, a process of re-securitization of regional development began against the backdrop of the resurgence of traditional Turkish regional policy issues such as the terrorist threat and Kurdish separatism (Kösebalaban, 2020). Third, a new phase of regional rivalry for leadership began between emerging regional "power centers" like Saudi Arabia, Iran, etc. Fourth, the nature and significance of conflicts in the region changed. The transformation of Türkiye's approach to foreign policy during this period is reflected in the following postulates: 1) pursuing a proactive foreign policy; 2) expanding Türkiye's global influence; 3) achieving the status of a power with global influence; and 4) autonomy of Turkish foreign policy.

These trends indicate a transformation of the foreign policy model of the early 2000s and a transition to the "Erdogan Doctrine," which has characterized Turkish regional policy in recent years. In the post-2016 period, associated with the failed military coup attempt, Turkish policy in the region has become characterized by 1) a heightened perception of regional threats from a national security perspective; 2) a new round of rivalry with regional players claiming leadership positions in the region; 3) the militarization of foreign policy instruments. 4) the implementation of unilateral and risky foreign policy steps; and 5) the establishment of situational alliances and interaction with tactical allies depending on national interests.

In terms of transforming the country's foreign policy toolkit, the primary focus is on strengthening import substitution capabilities and the autonomy of the national military-industrial complex (Özel Özcan & Şahin, 2025). The importance of not only ensuring domestic consumption but also promoting Türkiye as a significant arms exporter is emphasized.

As a result of the evolution from the "Davutoğlu Doctrine" to the "Erdoğan Doctrine," security has become central to Türkiye 's foreign policy, prompting a reconsideration of the approach to the use of military force as a foreign policy instrument. Moreover, the reluctance to abandon the already established resource of "soft power" has led to the development of a contradictory conceptual framework for Türkiye's contemporary foreign policy. While maintaining a high degree of importance for cultural and humanitarian cooperation, Türkiye is increasingly engaging in international processes within a proactive approach, including through military intervention. This transitional foreign policy model has proven effective in the face of the proliferation of new types of threats and is justified by the principle of "moral realism." Moreover, this dual reliance on hard and soft instruments exemplifies Ankara's attempt to transcend the traditional boundaries of middle power behavior, situating its activism within the broader literature on middle powers that seek to redefine their roles in a multipolar order.

TÜRKIYE'S VISION OF A NEW INTERNATIONAL ORDER: FROM GLOBAL JUSTICE TO NATIONAL AMBITION

R.T. Erdoğan has been promoting his own model of development of the international system named "The World is Greater Than Five" since 2013. This model is based on the idea of the need to change the international system that was formed following the Second World War, primarily by reforming the UN, in order to create a more "just" world (Aral, 2019).

Among the main problems of the existing system, it is noted (Erdoğan, 2021), firstly, the ineffectiveness of the UN in resolving humanitarian crises such as in Syria, Palestine, Afghanistan, Myanmar, Yemen, etc. and eliminating long-term threats to development like climate change, migration crisis, terrorism, poverty, famine, etc. Secondly, the paralysis of the main UN decision-making mechanism - the Security Council due to the limited number of participants, the presence of the principle of the need for unanimity of the permanent members of the UN Security Council when adopting any substantive resolution, the mandatory nature of Security Council resolutions and the recommendatory nature of the activities of all other UN bodies. Thirdly, the "crisis of justice" of the UN Security Council decision-making mechanism because of the results of World War II are the basis for distributing rights and powers and lack of representativeness due to failure to take into account the opinion of 75% of the world's population who are not permanent members of the Security Council, Islamophobia. Fourthly, the problem of UN legitimacy caused by the actions of the Security Council primarily humanitarian interventions.

To eliminate the identified problems, the Turkish side proposes a number of solutions united under the auspices of UN reform (Avatkov & Guzaerov, 2023). Firstly, R.T. Erdogan promotes the idea of the need to increase the number of permanent members of the UN (from 5 to 20). Secondly, it is proposed to elect these members by voting in the UN General Assembly. Thirdly, it seems necessary to expand the powers of the UN General Assembly. Fourthly, it is proposed to make the Security Council accountable to the GA. Fifthly, a necessary condition for the reform is the abolition of the veto right.

The Turkish approach to reforming the UN is positioned as based on a number of general principles, that is, not aimed at ensuring the narrow national interests of a limited group of states. The main principle is justice, which is understood as the absence of cultural, civilizational and religious discrimination. The second principle is equality, which is presented as an integral element of a fair system. The next principle is fair representation, the need for which is justified by the discrepancy between the system based on the results of World War II and the geopolitical realities existing today, as well as the modern demographic situation that led to the lack of levers of influence among the Islamic population of the planet, which exceeds 1.5 billion (Irkhin & Moskalenko, 2021). Also put forward as an important principle is the transparency of the decision-making process, which is not ensured in the context of the existence of secret diplomacy of the Security Council members. Another principle of the reform put forward by Türkiye is the accountability of the decision-making mechanism to the UN member states. The last principle is the preventive nature of possible conflicts of interest of the member states. From the point of view of all the listed principles, the main problematic element of the UN system is the fact of the existence and the mechanism of functioning of the Security Council.

While the 'The World is Greater Than Five' represents Türkiye's critique of the post-1945 international order and its call for a more just and representative global governance system, the concept of the 'Century of Türkiye' translates these normative ambitions into a comprehensive national strategy. Together, they illustrate how Ankara seeks not only to reform the rules of the global system, but also to consolidate the domestic and regional foundations necessary to claim a more prominent role within it

On the eve of the 100th anniversary of the Turkish Republic, R.T. Erdogan announced a new concept for the development of Türkiye and its foreign policy for the next hundred years, which he called the "Century of Türkiye". It is worth noting several key elements concerning the foreign policy line and international positioning of Türkiye, laid down within the framework of this concept.

It is worth starting with the desire of the Turkish leader to consolidate an autonomous model of foreign policy focused on the national interests of the country. The following can be identified as the main mechanisms for achieving this goal: 1) diversification of foreign policy relations through maintaining stable bilateral relations with the Russian Federation in the context of increasing Russian-Western confrontation, maintaining contacts with pro-Islamic forces in the countries of the Middle East and North Africa, strengthening cooperation with non-Western countries and representatives of the "global majority" or "global South", participation in alternative political projects and processes to the West, for example, the Astana format or an application for participation in BRICS, etc. (Gasparetto, 2021); 2) reducing the importance of the external element in priority sectors such as energy and the military-industrial complex (in 2023, the share of the national component in the Turkish military-industrial complex was 80%, while in 2002 this figure was 25%, alternative energy projects such as TANAP, TAP, etc. are being implemented); 3) unilateral actions that go beyond bloc interests like military operations in Syria " (Kutlay & Öniş, 2021a). At the same time, the need to reduce the influence of not only external "patrons", but also domestic political forces that limit freedom of action within the framework of foreign policy, such as the military or FETO, is emphasized. For example, during the period of the AKP's rule in Türkiye, the balance of military-civil relations in the country was radically changed. During this period, the main mechanisms of military influence on the political system were dismantled because the role of the National Security Council was reduced to an advisory level, structural personnel changes happened, subordination of the military leadership of various state institutions were given to civilian structures, the Ergenekon and Sledgehammer trials were organized, etc. (Shlykov, 2020).

R.T. Erdogan aims to make Türkiye one of the “top 10 countries in the world from an economic, political, technological, military and diplomatic point of view.” Thus, the Turkish leader seeks to transform Türkiye from a country following the EU and NATO into a leading power followed by the countries of the Muslim and Turkic world. Some authors say that this should ultimately lead to the formation of a certain axis consisting of countries friendly to Türkiye and ready to recognize its leadership (Ataman, 2023, p. 75). In this context, the period of Türkiye's Western-centric foreign policy before the AKP came to power is contrasted with the multi-vector policy of the period of R.T. Erdogan's party's rule. From Türkiye point of view, it is important to note the trend towards widening the gap between Türkiye and its Western partners (Dipama & Parlar Dal, 2024), represented by the US and the EU, which is confirmed by many examples, including Turkish-American contradictions regarding the Syrian Kurds and Türkiye 's subsequent conduct of a number of military operations in Syria that are contrary to US interests; the acquisition by Türkiye, a NATO member, of the Russian S-400 anti-aircraft missile system in response to the refusal to provide it with the American Patriot air defense system; Türkiye's actions towards EU countries during the 2015 migration crisis, etc.. It is worth noting that as a result of the implementation of a proactive regional policy of an extraterritorial nature, Türkiye has secured for itself the status of a gamechanger at the regional level in such events as in Libya in 2019, the Second Karabakh War in 2020, etc. Today, the Turkish Republic is striving to realize its own ambitions at the global level through proposals for UN reform, the desire to become a mediator between Russia and Ukraine, the implementation of the “Grain Deal”, etc. This is evidence of Türkiye's attempt to secure a more significant position at the global level and the transition from the implementation of regional initiatives to global ones.

THE KEY LIMITATIONS OF TÜRKIYE'S GLOBAL AMBITIONS

Despite Türkiye's increased foreign policy activism during the AKP's rule, its domestic political and socio-economic environment creates significant limitations to the strengthening of its international status. To start with, Türkiye is experiencing the systemic economic crisis in, in which the material base of the political regime does not correspond to its foreign policy ambitions. In the early 2000s Türkiye demonstrated rapid growth, positioning the country among the “emerging markets” but current financial instability, persistent inflation, and the volatility of the Turkish lira have eroded the state's ability to pursue greater international influence.

Thus, according to official data, in October 2022, inflation in Türkiye reached its highest level since the crisis of the 1990s - above 80% (Türkiye İstatistik Kurumu, 2022), which is also accompanied by the devaluation of the national currency.

Perhaps the main reason preventing Türkiye from curbing inflation is its significant trade deficit. External factors also played a role. First, increased geopolitical instability in neighboring regions led to higher global prices for energy and certain food products. Türkiye is energy-dependent, importing 93% of its oil and 99% (International Energy Agency, 2021) of its gas. This significantly widened Türkiye 's current account deficit. Second, the COVID-19 pandemic, as well as a number of regional crises, including the Iran-Israel war, disrupted global supply chains and caused a decline in several sectors crucial to the Turkish economy, primarily tourism. This led to higher prices for imported goods, which significantly increased Turkish budget expenditures while reducing revenues.

Furthermore, the Turkish lira has been devaluing since 2018, intensifying following the dismissal of the Central Bank governor and Recep Tayyip Erdoğan's proclamation of the "Turkish economic model" in 2021, as well as after the 2023 presidential elections. The key idea of the model is that, in a low-interest-rate environment, the depreciation of the national currency should increase the competitiveness of Turkish companies: their products will become cheaper, leading to increased exports. Growing exports will positively impact the foreign trade balance, resulting in a foreign exchange surplus and a current account surplus. Inflation is supposed to be contained by increasing domestic production, coupled with cheap labor. In reality, the implementation of the "Turkish economic model" has contributed to the growth of household indebtedness, as low interest rates primarily reduce the cost of borrowing for individuals and businesses. This, in turn, has contributed to increased consumption and demand for imports. Combined with the expansion of the money supply, this led to overheating of the Turkish economy and accelerated inflation.

All this led to a decrease in the standard of living of the population and an increase in social discontent and polarization in Turkish society. This is evidenced by the uncertain victory of R. T. Erdogan in the 2023 elections only in the second round and with a minimal advantage. Moreover, in the 2024 municipal elections, opposition candidates won in major cities like Istanbul, Ankara, and elsewhere. This confirms the trend of declining trust in the Turkish leader and the ruling party. According to MetroPOLL (2025), Erdoğan's public support has fallen by almost 5 percent over the past year, reaching 42.8 percent as of March 2025.

The situation got worse following the arrest of former mayor of Istanbul, Ekrem İmamoğlu, Erdoğan's main then potential opponent in case of early elections. On March 18, Istanbul University revoked Imamoglu's degree, making it impossible for him to run for president. He was then arrested on charges of participating in corruption schemes, organizing illegal economic activities, and having ties to the PKK, which is recognized as a terrorist organization in Türkiye. This provoked a negative reaction from a significant зart of the Turkish public, resulting in a wave of protests across the country. All this led to a to an increase in the level of social polarization. According to the results of a study conducted in 2020 by the German Marshall Fund together with Istanbul Bilgi University, 75% of respondents would not want their child to marry a supporter of the "most hostile" political party for them, and 72% of respondents would not want to do business with a supporter of the "most hostile" political party for them (German Marshall Fund of the United States, 2020). This means that a majority of Turkish citizens would not accept inter-party social relations such as marriage or business partnerships with members of rival political camps, highlighting the depth of polarization.

Given the problems that Turkish society and the state are experiencing, as well as the it's limited resources of the, it seems impossible to consider modern Türkiye as a classical great power, but it also seems necessary to reconsider the approach to the country as a middle power in the full sense of the term.

CONCLUSION

The case of Türkiye illustrates the complexity of positioning states within the contemporary multipolar international system. Türkiye under the rule of JDP goes beyond the conventional understanding of a middle power and tries to strengthen its international status. However, economic hardship, social polarization and structural problems of international system constrain Ankara's ability to do it, creating an ambition–capacity gap.

There are several scenarios of Türkiye's international status' evolution. The first one is optimistic that means Türkiye could become an emerging great power in the long term if: 1) succeeds in stabilizing its economy, reducing inflation, and sustaining high growth rates in order to accumulate the material foundation necessary for greater global influence; 2) consolidate the defense-industrial complex with self-sufficient critical technologies and competitive arms exports that would enhance strategic autonomy; 3) decrease the domestic polarization, enabling a more consensus-based foreign policy, that would present Türkiye as a reliable and predictable international actor; 4) further weakening of Western dominance or fragmentation of global governance institutions that would create the room for Ankara to project itself as a representative of the "global South." Under such conditions, Türkiye could evolve into an "emerging great power," though still below the level of such countries as USA or China.

The second scenario is more realistic and assumes that Türkiye could sustain the uncertain status of modified middle power between middle and great power in the medium term. In this case the economic situation could remain volatile, political polarization will continue, limiting the coherence of foreign policy but not preventing Ankara from pursuing regional activism. Türkiye will save the role of a gamechanger in the region. However, systemic constraints and limited resources will prevent it from translating regional influence into sustained global leadership. In accordance with this scenario, Türkiye continues to overact above its material resources but falls short of achieving the status of a great power.

The third scenario is the pessimistic one that assumes the weakening of Türkiye's international status. It would be in case of further economic decline, intensification of domestic discontent and weakening the legitimacy of the ruling elite. Social polarization could further erode political stability. At the same time, overstretch in multiple conflict zones may impose unbearable costs on Türkiye's economy and military. In this environment, Ankara would be forced to scale back its international ambitions and concentrate on domestic stabilization. Türkiye would remain an important regional actor, but its global initiatives would lose credibility. The state would effectively retreat to a more constrained version of middle power status, with reduced capacity to influence even its immediate neighborhood.

The long-term trajectory of Türkiye's international status depends on its ability to close the ambition–capacity gap. Economic stabilization and political consolidation are the critical domestic preconditions, while structural shifts in the global system provide the necessary external opportunities. Without these, Türkiye is likely to remain in the gray zone between a middle power and a great power, a state with notable regional influence but only limited capacity to shape the global order.

REFERENCES

Aktürk, Ş. (2020). Turkey's Grand Strategy as the Third Power: A Realist Proposal. *PERCEPTIONS: Journal of International Affairs*, 25(2), 152-177. https://dergipark.org.tr/en/pub/perception/issue/59437/853765

Aral, B. (2019). "The World Is Bigger than Five": A Salutary Manifesto of Turkey's New International Outlook. *Insight Turkey*, 21(4), 71–96. https://www.insightturkey.com/articles/the-world-is-bigger-than-five-a-salutary-manifesto-of-turkeys-new-international-outlook?utm_source=chatgpt.com

Arı, T. (2021). Orientation of Turkish Foreign Policy: Disengagement From or Re-Engagement to the West. In Arı, T. (Ed.), *Inter-State and Intra-State Conflicts in Global Politics: From Eurasia to China* (pp. 24–38)., https://www.academia.edu/43280142/The_revisiting_the_conceptual_and_theoretical_foundations_of_Turkish_foreign_policy DOI: 10.5040/9781666994384.ch-1

Ataman, M. (2023). The 'Century of Türkiye': A New Foreign Policy Vision for Building the Türkiye Axis. *Insight Turkey*, *25*(3), 73–96. DOI: 10.25253/99.2023253.6

Avatkov, V. A., & Guzaerov, R. I. (2023). «Mir bol'she pyati», ili spravedlivost' po-turecki [«The World is More than Five», or Turkish Justice]. *Contemporary Europe*, *1*, 194–201. DOI: 10.31857/S0201708323010163

Baklanov, A. G. (2022). Svet voskhodyashchej zvezdy? Novyj miroporyadok glazami Turcii [Light of the rising star?]. *Russia in Global Affairs*, *20*(6), 166–173. DOI: 10.31278/1810-6439-2022-20-6-166-173

Baklanov, A. G. (2022). Kakuyu igru vedet Turciya v Sirii? [What game is Türkiye playing in Syria?]. *Asia and Africa today,* 12, 23–30. DOI: 10.31857/S032150750023558-5

Benli Altunışık, M. (2020). *The New Turn in Turkey's Foreign Policy in the Middle East: Regional and Domestic Insecurities* (p. 113). https://www.iai.it/sites/default/files/9788833653501.pdf

Benli Altunışık, M. (2023). The trajectory of a modified middle power: An attempt to make sense of Turkey's foreign policy in its centennial. *Turkish Studies*, *24*(3-4), 658–672. DOI: 10.1080/14683849.2022.2141624

Botero, G. (1956). *The Reason of State*. Yale University Press.

Cagaptay, S. (2020). *Erdogan's Empire: Turkey and the Politics of the Middle East*. I.B. Tauris. DOI: 10.5040/9781838603465

Carr, A. (2014). Is Australia a middle power? A systemic impact approach. *Australian Journal of International Affairs*, *68*(1), 70–84. DOI: 10.1080/10357718.2013.840264

Cooper, A. (1997). *Niche Diplomacy: Middle Powers After the Cold War*. St. Martin's Press. DOI: 10.1007/978-1-349-25902-1

Cooper, A., Higgott, R., & Nossal, K. R. (2004). *Relocating Middle Powers: Australia and Canada in a Changing World Order*. UBC Press.

Cooper, A. F., & Flemes, D. (2013). Foreign Policy Strategies of Emerging Powers in a Multipolar World: An introductory review. *Third World Quarterly*, *34*(6), 943–962. DOI: 10.1080/01436597.2013.802501

Cox, R. W. (1989). Middlepowermanship, Japan, and Future World Order. *International Journal (Toronto, Ont.)*, *44*(4), 823–862. https://www.semanticscholar.org/paper/Middlepowermanship%2C-Japan%2C-and-Future-World-Order-Cox/3163877e1ab544eb9cef0500b8c5ab8851fb0aee. DOI: 10.1177/002070208904400405

Davutoglu, A. (2001). *Stratejik Derinlik: Türkiye'nin Uluslararası Konumu*. Küre Yayınları.

de Bhal, J. (2023). Rethinking 'middle powers' as a category of practice: Stratification, ambiguity, and power. *International Theory*, *15*(3), 404–427. DOI: 10.1017/S1752971923000118

Dipama, S., & Parlar Dal, E. (2024). Assessing the Impact of Turkey's Quest for Status Since the 2000s on Foreign Policy Change: Transformational or Transactional? *Uluslararası İlişkiler Dergisi*, *21*(81), 77–93. DOI: 10.33458/uidergisi.1406813

Efstathopoulos, C. (2017). Middle Powers and the Behavioural Model. *Global Society*, *32*(1), 47–69. DOI: 10.1080/13600826.2017.1351422

Erdoğan, R. T. (2021). *Daha Adil Bir Dünya Mümkün*. Turkuvaz Kitap.

Gasparetto, A. (2021). Transition and Middle Power: Turkey's Strategic Autonomy on the Atlantic Area Border with the Middle East, the Mediterranean and the Horn of Africa. In Attinà, F. (Ed.), *World Order Transition and the Atlantic Area. Global Power Shift*. Springer., DOI: 10.1007/978-3-030-63038-6_8

German Marshall Fund of the United States. (2020). *Dimensions of Polarization in Turkey 2020: Strategies and Tools for Mitigating Polarization in Turkey*. German Marshall Fund of the United States. https://www.turkuazlab.org/wp-content/uploads/2020/12/Dimensions-of-Polarization-in-Turkey-2020.pdf

Gilley, B., & O'Neil, A. (2014). *Middle Powers and the Rise of China*. Georgetown University Press. DOI: 10.2307/j.ctt7zswkb

Guzaerov, R. I. (2023). Turciya kak srednyaya derzhava v sisteme mezhdunarodnyh otnoshenij [Turkey as Middle Power in System of International Relations]. *Middle and Post-Soviet East*, *3*(3), 97–112. DOI: 10.31249/j.2949-2408.2023.03.06

Hale, W. (2000). Turki*sh* [Frank Cass.]. *Foreign Policy*, **•••**, 1774–2000.

Holbraad, C. (1971). The Role of Middle Powers. *Cooperation and Conflict*, *6*(2), 77–90. https://www.jstor.org/stable/45082994. DOI: 10.1177/001083677100600202

Holbraad, C. (1984). *Middle Powers in International Politics*. Macmillan. DOI: 10.1007/978-1-349-06865-4

International Energy Agency. (2021). *Turkey 2021 Energy Policy Review*. International Energy Agency. https://iea.blob.core.windows.net/assets/cc499a7b-b72a-466c-88de-d792a9daff44/Turkey_2021_Energy_Policy_Review.pdf

Irkhin, A. A., & Moskalenko, O. A. (2021). "Mir bol'she pyati". Stanovlenie Turcii v kachestve global'nogo aktora mirovoj politiki: perspektivy i vyzovy dlya Rossii ["The World is Bigger than Five". Turkey's Emergence as a Global Actor in World Politics: Prospects and Challenges for Russia]. *Vestnik RUDN. International Relations*, *21*(1), 91–107. DOI: 10.22363/2313-0660-2021-21-1-91-107

Jordaan, E. C. (2003). The Concept of a Middle Power in International Relations: Distinguishing Between Emerging and Traditional Middle Powers. *Politikon: South African Journal of Political Studies*, *30*(2), 165–181. DOI: 10.1080/0258934032000147282

Keyman, E. F. (2017). A New Turkish Foreign Policy: Towards Proactive "Moral Realism". *Insight Turkey*, 19(1), 55-69. https://www.insightturkey.com/articles/a-new-turkish-foreign-policy-towards-proactive-moral-realism

Kösebalaban, H. (2020). Transformation of Turkish Foreign Policy Toward Syria: The Return of Securitization. *Middle East Critique*, *29*(3), 335–344. DOI: 10.1080/19436149.2020.1770450

Kutlay, M., & Öniş, Z. (2021a). Turkish Foreign Policy in a Post-Western Order: Strategic Autonomy or New Forms of Dependence? *International Affairs*, *97*(4), 1085–1104. DOI: 10.1093/ia/iiab094

Kutlay, M., & Öniş, Z. (2021b). Understanding oscillations in Turkish foreign policy: Pathways to unusual middle power activism. *Third World Quarterly*, *42*(12), 3051–3069. DOI: 10.1080/01436597.2021.1985449

Larrabee, F. S., & Lesser, İ. O. (2003). *Turkish Foreign Policy in an Age of Uncertainty*. RAND. https://www.rand.org/pubs/monograph_reports/MR1612.html

Ongur, H., & Zengin, H. (2016). Transforming Habitus of the Foreign Policy: A Bourdieusian Analysis of Turkey as an Emerging Middle Power. *Rising Powers Quarterly*, 1(2), 117–133. https://rpquarterly.kureselcalismalar.com/quarterly/transforming-habitus-foreign-policy-bourdieusian-analysis-turkey-emerging-middle-power/

Öniş, Z., & Uluyol, Y. (2025). Middle Powers Between the West and the "Rest": Turkey During the Russian War on Ukraine. *Uluslararası İlişkiler Dergisi*, *22*(86), 5–25. DOI: 10.33458/uidergisi.1667320

Özel Özcan, M. S., & Şahin, E. (2025). The Historical Development and Strategic Importance of Türkiye's Defence Industry. *Anadolu Strateji Dergisi*, *7*(1), 151–166.

Riddell, R. G. (1948). The Role of Middle Powers in the United Nations. *External Affairs. Statements and Speeches.*, *48*(40), II.

Shlykov, P. V. (2019). Diskussii o spravedlivom miroporyadke v Turcii: sravnitel'nyj analiz koncepcij i popytok ih realizacii v 2000-e gody [Discussions on the Just World Order in Turkey: Comparative Analysis of Concepts and Foreign Policy Practices of Their Implementation in the 2000's]. *Comparative Politics Russia,* 10 (4), 34–51. https://doi.org/DOI: 10.24411/2221-3279-2019-10040

Shlykov, P. V. (2020). Armiya i voennaya elita v kontekste politicheskoj transformacii Turcii 2000-h i 2010-h gg [The Army and Military Elite in the Context of Turkey's Political Transformation in the 2000s and 2010s]. *Moscow University Bulletin*, 1, 33-54. https://cyberleninka.ru/article/n/armiya-i-voennaya-elita-v-kontekste-politicheskogo-razvitiya-turtsii-2000-h-i-2010-h-godov

Sucu, A. E., Safranchuk, I., Nesmashnyi, A., & Iskandarov, Q. (2021). Transformation of Middle Powers with the Decline of World Hegemony: The Case of Turkey. *Strategic Analysis*, *45*(4), 307–320. DOI: 10.1080/09700161.2021.1950409

Süsler, B. (2019). *Turkey: An emerging power in a changing world?* LSE IDEAS Strategic Update. https://www.lse.ac.uk/ideas/Assets/Documents/updates/LSE-IDEAS-Turkey-Middle-Power.pdf

Türkiye İstatistik Kurumu. (2022, Ekim). *Tüketici Fiyat Endeksi.* https://data.tuik.gov.tr/Bulten/Index?p=Tuketici-Fiyat-Endeksi-Ekim-2022-45799

Vershinina, V. V. (2020). «Derzhavy srednego urovnya» v mezhdunarodnyh otnosheniyah: sravnitel'nyj analiz konceptual'nyh podhodov [Middle Powers in International Relations: Comparative Analysis of Conceptual Approaches]. *Comparative Politics Russia*, 11(3), 25-40. https://doi.org/DOI: 10.24411/2221-3279-2020-10034

Waltz, K. (1979). *Theory of International Politics*. Addison-Wesley.

Yalçın, H. B. (2012). The Concept of "Middle Power" and the Recent Turkish Foreign Policy Activism. *Afro Eurasian Studies*, 1(1), 195-216. https://dergipark.org.tr/tr/pub/afes/issue/44785/557056

Youde, J. R., & Hoffman Slagter, T. (2013). Creating Good International Citizens: Middle Powers and Domestic Political Institutions. *Seton Hall Journal of Diplomacy and International Relations.* 36(52). 123-133. https://www.academia.edu/889757/Creating_Good_International_Citizens_Middle_Powers_and_Domestic_Political_Institutions

Zhukovskaya, T. Y. (2018), «Srednie derzhavy» kak element sovremennoj mirovoj sistemy: k voprosu o teoreticheskom osmyslenii koncepta ["Middle powers" as an element of the modern world system: on the issue of theoretical understanding of the concept]. *Vestnik TSU.* 1(171), 172-178. https://cyberleninka.ru/article/n/srednie-derzhavy-kak-element-sovremennoy-mirovoy-sistemy-k-voprosuo-teoreticheskom-osmyslenii-kontsepta

Chapter 16
Role of BRICS in the International Relations of the 21st Century:
A Critical Analysis Through the Lens of Multipolarity

Jipson Joseph
https://orcid.org/0009-0005-1795-5051
Christ University, India

ABSTRACT

Compared to the previous century, international relations in the 21st century are more intense and complex. The global order moved from multipolarity (pre-Second World War period) to bipolarity (post-Second World War period) to unipolarity (post-Cold War era). Although many believed that unipolarity would continue to exist for long under the superpower leadership of the USA, it was short-lived. Globalization, liberalization, and an open economy reshaped the international order that echoes interconnectedness and interdependence. Accordingly, the 21st century witnesses the revival of multipolarity. However, this period advances the emergence of developing countries to the global scenario, demanding active roles in policy-making and decision-making processes. The BRICS grouping is one such body. Consisting of ten emerging economies, it has a unique position to stand for the developing world's interests. From this perspective, this chapter critically examines the role of BRICS in 21st-century international relations through the lens of multipolarity.

DOI: 10.4018/979-8-3373-2342-8.ch016

1 INTRODUCTION

World history presents dualism in global governance: unipolarity and multipolarity, except during the Cold War period. The post-Westphalian period witnessed the growth of a multipolar international order with the emergence of nation-states that echo sovereignty and territorial integrity (Falk, 2025). However, this was primarily a prerogative of the Western countries, as most contemporary developing countries were their colonies. The aftermath of the Second World War redefined the global setting and favored the emergence of bipolarity. Although many colonies gained independence immediately after the period of war, many continued to align with the position of their colonial powers. During this period, the multipolar system of governance became confined to two power blocs under the leadership of the United States of America (USA) and the Union of Soviet Socialist Republics (USSR) (Cafruny et al., 2023). While the USA led the capitalist bloc, the USSR led the socialist bloc. A Non-Aligned Movement (NAM) existed in some countries along with these two blocs. However, the NAM countries had no significant role in the context of the power dynamics of the two blocs. The Cold War between these powerful blocs shaped world history for almost four decades. With the dissolution of the USSR, the Cold War ended, and the world immediately showed a tendency toward unipolar hegemony under the leadership of the USA (Vasconcelos, 2008).

A single central leadership is always preferred for efficient governance of any country. When there are many governance systems in a country, it complicates and weakens the system's effectiveness. However, such an understanding cannot be attributed to global governance. Each country has its desires, prejudices, anxieties, and interests. If the USA becomes the global leader, it will prioritize its interests, which we witness with the present Trump government. This article does not argue that the USA's politics and power dynamics are wrong, but claims that it may create confusion and disorder across the globe, as we are witnessing in the latest trade war. Multipolarity is the most suitable system of governance in the present context of increased globalization, liberalization, free market policy, and international relations (Stuenkel, 2015). Otherwise, global institutions like the United Nations (UN) should take up the decisive leadership role, where the representatives of each country have a unique role to play. However, the veto power of the Security Council members complicates this leadership role.

Many coalitions and intergovernmental organizations have originated in recent decades. Among them, BRICS is of special importance as it comprises the world's largest populous countries and presents the leading voice of the developing world. They are also the main markets of the developed countries. It evolved as BRIC in 2009 and became BRICS with South Africa's membership in 2010. BRICS is the acronym referring to the first five members: Brazil, Russia, India, China, and

South Africa. In 2024, four countries joined, and in 2025, one more country joined, enhancing the strength of this grouping. This intergovernmental organization's summits and ongoing discussions on various matters and its united stand at the international level enrich its importance as a group. It tries to stand united for the causes and concerns of the developing world. Such a perspective provides a scope for a multipolar global order.

In this perspective, this chapter critically analyzes the shift from multipolarity to bipolarity and then to a unipolar global order. Then, it examines the importance of regaining the multipolar system of governance for a balanced global order. The chapter will make this analysis in the context of the origin and growth of BRICS. The chapter's main objective is to critically explore multipolarity through the lens of the BRICS grouping. The developing countries cannot always be treated as subservient to the developed world's dictum. They have a unique role in international policy-making and decision-making processes, and the intergovernmental organization BRICS provides such a platform. This critical study will also explore the possibilities of BRICS in promoting a multipolar global order.

2 CONVENTIONAL GLOBAL ORDER – MULTIPOLARITY OR UNIPOLARITY?

The term 'world order' denotes "the arrangement of power and authority that provides the framework for the conduct of diplomacy and world politics on a global scale" (Falk, 2025). Although many small kingdoms existed from the dawn of civilization, they were either under or allies of some prevalent empires. The interconnectedness among the kingdoms was less due to a lack of transport and communication facilities. The Greek, Roman, Ottoman, and British empires affirm unipolarity in their space and time. However, this conventional framework changed with the emergence of nation-states in the 17th century. The Westphalian Treaty (1648) inspired the systematic shift to a multipolar global order (Chikvaidze, 2020). Multipolarity refers to many power centers that guide international order and interrelations, whereas unipolarity points to a single dominating power. The Congress of Vienna (1814-1815), convened after the defeat of Napoleon, strengthened the movement toward a balancing of powers. Although it was done in the context of Europe, it had a worldwide impact concerning multipolarity. Both unipolarity and multipolarity have their advantages and drawbacks. Unipolarity might lead to dictatorship, and multipolarity might cause conflicts and wars between the power-holders. The global order until the end of the Second World War was a mixture of unipolarity and multipolarity.

2.1 Influence of the Second World War

The Second World War originated from the ashes of the First World War. The Central Powers, consisting of Germany, Austria-Hungary, and Turkey, fought against the Allies, including France, Great Britain, Italy, Japan, Russia, and the USA (Showalter & Royde-Smith, 2025). The League of Nations, which was formed to address situations that can cause war, failed in its responsibility. This led to the Second World War, fought between the Axis Powers: Germany, Italy, and Japan, and the Allies: France, Great Britain, the Soviet Union, the USA, and China (Hughes & Royde-Smith, 2025). Both these wars point to bipolarity, as there are two power blocs. However, they existed as a coalition for the benefit of war and were not based on any specific ideologies. They were not permanent blocs like Japan and Italy, which were part of the Allies in the First World War, sided with Germany in the Second World War. Since the USSR followed communist ideology immediately after the First World War due to the Bolshevik Revolution, the USA did not want to spread it across Europe. Accordingly, when the Security Council was formed, the US believed the other four members could easily alienate the USSR. However, immediately after the War, China adopted communism and sided with the Soviet Union in 1949. This forced the US to increase its military strength in Europe to obstruct the spread of communism. On the other hand, the Soviet Union tried to restrict the spread of capitalism (Cafruny et al., 2023). It finally led to the period of the Cold War and bipolarity.

2.2 Bipolarity in the Form of Two Power Blocs

Immediately after the Second World War, global politics was divided into two blocs that aligned with two ideologies: capitalism and communism. The US led the group of capitalist countries, whereas the Soviet Union led the group of communist countries. Although these two blocs did not directly fight against each other, they indirectly fought in almost all fields. This confrontation is referred to as the Cold War. The US and its allies were called the First World or the Western Bloc, whereas the USSR and its allies were called the Eastern Bloc. While the Western Bloc functioned based on the NATO treaty, the Eastern Bloc adhered to the Warsaw Pact. Until the dissolution of the Soviet Union in 1991, this bipolar system of governance continued. During this time, many believed that this system of two superpowers and their allies would remain eternally, influencing global interactions. Military power was the most essential thing for world dominance during this period of bipolarity (Vasconcelos, 2008).

3 END OF BIPOLAR GLOBAL ORDER

The Western World accepted the collapse of the Soviet bloc and the Cold War with utmost happiness, believing it would lead to the dominance of Western democracy and its values and principles (Fukuyama, 1992). However, this optimism did not stand long as structural crises and readjustments initiated by the 'new globalization' changed the scenario (Vlados et al., 2022). The new globalization redefined the global structure due to the rise in information, advancements in healthcare, increasing transportation and communication facilities, and unprecedented global economic growth (Kieh, 2008). The US bloc believed it could establish its control worldwide by pushing Russia out of the new world order (Cafruny et al., 2023). It was possible for a shorter period. The scenario changed immediately, favoring the emergence of developing countries, multinational actors, and NGOs at the forefront. The period after bipolarity witnesses a short period of unipolarity and the resurgence of multipolarity.

3.1 Unipolar Hegemony

Global governance is primarily oriented toward creating an equitable social order (Dutta, 2019). It applies not only to people but also to countries. However, history testifies that just as some people enjoyed preference over others, some countries also enjoyed special provisions due to their economic and other advantages. Immediately after the Cold War, the US enjoyed the special status of a superpower, which continued to exist during the Bush senior and Clinton administrations (Vasconcelos, 2008). It was because the gap between the US and other countries was so huge that they could not significantly influence the international governance structure. The power disparity was significantly visible after the end of the Cold War. Many scholars called this period "the US and behind it the West." The US's economic, military, technological, diplomatic, and cultural supremacy was widely accepted during this period. This became more evident when they destroyed the Taliban, which was located 7000 miles away, immediately after the 09/11 attacks. It also caused a situation where even the allies of the former Soviet Union became united with the supremacy of the USA (Krauthammer, 2002/2003).

3.2 Advantages and Drawbacks of Unipolar Global Order

According to the UN framework, global governance aims to fulfill three obligations. Firstly, it should manage the trans-border issues among various sovereign countries. Secondly, it should ensure that a stable world order exists so that there is no confusion and insecurity across the globe. Thirdly, it should unite all countries to collectively address and solve global issues (Viswanathan & Soni, 2017). If a single center (unipolarity) leads and decides global governance matters, it would be easy to manage the trans-border problems, establish a stable order, and promote collective efforts. Besides, a non-biased superpower leadership can promote the welfare of all people. It can control interstate tensions without escalating into war.

However, these are not without any drawbacks. The UN and other international institutions should adhere to multilateral discussions and interactions. If a unipolar global order exists, its dictates would be final, affecting other members' choice-making and decision-making capacities. It will damage the UN principles and the genuine claims of developing countries (Antony, 2023). Even in the 21st century, where global interconnectedness has become so deep and the economies of developing countries are proliferating, the US claims that it is holding the world together (Biden, 2023). On the other hand, the globe has witnessed its favoritism on many occasions, like its voting in the UN against the ceasefire in Gaza and the embargo in Cuba (Cochrane & Zaidan, 2024). Against such hegemonic and biased approaches, the globe requires new forms of collaboration and principles (Nuruzzaman, 2022).

3.3 Shift toward Multipolarity

Globalization has redefined international relations, making the interconnection between countries more intense and complex regardless of economic status. Compared to previous centuries, the interdependence between countries has become crucial due to scientific and technological advancements and increased transport and communication facilities. This situation demands a vital global governance system. Global governance is the voluntary international cooperation of sovereign states to manage transnational issues (Viswanathan & Soni, 2017). The characteristic features of global governance are voluntary cooperation, sovereign states, management, and the transnational nature of issues. The UN and other international institutions have a significant role in managing transnational issues. However, if a single power holds control over the world, it cannot be considered a voluntary cooperation of the states; it would be nothing but a subjugation to the commands of the supreme power. There is also a high chance of favoritism that challenges the interdependence of countries. Voluntary cooperation always points to freedom and choice in making decisions concerning transnational issues with the support of one's allies. Regional cooperations, inter- and intra-continental collaborations, international institutions, NGOs, and multinational corporations also have specific roles in this multipolar system (Vasconcelos, 2008).

Paul Kennedy (1987) argued that from the ashes of the Cold War, a multipolar world should emerge that stands on four pillars: the US, the EU, Japan and China, and Russia. He may not have thought that developing countries would make significant economic growth. With the support of other countries in the Global South, Russia and China try to establish a unique position in global governance. Many regional and intercontinental groupings have been formed to support their members in trade, security provisions, and international decision-making. These groupings, formed based on the EU model, prompted the resurgence of a multipolar world order (Vasconcelos, 2008). Although researchers like Krauthammer (1990/1991) imagined that the US would continue to be a superpower for a long time, the drastic changes in the global landscape of the 21st century did not promote this move. Instead, it moved towards multipolarity. A multipolar global order would be impossible without strong and effective multilateral institutions like BRICS that proclaim the concerns of developing countries (Guterres, 2023).

4 BRICS: A RAY OF HOPE

The world first heard about BRIC through Golden Sachs economist Jim O'Neil's prophetic voice in 2001. It remained an idea without any practical measures until 2008, when the foreign ministers of these countries held a meeting in St. Petersburg. BRICs originated with the initiative of the four founding members — Brazil, Russia, India, and China — when the first Summit of BRICs was held in Yekaterinburg in 2009. These countries' resilience to the financial crisis of 2008 was the immediate inspiration behind the formation of this bloc (Stuenkel, 2013). South Africa joined the group in 2011, making it BRICS. Although there were many membership demands, it remained a bloc of five countries until 2024. Many argued that it should expand the circle of friends with more members to have a global impact (Sokolov et al., 2021). Accordingly, the second expansion of BRICS took place in 2024, adding four more members to the group: Egypt, Ethiopia, Iran, and the UAE. In January 2025, Indonesia also joined the group, extending its numbers to ten. They all have diverse interests and concerns. However, they all share anti-West ambitions and prefer a strong bloc against Western hegemony (Dutta, 2019).

The international political landscape is witnessing a paradigm shift as more emerging economies take the lead roles. Instead of being subjugated to the interests of the developed world, developing countries have started to establish their interests through various coalitions, like IBSA (India, Brazil, and South Africa), BASIC (Brazil, South Africa, India, and China), G-33, and ACP (African, Caribbean, and Pacific group). Compared to other groupings, BRICS has immense possibilities and opportunities to lead from the front as it includes all the leading emerging economies and influential actors of the Global South. It has also shown great capacity to form a non-Western coalition in the era of bloc building (Gowan, 2012).

Globalization has had a significant role in the formation of BRICS. Economic and regional integration is the force behind this powerful union in the Asia-Pacific region (Dutta, 2019). While the British and US economies took almost 150 and 50 years for meaningful economic growth, China and India took just 20 years, affirming the significance of the BRICS countries. They can promote bilateral trade and multilateral interactions among the members by sharing information, exchanging experiences and best practices, collaborating in research and capacity building, and coordinating policies (Joint Statement of the 7th Summit, 2015). Such methods can make it a powerful bloc that can assert the interests of developing countries. Besides, SDG 17 affirms the need for partnerships to realize other goals. Relying on this demand, BRICS countries propagate collaborative efforts and efficient co-operation to strengthen their attempts toward sustainable development and achieve a sustainable future for the developing world.

4.1 Power Dynamics of BRICS

BRICS is one of the most substantial power blocs across the globe. It consists of two permanent members of the UN Security Council, the two most populous countries, leading military powers, emerging economies, and countries with immense natural resources like crude oil. All of them are members of the UN and the World Bank. Although no one is a member of the G7 and OECD, almost all are members of the G20. Many of them are also members of regional integrations, like Mercosur (Southern Common Market), SAARC (South Asian Association for Regional Cooperation), SCO (Shanghai Cooperation Organization), and SADC (Southern African Development Community). Although some authors criticize BRICS for its attempts to occupy a unique position (Røren & Beaumont, 2019), the group members' strength and key roles in international scenarios affirm that it is no longer a mere aspiration but a strong claim. The BRICS members, Russia, China, and India, respectively, are just behind the USA in military power (Gupta, 2024). They also lead the table of agricultural producers like China #1, Brazil #3, India #4, and Russia #5 (Das, 2024). Besides, Russia #3, China #4, Iran #7, UAE #8, and Brazil #9 are among the top 10 oil-producing countries (Worldometer, 2024). All these affirm that they occupy crucial roles in global economic, military, industrial, agricultural, and service sectors and can influence the international order, pointing to the significance of multipolarity.

4.2 Economic Interactions of BRICS

While Jim O'Neil (2001) used the acronym 'BRICs' within the context of an economic setting, Wilson and Purushothaman (2003) predicted an uncontrollable economic growth of BRIC countries. This prediction seems right when we examine the present global economic interactions and trade scenario. They claimed that BRIC would become a strong opponent of G6 in the international economic setting, and the present data affirms this. With the bloc's expansion, its economic interactions are becoming larger. The financial strength of BRICS is robust in the present times, underlying Käkönen's (2014) argument that the world economy has shifted from the West to the emerging economies. Such a favorable scenario augments BRICS's economic interactions, both within and outside the group. The increased economic relations and international trade are the parameters of the present-day global prominence. The growing GDP rate is regarded as a measure of a prestigious position. BRICS countries affirm that they are even surpassing developed countries in this endeavor.

All BRICS countries had considerably low economic growth compared to developed countries due to their biased policies. However, in the last quarter of the 20th century, they all initiated a progressive approach in the economic sector to become on par with the developed world. This shift explicitly explains the influence of neoliberalism and the open economy. Countries like Brazil, India, and South Africa wanted to escape from the burden of the colonial past and exploitation through economic growth. Russia preferred economic development to address the backwardness caused by Marxist ideologies. China favored economic development to overcome problems like famine that it experienced between 1959 and 1961. All these show that despite having specific reasons for economic growth, they all underline one core element: significant policy changes. The state's policy intervention is the primary rationale for this progressive shift (Santiago, 2020). These countries' progressive governments prioritized their people's real concerns and intervened in the economic setting at the right time to strengthen the country's economic growth (Chatterjee & Naka, 2022). For instance, until the last decade of the 20th century, the Indian economic landscape was monopolized by the public sector, which affected the economic development of the country. However, the policy changes, favoring privatization, initiated a process of more foreign direct investment. It caused the initiation of several companies and industries, leading to more employment opportunities and GDP growth.

The BRICS group can strengthen its voice in the global setting mainly through its economic development and multilateral relations. To facilitate this move, they should mutually support and collaborate in financial transactions, the flow of capital and investments, fixing rates and tariffs, and assisting each other in emergencies. Without mutual support and collaborative functioning, the economic interactions among the BRICS countries and with others will not be significantly effective (Garcia & Bond, 2019). BRICS members know the importance of mutual economic interactions for their collective influence in the world economy. They accordingly initiate programs like joint trade ventures, upgrades of scientific and technical know-how, investments in basic infrastructure developments of member countries and other developing countries, promoting e-commerce, and focusing on the energy sector (Santiago, 2020).

One of the significant steps of BRICS in the global economic sector was the institution of the New Development Bank (NDB) in 2014. Nobody imagined that BRICS would make such a progressive step. It underlines the bloc's enthusiasm to become a powerful alternative to Western hegemony. Through the NDB, BRICS has become an aspirational bloc with a capital of USD 100 billion, almost half of the World Bank's capital. The bloc thus conveys a powerful message that if the World Bank or IMF is not supporting the developmental aspirations of BRICS or other developing countries, it has the potential to provide such assistance. It affirms that the developing world is no longer a mere recipient of loans and funds from developed countries and international financial institutions, but it can create capital to encourage its goals and objectives. Chatterjee and Naka (2022) argue that the institution of the NDB increases the financial flow and transactions among BRICS members, attracts other developing countries to the bloc, and ensures them that it can support and strengthen their reasonable developmental aspirations. Røren and Beaumont (2019) claim that this move also triggered cooperation among developing countries and increased their bargaining powers for more representation, voice, and power in international institutions and global governance. Undoubtedly, the NDB is a powerful mechanism to counterbalance the power politics of developed countries and can effectively bridge the gap between the Global North and the South (Steele, 2017).

Besides the NDB, BRICS also recommends using their currencies in cross-border financial transactions among the members to advance sovereignty and independence (Karataev et al., 2017). Russia and China have declared and initiated the de-dollarization process in their economic interactions (Arapova, 2019; Mohammed, 2024). Global trade transactions are primarily controlled by the dollar and the Euro (almost 77%) (Gouvea & Gutierrez, 2023). The Russian move of 'national currencies for trade' is strengthened in the context of the Russia-Ukraine crisis. The present-day 'tariff war' between the USA and China may also speed up the Chinese de-dollarization efforts. Arapova (2019) suggests that BRICS countries should prioritize their national currencies for trade interactions to increase their currency value and reduce the exchange rate. The feasibility of a common currency is debatable, and BRICS has not made any decision so far. However, Nach and Ncwadi (2024) argue that since the economies of BRICS countries are rapidly growing, it has the potential to surpass the G7 by 2050. This tendency has already been shown by surpassing the PPP GDP of the G7 from 2020 onwards and making steady progress thereafter (Jütten & Falkenberg, 2024).

4.3 BRICS and International Institutions

There were mixed opinions concerning the emergence of BRICs into the international scenario. Some considered it would have only a short existence, whereas others argued it could become a decisive bloc. The importance of BRICS can be evaluated based on its engagement in international institutions. Its role in counterbalancing the Western hegemony can be established only through its involvement in the global framework. The USA and other developed countries prompted the creation of the UN, the Bretton Woods Institutions, and the WTO. These institutions thus affirm the importance of Western hegemony (Hopewell, 2017). The political and economic landscape of the previous century prioritized the interests of the developed world. However, the present scenario affirms changes in the political and economic settings. Developing countries have become more powerful actors in the global economic market. Yet, their required roles and decision-making powers are not duly respected. Western prioritization is still visible in the various behaviors and decisions of the international bodies as they remain their major contributors. It forces them to downgrade the genuine concerns of developing countries (Käkönen, 2014). International institutions still practice outdated rules, inadequate representations, illogical voting methods, imprudent fund allocations, and explicit favoritism towards developed countries (Jütten & Falkenberg, 2024).

From the beginning, BRICS demanded an inclusive approach in international institutions like the UN and the Bretton Woods Institutions (Joint Statement by the 4th Summit, 2012). The present scenario is radically different from that of the formation of the UN. When the UN was formed just after the Second World War to establish peace and welfare across the globe (Mingst & Lynch, 2024), it was necessary to prioritize the then-leading powers in the decision-making process. The origin of the Veto power of the Security Council members can be justified accordingly. Although India and South Africa were among the 26 founding members of the UN, they were not given due significance as they were British colonies. The influence of the colonial powers and the leading actors of the Allies was visible throughout the formation and growth of the UN and its various institutions (Luard, 1982). Developing countries depended on the developed world for their socioeconomic development and scientific and technological support, forcing them to remain silent even when marginalized and rejected internationally (Medhat, 2020). However, the globe has made significant changes afterward, and developing countries are no longer mere colonies of the great colonial powers, as they have established themselves as powerful actors. It requires changes in the functioning of the UN and the Security Council memberships, considering the interests of the Global South (Joint Statement of the 5th Summit, 2013). A critical analysis of the voting choices of BRICS countries during 2006-2014 shows a lack of cohesion among the members (Hooijmaaijers &

Keukeleire, 2016). But, when all BRICS countries were simultaneously members of the UN Security Council in 2011, they jointly stood together for various causes (Jütten & Falkenberg, 2024).

The IMF claims to be a "quota-based" institution. Each member's quota is determined based on financial support to the IMF, borrowing capacity, and voting powers. Voting powers are essential for decision-making and are decided based on contributions to the IMF. Accordingly, the most significant contributor has more voting rights. It shows that developed countries control the IMF and the World Bank as they contribute more than developing countries. Although developing countries have significantly grown in GDP and economic interactions, their total voting rights are roughly 15% (Gouvea & Gutierrez, 2023). The financial institutions must also change their voting and decision-making formats, incorporating the interests and concerns of the Global South. Developing countries may not be in a strong position to donate funds to such institutions, but it does not mean their voice should not be respected in decision-making. (Käkönen, 2014). They also demand that global financial institutions' heads and other staff members be selected based on merit, not nationality (Joint Statement of the 2nd Summit, 2010). Such choices can promote diversity rather than being confined to the conventional unipolar perspective, prioritizing the developed world's interests. From its formation, the WTO prioritized the interests of the Western world in trade interactions. Even when the WTO affirms that its decisions are based on the consensus among its members, it is widely acknowledged that developed countries influence the decision-making process through their mini-group interactions. Wade (2003) sharply criticized developed countries for influencing the decisions of the WTO and unnecessarily interfering in the developing world's economic activities. Hopewell (2017) argues that from the 2008 Doha round meeting onwards, BRICS started to collaborate among themselves and with other developing countries to influence the decisions of the WTO, favoring the interests of the developing world. All BRICS countries are members of the Bretton Woods Institutions. Except for Iran and Ethiopia, all others are members of the WTO, affirming that their united stance can make significant changes in the decisions and functioning of these global institutions. The global march towards multipolarity will become realizable only from this perspective.

4.4 BRICS and the Developed World

Some think that BRICS countries prefer a "world without the West" (Barma et al., 2009). They criticize the increasing interconnection and collaboration of the developing countries, their prioritization of a multipolar global system, and the growing demand for significant roles in international institutions as open confrontations against the West. BRICS is not a bloc that stands in confrontation with the developed world. It just wants to prioritize the interests and concerns of the developing world without subordinating to the interests of developed countries. They prefer to establish themselves as powerful actors in the global scenario rather than confronting other actors. A stable political system, a developed economy, scientific and technological advancements, a low population, and a high GDP rate characterize developed countries. The World Population Review (2024) states that they own just 25% of the global population but occupy almost 80% of global wealth. On the other hand, the BRICS grouping has 42% of the global population but owns just 25% of the global economic output (UNCTAD, 2023). Undeniably, the present economic growth of the developed world is mainly due to the immense supply of natural resources from developing countries, which were colonies of the majority of present developed countries.

Some of the developed countries have changed their attitude towards developing countries. In contrast, others still try to influence their economic interactions and political decisions, leading to much confusion and developmental drawbacks (Wade, 2003). Unsound trade restrictions (Gray & Gills, 2016) and unequal exchange methods (Hickel et al., 2021) are the primary ways they continue to interfere with the developed world's internal matters and external interactions. Authors like de Matos-Ala (2017) and Tripathi (2021) criticize the tendency not to accept the contribution of knowledge from the Global South. They also criticize that the research on the Global South that is circulated in the developed world does not come primarily from the first-hand experiences of the local researchers, but from those of the developed world. It creates bias and prejudice rather than real awareness creation.

The BRICS group is responsible for voicing the concerns and interests of developing countries in their interactions with the developed world. Peaceful coexistence of the Global North and Global South is essential for global peace (Sergunin & Gao, 2018). However, this cannot be considered a mere responsibility of the developing countries. Both must strive for this objective. It would be possible only when there is a strong aspiration to restructure the hierarchical system of governance (Tripathi, 2021). Just as Pope Francis (2015) suggested a synodal way for the decision-making process of the Catholic Church, global governance also requires a synodal process. According to him, synodal refers to the process of walking together. Since the world's countries are sovereign powers without hierarchy, they require mutual respect and positive listening rather than commands and demands. The globe has plenty of resources for the meaningful lives of all its people, regardless of whether in the developed or developing world. However, unbalanced distribution patterns have caused profound insecurities in human life (UNDP, 1994). This necessitates that BRICS countries take the lead in striving for the real needs and interests of the developing countries against the priorities of the developed world. The Joint Statement of the 15th Summit (2023) underlined that BRICS prioritizes restructuring the global social, economic, and political order to become a fair, balanced, and representative order that promotes multilateralism and ensures international law principles.

4.5 BRICS and Developing Countries

When the origin of BRICS was officially announced, many believed that it would have the potential to become a powerful engine to unite the Southern Countries (Wilson & Purushothaman, 2003). Ayres (2017) claimed that within a short period, it emerged as a powerful voice of the Global South in the global economic and security forums. The developed world prioritizes its interests in international institutions like the UN, World Bank, IMF, and WHO. Many of these concerns were not compatible with the interests of the developing world. It necessitates counterbalancing the interests of the developed world. Such an initiative can be undertaken only when the developing countries have a strong coalition. BRICS provides a crucial framework wherein they can share their concerns and mutually collaborate to realize this objective (Dutta, 2019). Since all its members are from the Global South, this union is very sensitive to the issues of the developing world. It provides a platform for discussion, cooperation, and collaborative decision-making (Dutta, 2019).

According to the IMF reports, all BRICS countries belong to emerging or developing economies. They are the fastest-growing economies in the Global South. It empowers them to lead developing countries in the global scenario. Although the UN and other international institutions affirm the importance of equal status of countries in international relations, the divide between the developed and developing world is very much visible. The Global South is often marginalized and exploited. This necessitates unions like BRICS to voice the interests and concerns of developing countries in international settings. Since most of the members of the BRICS grouping are the prominent countries of the Global South, they can significantly raise their voices in international frameworks, affirming their collective efforts. Developing countries have become victims of the developed world's unjust and unfair activities and discrimination in the past. Many of their policies and positions in international settings are not favorable to developing countries, even now. For instance, they face severe injustice and discrimination concerning intellectual property rights that affect the availability of life-saving medicines, traditional medicine, and agricultural seeds. They become victims of the lobbying powers of the big MNCs and TNCs of the developed world. It demands that they stand together to ensure the rights of the farmers, the sick, and the indigenous people (Thakur, 2014). The BRICS group has always affirmed its role in confronting Western hegemony underlying the South-South cooperation for establishing a meaningful global order (Kipgen & Chakrabarti, 2022).

The new wave of economic growth initiated in the last quarter of the 20th century affirmed the importance of developing countries for global sustainability and peace. With the support of scientific and technological advancements, increased educational possibilities, efficient healthcare services, and sufficient capital flow, developing countries are actively engaged in international trade and economic interactions. It led to GDP growth and overall progress. It also helped them establish their unique position in the global economic order (Kniivilä, 2007; Joint Statement of the 1st Summit, 2009). Their outstanding growth and respectful position created confusion and problems as the global order was, until then, mainly controlled by the policies and decisions of the Western world. Developing countries require collaborative efforts and a united positioning to address this conflicting scenario and establish their rights and claims. BRICS acts as a prominent advocate that voices in favor of the developing world (Arapova & Lissovolik, 2021). It affirms the importance of promoting human rights, environmental protection, educational and employment opportunities, and healthcare possibilities without depending on the developed world. To facilitate such initiatives in developing countries, BRICS has formed the NDB, which financially supports such projects. These steps affirm BRICS's interest in protecting the interests and claims of the developing world (Kipgen & Chakrabarti, 2022).

4.6 BRICS and Diverse Interests

The Bretton Woods Institutions were formed with the conviction that one country's prosperity will lead to others' prosperity (Pehle, 1946). Similarly, the BRICS group is believed to provide prosperity to all its members and developing countries, underlying the scope of a multipolar world order. However, authors like Bremmer (2012) and Rolland (2013) criticize that since its members have diverse interests, it fails to establish a collective position in the international domain. Glosny (2010) notes that BRICS members could not make a joint position that could lead to an alternative model. Although there is progress in the functioning methods compared to the first few years of its formation, it still lacks a common strategy and united vision on international subjects and economic interactions. For instance, they do not exhibit any common standpoint concerning the Russia-Ukraine crisis or the US-China trade war, as no one wants to compromise their economic interests for the bloc's strength. Since all of them are growing economies, they cannot afford any trade barriers, economic blockades, or trade embargoes (Shambaugh, 2024). They prioritize economic interests, although they want to establish themselves as a strong opponent to Western hegemony. Balancing these two objectives becomes complicated due to the diverse and conflicting interests of the members. It devalues the possibilities of its cooperative functioning (Roberts, 2010).

As a reminiscence of the Cold War, Russia positions itself as a strong opponent to the US and the developed world. The position of China is always doubtful, as sometimes it shows its allegiance to the West, and sometimes it acts as a strong ally of Russia. India, Brazil, South Africa, and Indonesia are the founding members of the NAM, affirming that they do not align with any parties. Besides all these, they also compete with each other in economic interactions and international trade, as they all want to excel in economic growth. On the one hand, they are each other's leading trade partners. On the other hand, they are the leading opponents of each other in international trade as a significant portion of their market is in the developing world (Rolland, 2013). They also have conflicts and tensions, like China-India and China-Russia border issues and Egypt-Ethiopia Nile River water disputes (Jütten & Falkenberg, 2024). The Chinese attempts to overpower other members create challenges to this objective. They have achieved significant technological advancements, economic growth, and agricultural and industrial outputs, which condition their financial interests (Chatterjee & Naka, 2022). These do not perfectly align with the interests of other members, causing various challenges. China prefers to occupy leadership roles in international institutions to affirm its geopolitical position. Its preferred global acceptance has not yet been achieved due to its antagonism towards democracy (Flonk, 2021). The attempts to form "bypassing institutions" also failed in realizing their objective (Hooijmaaijers, 2021). It makes use of BRICS as a medium for the realization of this objective. All these underline a lack of unity (Hopewell, 2017) and a coherent vision for global governance (Beeson & Zeng, 2018).

To achieve its required global position, BRICS members must strive for collaborative and supportive functioning, putting aside their specific national interests. National interests are relevant for progress, but they should not become a barrier to their cooperative performance. They must also solve the conflicts and tensions among members to achieve a respectful position in the international landscape. The deep-rooted differences among them are explicit concerning political, economic, foreign policy, and security matters (Ayres, 2017), which must be solved through friendly discussions and commitment toward common goals.

4.7 BRICS and Multipolarity

de Vasconcelos (2008) states that multipolarity points to the emergence of a plurality of global actors, like the rise of China and India, the resurgence of Russia, and the increasing influence of Brazil against the concentration of power on the USA and the EU. According to him, all four founding members of BRICS have a significant role in transforming the world from a unipolar to a multipolar system.

Since its members are powerful countries in their regions, like Brazil in Latin America, Russia in Eurasia, India in South Asia, China in East Asia, South Africa in Southern Africa, Egypt in Northeastern Africa, Ethiopia in East Africa, Iran and UAE in West Asia, and Indonesia in Southeast Asia, they almost cover a good portion of the world and its population. These powers' cooperation and collective efforts can promote the attempts for multipolarity. Although they have diverse interests, as stated above, their unified position and vision have the potential to counterbalance Western hegemony (Dutta, 2019). The annual summits and the decision-making style can solve the diversity and conflicts among its members if properly employed. The BRICS bloc always arrives at decisions by consensus among members, affirming the importance of dialogue, mutual listening, and collaboration. Since many international institutions lack this functioning method, it puts forward a new style that should become the *modus operandi* of the multipolar global order.

Dutta (2019) argues that BRICS must address the trust deficit issue among its members to achieve its multipolarity objective. They should also increase the depth of intra-BRICS cooperation. The more collaboration there is, the stronger the bond will be. The attitude of the national leaders is also a vital concern for the growth of this bloc. If they support its cooperative functioning, it can change the design of South-South interactions and its role in international institutions. No individual country in the bloc could challenge the already established international framework controlled by the developed world. However, as a group, it would be able to make changes, challenging the power politics of the West. Besides, BRICS is characterized by ideology, issues, and institutions. Its ideology is to counterbalance Western dominance through collective efforts, but it lacks institutions to address the problems of its members and global issues (Saran, 2017). Although the bloc's expansion can affirm its inclusive and multipolar nature, it can complicate its attempts at convergence and consensus. However, if they can manage these complexities with openness and positivity, it can shift the globe from unipolarity to multipolarity.

Viswanathan and Soni (2017, p.12) claim that the "BRICS model of cooperation can provide the international community an example of a multilateral, inclusive, and open global system." BRICS countries have ensured cooperation in many areas, including multilateral trade, the 2030 development agenda, internet governance, and global taxation. The developed world is not interested in acknowledging the supremacy of the WTO in international trade governance since it follows the principle of 'one country, one vote.' While other international organizations prioritize the interests of developed countries through their biased voting rights, the WTO positions all countries on equal footing (WTO, n.d.). Accordingly, they promote mage-regional agreements to undermine the role of the WTO. However, BRICS accepts the WTO as the sole authority in international trade governance (Viswanathan & Soni, 2017). Two modes strengthen the BRICS stance in multilateral trade: a joint single window clearance system and trade in local currencies (Joint Statement of the 8th Summit, 2016). The BRICS members have consistently affirmed their commitment to the realization of SDGs. The institutions of NDB and other financial assistance to developing countries are oriented toward promoting sustainable development. Furthermore, the UN instituted a 25-member committee to revise the international taxation regime. However, the OECD coined the norms for global taxation without consulting the developing world, which is against the principles of justice, fairness, and equality. Internet governance is another vital area in which BRICS countries emphasize collaboration. Countries like China and Russia affirm that national laws should govern them, whereas India and Brazil insist on a multi-stakeholder approach (Viswanathan & Soni, 2017). Discussions are progressing toward a consensus among the members, which can benefit interactions among the members and lead to a multipolar perspective.

5 MULTIPOLARITY AND INTERNATIONAL RELATIONS: A WAY FORWARD

The unipolar world order has its advantages. However, its drawbacks suggest that the world requires a multipolar system for the smooth functioning of international relations. The present globe experiences immense economic growth, increasing interconnectedness, and wider recognition and promotion of values and principles like human dignity, human rights, justice, and security. This necessitates an in-depth relationship between the developed and emerging economies. Such positive cooperation is essential for multipolarity (Loo & Iqbal, 2019). While affirming that the post-2010 world is moving towards a pluralistic system, Papic (2021) argues that the concentration of power on one or two actors will not be beneficial in the long run. Accordingly, the multipolar global order is an inevitable demand of the present scenario (Stuenkel, 2015).

Realizing the importance of multilateralism and collaborative efforts in the international scenario, the UN General Assembly established the International Day of Multilateralism and Diplomacy for Peace (April 14) in 2018. Multilateralism refers to the cooperative functioning of at least three states. It revolves around consultation, inclusion, and solidarity. It is the guiding principle of the present international order (Dutta, 2019). Multilateralism and multipolarity are not synonymous. Multilateralism refers to the cooperative functioning of three or more states, whereas multipolarity points to more than two power centers. The interconnectedness and interdependence of nations in the present context insist that the globe requires multilateral relationships and policy-making methods for overall growth. These power blocs may be like OECD, G7, G20, G77, and BRICS. An increased number of blocs can create confusion in the global order. However, if systematically and respectfully used, these groups can engage in dialogue and collaboration aiming at global welfare. Accordingly, multilateralism is the rationale behind the understanding of multipolarity. Chikvaidze (2020, p.131) notes that "multipolarity without strong and accepted multilateral instruments is inherently unstable, volatile, and dangerous." The UN and other international institutions should function as mediators without partiality and prejudice to strengthen multilateral discussions in the multipolar world order. The globe should be ready to accept changes for peace and prosperity. The developed world should acknowledge the growth of developing countries by giving them more voice in policy-making and decision-making bodies. To deny the required position to the emerging powers is nothing short of an injustice.

The European Union, consisting of 27 countries, has shown the importance of multilateralism and multipolarity. Although there is a coordinating center, it respects the role and importance of each member regardless of power and economic status. The EU promotes the free movement of people, goods, capital, and services between members, affirming that they all contribute directly or indirectly to the growth of Europe and its people (Laatikainen, 2012). Such intra- and intercontinental groupings should be promoted to establish the true spirit of globalization and its interconnectedness. As the EU affirms, these groupings should adhere to the rule of law, human rights, and multilateral cooperation rather than sticking to violence and unbridled nationalism. However, the emergence of multiple actors with clashing interests must always be cautiously approached (Chikvaidze, 2020). Nuclear weapons are the biggest threat to multipolarity. Even in the recent Operation Sindoor, through which India retaliated against the Pakistan-sponsored Pahalgam terror attack, there were rumors that Pakistan might use nuclear weapons (Ahuja, 2025). The present atomic powers restrict other countries from acquiring nuclear weapons. Although many nuclear powers have reduced the number of their nuclear weapons, unless and until the complete disarmament of nuclear weapons takes place, it continues to be a massive threat to multipolarity.

6 CONCLUSIONS

People's understanding of the world has increased over time. The knowledge of the world was restricted to one's space and vicinity. Scientific and technological advancements improved people's transportation and communication facilities, and their perspectives concerning the world and its governance also changed. The understanding of unipolarity and multipolarity evolved accordingly. The post-Westphalian world echoed a multipolar order, pointing to nation-states' sovereignty and territorial integrity. The two consecutive world wars in the 20th century led to the evolution of bipolarity. It became evident in the aftermath of the Second World War, leading to almost forty years of the Cold War. However, with the dissolution of the Soviet Union, this period ended and led to the origin of unipolarity. It was a shorter period, and the 21st century witnessed the resurgence of multipolarity in the form of more regional integrations, multinational actors, NGOs, and intra-and intercontinental blocs. The BRICS bloc represents one of these multilateral groupings that promote a multipolar order. Such groups can ensure that the globe belongs to all and not the property of a few.

The BRICS grouping, with ten members and more expansion possibilities, has the potential to advance multipolarity. Since they are emerging economies, crucial military powers, leading producers of many goods and services, and top countries in the respective regions, they can promote multilateral cooperation and collaboration for the growth of developing countries. They are not enemies of the developed world, but prefer to establish their unique global position. Although they have diverse interests, their aspiration for sustainable development and a respectful position strengthen their collaboration. Such partnerships of countries (SDG 17) should be encouraged by international institutions and developed countries to ensure a world of multipolarity. Instead of seeing this bloc as a threat, the Global North should promote such groups to enhance solidarity and mutual respect, affirming universal brotherhood.

REFERENCES

Ahuja, N. (2025). 130 Nukes Aimed at You: Pak Minister's Open Threat to India as Tensions Flare. *India Today*. https://www.indiatoday.in/world/story/pakistan-minister-hanif-abbasis-open-threat-to-india-as-tensions-flare-130-nukes-aimed-at-you-2715738-2025-04-27

Antony, S. (2023). Diversification of BRICS: Emerging Economic and Geopolitical Shift. *Strategic Analysis,* 47(6), 565-570. https://www.tandfonline.com/doi/epub/10.1080/09700161.2024.2311475

Arapova, E. Y. (2019). The "BRICS Plus" as the First International Platform Connecting Regional Trade Agreements. *Asia-Pacific Social Science Review,* 19(2), 30-46. https://www.dlsu.edu.ph/wp-content/uploads/pdf/research/journals/apssr/2019-June-vol19-2/4-the-brics-plus-as-the-first-international-platform-connecting-regional-trade-agreements.pdf

Arapova, E. Y., & Lissovolik, Y. D. (2021). The BRICS Plus Cooperation in International Organizations: Prospects for Reshaping the Global Agenda. *Asia-Pacific Social Sciences Review,* 21(4), 192-205. https://animorepository.dlsu.edu.ph/apssr/vol21/iss4/14/

Ayres, A. (2017). How the BRICS Got Here. *Council on Foreign Relations*. https://www.cfr.org/expert-brief/how-brics-got-here

Barma, N., Chiozza, G., Ratner, E., & Weber, S. (2009). A World without the West? Empirical Patterns and Theoretical Implications. *The Chinese Journal of International Politics*, *2*(4), 525–544. https://www.jstor.org/stable/48615736. DOI: 10.1093/cjip/pop013

Beeson, M., & Zeng, J. (2018). The BRICS and Global Governance: China's Contradictory Role. *Third World Quarterly*, *39*(10), 1962–1978. https://www.tandfonline.com/doi/full/10.1080/01436597.2018.1438186. DOI: 10.1080/01436597.2018.1438186

Biden, J. (2023). Remarks by President Biden on the United States' Response to Hamas's Terrorist Attacks against Israel and Russia's Ongoing Brutal War against Ukraine. *The White House*. https://www.whitehouse.gov/briefing-room/speeches-remarks/2023/10/20/remarks-by-president-biden-on-the-unites-states-response-to-hamass-terrorist-attacks-against-israel-and-russias-ongoing-brutal-war-against-ukraine/

Bremmer, I. (2012). *Every Nation for Itself: Winners and Losers in a G-Zero World*. Portfolio.

Cafruny, A., Fouskas, V. K., Mallinson, W. D. E., & Voynitsky, A. (2023). Ukraine, Multipolarity, and the Crisis of Grant Strategies. *Journal of Balkan & Near Eastern Studies*, *25*(1), 1–21. https://www.tandfonline.com/doi/epdf/10.1080/19448953.2022.2084881?needAccess=true. DOI: 10.1080/19448953.2022.2084881

Chatterjee, M., & Naka, I. (2022). Twenty Years of BRICS: Political and Economic Transformations through the Lens of Land. *Oxford Development Studies*, *50*(1), 2–13. https://www.tandfonline.com/doi/full/10.1080/13600818.2022.2033191. DOI: 10.1080/13600818.2022.2033191

Chikvaidze, D. A. (2020). Multilateralism: Its Past, Present, and Future. *Cadmus*, 4(2), 127-133. https://cadmusjournal.org/files/journalpdf/Vol4Issue2/Vol4_Issue2.pdf#page=139

Cochrane, L., & Zaidan, E. (2024). Shifting Global Dynamics: An Empirical Analysis of BRICS+ Expansion and Its Economic, Trade, and Military Implications in the Context of the G7. *Cogent Social Sciences*, *10*(1), 2333422. https://www.tandfonline.com/doi/full/10.1080/23311886.2024.2333422. DOI: 10.1080/23311886.2024.2333422

Das, K. (2024). [Agricultural Producing Countries in the World. *GeeksforGeeks*. https://www.geeksforgeeks.org/agricultural-producing-countries-in-the-world/.]. *Top (Madrid)*, *10*, •••.

de Matos-Ala, J. (2017). Making the Invisible Visible: Challenging the Knowledge Structures Inherent in International Relations Theory in order to Create Knowledge Plural Curricula. *Revista Brasileira de Política Internacional*, *60*(1), e021. https://www.scielo.br/j/rbpi/a/cxMJg6m3HxkWzFXsFHqMfDc/?lang=en

de Vasconcelos, Á. (2008). 'Multilateralizing' Multipolarity. In G. Grevi & Á. de Vasconcelos (Eds.), *Partnerships for Effective Multilateralism: EU Relations with Brazil, China, India, and Russia* (pp. 11-32). Institute for Security Studies. https://op.europa.eu/en/publication-detail/-/publication/0f0a7d94-3d20-4983-89a3-91fee093c355

Dutta, A. (2019). Multilateral Diplomacy: Role of BRICS in Altering the Discourse of Global Governance. *International Journal of Scientific and Technology Research*, *8*(10), 1026–1031. https://www.ijstr.org/final-print/oct2019/Multilateral-Diplomacy-Role-Of-Brics-In-Altering-The-Discourse-Of-Global-Governance.pdf

Falk, R. (2025). World Order. *Encyclopedia Princetoniensis*. https://pesd.princeton.edu/node/696

Flonk, D. (2021). Emerging Illiberal Norms: Russia and China as Promoters of Internet Content Control. *International Affairs*, *97*(6), 1925–1944. https://academic.oup.com/ia/article/97/6/1925/6412472?login=false. DOI: 10.1093/ia/iiab146

Francis. (2015). Address of His Holiness Pope Francis During the Ceremony Commemorating the 50th Anniversary of the Institution of the Synod of Bishops. *The Holy See*. https://www.vatican.va/content/francesco/en/speeches/2015/october/documents/papa-francesco_20151017_50-anniversario-sinodo.html

Fukuyama, F. (1992). *The End of History and the Last Man*. Free Press.

Garcia, A., & Bond, P. (2019). Amplifying the Contradictions: The Centrifugal BRICS. *Social Register,* 55, 223-246. https://socialistregister.com/index.php/srv/article/view/30948

Glosny, M. A. (2010). China and the BRICS: A Real (but limited) Partnership in a Unipolar World. *Polity*, *42*(1), 100–129. https://www.journals.uchicago.edu/doi/10.1057/pol.2009.14. DOI: 10.1057/pol.2009.14

Gouvea, R., & Gutierrez, M. (2023). "BRICS Plus": A New Global Economic Paradigm in the Making? *Modern Economy,* 14, 539-550. https://www.scirp.org/journal/paperinformation?paperid=124945

Gowan, R. (2012). Asymmetrical Multilateralism: the BRICS, the US, Europe, and the Reform of Global Governance (2005-2011). In T. Renard & S. Biscop (Eds.), *The European Union and the Emerging Powers in the 21st Century: How Europe Can Shape a New World Order* (pp. 165-183). Routledge.

Gray, K., & Gills, B. K. (2016). South-South Cooperation and the Rise of the Global South. *Third World Quarterly*, *37*(4), 557–574. https://www.tandfonline.com/doi/full/10.1080/01436597.2015.1128817. DOI: 10.1080/01436597.2015.1128817

Gupta, C. (2024). Top 10 Most Powerful Countries in the World by Military Strength in 2024: Where Does India Rank? *The Indian Express*. https://indianexpress.com/article/trending/top-10-listing/top-10-most-powerful-countries-in-the-world-by-military-strength-in-2024-9382565/

Guterres, A. (2023). Secretary-General's Remarks at the BRICS Summit. https://www.un.org/sg/en/content/sg/speeches/2023-08-24/secretary-generals-remarks-the-brics-summit

Hickel, J., Sullivan, D., & Zoomkawala, H. (2021). Plunder in the Post-Colonial Era: Quantifying Drain from the Global South through Unequal Exchange, 1960-2018. *New Political Economy*, *26*(6), 1030–1047. https://www.tandfonline.com/doi/full/10.1080/13563467.2021.1899153. DOI: 10.1080/13563467.2021.1899153

Hooijmaaijers, B. (2021). China, the BRICS, and the Limitations of Reshaping Global Economic Governance. *The Pacific Review*, *34*(1), 29–55. https://www.tandfonline.com/doi/abs/10.1080/09512748.2019.1649298. DOI: 10.1080/09512748.2019.1649298

Hooijmaaijers, B., & Keukeleire, S. (2016). Voting Cohesion of the BRICS Countries in the UN General Assembly, 2006-2014: A BRICS Too Far? *Global Governance*, *22*(3), 389–407. https://www.jstor.org/stable/44860967. DOI: 10.1163/19426720-02203006

Hopewell, K. (2017). The BRICS — Merely a Fable? Emerging Power Alliances in Global Trade Governance. *International Affairs*, *93*(6), 1377–1396. https://academic.oup.com/ia/article-abstract/93/6/1377/4568590?redirectedFrom=fulltext. DOI: 10.1093/ia/iix192

Hughes, T. A., & Royde-Smith, J. G. (2025). World War II. *Britannica*. https://www.britannica.com/event/World-War-II

Joint Statement of the 15th Summit. (2023). Johannesburg II Declaration. South Africa. https://www.mea.gov.in/Images/CPV/Declaration_2408.pdf

Joint Statement of the 1st Summit. (2009). Joint Statement of the BRIC Countries' Leaders. Russia. http://www.brics.utoronto.ca/docs/090616-leaders.html

Joint Statement of the 2nd Summit. (2010). 2nd BRIC Summit of Heads of State and Government: Joint Statement. Brazil. https://brics2022.mfa.gov.cn/eng/hywj/ODS/202203/t20220308_10649518.html

Joint Statement of the 4th Summit. (2012). *Delhi Declaration*. https://www.mea.gov.in/bilateral-documents.htm?dtl/19158/Fourth+BRICS+Summit++Delhi+Declaration

Joint Statement of the 5th Summit. (2013). *Thekwini Declaration*. https://www.mea.gov.in/bilateral-documents.htm?dtl/21482

Joint Statement of the 7th Summit. (2015). Ufa Declaration. http://www.brics.utoronto.ca/docs/150709-ufa-declaration_en.html

Joint Statement of the 8th Summit. (2016). Goa Declaration. https://www.mea.gov.in/bilateral-documents.htm?dtl/27491/Goa+Declaration+at+8th+BRICS+Summit

Jütten, M., & Falkenberg, D. (2024). Expansion of BRICS: A Quest for Greater Global Influence. European Parliamentary Research Service. https://www.europarl.europa.eu/RegData/etudes/BRIE/2024/760368/EPRS_BRI(2024)760368_EN.pdf

Käkönen, J. (2014). BRICS as a New Power in International Relations? *Geopolitics, History, and International Relations,* 6(2), 85-104. https://www.jstor.org/stable/26805954

Karataev, S., Troshin, N., Bazhenov, I., & Josie, J. (Eds.). (2017). *Use of National Currencies in International Settlements: Experience of the BRICS Countries.* Russian Institute for Strategic Studies.

Kennedy, P. (1987). *The Rise and Fall of the Great Powers.* Random House.

Kieh, G. K. (Ed.). (2008). *Africa and the New Globalization.* Ashgate.

Kipgen, K. T., & Chakrabarti, S. (2022). The Politics Underpinning the BRICS Expansion. *Journal of Liberty and International Affairs, 8*(3), 445–458. https://e-jlia.com/index.php/jlia/article/view/773. DOI: 10.47305/JLIA2283445k

Kniivilä, M. (2007). Industrial Development and Economic Growth: Implications for Poverty Reduction and Income Inequality. In *Industrial Development for the 21st Century: Sustainable Development Perspectives* (pp. 295-332). UNDESA.

Krauthammer, C. (1990/1991). The Unipolar Moment. *Foreign Affairs, 70*(1), 23–33. https://www.foreignaffairs.com/articles/1990-01-01/unipolar-moment. DOI: 10.2307/20044692

Krauthammer, C. (2002/2003). The Unipolar Moment Revisited. *National Interest, 70*, 5–18. https://www.jstor.org/stable/42897438

Laatikainen, K. V. (2012). EU Multilateralism in a Multipolar World. In Jørgensen, K. E., & Laatikainen, K. V. (Eds.), *Routledge Handbook on the European Union and International Institutions: Performance, Policy, Power.* Routledge. DOI: 10.4324/9780203083642.ch33

Loo, M. K. L., & Iqbal, B. A. (2019). Global Competitiveness of BRICS and Canada: Implications for Business. *Transnational Corporations Review, 11*(2), 97–108. https://www.sciencedirect.com/science/article/pii/S1925209924002481?via%3Dihub. DOI: 10.1080/19186444.2019.1615360

Luard, E. (1982). *A History of the United Nations: Volume 1: The Years of Western Domination, 1945-1955.* Springer.

Medhat, A. (2020). A Critical Analysis of the United Nations' Performance in the Light of Contemporary Global Challenges. *SSRN.* https://papers.ssrn.com/sol3/papers.cfm?abstract_id=3564486 DOI: 10.2139/ssrn.3564486

Mingst, K., & Lynch, C. M. (2024). United Nations. https://www.britannica.com/topic/United-Nations

Mohammed, S. (2024). BRICS Plus: De-Dollarization and Global Power Shifts in New Economic Landscape. *BRICS Journal of Economics,* 5(1), 13-32. https://brics-econ.arphahub.com/article/117828/

Nach, M., & Ncwadi, R. (2024). BRICS Economic Integration: Prospects and Challenges. *The South African Journal of International Affairs*, *31*(2), 151–166. https://www.tandfonline.com/doi/pdf/10.1080/10220461.2024.2380676. DOI: 10.1080/10220461.2024.2380676

Nuruzzaman, M. (2022). Conflicts, Strategic Divergences, and the Survival of Economic Groupings: Will China-India Rivalry make BRICS Obsolete? *Asian Journal of Comparative Politics*, *7*(4), 1025–1044. https://journals.sagepub.com/doi/10.1177/20578911221108800. DOI: 10.1177/20578911221108800

O'Neil, J. (2001). Building Better Global Economic BRICs. *Global Economics Paper,* 66, 1-16. https://www.almendron.com/tribuna/wp-content/uploads/2013/04/build-better-brics.pdf

Pehle, J. W. (1946). The Bretton Woods Institutions. *The Yale Law Journal*, *55*(5), 1127–1139. https://openyls.law.yale.edu/bitstream/handle/20.500.13051/13339/61_55YaleLJ1127_1945_1946_.pdf?sequence=2&isAllowed=y. DOI: 10.2307/792757

Roberts, C. (2010). Challengers or Stakeholders? BRICs and the Liberal World Order. *Polity*, *42*(1), 1–13. https://www.journals.uchicago.edu/doi/abs/10.1057/pol.2009.20?journalCode=pol. DOI: 10.1057/pol.2009.20

Rolland, S. (2013). The BRICS' Contribution to the Architecture and Norms of International Economic Law. *Proceedings of the ASIL Annual Meeting,* 107, 164-170. https://www.jstor.org/stable/10.5305/procannmeetasil.107.0164

Røren, P., & Beaumont, P. (2019). Grading Greatness: Evaluating the Status Performance of the BRICS. *Third World Quarterly*, *40*(3), 429–450. https://www.tandfonline.com/doi/abs/10.1080/01436597.2018.1535892. DOI: 10.1080/01436597.2018.1535892

Santiago, F. (2020). The Role of Industrial Policies in the BRICS Economic Integration Process. *Inclusive and Sustainable Development Working Paper Series* (No. 1), UNIDO. https://downloads.unido.org/ot/16/53/16531301/WP_1_2020_FINAL.pdf

Saran, S. (Ed.). (2017). *A Decade of BRICS: Indian Perspectives for the Future*. Observer Research Foundation.

Sergunin, A., & Gao, F. (2018). BRICS as the Subject of Study of International Relations Theory. *International Organizations Research Journal,* 13(4), 55-73. https://iorj.hse.ru/en/2018-13-4/228932694.html

Shambaugh, G. (2024). Embargo. https://www.britannica.com/money/embargo-international-law

Showalter, D. E., & Royde-Smith, J. G. (2025). World War I. *Britannica.* https://www.britannica.com/event/World-War-I

Steele, P. (2017). BRICS Summit: An Opportunity to Lead Fairer, More Sustainable World. *International Institute for Environment and Development.* https://www.iied.org/brics-summit-opportunity-lead-fairer-more-sustainable-world

Stuenkel, O. (2013). The Financial Crisis, Contested Legitimacy, and the Genesis of Intra-BRICS Cooperation. *Global Governance, 19*(4), 611–613. https://www.jstor.org/stable/24526396. DOI: 10.1163/19426720-01904008

Stuenkel, O. (2015). *The BRICS and the Future of Global Order*. Lexington Books.

Thakur, R. (2014). How Representative Are BRICS? *Third World Quarterly, 35*(10), 1791–1808. https://www.tandfonline.com/doi/full/10.1080/01436597.2014.971594. DOI: 10.1080/01436597.2014.971594

Tripathi, S. (2021). International Relations and the 'Global South': From Epistemic Hierarchies to Dialogic Encounters. *Third World Quarterly, 42*(9), 2039–2054. https://www.tandfonline.com/doi/abs/10.1080/01436597.2021.1924666. DOI: 10.1080/01436597.2021.1924666

UNCTAD. (2023). BRICS Investment Report. https://unctad.org/system/files/official-document/diae2023d1_en.pdf

UNDP (United Nations Development Program). (1994). *Human Development Report.* https://hdr.undp.org/content/human-development-report-1994

Viswanathan, H. H. S., & Soni, S. (2017). BRICS Role in Global Governance Process. In Saran, S. (Ed.), *A Decade of BRICS: Indian Perspectives for the Future* (pp. 9–18). Observer Research Foundation.

Vlados, C., Chatzinikolaou, D., & Iqbal, B. A. (2022). New Globalization and Multipolarity: A Critical Review and the Regional Comprehensive Economic Partnership Case. *Journal of Economic Integration, 37*(3), 458–483. https://www.e-jei.org/journal/view.php?number=2013600276. DOI: 10.11130/jei.2022.37.3.458

Wade, R. (2003). What Strategies Are Viable for Developing Countries Today? The World Trade Organization and the Shrinking of 'Development Space.'. *Review of International Political Economy, 10*(4), 621–644. https://www.tandfonline.com/doi/abs/10.1080/09692290310001601902. DOI: 10.1080/09692290310001601902

Wilson, D., & Purushothaman, R. (2003). Dreaming with BRICs: The Path to 2050. *Global Economics Paper No. 99*. Goldman Sachs. https://www.goldmansachs.com/pdfs/insights/archive/archive-pdfs/brics-dream.pdf

World Population Review. (2024). Global North Countries 2024. https://worldpopulationreview.com/country-rankings/global-north-countries

Worldometer. (2024). Oil Production by Country. https://www.worldometers.info/oil/oil-production-by-country/

WTO. (n.d.). Whose WTO is it anyway? https://www.wto.org/english/thewto_e/whatis_e/tif_e/org1_e.htm

KEY TERMS AND DEFINITIONS

Bipolarity: Bipolarity refers to an international political governance system where two power blocs have decisive roles in the global landscape.

Economic Interactions: Economic interactions refer to the global commercial and trade activities between countries and people, intending to maintain financial security and sustainable development.

Globalization: Globalization refers to the increased interconnection between people and countries across the globe.

Multipolarity: Multipolarity points to an international economic and political governance system where more than two actors have decisive roles and powers.

Power-Dynamics: Power-dynamics refer to the balancing and interactions of global actors and nation-states in the international scenario to influence the activities of other actors.

SDGs: SDGs are the UN-designed international global objectives to transform the world to guarantee a sustainable future.

Unipolarity: Unipolarity refers to an international political governance system with only one hegemonic power.

Chapter 17
Triple Strategic Dynamics and Contestations of Quadrilateral Security Dialogue, China, and ASEAN in Southeast Asia Region

Tin Maung Htwe
https://orcid.org/0009-0002-3002-169X
Chiang Mai University, Thailand

ABSTRACT

Southeast Asia has emerged as a central arena in the evolving great-power competition between China and the Quadrilateral Security Dialogue (QUAD). As the QUAD consolidates its Indo-Pacific strategy, aimed at countering Beijing's expanding influence, China continues to entrench its economic and military presence in the region through a combination of economic statecraft, military posturing, and infrastructural expansion under the Belt and Road Initiative (BRI). This geopolitical contest has placed ASEAN in a structurally precarious position, compelling it to navigate security dilemmas, economic dependencies, and shifting alliances while striving to uphold its centrality and neutrality in regional governance. Framed Geopolitical Theory, this study examines the evolving strategic calculus of key regional actors. The QUAD seeks to construct a security and economic architecture that constrains China's ability to dictate the terms of engagement in the Indo-Pacific. In response, Beijing employs a dual-pronged strategy, combining coercive diplomacy with economic inducements to reinforce its influence. ASEAN, lacking the institutional

DOI: 10.4018/979-8-3373-2342-8.ch017

cohesion and military capabilities of major power blocs, finds itself entangled in this strategic rivalry, with internal divisions and external pressures threatening its ability to function as a cohesive geopolitical entity.

1. INTRODUCTION

Southeast Asia has long occupied a central position in global geopolitics, its strategic significance shaped by a confluence of factors: its vital maritime corridors, economic dynamism, and cultural diversity. The region's key maritime chokepoints of the Strait of Malacca, the South China Sea, and the Lombok and Sunda Straits serve as lifelines for international commerce and energy transportation (Bentley, 2023). This geographic importance has transformed Southeast Asia into an arena of great-power competition, where China and the Quadrilateral Security Dialogue (QUAD) vie for strategic influence (Cannon & Hakata, 2021). The study focus on how the economic, security, and institutional dynamics of the great-power rivalry between the Quadrilateral Security Dialogue (QUAD) and China influence ASEAN's strategic autonomy. By examining the economic drivers of this competition, such as China's Belt and Road Initiative (BRI) and the United States-led Indo-Pacific Economic Framework (IPEF), study shall mention that either create dependencies or offer diversification opportunities for ASEAN member states. By assessing how both China's military activities and the QUAD's naval exercises impact regional stability. The analysis will also assess the effectiveness of ASEAN's institutional mechanisms to manage these external pressures and upholding the bloc's principle of neutrality. Finally, the research will compare the varied strategic responses of different ASEAN countries to highlight the internal fragmentation that complicates a unified response to the growing geopolitical contest.

The geopolitical structure of Southeast Asia is defined by four interdependent dynamics: rapid economic expansion, persistent security dilemmas, intensifying great-power rivalry, and evolving institutional mechanisms. The fundamental dilemma facing ASEAN is how to maintain regional stability while managing the competing strategic interests of the QUAD and China. Economically, ASEAN has emerged as one of the fastest-growing economic blocs, drawing substantial foreign direct investment (FDI) from global actors such as China, the United States, Japan and the European Union (ASEAN Secretariat, 2023). However, these economic gains are offset by mounting security challenges, particularly in the South China Sea, where China's militarization through artificial island construction and aggressive naval patrols has fueled regional tensions. The United States has responded with Freedom of Navigation Operations (FONOPs) and strengthened security cooperation with ASEAN states, seeking to balance Beijing's growing assertiveness. The militarization of the region has led to heightened tensions, particularly with ASEAN members such as Vietnam and the Philippines (Rubel & Anderson, 2024).

China has positioned itself as the dominant external actor in Southeast Asia, employing a multifaceted strategy that integrates economic, military, and diplomatic tools. The Belt and Road Initiative (BRI) has been central to this approach, funding large-scale infrastructure projects that deepen China's economic foothold across ASEAN. Projects such as the China-Laos Railway, the Kyaukpyu deep-sea port in Myanmar, and hydropower initiatives in Cambodia and Laos underscore Beijing's ambition to weave Southeast Asia into its broader economic sphere (Zhao, 2023). Through trade agreements, infrastructure financing, and investment partnerships, China has solidified its role as ASEAN's principal economic partner, creating dependencies that limit the bloc's strategic autonomy. Yet China's engagement extends beyond economics. Its military presence in the South China Sea remains a significant flashpoint, with frequent naval deployments, military exercises, and island-building initiatives raising concerns over Beijing's long-term strategic objectives (Goh, 2013). Enforcement of its nine-dash line claims has led to repeated confrontations with ASEAN states, often involving coercion against fishing vessels and energy exploration efforts in contested waters. Meanwhile, Beijing has deployed a sophisticated soft-power strategy, utilizing Confucius Institutes, elite diplomacy, and media influence campaigns to shape regional narratives and cultivate pro-China sentiment within ASEAN (Gill & Huang, 2023). While these efforts have bolstered China's influence, they have also generated anxieties over debt dependency, political coercion, and the erosion of ASEAN's agency in regional affairs. The challenge for ASEAN states lies in balancing economic ties with China while preserving security partnerships with the QUAD, a delicate act that underscores the complexities of navigating great-power rivalry.

To counterbalance China's growing influence, the United States and its allies have deepened their engagement in the Indo-Pacific, with the QUAD emerging as a key pillar of this strategic realignment (Wenle, 2024). Comprising the United States, Japan, India, and Australia, the QUAD has sought to curb Beijing's regional dominance by reinforcing security partnerships, economic cooperation, and maritime stability (Wu, 2022). Meanwhile, ASEAN has attempted to preserve its centrality in regional governance by leveraging multilateral platforms such as the ASEAN Regional Forum (ARF), the East Asia Summit (EAS), and the ASEAN Defense Ministers' Meeting-Plus (ADMM-Plus). These institutions serve as diplomatic arenas for engagement with major powers, though they often struggle to prevent direct military confrontations (Yoshimatsu, 2022). At its core, the escalating strategic competition in Southeast Asia revolves around two competing forces: the QUAD's vision for a "Free and Open Indo-Pacific" (FOIP) and China's expanding geopolitical footprint. While the QUAD promotes an inclusive regional order grounded in economic resilience and maritime security, China continues to consolidate its influence through a combination of economic statecraft, military posturing, and strategic diplomacy. This power struggle presents both opportunities and risks for ASEAN, which must navigate these external pressures while safeguarding its strategic autonomy. Initially conceived as a security dialogue in 2007 and revitalized in 2017 amid growing concerns over China's assertiveness, the QUAD has since evolved into a formidable security, economic, and technological partnership. Militarily, the QUAD has expanded its influence through joint maritime exercises such as Malabar, intelligence-sharing frameworks, and capacity-building initiatives for ASEAN states. It efforts designed to counterbalance Beijing's maritime claims and coercive activities in the South China Sea (Qiao-Franco, Karmazin, & Kolmaš, 2024).

To address these challenges, ASEAN has prioritized security cooperation through mechanisms such as the ARF and ADMM-Plus, though these platforms remain constrained by their lack of enforcement mechanisms (Le Thu 2021). Institutional fragmentation, coupled with China's ability to leverage economic and political influence over certain ASEAN members, has further complicated efforts to establish a unified regional response. As strategic competition in Southeast Asia intensifies, ASEAN's ability to navigate this volatile environment will be critical in determining whether it can sustain regional stability or become increasingly subject to external pressures.

2. THIS LITERATURE REVIEW

Southeast Asia is emerging as a critical battleground in global geopolitics. Major powers are maneuvering to assert influence over regional security, economic dynamics, and diplomatic alignments. A strategic contest among China, the Quadrilateral Security Dialogue (QUAD), and the Association of Southeast Asian Nations (ASEAN) has created a complex web of geopolitical interactions that significantly impact the region's stability. Geopolitical Theory offers insights into the shifting balance of power in the Indo-Pacific. Stability in a given region is contingent upon the presence of a dominant power capable of providing order and economic leadership (Keohane, 1984). However, Southeast Asia presents a distinct case in which multiple competing actors contribute to a multipolar strategic environment that fosters both stability and contestation (Ikenberry, 2011). Mahan (1890)'s theory stresses the interdependence of a strong merchant marine for trade and commerce, a powerful battle fleet to defend sea lanes and defeat rival navies, and a network of overseas naval bases and colonies for coaling stations, repairs, and strategic resupply. China's rising economic and military power positions it as a potential regional hegemon, while the QUAD operates as a counterweight seeking to constrain Beijing's expansionist ambitions (Medcalf, 2020). ASEAN, in turn, plays a mediating role, though its consensus-driven model and internal divisions limit its effectiveness as a cohesive geopolitical actor.

Since its inception in 2013, the Belt and Road Initiative (BRI) has served as a primary mechanism for Beijing to project its economic influence across Southeast Asia through extensive infrastructure investments and the development of railways, ports, and special economic zones. This strategy has cultivated economic dependencies, particularly within Cambodia, Laos, and Myanmar. China's economic leverage has been instrumental in fostering internal divisions within ASEAN. It is hindering the organization's capacity to forge a unified response to shared security challenges. The alignment of certain member states with Beijing's interests has frequently obstructed the formation of a cohesive ASEAN position on South China Sea disputes. Consequently, this has generated scholarly concern regarding the potential erosion of the Association of Southeast Asian Nations' (ASEAN) strategic autonomy (Womack, 2023). Simultaneously, China militarization of artificial islands and assertive naval patrol actions in the South China Sea have escalated regional tensions (Zhang, 2022).

In response, the Quadrilateral Security Dialogue (QUAD) of the United States, Japan, India, and Australia has emerged as a key strategic counterweight to China's growing regional influence. Though not a formal military alliance, QUAD functions as a stabilizing force through enhanced security cooperation, economic partnerships, and technological collaboration (Pant, 2022). A central component of QUAD's strategy involves maritime security, where the United States and its allies conduct regular Freedom of Navigation Operations (FONOPs) to contest China's excessive territorial claims. Additionally, joint naval exercises such as the Malabar drills serve as deterrence mechanisms against Chinese maritime assertiveness (Koga, 2022). Beyond security, QUAD nations seek to reduce ASEAN's economic dependence on China by promoting alternative economic frameworks such as the Indo-Pacific Economic Framework (IPEF), which emphasizes resilient supply chains, digital trade, and clean energy initiatives. Japan and India have expanded infrastructure investments in Southeast Asia to counterbalance China's geoeconomic influence. ASEAN, for its part, adopts a strategic hedging approach, maintaining diplomatic flexibility while avoiding overt alignment with either China or QUAD (Acharya, 2021). The principle of ASEAN Centrality underpins its diplomatic engagement, reinforcing multilateralism as the foundation of regional governance (Goh, 2013). However, ASEAN's unity is frequently undermined by internal divisions over security and economic policies, particularly regarding responses to China's growing regional dominance.

Geopolitical Theory offers a framework for understanding the strategic rivalries, territorial disputes, and shifting power alignments that define Southeast Asia's security and economic landscape. Three primary areas of geopolitical contestation stand out: the South China Sea disputes, competing economic corridors, and evolving security alignments (Buzan & Wæver 2003). The South China Sea remains the focal point of geopolitical tensions, where China's expansive maritime claims conflict with ASEAN sovereignty concerns and QUAD's security imperatives. China's enforcement of its Nine-Dash Line claim, its militarization of contested islands, and its economic coercion against er ASEAN states have exacerbated regional frictions (Midford & Østhagen, 2024). Smaller states navigate between dominant powers within contested regions. The economic dimension of geopolitical contestation is equally significant. China's Belt and Road Initiative (BRI) has strengthened its economic influence across ASEAN, but concerns regarding debt-trap diplomacy and economic coercion have led some member states to seek alternative sources of infrastructure financing. Japan, India, and QUAD partners have responded by promoting initiatives. Japan's Partnership for Quality Infrastructure (PQI) and India's Act East Policy offer ASEAN states diversified economic options (Mohan, 2021: Wang, 2022).).

Southeast Asia's security architecture is also undergoing rapid transformation. China deepening defense ties with Cambodia and Myanmar, while QUAD members expand military partnerships with Vietnam, the Philippines, and Indonesia. ASEAN states actively participate in multilateral security frameworks with both China and QUAD, reflecting a pragmatic balancing strategy aimed at mitigating overreliance on any single power (Butcher, 2024: Gill et al., 2024). Therefore, Southeast Asia's geopolitical landscape is shaped by a dynamic contest between China, QUAD, and ASEAN, each pursuing distinct strategic objectives. ASEAN's role as a regional stabilizer remains critical, yet internal divisions continue to weaken its capacity to function as a cohesive strategic entity. As geopolitical competition intensifies, ASEAN's ability to maintain stability while preserving its strategic autonomy will be a decisive factor in shaping the future trajectory of the Indo-Pacific.

3. INDO-PACIFIC GEOPOLITICS IN FLUX: THE QUAD, CHINA, AND THE STRUGGLE FOR REGIONAL PRIMACY

3.1. The Quadrilateral Security Dialogue (QUAD) and Its Indo-Pacific Strategy

The Quadrilateral Security Dialogue (QUAD), comprising the United States, Japan, India, and Australia, has emerged as a pivotal strategic framework aimed at preserving a free, open, and inclusive Indo-Pacific. Its evolution reflects broader geopolitical shifts, particularly as a response to China's expanding influence and increasingly assertive foreign policy. While originally conceived as a security-oriented coalition, the QUAD has since broadened its scope to encompass economic resilience, supply chain diversification, and infrastructure development, reinforcing its role as a central actor in Indo-Pacific geopolitics (Bharti & Kumari, 2024). By integrating strategic initiatives in maritime security, economic frameworks, and technological cooperation, the QUAD not only reshapes regional stability but also influences ASEAN's strategic calculus, compelling Southeast Asian states to navigate the complex dynamics of great-power competition.

Initially established in 2007, the QUAD originated as an informal dialogue among the U.S., Japan, India, and Australia, with then-Japanese Prime Minister Shinzo Abe playing a crucial role in its conceptualization (Smith, 2022). The initiative was driven by mounting regional security concerns, particularly in light of China's growing assertiveness in the Indo-Pacific. Early QUAD activities included joint military exercises such as the Malabar naval drills, which sought to enhance maritime coordination and interoperability among member states. However, geopolitical realities soon tested the coalition's cohesion (Kratiuk, 2023). In 2008, Australia withdrew from the grouping, fearing potential economic repercussions on its extensive trade relations with China (Grare & Samaan, 2022). This period of dormancy highlighted the complexities inherent in balancing security imperatives with economic dependencies, a challenge that has remained a persistent feature of Indo-Pacific geopolitics. A decade later, shifting power dynamics and China's growing strategic ambitions in the Indo-Pacific necessitated the QUAD's revival. The re-emergence of QUAD 2.0 in 2017 was catalyzed by China's increasing military activities in disputed maritime zones, its expansive Belt and Road Initiative (BRI), and rising border tensions with India, including the Doklam standoff (2017) and the Galwan Valley clash (2020) (Chen & Liu, 2024). At the same time, the United States' Indo-Pacific Strategy reinforced the need for enhanced coordination among QUAD members to counterbalance China's regional influence. Since its reconstitution, the QUAD has gained momentum, with annual leaders' summits institutionalizing deeper cooperation in regional security, economic resilience, and technological collaboration. At the core of the QUAD's strategic agenda is maritime security, a domain that has become central to the balance of power in the Indo-Pacific (Tudoroiu, 2023).

The U.S. Navy's regular Freedom of Navigation Operations (FONOPs) in the South China Sea serve as a direct challenge to China's expansive territorial claims (Bateman, 2019). Other QUAD members, including Japan, India, and Australia, complement these efforts through joint naval patrols, increased diplomatic engagement, and enhanced security cooperation with Southeast Asian nations. India has expanded its naval footprint in the Indian Ocean. It is recognizing the strategic necessity of countering China's increasing influence over maritime trade routes and regional security dynamics (Bhattacharya, 2020). These initiatives underscore the QUAD's broader objective of preserving regional stability and deterring unilateral military aggression, signaling its enduring role as a counterweight to China's geopolitical ambitions (Dachi, Yurianto, & Purwanto, 2023). Beyond security, the QUAD is also reshaping Southeast Asia's economic landscape. The Indo-Pacific Economic Framework (IPEF) seeks to reduce ASEAN's dependency on China by fostering resilient supply chains, expanding digital trade, and promoting clean energy partnerships (Abadi & Al-Fadhat, 2023).

Another key dimension of QUAD cooperation involves technological security, particularly in sectors such as artificial intelligence (AI), cybersecurity, and critical infrastructure. With a growing emphasis on telecommunications, semiconductor manufacturing, and digital governance, QUAD nations aim to curb China's dominance in the technological sphere. However, ASEAN's engagement with the QUAD remains cautious. Many Southeast Asian nations are wary of entanglement in great-power rivalry and prefer to maintain diplomatic flexibility. While states such as Vietnam, the Philippines, and Indonesia have expressed openness to QUAD-led security initiatives, others, including Cambodia and Laos, remain aligned with China. This internal fragmentation complicates ASEAN's collective response to the QUAD-China contestation, rendering regional security dynamics increasingly volatile. As great-power rivalry continues to reshape the Indo-Pacific, the QUAD's trajectory will be defined by its ability to institutionalize deeper cooperation while maintaining strategic flexibility. Its expansion beyond security into economic and technological domains reflects an adaptive response to evolving regional challenges (Rai, 2022). However, the extent to which the QUAD can sustain cohesion among its members, navigate ASEAN's hesitations, and provide viable economic alternatives to China's initiatives will ultimately determine its effectiveness as a stabilizing force in the Indo-Pacific.

3.2. China's Expanding Influence in Southeast Asia: Economic and Military Strategies

China's engagement in Southeast Asia reflects a dual-pronged strategy that integrates economic statecraft with military assertiveness, designed to consolidate long-term regional dominance (Dosch, 2021). By leveraging vast investments in infrastructure, trade agreements, and financial institutions, China has positioned itself as a central economic actor within ASEAN. At the same time, Beijing has significantly expanded its military footprint, particularly in the South China Sea, where it employs both conventional forces and grey-zone tactics to solidify its territorial claims (Sarjito, 2024). These efforts are not only instrumental in advancing China's economic and security interests but also serve to counterbalance the influence of the United States and its regional allies, ensuring that Southeast Asia remains within Beijing's strategic sphere. A core objective of China's regional strategy is to integrate Southeast Asian economies into its own, fostering economic interdependence that translates into political leverage. This economic entanglement is driven by trade, foreign direct investment, and the role of financial institutions such as the Asian Infrastructure Investment Bank (AIIB). By creating economic dependencies, Beijing has shaped ASEAN policy decisions, particularly in states heavily reliant on Chinese trade and infrastructure financing. Beyond economic incentives, China exerts political influence through sustained diplomatic engagement, support for pro-China political elites, and strategic partnerships that align regional actors with its broader geopolitical vision (Shambaugh, 2020).

Militarily, China's objectives in Southeast Asia are closely linked to its strategic interests in the South China Sea. As a vital maritime corridor and a defensive buffer against U.S. influence in the Indo-Pacific, Beijing has pursued an aggressive approach that includes expanded naval patrols, military infrastructure development, and artificial island construction. Office of the Secretary of Defense (2024)'s The "Military and Security Developments Involving the People's Republic of China 2024" report delineates the People's Liberation Army's (PLA) escalating strategic posture in the Indo-Pacific The documented advancements reflect a calculated strategy to revise the regional security architecture. The PLA's adoption of a military-civil fusion (MCF) strategy is particularly salient, as it systematically leverages the civilian sector to enhance its military prowess. This institutional fusion allows the PRC to circumvent traditional military procurement bottlenecks and develop a "dual-use" capacity that strengthens both its economic and military power. The employment of "grey-zone" tactics, such as the persistent harassment of vessels in the South China Sea and aggressive military drills against Taiwan, serves to incrementally assert territorial claims and normalize a new, more coercive status quo without triggering a conventional conflict. These actions collectively represent a strategic challenge to the existing rules-based international order, compelling the United States and its regional allies to enhance their deterrence and security cooperation to maintain regional stability. By reinforcing its presence in contested waters, China strengthens its deterrence capabilities against regional adversaries while simultaneously extending its operational reach.

Beijing has deepened security cooperation with ASEAN states through arms sales, intelligence-sharing initiatives, and military agreements, further entrenching its strategic influence. The People's Liberation Army Navy (PLAN) plays a central role in China's military expansion, conducting joint exercises, increasing naval patrols, and demonstrating China's growing blue-water capabilities (Erickson, 2022). In addition to its formal naval presence, China extensively relies on its maritime militia and Coast Guard, which aggressively operate in disputed waters, frequently confronting ASEAN vessels in contested maritime zones (O'Rourke, 2025).

Furthermore, Beijing has expanded its security partnerships with Cambodia and Myanmar through arms sales and military assistance programs, further embedding its influence within Southeast Asia's security architecture (Cordesman & Hwang, 2021). China's military assertiveness is most visible in the South China Sea, where it claims nearly 90% of the waters under its controversial "Nine-Dash Line" doctrine (Hayton, 2014). This territorial claim has resulted in sustained disputes with Vietnam, the Philippines, Malaysia, and Indonesia, despite a 2016 ruling by the Permanent Court of Arbitration that invalidated China's assertions. Nonetheless, Beijing has continued to enforce its claims through military patrols, unilateral fishing bans, and coercive maritime behavior, escalating tensions with ASEAN nations over access to resource-rich waters. A key component of China's regional strategy involves the use of grey-zone tactics and coercive maneuvers that fall below the threshold of conventional military conflict but effectively intimidate and pressure regional actors. These include deploying maritime militias, using its Coast Guard to restrict ASEAN fishing and energy exploration activities, and enforcing maritime exclusion zones. China has transformed artificial islands such as Fiery Cross Reef, Subi Reef, and Mischief Reef into heavily fortified military installations, equipped with airstrips, missile systems, and advanced surveillance capabilities. The militarization of these outposts enhances China's ability to project power deep into the South China Sea, consolidating its control over the region's key maritime trade routes for economic advantages (Bentley, 2023).

China's economic strategy in Southeast Asia is largely embodied in the Belt and Road Initiative (BRI), its flagship foreign policy initiative designed to enhance regional connectivity through large-scale infrastructure development. Major BRI projects, such as the China-Laos Railway, the Jakarta-Bandung High-Speed Railway, and the Kunming-Singapore Rail Link, reinforce ASEAN's economic integration with China (Chirathivat, 2022). Simultaneously, strategic investments in deep-sea ports in Myanmar's Kyaukphyu Port and Cambodia's Sihanoukville Port along with energy projects such as hydropower plants in Laos and coal-powered facilities in Indonesia, further solidify China's economic presence in the region (Yu, 2024). Beyond physical infrastructure, Beijing's Digital Silk Road has expanded Chinese technological influence, particularly in telecommunications, 5G networks, and smart city initiatives across ASEAN (Koepp, 2022)Beyond conventional military posturing, hybrid warfare and cyber threats have become critical dimensions of strategic competition in the Indo-Pacific. China, Russia, and the U.S. engage in cyber operations targeting military networks, financial institutions, and critical infrastructure across Southeast Asia (Chauvin, 2024). China's information warfare tactics, including disinformation campaigns, represent an asymmetrical strategy designed to shape regional narratives and undermine adversarial coalitions (Hersman et al., 2022). Cybersecurity threats erode traditional hegemonic stability by enabling both state and non-state actors to challenge established power structures without direct military confrontation. The Gray Zone Conflict suggests that cyber-enabled operations, economic coercion, and disinformation campaigns serve as non-traditional tools of power projection (Mazarr, 2015). These tactics contribute to the evolving nature of great-power rivalry, where digital warfare plays an increasingly central role in shaping geopolitical outcomes (Brands & Cooper, 2022).

However, these economic engagements have raised concerns over China's strategic use of financial leverage, particularly in economically vulnerable states such as Laos, Cambodia, and Myanmar. The increasing debt burden on ASEAN states has heightened fears of economic coercion, allowing Beijing to exert influence over their political and economic decision-making (Dreher et al. 2022). Beyond sovereign debt, China has expanded its control over critical sectors such as telecommunications, energy, and agriculture, further embedding its economic dominance. This economic influence is reinforced through multilateral trade agreements, most notably the Regional Comprehensive Economic Partnership (RCEP), which has bolstered China's role as ASEAN's primary trading partner (Petri & Plummer, 2020). RCEP serves as a mechanism through which China consolidates regional economic integration while countering U.S.-led initiatives such as the Indo-Pacific Economic Framework (IPEF) (Breslin, 2021). The deepening of these economic linkages ensures that ASEAN states remain closely tied to China, complicating efforts to pivot towards alternative economic partnerships.

On the diplomatic front, China has cultivated strong ties with ASEAN, leveraging economic and political incentives to deepen regional engagement. The establishment of the China-ASEAN Comprehensive Strategic Partnership in 2021 marked a significant milestone in China's efforts to institutionalize its influence over ASEAN decision-making processes (Yeo, 2022). However, concerns persist over Beijing's ability to exert disproportionate control, particularly in relation to ASEAN's position on contentious issues such as the South China Sea disputes. A key pillar of China's diplomatic strategy has been its ability to exploit internal divisions within ASEAN, using economic inducements to align specific member states with Beijing's regional agenda (Mahbubani 2020). Cambodia, Laos, and Myanmar remain economically dependent on Chinese investments and frequently support China's positions through preventing ASEAN from formulating a unified stance on key security issues. This strategic fragmentation has weakened ASEAN's collective response to South China Sea tensions, allowing China to consolidate its position in the region with minimal resistance (Htwe, 2025). In parallel, China actively counters U.S.-led regional security initiatives such as the QUAD and AUKUS, perceiving them as attempts to contain its geopolitical ambitions. Through a combination of diplomatic engagement, development assistance, and elite influence campaigns, Beijing ensures that its strategic interests remain at the center of ASEAN's regional discourse. At the same time, China promotes ASEAN-led initiatives such as the ASEAN Outlook on the Indo-Pacific (AOIP) as a counterbalance to Western security frameworks, positioning itself as a cooperative regional leader while advancing its own geopolitical objectives (Malik, 2025)

China's expanding role in Southeast Asia highlights the structural challenges facing ASEAN as it seeks to maintain regional stability while navigating great-power competition. The entrenchment of China's economic influence, the assertiveness of its military strategy, and its ability to shape ASEAN's diplomatic orientation underscore the complexities of maintaining a balanced and independent regional order. As geopolitical rivalries intensify, the capacity of ASEAN to resist external pressures and assert its strategic autonomy will be decisive in shaping the future trajectory of Southeast Asia's political and security landscape.

3.3. Economic Dependence and Regional Stability in Southeast Asia

The economic landscape of the Indo-Pacific is increasingly defined by the competing hegemonic influences of China's Belt and Road Initiative (BRI) and the QUAD-aligned economic frameworks (Hall, 2021). Global economic stability is maintained when a dominant power provides public goods such as secure trade routes, financial stability, and infrastructure investment (Kindleberger, 1973). However, China's rapid economic rise has introduced a parallel system of influence, altering dependency structures across Southeast Asia (Breslin 2021,). While the BRI has facilitated economic development through extensive infrastructure investments, it has also created financial dependencies that expose recipient states to geopolitical coercion. The case of Sri Lanka's Hambantota Port, which was ceded to China due to debt insolvency, illustrates the risks of excessive reliance on Chinese capital (Abi-Habib, 2018). Similarly, BRI-backed projects in Cambodia, Laos, and Myanmar have raised concerns over debt sustainability, environmental degradation, and the erosion of national sovereignty, While these investments contribute to regional connectivity, they reinforce a model of asymmetric economic dependence that China can leverage to expand its strategic influence (Ferdinand, 2016).

China's economic expansions control over infrastructure and supply chains becomes a mechanism for expanding regional dominance In this sense, economic statecraft is not simply about development but serves as a means of consolidating geopolitical influence (Xi, 2021). In response, the QUAD and its allies have sought to counterbalance China's leverage through alternative economic initiatives. The Indo-Pacific Economic Framework (IPEF), spearheaded by the United States, focuses on enhancing trade transparency, strengthening digital governance, and promoting supply chain resilience to reduce Southeast Asia's reliance on China (Goodman et al. 2022). Similarly, Japan and India's Asia-Africa Growth Corridor (AAGC) represents an attempt to provide alternative connectivity solutions, mitigating China's monopolistic control over regional trade networks (Wang, 2022) Yet, despite these counterbalancing efforts, China's economic footprint remains unmatched, presenting ASEAN nations with a strategic dilemma: maintaining economic autonomy while simultaneously benefiting from both Chinese and QUAD-led investments.

As geopolitical rivalries intensify, the Indo-Pacific requires hybrid security frameworks that integrate military alliances with economic and diplomatic mechanisms. ASEAN-led security platforms, including the ASEAN Regional Forum (ARF) and the ASEAN Defense Ministers' Meeting-Plus (ADMM-Plus), attempt to provide a neutral forum for security dialogue. Therefore, ASEAN's long-standing principles of neutrality, non-interference, and consensus-based decision-making remain the foundation of its diplomatic posture. In an effort to reaffirm its agency, ASEAN introduced the ASEAN Outlook on the Indo-Pacific (AOIP) in 2019, positioning itself as a mediator rather than a participant in great-power competition. AOIP envisions a cooperative regional order that resists alignment with either the QUAD or China. However, internal divisions, economic dependencies, and external pressures continue to undermine ASEAN's ability to maintain this delicate balance. However, their effectiveness is often constrained by ASEAN's consensus-based decision-making process, which limits decisive action on emerging security threats. The ASEAN Outlook on the Indo-Pacific (AOIP) seeks to reinforce ASEAN's centrality in regional governance by emphasizing diplomatic engagement over military confrontation (Heiduk & Wacker 2020). However, regional organizations often struggle to maintain strategic autonomy when caught between rival hegemons. Countries such as Indonesia and Malaysia have prioritized preventive diplomacy and confidence-building measures to de-escalate tensions, particularly in the South China Sea, yet these initiatives are frequently undermined by external power rivalries (Qiao-Franco, Karmazin, & Kolmaš, 2024).

While geopolitical competition dominates regional security discussions, there remain limited opportunities for cooperation between QUAD nations and China in non-traditional security sectors (Gong, 2020). Maritime security initiatives toward counter-piracy operations and transnational crime prevention provide a potential avenue for engagement (Dian, 2022). Likewise, cybersecurity cooperation to safeguard critical infrastructure from cyber threats could serve as a mutually beneficial strategy, albeit constrained by geopolitical distrust (Lee & Hioe, 2022). Economic collaboration in digital trade regulations, supply chain security, and climate change mitigation also presents potential areas for diplomacy, reducing direct strategic confrontations (Jackson, 2023). However, without a comprehensive and inclusive security framework that accommodates both dominant and smaller regional actors, the Indo-Pacific will remain a contested geopolitical arena vulnerable to economic and military disruptions (Frühling & O'Neil, 2021).

Geopolitically, the Indo-Pacific remains a contested space, where maritime control, economic dependencies, and cyber domains serve as key areas of power projection. For regional actors, the challenge lies in fostering security cooperation, reducing economic vulnerabilities, and strengthening hybrid security mechanisms that integrate military, economic, and technological strategies. While QUAD and China remain strategic competitors, limited cooperation in non-traditional security sectors may provide opportunities for diplomatic de-escalation (Malik, 2025) Ultimately, the stability of the Indo-Pacific will depend on how effectively regional institutions, particularly ASEAN, can mediate between competing hegemons while preserving their strategic autonomy (Dian, 2015). Without an inclusive and adaptive approach to managing these rivalries, the region risks becoming an arena for prolonged geopolitical contestation, undermining both economic growth and security stability. A unipolar world order under a single dominant state ensures global stability by providing public goods such as security, free trade, and the enforcement of international norms (Kindleberger, 1973). In the Indo-Pacific, the United States has historically assumed this role through military alliances and security frameworks such as the U.S.-Japan Treaty of Mutual Cooperation and Security and the U.S.-Philippines Mutual Defense Treaty (Ikenberry, 2011). The U.S. employs Freedom of Navigation Operations (FONOPs) in the South China Sea (SCS) to deter China's maritime expansion and uphold international maritime law. However, China's assertive territorial claims through the "nine-dash line" and the militarization of artificial islands in South China Sea challenges U.S. maritime dominance and the principles of freedom of navigation (Budiana & Budiman, 2024). This contestation disrupts the stability traditionally ensured by U.S. hegemony, fostering a bipolar security environment where regional actors must balance between U.S. security guarantees and China's growing economic influence.

4. DISCUSSION: CONTESTATION AND STRATEGIC ALIGNMENTS

The Indo-Pacific is more than just a place on a map. It is a dynamic arena where powerful nations vie for influence and also a complex web of geopolitical tensions and strategic dilemmas. At the heart of this struggle is the contest between the established U.S.-led security framework and China's growing ambition to reshape the regional order. Instead of a single, dominant power, a multipolar environment where no one country can assert total control. This absence of a clear hegemon breeds instability drive a cycle of military buildup, economic pressure, and subtle, hybrid threats and challenge the existing rules of global order. The most significant tension for ASEAN is the split between its security and economic needs. Many ASEAN members rely on security partnerships with the United States and its allies in the Quad (U.S., Japan, Australia, and India) to counter China's military expansion.

At the same time, their economies are deeply intertwined with China, particularly through its Belt and Road Initiative (BRI), a massive infrastructure and investment project that offers an alternative to traditional Western-led financial systems. This economic reliance makes it difficult for them to take a unified stand against China on security issues. While ASEAN officially promotes a unified stance through frameworks like the ASEAN Outlook on the Indo-Pacific (AOIP), its members often have different priorities. Some members are more concerned with maritime security in the South China Sea, while others prioritize economic benefits from closer ties with China. These differing interests can undermine the bloc's ability to act as a cohesive force, making it vulnerable to external pressures and weakening its collective bargaining power. ASEAN's ability to maintain its autonomy and centrality and its role as the key diplomatic platform in the region hangs in the balance. Its success depends on its capacity to strengthen its own institutions. They must diversify its economic partners beyond China, and forge a collective strategy that allows it to manage external influence without sacrificing its sovereignty. The ultimate question is whether ASEAN can leverage this great-power rivalry to its advantage, or if it will be fragmented and absorbed into the competing spheres of influence. China's actions in the Indo-Pacific are often framed as a modern-day application of a classic geopolitical theory. Controlling key coastal regions is essential for global power for China. By extending its influence over the South China Sea and the Malacca Strait, China aims to secure the vital sea lanes that carry its energy imports and goods, enhancing its ability to project power and influence far beyond its borders. Therefore, this maritime assertiveness has triggered a direct and firm response from a coalition of states.

The Quadrilateral Security Dialogue (Quad) is a prime example. These nations conduct joint naval drills, like the Malabar exercises to counter China's growing naval strength and maintain a free and open Indo-Pacific. This creates a powerful geopolitical contestation where maritime security is a central point of rivalry (Shahzad and Khan 2022). The debate here centers on whether these maneuvers are a necessary defense of a rules-based order or an escalation of tensions that could lead to conflict. Beyond the military arena, the competition extends to the economic sphere. While the global economy has long been anchored by the U.S.-led order, China's Belt and Road Initiative (BRI) presents a significant and compelling alternative. Through massive infrastructure projects, the BRI forges economic dependencies in Southeast Asia and weaken the influence of U.S.-backed economic initiatives like the Indo-Pacific Economic Framework for Prosperity (IPEF) in long term. This economic rivalry isn't just about trade. It becomes a fundamental struggle over who sets the rules of global commerce. China's use of debt-financed projects in countries like Cambodia, Myanmar and Laos is a prime example of its economic statecraft (Kliman et al. 2021). Using financial power to gain strategic leverage and influence political decisions, this approach highlights a debate about the nature of aid and development, with Western nations countering with their own initiatives like the Partnership for Global Infrastructure and Investment (PGII), which emphasize transparency and sustainability as a contrast to China's model.

ASEAN's position is particularly precarious due to its internal divisions and members' varying levels of economic reliance on China. ASEAN's response remains fragmented, with nations such as the Philippines, Vietnam, and Malaysia challenging Beijing's claims, while Cambodia and Laos continue to align with China, obstructing ASEAN's ability to develop a unified position. While the bloc has attempted to manage disputes through diplomatic mechanisms like the Code of Conduct (CoC), these efforts are often undermined by a lack of enforcement and the disparate interests of its members. The differing approaches of the Philippines, which has used international law to challenge China and countries like Cambodia and Laos, which have prioritized economic benefits, highlight this internal schism. ASEAN's long-term survival as a cohesive and autonomous entity will depend on its capacity to leverage multilateral institutions, diversify its economic partnerships, and find a collective strategy that manages external influence without sacrificing its sovereignty. The ultimate question is whether the region will stabilize under a bipolar U.S.-China order or transition into a more complex multipolar framework. The outcome depends on the adaptability of regional institutions and the evolving role of economic and technological warfare in shaping the geopolitical landscape. Therefore, the Indo-Pacific remains a contested geopolitical landscape where hegemonic stability and strategic alignments continue to evolve. While a U.S.-led security architecture aims to uphold regional stability, China's expanding maritime and economic influence challenges the existing balance of power. By balancing security imperatives with economic interests, regional actors navigate these shifting dynamics.

A single dominant power may offer the best path to regional stability, but today's security environment is fragmented. In this complex balancing act among ASEAN, the Quad, and China, each plays a significant role. Economic ties between ASEAN states and China are deepening, making it difficult for these nations to lessen their dependency. At the same time, the U.S. faces geopolitical fragmentation as it attempts to counterbalance China. As tensions in the Indo-Pacific rise, the region will likely see an increase in military posturing, economic decoupling, and the evolving role of technology and cyber warfare in shaping the future geopolitical landscape of global technological rivalry. Whether the region stabilizes under a bipolar U.S.-China order or shifts to a multipolar security framework, the ultimate outcome will depend on several key factors. There are the adaptability of regional institutions, the strength of economic alternatives to Chinese investment, and the role of emerging technologies in shaping security and trade. Therefore, the challenge for ASEAN is clear. It must maintain regional stability without being pulled into great-power competition. ASEAN can achieve this by strengthening its security frameworks, diversifying its economies, and reinforcing its institutional resilience. If it fails to take decisive action, ASEAN risks becoming a peripheral actor in the larger geopolitical contest, jeopardizing its long-held goals of centrality and strategic autonomy in the Indo-Pacific.

5. CONCLUSION

Far from being a passive victim of great power competition, ASEAN actively demonstrates its agency by pursuing a strategic balancing act designed to safeguard regional autonomy and centrality. This approach recognizes that the Indo-Pacific's future hinges on the viability of a multipolar, not bipolar, order. ASEAN's effectiveness in this role, however, depends on its ability to transform internal divisions into a unified front on key security and economic issues, thereby reinforcing its collective influence.

To institutionalize this agency, ASEAN must proactively shape governance frameworks. This entails strengthening its own consultative mechanisms, such as the ASEAN Regional Forum and the East Asia Summit, to ensure they remain the primary platforms for security and diplomatic dialogue in the region. Policy recommendations must move beyond broad declarations to targeted actions. ASEAN should, for instance, coordinate a region-wide digital infrastructure policy to prevent over-reliance on a single external partner, and create a unified, transparent investment framework to attract a wider array of capital from both the QUAD and China.

The implications for the regional order are significant. ASEAN's successful navigation of these tensions can establish a new model for a stable, rules-based order not dictated by a single dominant power. It challenges the traditional great power politics paradigm and offers a pathway for medium-sized powers to maintain sovereignty and prosperity. Therefore, for the Indo-Pacific to achieve lasting stability, external powers must acknowledge and respect ASEAN's centrality, shifting their strategies from a zero-sum game of influence to one of constructive, multilateral engagement.

REFERENCES

Abadi, F. A., & Al-Fadhat, F. (2023). The influence of Indo-Pacific Economic Framework on peace stability in the ASEAN region. *Jurnal Global & Strategis, 17*(1), 33–50. DOI: 10.20473/jgs.17.1.2023.33-50

Abi-Habib, M. (2018, June 25). How China got Sri Lanka to cough up a port. The New York Times. https://www.nytimes.com/2018/06/25/world/asia/china-sri-lanka-port.html

Acharya, A. (2021). *ASEAN and regional order: Revisiting security community in Southeast Asia*. Routledge., DOI: 10.4324/9781003122333

Bateman, S. (2019). *Freedoms of navigation in the Asia-Pacific region: Strategic, political and legal factors*. Routledge., DOI: 10.4324/9780429199585

Bentley, S. (2023). *The maritime fulcrum of the Indo-Pacific: Indonesia and Malaysia respond to China's creeping expansion in the South China Sea*. Naval War College Press., https://digital-commons.usnwc.edu/cmsi-red-books/17/

Bharti, M. S., & Kumari, S. (2024). China's Belt and Road Initiative in Southeast Asia and its implications for ASEAN–China strategic partnership. [ARPE]. *Asia Review of Policy and Education, 3*(1), 22. DOI: 10.1007/s44216-024-00042-4

Bhattacharya, S. (2020). Countering China: India's Pacific predicament. Stosunki Międzynarodowe –. *International Relations, 56*(2), 164–243. DOI: 10.7366/020909612202002

Brands, H., & Cooper, Z. (2022). Danger zone: The coming conflict with China. W.W. Norton & Company. https://www.prio.org/journals/jpr/booknotes/310

Breslin, S. (2021). *China risen? Studying Chinese global power*. Bristol University Press., DOI: 10.1332/policypress/9781529215809.001.0001

Budiana, M., & Budiman, B. (2024). Sovereignty dynamics in the US-China geopolitical conflict in the South China Sea. Jurnal Sosial Sains dan Komunikasi, 3(1), 29–37. DOI: 10.58471/ju-sosak.v3i01.579

Butcher, J. D. (2024). Simply another practice among others? Analysing the rise of strategic partnerships in the Asia-Pacific region. *Australian Journal of International Affairs, 78*(4), 498–519. DOI: 10.1080/10357718.2024.2362143

Buzan, B., & Wæver, O. (2003). *Regions and powers: The structure of international security*. Cambridge University Press., https://ir101.co.uk/wp-content/uploads/2018/11/Buzan-Waever-2003-Regions-and-Powers-The-Structure-of-International-Security.pdf DOI: 10.1017/CBO9780511491252

Cannon, B. J., & Hakata, K. (Eds.). (2021). *Indo-Pacific strategies: Navigating geopolitics at the dawn of a new age* (1st ed., pp. 54–60). Routledge., DOI: 10.4324/9781003206934

Chauvin, E. (2024). Security regions: A heterogeneous world between conflicts and cooperation. In Beckouche, P., & Richard, Y. (Eds.), *Regionalization of the world: Comparing regional integrations* (pp. 111–126). Wiley., DOI: 10.1002/9781394284375.ch8

Chen, C., & Liu, R. (2024). "China-India border clash": Construction of event newsworthiness and discrepancies in Chinese and Indian news discourse. *SAGE Open*, *14*(4), 21582440241301472. Advance online publication. DOI: 10.1177/21582440241301472

Chin, G. T., & Zhu, J. (2022). Infrastructure at the G20. In The G20, development and the UN Agenda 2030 (1st ed., p. 20). Routledge. DOI: 10.4324/9781315608822-11

Chirathivat, S. (2022). China's Belt and Road Initiative and ASEAN connectivity in development: Can both bring synergy and opportunities together? In China's Belt and Road Initiative in ASEAN: Growing presence, recent progress and future challenges (pp. 153–182). DOI: 10.1142/12396

Cordesman, A. H., & Hwang, G. (2021, August 3). Updated report: Chinese strategy and military forces in 2021. Center for Strategic and International Studies (CSIS). https://www.csis.org/analysis/updated-report-chinese-strategy-and-military-forces-2021

Dachi, E. T., & Yurianto, M. (2023). The Indo-Pacific context: Maritime security challenges and diplomacy of ASEAN countries. [IJHESS]. *International Journal of Humanities Education and Social Sciences*, *2*(6), 1–36. DOI: 10.55227/ijhess.v2i6.509

Dian, M. (2015). The pivot to Asia, air-sea battle and contested commons in the Asia Pacific region. *The Pacific Review*, *28*(2), 237–257. DOI: 10.1080/09512748.2014.995124

Dian, M. (2022). The rise of China between Global IR and area studies: an agenda for cooperation. Italian Political Science Review/Rivista Italiana Di Scienza Politica, 52(2), 252–267. https://doi:DOI: 10.1017/ipo.2021.31

Dreher, A., Fuchs, A., Parks, B., Strange, A., & Tierney, M. (2022). *Banking on Beijing: The aims and impacts of China's overseas development program*. Cambridge University Press., DOI: 10.1017/9781108564496

Erickson, A. S. (Ed.). (2022). *Maritime gray zone operations: Challenges and countermeasures in the Indo-Pacific*. Taylor & Francis., DOI: 10.4324/9781003310723

Ferdinand, P. (2016). Westward ho—The China Dream and "One Belt, One Road": Chinese foreign policy under Xi Jinping. *International Affairs, 92*(4), 941–957. DOI: 10.1111/1468-2346.12660

Frühling, S., & O'Neil, A. (2021). *Alliances, nuclear weapons and escalation: Managing deterrence in the 21st century*. ANU Press., DOI: 10.22459/ANWE.2021

Gill, B.. (2024). *Geopolitics, military modernisation and the future of the Indo-Pacific*. Taylor & Francis., DOI: 10.4324/9781003283232

Gill, B., & Huang, Y. (2023). Sources and limits of Chinese 'soft power. In *Survival* (pp. 17–35). Routledge., DOI: 10.4324/9781003421801

Goh, E. (2013). The struggle for order: Hegemony, hierarchy, and transition in post-Cold War [Oxford University Press. https://www.politics.ox.ac.uk/publication/struggle-order-hegemony-hierarchy-and-transition-post-cold-war-east-asia]. *East Asia (Piscataway, N.J.)*, •••, 115–232.

Gong, X. (2020). Non-traditional security cooperation between China and Southeast Asia: Implications for Indo-Pacific geopolitics. *International Affairs, 96*(1), 29–48. DOI: 10.1093/ia/iiz225

Goodman, M. P., Reinsch, W., & Arasasingham, A. (2022, May 24). The Indo-Pacific Economic Framework: What it is—and what it isn't. Center for Strategic and International Studies (CSIS). https://www.csis.org/analysis/indo-pacific-economic-framework-what-it-and-what-it-isnt

Grare, F., & Samaan, J.-L. (2022). Australia and the ASEAN member states: From interest to commitment? In *The Indian Ocean as a new political and security region* (pp. 151–177). Springer International Publishing., https://link.springer.com/chapter/10.1007/978-3-030-91797-5_7 DOI: 10.1007/978-3-030-91797-5_7

Hall, T. (2021). The long game: China's grand strategy to displace American order. *International Affairs, 97*(6), 2023–2025. DOI: 10.1093/ia/iiab159

Hayton, B., & Torode, G. (2014). The South China Sea: The struggle for power in Asia. *Contemporary Southeast Asia, 36*(3), 467–469. DOI: 10.1355/cs36-3f

Heiduk, F., & Wacker, G. (2020). From Asia-Pacific to Indo-Pacific: Significance, implementation and challenges (SWP Research Paper 2020/RP 09). German Institute for International and Security Affairs (SWP). DOI: 10.18449/2020RP09

Hersman, R., Brewer, E., Sheppard, L., & Simon, M. (2022). *Influence and escalation: Implications of Russian and Chinese influence operations for crisis management*. Rowman & Littlefield., https://www.csis.org/analysis/influence-and-escalation-implications-russian-and-chinese-influence-operations-crisis

Htwe, T. M. (2025). China's strategic influence and rivalries in Southeast Asia: BRIC and China's geopolitical strategy. In Changing the global political economy: BRICS countries and alternative relations strategies IGI Global Scientific Publishing. https://www.igi-global.com/chapter/chinas-strategic-influence-and-rivalries-in-southeast-asia/365241

Ikenberry, G. J. (2011). *Liberal Leviathan: The origins, crisis, and transformation of the American world order*. Princeton University Press., DOI: 10.2307/j.ctt7rjt2

Jackson, V. (2023). *Pacific power paradox: American statecraft and the fate of the Asian peace*. Yale University Press., https://yalebooks.yale.edu/book/9780300257281/pacific-power-paradox/

Keohane, R. O. (1984). After hegemony: Cooperation and discord in world political economy. *International Affairs, 61*(2), 290–291. Advance online publication. DOI: 10.2307/2617490

Kindleberger, C. P. (1973). *The world in depression, 1929–1939*. University of California Press., https://www.ucpress.edu/books/the-world-in-depression-1929-1939/paper

Kliman, D., Kendall-Taylor, A., Lee, K., & Fitt, J. (2021). Global network competition: Emerging implications for national security. Center for a New American Security (CNAS). https://www.cnas.org/publications/reports/global-network-competition

Koepp, R. (2022). Locating the Digital Silk Road in the Belt and Road Initiative. In Gordon, D., & Nouwens, M. (Eds.), *The digital Silk Road: China's technological rise and the geopolitics of cyberspace* (pp. 13–25). Taylor & Francis., DOI: 10.4324/9781003390268-3

Koga, K. (2022). Introduction: ASEAN's strategic utility redefined. In Managing great power politics (pp. 1–18). Palgrave Macmillan. DOI: 10.1007/978-981-19-2611-2_1

Kratiuk, B. (2023). Strategic alliances and alignments in the Indo-Pacific. In Chacko, J., & Kazianis, H. T. (Eds.), *Handbook of Indo-Pacific studies* (pp. 248–266). Routledge India., DOI: 10.4324/9781003336143-16

Lee, K., & Hioe, B. (2022, March 12). Cybersecurity in the Indo-Pacific: Challenges and cooperation. The Diplomat. https://thediplomat.com/2022/03/cybersecurity-in-the-indo-Pacific-challenges-and-cooperation

Mahan, A. T. (1890). *The influence of sea power upon history, 1660–1783.* Little, Brown, and Company.

Malik, A. (2025). The Quad's implications for Indo-Pacific security (SSRN Scholarly Paper No. 5191457). Social Science Research Network. DOI: 10.2139/ssrn.5191457

Mazarr, M. J. (2015). Mastering the gray zone: Understanding a changing era of conflict. U.S. Army War College Press. https://press.armywarcollege.edu/monographs/428

Medcalf, R. (2020). *Contest for the Indo-Pacific: Why China won't map the future* (1st ed.). La Trobe University Press., https://researchportalplus.anu.edu.au/en/publications/contest-for-the-indo-pacific-why-china-wont-map-the-future

Mohan, C. R. (2021). A glimpse of the past. In *The elusive tipping point* (pp. 1–22). World Scientific Publishing., DOI: 10.1142/9789811225826_0001

O'Rourke, R. (2025). China's naval modernization: Implications for U.S. Navy capabilities (Congressional Research Service Report RL33153). Congressional Research Service. https://www.congress.gov/crs-product/RL33153

Office of the Secretary of Defense. (2024). Military and security developments involving the People's Republic of China 2024: Annual report to Congress (unclassified report). Department of Defense. https://media.defense.gov/2024/Dec/18/2003615520/-1/-1/0/MILITARY-AND-SECURITY-DEVELOPMENTS-INVOLVING-THE-PEOPLES-REPUBLIC-OF-CHINA-2024.PDF

Pant, H. V. (2022, March 20). India and the Quad: Chinese belligerence and Indian resilience. Observer Research Foundation. https://www.orfonline.org/research/india-and-the-quad

Petri, P. A., & Plummer, M. G. (2020, November 16). RCEP: A new trade agreement that will shape global economics and politics. Brookings Institution – Order from Chaos [Blog]. https://www.brookings.edu/articles/rcep-a-new-trade-agreement-that-will-shape-global-economics-and-politics/

Qiao-Franco, G., Karmazin, A., & Kolmaš, M. (2024). The Indo-Pacific and the next phase of ASEAN centrality. *Journal of Current Southeast Asian Affairs*. Advance online publication. DOI: 10.1177/18681034241307658

Qiao-Franco, G., Karmazin, A., & Kolmaš, M. (2024). The Indo-Pacific and the next phase of ASEAN centrality. *Journal of Current Southeast Asian Affairs*. Advance online publication. DOI: 10.1177/18681034241307658

Rai, M. S. (2022). Revisiting QUAD ambition in the Indo-Pacific leveraging space and cyber domain. arXiv. https://doi.org//arXiv.2209.04609DOI: 10.48550

Rubel, M., & Anderson, C. (2024). The South China Sea dispute and regional response. *Quest Journal of Management and Social Sciences*, *6*(1), 74–86. DOI: 10.3126/qjmss.v6i1.66297

Sarjito, A. (2024). China's gray zone strategy in the South China Sea: Tactics, objectives, and regional implications. [IJoMS]. *Indonesian Journal of Multidisciplinary Sciences*, *3*(2), 113–135. DOI: 10.59066/ijoms.v3i2.559

Secretariat, A. S. E. A. N. (2023). ASEAN investment report 2023: Fostering resilience amidst global challenges. ASEAN Secretariat. https://asean.org/wp-content/uploads/2023/12/AIR-Special-2023.pdf

Shahzad, S. M., & Khan, M. R. (2022). QUAD: The US strategic alliance for the Indo-Pacific region and the Chinese counterbalance. *Pakistan Journal of Multidisciplinary Research*, *3*(2), 56–72. http://pjmr.org/pjmr/article/view/329/72

Smith, J. M. (2022, September). The 'QuadFather': The legacy of Shinzo Abe and the Quad. ORF. https://www.orfonline.org/research/the-quadfather-the-legacy-of-shinzo-abe-and-the-quad/#_ednref80

Tudoroiu, T. (2023). *The geopolitics of China's Belt and Road Initiative* (1st ed.). Routledge., DOI: 10.4324/9781032616001

Wang, L. (2022). China–Japan competition in infrastructure investment in Southeast Asia: A two-level analysis. *Chinese Political Science Review*, •••, 1–26. DOI: 10.1007/s41111-022-00231-7 PMID: 40479399

Wenle, H. (2024). China in the Indo-Pacific: Perspectives and interests. In Josukutty, J. C. A., & Lobo, J. S. (Eds.), *The new world politics of the Indo-Pacific: Perceptions, policies and interests* (pp. 71–88). Routledge India., DOI: 10.4324/9781003479307-7

Womack, B. (2023). Continuities in China's Pacific Asian centrality. In *Recentering Pacific Asia: Regional China and world order*. Cambridge University Press., DOI: 10.1017/9781009393867.002

Wu, G. (2022). China's common prosperity program: Causes, challenges, and implications. The Asia Society Policy Institute. https://www.wita.org/wp-content/uploads/2022/03/ASPI_ChinaCommonProsp_report_fin.pdf

Xi, G. (2021). The future of the Indo-Pacific: Toward intensified geopolitical confrontation or enhanced economic integration? *China Quarterly of International Strategic Studies*, *7*(2), 219–242. DOI: 10.1142/S2377740021500093

Yeo, A. (2022). The state of Asian regionalism and current developments in the context of U.S.-China competition. In Hoo, T. B., & McKinney, J. M. (Eds.), *Chinese regionalism in Asia: Beyond the Belt and Road Initiative* (pp. 212–232). Taylor & Francis., DOI: 10.4324/9781003178965-2

Yoshimatsu, H. (2022). ASEAN and great power rivalry in regionalism: From East Asia to the Indo-Pacific. *Journal of Current Southeast Asian Affairs*, *42*(2), 186810342211392. Advance online publication. DOI: 10.1177/18681034221139297

Yu, H. (2024). *Understanding China's Belt and Road Initiative*. Springer Nature., DOI: 10.1007/978-981-99-9633-9

Zhang, S. (2022). Rise of China and its behaviours in the South China Sea: An analysis of defensive realism perspective. Liberal Arts and Social Sciences International Journal (LASSIJ), 6(1), 286–306. https://orcid.org/0000-0003-3217-5959

Zhao, M. (2023). Infrastructure Statecraft and Sino-U.S. Strategic Competition in the Indo-Pacific. *China Review*, *23*(1), 45–77. https://muse.jhu.edu/article/883826

Chapter 18
Miscalculation in Anarchy Iran's Strategic Ambiguity and the 2025 Iran–Israel Conflict: Hegemony in Global Governance

Mehmet Akar
https://orcid.org/0009-0008-1369-5936
European Studies, Dokuz Eylul University, Turkey

ABSTRACT

This chapter offers a case study of the 2025 Iran-Israel War which confirms the theoretical propositions of Offensive Realism but is limited by one particular assumption - that there are no miscalculations in the pursuit of power maximization. The country's pre-conflict policy - a deliberate pursuit of regional dominance supported by a nuclear ambiguity as close to breakout capacity as possible - demonstrates the theory's prediction that in an anarchic world, states pursue maximum power for their own survival. However, the conflict also reveals a major flaw - ambiguity creates uncertainty in strategic decisions – as seen 2025 Iran-Israel war it can also bring about a sudden conflict. This paper will rely on reports from the IAEA, professional assessments and conflict data to show that while Offensive Realism can explain a state's structural motivations - it cannot accurately predict miscalculations and/or failure mechanisms. The 2025 crisis clearly shows that rational power maximizing strategies are inherently risky when the uncertainty surrounding an adversary's resolve exists.

DOI: 10.4018/979-8-3373-2342-8.ch018

INTRODUCTION

By mid-2025, the Middle East balanced on a knife's edge - a disaster many saw coming. Years of rivalry between Iran alongside Israel – fought through secret operations, supporting different sides in conflicts, moreover a dangerous gamble over nuclear weapons – had built tension. Then, in June 2025, attempts to prevent war crumbled as both nations launched attacks targeting each other's infrastructure and nuclear facilities (Gambrell, Lidman, & Frankel, 2025; Rabinovich, 2024; ICG, 2018)

That twelve-day conflict wasn't sudden - it grew from increasing distrust between nations. Because "no central authority that sits above states and can protect them from each other," Moreover, they "can never be certain about other states' intentions" (Mearsheimer, 2001, p. 3).

The flare-up between Iran and Israel in 2025 throws light on how well offensive realism actually explains truly fierce fighting. It's a key example showing where the idea works - but also doesn't. War happens because the world lacks a boss to keep everyone in check - nations operate as they please (Mearsheimer, 2001, p. 3). Still, despite how often conflicts follow a pattern, their terrible results show we frequently misunderstand what others will do, fostering dangerous mistakes; therefore, even familiar conditions yield surprising outcomes.

Studies have thoroughly explored why Iran and Israel clash – recalling past wrongs, differing beliefs, alongside worries about safety (Gerges, 2013, pp. 42-43; Rabinovich, 2024). Likewise, much has been written regarding the nation's atomic efforts, examining its know-how, talks with others, also how it affects stability in the area (Dalton & Levite, 2024; IAEA, 2025, GOV/2025/8). Typically, scholars who look at international relations don't use John J. Mearsheimer's ideas about power to really dig into what might happen during a major war - a noticeable oversight.

Following Mearsheimer's idea, offensive realism suggests nations strive to "maximize its share of world power" - not just to stay safe, yet ultimately to "be the hegemon" (Mearsheimer, 2001, p. 2). This exploration uses a potential 2025 conflict as a test case, looking at whether Iran's secrecy, ambition in the region, alongside its progress toward nuclear weapons, fits with this thinking; however, it also points out where the theory falls short.

This chapter contends Tehran pursued a sensible, strength-focused nuclear path before 2025 - one fitting offensive realism - while also revealing the idea's flaw: even logical plans falter when others can't be trusted (Jervis, 1976, p. 52). Because true motives remain hidden, mistaking what another nation will tolerate is likely, shown by the disastrous attacks of June 2025 (Zurcher, 2025). The study explores this through these inquiries: initially, how does Iran keeping its aims unclear connect with the belief states want nuclear dominance to endure (Mearsheimer, 2001, p. 224)? How much did losing connections weaken Tehran's judgment before the fighting started in June 2025? Also, in what ways did actions by the U.S. and Israel take advantage of flaws in how Iran weighed risks - showing that secrecy doesn't always work against strong, determined opponents?

This research looks at the 2025 conflict using a specific approach: we test an existing idea against what actually happened. We draw evidence from several places - reports from the IAEA, what experts have said, current news - alongside the core concepts of offensive realism. Here's how this section unfolds. This work begins by laying out the core argument, predictions, then how we'll investigate them. Next, it dives into offensive realism – a way of seeing international relations – explaining its key ideas. Finally, these concepts get put to use examining Iran alongside its ambitions in the region. The report then follows the unfolding events toward the 2025 crisis. Next, it presents a military breakdown of what happened, followed by a gathering of those insights. Ultimately, the conclusion highlights what these developments mean for both theory and practical decisions.

2. THEORETICAL FRAMEWORK: OFFENSIVE REALISM AND REGIONAL POWERS

The research leans on John J. Mearsheimer's thinking about offensive realism – an idea detailing how global disorder influences what nations do. Seeing things from a structural realist angle, without anyone truly in charge, countries don't just try to get by; they constantly look for ways to become more powerful, bolstering their safety.

Iran, like other strong countries in the area, responds to dangers and chances while aiming for greater power. It begs the question – is Iran's unclear stance on nuclear weapons a calculated move, or driven by beliefs?

Looking at Iran's mixed signals alongside its work with nuclear technology using a realist viewpoint reveals how outside forces influence decisions, yet Iranian leaders still have control. Instead of seeing mistakes made in 2025 as one-off incidents, this perspective indicates they stemmed from fundamental motivations combined with ongoing safety concerns within a chaotic area.

Looking at things this way shows us how rivalry, feeling unsafe, alongside a constant need for protection built up until the 2025 fight between Iran and Israel. Consequently, what Iran did wasn't simply responding; rather, it was carefully planned – fueled by staying alive yet also wanting to change things in the area.

2.1 Structural Anarchy and Security Competition

States exist in a world without central authority, so they prioritize staying alive. Like similar ideas, it recognizes nations must look out for themselves and build strength. However, this view insists the structure of anarchy "to gain power at the expense of rivals, and to take advantage of those situations when the benefits outweigh the costs" (Mearsheimer, 2001, p. 21).

Without someone overseeing everything, countries feel they must build up strength just to stay safe. Consequently, even nations claiming peace often act aggressively abroad - holding back might expose them, given we can't truly know what others are planning. This systemic imperative is reinforced by three structural conditions: anarchy: "the absence of a central authority", "offensive military capability", and "never be certain about other states' intentions". So, "states recognize that the more powerful they are relative to their rivals, the better their chances of survival" (Mearsheimer, 2001, p. 3).

Even after the Cold War, big countries still compete for influence. We see this with ongoing American troops stationed in Europe and East Asia – a sign that nations worry about what Germany or Japan might do if left to their own devices (Mearsheimer, 2001, pp. 1-2). Because states never truly feel safe given others' strength coupled with hidden motives, they fall into a cycle where distrust breeds further distrust; essentially fearing one another. Moreover, "there is no mechanism, other than the possible self-interest of third parties, for punishing an aggressor" and "It is sometimes difficult to deter potential aggressors". So, "states have ample reason not to trust other states and to be prepared for war with them" (Mearsheimer, 2001, p. 32).

Mearsheimer cautioned against wishful thinking back in 2001, insisting on seeing reality instead. Despite American desires for a democratic China - a sort of massive Hong Kong accepting current global norms - he believed attempting friendly relations wouldn't work. Should China grow economically, a shift toward military might feel inevitable, with regional control in Northeast Asia likely becoming a goal - after all, nations often prioritize their own safety through influence. Consequently, America alongside partners would probably try to limit China's expansion, sparking rivalry and raising the specter of major conflict (Mearsheimer, 2001, p. 32).

The forecast fits what's happening now. Recently, at a gathering in Kuala Lumpur - the ASEAN summit - representatives from both the U.S. moreover China got together hoping to prevent their trade dispute from worsening, also to arrange talks between Trump then Xi. Discussions centered on China's broadened restrictions regarding rare earth materials - magnets included - coupled with the U.S.'s extensive list barring exports to numerous Chinese companies. Initial exchanges seemed promising; however, experts caution that failure to find common ground could worsen tensions. A temporary easing of trade barriers alongside collaboration in technology still feels within reach (Kok, 2025).

States live in a world without a central authority, so they constantly worry about each other. This unease won't simply vanish; instead, nations strive to become more powerful than rivals to ensure their own safety. Complete security, according to Mearsheimer, arrives solely with overall control – when no other nation poses a challenge. He notes "this situation, which no one consciously designed or intended, is genuinely tragic" (Mearsheimer, 2001, p. 3).

Bismarck, leading Brandenburg-Prussia during Germany's formation in the 1860s, voiced concerns about Poland. He believed a free Poland – though not yet independent – posed a serious danger because it might side with Prussia's rivals (McNeill, 2002, p. 552). Driven by this worry, Bismarck insisted on stripping Poles of power, reasoning that eliminating them as a political force guaranteed his nation's safety (Gall, 1986, p. 59; cited in Mearsheimer, 2001, p. 3). From 1795 to 1918, Poland existed as divided territory - politically broken up (Encyclopaedia Britannica, n.d.; Action Office, 2015). Consequently, nations striving for stability frequently perceive less powerful, uncertain countries nearby as potential dangers; this embodies the heart of the security dilemma. Without someone overseeing everything globally, countries naturally strive for strength simply to protect themselves. Therefore, Bismarck didn't act cruelly because he wanted to; instead, the chaotic state of global relations practically demanded it.

2.2 The Pursuit of Hegemony: Global and Regional Dimensions

Mearsheimer points out that the world lacks an overall governing power; nations operate as they see fit. Moreover, major global forces naturally have the means to wage war, posing a threat to one another. Thirdly, states "can never be certain about other states' intentions". Fourthly, "survival is the primary goal of great powers," which takes priority over other motives such as territory or ideology. Finally, great powers are "rational actors." In other words, "states pay attention to the long term as well as the immediate consequences of their actions." (Mearsheimer, 2001, pp. 29-32).

Mearsheimer challenges the idea - held by thinkers such as Milton Friedman - that a theory's usefulness stems solely from its ability to describe things. Instead, he argues "a theory based on unrealistic or false assumptions will not explain much about how the world works". He believed world politics should start with how things are, not how we wish they were. Therefore, striving for dominance - whether across the globe or just in one area - isn't foolish; instead, it's a sensible way to stay safe when there's no higher power to enforce rules (Mearsheimer, 2001, p. 30).

Hegemony can be global or regional as "one can distinguish between global hegemons, which dominate the world, and regional hegemons, which dominate distinct geographical areas." For example, the U.S. is a regional hegemon; as Mearsheimer (2001) notes "no other state in the Americas has sufficient military might to challenge it, which is why the United States is widely recognized as the only great power in its region" (Mearsheimer, 2001, p. 40).

Defensive realists believe attacking doesn't often work because international forces are too strong; ambitious nations typically face consequences (Carr, 1946, as noted by Mearsheimer, 2001). They suggest countries facing threats will team up to stop attackers, eventually defeating them. Because "offense-defense balance is usually heavily tilted toward the defense." So, defending is generally easier than conquering, expansion proves hard. Consequently, these thinkers recommend avoiding dangerous conflicts while maintaining a stable distribution of strength. In other words, "preserving the balance of power" may be key priority to maintain current stability (Mearsheimer, 2001, pp. 39–40).

However, some argue defensive views downplay opportunities for gain through force. They point to history - aggression doesn't always fail (Smith, 1986; Mearsheimer, 2001, p. 40). This view suggests attack works when circumstances are right. Looking at wars from 1815 to 1980, attackers prevailed in roughly sixty percent of cases (thirty-nine out of sixty-three) according to these thinkers (Clausewitz, 1976; Betts, 1997; Handel, 2001, Mearsheimer, 2001, p. 39). Throughout history, going on the attack has sometimes worked remarkably well. For instance, Otto von Bismarck forged Germany into a nation by winning wars versus Denmark (1864), Austria (1866), then France (1870) - a series of conflicts which demonstrably benefited him. Similarly, America grew substantially via taking land during the 1800s (Mearsheimer, 2001, p. 40).

Germany's story during the Nazi period isn't simple. They conquered Poland in '39, then France a year later; nevertheless, their campaign versus Russia from '41 to '45 ended in defeat. According to Mearsheimer, had Hitler stopped following his win over France, taking over everything might well have worked for the Nazis. History shows grabbing territory doesn't always pay off, however. Therefore, states need to be clever about building power - knowing both when to push forward also when to back down (Smith, 1986; Mearsheimer, 2001, pp. 39–40).

The Cold War finished, yet NATO stuck around. Rather than dissolve, it expanded toward the east. Nations consistently seek dominance, echoing offensive realism – they prioritize remaining powerful through competitive advantage. As one scholar noted, "the overriding goal of each state is to maximize its share of world power, which means gaining power at the expense of other states," Within a disordered world order, few nations settle for maintaining balance; typically, only a leading power attempts to preserve its control against challengers (Mearsheimer, 2001, p. 2).

2.3 Principles and Historical Evidence of Offensive Realism

Great nations constantly vie for dominance, according to Mearsheimer's 2001 ideas - a viewpoint stemming from how the world operates without anyone truly in charge. Similar to other theories, it recognizes countries prioritize staying safe by building strength because there's no global police force. Offensive realism differs from defensive realism regarding a state's ambition. While those favoring defense - like Waltz - believe nations primarily want safety, offensive realists think they strive for dominance (Waltz, 1989, p.40 as cited in Mearsheimer, 2001, p. 21).

Instead, offensive realism suggests powerful nations don't last long - the global landscape pushes countries to grab influence from competitors, eventually seeking total dominance. Mearsheimer asks "how do states maximize security?" or how nations best protect themselves. While defensive realists believe safety comes first, they disagree on how to get there (Snyder, 1991, pp. 11–12, as cited in Mearsheimer, 2001, p. 21). However, offensive realists insist security grows alongside a nation's overall strength "by maximizing their share of world power" (Mearsheimer, 2001, p. 21).

Mearsheimer draws a line between his take on realism - where states aggressively seek more influence - and the idea that people are naturally driven to dominate. Hans Morgenthau believed this drive for power was simply part of being human; he put it plainly, saying conflict exists everywhere, even within families, not just among nations. He argues that political behavior is driven by an inherent will to dominate, and that "a political policy attempts either to keep power, to increase power, or to demonstrate power" (Morgenthau, 1948, pp. 21–22). From this perspective, international politics is defined as "a continuing effort to maintain and to increase the power of one's own nation and to keep in check or reduce the power of other nations" (Morgenthau, 1948, p. 175).

Instead of believing nations naturally want to cause trouble – unlike what some think – John Mearsheimer suggests global politics itself drives their actions. He contends powerful countries aren't driven by a hunger for control; rather, the world order practically requires them to strive for strength. To put it simply, even if those in charge preferred peace, the chaotic nature of international relations compels rivalry, turning aggression into a reaction instead of a deliberate choice (Mearsheimer, 2001, p. 21).

Realist ideas differ because they disagree on what makes countries act as they do. Some believe it's simply how people are - a natural drive for power. Others think the international system itself forces nations to compete. One view insists states relentlessly strive for dominance, aiming to be top dog. However, another suggests countries seek stability through a balance of strength. Despite agreeing that states must look out for themselves when there's no global police force, these two ideas differ regarding how far nations will go to gain influence.

Looking at how major countries acted seems to back up the idea that they tend to be aggressive. For instance, Japan from 1868 to 1945, Germany during a similar period, likewise the Soviet Union throughout much of the twentieth century - each one consistently tried to grow its influence worldwide instead of staying put, as pointed out by Mearsheimer (2001). Nations operate as if constantly competing for dominance (Mearsheimer, 2001, p. 168). Take the U.S., seemingly focused on its own neighborhood, or Britain's global positioning - both behaved aggressively despite outward shows of moderation. This aligns with a straightforward view of international relations where strength is everything (Mearsheimer, 2001, pp. 170–171).

History keeps showing us how countries act according to a predictable pattern, backing up the idea that nations strive for dominance. Even when both sides knew a nuclear war meant everyone lost during the Cold War - the concept of "mutually assured destruction" (MAD) - major powers still tried to build more powerful weapons. This demonstrates a fundamental drive to gain an edge (Mearsheimer, 2001, pp. 232–233). Italy's willingness to seize chances internationally further backs up this idea. Repeatedly, throughout history - no matter the situation - nations act alike, demonstrating a drive for strength stemming from the international system itself, rather than internal issues (Mearsheimer, 2001, p. 233).

2.4 Nuclear Weapons and Offensive Realist Logic

Looking at how nations build nuclear weapons shows us a lot about what drives powerful countries - especially when viewed through the lens of one idea about international politics. This view suggests big players don't just settle for enough weaponry to deter attack, yet actively seek dominance in this area too. During the Cold War, both superpowers demonstrated this pattern. For instance, America in the fifties tried to outmaneuver Russia by preparing for a huge initial attack. Later, the 1983 Under the Single Integrated Operational Plan – 6 (SIOP-6) plan detailed attacks on fifty thousand locations - a strategy boosted by Multiple Independently Targetable Reentry Vehicle (MIRV) tech (Mearsheimer, 2001, pp. 225–228). Likewise, the Soviets grew their nuclear arsenal from 354 warheads in 1960 to 11,320 by 1989, focusing destructive power on enemy factories alongside their armed forces instead of population centers. Facing the threat of being wiped out together, both major powers-built defenses alongside plans for restricted use of nukes – attempts to move beyond guaranteed annihilation. These actions, logical responses to unpredictable tech or a potential enemy advantage (Mearsheimer, 2001, pp. 231–233), show nations prioritize strength to endure in a world lacking overall control. This arms build-up backs up the idea that countries strive for maximum power simply to stay alive.

According to Mearsheimer, major nations require both the ability to withstand a nuclear strike alongside robust military strength (Mearsheimer, 2001, p. 5). Should a country dominate through sheer nuclear might - outclassing competitors - traditional measurements of power become less important. Consequently, total control of nuclear weapons could reshape global influence. Countries with nukes - though they won't dominate the world - can really shake things up locally. Take Israel; keeping everyone guessing about their arsenal helps keep them safe in that part of the globe. However, if Iran gets nukes too, everything could change throughout the Middle East.

Great nations harbor mutual distrust and "great powers fear each other", a sentiment influencing how fiercely they compete for safety - also whether conflict erupts (Mearsheimer, 2001, pp. 42–44). This stems from a couple of consistent truths: countries have the means to project force, yet gauging another nation's aims remains uncertain. They realize that "one can never be certain that other states." Consequently, inherent anxieties plague international relations. Nuclear arms specifically amplify these worries due to their potential for immense harm; however, paradoxically, adversaries equipped with them tend toward peace (Mearsheimer, 2001, pp. 42–44). Deterrence, therefore, serves to lessen those fears.

Mearsheimer observed that nations possessing nuclear arsenals - ones able to withstand an initial attack yet still strike back - tend toward diminished apprehension when facing off against competitors. Why does having these weapons create a sense of ease? It's simple - nukes cause terrible damage, so nations are hesitant to start fights. However, Mearsheimer points out this doesn't eliminate worry altogether. Nuclear states continue to eye one another with suspicion, because a threat persists even between those who possess these weapons (Mearsheimer, 2001, p. 44). This reasoning probably eased tensions between major nations while the Cold War lasted. However, as Mearsheimer points out, it doesn't eliminate the risk of conflict - those with nuclear weapons continue to have cause for worry (Mearsheimer, 2001, pp. 43-44).

States cling to nuclear weapons - it's a matter of staying alive, also boosting their influence given the world's chaotic nature, much like realist thinkers have pointed out.

3. IRAN'S REGIONAL HEGEMONY STRATEGY: PURSUIT OF REGIONAL DOMINANCE

Considering how countries act when safety feels threatened, this section looks at Iran's efforts to become the dominant force in its region - a move that makes sense given ongoing feelings of being surrounded also cut off from others. Consequently, Iran broadened its reach throughout the Middle East utilizing unconventional methods, support for allies, moreover a deliberate strategy of keeping rivals guessing. This isn't simply about beliefs; it's about building strength to protect itself while discouraging attacks within a chaotic area.

3.1 Structural Imperatives and Regional Ambition

Because the world order doesn't have established guardians, nations naturally seek more influence. International relations are historically competitive - a hard reality. Consequently, building strength isn't simply aspiration; it's often what countries need to survive (Mearsheimer, 2001, p. 2).

Offensive realism suggests that without a global police force, nations equipped for battle, alongside uncertainty regarding others' goals, compel even normally calm countries to act warily and compete for strength. Essentially, greater power means improved odds of staying safe. Considering this, Iran – facing chaos in its region, pressure from the U.S. and Israel, moreover surrounded by opponents – has steadily built up its military, economy, and influence to protect itself (Judis, 2013). This isn't seen as simple aggression; instead, it's a sensible reaction to circumstances, fitting the idea that all nations aim to gain power when left to fend for themselves (Mearsheimer, 2001, pp. 2, 33). Ultimately "states recognize that the more powerful they are relative to their rivals. the better their chances of survival" (Mearsheimer, 2001, p. 3).

Iran doesn't just want to get by - it aims to dominate the Middle East. One school of thought suggests lasting safety comes from being utterly supreme (Mearsheimer, 2001, p. 2). Because, as some believe, losing now could mean disappearing later (Mearsheimer, 2001, p. 33).

Iran aims for dominance in the region using its nuclear work, support for allies, alongside building power among Shia communities. However, Tehran isn't simply reacting to global pressures; deeply held beliefs - its revolutionary spirit plus religious identity - drive its actions. Consequently, Iran manages external expectations while simultaneously justifying its growing role throughout the area via those very convictions.

Iran views its nuclear program as protection from enemies near and far, yet hasn't invaded another nation for over a century and a half - indeed, Iraq started their eight-year war. Though some find fault with Iranian backing of particular factions, there's reasoning behind those choices. To weaken Iran's influence could destabilize an already vulnerable area, with consequences for everyone (Gerges, 2013, pp. 42–43).

Offensive realism offers a useful way to analyze international politics by viewing nations as single entities focused on their own security (Mearsheimer, 2001, pp. 10–11)

- however, this approach falls short when examining Iran. Internal forces, specifically its revolutionary beliefs alongside the principle of religious leadership, actually amplify Iran's impact on groups like Hezbollah (Aarabi, 2019). Consequently, Iran's actions in the region aren't simply about defense. Instead, as Rabinovich contends, Iran blends ideological goals with ambitions rooted in past empires, broadening its power via allies throughout Lebanon, Iraq, moreover Syria. Iran's atomic efforts, alongside hostility toward Israel, serve to discourage rivals yet also extend influence. Its partnership with Russia in Syria has strengthened its foothold across the region (Rabinovich, 2024) - a development stemming from openings following the 2003 Iraq conflict, moreover conflicts within Syria and Yemen. Though opponents view Iran's growing strength as aggressive maneuvering, authorities there describe it as rectifying past wrongs (Sariolghalam, 2018).

The bruising war with Iraq from 1980 to 1988 really altered how Iran thought about safety. Feeling vulnerable in direct fights, they leaned into things like missile programs alongside supporting groups in other nations (International Crisis Group [ICG], 2018, pp. i-ii). Groups like Hezbollah, Syria's government, moreover the Houthis became key pieces of keeping Iran safe - tactic others frequently view as aggression. Though some claim bias toward one religious group over another, leaders in Tehran insist their backing of Palestinians stems from broad Islamic solidarity together with opposition to outside influence. Tehran often acts based on what works best at the moment – backing Armenia despite its Christian faith while Azerbaijan is largely Shia, working alongside groups such as Hamas and Islamic Jihad (both Sunni), also occasionally dealing with the Taliban and al-Qaeda (ICG, 2018, pp. i–ii). This shows a flexible approach to the region. However, Iran still presents itself as a protector of Shia Muslims globally.

Matsunaga's work from 2016 questions whether Iran truly aims to be the top power - a claim often made by Israel alongside Gulf states. He suggests Iranian foreign policy actually stems from resisting American influence. It's a position echoing both Ayatollah Ruhollah Khomeini's original ideas as well as current statements by Ayatollah Ali Khamenei, focused on supporting those harmed rather than controlling the region. Matsunaga suggests a nation prioritizes counterbalancing American power; its missiles alongside partnerships serve as defense, not attack (Matsunaga, 2016). Consequently, Iran seems focused on opposing dominance instead of seeking it. However, Rabinovich contends Iran's support for groups like Hezbollah, Hamas, and the Houthis stems from both safety worries also deeply held beliefs (Rabinovich, 2024). This policy isn't just reaction; it aims to reshape things in the area. Considering Iran's nuclear program alongside its support for groups - especially following events in Syria and the 2023 attacks by Hamas - suggests a slow slide into hidden conflict (Rabinovich 2024).

Offensive realism struggles with nuance; it doesn't quite grasp how things changed during the Cold War, for example (Mearsheimer, 2001, p. 11). Consider Iran: its use of allies, occasional progress on nuclear tech, even working with international inspectors after 2003 (IAEA, 2004, GOV/2004/11, pp. 2-3) - these actions aren't simply dictated by power dynamics. Practical needs together with beliefs played a role in those decisions.

Tehran acts much as expected when nations seek dominance - like Mearsheimer outlined - yet its choices aren't solely about power. Beliefs, history, even practical needs also matter. Consequently, Iran safeguards itself within global realities while bolstering its position in the region. Essentially, big picture theories explain some things, though grasping Iran fully demands looking at both broad forces alongside specific details.

3.2 Nuclear Ambiguity and International Oversight

Iran first explored atomic power in the 1950s, with help from a U.S. plan promoting peaceful uses of nuclear technology during the reign of the Shah (Vaez & Sadjadpour, 2013). Yet, talk of building bombs worried officials in America (U.S. Embassy Paris, 1974), so the effort stalled around 1975. After the 1979 revolution, the government decided these projects conflicted with religious principles, so they stopped them altogether. However, when war broke out with Iraq in 1980 – with help coming to Iraq from Western countries also Arab nations – Iran found itself alone. This led officials to look at nuclear tech once more.

Back in 2002, information released by a group called the People's Mujahedin Organization suddenly focused worldwide concern on secret nuclear work happening in Iran.

For years - since 2002, actually - watchdogs have grown worried about secret nuclear work happening in Iran. This includes hints of efforts toward building weapons. They haven't gotten clear answers from officials there when asked about experiments that could be tied to arms production; consequently, trust is eroding. A lack of openness, specifically around projects with a possible military purpose, hampers any ability to truly check what's going on (IAEA, 2011, GOV/2011/63, para. 38).

That very year, an Iranian Vice President voiced plans to develop their nuclear program. Consequently, a deal materialized allowing inspectors from the International Atomic Energy Agency - together with security specialists - to examine sites at Natanz moreover Arak (IAEA, 2003, GOV/2003/40, para. 3). This represented a key moment in diplomacy; rather than argument, they chose dialogue alongside direct facility checks.

3.2.1 Reporting Gaps and Erosion of Trust in 2003

Reports from 2003 indicated Iran hadn't completely met requirements set by their nuclear agreement. They didn't share details about uranium brought into the country in 1991 - information surfaced only twelve years later, initially incomplete. While admitting some work involving uranium, they withheld thorough accounts. Details about the Tehran Research Reactor, Jaber Ibn Hayyan lab, alongside sites in Esfahan arrived late; changes to designs followed. A lack of full cooperation with inspection requests raised questions concerning openness from Iran (IAEA, 2003, GOV/2003/40, Section D, paragraph 32).

Germany, Britain, alongside France – together known as the E3 – began talks with Iran. Thirteen years later, on July 14, 2015, they reached an agreement called the JCPOA. The deal included the five permanent members of the UN Security Council - America, the UK, China, France, Russia - with Germany also participating, as did the European Union. The deal aimed to keep Iran's atomic work non-military via tight controls alongside thorough checks. Following this, international penalties - those from the UN, Europe, and America - would disappear, allowing Iran back into world trade (European External Action Service, 2022).

The deal curbed how much uranium could be enriched, called for updates to the Arak reactor, moreover, set up thorough checks by the IAEA (The White House, 2015; Bedenko, Hesse, & Shin, 2022). So far, the 2015 JCPOA provides the deepest look into Iran's nuclear program ever achieved internationally (IAEA, 2017).

3.2.2 Iran's Nuclear Threshold in Mearsheimer's Framework

In May 2018, the United States - acting alone - left the JCPOA during Donald Trump's presidency. This move dramatically altered how the world monitored Iran's nuclear activities. Washington claimed the original agreement didn't address concerns about Iran's power in the region or its missiles; instead, they argued it simply bolstered Iran's troubling actions alongside delaying, rather than preventing, their pursuit of nuclear weapons (Trump, 2018). The pullout signaled a shift - Washington opted for strong-arm tactics instead of working with others, reinstating old penalties that threatened Iran's economy. Despite this, watchdogs kept observing things; they noted in May 2018 that Iran hadn't diverted any announced nuclear materials nor broken rules set by a UN resolution. Then, just two weeks after, these same observers confirmed Iran still wasn't enriching uranium beyond agreed limits, meaning everything was technically sound when the U.S. left (IAEA, 2018, GOV/2018/24). However, Britain, France, and Germany stood by the deal, believing it boosted global security (Smith, 2018). This split revealed a growing gap across the Atlantic; America aimed to limit Iran via sanctions, whereas Europe alongside the IAEA favored checks and talks to curb nuclear activity. In effect, leaving the arrangement broke down collaboration, ushering in hostility even though Iran was then demonstrably following the rules.

By 2025, Iran held nearly 275 kilograms of uranium refined to high levels (GOV/2025/8). Leaders claimed they could make a weapon if they chose to, yet insisted they weren't planning one (GOV/2025/10). A past nuclear official, Ali Akbar Salehi, stated Iran now has every ability needed. However, the present head, Mohammad Eslami, maintained their restraint stems from policy - not inability. This uncertainty, alongside a religious decree from Supreme Leader Khamenei's 2004 fatwa forbidding such arms, lets Iran appear to deter enemies without breaking international rules (Dalton & Levite, 2024).

According to Mearsheimer (2001), "that great powers fear each other is a central aspect of life in the international system," and "there is no night watchman to whom they can turn for help if another great power attacks them." In a world without central authority, "the probability that they will fight a war" always exists (Mearsheimer, 2001, p. 42) "Specifically, the more power a state possesses, the more fear it generates among its rivals." (Mearsheimer, 2001, p. 43). From a strategic realist perspective Iran's increasing capability signals a potential shift in the regional balance, intensifying fear among rivals despite the absence of declared intent.

Big countries seem scared of each other based on what they can do, not necessarily what they say they'll do. Essentially, a nation's power to cause trouble - which changes depending on the situation - is what really sets alarm bells ringing, according to one observation (Mearsheimer, 2001, p. 43). Nuclear weapon stockpiles - their scale alongside their resilience - matter, likewise does location, as well as how strength is spread globally. Realists who focus on strategy believe we can't truly know what others plan. Because there's no global police force, powerful nations react to each other's military might, not promises. This idea echoes earlier thinkers like Morgenthau, Niebuhr, and Meinecke; Frei also observed this tendency toward balancing power (Mearsheimer, 2001, p. 45).

3.2.3 Compliance Challenges under the NPT

Back in 2007, a report pointed out Iran wasn't following the rules - specifically agreements meant to ensure peaceful use of nuclear technology alongside UN demands. Though they accounted for all known nuclear material, inspectors couldn't get a complete picture because Iran didn't fully cooperate with extended checks nor adhere to specific technical requirements. Uranium got more concentrated - now at 4.8% U-235 - while work went on building the Arak reactor, also known as IR-40, alongside its heavy water facility. Because inspectors faced hurdles, they couldn't verify that Iran wasn't secretly pursuing nuclear weapons, which chipped away at trust in their stated goals (IAEA, 2007, GOV/2007/22).

Iran approaches its nuclear program driven by worries about safety alongside a willingness to adapt - it discourages attacks yet also helps with talks, fitting how countries seek more influence, according to one way of thinking about global politics.

3.2.4 Strategic Ambiguity: The Role of Amimut in Diplomacy and International Relations

Iran's approach to nuclear matters gains clarity when viewed alongside a time-honored practice in global affairs: purposeful uncertainty, termed *Amimut*. Nations often choose to remain unclear – this is *Amimut* – offering them leverage within tricky world politics. It means keeping intentions veiled, allowing for deterrence, adaptable negotiation, while also navigating challenges at home and abroad. When nations clash - over land, weapons, or deploying troops - a little uncertainty can actually help, making opponents hesitate. Yet relying on this tactic, called *Amimut*, isn't foolproof. Mistakes happen, tensions could worsen, trust erodes. Especially now, with technology changing how wars begin and unfold, things become even trickier (Youvan, 2024).

Amimut's story begins long ago, with how people negotiated across cultures. Think about the Oracle of Delphi - its unclear predictions allowed Greek cities wiggle room. Similarly, Rome and the Ottomans skillfully blurred lines in treaties to get what they wanted. Even Machiavelli noted this tactic, building on a practice still seen in today's world. *Amimut* gives countries options - a way to navigate tricky situations involving force or talks, discourage fights, and get ahead. However, used poorly, it could backfire (Youvan, 2024).

The former president's approach to Iran's nuclear program involved a deliberate mix of unclear messaging - diplomacy alongside veiled threats of war. Following reports about undisclosed Iranian nuclear work, he presented the U.S. as seeking talks, yet cautioned noncompliance would mean "massive conflict," keeping military intervention as an option (Northam & Hider, 2025). This push-pull between friendliness and pressure showed up distinctly in springtime discussions held in Oman then Rome (Ebrahim, 2025), shifting from hopeful signs to firm requirements like halting all uranium enrichment. Washington intentionally kept its options vague, hoping to force a reaction yet stay nimble. Instead, this secrecy made Tehran distrustful, worsening tensions in the region - showing how keeping things unclear can actually be policy, not just talk.

During retaliatory strikes on Iran, a two-pronged approach became clear. Even facing potential diplomatic fallout, former leadership disclosed to reporters they were aware of the impending action – "We knew everything." Though attempting to convince the Israeli Prime Minister to postpone things, they simultaneously issued Iran a sixty-day deadline for renewed talks. Even as the timeframe ended, Trump labeled Israel's attack "very successful" (Holland, 2025). It showcased a deliberate ambiguity – he spoke of keeping talks open with others, however signaled approval for his partner's actions. Consequently, Iran remained engaged in discussions, alongside ongoing force; nevertheless, allies grew uneasy regarding potential escalation throughout the region.

So, dealing with Iran under Trump meant walking a tightrope – trying to look strong while also talking peace. It worked okay for a bit, giving them some leverage. However, mixing talk of talks with threats of force was dangerous; people could easily get the wrong idea, leading to things spiraling out of control. This shows how a strategy built on keeping everyone guessing can backfire spectacularly when tensions are already high.

3.2.5 Iran's Nuclear Ambiguity Strategy

Iran's approach to nuclear power shifted - from showing off progress under the Shah, then embracing revolutionary religious ideas, ultimately settling on purposeful uncertainty exceeding simple technology. This change began when Iran joined the Nuclear Non-Proliferation Treaty in 1968, pledging commitment to peaceful uses of nuclear energy (France 24, 2015). Yet, the meaning behind this promise slowly altered. Back when Shah Mohammad Reza Pahlavi ruled, people - as Azodi notes - thought atomic power meant Iran was becoming modern, a sign of industry taking hold. It tied into wanting to be a major force in the region (Azodi, 2020). The Shah didn't just want electricity from reactors; Davenport points out he envisioned Iran showing off its tech skills while standing on its own two feet (Davenport, 2023).

The Shah presented his plans as progress without conflict, yet after the revolution things shifted - a deliberate ambiguity arose. Suddenly, Iran's nuclear efforts weren't just about power; they bolstered its position in the region while also acting as a warning to others. In 2010, Ayatollah Ali Khamenei offered a justification rooted in faith, hoping to counter rising global concerns (BBC Türkçe, 2010). He insisted nuclear arms went against Islam, maintaining Iran sought only peaceful applications. That same year, an IAEA report suggested the nation's nuclear work could be geared towards weapons development, also pointing to less willingness to work alongside the agency - raising doubts about earlier assurances (IAEA, 2010, GOV/2010/10). Ali Asghar Soltanieh, speaking for Tehran, dismissed the report as untrue, showcasing how Iran reacted to scrutiny from abroad (BBC Türkçe, 2010).

A 2010 report from the IAEA showed Iran hadn't misused announced nuclear resources; however, a lack of openness made verifying complete peaceful intent difficult. Specifically, failing to fully adopt key inspection measures alongside ongoing uranium enrichment - coupled with limited access to certain reactors - eroded confidence in how things were being checked. Khamenei bases authority on faith, yet offers no way to confirm claims - a problem when seeking acceptance globally. The head of the IAEA urges Iran to be open about its nuclear program; otherwise, trust won't develop (IAEA, 2010, GOV/2010/10). This reveals ongoing difficulty gaining clear assurances from Tehran regarding their work.

Iranian leaders shared comments in recent years – 2022 and 2024 – suggesting they now know how to build nukes, choosing instead to keep their capabilities hidden. For instance, Ali Akbar Salehi, who once led Iran's atomic program then served as foreign minister, stated in 2024 they've surpassed every limit, with each step intentionally designed for a specific reason; he signaled Iran can indeed make nuclear weapons (Iran International Newsroom, 2024). In 2022, Kamal Kharrazi, who advises Iran's leader and directs its foreign policy thinking, stated increasing enriched uranium to weapons-grade levels - going from 60% to 90% - presents no real challenge. Meanwhile, the nation's atomic energy director, Mohammad Eslami, made clear only Supreme Leader Khamenei will authorize such a move, highlighting how technical ability doesn't guarantee action; instead, everything depends on his choice. (Iran International Newsroom, 2024).

Reports from the IAEA show Iran's uranium supply is twenty-two times over the amount allowed by the 2015 agreement. Enrichment has also sped up, now reaching 60%. Though Rafael Grossi, who leads the IAEA, believes nothing technically stops them from creating a nuclear weapon, Iranian authorities - citing a religious decree against such arms - maintain they aren't pursuing one. David Albright, who knows a lot about nuclear issues, believes Iran might still build bombs. Even with a recent religious ruling against them, things are getting more secretive there - a situation where the desire to have weapons could grow. Back in 2022, they kicked out inspectors and made it harder to check what was happening, so we know less now. It seems Iran juggles its ability to make nuclear materials alongside public statements rooted in faith, which creates real danger for everyone. A May 2025 report indicates Iran now holds sufficient highly enriched uranium – at 60%, nearing weapons-grade 90% – for potentially building nine nuclear warheads (Murphy, 2025). Furthermore, because Tehran stepped away from the 2015 agreement, safeguards on their nuclear work have crumbled. For more than four years, without inspections stemming from that deal, vital data regarding their capabilities - like how much uranium they refine, plus details about machines and materials - has been lost, irretrievably so (IAEA, 2025, GOV/2025/24).

Iran halting cooperation - specifically, suspending a key agreement alongside refusing updates - makes inspecting facilities harder, diminishing openness. The nation now creates and stockpiles significantly enriched uranium, a troubling development since it is the sole country without nuclear weapons doing so (IAEA,

2025, GOV/2025/24). Consequently, trust in whether Iran's nuclear work is truly peaceful erodes; getting inspections back on track feels critical.

Iran hasn't built nukes, yet still aims to be the dominant force in its neighborhood by holding onto lots of refined uranium. Looking at things from a tough angle - where countries mostly look out for themselves - this makes sense. It lets Iran keep options open, discourage attacks, also lessen chances of outside meddling. As Mearsheimer (2001) notes, "a state has to know its limitations to survive in the international system," yet "great powers miscalculate from time to time because they invariably make important decisions on the basis of imperfect information," meaning that "they sometimes make faulty judgments and end up doing themselves serious harm" (Mearsheimer, 2001, pp. 38–39). Surprisingly, the 2025 Iran–Israel war showed that Iran's nuclear ambiguity, which was meant to give it more strategic flexibility, also turned into a risky and fragile situation.

3.3 Ideology vs. Pragmatism in Foreign Policy

Iran didn't quite live up to the rules of its nuclear agreement for quite some time. Investigations showed unreported uranium brought into the country in '91 and '93. Furthermore, they kept secret both uranium metal created from '99 to '02 - along with enriched uranium. Also unrevealed were details about importing UF_6, plus work separating plutonium, even concealing resulting waste. Iran didn't share details about places like Kalaye Electric or Lashkar Ab'ad. Moreover, they were slow - or didn't fully reveal - designs for the Jabr Ibn Hayan Laboratory alongside the Tehran Research Reactor. This behavior demonstrates a determined attempt to hide information, obstructing collaboration because of insufficient openness regarding their work with nuclear technology (IAEA, 2004, GOV/2004/83, Section A.2, paras. 85–86, p. 19).

Inspectors grew worried about Iran's work with uranium, specifically because what Iranian officials said kept changing. At first, they suggested certain procedures followed instructions from equipment providers; however, afterward they confessed to keeping quiet about small-scale uranium conversions happening from '81 to '93. Then, in August '03, Iran revealed prior, secret tests making UF_4 and UF_6 dating back to the nineties – a direct contrast to former reports. Digging deeper showed Iran brought in quite a bit of nuclear material from 1977 through 1991, yet didn't share what was happening when they should have. Later, in October 2003, they confessed the uranium went toward spinning tests at the Kalaye Electric site - something left out before (IAEA, 2003, GOV/2003/75, Annex 1, pp. 1–4). It highlights how Tehran's nuclear efforts weren't straightforward, lacking openness.

From late 2003 through early 2004, Iran worked with the IAEA in a way it hadn't before - agreeing to extra checks alongside halting some uranium work. Inspectors then visited sites like the research center in Tehran also the one at Natanz, sometimes showing up unannounced. Back in February 2004, Iran agreed to more checks, even letting inspectors take samples from areas linked to the military – a move toward building trust. However, details shared later that month needed further review; therefore, confirming everything wasn't finished (IAEA, 2004 GOV/2004/11, pp. 2-3).

Iran's approach to nuclear matters balances beliefs with practical goals. Repeated breaches of security protocols alongside secrecy eroded trust, yet allowed Iran to develop technology and strengthen its position. However, occasional collaboration - alongside brief openness - helped inspections occur, simultaneously offering Iran some influence despite penalties. Iran doesn't approach its nuclear aims with a single plan. Instead, it adapts, shifting strategies according to what happens. As a result, Tehran can still shape power dynamics in the region - all while pursuing its goals internationally.

4. THE PATH TO CRISIS: MISCALCULATION AND ESCALATION IN 2025

In 2025, tensions between Iran and Israel exploded. This happened because each country felt pressured, made faulty assumptions, also operated knowing things were unpredictable. Viewing events through a lens of power politics reveals both sides behaved predictably given the chaotic world they inhabit. However, misunderstandings alongside inherent uncertainties actually worsened the chance of conflict. What followed – initial assaults, payback strikes, widespread instability – demonstrates how striving for safety without rules can ironically create more danger, echoing a grim pattern previously observed.

4.1 Miscalculation and Strategic Ambiguity: The Path to Crisis in 2025

According to Mearsheimer (2001), nations - even those aiming for sensible choices - can stumble owing to incomplete data. This often results in poor decisions alongside substantial self-inflicted damage (Mearsheimer, 2001, pp. 38–39).

Jervis pointed out back in '76 that assuming nations always act logically isn't quite right. A country might want to steer clear of trouble, however mistakes happen - whether from seeing things wrong, ingrained thinking patterns, or misunderstanding what others are doing (Jervis, 1976, p. 52). This disconnects between goals and results shows how lacking full knowledge can lead to surprising, even risky situations globally.

By 2025, Tehran's approach to nuclear power proved dangerous. They didn't quite grasp how ready Israel was to attack first, nor did they fully believe that keeping their intentions unclear would stop anyone. Consequently, on June 13th, Israeli air raids hit sites at Natanz, Fordo, alongside Isfahan - effectively removing key leaders within the Islamic Revolutionary Guard Corps (IRGC). Nearly ten days passed before American planes hit those locations again - President Trump insisted they were utterly ruined (Gambrell, Lidman, & Frankel, 2025) However, Iran fired back at cities Tel Aviv, Haifa in Israel alongside a U.S. outpost in Qatar, achieving little gain yet highlighting flaws in their military and among allies. Simultaneously, Iran boosted uranium purification to 60%, well beyond the limit established years earlier (IAEA, 2025c), coupled with limits on inspections that raised alarms worldwide triggering strong reactions (IAEA, 2025b).

The current situation highlights how much influence Israel now wields throughout the area. Miller notes that recent Israeli actions toward Iran have altered things, positioning Israel as the dominant force in the region. Israel didn't just dismantle Iran's nuclear program; its show of force - supported by the U.S. - undermined Iran's influence alongside its allies, diminishing their power throughout the area. However, according to Miller, without a clear plan for what comes next, lasting peace remains doubtful. Netanyahu's government shows strength through military force, yet doesn't offer any real path toward peace - leaving Israel's growing power uncertain (Miller, 2025). Essentially, Miller (2025) believes Israel is becoming the dominant force in the region; however, this position isn't built to last because it depends more on winning battles instead of building agreements.

4.2. The 12-Day War of June 2025 and the Attacks of Iran and Israel

By June 2025, tensions flared between Israel then Iran - quickly becoming a focused twelve-day clash. Both sides exchanged missile and drone attacks, hitting cities alongside vital systems. This fight reshaped power dynamics across the Middle East. The clash revealed how far apart the armies are technologically, yet showed Iran's firm beliefs remain strong. Despite Israel harming Iranian bases, the conflict proved their struggle isn't over - it still complicates things in the region.

In mid-June 2025, Israel began attacks - dubbed "Rising Lion" - targeting Iranian nuclear sites, sparking fierce fighting. Netanyahu stated Iran neared building a bomb quickly, so he authorized the strikes. Iran labeled this a wartime threat, vowing to strike back. Their counterattack, "True Promise 3," met strong Israeli defenses; however, missiles flew for days. Iranian reports cite 224 deaths, meanwhile Israel acknowledges 24. Tensions flared quickly, soon becoming a larger problem for the region. With Tehran's nuclear sites heavily protected, President Trump considered a direct response, though doing so risked upsetting a fragile peace (Lam, Ferreira Santos, Lukiv, & Williams, 2025).

Come June 13th, 2025, Israel unleashed a massive aerial campaign - almost two hundred warplanes - targeting Iran's atomic program alongside key military installations. This offensive severely hampered their ability to enrich uranium, took out parts of the armed forces command, yet also dismantled much of Iran's anti-air protection. Beforehand, though, Israeli drones had quietly been put into play, meant to cripple Iranian long-range rockets and tracking networks (Tirpak, 2025). Israel demonstrated skillful use of tech alongside smooth teamwork. The attack weakened Iran's forces while shifting power dynamics throughout the area.

Iran fired numerous ballistic missiles at cities like Petah Tikva, Haifa, yet also Bnei Brak on June 16th; this caused eight deaths among civilians alongside roughly three hundred wounded. Though the American embassy office in Tel Aviv experienced slight harm - without casualties - Israel's military quickly retaliated by hitting missile sites plus nuclear locations within Iran (Fabian, 2025). Reports indicate Israeli troops carried out around 360 air attacks spanning twenty-seven Iranian regions, concentrating efforts near Tehran (Mehvar, 2025). Efforts focused on hindering the nation's atomic work alongside weakening its long-range rocket strength. Israel stopped about 86% of incoming missiles from Iran utilizing sophisticated defenses - Arrow, Iron Dome among them. Simultaneously, Israeli aircraft executed over 500 pinpoint attacks, guided by up-to-the-minute satellite data offering leaders greater maneuverability (Levaton, 2025; Mehvar, 2025).

On June 22nd, after American airstrikes hit Iranian nuclear facilities, Iran responded by firing numerous missiles toward Israel's north and center. The assault wounded a minimum of 86 people while also severely damaging buildings - especially in Tel Aviv and Nes Ziona. Haifa's defenses stumbled, revealing that even top-tier shields aren't foolproof (Euronews, 2025). Though Iran suffered serious blows to its army alongside its nuclear sites, the heart of its power - its beliefs and organizations like the IRGC - held firm. Israel carefully spared key religious figures, thus aiding the government in staying together. Instead of causing an uproar, the trouble seemed to bring many Iranians together, backing those in charge - a shared feeling of strength against outside pressure. That togetherness really helped the government hold on through everything (Raine, 2025; Balcı, 2025).

The attack on Haifa, Israel – a barrage of missiles from Tehran – highlights how this regional conflict is becoming increasingly about military force. Local officials report strikes hit two key locations within Haifa, where Israel keeps its naval fleet. Mayor Yahav appeared stunned by the missile strike, confessing his sadness. He urged Haifa citizens to heed official guidance - a plea born from the attack's emotional toll alongside practical concerns. News showed roughly twenty missiles hit Haifa also Beersheba, wounding two people (Newdick, 2025). Regarding the June 2025

Israel-Iran war, the following can be said: this war demonstrated that Israel could target Iran and reach Iran from a distance with aircraft, striking its infrastructure and some targets. But it was also an important indicator that Iran could also hit some important targets in Israel with its missiles and challenge Israel's defenses.

The fighting concluded with roughly 25 Israelis and 430 Iranians dead - a stark measure of how quickly things spiraled. Back-and-forth attacks showed a dangerous loop, driven by attempts to discourage further aggression alongside deep fears for survival (Fabian, 2025; Euronews, 2025). Tehran's atomic program hit hard times, yet wasn't defeated. Work started quickly to rebuild, alongside promises to keep enriching uranium. Officials insisted this was a guaranteed right according to agreements designed to prevent weapon building - though they stressed peaceful uses (Raine, 2025; Helmore, 2025). Iran quickly got its air defenses working again, using both weapons they built themselves – such as the Bavar-373 – together with Russian S-300 missiles. This speedy recovery showed how committed Tehran is to staying strong militarily (Daftari, 2025).

Iran held air defense practice – "Eqtedar 1403" – beforehand, displaying a boost in preparedness. The Majid missile system, built within the country, took down drones during those tests; they also ran through complex attack simulations involving command systems and monitoring (TABNAK, 2025). Yet, actual fighting showed gaps in Iran's defenses when confronted by Israel's stronger attacks alongside their intelligence work (Balcı, 2025).

Following the conflict, Iran pursued two paths - bolstering defenses alongside careful diplomatic efforts. With fresh nuclear discussions set to begin in Türkiye, officials in Tehran refused any calls for outright capitulation, maintaining that conditions after the attacks didn't permit forceful bargaining (Helmore, 2025; Daftari, 2025). Iran is stuck choosing a path forward: talk to America again, get tougher to discourage attacks, or keep everyone guessing. What they decide will really shake things up in the region – for better or worse (Balcı, 2025; Daftari, 2025).

Drawing from history, leaders frequently react to today's problems using what they remember most vividly. This helps explain how Iran might act in 2025. The lengthy, draining war with Iraq - where they fought a foe supported by the West - left a deep imprint. During that time, Iran cultivated an image of steadfastness; a way of enduring hardship. Consequently, their reaction to attacks from Israel and the United States in 2025 may echo strategies honed decades earlier, serving as a familiar pattern (Jervis, 1976, pp. 281-282).

Jervis noted that key lessons come from the 1980s Iran-Iraq War. These lessons can be road map for today's policymakers. During that war, Iraq had support from Western powers and Arab states. Iran, in turn, gained resistance experience both militarily and psychologically. So, we may think that Iran responded to Israeli and U.S. attacks in 2025 with resilience as a state and nation because of this experience.

But some thinking errors that may show up here. For one thing, we might stretch lessons from 1980s battles too far - conventional fighting then isn't quite the same as today's mix of cyberattacks alongside indirect conflict. Also, Iranian decision-makers may tend to see potential dangers based on what happened before, had overlooking other ways things could unfold. Decisions couldn't quite clear-headed because earlier hostility colored how people saw what was happening now. So, this could have blocked a complete understanding of wider effects, alongside how Tehran viewed things. Consequently, we may say that thinking became limited - a setback to sensible choices (Jervis, 1976, pp. 281-282).

Looking back at 2025, Iran's approach - shaped by lessons from the past - did a solid job of keeping things secure alongside boosting its ability to bounce back. However, this same method also left them vulnerable because of how they thought about things, snagged in patterns of belief.

The quick clash in June 2025 showed Israel's technological and operational superiority. However, it didn't diminish Iran's resolve nor halt their pursuit of nuclear power. Now, things have shifted - a long spell of animosity began after the clash, marked by Israel's steady force alongside Iran's stubborn pushback. Trouble hangs over the area because escalation still feels possible within this back-and-forth of threats (Raine, 2025; Mehvar, 2025).

Table 1. The 12-Day War of June 2025 – Iran-Israel Conflict Overview

Category	Summary & References
Duration & Scope	For nearly two weeks, fighting flared - around 360 aerial attacks by Israel hit 27 areas, especially targeting Tehran, according to reports from 2025 (Mehvar, 2025)
Key Iranian Strikes	June 16: Major missile assault on Petah Tikva, Haifa, and Bnei Brak (8 killed, 300 injured); June 22: retaliation after U.S. raids caused 86 injuries in Tel Aviv and Nes Ziona; ~20 missiles hit Haifa and Beersheba, targeting military and psychological symbols (Fabian, 2025; Newdick, 2025; Euronews, 2025)
Israel's Military Advantage	Missiles met resistance - systems like Arrow and Iron Dome stopped about 86% of attacks, despite a glitch in Haifa. Simultaneously, over five hundred drone raids benefited from up-to-the-minute satellite data (Levaton, 2025; Mehvar, 2025; Euronews, 2025)
Tehran's Military Damage	Nuclear sites alongside military installations suffered considerable harm, though Iran's Revolutionary Guard Corps - its commanders too - remained mostly unaffected (Raine, 2025; Balcı, 2025)
Iranian National Unity	When attacks happened, people rallied behind those in charge - a surge of unity that strengthened the government (Raine, 2025; Balcı, 2025)
Socio-Economic Impact in Israel	Rocket attacks forced roughly five thousand people from their homes. City leaders insisted on quick financial aid because daily expenses soared past 15 million NIS. Meanwhile, teamwork between regional and municipal governments faltered (Sokol, 2025)

continued on following page

Table 1. Continued

Category	Summary & References
Post-War Nuclear Status	The program stumbled, yet survived - a swift rebuild followed, positioning further development as a legitimate national pursuit (Raine, 2025; Helmore, 2025)
Air Defense Posture	Iran bolstered its air defense utilizing both the Bavar-373 alongside Russian S-300 systems. Earlier Eqtedar 1403 exercises hinted at preparedness, however actual conflict demonstrated weaknesses when facing Israeli intelligence operations plus accurate attacks (Daftari, 2025; TABNAK, 2025; Balcı, 2025)
Weaknesses Revealed	Israel faced successful, overwhelming strikes that bypassed safeguards, leaving cities struggling financially. Meanwhile, Iran's defenses showed cracks - even after practice runs (de Vega & Gutiérrez, 2025; Balcı, 2025; Sokol, 2025)
Diplomatic Response	Iran followed two paths at once - strengthening its armed forces alongside tentative negotiations about its nuclear program. It wouldn't accept demands for total capitulation (Helmore, 2025; Daftari, 2025; Balcı, 2025)
Long-term Outcome	Despite Israel's tech edge - yet unable to sway Tehran - the fighting simply deepened a pattern of standoffishness alongside ongoing animosity, according to Raine and Mehvar (2025) (Raine, 2025; Mehvar, 2025)

Source: Author's own compilation based on the content developed in this study.

5. MILITARY ANALYSIS: STRATEGIC BALANCE AND AIR DEFENSE LESSONS

The clash between Iran and Israel in 2025 wasn't just about flexing muscles; it showed how well modern defenses actually work. More than what happened on the battlefield, the event spotlighted weaknesses - even in top-tier technology - when swamped by numerous, simultaneous strikes. Modern air defenses face tricky contradictions. How well they work matters, naturally, yet so do things like keeping them supplied alongside a nation's ability to withstand disruption. Looking at defenses like Iron Dome, THAAD, plus SM-3 reveals dominance isn't just about tech; it requires blending technology seamlessly into how things operate, what industries support it, and even society itself.

5.1 The Paradoxes of Air Defense: Strategic Lessons from the 2025 Iran-Israel Conflict

The idea that having the best technology in modern warfare mean complete security right or not? The fighting between Iran and Israel in June 2025 proved that wrong - a harsh lesson showing what happens when ideas meet reality. Really, whether defenses work isn't just about how well they work, it's tied to things like money, supplies, plus broader social and political situations. Looking at defenses like

Iron Dome, THAAD, yet also SM-3, this work shows tech improvements sometimes move faster than long-term stability. Moreover, keeping a country safe now seems closely linked to cities holding strong. The fighting June 2025 revealed a tricky problem with current missile shields – they struggle with balancing cutting-edge features, expenses, alongside practical supply lines.

5.2 The Fragility of the Iron Dome: High Technology under Saturation Strategies

Iron Dome, usually quite effective at stopping rockets – around 86-90% according to reports – faced a different challenge this time (American Jewish Committee [AJC], 2025). It wasn't about tricky technology; instead, sheer numbers overwhelmed the system. Iran sent so many drones alongside missiles that Israel's usual advantages didn't matter much. Consequently, some attacks succeeded, hitting places like Tel Aviv and a refinery near Haifa, demonstrating how even top defenses struggle against massive, well-timed assaults. De Vega and Gutiérrez noted how this tactic resembled Russia's in Ukraine – cheaper drones wore down defenses prior to bigger missile strikes (de Vega & Gutiérrez, 2025). Even with $14.3 billion in U.S. support from 2024 bolstering Israel's layered Iron Dome, David's Sling, and Arrow 3 systems (AJC, 2025), complete shielding proved impossible when facing an enemy deliberately aiming to overwhelm resources. Consequently, the fighting highlighted the need to keep evolving defenses alongside ongoing funding.

5.3 Logistical Bottlenecks: Constraints Beyond the Strategy in THAAD and SM-3 Systems

The war showed something surprising: even great tech isn't much use without supplies and factories to back it up. For instance, America sent its THAAD missile defense system to help Israel. During the fighting, around 150 THAAD interceptors were fired – almost a quarter of everything the U.S. had in stock (Trevithick, 2025). A mere hundred missiles roll off the Lockheed Martin line each year, creating a real problem. Replacing those used in conflict might demand four years. It isn't just about whether they work; keeping supplies steady is vital.

Replacing those used in conflict might demand four years. It isn't just about whether they work; keeping supplies steady is vital. This situation showed us the vulnerability of deterrence in the future conflicts, such as potential Taiwan Strait issue. So, we can think that the victory may hinge on how the parties can build quick and more ammunitions.

The SM-3 Block IIA missile, vital for shipborne defenses, presents a tricky problem. Each one costs $37 million (Trevithick, 2025) - a hefty price when facing numerous attacks, pushing budgets to their breaking point. States face a real bind: keeping people safe costs money. What once showed far-reaching plans now comes down to budget concerns - getting things done cheaply, building them quickly, and making enough of them.

5.4 The Local Cost of Security: The Socio-Economic Front of Defense

The fighting wasn't just about intercepting rockets; it hit cities hard, testing how well they could bounce back. After Tehran struck, towns bore the brunt of things. By mid-June 2025, helping around 5,000 people who'd lost homes or were otherwise impacted ran over 15 million shekels a day - roughly $4.3 million. Mayors signaled funds wouldn't last much longer (Sokol, 2025). Nowadays, warfare extends beyond battlefields - it disrupts city systems, strains local resources, likewise imperils citizens. Collaboration between national and city authorities isn't simply red tape; rather, it is now essential for keeping the country safe.

5.5 Conclusion: Toward a Post-Technological Strategy

By 2025, fighting between Iran and Israel spotlighted some tricky contradictions at the heart of today's defenses against airborne attacks

1. How well things are built versus how smoothly they keep running
2. Expensive options versus being able to quickly change plans
3. What a nation can build versus what it actually faces.

Looking ahead, designing defenses requires more than just better tech. A strong plan joins technology to reliable supplies, sensible budgets, also ways to shield communities - essentially, keeping people safe within cities. What matters now isn't just stopping missiles, yet how quickly life gets back to normal after an attack. How well defenses work will depend less on specs, more on fitting into a bigger recovery plan (Trevithick, 2025; de Vega & Gutiérrez, 2025; Sokol, 2025).

Table 2. Strategic Assessment of Modern Air Defense Systems in the 2025 Iran-Israel Conflict

System	Strategic Role	Effectiveness	Key Limitations	Reference
Iron Dome	Short-range rocket and UAV* interception	During fighting, they stopped around 86 to 90 out of every 100 attacks, thereby lessening harm to cities	Exposed when many drones or missiles strike at once - important places like Tel Aviv and oil refineries could be hit. It struggles when overwhelmed, also needing other defenses to work well	American Jewish Committee (AJC), 2025; de Vega & Gutiérrez, 2025
THAAD	Shielding against missiles launched from way up high	They got them into position - about 150 missiles sent off	About a quarter of available stock in the US is gone. Production crawls - only around one hundred items yearly - so getting more takes four years	Trevithick, 2025
SM-3 (Block IIA)	The Navy's system to intercept missiles from the ocean. It reaches far	Strong defenses versus critical dangers	Each piece costs $37 million, a price that won't last if we keep using them heavily. Getting our hands on them takes far too long	Trevithick, 2025
Integrated Systems (Iron Dome + David's Sling + Arrow 3)	Layered regional defense through U.S.-Israel cooperation	Better teamwork across security layers	Despite interwoven defenses, a determined, large-scale assault still poses a threat. Reliance on financial support from the United States - $14.3 billion authorized this year - complicates matters, alongside tangled supply chains	AJC, 2025; de Vega & Gutiérrez, 2025
Socio-Economic / Civilian Impact	Communities getting prepared, keeping people safe, alongside ways to make things right	People demanded quick help after being forced from their homes - about five thousand of them. This situation really highlighted how crucial it is to keep civilians safe	City expenses are sky-high - over 15 million NIS each day. Getting everyone on the same page, from city hall to local areas, is key. Existing shelters won't hold up against big bombs (500 to 1,000 kilograms). Even with tech solutions, people will still struggle financially	Sokol, 2025; de Vega & Gutiérrez, 2025

* Unmanned Aerial Vehicle

Source: Author's own compilation based on the content developed in this study.

6. ANALYSIS AND SYNTHESIS: OFFENSIVE REALISM AND THE FRAGILITY OF THE 2025 CRISIS

Looking at a possible 2025 clash between Iran and Israel using ideas from John Mearsheimer, this explores how Iran sought power - via weapons, allies, and ambition - in a world without central control. It also considers whether any peace holds, alongside what that means for safety across the region.

6.1 The Nuclear Threshold: Deterrence and its Discontents

In a world lacking global authority, nations act as Mearsheimer described – they seek security by growing stronger. They build up their forces, even developing nuclear arms, hoping to reshape influence within their areas (Mearsheimer, 2001, pp. 21, 30–31, 224). This drive for dominance stems from a basic need to endure (Mearsheimer, 2001). Without anyone truly in charge, coupled with distrust among nations, powerful countries feel they must aggressively pursue dominance. Consequently, they strive for an edge - even aiming to have more nuclear weapons than others - as a way to secure themselves (Mearsheimer, 2001, pp. 168, 224).

History backs up this idea quite well. Consider how nations like Japan, Germany, the Soviet Union, moreover Italy acted – they weren't content with things as they were; instead, they actively sought more influence (Mearsheimer, 2001, pp. 169–209). This demonstrates that when there isn't a central authority, building strength simply makes sense.

Iran's approach to nuclear matters shows how things work. They boost uranium refinement yet steer clear of openly building weapons, aiming to discourage enemies without inviting attack. Tehran's ability to produce enriched material was almost at a critical point by 2025. Alongside this, continued disregard for international inspection rules - like limiting where inspectors could go, alongside questions remaining about places such as Varamin - suggested a deliberate effort to stay hidden (IAEA, 2024, GOV/2024/61; IAEA, 2025, GOV/2025/8; IAEA, 2025c). This aligns with thinking that nations are always unsure what others truly plan, evidenced further by Tehran declining to follow agreed-upon verification measures (Mearsheimer, 2001, p. 31; IAEA, 2024, GOV/2024/61; IAEA, 2025, GOV/2025/8).

Iran pursues nuclear capabilities logically, aiming to bolster its position given the world's lack of central control. It echoes the idea that powerful nations deliberately maintain uncertainty around their weapons to discourage rivals and alter influence in their area - a concept still relevant today when examining how countries act regarding nuclear arms.

6.2 Anarchy, the Security Dilemma, and the Inevitability of Future Conflict

Iran's nuclear policy is inseparable from its broader ambition for dominant influence, a rational goal under offensive realism, "those rival nuclear powers will not simply accept mutual assured destruction (MAD) but instead will strive to gain nuclear superiority over the other side" (Mearsheimer, 2001, pp. 171-172). According to offensive realism, "the pursuit of regional hegemony is not a quixotic ambition", (Mearsheimer, 2001, p. 213) but "the best way for a state to survive in anarchy is to take advantage of other states and gain power at their expense. The best defense is a good offense" (Mearsheimer, 2001, p. 36).

Iran attempts to extend its reach throughout the Middle East. It does so via its nuclear program alongside military strength - the Quds Force, missile technology, groups like Hezbollah - thereby confronting rivals including Israel moreover the United States (Mearsheimer, 2001, pp. 231–233; Burke, 2024). According to one view, nations naturally strive for greater power through growth (Mearsheimer, 2001, pp. 209-210). Iran seems to follow this pattern, building alliances to discourage opposition while reshaping the region (Mansour, Al-Shakeri, & Haid, 2025). Opposing Israel, Saudi Arabia, alongside American power in the Middle East, the Axis of Resistance isn't a single entity - rather, it's a collection. Groups like Hezbollah, Hamas, Palestinian Islamic Jihad, various Iraqi factions, then the Houthis operate somewhat on their own yet receive backing from Iran. This assistance takes shape as weaponry, instruction, reciprocal aid, orchestrated by Iran's IRGC (Zeidan, 2025).

By 2025, Tehran navigated a tough spot: easing of some restrictions alongside closer bonds with Russia seemed a calculated move against the West, boosting influence even with limited collaboration in 2024 (IAEA, 2024). Yet, significant losses for allies – Hamas faltering, Hezbollah crippled, Assad ousted by year's end – dashed hopes of dominance, pushing Iran toward relying more on its own nuclear strength and missiles (Burke, 2024; Gambrell, Lidman, & Frankel, 2025). It echoes a simple truth about power, as one scholar put it, wanting control doesn't guarantee having the means to achieve it (Mearsheimer, 2001, p. 37).

6.3 Offensive Realism and the Fragility of the 2025 Israel-Iran Ceasefire

A truce took hold June 24, 2025, halting conflict between Israel and Iran - with help from then-President Trump. This outcome mirrors an idea from political scientist John Mearsheimer: strong nations don't recklessly seek power, nor do they fight battles they can't win (Mearsheimer, 2001, p. 37). Indeed, when Iranian officials signaled, they'd halt further attacks should Israel back down ("We have no intention to continue…if Israel stops," said Foreign Minister Araghchi), it showed a calculated move to safeguard what remained of their strength despite facing disadvantages Zurcher, 2025). Though Trump announced a ceasefire - "It's now in effect! Don't break it!" - both sides spun the outcome as a win. Iran highlighted their missile strikes as strong-arm tactics; meanwhile, Israel portrayed Operation Rising Lion as wiping out two major dangers (Folk & Ray, 2025). This behavior aligns with how countries focus on appearing stronger than others alongside satisfying internal audiences.

Systemic constraints further shaped outcomes. Despite U.S. claims of "complete destruction" of Iran's nuclear facilities at Fordo, Natanz, and Isfahan (Mackintosh & Yousif, 2025), Tehran's retaliatory strikes revealed enduring deterrent capacity, illustrating offensive realism: "a state's military power is usually identified with the particular weaponry at its disposal, although even if there were no weapons, the individuals in those states could still use their feet and hands to attack the population of another state" (Mearsheimer, 2001, pp. 30–31). Tehran's sway diminished because its allies faltered - Hezbollah, Hamas, for instance - while assistance from Russia and China proved insufficient. Meanwhile, the EU attempted talks to avert a nuclear crisis, demonstrating how global cooperation can temper aggressive ambitions (EEAS, 2025).

EU officials made clear Iran shouldn't build nukes, believing talks offer the best long-term solution. Despite a shaky truce, now is the moment to restart conversations. Officials urged a swift restart to discussions, desiring UN watchdogs back on the ground. The EU restated its willingness to talk things over (EEAS, 2025b).

Barely had a truce taken hold when trouble flared – Israel blamed Iran for breaking it, swiftly followed by retaliatory attacks (Folk & Ray, 2025). Not mincing words, President Trump lashed out at everyone involved, especially Israel: "Israel, just don't use those bombs...". "Get your pilots back immediately!" declared. An Israeli official, claiming Iran broke the truce with missile fire. Tehran countered, blaming Israel for ongoing assaults after the agreement began. Despite citizens on each side feeling some ease - a glimmer of peace - disagreements over what happened cast a shadow on whether this calm will last. It showed just how easily talks can unravel in unstable areas like this one (Cornwell, Holland, & Hafezi, 2025).

According to Mearsheimer, major nations are wary - they distrust one another, anticipating potential conflict. Nations expect trouble. Consequently, they don't easily believe each other (Mearsheimer, 2001, p. 32).

By June 2025, fighting between Iran and Israel - fueled by American participation - ended with a Qatari-brokered truce. Yet skirmishes continued, suggesting this wasn't real peace so much as a breather for everyone to regroup. Iran appeared stronger diplomatically, Israel bolstered its image at home alongside its defenses, whereas the U.S. calmed oil prices yet sent signals both worldwide and internally. The show depicts how people - even when acting logically - sometimes dial things down briefly during conflict as a strategy when they're weaker. However, this pause doesn't fix deep-rooted problems; instead, it sustains distrust alongside ongoing friction because there's no overarching authority enforcing peace (Bukhari & Mujaddid, 2025, pp. 146-147, 154-155).

U.S. intelligence indicates airstrikes against Iran's nuclear work set things back just briefly – perhaps a couple of months. That clashes with statements from the President alongside his Defense Secretary, who insisted the program was utterly destroyed. Officials now say Iran might restart activity soon, yet the White House disputes this claim. Some experts caution satellite photos don't show everything at underground locations. Intelligence reports clashed sharply with what politicians stated about how well the strikes worked (Landay, Slattery, Ali, & Stewart, 2025). The DIA believed the attacks merely set back Iran's nuclear program a little - just months - because many machines survived, alongside moved nuclear material. Yet President Trump plus Defense Secretary Hegseth insisted Iran's nuclear work was completely ruined. Though, specialists pointed out the vital underground parts weren't hit; mainly surface buildings took heavy damage. Reports suggest Iran maintains hidden nuclear sites untouched by recent attacks. Israel stated minimal harm occurred at Fordow, yet claimed joint efforts with the U.S. set back Iranian nuclear work two years. These clashing accounts highlight secrecy regarding what actually happened, showcasing a divide between official statements and real information. The problem could skew how we understand what happened (Bertrand, Lillis, & Cohen, 2025). Therefore, further research should scrutinize the war's consequences.

Table 3. Offensive Realism & Fragility of 2025 Ceasefire

Aspect	Details & References
Ceasefire Mediation	On June 24th, 2025, Donald Trump, then U.S. President, helped arrange this (Zurcher, 2025).
Iran's Conditional De-escalation	Foreign Minister Araghchi: no further response if Israel stops aggression (Zurcher, 2025)
Public Messaging & Narratives	According to reports, Iran stated its missiles hit their targets. Meanwhile, Israel asserted they eliminated a significant danger to their survival (Folk & Ray, 2025)
Proxy Network Decline	Weakened Hezbollah and Hamas reduced Tehran's regional leverage (Burke, 2024; Mansour et al., 2025)
External Support Limits	Limited Russian and Chinese support constrained Tehran's power (EEAS, 2025; Mearsheimer, 2001, p. 30)
EU Diplomatic Role	Iran was called on to stop its pursuit of nuclear arms, alongside a request to restart discussions likewise allow checks by the IAEA (EEAS, 2025b)
Ceasefire Violations	Within hours, claims of wrongdoing surfaced - the U.S., notably, rebuked Israel following its airstrikes (Folk & Ray, 2025; Cornwell et al., 2025)

continued on following page

Table 3. Continued

Aspect	Details & References
Structural Anarchy & Security Dilemma	Mearsheimer: "states in the international system also aim to guarantee their own survival. Because other states are potential threats, and because there is no higher authority to come to their rescue… Each state tends to see itself as vulnerable and alone, and therefore it aims to provide for its own survival" (Mearsheimer, 2001, pp. 33)
Intelligence vs Political Claims	The Defense Intelligence Agency reported program setbacks lasting just a few months - a far cry from the extensive damage claimed by Trump and Hegseth (Landay et al., 2025; Bertrand et al., 2025).

Source: Author's own compilation based on the content developed in this study.

7. CONCLUSION

Looking at the 2025 clash between Iran and Israel, it really shows how useful - yet also troubling - the idea of offensive realism is. This concept keenly illuminates why Iran has sought power for so long, shedding light on what motivated them. It also shows how structures shape what countries do. Consequently, we see even powerful nations aren't entirely free; instead, Iran struggles to combine force with talks - a challenge for any country where there's no global authority.

Because the world lacks a central authority, given past dangers, alongside doubts about arms control efforts, Iran's ambition for greater strength feels less like a surprise, more like a natural reaction to circumstances. Their tactic – getting close to building nukes yet holding back – functioned as a way to discourage attacks, gain leverage during talks, also project influence without instantly provoking war. Ultimately, this situation could support the idea that nations prioritize their own safety by accumulating power, with nuclear weapons being the most potent means in this unfortunate rivalry.

The trouble isn't just disagreement; it reveals how shaky even careful thinking can be. A focus on pure reason, as some believe nations operate, ignores the uncertainty of a world without central control. Instead of craving dominance, Tehran simply got its assessment wrong - it didn't understand how its strength stacked up against others' determination. Losing its hidden support system diminished crucial defenses, so it depended too much on uncertain nuclear power. That uncertainty, meant to protect it, actually made things worse. Rivals figured they could hit the nuclear facilities with regular weapons without causing a full nuclear response – a gamble they took as Iran neared completion of its work.

Things don't look good for a peace that sticks. This unsteady truce, arranged with help from the United States, quickly fell apart as both sides blamed each other for breaking the agreement – a classic example of how trying to ensure one's own safety can make everyone less secure. Iran seems set to become even harder to read, keeping its nuclear work hidden yet spread out instead of obviously fortifying old locations. It's a way to hold onto power without directly inviting attack. Meanwhile, Israel will keep sharpening its plans for striking first, also improving defenses against a goal that grows increasingly difficult to pinpoint. Distrust lingers, alongside a relentless contest for power – the root issues haven't shifted. The conflict in 2025 didn't end the chaos; instead, it underscored how bleak things are, restarting the rivalry with escalated risks.

Offensive realism gets at why nations act as they do – a constant hunger for strength – yet doesn't reliably tell us when trouble will actually flare up. It spots the danger, however misses the ignition point. What happened in 2025 revealed that amidst global chaos, even careful leaders can blunder into war, showing power seeking isn't always secure.

8. REFERENCES

Aarabi, K. (2019, March 20). *What is velayat-e faqih?* Tony Blair Institute for Global Change. https://institute.global/insights/geopolitics-and-security/what-velayat-e-faqih

Action Office. (2015, June 11). *Poland: Forging the Polish nation nonviolently, 1860s–1900s.* https://actionoffice.org/en/2015/06/11/imaging-polish-nation/ and Encyclopaedia Britannica. (n.d.). *Partitioned Poland.* https://www.britannica.com/topic/history-of-Poland/Partitioned-Poland

American Jewish Committee. (2025, July 22). *6 things you need to know about Israel's Iron Dome defense system.* https://www.ajc.org/news/6-things-you-need-to-know-about-israels-iron-dome-defense-system

Azodi, S. (2020, December 8). *A history of continuity in Iran's long nuclear program.* Atlantic Council. https://www.atlanticcouncil.org/blogs/iransource/a-history-of-continuity-in-irans-long-nuclear-program/

Balcı, Ç. (2025, July 1). *The 12-day war from the perspective of Iran.* Daily Sabah. https://www.dailysabah.com/opinion/op-ed/the-12-day-war-from-the-perspective-of-iran

BBC Türkçe. (2010, February 19). *İran'ın dini lideri Hamaney: Nükleer silah geliştirmiyoruz.* https://www.bbc.com/turkce/haberler/2010/02/100219_iran_khamanei

Bertrand, N., Lillis, K. B., & Cohen, Z. (2025, June 24). *Exclusive: Early US intel assessment suggests strikes on Iran did not destroy nuclear sites, sources say.* CNN. https://edition.cnn.com/2025/06/24/politics/intel-assessment-us-strikes-iran-nuclear-sites

Betts, R. K. (1997). Should strategic studies survive? *World Politics*, *50*(1), 7–33. DOI: 10.1017/S0043887100014702

Bukhari, S. R. H., & Mujaddid, G. (2025). *Strategic Ceasefire or Tactical Deception: A Geopolitical Analysis of the Iran, Israel*, U.S. Crisis in 2025. *Qlantic Journal of Social Sciences*, *6*(2), 146–156. DOI: 10.55737/qjss.vi-ii.25354

Burke, J. (2024, September 29). *The Middle East in crisis: 7 October, the day that changed the world.* The Guardian. https://www.theguardian.com/world/2024/sep/29/the-middle-east-in-crisis-7-october-the-day-that-changed-the-world

Carr, E. H. (1946). *The twenty years' crisis, 1919–1939: An introduction to the study of international relations* (2nd ed.). Macmillan. DOI: 10.1007/978-1-349-15208-7

Cornwell, A., Holland, S., & Hafezi, P. (2025, June 24). *Trump says both sides violate ceasefire, tells Israel: 'Do not drop those bombs'.* Reuters. https://www.reuters.com/world/middle-east/trump-announces-israel-iran-ceasefire-2025-06-23/

Daftari, A. (2025, July 21). *Iran's Army repairs air defenses for new war.* Newsweek. https://www.newsweek.com/iran-air-defence-restored-war-nuclear-talks-europe-2101563

Dalton, T., & Levite, A. E. (2024, May 23). *Iran's nuclear threshold challenge.* War on the Rocks. https://warontherocks.com/2024/05/irans-nuclear-threshold-challenge/

Davenport, K. (2023, January). *Timeline of nuclear diplomacy with Iran, 1967–2023.* Arms Control Association. https://www.armscontrol.org/factsheets/timeline-nuclear-diplomacy-iran-1967-2023

de Vega, L., & Gutiérrez, Ó. (2025, June 18). *Iran finds cracks in Israel's missile defense system.* El País. https://english.elpais.com/international/2025-06-18/iran-finds-cracks-in-israels-missile-defense-system.html

Ebrahim, N. (2025, April 22). *The US and Iran will resume nuclear talks on Saturday. Here's what we know.* https://edition.cnn.com/2025/04/18/middleeast/us-iran-nuclear-talks-what-we-know-intl

Euronews. (2025, June 22). *Iran launches wave of missiles at Israel following US bombing of nuclear sites. Euronews with AP.* https://www.euronews.com/2025/06/22/iran-launches-wave-of-missiles-at-israel-following-us-bombing-of-nuclear-sites

European External Action Service. (2025, July 15). *Foreign Affairs Council: Remarks by High Representative Kaja Kallas at the press conference.* https://www.eeas.europa.eu/eeas/foreign-affairs-council-remarks-high-representative-kaja-kallas-press-conference-1_en

European External Action Service. (2025, June 23). *Foreign Affairs Council: Remarks by High Representative Kaja Kallas at the press conference.* https://www.eeas.europa.eu/eeas/foreign-affairs-council-remarks-high-representative-kaja-kallas-press-conference-0_en

European External Action Service (EEAS). (2022, April 28). *Joint Comprehensive Plan of Action (JCPOA).* https://www.eeas.europa.eu/delegations/vienna-international-organisations/joint-comprehensive-plan-action-jcpoa_en?s=66

Fabian, E. (2025, June 16). *8 killed, nearly 300 injured as Iranian ballistic missiles strike central Israel, Haifa. The Times of Israel.* https://www.timesofisrael.com/8-killed-nearly-300-injured-as-iranian-ballistic-missiles-strike-central-israel-haifa/

Folk, Z., & Ray, S. (2025, June 24). *Israel And Iran Confirm Ceasefire Is In Effect—Trump Says 'Please Do Not Violate It' (Live Updates). Forbes.* https://www.forbes.com/sites/zacharyfolk/2025/06/24/israel-and-iran-confirm-ceasefire-is-in-effect-trump-says-please-do-not-violate-it-live-updates/

France 24. (2015, July 14). *Timeline: A history of Iranian nuclear diplomacy.* https://www.france24.com/en/20150713-timeline-history-iranian-nuclear-diplomacy

Frei, C. (2001). *Hans J. Morgenthau: An intellectual biography.* Louisiana State University Press.

Gall, L. (1986). *Bismarck: The White Revolutionary* (Vol. I: 1851–1871, Trans. J. A. Underwood). London: Unwin Hyman. As cited in Mearsheimer, J. J. (2001). *The tragedy of great power politics.* W. W. Norton & Company. p. 3.

Gambrell, J., Lidman, M., & Frankel, J. (2025, June 18). *Israel strikes Iran's nuclear sites and kills top generals. Iran retaliates with missile barrages.* The Associated Press. https://apnews.com/article/iran-explosions-israel-tehran-00234a06e5128a8aceb406b140297299

Gerges, F. (2013). *Ortadoğu Uluslararası İlişkiler Çalışmaları: Tarih, Teori ve Metodoloji Üzerine Bir Haşiye* (Z. T. Kor, Trans.). London School of Economics Ortadoğu Merkezi. (Orijinal çalışma 1 Haziran 2013 tarihinde yayımlanmıştır)

Handel, M. I. (2001). *Masters of war: Classical strategic thought* (3rd ed.). Frank Cass.

Helmore, E. (2025, June 29). *Iran's nuclear enrichment 'will never stop', nation's UN ambassador says.* The Guardian. https://www.theguardian.com/world/2025/jun/29/iran-nuclear-enrichment-un-ambassador

Holland, S. (2025, June 13). *"We knew everything," Trump tells Reuters about Israel's strikes on Iran.* Reuters. https://www.reuters.com/world/middle-east/trump-tells-reuters-its-unclear-if-iran-still-has-nuclear-program-2025-06-13/

IAEA. (2024, November 19). *Verification and monitoring in the Islamic Republic of Iran in light of United Nations Security Council Resolution 2231 (2015)* (GOV/2024/61). https://www.iaea.org/sites/default/files/24/11/gov2024-61.pdf

IAEA. (2025, February 26). *NPT Safeguards Agreement with the Islamic Republic of Iran: Report by the Director General (GOV/2025/10).* https://www.iaea.org/sites/default/files/gov2025-10.pdf

IAEA. (2025, February 26). *Implementation of the NPT Safeguards Agreement in the Islamic Republic of Iran* (GOV/2025/8). https://www.iaea.org/sites/default/files/25/03/gov2025-8.pdf

IAEA. (2025, March 3). *IAEA Director General's introductory statement to the Board of Governors.* https://www.iaea.org/newscenter/statements/iaea-director-generals-introductory-statement-to-the-board-of-governors-3-march-2025

International Atomic Energy Agency. (2003, June 6). *Implementation of the NPT safeguards agreement in the Islamic Republic of Iran* (GOV/2003/40). https://www.iaea.org/sites/default/files/gov2003-40.pdf

International Atomic Energy Agency. (2003, November 10). *Implementation of the NPT safeguards agreement in the Islamic Republic of Iran (GOV/2003/75).* https://www.iaea.org/sites/default/files/gov2003-75.pdf. Annex 1.

International Atomic Energy Agency. (2004, November 15). *Implementation of the NPT safeguards agreement in the Islamic Republic of Iran* (GOV/2004/83). https://www.iaea.org/sites/default/files/gov2004-83.pdf. Section A.2, paras. 85–86.

International Atomic Energy Agency. (2004, March 1). *Implementation of the NPT safeguards agreement in the Islamic Republic of Iran* (GOV/2004/11). https://www.iaea.org/sites/default/files/gov2004-11.pdf

International Atomic Energy Agency. (2007, May 23). *Implementation of the NPT safeguards agreement in the Islamic Republic of Iran (GOV/2007/22).* https://www.iaea.org/sites/default/files/gov2007-22.pdf

International Atomic Energy Agency. (2010, February 18). *Implementation of the NPT Safeguards Agreement and relevant provisions of Security Council resolutions 1737 (2006), 1747 (2007), 1803 (2008) and 1835 (2008) in the Islamic Republic of Iran (GOV/2010/10).* https://www.iaea.org/sites/default/files/gov2010-10.pdf

International Atomic Energy Agency. (2011, November 8). *Implementation of the NPT safeguards agreement and relevant provisions of Security Council resolutions in the Islamic Republic of Iran* (GOV/2011/63). IAEA Board of Governors. https://www.iaea.org/sites/default/files/gov2011-63.pdf

International Atomic Energy Agency. (2017, November 14). *Director General's speech on Iran, the JCPOA and the IAEA.* https://www.iaea.org/newscenter/statements/director-generals-speech-on-iran-the-jcpoa-and-the-iaea

International Atomic Energy Agency. (2018). *Verification and monitoring in the Islamic Republic of Iran in light of United Nations Security Council resolution 2231 (2015)* (GOV/2018/24). https://www.iaea.org/sites/default/files/gov2018-24.pdf

International Atomic Energy Agency. (2025, May 31). *Verification and monitoring in the Islamic Republic of Iran in light of United Nations Security Council resolution 2231 (2015) (GOV/2025/24)*. https://www.iaea.org/sites/default/files/gov2025-24.pdf

International Crisis Group. (2018, April 13). *Iran's priorities in a turbulent Middle East* (Middle East Report No. 184, pp. i–ii). International Crisis Group. https://www.crisisgroup.org/middle-east-north-africa/gulf-and-arabian-peninsula/iran/184-irans-priorities-turbulent-middle-east

Iran International Newsroom. (2024, February 12). *Iran signals it is closer to building nuclear weapons*. https://www.iranintl.com/en/202402123916

Jervis, R. (1976). *Perception and misperception in international politics*. Princeton University Press. (2017 new ed. with preface).

Judis, J. (2013, October 1). *Netanyahu's shockingly bad Iran speech*. New Republic. https://carnegieendowment.org/posts/2013/10/netanyahus-shockingly-bad-iran-speech?lang=en

Kok, X. (2025, October 25). US, China seek to avoid trade war escalation, salvage Trump-Xi meeting in Malaysia talks. Reuters. https://www.reuters.com/world/china/us-china-seek-avoid-trade-war-escalation-salvage-trump-xi-meeting-malaysia-talks-2025-10-25/

Lam, L., Ferreira Santos, S., Lukiv, J., & Williams, N. (2025, June 19). *Israel-Iran: How did latest conflict start and where could it lead?* BBC News. https://www.bbc.com/news/articles/cdj9vj8glg2o

Landay, J., Slattery, G., Ali, I., & Stewart, P. (2025, June 24). *US strikes may have set back Iran nuclear program only months, sources say*. Reuters. https://www.reuters.com/world/us-strikes-may-have-set-back-iran-nuclear-program-only-months-sources-say-2025-06-24/

Levaton, S. (2025, July 1). *Israel's 12-day war with Iran was a test of technological dominance*. The Times of Israel. https://www.timesofisrael.com/israels-12-day-war-with-iran-was-a-test-of-technological-dominance/

Mackintosh, T., & Yousif, N. (2025, June 22). *What we know about US strikes on three Iranian nuclear sites*. BBC News. https://www.bbc.com/news/articles/cvg9r4q99g4o

Mansour, R., Al-Shakeri, H., & Haid, H. (2025). *The shape-shifting 'axis of resistance': How Iran and its networks adapt to external pressures.* Chatham House. https://www.chathamhouse.org/2025/03/shape-shifting-axis-resistance

Matsunaga, Y. (2016, March 18). *Is Iran seeking regional hegemony?* Atlantic Council. https://www.atlanticcouncil.org/blogs/iransource/is-iran-seeking-regional-hegemony/

McNeill, W. H. (2002). *Dünya tarihi* (A. Şenel, Çev.; 6. baskı). İmge Kitabevi Yayınları. (Orijinal eser 1967'de yayımlanmıştır).

Mearsheimer, J. J. (2001). *The tragedy of great power politics.* W. W. Norton & Company.

Mehvar, A. (2025, July 4). *Q&A | Twelve days that shook the region: Inside the Iran-Israel war.* Armed Conflict Location & Event Data Project (ACLED). https://acleddata.com/qa/qa-twelve-days-shook-region-inside-iran-israel-war

Meinecke, F. (1984). *Machiavellism: The doctrine of raison d'état and its place in modern history* (Scott, D., Trans.). Westview. (Original work published 1924)

Miller, P. D. (2025, July 28). *The era of Israeli hegemony?* Law & Liberty. https://lawliberty.org/the-era-of-israeli-hegemony/

Morgenthau, H. J. (1948). *Politics among nations: The struggle for power and peace.* Alfred A. Knopf.

Morgenthau, H. J. (n.d.). *Scientific man.* (Source provides title only; publication details needed for full reference.)

Murphy, F. (2025, June 25). *UN nuclear chief says it's possible Iran's highly enriched uranium 'is there'.* Reuters. https://www.reuters.com/world/europe/iaea-chief-returning-iranian-sites-is-top-priority-2025-06-25/

Newdick, T. (2025, June 20). *Iranian Ballistic Missiles Hit "Strategic Points" In Israeli Port City Of Haifa (Updated).* The War Zone. https://www.twz.com/news-features/iranian-ballistic-missiles-hit-strategic-points-in-israeli-port-city-of-haifa

Niebuhr, R. (1932). *Moral man and immoral society.* Scribner's.

Northam, J., & Hider, J. (2025, June 12). *Trump warns a strike on Iran "could very well happen" if no nuclear deal is signed.* NPR. https://www.npr.org/2025/06/12/nx-s1-5431758/trump-iran-strike-nuclear

Rabinovich, I. (2024, Spring). *Iran's quest for regional hegemony.* Horizons, (26). Center for International Relations and Sustainable Development (CIRSD). https://www.cirsd.org/en/horizons/horizons-spring-2024--issue-no-26/irans-quest-for-regional-hegemony

Raine, J. (2025, July 23). *How 12 days have changed Iran. International Institute for Strategic Studies.* https://www.iiss.org/online-analysis/online-analysis/2025/07/how-12-days-have-changed-iran/

Sariolghalam, M. (2018, February 20). *Prospects for change in Iranian foreign policy. Carnegie Endowment for International Peace.* https://carnegieendowment.org/research/2018/02/prospects-for-change-in-iranian-foreign-policy?lang=en

Smith, B. (2018, May 10). *Iran nuclear deal: What next?* UK Parliament, House of Commons Library. https://commonslibrary.parliament.uk/iran-nuclear-deal-what-next/

Smith, M. J. (1986). *Realist thought from Weber to Kissinger.* Louisiana State University Press.

Snyder, J. (1991). *Myths of Empire: Domestic Politics and International Ambition.* Ithaca, NY: Cornell University Press. cited in Mearsheimer, J. J. (2001). *The tragedy of great power politics.* W. W. Norton & Company.

Sokol, S. (2025, June 18). *Mayors demand government take quick action to compensate victims of Iranian strikes.* The Times of Israel. https://www.timesofisrael.com/mayors-demand-government-take-quick-action-to-compensate-victims-of-iranian-strikes/

TABNAK. (2025, February 4). Iranian Army kicks off main phase of 'Eqtedar 1403' air defense drill in south western areas. https://www.tabnak.ir/en/news/5932/iranian-army-kicks-off-main-phase-of-%E2%80%98eqtedar-1403%E2%80%99-air-defense-drill-in-south-western-areas

The White House. (2015, July 14). *Key excerpts of the Joint Comprehensive Plan of Action (JCPOA).* https://obamawhitehouse.archives.gov/the-press-office/2015/07/14/key-excerpts-joint-comprehensive-plan-action-jcpoa. Bedenko, V., Hesse, V., & Shin, J. (2022, December 12). *Learning from the JCPOA experience: Restarting dialogue aimed at crisis resolution.* Open Nuclear Network. https://platform.opennuclear.org/thoughtroom/research-reports/learning-from-the-jcpoa-experience-restarting-dialogue-aimed-at-crisis-resolution

Tirpak, J. A. (2025, June 14). *Israel launched an attack with 200 fighters. Could the US?* Air & Space Forces Magazine. https://www.airandspaceforces.com/u-s-air-force-would-be-challenged-to-match-israeli-strike-given-readiness-slide/

Trevithick, J. (2025, July 25). *150 THAAD ballistic missile interceptors fired by U.S. during Iran's barrages on Israel: Report*. The War Zone. https://www.twz.com/land/150-thaad-ballistic-missile-interceptors-fired-by-u-s-during-irans-barrages-on-israel-report

Trump, D. J. (2018, May 8). *President Donald J. Trump is ending United States participation in an unacceptable Iran deal*. Trump White House Archives. https://trumpwhitehouse.archives.gov/briefings-statements/president-donald-j-trump-ending-united-states-participation-unacceptable-iran-deal/

U.S. Embassy Paris. (1974, June 24). *Interview with Shah (Cable 15305)*. U.S. Department of State. https://nsarchive2.gwu.edu/nukevault/ebb268/doc01a.pdf

Waltz, K. N. (1993). *Origins of War in Neorealist Theory*. In R. L. Rothstein (Ed.), *The Evolution of Theory in International Relations* (pp. 39–52). Columbia: University of South Carolina Press. cited in Mearsheimer, J. J. (2001). *The tragedy of great power politics*. W. W. Norton & Company.

Youvan, D. C. (2024). *Amimut (Ambiguity): The Strategic Use of Uncertainty in Diplomacy and International Relations*. DOI:DOI: 10.13140/RG.2.2.16161.01127

Zeidan, A. (2025, June 23). *Axis of Resistance*. Encyclopædia Britannica. https://www.britannica.com/topic/Axis-of-Resistance

Zurcher, A. (2025, June 24). *With possible Iran-Israel ceasefire, Trump's high-risk strikes may pay off*. BBC News. https://www.bbc.com/news/articles/cdr3yxgjd6ro

Chapter 19
Language, Identity, and Geopolitics: Multilingual Education in Kazakhstan

Suat Beylur
https://orcid.org/0000-0002-1508-8477
Eurasian Research Institute, Khoja Akhmet Yassawi International Kazakh-Turkish University, Kazakhstan

ABSTRACT

Kazakhstan, like many other post-Soviet states, possesses a multicultural and multilingual social structure. Its long shared border with Russia and the relatively large proportion of Russian-speaking ethnic communities within its population distinguish it from other countries in the region. The status of the Kazakh language, which had been disadvantaged prior to independence, has significantly improved through language policies implemented since 1991. With the adoption of the Trilingual Education initiative in 2007, the state aimed to integrate Kazakh, Russian, and English into the national education system. However, experience and findings accumulated over time indicate that the initiative has not fully achieved its intended objectives. Adopting an interdisciplinary approach, this chapter analyzes Kazakhstan's current language policy and its implications for identity formation and geopolitics, offering a theoretical framework for understanding multilingual education in post-Soviet contexts alongside practical recommendations for policymakers.

DOI: 10.4018/979-8-3373-2342-8.ch019

INTRODUCTION

The Kazakhs emerged as a distinct political entity in the 15th century following the dissolution of the Golden Horde. For several centuries, they maintained control over a vast steppe territory. However, during the 18th century, continuous conflicts with regional powers, particularly the Dzungars, weakened the Kazakh state. This decline eventually compelled the Kazakh leadership to seek Russian protection, initiating a gradual process of political dependence. By the mid-19th century, through a combination of military campaigns and diplomatic strategies, all three Kazakh jüz (hordes) were fully incorporated into the Russian Empire (Akimbekov, 2023).

Unlike the more urbanized khanates of southern Central Asia, Kazakhstan's vast open steppes made it a prime location for large-scale settler colonization. Russian authorities encouraged agricultural migration and established military outposts across the region, which dramatically transformed the sociopolitical landscape (Dave, 2007). These policies laid the foundation for Russification, a systematic effort to assimilate the local population into the imperial structure.

Russification relied not only on political and military control but also on cultural and linguistic assimilation. Russian-language schools were established, and participation in public administration increasingly required fluency in Russian (Kudaibergenova, 2019). This linguistic hierarchy positioned Russian as the language of prestige and power while gradually marginalizing Kazakh from formal education and governance. These colonial legacies continue to shape Kazakhstan's contemporary language policies, influencing both nation-building strategies and the challenges of balancing Kazakh revival with the enduring role of Russian.

In this context, language functioned as a key instrument of power: although early Russian administrators initially allowed the use of local languages in judicial and religious affairs, their long-term objective was to gradually reduce their public role. In Kazakhstan, this process unfolded slowly but profoundly, as Russian increasingly replaced Kazakh in education and governance.

Despite these pressures, the early 20th century witnessed the emergence of a vibrant Kazakh intellectual movement inspired by Alash ideas, modernist, and anti-colonial currents. Figures like Ahmet Baitursynov, Alikhan Bokeikhanov, and Mirjaqip Dulatov advocated for educational reform, national revival, and linguistic empowerment through the Jadidist movement (Smagulova, 2006). Their efforts included modernizing Kazakh-language education, reforming the Arabic script, and creating vernacular print culture to promote national consciousness.

Following the Bolshevik Revolution of 1917, many of these intellectuals initially aligned with Soviet ideals, hoping for cultural autonomy and language rights. However, by the late 1920s and 1930s, Stalinist purges decimated the Kazakh intelligentsia, and policies shifted from korenizatsiya (indigenization) to intensified

Russification. During this period, Russian became the dominant language in higher education, science, and administration, while Kazakh was relegated to rural and informal domains (Fierman, 2006).

Under Soviet rule, language policy was tightly linked to ideological control. While official doctrine paid lip service to the equality of nations, the practical outcome was a linguistic hierarchy with Russian at the apex. This resulted in a gradual erosion of Kazakh usage in public life and a generational decline in fluency. By the 1980s, a significant portion of ethnic Kazakhs, especially in urban areas, were more proficient in Russian than in their native language (Dave, 2007).

As a result, the majority of the Kazakh intelligentsia received their education in Russian and produced their scholarly and literary works in the same language. Following independence, the first major policy initiative to redress this linguistic imbalance was undertaken in 1993, when Kazakh was declared the official state language. However, due to political sensitivities and resistance from the Russian-speaking population, the 1995 Constitution granted Russian the status of an official language as well. A subsequent legal amendment in 1997 mandated that all citizens must attain functional proficiency in Kazakh, the state language. By 2010, knowledge of Kazakh had become a formal requirement for employment in public institutions.

Currently, Kazakhstan promotes trilingual education model encompassing Kazakh, Russian, and English. Despite these efforts, Russian remains the dominant language of daily communication. In his 2011 State of the Nation address, President Nazarbayev announced the goal of raising the proportion of Kazakh-speaking citizens to 95%. As part of this vision, the "Kazakhstan 2050 Strategy" emphasized the adoption of the Latin alphabet as a key step in the modernization of the Kazakh language (Beylur, 2019). Efforts toward modernization also included large-scale terminology development and targeted programs to strengthen Kazakh in public life. Nevertheless, the language continues to be underutilized in education, academic publishing, and mass media. Russian-language television channels and entertainment programs, in particular, continue to attract a large audience nationwide (Burkhanov, 2017).

This chapter aims to examine Kazakhstan's language policies in the post-independence period through the lenses of nation-building and geopolitics. The preservation of the multilingual structure—shaped by historical developments and reinforced by post-independence policies—serves as a tool for social cohesion and communication. However, it simultaneously presents challenges to the full establishment of the Kazakh language as a comprehensive language of science and culture, particularly in the context of identity formation and nation-building.

Closely related to these internal dynamics is the role of language policy in Kazakhstan's foreign policy orientation. As a reflection of its multi-vector foreign policy, Kazakhstan promotes the development and dissemination of the Kazakh language domestically while continuing to use Russian extensively, given its enduring dominance in the region. On the other hand, in line with the importance Kazakhstan attaches to its relations with the West - particularly the European Union and the United States - it also places significant emphasis on the advancement of English within the educational system.

Drawing on national reports and policy documents, official statistics, academic research, and field research conducted in this area, this chapter adopts an interdisciplinary, critical, and comparative approach to analyzing Kazakhstan's multilingual education policies.

THEORETICAL BACKGROUND

Language is not only a tool of communication but also a foundational element of identity, belonging, and legitimacy. In post-imperial and post-colonial states such as Kazakhstan, language becomes a central arena in which nation-building strategies are negotiated. The post-Soviet experience has necessitated the reimagining of national identities, often through the elevation or institutionalization of titular languages as markers of sovereignty, authenticity, and cultural revival.

Will Kymlicka's theory of multicultural citizenship (1995, 2001) provides one of the most influential frameworks for examining language rights and minority inclusion. He argues that national minorities require differentiated rights—particularly in the domains of education, language, and culture—to ensure fair participation in society. In Kazakhstan, balancing Kazakh, Russian, and English within the education system can be interpreted as an attempt to harmonize nation-building with multicultural accommodation.

Anthony D. Smith's ethnosymbolist approach suggests that modern nations are rooted in pre-modern ethno-cultural ties and symbols (Smith, 2009). From this perspective, the revival of the Kazakh language following independence is not merely administrative but deeply symbolic, aimed at restoring continuity with the pre-Soviet cultural and linguistic heritage. Similarly, Bhikhu Parekh's (2006) views on multiculturalism emphasize the need to maintain diversity while fostering a shared civic identity.

Charles Taylor's notion of 'recognition' (1994) and Stuart Hall's (1996) theory of identity as positional and constructed through discourse also offer relevant insights. Taylor emphasizes that the denial of cultural recognition can inflict harm and marginalization, which is pertinent in the context of Kazakh language revitalization. For Hall, identity is shaped by history, language, and power—a dynamic that resonates strongly in Kazakhstan's trilingual education policies.

Erik Erikson's (1968) psychosocial theory underscores the developmental role of mother tongue education in forming stable identities. When young learners are educated in their native language, they not only perform better cognitively but also develop a secure cultural identity. This insight is vital in evaluating Kazakhstan's trilingual education model, which aims to balance functional proficiency in three languages with national identity formation.

The theoretical frameworks discussed above illuminate the complex interplay between language, identity, and power in post-Soviet Kazakhstan. Kymlicka's emphasis on differentiated minority rights, Smith's focus on symbolic continuity, Parekh's advocacy for multicultural cohesion, Taylor's theory of recognition, Hall's discourse-centered identity model, and Erikson's psychosocial insights collectively frame language not merely as an instrument of instruction, but as a deeply political and cultural medium. Together, these perspectives underscore that multilingual education in Kazakhstan is embedded in broader processes of post-colonial transformation, identity negotiation, and geopolitical alignment. Rather than being an isolated policy choice, the trilingual model reflects Kazakhstan's attempt to reconcile its Soviet past, ethno-cultural composition, and global aspirations—rendering language policy a critical site of both domestic identity-making and international signaling.

LANGUAGE POLICIES IN THE POST-SOVIET SPACE

The collapse of the Soviet Union in 1991 brought about significant transformations in the linguistic landscapes of the newly independent states. The Soviet legacy had left behind a complex multilingual environment where Russian was the dominant language of administration, education, and interethnic communication, while titular languages were marginalized, particularly in urban and elite spheres. In the post-Soviet period, each state undertook distinct language policies shaped by demographic factors, political priorities, and national identity discourses. This section explores the language policies of Russia, Uzbekistan, and Kyrgyzstan, analyzing their legal and institutional frameworks and the implications for nation-building, ethnic relations, and political stability.

Russia: Linguistic Unity or Cultural Hegemony?

Russia's post-Soviet language policy presents a complex interplay between constitutional guarantees of linguistic diversity and a political trajectory increasingly oriented toward centralization and Russification. Article 26(2) of the 1993 Russian Constitution affirms every citizen's right to use their native language in daily life, including in education. Furthermore, Article 68 allows republics within the Russian Federation to declare their own official languages alongside Russian. Initially, these provisions enabled ethnic republics such as Tatarstan and Bashkortostan to implement bilingual education and assert a degree of cultural autonomy (Council of Europe, 2021).

However, constitutional reforms introduced in 2020 redefined Russian as "the language of the state-forming people" and mandated its use across all levels of government, even in republics with their own state languages (RF Constitution, 2020). This shift was reinforced by legal amendments to the Education Law in 2018, which reclassified indigenous languages as optional while making Russian instruction mandatory at all pre-primary and primary schools (RF Education Law, 2022). The central government justified this change by citing a shortage of qualified teachers for minority languages, yet it was widely perceived as a blow to linguistic diversity (Jankiewicz et al., 2020).

Although federal laws such as the Law on the State Language and the Law on Languages of the Peoples of Russia formally recognize and protect linguistic plurality—including the development of non-written languages—actual implementation has been uneven. While 37 languages have official status in various federal entities, only 24 are used in education, and just 16 serve as the primary language of instruction in select schools (Council of Europe, 2021).

These developments reflect a gradual but consistent narrowing of linguistic space for non-Russian communities, despite Moscow's claims of supporting ethnocultural traditions. Russia's efforts to maintain Russian linguistic dominance—both within its borders and across the post-Soviet space—suggest a shift from federal multiculturalism toward a model of centralized linguistic hegemony (Carlson, 2015; Fierman, 2006; Topsakal, 2010).

Uzbekistan: The Pursuit of Cultural Realignment

Uzbekistan's post-independence language policy has centered on promoting Uzbek as a cornerstone of national identity and cultural sovereignty. The 1995 Law on the State Language, along with subsequent amendments, declared Uzbek—written in the Latin script—as the sole official language of the Republic. This legislation marked a definitive break from the Soviet-era legacy of Russian linguistic dominance and symbolized a broader effort to assert cultural autonomy. However, the implementation of Uzbek as the primary language in state institutions, education, and media has been gradual and uneven. In practice, Russian continues to play a significant role in urban administration, higher education, and commercial life (Zaborona, 2023).

Recent language reforms have signaled the government's renewed resolve to strengthen Uzbek language policy. A 2020 draft law proposed curbing the use of Russian in official settings, though it was later softened in response to public concern. Nevertheless, the initiative reflected a broader ideological shift toward linguistic indigenization. The ongoing campaign to complete the transition to the

Latin alphabet by 2023—originally launched in the 1990s—has also been promoted as a strategic effort to distance Uzbekistan from Russian cultural hegemony and foster deeper integration with the Turkic world (RFE/RL, 2020).

Despite these assertive policies, challenges remain. Russian-speaking minorities, especially in Tashkent and other metropolitan areas, express concerns over social exclusion and the diminishing role of Russian in public life. Critics argue that overly rigid language policies risk undermining social cohesion in a multiethnic society. While Uzbekistan's strategy aims to cultivate a unified civic identity through the elevation of Uzbek, the state must carefully balance cultural revival with inclusive governance. Thus, the evolving language policy landscape in Uzbekistan illustrates the tensions between nation-building, linguistic autonomy, and social pluralism.

Kyrgyzstan: Between Pragmatism and Identity

Kyrgyzstan's post-independence language policy reflects a pragmatic balancing act between the promotion of titular identity and the accommodation of linguistic diversity. The 1993 Constitution established Kyrgyz as the state language, while granting Russian the status of an official language—a recognition of the country's multiethnic composition and the widespread use of Russian, particularly in urban centers and northern regions (Carlson, 2015). This dual-language arrangement has remained largely intact, serving both symbolic and functional purposes.

Throughout the 1990s and early 2000s, Russian maintained a dominant position in higher education, administrative communication, and national media. While this linguistic landscape facilitated continuity in governance and interethnic interaction, it also raised questions regarding the visibility and institutionalization of Kyrgyz. In response to growing nationalist discourse, particularly in the aftermath of political upheavals in 2005 and 2010, there have been incremental efforts to strengthen the status of Kyrgyz. Notably, a 2023 law mandated the use of Kyrgyz in all official functions and required civil servants to demonstrate language proficiency (Caravanserai, 2023). This measure, although perceived by some as potentially exclusionary, was justified by proponents as a necessary step toward consolidating national sovereignty and cultural identity.

Unlike Uzbekistan, however, Kyrgyzstan has refrained from implementing radical linguistic reforms such as script changes or the marginalization of Russian. This cautious, adaptive approach has helped maintain social cohesion in a linguistically heterogeneous society. At the same time, it underscores the tension between symbolic nation-building and the practical considerations of multilingual governance. Language policy in Kyrgyzstan thus reveals an ongoing negotiation between ethnonational aspirations and the imperatives of inclusive statecraft in a post-Soviet context.

The post-Soviet space reveals divergent approaches to language policy. While Russia centralizes linguistic authority and limits minority language rights, Uzbekistan pursues a nationalizing strategy centered on the titular language and script reform. Kyrgyzstan, meanwhile, adopts a hybrid model that balances ethnic identity with practical multilingualism. From the perspective of identity politics, these policies reflect broader strategies of nation-building. In Russia, language functions as a tool for reasserting national unity under a centralized state ideology. In Uzbekistan, it is a marker of cultural independence and differentiation. In Kyrgyzstan, it is a gradual project of cultural reaffirmation conducted within a bilingual framework.

In terms of social cohesion, aggressive language policies may risk alienating ethnic minorities, especially where Russian still serves as a lingua franca. By contrast, more inclusive or gradual approaches appear more conducive to maintaining stability, though they may delay full linguistic indigenization. These cases also offer relevant contrasts and parallels for understanding Kazakhstan's trilingual education policy and its balancing act between identity formation, civic inclusiveness, and geopolitical alignment, which is further discussed in subsequent sections.

TRILINGUAL EDUCATION IN KAZAKHSTAN: POLICY AND PRACTICE

Kazakhstan's trilingual education model has developed in phases since independence in 1991, reflecting changing laws and priorities. During the early independence period (1991–2000), the government focused on elevating the Kazakh language's status while preserving Russian for interethnic harmony. The 1995 Constitution declared Kazakh the state language and Russian the official language for interethnic communication. The 1997 Law on Languages reinforced this framework: it mandated Kazakh for official use but guaranteed citizens' rights to use Russian and other minority languages.

In the 1990s, the government prioritized "Kazakhization" of public life, notably by expanding Kazakh- medium schools as part of post-Soviet nation-building. At independence, only about one-third of primary students were taught in Kazakh; by 2000, the share of Kazakh-medium schools had risen sharply. This shift was driven by both policy and demographic changes. The ethnic Kazakh population (the primary custodians of the Kazakh language) grew from 39.7% in 1989 to over 53% by 1999, increasing demand for Kazakh education. Meanwhile, Russian-medium education, though still widespread, began a gradual decline as many Russian-speaking families emigrated and the government promoted Kazakh as the language of state-building. By the late 1990s, Kazakhstan had effectively established a bilingual framework:

Kazakh was used for state functions, and Russian served as a lingua franca for its diverse population (Makhanov, 2023).

During the 2000s, Kazakhstan's leadership broadened its language-in-education policy from bilingualism to trilingualism. Then-president Nursultan Nazarbayev introduced the vision of a "Trinity of Languages" (Kazakh, Russian, English) as a cultural project to bolster the country's competitiveness and unity. He first hinted at this idea in a 2006 speech at the Assembly of the People of Kazakhstan. The concept was formally articulated in his 2007 annual address "New Kazakhstan in a New World," which proposed gradual implementation of trilingual education nationwide. In a 2008 address, Nazarbayev urged accelerating the initiative and improving Kazakh language teaching quality "as the state language that unites our entire society." The inclusion of English – the global lingua franca – alongside Kazakh and Russian was justified as critical for accessing scientific and economic opportunities in a globalized world.

By the end of the 2000s, policy discourse in Kazakhstan fully embraced the idea that young citizens should be fluent in all three languages: Kazakh for national identity, Russian for interethnic communication, and English for international integration. This vision aligned with the country's development strategy "Kazakhstan–2030/2050," which framed language skills as key to national progress. Notably, the push for trilingualism did not mean abandoning Russian; rather, it institutionalized a balance – elevating Kazakh's role without disenfranchising Russian speakers, and adding English to the mix for global connectivity (Armurzin et al., 2024).

By 2010, Kazakhstan had thus shifted from a bilingual education paradigm to an officially trilingual one, setting ambitious goals for language learning in the coming decade. Since 2011, the trilingual education policy has been codified through a series of state programs and legal measures. In 2011 the President issued Decree No. 110 approving the State Program for the Development and Functioning of Languages 2011–2020, which set concrete targets for trilingual proficiency. This program, overseen by the Ministry of Culture, aimed to ensure that by 2020 15% of Kazakhstan's population would speak all three languages. It also projected that 95% of citizens would know Kazakh by 2020 (a goal later extended to 2025) and that English proficiency would reach 20% of the population.

Parallel to the language-use program, the government launched education-specific roadmaps. The State Program of Education Development 2011–2020 (adopted in 2010) and its successor, the State Program of Education and Science Development 2016–2019, both included trilingual education as a strategic priority. In 2015, Kazakhstan's "100 Concrete Steps" National Plan reinforced these efforts: one of the steps explicitly called for the phased introduction of English as a medium of instruction in upper secondary schools (for science subjects) by 2019, while strengthening Kazakh in humanities and maintaining Russian instruction where appropriate (Lee, 2015).

To guide implementation, the Ministry of Education and Science (MoES) issued a detailed "Roadmap for the Development of Trilingual Education 2015–2020," which scheduled the rollout of trilingual curricula across all levels of education. By policy design, 2019–2020 was a milestone: high schools nationwide were to begin teaching subjects like chemistry, biology, physics, and ICT in English, Kazakh language and history in Kazakh, and continue offering Russian language and literature in Russian (Lee, 2015).

By the 2020s, Kazakhstan's language-in-education landscape had undergone a significant transformation: Kazakh had become the dominant language of instruction, English was introduced in primary education, and Russian-language schools, while still present, were steadily transitioning toward bilingual or trilingual formats (Makhanov, 2023). During the presidency of Kassym-Jomart Tokayev, a more nuanced shift in the implementation of trilingual education emerged. Departing from his predecessor's assertive promotion of English-medium STEM instruction, Tokayev advocated a sequential approach—prioritizing solid bilingual proficiency in Kazakh and Russian before introducing English, contingent upon student and teacher readiness (Karabassova, 2020).

Institutional Arrangements for Implementation

Implementing trilingual education on a national scale required significant institutional coordination. The lead agency MoES, responsible for curriculum standards, teacher training, and school administration, making it the primary driver of trilingual curriculum reform. Indeed, educational institutions have been explicitly identified as "the main organs responsible for the implementation of the 'Trinity of Languages' policy" (Klyshbekova, 2020). Within the MoES structure, key units include the National Curriculum Center and the National Testing Center, which have integrated trilingual goals (e.g. developing new subject standards and exam options in Kazakh, Russian, and English). The Ministry of Culture played a supporting role by overseeing broader language promotion programs (such as the 2011–2020 Languages Development Program) aimed at adult language learning and preserving minority languages. Other government bodies, like the Assembly of the People of Kazakhstan (an advisory council on interethnic relations), have also supported multilingual initiatives – for instance, through cultural programs and community language courses – to complement formal education efforts (Klyshbekova, 2020).

Specialized institutions and pilot programs have been crucial in translating policy into practice. Foremost among these are the Nazarbayev Intellectual Schools (NIS) – a network of elite public schools for grades 1–12 established in 2008 with a mandate to innovate and model new educational approaches. The NIS network was designed to adopt and test best global educational practices and translate them to the broader school system. They serve as laboratories for trilingual education: students learn in Kazakh, Russian, and English, and subjects like science are taught using Content and Language Integrated Learning (CLIL) methods (Shamshidinova, Ayubayeva, & Bridges, 2014).

NIS are funded and managed separately from regular public schools, allowing them to pioneer trilingual pedagogies that are later shared nationally. For example, NIS developed textbooks and teacher guides in English for math and science and demonstrated that students can master subject content in a foreign language given proper support. Their experience informed MoES's rollout of trilingual instruction through teacher training and curriculum dissemination (Makhanov, 2023).

Alongside NIS, the Daryn network of specialized schools for gifted children embraced trilingual education. By 2015, at least 33 Daryn schools were teaching in three languages and achieving notable results (Lee, 2015). In addition to these two exemplary cases, some internationally affiliated educational institutions have also successfully implemented trilingual instruction (Suleimenova & Akanova, 2023).

To support the trilingual initiative, the MoES, often in collaboration with NIS and international experts, created new standards. The National Academy of Education named after Y. Altynsarin contributed to syllabus design. Institutions like Orleu and the NIS Center of Excellence retrained thousands of teachers in bilingual methods and English proficiency. The government set a target of having 15% of (science, technology, engineering, mathematics) STEM teachers proficient in three languages by 2020. Universities such as Nazarbayev University became part of the ecosystem producing educators and conducting policy-relevant research (Makhanov, 2023).

In sum, Kazakhstan's approach has been highly institutionalized: a top-down policy steered by ministries and enriched by experimental schools, with structured feedback loops to expand successful practices. This robust institutional framework has been a key factor in sustaining the trilingual education reform over the past 15+ years.

The 2007 Trilingual Education Policy: Objectives, Implementation, and Consequences

The official launch of Kazakhstan's three-language education policy in 2007 by Nazarbayev marked a strategic turning point in the nation's language planning. At its core, the policy seeks to reconcile nation-building with globalization. Nazarbayev framed the initiative as essential for "the success of every Kazakhstani" and for enhancing the country's competitiveness. The objective was to cultivate a generation fluent in Kazakh, Russian, and English, thereby strengthening civic unity and enabling full participation in both regional and global spheres.

Each language was assigned a distinct role:

- Kazakh: as the state language, serving as the cornerstone of national identity and an integrative force uniting all ethnic groups.
- Russian: as the language of interethnic communication, retained due to Kazakhstan's sizable Russian-speaking population and Soviet legacy, helping to preserve social cohesion.
- English: as the language of science, technology, and global communication, facilitating Kazakhstan's integration into the global economy (Klyshbekova, 2020).

The policy rationale was that proficiency in three languages would connect Kazakhstanis to global knowledge flows while leveraging the country's Eurasian heritage to project a modern, globally connected identity (Nazarbayev, 2007, 2009, as cited in Baiturzhanova, 2015). It was framed as a "unity-through-diversity" strategy: multilingualism fostering mutual respect in a multiethnic society. Thus, the 2007 policy had two central goals:

- Enhance human capital by equipping students with Kazakh, Russian, and English skills.
- Reinforce civic unity and identity by elevating Kazakh without marginalizing other languages (Klyshbekova, 2020).

These objectives were integrated in national strategies such as Kazakhstan–2050, which set a goal for 95% of the population to speak Kazakh by 2025, alongside promoting English for global opportunities.

The trilingual policy has been rolled out incrementally over 15+ years through curricular reforms, pilot programs, and capacity-building. A key early step was introducing trilingual instruction in select schools. From 2007, NIS and other urban high schools taught science and math in English, history and social sciences in Kazakh, and retained Russian for other subjects, modeling the policy via Content and Language Integrated Learning (CLIL) (Lee, 2015).

After 2013, the Ministry of Education and Science (MoES) mandated in a standard curriculum that all secondary schools gradually offer instruction in three languages. Primary schools focused on Kazakh and Russian, introducing English by Grade 3 (or even Grade 1). Middle schools taught all three languages as subjects. High schools were to teach core subjects in English, while maintaining Kazakh in humanities and Russian in select disciplines. By 2019, 153 pilot schools beyond NIS were teaching at least one subject in English (Karabassova, 2020).

Preschools were also integrated: by 2018, many kindergartens introduced Kazakh, Russian, and English in play-based formats. New textbooks and resources supported this shift: trilingual glossaries, English-language science texts with

Kazakh/Russian support, and Kazakh-language materials for subjects previously taught only in Russian.

The biggest hurdle—teacher readiness—was met with intensive professional development. Thousands of teachers completed English and CLIL training. The Bolashak scholarship program sent educators abroad to develop language and subject-teaching skills. The goal was a workforce capable of delivering content in Kazakh, Russian, or English. By 2020, 35% of high school STEM teachers had attained at least B2-level English (Karabassova, 2020). Higher education also adapted: many universities opened English-medium programs and required graduate students to master English. Some required doctoral theses in Kazakh or English. These measures slowly shifted Kazakhstan's academic language culture.

Implementation outcomes reflect the policy's goals. One success is strengthened civic unity in a multiethnic state. By retaining Russian and adding English, the policy avoided marginalizing minorities. Russian-language schools remain available (over 1,000), and the state supports minority-language schools (e.g., Uzbek, Uyghur, Tajik), preserving diversity (Suleimenova & Akanova, 2023). Surveys show strong public support for the trilingualism concept, perceived as a national asset (Smagulova, 2020). Nazarbayev called it a "collective identity that transcends ethnic boundaries."

Human capital has also improved. English is now widely taught from early grades, and younger Kazakhstanis are far more proficient than Soviet-era cohorts. More students study abroad, supported by growing access to English-medium programs like Nazarbayev University or Kazakh-British Technical University. The policy spurred curricular innovation. New methods (e.g., CLIL) were adopted. NIS students, taught in all three languages, excelled in Olympiads and gained admission to top global universities, validating the trilingual, inquiry-based curriculum (Shamshidinova et al., 2014).

The role of the Kazakh language has increased significantly. Demand for Kazakh-medium education has surged, even among ethnic Kazakhs in cities who previously preferred Russian-language schools. This shift reinforces Kazakh as the core of national identity; it was emphasized as a *"main factor of unity."* As a result, today's younger generation is far more fluent in Kazakh than previous cohorts.

Meanwhile, Russian remains strong: most graduates are still bilingual and continue to access its vast scientific and cultural corpus. Together with Kazakh and English, this is creating an emerging trilingual generation. Scholars argue that these trends enhance Kazakhstan's regional cooperation and global positioning (Smagulova, 2018).

National test data affirms these trends. In 2014, 70% of graduates took the Unified National Test (UNT) in Kazakh; by 2024, it was 75%, with 25% in Russian and 0.2% in English. Census data shows 94.5% of citizens report Russian proficiency, 82.3% Kazakh, and 16–18% English (Suleimenova & Akanova, 2023).

In summary, the 2007 policy's phased implementation and institutional support have delivered measurable gains in language proficiency, national unity, and educational innovation. Kazakhstan's trilingual model stands as a rare example of inclusive multilingual nation-building in the post-Soviet space.

Challenges and Shortcomings

Despite these advances, the trilingual education policy has faced significant challenges during implementation. A major difficulty was rolling out multiple large-scale reforms simultaneously - including a comprehensive curriculum overhaul and new assessment systems in the mid-2010s - which placed tremendous pressure on schools and teachers. Many educators felt overwhelmed by the rapid pace of change (Kurmangaliyeva & Zhidebekkyzy, 2016).

One critical challenge has been the shortage of teachers qualified to teach content in English. Although the policy mandated English-medium instruction for STEM subjects, many teachers - especially outside elite institutions like the NIS - lacked sufficient proficiency (Nazarbayev University, 2023; ETS Global, 2023). As a result, some schools resorted to superficial compliance strategies, such as teaching only key terminology in English while explaining concepts in Kazakh or Russian. However, this hybrid approach often compromised both subject mastery and language learning, producing students with weak skills across all three languages (Smagulova, 2020).

The gap between elite and mainstream schools further exacerbated these issues. While NIS and urban institutions possessed the financial and human resources to implement the trilingual model, rural and underfunded schools struggled. This inequality led the government to postpone the full STEM-English transition in non-elite schools after 2019 (Dosmagambetova, 2019). The disparity continues to threaten the inclusivity and equity of the policy's long-term goals.

Another pedagogical concern has been the monoglossic approach embedded in earlier iterations of the policy, which treated each language as functionally isolated. Research by Mehisto et al. (2014) showed that such separation undermined effective learning by ignoring translanguaging strategies commonly used by teachers. While recent policy revisions have started to promote bilingual methods (Karabassova, 2021), implementation remains uneven.

Beyond pedagogical matters, the multilingual education policy has also raised broader societal sensitivities. Some Kazakh language advocates worry that the dominant role of English and Russian in academic domains risks marginalizing Kazakh, particularly in science and higher education (Suleimenova, 2019). Concurrently, some ethnic minorities have expressed concern over Kazakh language proficiency requirements for public service and education, highlighting the challenge of balancing national integration with minority rights. Perhaps most importantly, there is growing concern that students are acquiring second and third languages without first achieving academic fluency in Kazakh, the titular language. Linguists argue that this sequencing may hinder cognitive development and later academic performance, especially in knowledge production and conceptual learning (Cummins, 2000; Heugh, 2011; Smagulova, 2020).

At independence, Kazakh was not yet fully institutionalized in formal education due to the prior dominance of Russian. Many children, particularly in urban or bilingual households, entered school with limited Kazakh proficiency (Smagulova, 2006). The post-2007 trilingual policy—while ambitious—added further complexity, especially for rural and minority students with less access to linguistic resources (Aidarbekova, 2015; Armurzin et al., 2024). A major risk has been "premature language layering," where English is introduced as a medium of instruction before foundational fluency in Kazakh or Russian has been achieved. This has led to reduced content comprehension and diminished student confidence in both subject matter and language (Karabassova, 2020).

These issues challenge Kazakhstan's nation-building goal of a unified Kazakhstani identity anchored in the state language. Scholars such as Suleimenova (2019) and Smagulova (2020) caution that without strong early literacy in Kazakh, Russian and English may remain dominant in academic and scientific domains. This could undermine the cultural status of Kazakh and efforts to develop original knowledge in the national language.

To mitigate these issues, experts have called for a phased and differentiated model of multilingual education. In such a model, students would begin their schooling primarily in Kazakh, with Russian and English gradually introduced through subject-based or immersion approaches at later stages. This aligns with the mother tongue-based multilingual education (MTB-MLE) framework endorsed by UNESCO (2016), which has been shown to improve cognitive outcomes and language retention when supported by adequate teacher training and curricular materials.

However, successful implementation of such a model in Kazakhstan is hindered by persistent structural inequalities. Elite urban schools are far better positioned to support trilingual instruction than under-resourced rural institutions. If these disparities are not addressed, they may entrench linguistic and educational stratification - with only a small subset of students becoming truly trilingual, while others fall behind in both content and language competence (Armurzin et al., 2024; Lee, 2015).

Consequences for National Identity and Scientific Development

The strengths and challenges discussed reveal how Kazakhstan's trilingual education policy, while fostering unity, also introduces tensions in identity-building and scientific advancement. On one hand, the policy undeniably contributes to civic unity. It projects an inclusive national identity – often phrased as the "Kazakhstani identity" – in which every citizen, regardless of ethnicity, is expected to share in the state language (Kazakh) but also values Russian and English. This has symbolic power: multilingualism is cast as a cornerstone of Kazakhstan's modern nationhood (Royal Thai Embassy, 2024). The fact that schoolchildren learn the state language together (even if some speak Russian at home) helps inculcate a sense of belonging to a common civic space. Additionally, the policy's respect for Russian mitigated what could have been a source of ethnic tension; instead, language has become a less divisive issue in Kazakhstan compared to some other post-Soviet states.

On the other hand, the dilemmas are evident. In terms of national identity, there is an ongoing debate: should Kazakhstan eventually gravitate toward Kazakh dominance in all spheres (with Russian and English as mere supplements), or continue a balanced trilingualism indefinitely? The trilingual policy, as it stands, somewhat postpones this choice by keeping all three at play, but as decolonization discourse gains strength domestically, pressures mount to further "Kazakhize" higher education and science (Eurasian Research Institute, 2024).

Some intellectuals argue that young children should be educated primarily in Kazakh in the early years to solidify their national identity, only learning Russian and English later. They fear early exposure to the other languages could dilute Kazakh proficiency. Others counter that early multilingual education is beneficial and that Kazakhstan's identity is inherently multicultural and multilingual. This philosophical split underscores the policy's balancing act: celebrating multilingualism while ensuring Kazakh's primacy.

Regarding science and development, the introduction of English is a double-edged sword. In principle, teaching science in English connects students to global scientific literature and facilitates international collaboration. Indeed, English-medium programs at institutions like Nazarbayev University have enabled local researchers to publish more widely and engage in international projects. However, the transition also poses a risk of short-term learning losses in science and math, as students and teachers adjust to new languages of instruction. If not managed carefully, this could hamper deep understanding of STEM subjects across a cohort.

The government's cautious approach — delaying the full English-medium switch until teachers are ready — reflects awareness that scientific proficiency should not be sacrificed for language goals. There is also the question of knowledge production in Kazakh: much high-level instruction and research still occurs in Russian or English. If Kazakh is to become a language of science (part of national development goals), significant effort is needed to expand its scientific vocabulary and produce quality textbooks and research in Kazakh. The trilingual policy alone does not guarantee this shift; it could even reinforce English and Russian linguistic dominance in science unless deliberate measures are taken. Authorities have started addressing the gap by commissioning Kazakh translations of university textbooks and planning for more Kazakh-medium study tracks in technical universities (Ministry of Science and Higher Education, 2023).

The long-term consequences of the trilingual policy will depend on how these identity and science issues are navigated. Will Kazakhstan successfully produce a truly trilingual elite that strengthens the state language and drives scientific innovation? Or will divisions emerge — for example, between English-educated urban elites and Kazakh-educated rural populations? So far, evidence suggests cautious optimism. Public opinion remains generally favorable to multilingual education, and incremental gains are evident in all three languages among youth. The policy has become a defining feature of Kazakhstan's education system and is often cited internationally as a unique model of trilingual nation-building. As one analysis noted, implementing trilingual education has been *"highly controversial"* at times, yet it is a *"strategically significant phenomenon"* for Kazakhstan. In conclusion, since 2007 Kazakhstan's trilingual education policy has played a critical role in forging a cohesive national identity in a multilingual society and in preparing new generations for a globalized, knowledge-based economy. It stands as an ambitious social project that has achieved considerable success in expanding Kazakh language use and multilingual competence, even as it continues to grapple with practical challenges and the delicate balance between unity and diversity, tradition and modernity (Eurasian Research Institute, 2024).

LANGUAGE AND FOREIGN POLICY: REFLECTION OF MULTIVECTOR FOREIGN POLICY

Since gaining independence in 1991, Kazakhstan has pursued a "multivector" foreign policy designed to balance relations with all major powers rather than align exclusively with any single bloc (Republic of Kazakhstan, 2020; Yuneman, 2023). This approach ensures national security and economic development by engaging immediate neighbors like Russia and China, as well as Western countries and the broader Islamic and Turkic worlds.

It also allows Kazakhstan to avoid falling under any one country's hegemony, maintaining flexibility and sovereignty amid competing regional influences. The official doctrine defines multivectorism as "a diplomatic strategy based on building relations with the international community in general, and with neighboring states in particular, on a pragmatic and balanced basis," emphasizing pragmatic partnerships across the geopolitical spectrum (Republic of Kazakhstan, 2020). Over the past three decades, this strategy has established Kazakhstan as a bridge between East and West, exemplified by its membership in Russian-led alliances (like the

Eurasian Economic Union and Collective Security Treaty Organization) alongside deepening ties with Western institutions (such as hosting the OSCE Summit in 2010 and signing the Enhanced Partnership and Cooperation Agreement with the European Union in 2020; European Commission, 2020).

Kazakhstan's strategic geography and multiethnic composition necessitate this inclusive diplomacy. By engaging all major powers, Kazakhstan avoids the orbit of any single great power and instead navigates a middle path that leverages the strengths of various partners while guarding its independence. Its domestic language policy actively supports this multivector stance: the promotion of Kazakh, retention of Russian, and adoption of English all mirror a deliberate effort to engage multiple global centers of power.

Kazakhstan–Russia Relations and Language Policy

Kazakhstan's relationship with Russia is arguably the most complex and deeply entwined component of its multivector policy. Linguistically, Russian holds a powerful position: over 83% of Kazakhstan's population is proficient in Russian (Agency for Strategic Planning and Reforms, 2023), and the language retains constitutional status as an official language for interethnic communication. This reality serves as a cultural bridge to Russia and facilitates Kazakhstan's participation in Moscow-led initiatives. Russian remains the dominant language of urban business, media, and higher education in Kazakhstan, reflecting Russia's historical influence and ongoing soft power. Indeed, the Russian language itself serves as a significant soft power tool in Central Asia, embodying Russia's historical, cultural, and political hegemony in the region (Gafarli, 2020). Shared Russian-language media and educational content contribute to a common information space: for example, surveys indicate that two-thirds of Kazakhstan's residents still read Russian-language press at least occasionally, ensuring that Russian perspectives retain substantial sway in Kazakhstani public opinion (Beishalieva, 2024).

In this way, Moscow continues to wield outsized cultural influence, using language and media to project its worldview and maintain its dominance in what it considers its "near abroad." As one observer noted, Russia remains the most dominant external power in Central Asia and actively leverages soft power to protect its economic, political, and military interests (Gafarli, 2020).

At the same time, Kazakhstan carefully manages its linguistic sovereignty to assert national identity without alienating Russia. The government has consistently affirmed the importance of the Russian language for social cohesion and regional integration, and it collaborates with Russia on educational initiatives and cultural exchanges. Yet, Kazakhstan has also taken symbolic steps to dilute the legacy of Russian linguistic domination. One landmark move is the planned transition from Cyrillic to a Latin-based Kazakh alphabet by 2031, a reform then-President Nazarbayev announced in 2017 as part of Kazakhstan's modernization and a "course toward the future." This shift carries geopolitical overtones: it aligns Kazakhstan more closely with the Turkic world and global norms, while creating subtle distance from Russia's Cyrillic-centric orbit. Notably, the announcement of the Latin script transition was met with unease in Moscow, which perceived it as a potential threat to its influence in the region (Gafarli, 2020).

Russian commentators saw the alphabet change as Kazakhstan stepping out from under Russia's cultural umbrella – a clear example of how even orthographic choices can become geopolitical statements. Kazakhstani officials, however, framed the reform as a natural progression for a society looking to integrate with the global economy and digital world (where Latin scripts dominate), and they reassured that Russian's status within Kazakhstan would remain unchanged. Then-President Nazarbayev underscored that the role of Kazakh is increasing and that all citizens, especially youth, must know the state language to fully participate in national life, even as Russian continues as a key language of daily use. This dual messaging reflects Kazakhstan's balancing act: asserting its cultural autonomy (and thus statehood) through Kazakh, without provoking Russia by marginalizing the Russian language.

In practice, Kazakhstan has maintained Russian-medium schools and media alongside aggressive Kazakh language revitalization, seeking a bilingual equilibrium. The result is a nuanced form of linguistic dual allegiance – using Russian to uphold strategic partnership and internal stability, while promoting Kazakh to solidify sovereignty and identity. This careful management of language vis-à-vis Russia exemplifies how Kazakhstan negotiates the power dynamics of a former metropole and its post-colonial state: language policy becomes a barometer of geopolitical orientation, signaling both deference to Russian influence and the limits of that influence in a proudly independent Kazakhstan.

Relations with the Turkic World

Kazakhstan's engagement with the Turkic world forms another pillar of its multivector foreign policy, intertwining language policy with geopolitics and cultural realignment. As a Turkic-speaking nation, Kazakhstan shares deep linguistic, historical, and religious ties with countries like Türkiye, Azerbaijan, Kyrgystan, Uzbekistan, Turkmenistan, and others across Eurasia.

Then-President Nazarbayev often emphasized Kazakhstan's identity as part of the broader Turkic and Islamic civilization, alongside its post-Soviet and modern state identity. Since the establishment of the Organization of Turkic States (OTS) in 2009 (formerly the Turkic Council), Kazakhstan has actively promoted Turkic cooperation. Language is central to this effort: initiatives such as the creation of a

Common Turkic Alphabet and increased cultural exchanges underscore a vision of Turkic unity transcending Soviet-era divisions (Abuova, 2024). In September 2024, the OTS announced a 34-letter Latin-based common alphabet to foster linguistic unity among Turkic nations—a historic step aimed at easing communication and strengthening cultural bonds (Turkic Academy, 2024). Kazakhstan's own shift to a Latin script dovetails with this regional trend. By aligning Kazakh orthography with that of other Turkic languages, Kazakhstan not only preserves its linguistic heritage but also symbolically pivots away from the Russian sphere of influence in favor of Turkic integration (Turkic Academy, 2024).

Relations with Türkiye have been particularly influential. Türkiye is often described in Kazakhstan as a "brotherly nation" – a recognition of common Turkic roots and a shared aspiration for regional leadership. The two countries have enhanced cooperation in education (e.g., Khoja Akhmet Yassawy International Kazakh-Turkish Univeristy (Turkistan), Yunus Emre Cultural Centre (Astana), and other institutions in which Turkish is thought), trade, and even military training. The alignment of language policies – such as Kazakhstan's Latinization mirroring Türkiye's earlier script reforms – strengthens this partnership and bolsters Kazakhstan's role in the Turkic-Islamic world. It allows Kazakhstan to project a multi-civilizational identity: not only a close partner of Russia and China, but also an integral member of the Turkic world with its own civilizational clout. Embracing a Turkic linguistic kinship provides an alternative source of soft power for Kazakhstan that balances against Russian cultural hegemony.

For instance, joint cultural projects (like Turkic history textbooks and language programs) and high-level forums (such as the regular OTS summits) showcase a shared heritage and future. By championing Turkic unity, Kazakhstan helps create a multipolar cultural landscape in Central Asia—one where Russia's influence is counter-weighted by a resurgent Turkic identity and cooperation. This does not mean Kazakhstan seeks to replace Russian ties with Turkic ones, but rather to diversify its cultural diplomacy.

The Turkic-language media exchanges, student programs, and common heritage celebrations foster a sense of solidarity and collective strength among these nations, which can serve as a buffer to external hegemonic pressures. In short, Kazakhstan's linguistic pivot toward the Turkic world is both an embrace of its deeper roots and a strategic hedge: it elevates a regional identity that connects Central Asia internally, reducing sole dependence on Russian or Western narratives. This balanced cultivation of Turkic links exemplifies multivectorism in the cultural realm—enabling Kazakhstan to situate itself as a key player in a community of kindred nations, thereby enhancing its strategic autonomy.

Relations with the West and Role of English

Parallel to its Eurasian engagements, Kazakhstan has steadily built strong relations with the West, and here the English language becomes a critical conduit. The European Union is Kazakhstan's largest trading partner and a significant source of investment and technology. The entry into force of the EU-Kazakhstan Enhanced Partnership and Cooperation Agreement (EPCA) in March 2020 marked a milestone in broadening ties across nearly 30 sectors (European Commission, 2020). Culturally and educationally, Kazakhstan has opened itself to Western influence to modernize its economy and society. English, as the lingua franca of globalization, is central to this opening. Kazakhstan's "Trinity of Languages" policy explicitly includes English as a third pillar (alongside Kazakh and Russian) to equip younger generations for global competitiveness. This policy resulted in a nationwide push for English instruction in schools, scholarships like Bolashak enabling thousands of Kazakh students to study at Western universities, and the establishment of English-medium institutions at home (for example, Nazarbayev University). Mastery of English is seen as a gateway to the world's knowledge economy and an essential skill for engaging with multinational companies, international diplomacy, and global science.

In geopolitical terms, English represents Kazakhstan's link to the West and the U.S.-led international order. By promoting English, Kazakhstan signals its commitment to being a part of the global community and not just the post-Soviet sphere. This is not without its own power dynamics: one could argue that English-language dominance worldwide is a form of Western cultural hegemony, sometimes termed linguistic imperialism. Kazakhstani policymakers, however, approach English pragmatically as a neutral tool of modernization rather than an ideological threat. The emphasis is on using English to access cutting-edge science, diversify the economy, and amplify Kazakhstan's voice in international forums. At the societal level, Western cultural presence in Kazakhstan has grown via media, education exchanges, and tourism, but it remains carefully managed. Programs like Erasmus+, the presence of the British Council and Alliance Française, and American Corners reflect a controlled opening that enriches Kazakhstan's human capital. English proficiency among young Kazakhs has risen steadily (Beishalieva, 2024). This emerging trilingual generation – fluent in Kazakh, Russian, and English – is a cornerstone of Kazakhstan's nation-building vision: citizens who are rooted in their national culture, able to communicate across the post-Soviet region, and fully capable of engaging the wider world.

The government's language strategy thus mirrors its foreign policy triangulation. Culturally, just as Kazakhstan balances Russian and Chinese influence with Western partnerships, linguistically it balances Russian heritage with Kazakh revival and Western modernity through English. Each vector reinforces the others. For example,

English-speaking Kazakhstani diplomats and businesspeople can interface with European and American partners to attract investment and security cooperation, while Russian-speaking officials and citizens maintain close ties with Moscow and other CIS states. This multilingual agility increases Kazakhstan's value as a mediator and a hub (one practical outcome: Astana [Nur-Sultan] has hosted several high-profile international talks, from OSCE meetings to Syrian peace negotiations, bolstering its image as a neutral ground). Kazakhstan's embrace of English also subtly diversifies the cultural influences on its population, ensuring that no single external narrative – not even Russia's – can fully dominate the information space or educated discourse. In effect, proficiency in English provides Kazakhstan with another channel of knowledge and soft power, balancing the Russian-centric media sphere with global perspectives.

CONCLUSION

In Kazakhstan's post-Soviet journey, language policy has been a central pillar of nation-building and a reflection of its geopolitical balancing act. Kazakhstan has embraced a multilingual model – elevating Kazakh as the heart of civic identity while preserving Russian as a practical interethnic lingua franca and introducing English to link the country globally. This trinity of languages has been pursued both as a symbolic affirmation of independence and as a pragmatic strategy of international engagement.

This strategy is rooted in Kazakhstan's historical and theoretical context. After decades of Russification under imperial and Soviet rule, nearly all urban Kazakhs became more comfortable in Russian than in their native tongue. Independence in 1991 thus presented both an opportunity and a challenge: on one hand, elevating Kazakh was urgent to heal the cultural rupture of colonialism; on the other, drastic language purges could inflame ethnic tensions and isolate the country. The Kazakh government pursued a centrist and cautious language policy to avoid both extremes.

The comparative survey underscores how Kazakhstan's model differs from its neighbors. Unlike Uzbekistan's drive toward Uzbek-exclusive identity or Russia's recent reassertion of Russian-only policy, Kazakhstan has consciously chosen inclusion over exclusion. It has not discarded Russian even as it strengthens Kazakh – a pragmatic recognition that over 80% of citizens speak Russian (Smagulova, 2006). It also learned from Kyrgyzstan's caution: Russia was granted official status in Kyrgyzstan to avoid social polarization.

The implementation of trilingual education has produced both gains and strains. On the positive side, Kazakh usage has visibly expanded. In the 1990s, Kazakh-medium schooling was rare, but today a majority of students learn in Kazakh or in bilingual programs. The percentage of university entrants taking national exams in Kazakh has risen substantially. Proficiency data confirm the shift: roughly 80% of Kazakhs now speak Kazakh proficiently, up from far lower Soviet-era levels, and 35% claim to understand English (Committee on Statistics, 2021).

Crucially, social cohesion has been largely maintained. By accommodating Russian-speakers and minority communities (who still enjoy schools in Uzbek, Uyghur, or other languages), the trilingual framework has defused what might otherwise be an ethnic flashpoint. Many Kazakh citizens – including ethnic Kazakhs who had grown up speaking Russian – have embraced Kazakh as part of a shared Kazakhstanstani identity. As one analysis notes, language in Kazakhstan has become "a collective identity that transcends ethnic origin" (Smagulova, 2006).

However, there are ongoing challenges and tensions. The ambition of fully implementing trilingualism collided with resource realities. Many rural and ordinary schools struggled to find qualified English teachers. While elite schools and cities produced fully trilingual students, many others resorted to partial compliance (e.g. glossing terms in English but explaining in Russian). Disparities remain: a child in Almaty or at a Nazarbayev school can attain fluent English and Kazakh, while others lag.

Moreover, language policy in Kazakhstan is inseparable from identity debates. The trilingual model implicitly postpones a decision on whether Kazakhstan will ever truly favor one language above the others. Some Kazakh nationalists worry that Russian and English still occupy too much space, fearing Kazakh could remain second-tier in science and technology. Conversely, some minority groups worry about Kazakhization pressures and welcome the retention of Russian. These debates surfaced around specific issues, such as the Latinization of Kazakh, perceived by some as a step away from Russian.

Finally, this multilingualism dovetails with Kazakhstan's multivector foreign policy. By design, each language corresponds to a strategic vector. Russian preserves a bridge to Russia and the Eurasian bloc; Kazakh emphasizes Kazakhstan's sovereignty and Turkic-Islamic heritage; English connects with the West and global markets. This is not mere rhetoric. Kazakhstan remains active in Russian-led organizations (like the Eurasian Economic Union) in large part thanks to the shared language, while simultaneously courting English-speaking institutions like the World Bank and EU.

In conclusion, Kazakhstan's multilingual education policy has been a bold experiment with far-reaching impacts. On one hand, it has strengthened national unity by making Kazakh the glue of public life without excluding minorities, and it has expanded global engagement by imparting English skills. The broad gains – high rates of bilingual Kazakh/Russian proficiency, the emergence of trilingual elites, and positive public attitudes toward the policy – suggest that this model has largely succeeded in its twin goals.

Kazakhstan's journey illustrates that language policy in a multiethnic state is never a purely technical matter of curriculum, but a reflection of identity and power. The coming decade will likely show whether the balance Kazakhstan has struck endures: will it gradually crystallize into a truly trilingual society, or will one language emerge dominant as demographics shift? The answer will influence not only schoolyards, but the very character of Kazakhstan's nationhood and its place in the world. Thus, a careful recalibration of language policy – reinforcing Kazakh without marginalizing others – remains essential.

This study contributes theoretically by linking Kazakhstan's trilingual education model to Kymlicka's framework of multicultural citizenship and drawing on complementary perspectives from Smith and Taylor, demonstrating how language policies can function as tools of both inclusion and symbolic nation-building. Practically, the findings underscore the need for targeted teacher training and equitable resource distribution to ensure that trilingual education achieves its intended goals of social cohesion and global competitiveness.

REFERENCES

Abuova, N. (2024, September 23). Turkic States revive Latin-based alphabet to preserve linguistic heritage. *The Astana Times*. https://astanatimes.com/2024/09/turkic-states-revive-latin-based-alphabet-to-preserve-linguistic-heritage/

Aidarbekova, A. (2015). *Trilingual education in Kazakhstan: Problems and perspectives*. Ministry of Education and Science of the Republic of Kazakhstan.

Akimbekov, S. (2023, March 15). *The Kazakh Khanate and the Russian Empire*. Qalam. https://qalam.global/en/articles/the-kazakh-khanate-and-the-russian-empire-en

Armurzin, Y., Amanzhol, N., Toleubayeva, K., Baimukhanova, S., & Karimov, R. (2024). Challenging aspects of Kazakhstan's trilingual education policy: Evidence from a literature review. *Asia Pacific Education Review*, *25*, 801–811. DOI: 10.1007/s12564-023-09823-7

Beishalieva, C. (2024, July 16). Echoes of empire: The resilience of Russian in Central Asia. *Eurac Research – Mobile People & Diverse Societies Blog*. https://www.eurac.edu/en/blogs/mobile-people-and-diverse-societies/echoes-of-empire-the-resilience-of-russian-in-central-asia

Beylur, S. (2019). Sosyal değişim sürecinde Kazakistan'da din-devlet ilişkileri (Üniversite öğrencileri örneği) [Doctoral dissertation, Ankara Yıldırım Beyazıt Üniversity]. YÖK Ulusal Tez Merkezi.

Bridges, D. (Ed.). (2014). *Educational reform and internationalisation: The case of school reform in Kazakhstan*. Cambridge University Press.

Burkhanov, A. (2017). Kazakhstan's national identity building policy: Soviet legacy, state efforts, and societal reactions. *Cornell International Law Journal*, *50*(1), 1–17.

Carlson, C. F. (2015). Nation-building in Central Asia through language legislation. *Manas Journal of Social Studies*, *4*(4), 22–30.

Cummins, J. (2000). *Language, power and pedagogy: Bilingual children in the crossfire*. Multilingual Matters.

Dave, B. (2007). *Kazakhstan: Ethnicity, language and power.* Routledge. DOI: 10.4324/9780203014899

Dosmagambetova, S. (2019). Reforming STEM education in Kazakhstan: The implications of trilingual policy. *Journal of Language and Education*, *5*(4), 45–52. DOI: 10.17323/jle.2019.9342

Erikson, E. H. (1968). *Identity: Youth and crisis*. W. W. Norton & Company.

European Commission. (2020, February 28). Entry into force of the EU-Kazakhstan Enhanced Partnership and Cooperation Agreement on 1 March [Press release]. https://eeas.europa.eu/delegations/kazakhstan/75956/

Fierman, W. (2006). Language and education in post-Soviet Kazakhstan: Kazakh-medium instruction in urban schools. *The Russian Review*, *65*(1), 98–116. DOI: 10.1111/j.1467-9434.2005.00388.x

Gafarli, T. (2020, July 6). Is Russian cultural hegemony in Central Asia finally over? *Politics Today*. https://politicstoday.org/is-russian-cultural-hegemony-in-central-asia-finally-over/

Global, E. T. S. (2023). *English proficiency report: Kazakhstan*. https://www.etsglobal.org/

Hall, S. (1996). Introduction: Who needs identity? In Hall, S., & du Gay, P. (Eds.), *Questions of cultural identity* (pp. 1–17). SAGE Publications.

Heugh, K. (2011). Theory and practice—Language education models in Africa: Research, design, decision-making, and outcomes. In Ouane, A., & Glanz, C. (Eds.), *Optimising learning, education and publishing in Africa: The language factor* (pp. 105–156). UNESCO.

Jankiewicz, S., Knyaginina, N., & Prina, F. (2020). Linguistic rights and education in the republics of the Russian Federation: Towards unity through uniformity. *Review of Central and East European Law*, *45*(1), 59–91. DOI: 10.1163/15730352-bja10003

Karabassova, L. (2021). Teachers' conceptualization of content and language integrated learning implementation: Insights from trilingual contexts in Kazakhstan. *Language Learning Journal*, *49*(5), 631–644.

Klyshbekova, M. (2020). *The trilingual education policy in Kazakhstan: Language choices for teaching-learning purposes in the classroom* [Master's thesis, Nazarbayev University, Graduate School of Education].

Kudaibergenova, D. T. (2019). *Toward nationalizing regimes: Conceptualizing power and identity in the post-Soviet realm*. University of Pittsburgh Press.

Kurmangaliyeva, G., & Zhidebekkyzy, A. (2016). Curriculum reform in Kazakhstan: Teachers' experiences and perspectives. *Procedia: Social and Behavioral Sciences*, *228*, 175–181.

Lee, D. (2015, October 13). Experts discuss challenges of introducing trilingual education system in schools. *The Astana Times*. https://astanatimes.com

Makhanov, K. (2023). The trends of language shift in education in Kazakhstan. *Eurasian Research Institute Bulletin, 8*(4), 1–4.

Mehisto, P. (2015). Kazakhstan: From 20 trilingual schools to thousands? In P. Mehisto & F. Genesee (Eds.), *Building bilingual education systems: Forces, mechanisms and counterweights* (pp. 109–130). Cambridge University Press.

Mehisto, P., Kambatyrova, A., & Nurseitova, K. (2014). Three in one? Trilingualism in policy and educational practice in Kazakhstan. In Bridges, D. (Ed.), *Educational reform and internationalisation: The case of school reform in Kazakhstan* (pp. 152–177). Cambridge University Press.

Nazarbayev, N. A. (2007, February 28). *New Kazakhstan in a new world.* Address to the people of Kazakhstan.

Nazarbayev, N. A. (2011, January 28). *Building the future together.* Address to the people of Kazakhstan.

Nazarbayev University. (2023). *Policy brief: English-medium instruction and teacher readiness in Kazakhstan.* Graduate School of Education.

Parekh, B. (2006). *Rethinking multiculturalism: Cultural diversity and political theory* (2nd ed.). Palgrave Macmillan. DOI: 10.1007/978-0-230-20425-6

Republic of Kazakhstan. (2020). *Foreign policy concept for 2020–2030.* Ministry of Foreign Affairs. https://www.akorda.kz/en/legal_acts/decrees/on-the-concept-of-the-foreign-policy-of-the-republic-of-kazakhstan-for-2020-2030

RFE/RL. (2020). Uzbekistan moves to quicken transition to Latin alphabet. *Radio Free Europe/Radio Liberty.* https://www.rferl.org/a/uzbekistan-latin-alphabet-transition/30473142.html

Smagulova, J. (2006). Kazakhstan: Language, identity and conflict. *Innovation (Abingdon), 19*(3–4), 303–320. DOI: 10.1080/13511610601029854

Smagulova, J. (2018). Language policy in Kazakhstan: Trilingual education for unity and modernization. *Language Problems and Language Planning, 42*(3), 230–250.

Smagulova, J. (2020). Trilingual education and social inequality in Kazakhstan: A critical sociolinguistic perspective. *Current Issues in Language Planning, 21*(5), 469–487. DOI: 10.1080/14664208.2020.1771037

Smith, A. D. (2009). *Ethno-symbolism and nationalism: A cultural approach.* Routledge. DOI: 10.4324/9780203876558

Suleimenova, E., & Akanova, A. (2023). Trilingual education in Kazakhstan: Current progress and future directions. *International Review of Education, 69*(1–2), 87–104.

Suleimenova, E. D. (2010). Language situation and language policy in Kazakhstan. In *Proceedings of the International Conference on Linguistic Rights and Language Policy* (pp. 35–42). Almaty, Kazakhstan: Kazakhstan Academy of Sciences.

Suleimenova, E. D. (2019). The sociolinguistic aspects of multilingual education in Kazakhstan: Between ideology and practice. *Eurasian Journal of Educational Research, 81*, 43–60. DOI: 10.14689/ejer.2019.81.3

Suleimenova, E. D., & Akanova, D. (2023). Russian language in the dominant communicative sphere of education in Kazakhstan. *Chinese Journal of Slavic Studies, 3*(1), 68–85.

Taylor, C. (1994). *Multiculturalism: Examining the politics of recognition*. Princeton University Press. DOI: 10.2307/j.ctt7snkj

Turkic Academy. (2024). *Common Turkic alphabet adopted in 2024*. https://turkicacademy.org/

UNESCO. (2016). If you don't understand, how can you learn? Policy paper 24, Global Education Monitoring Report. Paris, France: UNESCO.

Yuneman, R. A. (2023). Kazakhstan's multi-vector foreign policy: A case study of voting on UNGA resolutions. *Russia in Global Affairs, 21*(2), 141–162. DOI: 10.31278/1810-6374-2023-21-2-141-162

Zaborona. (2023). *How Central Asian countries are abandoning the Russian language*. https://zaborona.com/en/how-central-asian-countries-are-abandoning-the-russian-language/

Zubok, V. M. (2021). *Collapse: The fall of the Soviet Union*. Yale University Press., DOI: 10.2307/j.ctv1zvccnm

KEY TERMS AND DEFINITIONS

Bilingual Education: An educational approach in which two languages are used systematically for instruction and assessment, aiming to develop academic proficiency in both. In Kazakhstan and wider Central Asia, it often refers to the coordinated use of Kazakh (or another titular language) and Russian to balance nation-building with social cohesion.

Central Asia: Although there are different views regarding its designation and geographical scope, in this study, Central Asia refers to Kazakhstan, Kyrgyzstan, Tajikistan, Turkmenistan, and Uzbekistan. These countries, located at the center of Asia, share numerous common cultural values - particularly in terms of language and religion - arising from their deep and interconnected historical heritage.

Hegemony: A form of dominance in which power is maintained not only through coercion or law but also through cultural, linguistic, and ideological leadership that normalizes one group's preferences as "common sense." In language policy, hegemony appears when a prestige language structures access to knowledge, status, and institutions.

Identity Formation: The dynamic, lifelong process through which individuals and groups construct a sense of "who we are" by drawing on history, language, symbols, and power relations.

Kazakhstan: Kazakhstan is a Central Asian country bordered by Russia to the northwest and north, China to the east, Kyrgyzstan, Uzbekistan, and Turkmenistan to the south, with the Aral Sea along its southern boundary and the Caspian Sea to the southwest. As the largest state in Central Asia and the ninth largest in the world by land area, Kazakhstan has a diverse and multiethnic population shaped by centuries of migration, imperial legacies, and Soviet influence. Its sociocultural landscape is characterized by a multilingual environment where Kazakh, Russian, and increasingly English play vital roles in education, governance, and public life, reflecting the country's efforts to balance nation-building with interethnic harmony and global engagement.

Kazakh Language: A Kipchak Turkic language and the state language of Kazakhstan, central to symbolic sovereignty and cultural continuity.

Language Policy: The set of state and institutional decisions-laws, curricula, standards, and practices—that regulate language status, use, and acquisition in society.

Nation-Building: Intentional state-led processes that cultivate a shared civic identity, institutions, and symbols capable of binding diverse populations.

Trilingual Education: A structured model that develops proficiency and academic literacy in three languages assigned complementary functions-typically Kazakh (state/identity), Russian (interethnic/regional), and English (global/scientific).

About the Contributors

Merve Suna Ozel Ozcan is an Associate Professor of International Relations at Kirikkale University, Türkiye. She is also vice chair of the International Relations Department. She graduated from Gazi University with a double major in International Relations and History.She received her first Master's degree from Gazi University's Department of Political and Social Sciences, with a thesis on Russian nationalism.She completed her PhD in International Relations at Kırıkkale University. She later earned a second Master's degree in the Department of History at Kırıkkale University, specialising in Türkiye's stability diplomacy. Her research interests include Russian studies, great power politics, energy security, and international relations in Eurasia.Özcan is the author of the books Empires: Great Powers from Past to Present and Unlimited Power of Russia, and has edited several academic volumes, including Russia–Eurasia Relations: Actors, Issues and Challenges,Analysing Energy Crises and the Impact of Country Policies on the World.Her expert commentary on contemporary geopolitical developments is frequently featured in national and international media.

***

Mehmet Akar is a PhD candidate in European Studies at Dokuz Eylul University, specializing in international security, conflict resolution, and Middle Eastern geopolitics. He holds a Master's degree in Conflict Resolution and has over 30 years of professional experience in aviation. His research focuses on nuclear nonproliferation, great power competition, and regional security dynamics.

Andi Asrifan, S.Pd., M.Pd. is a senior lecturer in the Doctoral Program in English Language Education at the Graduate School of Universitas Negeri Makassar (UNM), Indonesia (unm.ac.id). With a Doctor of Education in English Language Education, he has demonstrated a consistent commitment to advancing research in

English as a Foreign Language (EFL), digital pedagogy, and the integration of artificial intelligence (AI) in language instruction. Dr. Asrifan previously served as Head of the Institute for Cooperation and International Affairs at Universitas Muhammadiyah Sidenreng Rappang and continues to collaborate across academic institutions, both nationally and internationally, actively. Over the past two years, Dr. Asrifan has led several research initiatives focused on AI-driven curriculum development, bilingual education in Southeast Asia, and digital parenting in urban Indonesia. He is frequently invited as a keynote speaker at international conferences and serves as a reviewer and editorial board member for various Scopus-indexed journals. His publications have appeared in high-impact outlets and span the disciplines of education, linguistics, and cultural studies.

Ejazul Haq Ateed is a PhD student in the Department of International Relations at Kirikkale University, Türkiye. He holds a master's degree in International Relations from Kirikkale University and a bachelor's degree from the International Islamic University, Islamabad, Pakistan. His research experience includes collaborations with the Center for Research and Security Studies (CRSS) and the International Institute for Global Strategic Analysis (IIGSA). He has also worked on projects funded by Bilimsel Araştırma Projeleri (Academic Research Projects, BAP) at Kirikkale University.

Aslan Azimzadeh, In 2015-2019, he received a bachelor's degree in World Economy at Azerbaijan State University of Economics (UNEC). In 2019-2021, he graduated with honors from Azerbaijan State University of Economics (UNEC) with a master's degree in "International Finance and Currency Credit Relations" majoring in "World Economy". He is a member of the Chinese Economists Society. He is a researcher at "One Belt One Road" research center. Since 2021, he has been a lecturer at the UNEC Department of Economics. Also since 2021, he has been a lecturer at the Odlar Yurdu University Department of Economics and Economic Relations. Field of research: Chinese economy, Macroeconomic Proportions, Investment, Techno-economic paradigms, Innovation

Suat Beylur is the Director of the Eurasian Research Institute at Khoja Ahmed Yassawi International Kazakh-Turkish University. He holds a PhD in Sociology from Ankara Yıldırım Beyazıt University and an MA in International Relations from Hacettepe University. His research focuses on multiculturalism, social change, youth, and state–religion relations in Central Asia, alongside language policy, identity, and modernization in the post-Soviet context. Dr. Beylur has published in SSCI- and Scopus-indexed journals such as Bilig, Golden Horde Review, and Turkish Studies, and edited several academic volumes. He serves as editor of Eurasian Research

Journal and Asya-Avrupa Journal, and has led nationally and internationally funded research projects. Prior to his current position, he held advisory and administrative roles in Türkiye's public institutions, including the Grand National Assembly and the Presidency for Turks Abroad (YTB).

Hurşit Dingil He graduated in 2017 as the top-ranking student from the Department and Faculty of Political Science and International Relations at Niğde Ömer Halisdemir University. During his undergraduate and graduate studies, he completed internships at various public institutions, including the Ministry of Foreign Affairs, Ministry of Treasury and Finance, Ministry of Trade, Turkish Cooperation and Coordination Agency (TİKA), Grand National Assembly of Turkey (TBMM), Presidency's Directorate of Communications, Central Bank of the Republic of Türkiye, Turkish Competition Authority, and TRT. His primary research interests include national security strategies and doctrines, Great Power Competition, asymmetric and hybrid threats, and rising threats (Ballistic Missiles, Hypersonic Missiles, Kamikaze UAVs, and S/UAVs). He has published numerous book chapters, research reports, and scholarly articles on these subjects at national and international levels. Furthermore, he serves as a reviewer for various national and international peer-reviewed journals, and his commentary, analysis, and evaluations on security and foreign policy issues are frequently featured in national and international media outlets and TV programs.

Emre Erdemir received his BA degree in International Relations from Akdeniz University in 2015 and his MA degree in EU Politics and International Relations from Marmara University Institute of European Studies in 2018. He holds a PhD in European Union politics and international relations from the Marmara University Institute of European Studies in 2024. Between 2022 and 2025, he worked as a project assistant in the TÜBİTAK 1001 project titled "Cultural Foundations of Foreign Policy: A Cross-Country Quantitative Research with an Original Data Set" at Antalya Bilim University. His research interests include EU foreign policy, Chinese foreign policy, energy security policy, and international relations theories.

Cihan Günyel graduated from Istanbul University's European Community Department in 2002 and Kadir Has University's International Relations and Globalisation Master's programme in 2011. In 2021, he completed his doctorate at Istanbul Gelişim University, Department of Political Science and International Relations, with a thesis titled "The Role of Black Sea Security in NATO's Identity Formation". He researches NATO, European security architecture, identity, post-structuralism and social constructionism. He has national and international publications.

Damir Islamov is a Research Fellow at the Centre for Mediterranean Studies of the National Research University Higher School of Economics (Russia). He conducts analytical work and is responsible for organizing and participating in conferences and seminars. He earned his Bachelor's and Master's degrees in the Department of International Relations at Kazan Federal University. In 2024, he received his PhD in History with a thesis titled "The European Union and Türkiye's Foreign Policy in the Western Balkans from 2008 to 2021". His research interests include Turkish foreign policy, Russian-Turkish relations, the Türkiye-NATO-EU triangle, Türkiye's role in Southeastern Europe, the foreign policies of Central Asian and South Caucasus countries, as well as international relations in the Wider Black Sea region and the Eastern Mediterranean.

Jipson Joseph has a PhD in Ethics from DVK Bangalore. Currently, he is a Research Scholar at School of Law, Christ University, Bangalore, India. His research interests are in the fields of ethics, gender studies, constitutional law, human rights, human security, environmental justice, SDGs, developmental policies, emerging economies, BRICS bloc, and global poverty. He has published 6 books, co-edited one book, and contributed scholarly articles to many international and national journals and edited volumes including IGI Global Scientific Publishing's edited books.

Pranjal Khare is an ardent researcher and a lawyer. He is currently working as an Assistant Professor of Law at OP Jindal Global University, India.

Nubara Kuliyeva is a Junior Research Fellow at the Centre for Comprehensive European and International Studies of the National Research University Higher School of Economics(HSE) in Russia. She is also a visiting lecturer at the Department of the Institute of Oriental Studies of the Russian Academy of Science of Faculty of World Economy and International Affairs at the HSE. She participates in research projects, prepare analytical materials, organize and participate in scientific events. She earned her Bachelor's Degree and Master's degree at Faculty of World Economy and International Affairs at HSE. Now, she is a PhD candidate at School of International Regional Studies of HSE and is working on her thesis titled "The Evolution of Türkiye's Policy in the MENA region under the Justice and Development Party's Rule (2002–2023)". Her research interests are Turkish and Middle Eastern studies and international relations in the MENA, Central Asia and South Caucasus regions.

Le Hoang Kiet is a researcher in the field of International Relations in Vietnam. He currently holds a BA in Political Science, a MA in Public Policy from Can Tho University (Vietnam) and is a PhD student in International Relations from the University of Social Sciences and Humanities, Hanoi (Vietnam). He has experience in researching international relations with more than 50 studies published in Vietnam and internationally. His research interests focus on Europe and the Indo-Pacific. It focuses on issues of power competition between major powers. He has published many research articles in famous and prestigious SCOPUS/WOS journals such as Vestnik Novosibirskogo Gosudarstvennogo Universiteta, Seriya, Современная Европа научный журнал, Journal of Educational and Social Research, Vestnik of Saint Petersburg University, Contemporary Chinese Political Economy and Strategic Relations, Przegląd Strategiczny, Australian Journal of Maritime & Ocean Affairs, The Russian Journal of Vietnamese Studies, Academic Journal of Interdisciplinary Studies...

Dana-Marie Ramjit is an experienced scholar and researcher specializing in postinternational governance and multilevel politics. Dana-Marie's research explores the intricate dynamics between globalization, localization, and governance structures in a world marked by turbulence and complexity. With a focus on collaborative governance, heterarchy, and policy innovation, Dana-Marie has contributed significantly to understanding how states and non-state actors navigate the challenges of the modern political landscape.

Rismawati Sudirman is a distinguished academic and consultant with a robust focus on sustainability reporting. She currently holds the position of lecturer and Head of the Quality Assurance Institute at Universitas Muhammadiyah Palopo, where she has been pivotal in ensuring the quality of university processes and outputs since February 2020. Additionally, she serves as an Assurer for Sustainability Reporting at the National Center for Sustainability Reporting in Jakarta, specializing in the evaluation of sustainability reports for mining companies across Indonesia. Her academic qualifications are extensive, comprising a Bachelor's degree in Economics and Accounting, a Master's degree in Accounting Science, and a Doctorate in Accounting from Universitas Brawijaya, Malang. Rismawati is also a certified specialist in sustainability reporting, risk management, and tax planning, holding several prestigious certifications including Certified Sustainability Reporting Specialist (CSRS) and Certified Risk Management Practitioner (CRMP). In her professional capacity, she has provided consultancy services in financial management and tax compliance for companies such as PT. Reski Barito Timur and PT. Helay Raya. Furthermore, she has authored multiple publications on taxation and management, contributing significantly to the academic community. Her interests in reading, writing, and travel reflect her commitment to lifelong learning and professional growth in her field.

Göran Roos is an independent trustee at the University of Buckingham and Visiting Professor at Cranfield School of Management. He is a fellow of both the Australian Academy of Technological Sciences and Engineering and the Royal Swedish Academy of Engineering Sciences. A pioneer of modern intellectual capital science, Professor Roos has advised government bodies in more than 50 countries on industry policy, innovation systems and strategy. His current work focuses on the transition towards digital and low environmental footprint economies at corporate, regional and national levels. He holds degrees from Chalmers University of Technology, INSEAD, Henley Management College and the University of South Australia, and has authored over 300 publications with approximately 19,000 citations, establishing him as a leading authority on the transformation of economic, technical, and structural systems.

Ramazan Safa is a PhD candidate in Political Science and International Relations at Adam Mickiewicz University in Poland, where he also serves as a fourth-year assistant researcher. His academic journey began with a BA in International Relations from Selcuk University, followed by an MSc in Political Science from the European University of Lefke. Safa's research interests encompass international development, comparative politics, and the politics of international organizations, with a particular focus on the Eastern Mediterranean region. He has presented at international conferences and published scholarly articles, including works on the Cyprus conflict.

Ezgi Şahin is a master's student at Kırıkkale University and is currently in the thesis stage of her studies. Her research focuses on international security, international relations theories, and regional studies. Specifically, she is interested in geopolitical dynamics, security policies, and great power competition in strategic regions such as the Arctic and the South China Sea.

Tran Xuan Hiep is a scholar and researcher currently working at Falcuty of History, University of Science and Education, University of Da Nang, Vietnam. He is a leading International Relations researcher in Vietnam. With a prolific academic record, he has published over 160 scholarly works including books, book chapters, and articles, with nearly 40 publications indexed in SCOPUS/ISI databases.

Yusuf Abubakar Wara was born in 1982 at Wara district in Kebbi state of Nigeria. He was educated at Federal Government College Ilorin between 1988-1993. He graduated from Ahmadu Bello University, Department of Political Science, in 2010. He completed his master's degree in Gazi University Department of International Relations in 2015 and his Ph.D. in Political and Social Sciences in 2021. He is an analyst in Political Science, Good Governance and Diplomacy at Kastamonu University, Türkiye.

Index

A

B

C

D

E

F

G

H

I

J

K

L

M

N

O

P

R

S

T

U

V

W

www.ingramcontent.com/pod-product-compliance
Lightning Source LLC
LaVergne TN
LVHW062338300926
849161LV00007B/1738